LONGMAN LINGUISTICS LIBRARY

HISTORY OF LINGUISTICS VOLUME II

# LONGMAN LINGUISTICS LIBRARY

General editors
**R. H. Robins** *University of London*
**Martin Harris** *University of Manchester*
**Geoffrey Horrocks** *University of Cambridge*

**A Short History of Linguistics**
Third Edition
R. H. ROBINS

**Text and Context**
*Explorations in the Semantics and Pragmatics of Discourse*
TEUN A. VAN DIJK

**Introduction to Text Linguistics**
ROBERT-ALAIN DE BEAUGRANDE
AND WOLFGANG ULRICH DRESSLER

**Psycholinguistics**
*Language, Mind, and World*
DANNY D. STEINBERG

**Principles of Pragmatics**
GEOFFREY N. LEECH

**Generative Grammar**
GEOFFREY HORROCKS

**The English Verb**
Second Edition
F. R. PALMER

**A History of American English**
J. L. DILLARD

**English Historical Syntax**
*Verbal Constructions*
DAVID DENISON

**Pidgin and Creole Languages**
SUZANNE ROMAINE

**General Linguistics**
*An Introductory Survey*
Fourth Edition
R. H. ROBINS

**A History of English Phonology**
CHARLES JONES

**Generative and Non-linear Phonology**
JACQUES DURAND

**Historical Linguistics
Problems and Perspectives**
EDITED BY C. JONES

**Modality and the English Modals**
Second Edition
F. R. PALMER

**Semiotics and Linguistics**
YISHAI TOBIN

**Multilingualism in the British Isles I: the Older Mother Tongues and Europe**
EDITED BY SAFDER ALLADINA AND VIV EDWARDS

**Multilingualism in the British Isles II: Africa, Asia and the Middle East**
EDITED BY SAFDER ALLADINA AND VIV EDWARDS

**Dialects of English**
*Studies in Grammatical Variation*
EDITED BY PETER TRUDGILL AND J. K. CHAMBERS

**Introduction to Bilingualism**
CHARLOTTE HOFFMANN

**Verb and Noun Number in English**
*A Functional Explanation*
WALLIS REID

**English in Africa**
JOSEF S. SCHMEID

**Linguistic Theory**
*Discourse of Fundamental Works*
ROBERT DE BEAUGRANDE

**Aspect in the English Verb**
*Process and Result in Language*
YISHAI TOBIN

**The Meaning of Syntax:**
*A Study in the Adjectives of English*
CONNOR FERRIS

**History of Linguistics**
*Volume I: The Eastern Traditions of Linguistics*
*Volume II: Classical and Medieval Linguistics*
EDITED BY GIULIO LEPSCHY

# History of Linguistics

## Volume II: Classical and Medieval Linguistics

edited by Giulio Lepschy

LONGMAN
LONDON AND NEW YORK

**Longman Group UK Limited**
Longman House, Burnt Mill,
Harlow, Essex CM20 2JE, England
*and Associated Companies throughout the world*

*Published in the United States of America
by Longman Publishing, New York*

English translation first published 1994
Chapter 2 translated by Emma Sansone

ISBN 0–582–09490–9 CSD
ISBN 0–582–09491–7 PPR

British Library Cataloguing-in-Publication Data

A catalogue record for this book is
available from the British Library

Library of Congress Cataloging-in-Publication Data

Storia della linguistica. English.
History of linguistics / edited by Giulio Lepschy.
p. cm.
Includes bibliographical references and index.
Contents: v. 1. The eastern traditions and linguistics—v.
2. Classical and medieval linguistics.
1. Linguistics—History. I. Lepschy, Giulio C. II. Title.
P61.S513 1994
410′.9—dc20 93–31169
CIP

Set by 15M in 10/11 pt Times
Produced by Longman Singapore Publishers (Pte) Ltd.
Printed in Singapore

# Contents

# Introduction

This work originated in the discussions held by a group of advisors for linguistics of the Italian publishers il Mulino. Examining the areas in which new and useful initiatives could be encouraged, it was thought that a large-scale history of linguistics would meet a widely felt need, and I was asked to elaborate a plan for such a work. The preparation and completion of the project took about ten years, and the work, written by scholars from different countries, began appearing in Italian in 1990. This English edition has been reorganized into four volumes. In this introduction I shall say something about the nature and contents of this work, and its place within the present panorama of linguistic historiography.

What I had in mind was a history of linguistic thought, rather than an account of the development of linguistic science. In other words, for different societies and in different periods, I wanted to have a presentation of the prevailing attitudes towards language: its social, cultural, religious and liturgical functions, the prestige attached to different varieties, the cultivation of a standard, the place of language in education, the elaboration of lexical and grammatical descriptions, the knowledge of foreign idioms, the status of interpreters and translators, and so on.

This implies of course a 'view from within', that is, presenting the linguistic interests and assumptions of individual cultures in their own terms, without trying to transpose and reshape them into the context of our ideas of what the scientific study of language ought to be. The purpose is an understanding of what certain societies thought about language, rather than an assessment of their ideas on a scale of scientific progress.

The problem is familiar to historians of science and the line I am following does not necessarily imply a lack of confidence in the possibility of obtaining reliable findings in linguistic study. Whether 'science' is the most suitable term for what linguistics does, is of course open to debate: see Chomsky (1969, 56) and Graffi (1991b). In any case, the authors of different chapters were also encouraged not to enlarge on methodological problems posed by linguistic historiography but to concentrate instead on the presentation of facts, on the interpretation of texts which they considered relevant and interesting for the periods and cultures they were discussing. But, after obtaining the agreement of my authors concerning the general aims, I left them completely free to organize their chapters as they thought fit, without trying to impose a unifying format, because I thought that differences of perspective and treatment would contribute to highlighting specific features of individual traditions. For instance, the chapters on Indian and Arabic concentrate on the elaboration of grammatical analysis, in both cases an important contribution of these civilizations, whereas the Hebrew chapter places more stress on the theological, mystical and philosophical context of Jewish reflections on language.

The content of the four volumes of the English edition is as follows: Volume I includes the ancient traditions, each of which develops in a manner which is, from a viewpoint both cultural and chronological, largely independent, apart from obvious connections, like those between Arabic and Hebrew thought in the Middle Ages. (The Graeco-Roman tradition, which is the basis of those reflections on language which we present chronologically in Volumes II–IV, appears at the beginning of the second volume.) Chapter 1, by Göran Malmqvist, of Stockholm University, describes the development of Chinese linguistics, analysing the relevant lexicographical and grammatical works, and throwing light on the particular shape imposed on phonological analysis by the logographic nature of Chinese script. Chapter 2, by George Cardona, of the University of Pennsylvania, presents the Indian grammatical tradition, its cultural and religious implications, and particularly the contribution of Pāṇini, illustrating its systematic character and its attention to detail. Chapter 3, supervised by Erica Reiner, of the University of Chicago, presents and interprets the documents which bear witness to linguistic interests and knowledge in the civilizations of the ancient near East; the chapter is divided into three sections, devoted to Ancient Egyptian (by Janet Johnson), Sumerian (by Miguel Civil), and Akkadian (by Erica Reiner). Chapter 4, by Raphael Loewe, of the University of London, examines the place of language within the Hebrew tradition, from the Biblical period, through the Talmudists, the mystics, the enlightenment, down to the rebirth of Hebrew as an everyday language, paying particular attention to the philosophical and cultural implications of these trends. Chapter 5, by the late Henri Fleisch, of Saint Joseph University in Beirut, probably the last essay to flow from the pen of this eminent scholar, deals synthetically with the original system of grammatical analysis elaborated by the great Arabic civilization of the Middle Ages.

The following volumes present the main stages of the European tradition, in their chronological succession. They include two chapters each. In Volume II, the first chapter, by Peter Matthews, of Cambridge University, deals with classical linguistics and offers a reading of the main texts of the Graeco-Roman world which elaborate the grammatical categories on which we still base our analysis of language. The second chapter, by Edoardo Vineis, of Bologna University, and (for the philosophy of language) by Alfonso Maierù, of Rome University, present a detailed discussion of language study from the end of the sixth to the end of the fourteenth century, not limited to the late medieval period which has received most attention in recent years (with particular reference to Modistic philosophy), but extending to the less frequently studied early Middle Ages.

In Volume III, the first chapter, by Mirko Tavoni, of Pisa University, covers the fifteenth and sixteenth centuries, and is completed by two sections, one on *Slavia Romana*, by M. D. Gandolfo, and one on *Slavia Orthodoxa*, by S. Toscano; the bibliography of this chapter takes advantage of the great Renaissance Linguistic Archive set up by M. Tavoni at the Istituto di Studi Rinascimentali in Ferrara. The second chapter, by Raffaele Simone, of Rome University, offers a helpful map of the varied terrain constituted by seventeenth- and eighteenth-century culture, in which many of the roots are found from which the great plant of later comparative linguistics derives its nourishment; R. Simone, who is a professional linguist, keeps in mind the philosophical perspective that is particularly relevant for this period.

In Volume IV, the first chapter, by Anna Morpurgo Davies, of Oxford University, examines the flowering of historical and comparative linguistics in the nineteenth century, stressing in particular some aspects which traditional presentations, focusing on the Neogrammarians, sometimes leave in the shadow, like the interest in typological classifications, and the importance for comparative philology of the newly constituted German university system in the first three decades of the century. The second chapter, by the editor of this work, offers a synthesis of the main developments in twentieth-century linguistics, extending from the progress of comparative studies to linguistic theory, philosophy of language, and

the investigation of language use in different areas, from literature
to social communication. The Italian edition also includes a chapter
on the history of Italian linguistics and dialectology, by Paola
Benincà, of Padua University, which has been omitted from the
English edition.

Let us briefly look at the present state of linguistic historiography. Over the last three decades there has been a considerable
revival of interest in this field. In 1974 Konrad Koerner, a German
scholar teaching in Canada, founded the journal *Historiographia
Linguistica*, which has become a forum for international discussion
on the history of linguistics; in 1978 he was the organizer of the
first international congress on the history of linguistics (the meetings continue at three-yearly intervals). There are also several other
associations devoted to the history of linguistics, like the Société
d'histoire et d'épistémologie des sciences du langage, created in
1978, presided over by S. Auroux, which publishes a Bulletin and
the journal *Histoire Épistémologie Langage* (1979–); the Henry .
Sweet Society for the History of Linguistic Ideas, founded in 1984
on the initiative of Vivian Salmon, which organizes regular meetings
and publishes a *Newsletter*; the North American Association for
the History of the Language Sciences, founded in 1987. The interest
in the history of linguistics over this period is also indicated by the
publication of monographs and collections of studies, such as
Hymes (1974), Parret (1976), Grotsch (1982), Schmitter (1982),
Chevalier and Encrevé (1984), Bynon and Palmer (1986), Formigari
and Lo Piparo (1988), and by the two tomes devoted to the
historiography of linguistics by Sebeok (1975).

A separate study would be necessary to examine the main available histories of linguistics, from the great works of the nineteenth
century devoted to Classical linguistics by Steinthal (1863), to
Oriental philology by Benfey (1869), and to Germanic philology by
R. von Raumer (1870). Subsequent studies witness the triumph of
Neogrammarian comparative philology, from Delbrück (1880) to
Meillet (1903) to Pedersen (1924). Since the 1960s numerous historical presentations have been published, from the large and well-
informed work by Tagliavini (1963), lacking however in historical
perspective and theoretical insight, to the two-volume contribution
by Mounin (1967–72), the neat and well-balanced book by Robins
(1967), the acute and comprehensive synthesis by Law (1990), the
disappointing attempts by Malmberg (1991) and Itkonen (1991).
Large-scale works have also started appearing in the last few years,
under the direction of Auroux (n.d.) and of Schmitter (1987).
There is no space to mention in this context the great many studies
devoted, since the 1960s, to individual periods and problems in the

history of linguistics, although they often provide the detailed groundwork that makes possible overall synthetic assessments (some titles will be quoted in the list of references).

What is the place of our history of linguistics against this background? To me it seems to be placed in an advantageous position, in the middle ground between the concise, one-author profiles on the one hand, and the extended, multi-authored, multi-volume series on the other. Compared to the former, it has the greater richness of detail, which is made possible by the larger space available and the higher degree of reliability that derives from the authority of contributors who are specialists in the individual areas; compared to the latter, it is more compact and coherent in perspective and basic assumptions, and it can not only be consulted for single questions, or studied in individual sections, but also be read in its entirety.

If I were asked to present a schematic précis of the main features which I see as inspiring this work and characterizing its realization, I would list the following points:

1. A perspective directed towards understanding the past, rather than dealing with present-day concerns. The aim is to reconstruct and illustrate different epochs and traditions within their own context and on the basis of their own values, rather than of their appeal to present-day preoccupations; to highlight their linguistic interests, rather than our own.

2. This is a history of linguistic thought, of interests and attitudes toward language. These may or may not find a place within the elaboration of a 'scientific' study of language (however we may want to define it), but in any case I feel that an account of the preoccupations with linguistic matters in different societies proves to be an interesting and worthwhile object of historical investigation.

3. I have considered it essential, in my choice of authors for individual chapters, that they should be specialists, able to analyse the relevant texts in the original languages, and to present them to a lay readership. I aimed at obtaining not an account of what is known, derived from current literature, but a series of original contributions based on first-hand study of the primary sources.

4. From what precedes it is clear that this work is prevalently concerned with a historical and philological study of ideas, texts from the past, rather than with methodological and theoretical problems posed by historiography. It is an 'extroverted', rather than an 'introverted' history, dealing with the

facts it analyses, rather than with the theoretical and ideological assumptions which lie behind the work of the historian. This obviously does not imply that methodological questions are not a legitimate object of study; but I believe that it is possible to offer useful contributions on the history of linguistics, without dealing in the first instance with the theory of historiography.

5. One of the main linguists of our times, Yakov Malkiel, observed some years ago (Malkiel and Langdon 1969) that to produce good work on the history of linguistics it is not enough to be a linguist: one has also to be a historian, and to fulfil the expectations normally raised by a historical essay. Here, of course, one can only observe that the ability to set some episodes of the history of linguistics within their social and cultural context, is the exception rather than the rule (examples that come to mind are those of Dionisotti (1967a,b, 1972) or Timpanaro (1963, 1965, 1972, 1973)). What I had in mind for this history of linguistics was the more modest aim of providing information about ideas on language, in different periods and societies, which are not easily (and in some cases not at all) accessible elsewhere.

I know from direct experience that linguists feel the need for a work of this kind, and I hope it may also appeal to readers who are interested to know how people, at different times and within different cultural traditions, have looked at one of the most essential and challenging features of our common humanity – that is, language.

G. C. Lepschy

## References

AARSLEFF, H. (1982) *From Locke to Saussure. Essays on the Study of Language and Intellectual History*, University of Minnesota Press, Minneapolis.

AMIROVA, T. A., OL'KHOVIKOV, B. A. and ROŽDESTVENSKIJ, JU. V. (1975) *Očerki po istorii lingvistiki*, Nauka, Moskva (German tr. *Abriss der Geschichte der Sprachwissenschaft*, Veb Bibliographisches Institut, Leipzig 1980).

AUROUX, S. (ed.) (n.d.) *Histoire des idées linguistiques. Tome 1: La naissance des métalangages. En Orient et en Occident*, Mardaga, Liège/Bruxelles.

AUROUX, S. (1992) *Histoire des idées linguistiques. Tome 2: Le développement de la grammaire occidentale*, Mardaga, Liège.

BENFEY, T. (1869) *Geschichte der Sprachwissenschaft und orientalischen Philologie in Deutschland, seit dem Anfange des 19. Jahrhunderts mit einem Rückblick auf die früheren Zeiten*, Cotta, München.

BORST, A. (1957–63) *Der Turmbau von Babel. Geschichte der Meinungen über Ursprung und Vielfalt der Sprachen und Völker*, Hiersemann, Stuttgart.

BRINCAT, G. (1986) *La linguistica prestrutturale*, Zanichelli, Bologna.

BYNON, T. and PALMER, F. R. (eds) (1986) *Studies in the History of Western Linguistics. In Honour of R. H. Robins*, Cambridge University Press, Cambridge.

CHEVALIER, J.-C. and ENCREVÉ, P. (eds) (1984) *Vers une histoire sociale de la linguistique* (Langue Française, 63), Larousse, Paris.

CHOMSKY, N. (1966) *Cartesian Linguistics. A Chapter in the History of Rationalist Thought*, Harper and Row, New York.

CHOMSKY, N. (1969) Linguistics and Philosophy, in *Language and Philosophy. A Symposium*, edited by S. Hook, New York University Press, New York, 51–94.

DELBRÜCK, B. (1880) *Einleitung in das Sprachstudium. Ein Beitrag zur Geschichte und Methodik der vergleichenden Sprachforschung*, Breitkopf und Härtel, Leipzig.

DIONISOTTI, C. (1967a) La lingua italiana da Venezia all'Europa. Il Fortunio e la filologia umanistica. Niccolò Liburnio e la letteratura cortigiana, in *Rinascimento europeo e Rinascimento veneziano*, edited by V. Branca, Sansoni, Firenze, 1–46.

DIONISOTTI, C. (1967b) *Geografia e storia della letteratura italiana*, Einaudi, Torino.

DIONISOTTI, C. (1972) *A Year's Work in the Seventies. The Presidential Address of the Modern Humanities Research Association delivered at University College, London, on 7 January 1972*, reprinted from *The Modern Language Review*, Vol. 67, No. 4.

FORMIGARI, L. and LO PIPARO, F. (eds) (1988) *Prospettive di storia della linguistica*, Editori Riuniti, Roma.

GRAFFI, G. (1991a) *La sintassi tra Ottocento e Novencento*, il Mulino, Bologna.

GRAFFI, G. (1991b) Concetti 'ingenui' e concetti 'teorici' in sintassi, *Lingua e Stile*, 26, 347–63.

GROTSCH, K. (1982) *Sprachwissenschaftsgeschichtsschreibung. Ein Beitrag zur Kritik und zur historischen un methodologischen Selbstvergewisserung der Disziplin*, Kümmerle Verlag, Göppingen.

HYMES, D. (ed.) (1974) *Studies in the History of Linguistics*, Indiana University Press, Bloomington.

ITKONEN, E. (1991) *Universal History of Linguistics*, Benjamins, Amsterdam.

KOERNER, K. (1978) *Towards a Historiography of Linguistics. Selected Essays*, Benjamins, Amsterdam.

KOERNER, K. (1989) *Practicing Linguistic Historiography. Selected Essays*, Benjamins, Amsterdam.

LAW, V. (1990) Language and Its Students: the History of Linguistics, in

*An Encyclopedia of Language*, edited by N. E. Collinge, Routledge, London/New York, 784–842.

LEPSCHY, G. (ed.) (1990) *Storia della linguistica*, vol. 1 and 2, il Mulino, Bologna.

MALKIEL, Y., LANGDON, M. (1969) History and Histories of Linguistics, *Romance Philology*, 22, 530–74.

MALMBERG, B. (1991) *Histoire de la linguistique de Sumer à Saussure*, Presses Universitaires de France, Paris.

MEILLET, A. (1903) *Introduction à l'étude comparative des langues indoeuropéennes*, Hachette, Paris (eighth edition, 1937).

MOUNIN, G. (1967—72) *Histoire de la linguistique*, 2 vols, Presses Universitaires de France, Paris.

OL'KHOVIKOV, B. A. (1985) *Teorija jazyka i vid grammatičeskogo opisanija v istorii jazykoznanija. Stanovlenie i evolucija kanona grammatičeskogo opisanija v Evrope*, Nauka, Moskva.

PARRET, H. (ed.) (1976) *History of Linguistic Thought and Contemporary Linguistics*, de Gruyter, Berlin.

PEDERSEN, H. (1924) *Sprogvidenskaben i det Nittende Aarhundrede. Metoder og Resultater*, Gyldendalske Boghandel, København (English tr. *Linguistic Science in the Nineteenth Century*, Harvard University Press, Cambridge, Massachusetts 1931; and with the new title *The Discovery of Language. Linguistic Science in the Nineteenth Century*, Indiana University Press, Bloomington 1962).

RAUMER, R. VON (1870) *Geschichte der germanischen Philologie vorzugsweise in Deutschland*, Oldenbourg, München.

ROBINS, R. H. (1967) *A Short History of Linguistics*, Longman, London (third edition, 1990).

SALMON, V. (1979) *The Study of Language in Seventeenth-Century England*, Benjamins, Amsterdam.

SCHMITTER, P. (1982) *Untersuchungen zur Historiographie der Linguistik. Struktur – Methodik – Theoretische Fundierung*, Narr, Tübingen.

SCHMITTER, P. (ed.) (1987) *Zur Theorie und Methode der Geschichtsschreibung der Linguistik. Analysen und Reflexionen* (Geschichte der Sprachtheorie, 1), Narr, Tübingen.

SEBEOK, T. (ed.) (1975) *Historiography of Linguistics* (Current Trends in Linguistics, 13), Mouton, The Hague.

STEINTHAL, H. (1863) *Geschichte der Sprachwissenschaft bei den Griechen und Römern mit besonderer Rücksicht auf die Logik*, Dümmler, Berlin (second edition, 1890–91).

TAGLIAVINI, C. (1963) *Panorama di storia della linguistica*, Pàtron, Bologna.

TIMPANARO, S. (1963) *La genesi del metodo del Lachmann*, Le Monnier, Firenze (new edition, Liviana, Padova 1985).

TIMPANARO, S. (1965) *Classicismo e illuminismo nell'Ottocento italiano*, Nistri Lischi, Pisa (second, enlarged edition, 1969).

TIMPANARO, S. (1972) Friedrich Schlegel e gli inizi della linguistica indoeuropea in Germania, *Critica Storica*, 9, 72–105.

TIMPANARO, S. (1973) Il contrasto tra i fratelli Schlegel e Franz Bopp sulla struttura e la genesi delle lingue indoeuropee, *Critica Storica*, 10, 53–90.

# Acknowledgements

In the preparation of the Italian edition I availed myself of the advice of many friends and colleagues. For Volume I, I should like to thank in particular Zyg Barański, Verina Jones, Anna Morpurgo Davies, Joanna Weinberg (Introduction); Michael Halliday and Michael Loewe (Chapter 1); Anna Morpurgo Davies (Chapter 2); Arnaldo Momigliano (Chapter 3); Ada Rapoport and Joanna Weinberg (Chapter 4); Bernard Lewis (Chapter 5); for Volume II, Tullio De Mauro (Chapter 2); for Volume III: Giuseppe Dell'Agata (Chapter 1), Tullio De Mauro (Chapter 2). I am grateful to Emma Sansone, who has sensitively and helpfully performed the difficult job of translating into English chapters originally in other languages (Volume I, Chapter 5; Volume II, Chapter 2; Volume III, Chapters 1 and 2; Volume IV, Chapter 2). I should also like to thank the series' editors for their advice and comments during the preparation of the English edition. The English version introduces some updatings and improvements on the previous Italian edition. In particular Volume I, Chapter 4 includes a more detailed discussion of Hebrew grammatical ideas. For help and advice concerning the history of Arabic linguistics (Volume I, Chapter 5) I am grateful to Professor E. Ullendorff and Professor A. F. L. Beeston. I am grateful to Emma Sansone for her assistance in preparing the Index of Volume II, and to Rolando Ferri for help in correcting the proofs.

# Notes on the contributors

**George Cardona** received a BA from New York University and an MA and PhD in Indo-European Linguistics from Yale University. He has spent several years studying texts of traditional śāstras with paṇḍitas in India (Vadodra, Varanasi, Madras). Since 1960 he has taught at the University of Pennsylvania, first in the Department of South Asian Studies, then (since 1965) in the Department of Linguistics. His major fields of interests and research are ancient Indian grammatical thought, Indo-Aryan, and Indo-Iranian. Among his works are *A Gujarati Reference Grammar* (Philadelphia 1965), *Pāṇini, a Survey of Research* (The Hague 1976; reprinted Delhi 1980), and *Pāṇini's Grammar and its Traditions. Volume 1: Background and Introduction* (Delhi 1988).

**Miguel Civil** born in Sabadell (Barcelona, Spain) studied Assyriology in Paris (École Pratique des Hautes Études and Collège de France). He worked with Professor S. N. Kramer in Philadelphia for several years and then joined the staff of the Oriental Institute of the University of Chicago. His speciality is Sumerian texts and grammar, with emphasis on lexicography. He is co-editor of *Materials for the Sumerian Lexicon* and member of the editorial board of the *Chicago Assyrian Dictionary*.

**Henri Fleisch** (1904–85) born in Jonville (France); a Jesuit, he studied in the schools of his Order and in Paris, École de Langues Orientales Vivantes (1934–36) and at the Sorbonne. In 1938 he was appointed Professor of Arabic Philology at the Institut de Lettres Orientales in Beirut, and then Director of the Prehistory Museum, and Scriptor at the Saint-Joseph University. Among his works: *Introduction à l'étude des langues sémitiques* (Paris 1947); *L'Arabe* *classique. Esquisse d'une structure linguistique* (Beirut 1956), *Traité de philologie arabe* (Beirut, vol. 1, 1961, vol. 2, 1979); *Études d'arabe dialectal* (Beirut 1974).

**Maria Delfina Gandolfo**, born in Rome, graduated in Genoa in Russian Language and Literature, with a thesis on the history of alphabets in the Slavic world. She took an MA and an MPhil at Yale University, and is preparing a PhD dissertation on the orthographic questions in the Slavic tradition.

**Janet H. Johnson**, born in Everett, Washington, studied at the University of Chicago and is now Professor of Egyptology at the Oriental Institute at that University. Her major philological interests are in Demotic (Egyptian) and the synchronic and diachronic studies of the ancient Egyptian language. She has written *The Demotic Verbal System* (Chicago 1976), *Thus Wrote 'Onchshes-honqy: An Introductory Grammar of Demotic* (Chicago 1986), and numerous articles on the grammar of various stages of Egyptian, including the summary and overview in *Crossroads: Chaos or the Beginning of a New Paradigm*, Papers from the Conference on Egyptian Grammar held in Helsingør, 28–30 May 1986.

**Giulio Lepschy**, born in Venice, studied at the Universities of Pisa (Scuola Normale Superiore) and Zürich, Oxford, Paris and London. He is Professor in the Department of Italian Studies at the University of Reading, and a Fellow of the British Academy. His research work is mainly on Italian linguistics and dialectology, and on the history of linguistics. Among his publications are: *A Survey of Structural Linguistics* (London 1970); (with Anna Laura Lepschy) *The Italian Language Today* (London 1977); *Saggi di linguistica italiana* (Bologna 1978); *Intorno a Saussure* (Turin 1979); *Sulla linguistica moderna* (Bologna 1989); *Nuovi saggi di linguistica italiana* (Bologna 1989); *La linguistica del Novecento* (Bologna 1992).

**Raphael Loewe** studied classics at Cambridge before 1939 and semitics (also subsequently in Oxford) after the War. He held teaching posts and fellowships at Leeds, Cambridge, Providence, Rhode Island, and at University College, London, whence he retired from the Goldsmid Chair of Hebrew in 1984. He has concerned himself mainly with the impact of Jewish biblical exegesis and legend on European scholasticism, and with Hebrew poetry in Spain. His publications include: The Medieval History of the Latin Vulgate, in *The Cambridge History of the Bible*, 2 (Cambridge

1969); *The Rylands Haggadah* (London 1988); *Ibn Gabirol* (London 1989).

**Alfonso Maierù** studied at the University of Rome La Sapienza, where he teaches History of Medieval Philosophy. He has worked mainly on medieval logic (*Terminologia logica della tarda scolastica*, Rome 1972), dealing with some of its problematic aspects (he has written several essays on Trinitarian theology and logic). Since 1978 he has also been working on scholastic institutions and teaching techniques, and on philosophical terminology in Dante.

**Göran Malmqvist**, Professor of Chinese at the University of Stockholm and a member of the Swedish Academy. He taught Chinese at the School of Oriental and African Studies in London (1953–5); served as Cultural Attaché to the Swedish Embassy in Peking (1956–8) and as reader and subsequently professor in Chinese at the Australian National University in Canberra in 1956–65. He has published in the fields of Chinese dialectology, classical and modern Chinese syntax, Chinese metrics and textual criticism. He has also translated a number of Chinese literary works into Swedish. Among his publications are: The Syntax of Bound Forms in Sich'uanese, *BMFEA* (*Bulletin of the Museum of Far Eastern Antiquities*), 33, 1961, 125–99; Studies in Western Mandarin Phonology, *BMFEA*, 34, 1962, 129–92; *Problems and Methods in Chinese Linguistics* (Canberra 1962); *Han Phonology and Textual Criticism* (Canberra 1963); Studies on the Gongyang and Guuliang Commentaries, I, *BMFEA*, 43, 1971, 67–222; II, *BMFEA*, 47, 1975, 19–69; III, *BMFEA*, 49, 1977, 33–215.

**Peter Hugoe Matthews**, born near Oswestry in England; graduated at the University of Cambridge 1957; has taught general linguistics at Bangor, North Wales, at Reading, and, since 1980, at Cambridge, where he is at present Professor of Linguistics and Fellow of St John's College. He is a Fellow of the British Academy. Principal research interests in syntax, morphology and the history of linguistics. His main publications are: *Inflectional Morphology* (Cambridge 1972); *Morphology* (Cambridge 1974); *Generative Grammar and Linguistic Competence* (London 1979); *Syntax* (Cambridge 1981); *Grammatical Theory in the United States from Bloomfield to Chomsky* (Cambridge 1993).

**Anna Morpurgo Davies**, born in Milan, graduated at the University of Rome before spending a year at Harvard University. She is Professor of Comparative Philology at the University of Oxford, and taught at Yale, Pennsylvania, and other American universities. She is a Fellow of the British Academy. She works on Indo-European comparative grammar (particularly Mycenean, Ancient Greek, ancient Anatolian languages), and on the history of nineteenth century linguistics. She has published *Myceneae Graecitatis Lexicon* (Rome 1963); she has edited with Y. Duhoux, *Linear B: A 1984 Survey* (Louvain 1985), and she has written articles in British, Italian, German, French and American journals.

**Erica Reiner**, born in Budapest, studied Linguistics and Assyriology at the École Pratique des Hautes Études, Paris, and at the University of Chicago (PhD 1955). She is Professor at the University of Chicago and Editor-in-Charge of the Chicago Assyrian Dictionary. Her major interests are the language and literature of ancient Babylonia and Assyria. Her main publications are: *A Linguistic Analysis of Accadian* (The Hague 1966); *The Elamite Language* (Handbuch der Orientalistick, II-2, Leiden 1969); (with D. Pingree) *Babylonian Planetary Omens*, 1 and 2 (Malibu 1975 and 1981); *Your Thwarts in Pieces, Your Mooring Rope Cut: Poetry from Babylonia and Assyria* (Ann Arbor 1985).

**Raffaele Simone**, born in Lecce, is Professor of General Linguistics at the University of Rome La Sapienza. He works on the history of linguistics, on Italian linguistics, on theory of grammar and on textual linguistics. Main publications: Introduction to and translation of *Grammatica e Logica di Port-Royal* (Rome 1969); with R. Amacker, Verbi modali in italiano (*Italian Linguistics*, 3, 1977); *Maistock. Il linguaggio spiegato da una bambina* (Florence 1988); *Fondamenti di linguistica* (Bari/Rome 1990); *Il sogno di Saussure* (Bari/Rome 1992).

**Mirko Tavoni**, born in Modena, studied at the Scuola Normale Superiore of Pisa, taught at the University of Calabria, and is now Associate Professor of the History of the Italian Language at the University of Pisa. He works mainly on the history of Medieval and Renaissance linguistic ideas. Principal publications: *Il discorso linguistico di Bartolomeo Benvoglienti* (Pisa 1975); *Latino, grammatica, volgare. Storia di una questione umanistica* (Padua 1984); *Il Quattrocento*, in the series «Storia della lingua italiana» (Bologna 1992). He is the co-ordinator of the bibliographical project *Renaissance Linguistic Archive* at the Istituto di Studi Rinascimentali in Ferrara.

**Silvia Toscano** studied at the Universities of Pisa and V. Trnovo;

she is a researcher at the Istituto di Filologia Slava of the University of Pisa. She works mainly on Slavic linguistics. Among her recent works are: *L'«articolo» nel trattato slavo Sulle otto parti del discorso* (Rome 1984); *I «modi verbali» nel trattato slavo Sulle otto parti del discorso* (Rome 1988).

**Edoardo Vineis**, born at Broni (Pavia), he studied at the University of Pisa (Scuola Normale Superiore). He teaches Linguistics at the University of Bologna. He works on Latin linguistics, history of the Italian language, and history of linguistics. His main publications are: *Studio sulla lingua dell'«Itala»* (Pisa 1974); (with P. Berrettoni) annotated edition of A. Manzoni and G. I. Ascoli, *Scritti sulla questione della lingua* (Turin 1974); Grammatica e filosofia del linguaggio in Alcuino, *Studi e Saggi Linguistici*, 28, 1988, 403–29; Latino, in *Le lingue indoeuropee*, ed. by A. Giacalone Ramat and P. Ramat (Bologna 1993, 289–348).

# Chapter 1

# Greek and Latin Linguistics

*Peter Matthews*

## 1.1 Introduction

Two basic difficulties confront the student of linguistics in antiquity. First, there is a problem of deciding what should count as linguistics. Second, there are crucial deficiencies in our sources. Similar problems will at times afflict the contributors of later chapters. But in our period they are much more serious, and both merit more than casual mention.

### 1.1.1 The term 'grammar'

The term 'linguistics' dates from the early nineteenth century, and there is no ancient term which corresponds to it. In late antiquity the grammarians, in particular, give descriptions of Greek and Latin which are the distant forerunners of a modern descriptive grammar. They divide words into classes which are close to those that we still recognize: noun, verb, pronoun, adverb, and so on. They identify familiar morphological categories such as case, number and tense. They give rules, occasionally systematic though more often sporadic, for what we now call inflection and word formation. They distinguish what is correct from what is incorrect and in the works of two grammarians, Apollonius Dyscolus in the second century AD and Priscian at the beginning of the sixth, we find the earliest extant treatments of syntax. There is therefore a temptation to see the history of linguistics as equivalent to the history of grammar. On this view, it would begin in earnest in the centuries just before the Christian era, when ancient grammar emerged as an independent scholarly discipline.

But the ancient discipline of 'grammar' (Gk. *grammatikḗ*, Lat. *grammatica*) had neither the same scope nor the same role as its modern descendant. The term itself derives from the Greek word for a letter of the alphabet (*grámma*, stem *grammat-*), and when Plato, in the fourth century BC, first talks of a *tékhnē grammatikḗ* (a craft, skill or art of grammar) its subject matter is the names of letters, their classification, and so on.[1] Before the third century BC a professional *grammatikós* or *grammatistḗs* was simply someone who taught writing and reading; the first word was also used of a lettered or educated man, as opposed to an illiterate (*agrámmatos*, with the negative prefix *a-*, 'unlettered').[2] From the beginning of the third century, *grammatikḗ* or 'grammar' was given a new sense, in which it referred more widely to the whole of what we might now call philology and criticism. According to the definition of Eratosthenes (c.275–194 BC), grammar is a general expertise in literary texts.[3] In a later definition by Dionysius Thrax (c.170–c.90 BC) it is, in general, the study of literary usage. It has six parts, some of which we will consider further in subsection 1.5.3; but the last and finest is poetic criticism.[4]

It is from this literary and textual discipline that the grammatical tradition of antiquity eventually emerges. But plainly these are not modern definitions, and neither is that given, in the first century AD, by the Roman rhetorician Quintilian. According to Quintilian, *grammatica* or grammar has two parts. The first is the knowledge of correct usage (in his account both spoken and written). The second is the reading or expounding (*enarratio*) of poets and other authors.[5] In his sketch of its subject matter, the first part embraces the study of sounds and letters, of 'parts of speech' or word classes, of inflectional and other grammatical categories. But it also includes a standard classification of 'faults and virtues of discourse' (*vitia et virtutes orationis*) which has no modern equivalent and which covers topics such as (under 'virtues') the definitions of the figures of speech, which are now seen as belonging elsewhere. The same two-part definition is given by the grammarians themselves, and refers above all to their role in the contemporary educational system. The *grammaticus* was by then a secondary school teacher, and those whose pedagogical or scholarly treatises are known to us are a small fraction of the grammarians teaching in cities throughout the empire. Unlike the *grammatikós* in classical Greece, he took pupils who were already literate, and the scope of his instruction was indeed as this definition implies. In the fourth century AD Donatus is the author of two important elementary texts, both dealing in large part with grammar in the modern sense. But the fuller of the two includes the 'faults and virtues of discourse', and he also wrote detailed commentaries on Virgil and Terence, two of the authors regularly selected for exhaustive study in the schoolroom.[6]

Even when the place of grammar was established, the grammarians were not the only students of language. Their pupils passed from them to the rhetorician, who taught the effective use of language for, in particular, advocacy. It was this branch of study that was concerned with, among other things, sentence rhythm and the choice of word order. Another adjacent field was that of logic or dialectic. It was the dialectician rather than the grammarian who distinguished different types of utterance or, as we might now say, speech act: those which were true or false and others, such as commands or wishes, which he then excluded from his field. In a wider sense, there is as much 'linguistics' in the unfinished dialectical treatise of Augustine (354–430 AD) as in either of the grammatical manuals which the manuscript tradition also ascribes to him.[7] By the end of our period grammar, rhetoric and dialectic already formed the 'trivium' or first three of the seven 'liberal arts'.[8] None was wholly concerned with what we now call linguistics. But none was wholly unconcerned with it.

There are similar difficulties in the period before grammar was established. Some linguistic terms, such as those for 'letter' and 'syllable', are prehistoric. If we ask, more generally, when linguistic analysis began, one answer would put it as early as 1000–800 BC, with the insights into the phonological structure of Greek that underlay the invention of the alphabet. Other categories, such as gender or tense, are identified from the fifth century BC onwards; many by, in particular, the middle of the third. The treatment of individual topics in grammar, and in some cases the definitive treatment, precedes its formal institution. There are also early signs of theoretical speculation. One persistent preoccupation of ancient scholarship is the search for etymological motivation for the meanings of words: this is familiar to Latinists from the encyclopaedic surveys of Varro (116–27 BC) and, at the very end of our period, of Isidore of Seville, and its validity or non-validity is still a topic for Augustine in the late fourth century AD. But the practice itself is already evident in the earliest Greek poetry, especially in attempts to explain the names of Gods.[9] If we seek the origins not of grammar but of theoretical linguistics, a possible answer is that it begins as soon as we can see such interest in the nature of the vocabulary. Yet another answer – and this is arguably the best – would date it from the formulation of serious problems in the philosophy of language. That is due, in particular, to the Sophists in the fifth century BC and to Plato (c.429–347 BC), who argued against them.

But the academic framework, where there is one, is simply that of 'philosophy' (*philosophía*). In origin a philosopher was literally a lover (*philo-*) of wisdom (*sophía*); and, as Plato makes clear in the *Republic*, his interest was in *sophía* as a whole, and not merely in one aspect or another. In the truest sense he is a contemplator of truth.[10] Both Plato and Aristotle (384–322 BC) are rightly seen as major figures in the early development of our subject. But the former, in particular, deals with questions of language in contexts that, in modern and not just in ancient terms, are philosophical and not linguistic. In calling himself a *philósophos* or philosopher, Plato was particularly concerned to distinguish his aims and those of his teacher Socrates (469–399 BC) from what, in his representation, were the mercenary objectives of the sophists. But the term *sophistês* or 'sophist' is another transparent derivative of *sophía* (compare *grammatistês* from *grámma*) and referred to a teacher of practical wisdom, especially of verbal expertise in argument.[11] Where their theories are important to us, it is precisely because they too are 'philosophical'.

Two or three generations after Aristotle, philosophy was divided by Zeno of Citium (335–263 BC) into three parts: the first is 'logic' (*tò logikón* 'the logical [part]') and the others ethics and physics (*tò ethikón, tò phusikón*).[12] Zeno's followers were the Stoics, and it is within Stoic logic, particularly that of Chrysippus (c.280–207 BC), that much of the analysis that was later incorporated into the grammatical tradition has its origin. But the term which refers to this part of philosophy is derived from a base (*lógos*) whose modern translations are Protean, and neither it, nor its own parts and sub-parts as the Stoics conceived them, will fit into any later scheme of disciplines. On one view it is to be regretted that the study of language developed within philosophy, and within logic in particular. According to some commentators, ancient linguistics never freed itself from this initial contamination. But it would be as reasonable or as unreasonable to claim that ancient logic is contaminated by linguistics. In the later period grammar is a discipline concerned with language, to be distinguished from dialectic and rhetoric, which were also concerned with language. Our problem is simply that none of these terms meant in antiquity exactly what they mean now. For the Stoics and their predecessors the only comparable subject is one which subsumed all three. Within it what we now call logic and what we now call grammar are not distinct.

### 1.1.2 The sources

Our second problem is that of sources, and for this purpose we can adopt a conventional division of antiquity into three periods. The first or Classical period ends with the death of Alexander the Great in 323 BC; its intellectual history is that of the original Greek-speaking states, and is centred above all in Athens. The Hellenistic period ends with the battle of Actium in 31 BC, which brought the last of the successor states to Alexander's empire under direct Roman rule. In this period Greek civilization was extended to areas that were not originally Greek-speaking, and Alexandria, in particular, is another major intellectual centre. The third or Imperial period may conveniently be said to end with the abandonment of Latin in the administration of the Eastern empire. From then on the Greek tradition has little direct influence on the study of Latin until the Renaissance.

For the Imperial period we have important works from the first century AD onwards. We have already referred to the *Institutio Oratoria* or 'Training of a Public Speaker' of Quintilian, in which, at the beginning, the place and scope of grammar are already firmly established. In the next century the works of Apollonius Dyscolus survive in part: in particular, the bulk of his four books on syntax (*perì suntákseōs*), and shorter monographs on pronouns, adverbs and conjunctions. Where his doctrine is not known directly, the gap is often supplied by the Latin grammar of Priscian, writing in Constantinople in the early sixth century, who takes Apollonius as his model. We also have an extensive series of shorter Latin grammars, of which the two by Donatus, in the fourth century, subsequently achieved remarkable fame and influence. The scope and material of grammars in this tradition show a strong family resemblance, down to detailed wording and the choice of examples. It is therefore possible to reconstruct their chronology and other relationships between them, by methods not unlike those applied to manuscript traditions. Various grammarians also refer by name to predecessors whose work is lost; on this evidence, the content of grammatical instruction in the West can to a fair extent be traced back to its beginning, in a comprehensive grammar by Remmius Palaemon, which we know from Quintilian and others to have been composed in the first century AD.[13]

For the Classical period we have, in particular, the dialogues of Plato. His *Cratylus* deals specifically with the relation between words and things, and is the only complete text on the philosophy of language that has come down to us. But there are important passages in other dialogues, notably the *Sophist*. For Plato's contemporaries and immediate predecessors we depend on his own testimony and that of others to whom their writings and oral teaching were still familiar. We therefore see them largely through the eyes of their critics, whose own theories, in consequence, are partly disembodied. Nevertheless, we are fortunate in having texts of such significance which stand so close to the beginnings of rational

inquiry in our field. In the next generation, the surviving works of
Aristotle include two summary treatises, the *Poetics* and the *De
Interpretatione* (*perì hermeneías* or 'On Exposition') with important
paragraphs on the theory of the sentence and its parts. Aristotle's
contributions to the theory of language, here and elsewhere, are
very brief. But they are a starting point for the work of later
philosophers, and we are again fortunate in having them. From the
early period we also know of arguments on the origin of language
by Democritus (born c.460 BC), one of the two founders of the
atomic school of philosophy. But his works are lost, and we
depend on a late commentator.

When we turn to the Hellenistic period, this is unfortunately our
usual predicament. Among the followers of Democritus we have a
summary paragraph by Epicurus (341–270 BC) on the origin of
language; this can be linked with other accounts, especially that of
the Roman poet Lucretius (94–55 BC). But for the Stoic school,
whose work on grammatical categories in particular is crucial to the
history of this period, we depend entirely on secondary testimony.
Our main source, and our only connected exposition, is in a textbook
compilation on the lives and theories of eminent philosophers,
written by Diogenes Laertius (probably third century AD). This was
itself composed on the basis of earlier secondary sources, and is safe
only to the extent that they are safe.[14] For the origin of grammar as
such we have a text traditionally ascribed to Dionysius Thrax which,
if genuine, is vitally important. We have already cited its definition
of grammar, which is generally accepted. But the sections which
follow deal with letters, syllables, nouns, verbs and other parts of
speech in a way that is not only unrelated to this definition, but also
strikingly similar to their treatment by Donatus and other grammarians of the late Empire. If they are genuine, then grammatical
description had already been fixed at least in one tradition, by the
end of the second century BC, and the subsequent history is largely
that of sheep following sheep. But an alternative explanation is that
this material was attached to Dionysius' name, perhaps by a process
of rewriting or mangling an existing treatise, in the period after
Apollonius Dyscolus. As a compendium it is very neat and, like the
grammars of Donatus, it has had immense influence. But it is not
safe to take it as evidence for Dionysius' own time.[15]

If this text is rejected, the only substantial source for linguistic
analysis in this period is the *De Lingua Latina* ('On the Latin
Language') of Varro, from the mid first century BC. Only a
fragment survives (six books, with lacunae, of an original 25), and
we are obliged to read it largely out of context, except for that
which Varro himself supplies.

Given the deficiencies in our sources, and the discrepancies between ancient categories of inquiry and our own, no survey of ancient linguistics can entirely escape a charge of distortion. A balanced history is not possible, or possible only at a general level.[16] It is clear, for instance, that the earliest grammarians borrowed many categories from Stoic philosophy. But it is hard to say in detail what they borrowed and what adaptations they made: our sources for Stoic doctrine are inadequate, the earliest grammatical texts are arguably three centuries after the event, and no ancient doxographer himself addresses this issue. One has the sense that Apollonius Dyscolus was an original scholar, who did not merely sort through and rearrange existing lore. But what of his predecessors? Some of them are named in argument; but although this tells us what they thought when Apollonius does not agree with them, we do not know how much of that which he presents uncontroversially was common property. These are problems arising purely from our lack of primary sources, and both lie within the central field of grammar. But we also have to consider the scope of our inquiry. We can scarcely include a full account of ancient rhetoric. But if we then deal with some parts of rhetorical theory, we are tearing them out of context. And which parts should be covered? The analysis of language is concerned not only with the sentence, but also with long stretches of discourse. Should we therefore consider the ancient division of forensic speeches, into a prooemium, a narrative section, and so on? Within the sentence, our modern discipline is concerned with word order. But should ancient linguistics, or the projection onto ancient scholarship of what we now call linguistics, be taken to include the ordering of words as dictated by euphony? In other cases both our sources and our categories of thought may be an obstacle. We do not know exactly what place the classification of grammatical categories played in Hellenistic literary scholarship. It may be that, because these scholars called themselves grammarians, our whole perception of this period is anachronistic. But we have too little evidence either to confirm this or to remedy it.

There is no ideal solution to these difficulties. A partial solution, however, is to stay as close as possible to the texts that do survive, and in particular to those that are important either as primary contributions or for their influence in later periods. An example of the former is Plato's *Cratylus*, which we will discuss in section 1.3; of the latter, the *Ars Minor* and *Ars Maior* of Donatus, whose contents will be summarised in subsection 1.6.1. We may then adopt a plan which is in part historical and in part thematic. The short section which follows (1.2) deals with ancient treatments of phonetics and phonology. This is taken first because that aspect of language was apparently the first to be analysed. But it is a field in which there is little discernible history, and we will therefore draw equally on sources from Plato, in the early fourth century BC, to Priscian, in the early sixth AD. Section 1.3 is concerned with the relationship of words to things and with the connected topics of etymology and the origin of language. This concentrates on Plato, the other primary contributions run effectively from the fifth century BC to the first. We then deal, in section 1.4, with the analysis of the sentence into parts, first in a philosophical context (here our starting point will again be Plato) and subsequently, and for different reasons, in grammars. In the course of this, we move decisively out of the classical period, and out of the period in which the study of language is an undefined aspect of *philosophia* or intellectual inquiry in general. We will then grasp a nettle which, in a survey of this length and character, we are virtually obliged to grasp, and concentrate, for the bulk of the last two sections, on ancient grammar. In section 1.5 we are concerned with its origins in Hellenistic scholarship: in particular with the Stoics, with the literary grammarians themselves, and with the wider status of Greek in this period. Finally, in section 1.6, we will examine selected grammatical texts from the Empire. This section is necessarily longer than the others, since there is no other period from which so much material survives.

At the very end of this survey subsection (1.6.2) we will try to extract and summarize an ancient model for the description of language. It must be stressed, however, that if there was no discipline that we can properly equate with linguistics, still less was there any distinct concept of linguistic theory. A Greek grammarian was simply concerned with Greek, not with language or languages generally. When Apollonius Dyscolus, for example, proposes a semantic explanation for phenomena in Greek syntax (see the latter half of subsection 1.6.1), his account is internal to that language and, as a theory of wider application, is often invalidated even by Latin. Indeed there is no reason to suppose that Apollonius knew Latin: when the Romans conquered the Eastern Mediterranean Greek remained the normal working language and the sole language of ordinary education, and continued so throughout the Empire. In the West Greek was, in principle, taught alongside Latin and it was a mark of education to be 'eloquent in both languages'.[17] The Latin grammarians could accordingly make practical use of Greek (for example, to distinguish by translation different senses of Latin words); they occasionally compare grammatical categories in Latin with those of Greek; and, more seriously, their analyses are adapted, directly or ultimately, from a Greek original. But what resulted from this transferral was, again, simply a grammar of Latin.

Nor was there any occasion, until some centuries after our period, to adapt the model of either Greek or Latin grammar to any other language. The Hellenistic states had one official language, which was Greek, and the Roman Empire just two, which were Greek and Latin. Therefore the grammarians, who became part of the official educational system, were concerned with linguistic and literary training in these languages only. Nor did they have to teach then to beginners: their pupils were members of an urban community which spoke Greek or Latin already and who had already attended primary classes. This too does not change until some centuries after the collapse of the Western Empire, when the tradition of Latin grammar had to be adapted in areas where the native language was entirely Germanic.[18] Other languages were still spoken locally in many provinces. But neither a grammarian nor any other educator had the slightest professional reason to be interested in them.

In these respects the Roman Empire is very different from the colonial empires of the post-medieval period. From the sixteenth century onwards there is a natural connection between the grammatical tradition and the description and reduction to writing of unfamiliar languages. One thinks immediately of the way in which the Spanish grammar of Nebrija was used as a model by missionaries in Central and South America. It is also natural to think of a grammar book as an aid to learning a new language. But such connections would have seemed strange to the scholars and schoolmasters by whom the tradition was originally developed and transmitted. Between the different parts of what we now think of as linguistics and the applications of linguistics there was, once again, no continuity.

## 1.2 Phonetics and phonology

The Greek alphabet is the first script which has independent letters for both consonants and vowels. Its precursor was a North Semitic script which represented consonants only; and the crucial step in its invention was to dispense with certain unneeded consonant symbols and use them for vowels instead. Whoever did this had a clear appreciation of the exigencies of the Greek language; there are many words which would be null or unrecognizable if the vowels were omitted. In its developed form the alphabet also represented a series of consonantal distinctions that are peculiar to Greek, between aspirated $p^h$, $t^h$ and $k^h$ (both the first and the last required new letters) and unaspirated $p$, $t$ and $k$. Conversely, it tended to suppress letters which did not mark distinctions; the most persistent was the symbol for a Semitic uvular stop, whose continuation is the Roman 'q'. The Classical Greek alphabet still falls short of a complete phonemic transcription. It originally had no symbols for the accent or initial $h$; it included letters such as ξ (Roman $x$) which were known to represent a cluster of two elements; length was distinguished for only two of the five vowel qualities. Nevertheless, both it and the Semitic systems which preceded it show remarkable practical insights.[19]

The societies which used the Greek and subsequently the Latin alphabet became increasingly literate. Writing was not a preserve of priests and professional scribes; in the sixth century Greek mercenaries left their names as graffiti on a building in Egypt, and Athenians voted for the expulsion of a citizen by writing his name on a potsherd. Under the Roman Empire literacy was a requirement for service in the legions. They were therefore societies in which the analysis of speech by writing exerted an early and continuing influence on thought. A hundred years before Plato, the Pythagoreans appear to have developed a hierarchy of musical units in which the levels were compared to those of speech, the *sumphōníai* or concordant intervals to syllables, and the *harmoníai* (musical modes or styles) to word types.[20] Plato himself uses the terms for syllable and speech-elements (*sullabé, stoikheîon*) without explanation; presumably they could be taken for granted in educated conversation. In an important passage, Socrates is represented as arguing that whereas syllables can be explained in terms of speech sounds (thus the first syllable of his own name can be analysed into $s$ and $ō$), the speech elements themselves have no explanation ($s$ and $ō$ are individually unanalysable). How can there be elements of elements?[21] The term *stoikheîon* 'speech element' is from a noun *stoîkhos*, which referred to a line or file of people; the allusion is precisely to the linear arrangement of letters. But the unanalysability of letters provided a model for the similarly unanalysable elements of physics, and both it and the Latin *elementum*, which is also a term derived from writing, have both senses. It is a striking instance of a notion that is originally linguistic extending into a much wider field.[22]

Plato also employs a basic classification of letters or speech elements into sounding (*phōnḗenta*) and non-sounding (*áphōna*). In the grammarians these terms are part of a settled taxonomy, in which the primary criterion is whether a letter can form a syllable on its own. Those that can are *phōnḗenta* 'vowels' (Lat. *vocales*);

those that cannot are consonants (*súmphōna*, Lat. *consonantes*; literally 'sounding in conjunction'). A secondary criterion is whether a letter is physically pronounceable in isolation. Vowels are; but so are consonants such as *s* or Latin *f*, the 'liquids' *l*, *m*, *n* and *r*, and 'double letters' such as *x* [ks] and Greek *ψ* [ps]. These are therefore 'half vowels' (*hēmíphōna*, Lat. *semivocales*). The *áphōna* (Lat. *mutae* 'mute' or 'silent' consonants) are those that can neither form a syllable nor be pronounced on their own: thus stop consonants such as *p* or *b* (also the Latin *h*). The classification is evidently old. All three terms are in Aristotle, the vowels and half-vowels both having an audible sound and the mutes and half-vowels both having a constriction (*prosbolé*).

He does not use the term 'half vowel', but draws what is apparently a similar distinction between *áphōna* that are also *áphthogga*, 'speechless' and those that are not 'speechless' (conversely, those that are 'noises' and those that are not even 'noises').[23]

For the rest we can begin where ancient writers themselves began, with vocal sound (*phōné*, *vox*) in general. This is defined either physically, as air that is struck or set in motion, or as perceived by the hearer: a formulation in these terms is cited from the Stoic Diogenes of Babylon (c.240–152 BC), and the properties are similarly combined in the definition given by the Latin grammarians Charisius and Diomedes (fourth century AD), the latter mentioning the Stoics as his source. Democritus had earlier defined it as a stream of atoms. Vocal sound in man differs from that of animals. According to Diogenes of Babylon, the latter is air set in motion 'under an impulse'; the former is articulate (literally 'jointed' or 'having distinct members') and is set in motion by thought. The grammarians generally define 'articulate' as 'representable by letters'; a sound that cannot be written down is non-discrete or 'inarticulate'. Priscian has a more elaborate classification in which, for example, a human whistle is at once articulate, since it signifies something in the mind of the whistler, but not representable by writing.[24]

Our source for Diogenes of Babylon also cites a form that became the standard theory of the letter. According to this a letter has three aspects. One is its name: for example, the Greek letter *α* has the name *álpha*. Another is its written shape or character (Lat. *figura*). The third is its 'power' or 'value' (Lat. *potestas*). In Priscian's account this includes both its pronunciation and its distribution (*ordo*). Thus 'u' can be pronounced either long or short; it can also have the value of a consonant ([w] as in *uis* 'force'); and it can form the second member of the diphthongs *au* and *eu*. It is because of the pronunciations, Priscian remarks, that both the name and the written shape are invented.[25]

Name, shape and power are variable properties of the letter, in the same sense that case and number, for example, are variable properties of the noun. The letter itself is identified effectively in two ways. The basic definition of the grammarians equates it with the *stoikheîon* or speech element: the 'smallest part' or 'element' (Charisius) of an articulate vocal sound. Similarly, in our source for Diogenes of Babylon, the elements of speech are 'the twenty-four letters'. It is accordingly a unit of sound, comparable – at least in respect of indivisibility – to the modern 'phoneme'. This tradition continues well into the modern era. But a letter is also a written mark: the 'mark of the speech element' or 'an image as it were' of the vocal sound (Priscian). The terms 'letter' and 'element' are therefore strictly distinguishable. As Priscian explains, the statement that a syllable cannot begin with *rp* is not, properly speaking, a statement about letters. We can write such a sequence with no difficulty. It is a statement about the pronunciations: we cannot utter an [r] and a [p] together unless the order is reversed. These pronunciations are the elements.[26]

In fact, as Priscian says, the confusion is general. His own initial definition of the letter is in the standard tradition: 'the smallest part of a vocal sound that is representable by letters'. Our text of (pseudo-) Dionysius Thrax has a section headed 'On the speech-element' (*perì stoikheíou*), which begins 'there are twenty-four letters (*grámmata*) . . .'[27] For a treatment comparable to that of Priscian we can turn to Diomedes. Like the other grammarians, he begins by defining the letter as the smallest part of an articulate vocal sound; he adds that it 'has its origin in an element (*elementum*) and can be marked by a single shape (*figura*)'. The *elementum* is then defined as the 'smallest force and indivisible substance of an articulate vocal sound'; as an alternative, he gives the definition of elements in general. 'Its shape', he continues, 'is called a letter, and all the shapes of letters number twenty three; but their values (*potestates*), which we call elements, are understood to be many more'. Like Priscian, he ends by reinforcing the distinction. The element is 'the force itself and the value', while the letter is the shape corresponding to the value. Accordingly, 'what is understood is the element, what is written is the letter'.[28]

In short, the grammarians were trying to maintain a distinction between speech and writing, but within a tradition in which the letter had been defined indiscriminately. In consequence, both *littera* and *elementum* have a certain resemblance to the twentieth-century 'phoneme'. But for neither is the translation wholly appropriate. On the one hand, the letters of the alphabet did not give a complete phonemic transcription. On the other hand, the elements were said to include varying phonetic values: for example, the pronunciation of a vowel when accented or unaccented.

The treatment of phonetics is likewise only partially successful. In the late first century BC a rhetorical writer, Dionysius of Halicarnassus, gives a reasonably clear description of many of the Greek consonants. For example, in the pronunciation of *m* the mouth is 'pressed together at the lips' and the breath is 'partly through the nostrils'. In particular, he distinguishes three positions of articulation for stop consonants: 'from the extremity of the lips', 'with the tongue pressed against the front of the mouth at the upper teeth', 'with the tongue rising to the palate near the throat'. In each position there is the same distinction into three types ($p/p^h/b$, $t/t^h/d$, $k/k^h/g$). Dionysius also gives a partial account of the articulation of long vowels. The long $\bar{a}$, he says, is the most euphonious, 'the mouth being opened to the maximum and the breath carried up towards the palate'. The $\bar{\imath}$ is the least euphonious: 'the breath is set in motion in the area of the teeth with the mouth opened to the minimum and the sound unadorned by the lips'.[29] In the next century Quintilian points out that there are phonetic distinctions that are not shown by the Latin orthography: for example, the second vowel in *optimus* 'best' is between *u* and *i* (perhaps [*i*]). There is also some recognition of what we would now call allophones. Quintilian remarks that *m* is 'barely expressed' in final position before a vowel; and Priscian cites Pliny the Elder (25/24–79 AD) for a distinction between three forms of *l*, a 'thin' pronunciation – the term is also used of front vowels – when doubled intervocalically, a 'full' pronunciation – a term also used of back vowels – at the ends of words or syllables, and an intermediate pronunciation elsewhere.[30]

But there are clear inadequacies, of which the most striking was a failure to understand the mechanism of voicing. Of the nine Greek plosive consonants, three were aspirated ($p^h$, $t^h$ and $k^h$) and three unaspirated (*p*, *t* and *k*). In ancient terminology the former were 'rough' (*dasús*), and are described by Dionysius of Halicarnassus as having added breath; the latter are 'smooth' (*psilós*). These terms were also used for the presence or absence of [h] before vowels (called 'rough' and 'smooth breathings'). The *b*, *d* and *g* were then classed as 'intermediate' (*mésos*). In the formulation of (pseudo-) Dionysius Thrax, they are 'rougher than the smooth and smoother than the rough'. The assumption must be that they were voiced, but this account offers scant evidence for it. In Latin there were two stop consonants in each series, which corresponded phonetically to the 'smooth' (voiceless) and 'intermediate' (voiced) in the Greek system. In ignorance of the true distinction – an ignorance that was to continue until the modern era – the grammarians sometimes grope for supralaryngeal differences. For example, Terentianus Maurus, whose verse treatises on letters, syllables and metres were composed in the late second century AD, says that *t* should be pronounced at the top of the teeth and *d* as a true dental, with the tongue curving from the lower teeth to the upper.[31]

Nor do the grammarians give what we would consider a satisfactory account of the syllable. Both Latin and Greek distinguished what are traditionally called 'long' and 'short' syllables. For example, in Latin *arma* 'weapons' the first syllable is long because it ends in a consonant (*ar*-); it is also long in *rēte* 'net', in this case because it ends in a long vowel (*rē*-). But in *mare* 'sea' it is short, because it ends in a short vowel (*mă*-). This is a modern account whose only defect is that the same terms are traditionally used for both syllable length and vowel length. But ancient treatments are rather different. On the one hand, the Roman grammarians did in practice have a richer terminology: whereas a syllable is either *longa* 'long' or *brevis* 'short', its vowel, which in Latin had the same written shape whatever its quantity, is usually described as either 'drawn out' (*producta*) or 'abbreviated' (*correpta*). On the other hand, the rules do not refer to the divisions between syllables. In the summary account of Donatus, the first syllable of *arma* is long because the vowel, though 'abbreviated', is followed by two consonants. It is likewise long in *axis* 'axle', because the *a* is followed by a 'double' consonant, one which corresponded to two 'elements' [ks]. In such cases the syllable is said to be long 'by position', whereas syllables which contained a 'drawn out' vowel or diphthong were long 'by nature'. In *mare* the first syllable was short because the abbreviated *a* is followed by only one consonant. Similarly, the syllable of *et* would be short in *et arma* 'and weapons' (*e* followed by the single consonant *t*), but long in *et mare* 'and the sea' (*e* followed by *t* plus *m*). Donatus does not in fact say anything about the actual syllable boundaries (*ar-ma* and so on).[32]

Other grammarians do. For example, Charisius gives the same rule for a vowel followed by two consonants, adding that sometimes they are both in the same syllable (*ars* 'art') whereas in *arma*, for instance, they are in two different syllables. But syllabification and quantity were for the most part treated independently. The latter was of particular importance because it formed the basis for classical verse metre; the rules we have cited are good practical indications by which, provided the length of vowels is known, a pupil can learn to scan lines correctly. They are regularly followed by cases where a syllable could, in verse, be scanned as either long or short (for example, the first syllable of *lacrimae* 'tears'), and in Donatus the next section deals with metrical feet. Here as elsewhere we must remember that the origins of grammar lie in literary education, and not in a disinterested structural analysis of the language. Syllabification is of practical importance mainly for dividing words at the end of lines. The implied criterion was whether the sequence of consonants could begin an initial syllable: *rm* cannot and therefore *arma* was divided *ar-ma*; but *gr*, for example, could and therefore a word like *agrī* 'fields' was seen as syllabically *a-grī*. Similarly, Charisius has *a-mnis* 'river' and *a-xis* 'axle'. In fact, so far as Latin is concerned, initial *mn* and *x* are found only in loan words from Greek.[33]

Finally, it has to be noted that in the late Imperial period the grammarians were describing a written language whose spoken form had already diverged markedly. In the Classical period Greek had a distinction between a high pitch in, for example, *moûsās* (accusative plural of the word for 'Muse') and a falling pitch in, for example, *moûsa* (nominative singular); in the Alexandrian period these were marked in writing, as shown, by the acute accent and the circumflex. But the Roman tradition then talks of an acute and circumflex in Latin: Priscian, for example, draws a similar distinction between the dative/ablative plural and the nominative singular of the word for 'hook' (*hámīs*, with a long vowel in the final syllable, but *hâmus*, with a short). Now it is conceivable that the Latin stress was realized in that way. But there is no other evidence that it was so, and it is generally assumed that the grammarians were simply imitating their Greek models. They were therefore teaching something which in Latin itself was quite artificial. But in extenuation it is worth remarking that a grammarian such as Priscian would not have heard the contrast which was still being inculcated by his Greek counterparts. For, on evidence from the late fourth century, the Greek language had already developed a single stress accent in place of both the earlier pitch phonemes.[34]

## 1.3 The status and origin of words

If the first Greek 'linguists' were the unknown men who developed the alphabet, our first 'linguistic' text is Plato's *Cratylus*, composed at some time (its place in Plato's *oeuvre* is not certain) in the first half of the fourth century BC.[35] At the beginning of the dialogue, Socrates joins two contemporaries, Hermogenes and Cratylus, who are disputing the relationship of language to reality. The dispute should be seen in the context of a general opposition in fifth

century thought, between 'law' (*nómos*) and 'nature' (*phúsis*). Cratylus takes the view that words or names are correct 'by nature'
(*phúsei*); the principles of correctness are accordingly the same for
all societies, Greek and non-Greek. Similarly, the view could be
held that there are principles of conduct which transcend the laws
made in particular circumstances. But Hermogenes cannot be per-
suaded that the correctness of words has any basis other than
convention and agreement (*suntheke, homología*); no word is given
by nature, but by the law and custom (*nómoi, éthei*) of those who
habitually use it.[36]

The ensuing discussion falls into two physically unequal parts. In
the first three-quarters of the dialogue Socrates articulates against
Hermogenes the theory that words are not, as we would now say,
arbitrary. In the last quarter he turns to Cratylus and argues, in
particular, that they cannot be an adequate guide to things. The
*Cratylus* is not an easy work and has had varying interpretations.
But in the context of Plato's general philosophy this last point is
vital.

### 1.3.1 The argument of 'Cratylus'

The extreme form of what we may call the Hermogenean view is
that, even if someone uses a word differently from the rest of his
community, for example by calling a 'man' what everyone else calls
a 'horse', that usage is correct for him privately. Socrates argues
against this that if statements are true or false their smallest parts,
which are the words, must also be true or false. He also connects it
with the view that the existence of things is relativistic: in the
famous dictum of the sophist Protagoras (c.490–420 BC), 'man is
the measure of all things'. Hermogenes agrees that this must be
wrong.[37]

Socrates then argues that speech is an action, like lighting a fire
or weaving. But actions are also part of reality, and are performed
not arbitrarily, but with their correct instruments. In the case of
speech these are words: a word is an instrument for giving information and separating forms of reality, just as, in weaving for example,
a shuttle is an instrument for dividing the web. Now shuttles are
made by a craftsman who is skilled in that work. In making them
he has in mind their function; his blueprint is something suited by
nature (*phúsei*) to be a shuttle. Similarly, there must be a craftsman
who makes words. Since, according to Hermogenes, words are a
matter of law (*nómos*), this must be the 'law-giver' (*nomothétes*).
Such a craftsman makes words for the imparter of information just
as a carpenter makes shuttles for the weaver, and, just as there are
different specific shuttles for specific kinds of cloth, so, as Cratylus

maintains, there are specific words, in Greek and in any other language, which are correct by nature for specific things. Finally, the craftsman must work to the instructions of a competent user. In the case of shuttles this is the weaver. In the case of words it is the *dialektikós* or 'dialectician', a man skilled in the practice of argument.

Hermogenes swallows all this, but would still like to be shown what is this 'correctness of words by nature'. Socrates first makes clear that he has no authority in the matter. But he begins, in a spirit of inquiry, by looking at proper names. In Homer's *Iliad* the son of Hector ('holder') is variously called Astyanax ('ruler of the city') and Scamandrios ('of the river Scamander'); but the first he argues, is more appropriate, on the principle that just as lions give birth to lions and horses to horses, so a human father will tend to beget a son whose character is like his own. 'Hector' and 'Astyanax' effectively mean the same, even though, as Socrates points out, the letters are largely different. Similarly, Iatrocles ('famous as physician') and Acesimbrotos ('healer of mortals') are both suitable names for a doctor.

Socrates is now seized by a fit of inspiration, and overwhelms Hermogenes with a flood of etymological explanations. The word for 'god' (*theós*) is from *theîn* 'to run'. The reason for this is that the first Greeks, like many foreign nations, took as their gods the sun and moon and so on; these were seen to be in constant motion (*théonta* 'running'), and therefore by their nature were called *theoí*. Man is an animal who examines and reflects on what is perceived; hence the word for 'man' (*ánthrōpos*) is appropriately derived from *anathrôn hà ópōpe* 'examining what it has seen'. Poseidon is the god of the sea, an element that restricts movement. He has, as it were, a shackle (*desmós*) on his feet (dative *posí*), and his name was thus appropriately based on *posídesmos*. The *e* is added for the sake of appearance. Other explanations are that he is a god 'knowing many things' (*pollà eidōn*); one need only replace the double *ll* with *s*. He is also the god who causes earthquakes and, if we add a *p* and *d*, can be seen as [*p*]*hò seî*[*d*]*ōn* 'the shaker'. The word for 'justice' (*dikaiosúnē*) is from *dikaíou súnesis* 'comprehension of [what is] just', and *díkaion* 'just' is in turn from *diaïón* 'penetrating', with a *k* for euphony. *Tékhnē*, 'skill' is from *héxis noû*, 'condition of mind'. The form is somewhat different, but Hermogenes must understand that the original words have been altered later for the sake of ornamentation, with letters added or deleted and so on. A final example is the derivation of *ón* 'being' from *ión* 'going'. This is one of many that are designed to fit the theory of Heraclitus (fl. 500 BC), whose most famous aphorism is

that 'Everything is in motion' (*pánta rheî*). Cratylus, whose side of
the argument Socrates is now taking, was a follower of Heraclitus.[38]

Opinions have differed as to how far Plato meant such derivations to be taken seriously. They have parallels in literary contexts:
for example, a character in a tragedy by Euripides (c.485–406 BC)
relates the name of the goddess of love, Aphrodite, to *aphrosúnē*,
'folly'.[39] In another dialogue Plato himself derives *érōs*, 'sexual
love' from *rhṓmē*, 'physical strength' and *mantikḗ*, 'prophecy'
from *manikḗ*, 'madness'.[40] But there are indications throughout
this section that Socrates does not believe what he is saying. He has
been listening that morning to a seer called Euthyphro; it must be
from him that he has contracted such miraculous wisdom. Tomorrow he will cure himself of it. His insights are so ingenious that he
is in danger, if he does not watch out, of becoming cleverer than he
ought to be. Hermogenes says that there is a chance that he has got
the god Hephaestus right – unless some other idea is going to occur
to him. Socrates replies that, to avoid this, he had better ask about
Ares, the god of war, instead.[41] We have, in addition, the evidence
of the etymologies themselves, which are as preposterous as anyone
might devise. The most convincing interpretation of this part of the
argument is that the practice of haphazard etymologizing was
usual at the time, that others had taken it seriously, especially in
the context of religion, and that Plato's object, in devoting nearly
half of the dialogue to illustrations of the sort that have been cited,
was to parody it into disrepute.

Inspired though he may be, Socrates cannot find appropriate
derivations for every word. In the case of 'fire' (*pûr*) the 'Muse of
Euthyphro' abandons him; he can only suggest that it might have
been borrowed from another language, perhaps Phrygian. Similarly
for *kakós*, 'bad'.[42] Other words may now be altered out of recognition. But appeals of that kind cannot finally solve the problem.
When all derived words have been traced to their sources, we will
be left with a set of simple words that cannot themselves be
analysed in the same way. These are elementary words (*stoikheîa*).
If they too are to be explained, some new approach is needed.

The answer, according to Socrates, must lie in a sophisticated
form of onomatopoeia.[43] If we were not able to speak we would
imitate things by gestures, raising up our hands to indicate lightness
or upwardness, mimicking the galloping of a horse, and so on.
Perhaps then words are vocal imitations. Now they are not so in a
crude sense: we do not utter the word for 'sheep' when we mimic
the sound 'baa'. But just as a painter mixes colours to represent the
colour of the objects he paints, so the original maker of words

(*onomastikós*) must have combined letters and syllables to represent the essence of the things referred to. A laughable idea, as Socrates admits; and neither he nor Hermogenes can understand how it might have been done. But we have to suppose this, if the theory of the correctness of words is to be defended. Socrates therefore suggests that *r*, for example, is a means of representing movement: thus *rheîn*, 'to flow' and *rhoé*, 'river', *trékhein*, 'to run'; also words like *kroúein*, 'to strike' or *thraúein*, 'to shatter'. This is because the tongue is shaken about and is not still (on this and later evidence a trilled [r]). The letter *i* is for small things, which can go through anything: hence *ienai* 'to go', whose participle (*ión*) we met earlier as the source of 'being' (*ón*). Breathy letters like *s* imitate, for example 'shaking' (infinitive *seíesthai*) or 'cold' (adjective *psukhrós*). In *d* and *t* the tongue is compressed and resistant: thus *desmós*, 'bond, shackle' and *stásis*, 'state, condition'. In the production of *l* it slips or glides: thus, for example, *liparós*, 'oily' or *kollódēs*, 'glutinous'; also, complemented by *g*, in *glískhros*, 'sticky' or *glukús*, 'sweet'. The letters *a* and *ē* are found in words for 'big' (stem *megál-*) and 'length' (*mêkos*) because they are big letters. This is how a *nomothétēs* or word-maker must have proceeded.[44]

After this brilliant tour de force Plato makes Cratylus speak for the first time. He is, of course, delighted with the way the argument has gone, whether Euthyphro or some other Muse has inspired it. But Socrates himself has misgivings about his own wisdom, and wants to check it carefully. The first point, they agree, is that words are correct in as much as they reveal the nature of things. Their function is to instruct, and that skill is practised by craftsmen who have been described as law-givers. But some craftsmen – for example, some painters – are better than others; is that not true of law-givers also? Cratylus denies that any law is superior to any other. Likewise for words: all words are correct or else they are not words at all. Nor can anyone speak falsely. One can say what is so but it is impossible to say what is not so. Suppose that someone were to greet him as Hermogenes. According to Cratylus he would be making pointless noises, banging a kettle.[45]

Socrates returns to the notion of imitation. Words, they agree, are imitations of things. So are paintings; but one might, for instance, mistake a painting of a man for that of a woman. Just as the painting has been connected with the wrong object, so, when we lie, we apply a word to the wrong object. Cratylus does not accept the parallel. But Socrates insists. If I say to someone, 'This is your portrait', perhaps it is or perhaps it is not. Similarly, if I say to someone, 'This is your name'. He then points out that by combining shapes and colours a painter may produce either a good or a poor likeness. Likewise our law-giver might, by combining letters and syllables, produce either a good or a poor word. Once more, there are good workmen and bad workmen. Cratylus replies that either the letters of a word are arranged correctly or, once again, what is written is not a word at all. But, says Socrates, any image must to some degree be imperfect. Suppose that a god were to make something identical in every respect with Cratylus. It would not be an image of him; there would simply be two Cratyluses instead of one. Still less can words be perfect images. If they were, we would have no way of telling which was word and which was thing. It is not necessary that every letter in a word should be appropriate, or every word in a discourse. A thing is still referred to if its general outline (*túpos* 'impression, cast, sketch, model') is there.[46]

Though not wishing to be fractious, Cratylus still does not accept that imperfect words can be words. But Socrates returns to their premises. A word (they agree) is an indication of a thing; some words are derived and some are primitive, and those that are primitive must indicate by resemblance. The only alternative is the view put forward by Hermogenes. The resemblance must lie in individual letters: for example, it had been suggested that *r* represents motion and hardness and *l* smoothness and softness. What then of the word for 'hardness'? In Athens one says *sklerótēs*, in Eretria *sklerotér*, but whether it has final *s* or *r* it is still understood. And it is understood as 'hard' even though the *l* should indicate the opposite. Cratylus replies that, as Socrates himself had argued earlier, letters can get altered in the course of time. But in that case the word 'hard' must be understood through custom (*éthos*), and how does that differ from convention (*sunthékē*)?[47] In such cases words do not indicate entirely by resemblance. In part at least, convention also comes in.

Socrates again asks Cratylus about the basic function of words; Cratylus repeats that it is to instruct, in the quite straightforward sense that someone who understands the words understands the things as well. Indeed it is the best and only way to know them; also to find out about them if they are not known already. But what, asks Socrates, if whoever made the words did not himself understand the nature of things? Cratylus replies that this is impossible: if the maker had been ignorant then, as he has said before, the words would not be words at all. Moreover, there is evidence that he was not mistaken, since all words have been seen to point in the same way. Cratylus is here alluding to the theory of Heraclitus, which Socrates' earlier etymologies had supported.

Socrates retorts that that is no argument: they might all reflect the same initial error. He then says that there are other words which do not support the theory of flux or motion. The word for 'knowledge' (*epistḗmē*) is from the verb 'to set' or 'to stand': it fixes (*hístēsi*) the mind on (*epí*) things. Likewise 'inquiry' (*historía*) fixes what was in flux, and *pistós*, 'trustworthy', means 'to stand firm' (*histán*) in all things. It is the words for bad qualities like stupidity (*amathía*) that point the other way: this refers to the course of someone 'going along with a god' (*háma theõi ióntos*).[48] Socrates thinks there are many other words which would suggest that their inventor signalled things not as moving but as standing still. He then asks how the original maker of words could himself have understood the nature of the things that they were to refer to. Cratylus answers that some superhuman power must have been responsible. But how can we now discover whether the true words are those which indicate that the world is static or those which indicate that it is in flux? There must be a way to learn about things other than through words; and if there is, that way must surely be better. Why learn from what is at best an image, rather than from the original directly? For Socrates the Heraclitean view cannot in any case be correct: there are unchanging ideals of beauty, of goodness and of all other forms of being, and it is of these alone that knowledge, which must itself be unchanging, is possible. But whichever view is correct, it would be senseless to trust in words for guidance.

### 1.3.2 The origin and nature of language

I have summarized the *Cratylus* consecutively, in the hope that I will have brought out both the flavour of the dialogue (frustrating or not, it is an enjoyable specimen of dialectic) and the range of issues that are in question. It has often been seen wrongly as a treatment of the origin of language.[49] However, the myth of an original name-giver, comparable to a partly legendary law-giver such as Solon, is introduced as a basis for argument. It is not simply a discussion of (in modern terms) the 'arbitrariness of language'. At the end of the dialogue Plato relates the argument to his theory of ideal forms or 'ideas', and he is at pains, as we have seen, to refute the belief that words are a way of getting at reality. Another important aspect of what we may call the Cratylean view is that it is impossible to speak falsely; this is a point we will return to at the beginning of the next section. But it is a tribute to Plato's success, in this and other dialogues, that no later generation had to grapple with the problem of language and reality in quite such a radical form. Many difficulties remained, but in the period after

Plato it is easier to distinguish separate lines of inquiry, of which some are in modern terms philosophical and others more clearly scientific.

One scientific problem is that of the historical origin of language. Greek religion has no developed myth which explains it – or, if there was one, it has not been preserved.[50] But a natural explanation is first attested in Plato's *Protagoras*. According to the view which Plato puts into the mouth of Protagoras, and which there is no reason to believe that he did not in fact hold, sounds and words, like buildings, beds or clothing, were the product of a technical wisdom (*éntekhnos sophía*) which distinguished man from other forms of creation. In the dialogue this forms the prelude to a general account of the evolution of societies.[51] A similar theory is presented as traditional in the general history of Diodorus Siculus (first century BC). Men were originally solitary and bestial; but to protect themselves from predators they began to band together and to recognize each other's character. Starting from a vocal expression that was meaningless and confused, they gradually articulated words and agreed on a token for every object, so that there was an accepted form of communication. This happened separately in many different places, and therefore there exist forms of speech (*diálektoi*) of diverse kinds. Diodorus then passes to the gradual invention of fire, buildings, agriculture and so on, to which man was driven by further experience and necessity.[52]

A fuller explanation was developed within the atomist tradition of natural philosophy. The views of its founders can only be inferred; but that of Epicurus is given briefly in a summary of his physical theories, reproduced by Diogenes Laertius.[53] In the beginning words were not created through conscious decision (*thései*), but in every community human nature produced sounds in an individual way in response to individual conditions and individual sense impressions. At a later stage such individual sounds were adopted generally in each society, so that things could be explained more briefly and with less ambiguity. Some were also aware of invisible things and introduced sounds for these, either under an impulse or on the most appropriate analogy. The first of these stages is further elaborated in the didactic poem by Lucretius, *De Rerum Natura* ('On the Nature of Things').[54] He points out that animals make different sounds in different circumstances: for example, a dog when it is growling or when it is barking, when it is with its young, or alone in the house, or being whipped; a stallion when in rut or in battle; birds when fighting or otherwise, or in different weathers. 'If varying feelings can force animals, dumb though they are, to emit varying sounds, how much more natural that man, with voice in full strength, should have been able to distinguish different things by one or another expression!'

Lucretius is arguing against the view that language was invented by a particular individual. For that he has no respect. How was this one man able to distinguish all things vocally when his contemporaries could not? If no other person had already made such use of vocal expression, how was the idea implanted in his mind and how did he initially grasp what he wanted to do? And how could he alone have made everyone else want to learn the words he had invented? It is not easy to teach the deaf; nor would it have been easy to get the rest of the community to attend to unfamiliar noises. In a similar vein Diogenes of Oenoanda, in the second century AD, ridicules the notion that some man could have gathered people together, in an age when there were no rulers, and taught them the meanings of sounds when no sounds or letters yet existed.[55] At the beginning of his argument Lucretius compares the gestures by which infants point out things. Like the young of other species they anticipate the use of their faculties. This is not so different from the way in which men were first driven into speech by nature and the exigencies of their situation.

For commentators of the Imperial and later periods, the issue is precisely whether words exist by nature (*phúsei*) or by imposition (*thései*, literally 'placing').[56] But it is important to distinguish the Epicurean theory of the evolution of language from the philosophical controversy in the *Cratylus*. As we have seen in our summary of Plato's dialogue, one possible view is that words are suited to things by nature (*phúsei*) because they were first created by an individual (Socrates' *nomothétēs*, literally 'law-placer')[57] with the necessary understanding. But it is logically possible for someone to invent and impose words whose relation to things is entirely conventional. As we can now see from the account of Epicurus, the view that language had its origin by nature (*phúsei*), in the way suggested by Lucretius, does not preclude some later social contract, whereby communication is determined for particular societies. Its proponent could in principle agree with Hermogenes, that in languages as they have finally evolved words are not correct by nature (*phúsei*), but only by agreement and convention. This may indeed have been the view of Democritus: we are told by the Neoplatonist Proclus (fifth century AD) that he was a conventionalist as regards the relation between words and things, on the grounds, for example, that the same form could be used of things which were different.[58]

On that issue it is the Hermogenean view that was eventually to triumph. For Aristotle an *ónoma* ('name', 'noun' or 'word' – the terms are not at this stage distinguished) is a token (*súmbolon* or symbol). Speech (*lógos*) 'is composed of words and each word is a token'. A noun in particular is 'a vocal sound signifying according to a convention' (*katà sunthḗkēn*); for they do not exist by nature (*phúsei*) but when a token is created. Aristotle compares inarticulate sounds, such as those of animals, in which there are no words.[59] The phrase *katà sunthḗkēn* 'according to a convention' picks up one of the terms used by Hermogenes at the beginning of Plato's *Cratylus*, and itself stands at the head of a long tradition. In late antiquity Boethius (c. 480–524 AD) gives the rendering *secundum placitum*, 'according to an agreement', and the medieval interpretation *ad placitum* ('secondo che v'abbella' in the mouth of Adam in the *Divine Comedy*) leads through the Renaissance to the modern concept of arbitrariness.[60] Although ideas and interpretations have varied, the terminological tradition has been continuous. Nor has the Cratylean side of the argument, which Aristotle appears to discount without further discussion, had any reputable modern successor.

But in antiquity the Stoics also posited a natural relationship between expressions and the meanings that they express, and in later scholarship the techniques of ancient etymology, in particular that of explaining the sense of one word by connecting its form to that of another word, continued to flourish. For the Stoics our sources are barely sufficient.[61] But the principles are amply illustrated, two centuries later, in the surviving work of Varro. According to Varro the study of a language has three parts, of which the first deals with the way in which words are assigned (*imposita*, translating the Greek sense of *thésis* or 'placing') to things. The books which justified his theory are among the many that are lost; his practice, however, could be cited at some length. For example, the word *caelum* 'sky' is derived from the adjective *cavum* 'hollow'; so too, among others, is *caverna* 'cave'. For the first Varro mentions but rejects alternative derivations proposed by Lucius Aelius Stilo (fl. 200 BC), one from *caelare* 'to raise up' (it might perhaps seem better if the connection were reversed) and the other from *celare* 'to hide' (because the sky is not hidden). *Terra* 'earth', and here he follows Aelius, is so called because it is trodden down (*teritur*); likewise *iter* 'way', and just as an *actus* 'cattle drove' is a way worn down by driving (*agendo*) so a *via* 'road' is worn down by transporting (*vehendo*). The god Jupiter is the father (*pater*) because he makes visible (*patefacit*) the semen, and his consort Juno 'helps' (*iuvat*) 'together with' (*una*) him. *Testudo* 'tortoise' is from *testa* ('pot, shell'); less reasonably, *lolligo* 'squid' is an alteration of *volligo*, so called because it 'flies underneath' (*subvolat*). An otter (*lutra*), whose behaviour is confused with that of the beaver, is an animal which 'looses' (*luit*) trees from the bank. These examples are from the opening sections of a systematic survey of the Latin vocabulary, whose first part deals with space and objects occupying space (the world in general, physical features, place names, names of gods, of animals, and so on) and second part with time and actions taking place through time.[62] At the outset Varro says that he will deal both with what the Greeks call *etumología*, the study of the 'true' sense of words, and with meanings (*sēmainómena*, 'things signified'), concentrating on the former.[63] It is clear from his own treatment, from his references to earlier writers, including both Stoics and Alexandrians,[64] that such explanations illustrate a serious and continuing tradition.

We also find a continuing interest in sound symbolism and other symbolic explanations. We are told, for example, that the Roman scholar Publius Nigidius Figulus, a contemporary of Varro, proposed a gestural account of the Latin words for 'we' (*nos*) and plural 'you' (*vos*). In the latter, which was phonetically [wo:s], we gradually protrude the edges of our lips and direct our breath forward towards the people with whom we are talking. But in the former we do not protrude the lips and the breath is not poured forth and directed; instead we restrain the lips and breath 'as it were within ourselves'. In this way the movements of the mouth and air are suited to the opposite senses. Our source selects this as an attractive and witty example, from among many arguments which purported to show that words were constituted by nature (*naturalia*, by *phúsis*) and were not arbitrary (*arbitraria*, by *thésis*).[65]

A modern reader will find such explanations less witty than ridiculous. It is also very easy to disparage the ancient practice of etymology, which from the viewpoint of historical etymology as we have known it since the nineteenth century was opportunistic and without system. But we must consider carefully where the error lies. Ancient etymology was not intended to be historical, and in that sense does not represent a bad practice that has been supplanted in modern times by good practice. It was an attempt to discover the true relation (the adjective *étumos* means 'true' or 'genuine') between an expression and its content. However we may criticize the practice, the basic fault lay in the theoretical assumption that such truths are there to be discovered.

## 1.4 Elements of the sentence

One of the most puzzling side issues in the *Cratylus*, at least to a layman or to a philosopher of any later period, is the insistence by

Cratylus that, just as words are either correct by nature or not words at all, so anything said is either true or else a series of meaningless noises. We can connect this with an argument by Socrates, towards the beginning of the dialogue, that if statements are true or false their parts must also be true or false.[66] In both cases there is a failure, as we would now see it, to distinguish the character of terms from that of propositions. Plato's remedy of this confusion forms one episode in his later dialogue *The Sophist*, and involves the earliest attested analysis of a sentence construction. It is therefore connected by most commentators with the later development of what were called in antiquity the 'parts' or 'elements of a sentence' (*mérē lógou*, Lat. *partes orationis*) or, in the far less perspicuous translation which is usual in the modern tradition, the 'parts of speech'.

We will deal first with the philosophical problem; then with the subsequent emergence of parts of speech systems; then with the system as we find it in the extant work of the grammarians.

### 1.4.1 The philosophical context

The argument that one cannot speak falsely seems to have been widespread in the fifth century. It is ascribed by Aristotle to Antisthenes (c.455–c.360 BC), with the corollary that one cannot contradict.[67] In Plato's *Euthydemus* these views are put into the mouths of two low-grade sophists, Euthydemus and Dionysodorus; in questioning them, however, Socrates remarks that he has heard their argument from many people, that the followers of Protagoras made great use of it, and that others had used it before him. In the *Cratylus* itself, he says that the notion that one cannot lie has been held by 'many people, both now and in the past'.[68] Our sources for this argument and for the sophists' other problems with language are secondary and incomplete. But it does seem that they had stumbled into a genuine philosophical difficulty.[69]

The problem is one of many that sprang, wholly or in part, from a failure to discriminate different senses of the Greek verb 'to be'. Its basic uses were as a copula or in the sense of English 'there is': 'The wine is sweet', 'There is a city which . . .' But in philosophical writing it had developed an absolute sense: 'There are (no) gods', 'Gods (do not) exist'. The consequences of not distinguishing these were serious for Presocratic philosophy generally, but are illustrated in a particularly naive form by the passage immediately before the argument in the *Euthydemus*. Socrates would like the boy Clinias to be taught to be wise, and therefore 'to be not ignorant' (*amathê mề eînai*). But, according to Dionysodorus, that means that he would like Clinias 'no longer to be' (*mēkéti eînai*). That is, he

would like him to be dead.[70] The mistake that we are concerned
with is more subtle. But part of the difficulty is that a true
statement was seen holistically as a statement about 'that which is'.
Accordingly, a false statement would be about 'that which is not'.
That is, it would be about the non-existent.

Another difficulty is that the term *lógos*, which I have just
translated 'statement', had in fact a very much wider sense.[71] In
form it is related, by a transparent change of vowel, to the root of
*légein* 'to say', and in the later grammatical tradition can easily be
rendered by the modern 'sentence'. That is how I have translated it
in the collocation *mérē lógou* 'elements of a sentence' in the first
paragraph of this section. But 'something said' may be an argument: for example, we are now dealing with the argument (*lógos*)
that a statement (*lógos*) cannot be false. It may also be an explanation: in a passage cited earlier from the *Theaetetus*, a minimal
speech element, such as *s*, is shown to have no explanation (*lógos*)
in terms of its parts. In place of 'explanation' we could have used
the vaguer words 'description' or 'account'.[72] So, to return to the
argument, a *lógos* which is true is an account of 'that which is'. In
the words that Plato puts into the mouth of Euthydemus, someone
who 'says those things that are' (*légei tà ónta*), 'says those things
that are true' (*légei t'alēthê*). A false *lógos* would be an account
of 'that which is not'. But 'that which is not' does not exist; so,
someone who 'said that which is not' would be giving an account
of nothing. In the *Euthydemus* there is a subsidiary confusion
between two senses of the verb *poieîn*, 'to do' and 'to make'. To
speak is to do something; that is, to make something. Someone
who 'said that which is not' would also be making something. But
that is impossible, since he would be making something non-existent. Given that one cannot speak falsely, it is easy to see why, in
addition, one cannot contradict. For if two people appear to
contradict each other either they are talking about different things,
or one of them is talking about nothing whatever.[73]

We have a glimpse here of the teething problems of the philosophy of language, and it is very easy both to smile at the sophists'
difficulties and to undervalue Plato's very considerable achievement
in removing them. In the *Euthydemus*, Socrates argues merely that
the view of Euthydemus and Dionysodorus is self-refuting. For if
they are right the opposite contention, that they are wrong, cannot
be contradicted. In the *Sophist*, which belongs to a later group of
dialogues, the dominant figure is not Socrates, but a visitor from
the philosophical school of Elea. His main aim, which need not
concern us, is to characterize the sophist as a type; however, in the
episode before the one which is directly relevant, he points out that

we are not speaking in the same way when we say that something
'is' in itself the same and when we say that, in a relative sense, it 'is
not' or is no longer the same.[74] This effectively removes the main
philosophical difficulty with 'to be'. Thus, to return to the naive
illustration from the *Euthydemus*, to say that Clinias would at one
time be ignorant and at another time be not ignorant is not to deny
that he would, in himself, be the same Clinias.

In the episode which follows, the crucial step is to identify a
sentence (*lógos*) as having a noun element and a verb element. As
the visitor explains, these are two different kinds of indication of
reality. A verb (*rhêma*) is an indication of actions; examples are
'walks', 'runs', or 'sleeps' (third singular present indicative *badízei,
trékhei, katheúdei*). A noun (*ónoma*) is a sign of those that
perform actions: thus 'lion', 'deer' or 'horse' (nominative singular
*léōn, élaphos, híppos*). There can be no *lógos* unless both these
elements are present. Hence the smallest and most primitive *lógos*
joins together a single noun and a single verb: for example, 'man'
and 'learns' (*ánthrōpos manthánei*). Such an expression does not
merely name things – thus naming a man or naming learning – but
'achieves something' (*ti peraínei*) in combining verbs with nouns.
And just as things do or do not fit together, so do vocal signs.
Sentences are formed by those that do fit.

To be a *lógos* as such, an expression must then be 'of something'.
The visitor, who is talking to Theaetetus, takes for illustration the
sentence 'Theaetetus is sitting down'. Who is that sentence of or
about? Obviously, Theaetetus answers, it is about me. Then let us
take another: 'Theaetetus is flying.' Who is that about? Again,
Theaetetus answers, it is about me. But one sentence is true and the
other untrue. The true one says about Theaetetus 'the things that
are as they are'. The one which is untrue says about him 'things
other than the things that are'. It says 'what is not so as if it were
so.' Thus, to sum up, we can have an expression which is of or
about something that exists, which is therefore a *lógos* and which
combines a noun and verb in the same way as a *lógos* which would
be true; but, because what it says of that entity is not the same as
what is in fact the case, it is a false *lógos*.[75]

An historian of linguistic thought must read this passage in two
ways. In its own time it was the solution to a very nasty philosophical puzzle and, since it did solve it, it was one which Plato's
successors no longer had to struggle with. But it is also the source
of an analysis which is basic to the Western grammatical tradition,
in which a sentence consists minimally of a noun – in modern
terms the subject – and a verb which, to use another later term, is
predicated of it. The division between noun and verb is also the

most primitive division between word classes, and it will be noted that the visitor's criterion for it was that of denotation. A verb (*rhêma*, literally 'something said') is an indication (*dêlōma*) of actions. A noun (*ónoma*, in the most basic sense 'a name') is a sign (*sēmeîon*) of those that perform actions.[76]

### 1.4.2 The theory of parts of speech

The subsequent development of the 'part of speech' system cannot be wholly or safely reconstructed. The collocation *mérē tês léxeōs* 'parts of the utterance' appears in a technical sense in Aristotle's *Poetics*; the term which is here translated 'utterance' is another derivative of *légein* 'to say'. But Aristotle's list is one of linguistic elements generally, starting from the *stoikheîon*, which we discussed in section 1.2, and ending with the sentence. The *stoikheîon* is an indivisible vocal sound, and is classified into vowel, 'half-vowel' and 'mute', with an allusion to other phonetic variables. The next element is the syllable, a vocal sound without meaning which, unlike the *stoikheîon*, is composite. The next two are the *súndesmos* (literally, a 'binder together') and the *árthron* (literally 'joint'). In the later tradition these are the terms for conjunction and article (Lat. *coniunctiò, articulus*); but our text is at this point so corrupt and jumbled that we cannot confidently say what Aristotle meant. It seems that these, too, were 'without meaning' (*ásemoi*); according to the text, the first would include the sentence particles *mén, étoi* and *dé* (commonest translations 'on the one hand', 'either . . . or', 'on the other hand'), and the second the prepositions *amphí* and *perí* ('about, concerning, . . .'). But the preceding explanations, though translatable, make no real sense.[77]. A further difficulty is that the term *árthron* ('article') is not found elsewhere in Aristotle's work. *Súndesmos* is and, appropriately to its etymology, such elements are said to 'make many things one'.[78]

The next two elements are the noun and verb, which are defined both here and in the introductory chapter of the *De Interpretatione* as vocal sounds 'with meaning' (*sēmantikaí*), whose parts do not themselves have meaning. Even in a compound such as *Theódōros* (personal name from *theós*, 'god' and *dôron*, 'gift') no meaning attaches to *dōros*. A verb 'has an additional meaning of' (*prossēmaí-nei*, 'consignifies') time, whereas a noun has meaning 'without time'. For example, *ánthrōpos*, 'man' and *leukós*, 'white' do not signify 'when'; but *badízei*, 'walks' and *bebádiken*, 'have walked' additionally signify, respectively, present time and past time. In the *De Interpretatione* Aristotle compares the derivationally related *hugíeia*, 'health' and *hugiainei*, 'is healthy', the latter again with the additional meaning of 'being the case now'. He adds that a verb always has the meaning of things that are so: thus, things that are so of the subject. The next element is the *ptôsis* (literally, 'falling'), which in modern terms can most nearly be rendered by 'inflectional modification'. In defining nouns Aristotle gives examples in the nominative singular, and in the *De Interpretatione* he makes clear that forms like *Phílōnos* 'of Philo' and *Phílōni* 'to Philo' are not nouns but *ptóseis* 'inflectional modifications' of nouns. Similarly, verbs are forms in the present indicative; a future such as *hugianeî*, 'will be healthy' is not a verb but a *ptôsis* of a verb. In the *Poetics* Aristotle again mentions modifications for 'of' and 'to'; other examples are forms for many versus one (plural *ánthrōpoi*, 'men'; singular *ánthrōpos*, 'man'), and verb forms used in a question (*ebádisen?*, 'Did [he] walk?' – in this case there is no specific inflection) or a command (imperative *bádize*, 'walk!').[79].

The final element is the sentence (*lógos*). This is a composite vocal sound which has meaning and some of whose parts also have meaning. The second criterion distinguishes it from nouns and verbs; and in the *De Interpretatione* Aristotle adds that only a sentence can have the meaning of an assertion (*katáphasis*) and not simply of an expression (*phásis*). For example, the noun *ánthrōpos*, 'man' has meaning, and in that respect is different from its constituent syllables, which are merely vocal sounds. But *ánthrōpos* on its own has no meaning of being so or not being so; there will be no assertion or denial (*apóphasis*) unless something is added to it. A sentence with a propositional meaning (*apophantikós*) is one which is either true or false, and it is these that Aristotle discusses further. In the next paragraph of the *De Interpretatione* he says that the most elementary proposition is an assertion, and the next is a denial; others are 'made one by conjunction' (*sundésmōi*). He also says that a proposition must contain either a verb or its 'inflectional modification' (*ptôsis*). But not all sentences are propositional. For example, a prayer is a sentence, but is neither true nor false. If we define a man as 'a land animal with two feet', that too is a sentence; but it has no verb and becomes a proposition only if 'is' or 'will be' or 'was' is added.[80]

Aristotle's analysis is the earliest of its kind, and the first which sets the terms for at least two of the traditional 'parts of speech' within what can be reasonably called a grammatical theory. Difficult though both passages are, they are fundamental for what follows. But after Aristotle we have no direct information for at least two centuries. If we discount the text of (pseudo-) Dionysius Thrax our next primary source is the surviving work of Varro in the first century BC. Our other sources for the Hellenistic period are secondary; although the account that is given can in substance be traced back to the first century BC, we are mostly dealing with later recensions.

We can begin with the version ascribed to Apollonius Dyscolus (second century AD), who appears in turn to be indebted to Tryphon (late first century BC).[81] According to this, the Peripatetics or followers of Aristotle distinguished just two elements of the sentence, the noun and the verb. We have already seen that these and their 'modifications' (*ptóseis*) are the only words which Aristotle saw as meaningful, and the only ones to be defined in the *De Interpretatione*. According to Apollonius, the other types of word were seen not as parts or elements, but as having the function of a glue or binding agent. Similarly, it was said, the parts of a ship are the sides, the rudder and the sail; pitch, tow and nails are not parts but things that bind and glue the parts together. Moreover, just as a boat can be made of a single piece of wood, without glue or binding agent, so a sentence can consist of just a noun and a verb, without words of any other type. But a sentence cannot be formed with no noun or with no verb, just as, by implication, no boat can consist just of pitch, tow and nails.

This analysis is expounded and then criticized. The objections are, first, that the other elements have their own semantic roles (*sēmasíai*, Lat. *significationes*) and do not, in fact, bind together nouns and verbs. Thus in 'The man walks about' (*ho ánthrōpos peripateî*) the article *ho*, 'the', bears a relationship to the noun, but none whatever to the verb. Conversely, in 'The man walks about beautifully' (*ho ánthrōpos kalôs peripateî*) the adverb *kalôs*, 'beautifully', bears a relationship to the verb but none whatever to the noun. Even the words that we actually call 'binders' (*súndesmoi* 'conjunctions') do not bind together a noun and a verb. One does not say, for example, 'Tryphon and reads' (*Trúphōn kaì anagignōskei*). Instead they bind a noun and a noun ('Theon and Tryphon'), a verb and a verb ('[I] write and read'), or generally elements that are similar: thus pronouns and a noun in 'I and you and Apollonius'. As to semantic roles, an article is anaphoric; it signifies a 'referring back' (*anaphorá*). A pronoun is either anaphoric or deictic; in the latter case it signifies a 'pointing out' (*deîxis*). These roles are explained in Apollonius' other works (Section. 1.6.1 below) and are peculiar to these elements; nouns and verbs do not share them. Again, it is one thing to say 'I go' (*baínō*) and another to say 'I go down' (*katabaínō*) or 'I go over' (*huperbaínō*); this shows that prepositions such as *katá*, 'down' or *hupér*, 'over', also vary the meaning. So do adverbs; in *kalôs peripateî*, 'walks about beautifully', the adverb contributes a quality (*poiótēs*, literally 'what-sort-ness') to the meaning. Even conjunctions have a semantic role that is not present in nouns and verbs. *Gráphō*, 'I write', is a complete utterance. In *kaì gráphō*, 'I also write, I even write', the conjunction *kaí*, 'and, also, even', adds confirmation, and the utterance does not call for completion. By contrast, *gráphō mén* and *grápheis dé* ('On the one hand I write', 'On the other hand you write'), with the different conjunctions *mén* or *dé*, are each incomplete.[82]

The second objection is to the argument that only a noun and a verb are needed to form a complete sentence. That is so: but similarly, a man, for example, may be without hands or feet but cannot be without a brain or a heart. One does not then say that hands and feet are not parts of a man. Likewise it does not follow that the other elements are not parts of a sentence; merely that the noun and the verb are the pre-eminent parts. This is the general view of the grammarians. Donatus says that the noun and verb are the 'principal' elements of the sentence, and the corresponding passage of Consentius (fifth century AD) adds that this is because when joined together they form an utterance (*coniunctae efficiunt locutionem*).[83] Priscian's terms are 'principal and pre-eminent', and, following Apollonius, he lists them as the first two elements. In support he reproduces an example from Apollonius' *Syntax* which contains all elements bar the conjunction:

| idem | homo | lapsus | heu | hodie | concidit |
|------|------|--------|-----|-------|----------|
| 'the same | man | having slipped | alas | today | fell down' |
| (Pronoun | Noun | Participle | Interjection | Adverb | Preposition + Verb) |

and shows that neither the noun nor the verb can be deleted. Thus if one says *idem lapsus heu hodie concidit* the sentence, according to Priscian, is incomplete because it lacks a noun, and if one says *idem homo lapsus heu hodie* it is incomplete because it lacks a verb. But one can delete the adverb (*idem homo lapsus heu concidit*, 'The same man having alas slipped fell down'), the preposition (substitute simple *cecidit* 'fell' for the compound *con-* + (*ce*)*cidit*) and all the others without the sentence becoming incomplete.[84]

These arguments come from a tradition which is some centuries later than the texts of Aristotle with which we began this subsection. Aristotle's concerns were basically those of logic or dialectic and his wording is problematic even where the text is sound. In contrast, Apollonius and his followers are writing as specialized linguistic scholars and their observations are readily expounded in our own terms. It is worth reflecting on this difference whenever we are forced to rely on the grammarians and their contemporaries as

secondary sources. We might easily misapprehend Aristotle if all
we had was this account of Peripatetic teaching generally. In the
case of the Stoics, who are the leading figures in the century that
follows, only secondary sources have survived. These also tend to
cite the Stoic school in blanket fashion, without distinguishing
particular members. In these circumstances the risk of misapprehen-
sion is real.

What our sources tell us is, first, that the Stoic 'parts of speech'
belonged to a branch of dialectic which was concerned with vocal
sound or expression (*phōnḗ*). Its other branch was concerned with
the meaning that is expressed (*tò lektón*, 'what is said'). In the
definition of Diogenes of Babylon, vocal sound is 'air that is set in
motion' and a *léxis*, 'utterance', is a vocal sound that is articulate
or representable by letters. The elements of the utterance (*tês
léxeōs stoikheîa*) are thus the twenty four letters of the Greek
alphabet. A sentence (*lógos*) is a vocal sound that, in addition, has
meaning: by contrast, *blíturi*, which means nothing in Greek, is an
utterance (*léxis*), since it consists of *b* plus *l* and so on, but, being
meaningless (*ásēmos*), is not a *lógos*. The parts of a *lógos* are
accordingly divisions of a material signifier (*sēmaínōn*, 'signifying')
whose signification (*sēmainómenon*, 'that being signified') is an
immaterial entity which formed a separate object of study. The
branch of dialectic concerned with the vocal sound also included
the topic of good and bad speech according to Diogenes Laertius,
whose summary we must either take or leave, other subjects included the definitions of a rhythmical or poetical phrase, of division
into genus and species, and of ambiguity. But it did not include for
example, cases and tenses. In grammars these are handled under
individual parts of speech. In Stoic philosophy the categories that
correspond were dealt with separately, as part of the study of 'what
is said' (*tò lektón*).[85]

Within this scheme, our sources say that the Stoics recognised
five parts of speech.[86] Where the grammarians speak of a single
class of nouns, they made a distinction between an individual name
(*ónoma*) and what was called a *prosēgoría* or 'naming' in general.
The latter is the ancient term for what we now call a common noun
(Lat. *appellatio* or *nomen appellativum*), and Diogenes of Babylon
is said to have defined it as an element of a sentence 'signifying a
quality in common' (*sēmaînon koinḕn poiótēta*). The former was
later called a proper noun (*ónoma kúrion*; Lat. *nomen proprium*,
'specific noun'), and was defined correspondingly as an element of
a sentence 'indicating an individual quality' (*dēloûn idían poiótēta*). According to the account by Apollonius which we were
citing earlier, the reasons for making this a major division were,

first, that proper nouns and common nouns had different declensions (in fact, he points out, there are similar inflections in both classes) and, secondly, that whereas one can derive a patronymic from a proper name (*Hómēros*, 'Homer'; *Homērídēs*, 'son of Homer') one does not, for instance, say *anthrōpídēs*, from the common noun *ánthrōpos*, 'man'. To the latter argument he replies that this could only mean 'son of mankind' in the plural, which is biologically impossible.[87]

The three other parts of speech were the verb, the conjunction or 'binding' element (*súndesmos*), and the article or 'joint' (*árthron*). In the reported definition of Diogenes of Babylon, a verb is an element of a sentence 'signifying a simple predicate' (*semaînon asúntheton katēgórēma*); others, we are told, defined it as an element without case (*áptōton*), 'signifying something construed of one or more entities' (*semaînon ti suntaktòn perí tinos ḕ tinôn*). According to Apollonius, it included, as a mood or inflection of the verb (*égklisis*), the nominal forms that he and other grammarians classify separately as participles. The *súndesmos* or conjunction was defined as an element 'binding together the elements of the sentence' (*sundoûn tà mérē toû lógou*); according to Apollonius it included the grammarians' prepositions as well as their conjunctions.

But he adds that the preposition (*próthesis*) was distinguished as a 'prothetic' conjunction (*prothetikós*, 'placed before') because of its distinctive syntax.[88] Finally, the *árthron* included a definite and an indefinite sub-type: those which are indefinite (*aoristṓdē*) are those called *árthra*, 'articles' in the later tradition, those which are definite (*hōrisména*) are the pronouns.[89] The *árthron* was distinguished as an inflected word with noun-like characteristics; according to Dionysius of Halicarnassus, its separation from the *súndesmos* was specifically Stoic (this would imply that its appearance in the text of Aristotle's *Poetics* is itself a corruption), and was earlier than the division of proper noun and common noun.[90]

Diogenes Laertius ascribes the five parts of speech to Chrysippus and Diogenes of Babylon; he adds that Antipater, who succeeded Diogenes as head of the school in the second century BC, introduced a further element called the *mesótēs* (literally, 'the middle').[91] Grammatical and rhetorical sources refer simply to 'the Stoics'; it is therefore hard to say how much of the detailed argument transmitted by Apollonius Dyscolus (such as the treatment of prepositions as a subdivision or the grounds for distinguishing proper nouns and common nouns) is original and how much derives from later polemic and exegesis. But, on the evidence we have, the Stoics were the main inventors of what was to become

the standard parts of speech system. They were the first to distinguish consistently between phonetic elements (the *stoikheîa tês
léxeōs*, 'elements of the utterance') and what we would now call
elements of the grammatical construction, and they referred to the
latter specifically as 'parts' (*mérē*) or – the term is also used by
them and sporadically later – as 'elements' (*stoikheîa*) of a meaningful utterance or sentence (*lógos*). They seem to have established
most of the traditional elements, either as main classes or as sub-
classes. For this and other aspects of Stoic grammar, the contribution of Chrysippus, a generation or two before Diogenes of Babylon, appears to have been particularly important. His works were
notoriously voluminous and tiresome; but a great deal might be
clearer if we could read them.[92]

The grammarians and rhetorical writers mention other systems,
none of which differ strikingly from the one that eventually
achieved canonic status. That scheme itself is possibly Alexandrian:
Quintilian says that Aristarchus (c.217–145 BC) distinguished eight
parts, and a date before the first century would be certain if the
text of (pseudo-) Dionysius Thrax could be accepted as genuine. But
it should be noted that Dionysius of Halicarnassus, who normally
adopts a scheme of nine parts, does not seem to have known it.
Quintilian also says that eight were distinguished, in his own time,
by Remmius Palaemon; we assume that these are the eight of the
later Roman tradition.[93] Other schemes are invincibly anonymous.
One with nine parts is attested in papyri of the Imperial period; it is
identical to what we think of as the standard scheme except that it
continues the Stoic division of *ónoma* and *prosēgoría*.[94] According
to Quintilian the specific contribution of Aristarchus had been to
reduce these to a single main class. Others drew a three-fold
distinction between, in Latin, the *nomen* or proper noun, the
*vocabulum* (a common noun which refers to something visible and
tangible) and the *appellatio* (a common noun such as 'wind' or
'virtue' which refers to something either invisible or intangible).[95]
Another proposed division was between verbs (*sc.* finite verbs) and
infinitives; according to the fragment ascribed to Apollonius, one
system of 11 elements included both this and the division between
proper and common nouns, with a further separation of *skhetliastiká* or 'expostulations' (for example, the emphatic *nḗ* in *nḕ tòn
Día*, 'Yes by Zeus') from adverbs. The Roman tradition also
included interjections as a distinct class, and we are told by Priscian
that some Greek grammarians also dealt with them similarly.[96]

The picture which our sources present is of a fluctuating refinement of the Stoic system, promoting to separate elements things that
they had treated as subdivisions (prepositions and conjunctions,

pronouns and articles, verbs and participles), reducing to a sub-division their distinction between proper and common nouns, establishing the adverb as a full element, sometimes dividing further (finite verbs and infinitives, concrete nouns and non-concrete, adverbs and interjections), until the standard schemes became fixed. But there is at least one system which the doxographic tradition does not mention, but which is applied to Latin in the extant books of Varro.[97] Its context is the treatment of inflection or, more generally, word formation; and the first division that Varro makes is between what we might now call modifiable and unmodifiable words. The former are 'fertile', in that, by inflectional or other modification, they give birth to many different forms. For example, *lego*, 'I read', gives birth to *legis*, 'you read'; *legebam*, 'I was reading', and so on. The others are 'sterile'; they give birth to nothing. For example, nothing can be derived from *et*, 'and', or *cras*, 'tomorrow'.[98]

Varro then takes, as a further criterion, the distinction between case inflection and tense inflection. At first the variable words are said to include two parts of speech: one 'additionally signifies' cases (*adsignificat casus*) and the other times. The first is the *vocabulum*, which in this context we must translate by 'noun'; the second the verb (*verbum*). For authority he refers to Aristotle, who had given the same criterion for verbs in the passages which we have cited earlier.[99] But in a later section Varro adopts a more elaborate system which divides the variable words into four main parts. The first has cases but not tenses; this corresponds to what was first called the *vocabulum*. The second covers finite and infinitive verbs, which have tenses but not cases. The third has neither cases nor tenses: the examples given are the adverbs *docte*, 'learnedly' and *commode*, 'appropriately'. The fourth are participles, which have both cases and tenses. According to Varro, some scholars have called these four parts those of 'naming' (*appellandi*), of 'saying' (*dicendi*), of 'supporting' (*adminiculandi*) and of 'joining' (*iungendi*).[100] But whatever the names, the criteria are consistently inflectional. The divisions are also expounded, somewhat inconsequentially, in the books dealing with etymology: at that point Varro talks not of parts of speech (*partes orationis*), but simply of 'four types of word modification' (*verborum declinatuum genera . . . quattuor*).[101]

The 'naming' words are then subdivided into four types by a criterion of increasing definiteness. Words such as *quis* ('who' or 'which') are maximally indefinite (*infinitum*), while others, such as *hic* 'this', are maximally definite (*finitum*). But between these extremes there are words like *scutum* 'shield' or *gladius* 'sword' which are 'quasi-indefinite' (*ut infinitum*) and others like the personal names *Romulus* and *Remus* which are 'quasi-definite' (*ut finitum*). According to Varro, the two middle types are the *vocabulum* (here meaning 'common noun') and the *nomen* ('proper noun'); together they are called *nominatus* ('nouns'). The two extreme types are together called *articuli* ('articles'), the maximally indefinite is the *provocabulum* ('pro common noun') and the maximally definite the *pronomen* ('pro proper noun').[102] We can accordingly represent the system as a whole as having four levels. At the highest level, words are divided into the modifiable type and the unmodifiable (*fecundum, sterile*). At the next level modifiable words belong to one of the four parts of speech: of naming, of saying, of supporting, of joining (*appellandi, dicendi, adminiculandi, iungendi*). At the third level, words of naming are divided into the major types of noun and article (*nominatus, articulus*). Finally, at the fourth level, nouns are divided into the sub-types of common noun and proper noun (*vocabulum, nomen*) and articles into the sub-types of 'pro common noun' and 'pro proper noun' (*provocabulum, pronomen*). The only other subdivisions, at least in the extant text, are within paradigms.

It seems clear that Varro's doctrine comes from various sources. He says at one point that just as the Greeks have an *oratio* divided into four parts, so do the Romans; this implies that he is applying to Latin an analysis of Greek that, on his understanding, was already current.[103] He refers anonymously to earlier scholars for the names both of the four parts and of the successive divisions of the first part. He also refers to the Alexandrian philosopher Dion, who had visited Rome in a diplomatic mission in 56 BC, for a scheme with three parts: one with cases, one with tenses and a third with neither.[104] The problem for the historian is whether Varro has understood all or any of these sources correctly. If his grasp of contemporary Greek scholarship was sound, then at least one grammarian had fastened on the criteria of case and tense inflection and pushed them to a logical conclusion, and at least one (not necessarily the same) had extended the criterion of finiteness and applied it to nominal words in general with some acumen.

Unfortunately, Varro's mind is not as good as a modern summary of his doctrine may suggest, he is writing in what may still be the formative period of Greek linguistics (see end of section 1.5) and both systems may be generated by misunderstanding. Certainly we have no other evidence for them. The partial survival of Varro's work must therefore serve above all as a reminder that our knowledge is fragmentary, and that much of what we do know, or think we know, depends on a doxographic tradition which is polemic and transmitted from the standpoint of the canonic system.

Schemes which did not fit into the argument may simply have been
left out.

### 1.4.3 Canonical schemes

Once the standard systems were established, there is virtually no
change, in antiquity and throughout the early Middle Ages. The
Greek tradition recognized eight elements of the sentence (*mérē
toû lógou*): the noun (*ónoma*), verb (*rhêma*), participle (*metokhê*),
article (*árthron*), pronoun (*antōnumía*), preposition (*próthesis*),
adverb (*epírrhēma*) and conjunction (*súndesmos*). This is the order
in which they are expounded in the summary account of (pseudo-)
Dionysius Thrax and which is justified in detail by Apollonius
Dyscolus.[105] The noun and verb appear first, as the principal or
necessary elements: the noun before the verb, on the grounds that
entities exist before the actions that they perform or undergo.
Participles follow the verb, because they are derived from it. The
article, which comes next, is syntactically relatable to nouns ('the
man'), to participles ('the person walking', literally 'the walking')
and also to the infinitive form of verbs (literally 'the to-walk'). It
precedes the pronoun, because pronouns are not related to nouns
but substituted for them; as Apollonius remarks, the pronoun
could almost have taken its place directly after the first element. Of
the remainder the preposition, which is syntactically preposed to
the first element, comes after the adverb, which is syntactically
related to the second. The conjunction comes last, since it has no
meaning except through its relationship to the others. This passage
forms part of the opening sections of Apollonius' work on *Syntax*,
which we will examine in some detail in subsection 1.6.2. His
arguments remind us that the analysis into word classes had a
fundamentally syntactic purpose.

The Latin tradition also recognized eight elements, but with two
substantive differences. In the different order in which they are
listed by Donatus and other Roman grammarians, these are the
noun (*nomen*), pronoun (*pronomen*), verb (*verbum*), adverb (*adverbium*), participle (*participium*), conjunction (*coniunctio*), preposition
(*praepositio*) and interjection (*interiectio*). Whatever the justification
for this, it is abandoned by Priscian for an arrangement that comes
as near as possible to that of Apollonius: noun, verb, participle,
pronoun, preposition, adverb, interjection, conjunction.[106] Apart
from the order which was a serious topic at least for grammarians
such as Apollonius and Priscian, the differences are as follows.
First, the Romans recognized that, where Greek had a definite
article which was functionally distinct from the pronouns, Latin
did not.[107] Secondly, they followed a tradition in which interjec-

tions, which form various classes of adverbs in, for example, (pseudo-) Dionysius Thrax, were distinguished as a separate element. The ground is given by Donatus and others: this type of word 'is not immediately subordinate to the verb'. Priscian, writing in Constantinople in the sixth century, explains that the Greek grammarians had seen them as subordinate to a verb which could be understood. For instance, *papae* (an expression of delight) has in itself a verbal sense, even if *miror*, 'I admire' is not added. But he then says that this was the main reason for the Roman grammarians treating them separately.[108]

The criteria which underlie the remainder of the system are summarised towards the beginning of Priscian's work. The number of elements of the sentence will not be correctly determined, he says, unless we pay attention to the individual semantic character (literally the 'characteristics of the significations') of each.[109] Only thus will we resolve the conflict between alternative systems, some with five elements, some with nine, some with ten, and so on, which we reviewed earlier. Let us therefore take this account, which is brief and easily accessible, as a framework for the grammatical tradition generally.

The distinguishing characteristic of the noun, Priscian says, is to signify substance and quality (*substantiam et qualitatem*). This is true not only of proper nouns but also of the two types of common noun (the *appellatio* and *vocabulum*) that others had treated separately; therefore, he says, all three are a single element. The criterion also fits with a distinction that Apollonius draws between the noun and the pronoun. The former is said to signify substance with quality: more literally, 'being with what-sort-ness' (*ousían metà poiótētos*). The latter signifies substance alone.[110] Priscian says that the distinguishing characteristic of the pronoun is that it is 'used in place of a proper noun and signifies specific persons' (first/second/third person). He then points to words like *quis*, 'who'/'which' or *qualis* and *talis*, 'of what sort', 'of that sort' which the tradition in general also treats as pronominal. Some of these resemble pronouns in their inflections; but on semantic grounds, following Apollonius for Greek words whose functions are partly similar, he says that they would be better classed as nouns. The reasons are partly that they do not meet either of his defining criteria, and also that they too have 'substance, however indefinite (*infinitam*), and quality, however general', which is the distinctive property of nouns.[111]

The definitions of the noun all refer, in addition, to the property of case. That of Priscian is the Latin equivalent of a Greek definition ascribed by a scholiast to the school of Apollonius:

according to this, a noun is 'an element of the sentence with case, which assigns to every underlying object or thing a common or an individual quality'. The scholiast mentions others who spoke of substance instead of quality. For 'object or thing' (*corpus aut res*, Gk. *sôma ê prâgma*) compare the formulation of, for example, Donatus and (pseudo-) Dionysius Thrax: 'an element of the sentence with case, which signifies an object or thing either individually or in common'. Another variant, which we can cite from Charisius, speaks equivalently of a 'material or non-material thing' (*res corporalis aut incorporalis*) and also makes explicit that a noun does not have tense.[112] Finally, the formula 'individually or in common' (Donatus' *proprie communiterve*) introduces the subsidiary distinction between proper and common nouns, which for all grammarians was the first subdivision. Like the material *vocabulum* and the non-material *appellatio*, these had once been treated as independent elements. The definitions are thus designed to underline the unity of the class, as the Alexandrians and their successors saw it.

For the pronoun, the simplest formulation is given by (pseudo-) Dionysius: this says that 'a pronoun is a word used in place of a noun, which indicates specific persons'. This is effectively the definition of Apollonius.[113] Priscian, both in the passage cited and in the definition which begins his detailed treatment of the element, differs in that it is said to stand specifically for a proper noun. The same view is ascribed by a scholiast to Stephanus, a student of Greek who was probably Priscian's contemporary. The reason is that a pronoun, like a proper noun, seeks to identify a single individual; while other nouns have an undefined reference, unless the article 'the' is also included. An alternative, which we will find in Apollonius' *Syntax*, is to say that a pronoun stands for article + noun, not for a noun alone.[114] In addition, some definitions do not refer to the category of 'persons'. One version can be cited from Charisius: according to this, the pronoun is an element of the sentence which is 'put in place of a noun and, although less fully, nevertheless signifies the same'. For the wording compare that of Donatus: 'put in place of a noun and almost signifies as much'. But Donatus does also refer to persons.[115]

The verb, it will be recalled, is the second of the 'principal' elements of the sentence. In one short definition it is simply distinguished as such: 'a leading element of the sentence without case'.[116] This opposes it to the noun, which does have case. But in the passage of Priscian with which we began this survey the 'semantic characteristic' of the verb is stated more elaborately. First, it signifies 'something done and/or experienced' (*actionem sive passionem sive utrumque*); the formulation thus refers explicitly to both the 'doing' sense of the active verb and the 'experiencing' (literally 'suffering') sense of the passive. Second, it signifies 'with moods and [derived] forms and tenses' but without 'case'. Priscian points out that these characteristics cover both finite verbs and infinitives, which some had wished to separate; but they exclude participles, which do have cases – also genders like nouns – and do not have moods. Definitions in general follow broadly the same strategy. The one which Priscian himself gives later is very close, but omits the superfluous reference to derived forms. Others add that the verb has persons and numbers. An example is that of (pseudo-) Dionysius: 'a word without case, admitting tenses and persons and numbers [and] representing something done or experienced' (enérgeian è páthos). Another is the more complicated definition of Apollonius, which is cited and praised by the Byzantine commentator Heliodorus. This makes clear that tenses are combined with moods (Heliodorus says that this is to distinguish verbs from temporal adverbs) and includes a formula which makes clear (again according to the commentator) that person and number are not found in infinitives. In place of 'something done or experienced', the formula of Charisius refers more simply to an *administratio rei*, literally 'handling of a thing'.[117] But it will be seen that the general tendency of these definitions, like those of the noun, is to add together the properties of different sub-classes of a main class, rather than look for criteria which would be minimally sufficient.

The participle comes after the verb in the Greek ordering, because its forms are inflectionally derived from verbs and because it shares the characteristics of both the two principal elements. These are the reasons given by Apollonius, and are the basis for the Latin definition of Priscian: according to this, a participle is 'an element of the sentence which is admitted in place of a verb, is regularly (*naturaliter*) derived from the verb, and has both gender and case like nouns and all the properties of the verb except persons and moods'.[118] By name it is a 'sharing' element (Gk. *metokhḗ* from *metékhein*, 'to share') and another definition simply makes this explicit: in the formula of (pseudo-) Dionysius, 'a word sharing (*metékhousa*) the character of verbs and nouns'. The shared properties are 'the same as the noun' and again 'the same as the verb except for persons and moods'. But a minimal definition, which we have already met in Varro, is cited by Charisius from another fourth century grammarian, Cominianus. According to this, it is 'an element of the sentence with tense and case'.[119]

Having given reasons for separating the noun, verb, participle and pronoun, Priscian's synthetic account turns briefly to the semantic characteristics of the other elements. Since he is dealing with Latin the article, which came between the participle and the pronoun in Apollonius' list, is not included. For Greek it is defined by (pseudo-) Dionysius as 'an element of the sentence with case, which is placed before or after the inflection of the nouns'; by referring to postposition the definition includes the partly homonymous relative pronoun (masculine *hós*) as well as the article proper (*ho*).[120] The distinguishing characteristic of the adverb, which Priscian takes next, is 'to be placed with a verb, without which it cannot have a complete meaning'. In the formula of the earlier Latin grammarians, it is 'added to a verb to fill out and make clear its meaning'. Priscian's later definition adds that it is indeclinable. According to Apollonius, whose characteristically elaborate account Priscian is in part reproducing, an adverb is a word which is indeclinable, which is applied to all or some of the inflections of a verb (the point here is that some adverbs do not collocate with the entire paradigm) and which will not complete the sense without it. Apollonius and Priscian compare the syntax of adverbs with that of adjectives. The latter are a sub-class of nouns (Lat. *nomina adiectiva*) which are added (*adiecta*) to other common nouns. The corresponding adverbs are the indeclinable forms which they assume when they are added to verbs.[121]

The difference between adverbs and prepositions, as Priscian explains it, is that an adverb can be added before or after the verb and with or without an element inflected for case; as an independent word, a preposition is used only with elements inflected for case and always comes before them. However, it can also be used in compounds such as *indoctus* 'unlearned' (where the grammarians saw a preposition in the prefix *in*), *intercurro* 'I run between' (with preposition *inter* 'between') or *proconsul* 'proconsul' (with preposition *pro* 'in place of'). So, in the definition that Priscian gives later, a preposition is 'an indeclinable element which is placed before all other elements either in construction (*appositione*) or in compounding'. The earlier Roman grammarians refer to its effect on the element to which it is preposed: in the formula of Donatus, it is 'an element of the sentence placed before other elements of the sentence which either changes or fills out or diminishes their meaning'.[122] In the passage which we have taken as our framework, Priscian also underlines the difference between prepositions and conjunctions. The characteristic of the latter is to 'join together different nouns or any words inflected for case, or different verbs or adverbs'. Prepositions cannot do this; nor are conjunctions compounded with verbs; nor, as separate words, are they limited to the position before a word inflected for case, but appear either before or after words of any type. The simplest definition of the conjunction is one given by various Roman grammarians: 'an element of the sentence tying together and ordering the sense'.[123]

The interjection is not included in Priscian's synthetic introduction and is discussed later, without formal definition, only in an appendix to his book on adverbs. In this, as in other matters, he adheres closely to the Greek tradition. But from the earlier Roman tradition Charisius cites three definitions, all of which say that an interjection is an element of the sentence which 'signifies an emotion' (*motum* or *adfectum animi*). In one definition, Donatus adds that it is 'inserted' (*interiecta*) among other elements of the sentence; the definition is thus related to the name (*interiectio*) in the same way that the preposition (*praepositio*, Greek *próthesis*) is said to be 'preposed' (*praeposita*, *protitheméne*) to other elements, or the conjunction (*coniunctio*, *súndesmos*) is presented in another formulation as 'conjoining' (*coniungens*, *sundéousa*). Another addition, found also in Diomedes, is that interjections are uttered with an 'indistinct vocal sound' (*voce incondita*).[124]

It will be clear from these definitions that, even in late antiquity, we are not dealing with an entirely homogeneous tradition. The status of the interjection was barely resolved; it so happens that the extant Greek writers jump one way while the Romans jumped the other. Nor do the definitions follow an entirely consistent strategy. Some, which we have cited from time to time, are maximally economical; others, especially those of Apollonius Dyscolus, try to cover as many characteristics as possible. Nor can we reconstruct a continuous historical movement. The later grammarians seem to have inherited a stock of variant formulae, from which they could select, conflate and adapt as they thought fit. Of the scholars who may have been the originators of the formulae, only Apollonius (still excepting the text ascribed to Dionysius Thrax) can be read extensively, and then only in part. Those who lie behind him in the Greek tradition (such as Tryphon), or behind grammarians like Charisius in the Roman tradition (notably Remmius Palaemon), are known, or known explicitly, only through cited fragments.

## 1.5 The prehistory of grammar

Many familiar grammatical categories make their first appearance in antiquity before the constitution of grammar as a separate field of study. Chief among them are the terms for parts of speech, whose development we have considered in the last section. We have also noted the early appearance of the terms for letter and syllable, and the division of letters into vowels, 'mutes' and 'half-vowels'. In the fifth century, the sophist Protagoras is said to have distinguished four types of utterance (wish, question, answer and command); our source, Diogenes Laertius, tells us that he was the first to make such an analysis.[125] Protagoras is also said by Aristotle to have argued that certain nouns (*mênis*, 'anger', *pélēx*, 'helmet') should rightly be masculine instead of feminine. Although the grounds are not explicit (it may be that the concepts have male associations, or it may have to do with the inflectional endings), this is our first reference to the grammatical category of gender. In the same passage Aristotle himself identifies the regular endings of the three Greek genders (masculine -*os*, feminine -*ē*, neuter -*o* or -*on*), and remarks that whereas a word like the neuter *xúlon*, 'wood', has the right ending for an inanimate object, others such as the masculine *askós*, 'wineskin', or the feminine *klínē*, 'bed', do not. This is the first extant acknowledgement of a discrepancy between grammatical gender and the corresponding real-world categories.[126] From the *De Interpretatione* we have already cited Aristotle's observation that a verb 'additionally signifies time'; the word translated 'time' (*khrónos*) is equally the term for 'tense'. Among other irrelevant and jumbled information, Diogenes Laertius also tells us that Protagoras was the first to distinguish 'parts of time'.[127] Such scattered fragments have survived in part by chance, and may hint at a richer whole. But they are not articulated into an organized body of grammatical analysis, as we find it in later centuries. How then and why did grammars subsequently emerge?

These questions can be answered only in vague and speculative terms. The reason, once more, is that we lack extended first-hand sources and must frequently rely on secondary or tertiary testimony which is bitty and sometimes very late. But if we cannot reconstruct a detailed history, certain major factors can nevertheless be identified.[128]

### 1.5.1 The analysis of the Stoics

The first and one of the most important is the analysis of language within the framework of Stoic dialectics. We have already noted that the Stoics divided this sub-branch of philosophy into two parts. One dealt with 'vocal sound' (*phōnē*), with the 'air set in motion' that served as a signifier. It was under this heading that Diogenes of Babylon is said to have defined the properties of letters; that the meaningful *lógos* 'sentence' is distinguished from the merely phonetic *léxis* 'utterance'; and that Chrysippus in particular appears to have developed the five-part system of *mérē lógou* 'parts of a sentence'. The other branch of Stoic dialectics dealt with the thing signified, an incorporeal entity which, on the one hand, bore an isomorphic relation to the material signifier, and, on the other hand, could be related to the concrete event or circumstance (*tò tugkhánon*) that was referred to. At that level, the Stoics were concerned with the analysis of the *lektón*, 'the thing said'. A predicate, such as *gráphei*, 'writes', is described in our sources as an incomplete *lektón* (the 'thing said' of some individual who remains unspecified). If we also say who is writing it becomes a complete *lektón*, and the particular concern of Stoic logic, in the modern sense of 'logic', was the type of complete *lektón* called an *axíōma* ('judgment'), which was capable of being true or false. But not every complete *lektón* is an *axíōma*. Under the same heading, therefore, the Stoics also developed a more elaborate typology of 'things said', in which 'judgments' are distinguished from commands and wishes (*prostaktiká, euktiká* – later the normal terms for imperative and optative), from enquiries that call for an explanatory answer ('Where does Dion live?'), from questions calling merely for assent or dissent ('Is it daytime?'), and so on. They also began the detailed analysis of certain other semantic categories: in particular, those of case, tense and voice.[129]

The term translated 'case' (*ptôsis*) is one that we have already met in Aristotle, where it referred to nouns and verbs that have been altered, by inflectional modification, from the form they take in simple two-word statements. Stoic usage is and is likely to remain problematic; but in the specific sense with which we are now concerned the term was at once restricted to a semantic role of nouns and extended to include that of the nominative (which for Aristotle had been the noun itself and not a *ptôsis* of a noun) as well as the others. The nominative was then called the 'straight' case (*ptôsis orthé* or 'upright falling'); the genitive, dative and accusative were oblique cases (*ptôseis plagíai* or 'sideways fallings'). The terms for these four members of the category are also Stoic. The nominative is etymologically the 'naming' case (*onomastikē*), the one which identifies or names an individual. The genitive, which came next in the order which we later find in the grammarians, is referred to by the term which usually means 'generic' (*genikē*, from *génos* 'genus'). Its original sense is very doubtful, and the Latin translation *genetivus*, which derives from the notion of 'birth', suggests that it was already obscure some two centuries later. The dative is more transparently the 'giving' case (*dotikē*). Finally, the accusative (*aitiatikē*) was mistranslated into Latin as the 'accusing' case (*accusativus*); although the word itself will bear this interpretation, the standard and more perspicuous explanation derives it from the Aristotelian term for an 'effect' (*aitiatón*) as opposed to a 'cause' (*aítion*). The Stoics are also said to have recognized a fifth case – possibly the vocative, though we are not told so.[130]

The Stoic analysis of case appears to be the direct source for what is later found in grammars. But that of tense is interesting as much for the things that the later tradition did not take over as for those that it did. For the grammarians at least, the primary division was that of present, past and future (enestṓs, parelēluthṓs, méllōn). The past was then divided into four: imperfect (paratatikós, 'extending'), perfect (parakeímenos, 'lain down'), pluperfect (hupersuntélikos, 'over-completed'), and aorist (aóristos, 'indeterminate'). In applying a similar analysis to Latin, Priscian comments that the reason why the past is subdivided (in Latin into the three categories of imperfect, perfect and pluperfect) is that there is much more past time that we can talk about. But in the brief account of (pseudo-) Dionysius Thrax we are also told that there are three kinships or family relationships among tenses. One is that of the present to the imperfect; the second that of the perfect to the pluperfect; the third that of the aorist to the future.[131]

In explaining the family relationships a commentator makes clear that the first two at least are of Stoic origin.[132] The first pair (present and imperfect) were, in the Stoic account, the 'present extending' (enestṑs paratatikós) and the 'past extending' (parōikhēménos paratatikós). In the case of the present we are told that this is because the action extends into both the past and the future: since the present moment is fleeting, if one says 'I am doing something' one indicates both that one was doing it in the immediate past and that one will be doing it in the immediate future. For the imperfect, the reason given is that, although most of the action has been performed, there is still a little left. As for the second pair, the perfect was called not a past but the 'present completed' (enestṑs suntelikós, also téleios enestṓs)[133] and the pluperfect was said to be the past corresponding to it (by implication, the 'past completed' or parōikhēménos suntelikós). Because of these semantic parallels, the words involved are formally similar. In the 'present extending' túptō, 'I am hitting' and the 'past extending' étupton, 'I was hitting', the stem ends with the consonants -pt-, while in the 'present completed' tétupha, 'I have hit' and the 'past completed', etetúphein, 'I had hit', the stem ends in -ph- and the -t- is reduplicated. In the case of the grammarians' third pair (aorist and future), the explanation given is that both are indefinite. The Greek term 'aorist' means 'indefinite' (aóristos; Lat. infinitum), and the commentator points out that the form can be made specifically perfect or pluperfect in sense by adding suitable adverbs. Thus epoíēsa árti, 'I did (aorist) just now' is equivalent to pepoíēka, 'I have done' and epoíēsa pálai, 'I did long ago' is equivalent to epepoiḗkein, 'I had done'. Similarly, he says, the future poiḗsō, 'I will do', leaves the extent of future time indefinite. It will be seen that both the aorist and the future have forms in -*s*-.[134]

There have been various attempts to reconstruct a Stoic system of tenses on the basis of this scholium.[135] But although the system as a whole may elude us, it does seem clear that, in the first two of the pairs set out by (pseudo-) Dionysius, the temporal opposition between present and past is criss-crossed by another opposition that we would now describe as aspectual, between continuing or 'extending' actions and actions that are completed. A similar and wider distinction of aspect is implied by Varro, who insists that 'perfects' such as *didici*, *didiceram* and *didicero* ('I have learned, had learned, will have learned') form a different inflectional paradigm from that of 'non-perfects' (*infecti*) such as *disco*, *discebam* and *discam* ('I am learning, was learning, will learn').[136] But the tradition enshrined by the grammarians is evidently one in which the Stoic 'present complete' or perfect was reclassified as past. There were then three pasts where the Stoics saw two: the 'past extending' or imperfect; the one which the Stoics themselves called 'past complete'; and a third which was also 'complete'. The way out was to describe the Stoics' past complete as 'over-completed' or, in the Latin terminology, 'more than perfect' (*plusquam-perfectum*).

Finally, the Stoics drew distinctions between predicates which correspond, in their semantic scope at least, to the category that is later called voice. For the grammarians voices are 'conditions' or 'dispositions' (*diathéseis*) of a verb, and in the summary of (pseudo-) Dionysius Thrax there are three: that of 'activity' (active), that of 'experience' (passive), and a third which is intermediate (middle). The last refers to forms such as *epoiēsámēn*, 'I made for myself', which formally resemble passives more than actives, but are said to indicate 'at one time an activity and at another time an experience'. This three-term system is the simplest. Other grammarians make further distinctions, in particular between a verb which has both active and passive forms (*túptō*, 'I hit'; *túptomai*, 'I am hit') and an intransitive such as *zô*, 'I live', which was described as neutral (*oudéteros*, 'neither'; in the traditional Latin terminology, 'neuter').[137]

The Stoics, to repeat, were concerned with types of predicate; and their analysis only partly corresponds to that established later. However, it appears that they distinguished between 'straight' predicates (*katēgorémata orthá*), in which an active verb is construed with one of the three oblique cases, and 'reversed' predicates (*húptia*), in which the verb is passive. A third type was again 'neutral' (*oudéteros*). Diogenes Laertius also tells us that the reversed predicates included some which were 'reflexive' (*anti-peponthóta*): his example is the middle *keíretai*, 'cuts his hair' or 'has his hair cut', in which 'the cutter includes himself' in the action. Reflexive predicates are said to be at once 'reversed' and 'activities'. Predicates of all these types are said to be subdivisions of a larger category called the *súmbama*, a term peculiar to Stoic semantics which seems to have referred to any predicate that is construed with a nominative subject. The *súmbama* was in turn distinguished from a *parasúmbama* (literally 'at the side of the *súmbama*'), which we are told was an impersonal.[138]

This is effectively all we are told about the Stoic treatment of specific semantic categories. The importance of their work is evident: if other categories were analysed with similar insight, Stoic dialectic must have been a principal source not just for the system of parts of speech (Subsection 1.4.2), but for the grammatical description of Greek in general. However, it is also evident that, in taking these analyses over, the grammarians made important modifications. In their terms, a category such as case or tense is one of the variable 'concomitants' (*parepómena*, Lat. *accidentia*) of the parts of speech. A grammar will therefore have a chapter on nouns which will include a section on cases, a chapter on verbs including a section on tense, and so on. A part of speech and a 'concomitant' of a part of speech are constructs of the same level; moreover, both are categories of words, and it is on the word (as we will note in greater detail in Subsection 1.6.2) that the account of grammar is based. But for the early Stoics the levels were different. As we have seen, the parts of speech belonged with other topics to the branch of dialectic which was concerned with 'vocal sound' (*phōné*, the physical expression or signifier). But the categories which we have discussed belong to the analysis of 'what is said' (that which is *sēmainómenon* or signified). Furthermore, although the parts of speech are words and the word seems a natural unit at the level of expression, the analysis of meaning was based on sentence meanings and predicates. The Stoic distinctions between *ptóseis* or 'cases' are later used to label an inflectional category; but one suspects that in its original context 'complements' or 'valents' might be a nearer modern translation. Voice, or what we now call voice, was a category of predicates, and the apparent precursor of what the grammarians call mood was a typology of speech acts or sentence modalities.

This last category, in particular, may serve as a warning not to over-interpret our late and solitary information on Stoic tenses. According to another late grammarian, the Stoics called the indicative the 'straight' mood, 'like the nominative', and the others the oblique moods.[139] As subsidiary testimony this is interesting, since, as we have seen, the same term 'straight' was also used, in opposition to 'reversed', in the classification of voices. But on its own it could be taken to imply that the Stoics established moods as a category of words. In the case of tenses our only sources are two late grammarians, and they deal with the matter within their own framework. But we know that this was not the framework of the Stoics themselves, and it would therefore be imprudent to assume that they too saw distinctions such as that of 'extending' and 'completed' (assuming that these have been reported correctly) as matters of word meaning. A plausible interpretation would again assign them to the description of the *lektón*, the predicate or proposition that is the 'thing said'.[140]

### 1.5.2 Linguistic norm

A second factor which entered into the development of grammar was a growing concern for correct Greek (*hellēnismós*, literally 'Greekness'). The conquests of Alexander greatly extended the area in which Greek was spoken. His own state of Macedon was already one in which a Hellenising monarchy, which had adopted the Greek dialect of Athens as its court language, ruled a population that to the Greeks themselves was 'barbarian' or foreign-speaking. Its expansion established the same conditions over the whole of the Near East, in Egypt, Anatolia, Syria, Mesopotamia and beyond. The Athenian or Attic dialect also assumed a similar role within the original Greek homeland. The local varieties, including that of Athens, had once been those of separate city states. But many cities had already lost their freedom, in particular those that had come under Athenian domination in the fifth century. That in itself had led to a limited expansion of Attic. With the conquest of Philip of Macedon, Alexander's father, the independence of the city states was finally effaced. In the wake of this political change, the other local dialects became merely local; while Attic, the language of the conquering dynasty, which was already spoken over a larger area and had transcendent literary prestige, developed in the third century into the common speech (or *koinē*) of the Greek homeland as well as the enormous new territories into which Greek intellectual culture now extended.[141]

It naturally became the mark both of education and of cultural unity. After Alexander's death the empire had split into three, with capitals such as Alexandria (a new city founded by Alexander himself) in places that had not previously been Greek-speaking. Politically, the Eastern Mediterranean was to remain divided until, in the late first century, it was unified by Rome. But intellectually it was one. An educated man was at home, at his own level, through-out the Greek world.

At the same time his level was that of an urban elite, within a larger population that continued to speak other languages and in part clung to other cultures. He may himself have come from an area where Greek civilization was thin. Among the Stoics Zeno, who founded the school, was from Citium in Cyprus and of Phoenician extraction. This implies that he may have learned Greek as a second language. Chrysippus, without whom, it was said, there would have been no Stoa,[142] came from the former colony of Soli in Cilicia, a part of what is now Southern Turkey. Diogenes 'of Babylon' was born in Seleucia on the Tigris, founded only a generation earlier as the abortive capital of one of the successor kingdoms. The Stoic school took root in Athens. But the new intellectual centres were themselves in formerly 'barbarian' areas.

Neither the situation nor the events that gave rise to it have an exact modern parallel. But from partly similar instances it is easy to imagine both the importance that citizens of the Greek states will have attached to mastery of the common language and the new concepts of education that this will have led to. For Aristotle to 'speak correct Greek' (hellēnízein) was already the foundation of good style, and we are told by Cicero that Aristotle's successor Theophrastus (born c.370 BC) distinguished four 'virtues' of speech. The first was correctness, and the other three were clarity, appropriateness and elegance.[143] By the end of the next century the classification of both good and bad features had been elaborated by the Stoics. According to Diogenes Laertius, whose account we are following, this formed part of the branch of dialectic which was concerned with the physical expression of speech, and his particular source, or that transmitted by his own sources, appears to be a treatise on vocal sound (tékhnē perì phōnês) by Diogenes of Babylon. The 'virtues' (aretaí) of 'meaningful speech' (lógos) again begin with hellēnismós or 'Greekness', which is defined as speech 'faultless in respect of rules and without careless usage'. The other virtues are said to be clarity, brevity, appropriateness and elegance. By appropriateness is meant the suiting of speech to the subject matter; elegance (kataskeuḗ) is defined as the avoidance of 'colloquialism' (idiōtismós). Two 'vices' or faults (kakíai) are distinguished, both of which are etymologically the opposite of hellēnismós. 'Barbarism', already defined by Aristotle as the use of wrong vocabulary, is speech 'contrary to the custom of Greeks of good repute'. To speak 'barbarically' is by implication the opposite of to speak 'Greekly'. Soloikismós or 'solecism', also an older term, refers to meaningful speech 'put together incongruously'.[144]

From the first century BC we know of specific treatises 'on Hellenism' (*perì hellēnismoû*); among early authors were the Alexandrian scholar Philoxenus and Tryphon, whom we have already met in subsection 1.4.2 as one of the sources for the part of speech system. The Latin calque on *hellēnismós*, (*Latinitas* or 'Latinity') is first attested early in the same century, and works on 'Latin speech' (*De sermone Latino*) were composed by Varro and his contemporary Antonius Gnipho.[145] But as we pass into the period of the Empire the problem of good Greek is more and more that of written 'speech' in particular. The 'koine' of the Eastern Mediterranean, though derived from Attic, changed as all languages change and became increasingly removed from that of the great writers of the classical period. Certain grammatical features familiar in modern Greek are already found or foreshadowed in the texts of the New Testament, from the first century of the Imperial era. The response of the literary elite was to return to classical usage, and this way institute an 'Atticizing' movement which suppressed features of the spoken language and imposed a literary standard that was to last until the decline of the Byzantine empire in the late eleventh century. In Latin, a similar standard was set by writers such as Cicero and Virgil. But Latin also changed, and by the late Empire the written and spoken languages were diverging at all levels. In both languages, the maintenance of the standard naturally became a primary educational concern.[146]

The concern of grammar with correct usage is made explicit in the definition by Quintilian, from the first century AD, which we cited in section 1.1. According to this, the first of two parts of grammar is 'the knowledge of correct speech' (*recte loquendi scientia*); this is also taken to subsume the 'knowledge of correct writing', which is dealt with in a separate section. Under correct speaking the subjects covered are very similar to those that belonged to the Stoic treatment of vocal expression. First comes the study of letters, then of the parts of speech. Next, pupils 'must know the inflections of nouns and verbs' (*nomina declinare et verba ... sciant*), without which, Quintilian says, they will be unable to understand what follows. This was not a Stoic topic (at least if our information is not deficient), and its source will particularly concern us in the next subsection. According to Quintilian, a keen instructor will point out, among other things, discrepancies between genders and endings (the man's name *Murena* ends with an -*a* that is characteristic of feminines, the girl's name *Glycerium* with an -*um* that is characteristic of neuters); the derivation of names such as *Rufus* (literally, 'the red') or *Plautus* ('flat-footed'); the question whether, in an instrumental use of the ablative (*hasta*, 'with a spear'), we should recognize the 'force of a sixth case'; the existence of defective verbs such as impersonals.[147] Such topics are common in grammars, conceived still as a medium for teaching correct speech, for centuries to come.

The virtues and faults of speech form the remainder of this first part. First, speech (*oratio*) should be free of error (*emendata*), a requirement equivalent to that of *hellēnismós* in the account ascribed to the Stoics. In addition, it should be clear (*dilucida*) and elegant (*ornata*, 'embellished'); many authorities, Quintilian explains, include appropriateness under elegance. These are the three virtues, and the faults are their opposites. However, in classifying both good and bad features, Quintilian draws a major distinction between cases which involve just one word and those which involve several. When a single word is wrong the fault is classed as a barbarism: for example, it may be imported from a foreign language, it may be rude or threatening, sounds may be altered or in the wrong place, or it may have an incorrect accent. When the fault involves two or more words it is a solecism. Quintilian's first example is of an adjective whose gender agrees wrongly: were it not that Virgil had written both, either *amarae corticis*, 'of bitter bark' (where *amarae*, 'bitter' is feminine) or *medio cortice*, literally 'in the middle bark' (where *medio*, 'middle' is masculine) would have to be corrected. One classification which he reports divided solecisms into four types, the first involving addition (pleonasms such as *nam enim*, 'for for'), the second deletion (ellipses such as *Aegypto venio*, with no initial preposition, for 'I come from Egypt'), the third transposition (for example, the jumbled word order in *quoque ego*, 'also I' for *ego quoque*), and the fourth substitution (thus, in the examples from Virgil, either *amarae* for masculine *amari* or *medio* for feminine *media*). There is a similar mechanical classification at the level of barbarism: incorrect addition of letters (as *choronae*, 'crowns' for *coronae*), and so on.[148]

The text which we are citing belongs to a period when the tradition of prescriptive grammar was securely established. The distinction between barbarism and solecism is standard in the grammarians, and from their detailed classification it is obvious that, by Quintilian's time, these matters had been extensively worked over. In the next century, the principles underlying correct syntax are systematically explored by Apollonius Dyscolus (section 1.6.1). But since we lack continuous evidence for the Hellenistic period, our only resource is to compare the tradition which historically emerged with such information as we have on the Stoics and others, and to try to relate this to the linguistic situation of the Greek world at the time when grammar originated. The evidence points to a new concern with language as the domain of correctness and conformity. To anyone familiar with prescriptive grammar in the modern period, the collocation of topics in the first part of Quintilian's account of grammar, in which the parts of speech and noun and verb inflection are the principles which underlie the identification of grammatical errors, and the avoidance of these is set alongside the requirement that speech should be lucid and elegant, may seem entirely natural. In another passage, which we will cite in context in the next section, Quintilian assesses the conflicting claims of *ratio* (logic or regularity) and *consuetudo*, 'usage' as criteria for correctness. That too is a familiar issue. But this is precisely because, in this as in many other matters, we are ourselves the inheritors of Hellenistic concepts. In the case of grammar, the origin of these concepts is plausibly sought in the quite new problems of a standard cultural and administrative language, and the new educational needs attendant on them.

### 1.5.3 The Alexandrian scholars

A third factor is the development of Alexandrian literary scholarship. In Greek literary history the end of the fourth century BC is marked by the emergence of scholar poets, writing in a learned and artificial style. The first was Philetas, famous both for his elegies and for an extensive glossary of archaic and other rare words. One of the pupils of Philetas was the effective founder of the Alexandrian library, Ptolemy II. Another was Zenodotus (born c.325 BC), who in the mid-280s became its first head. Zenodotus was a pioneering editor of the texts of Homer and other earlier poets, and seems incidentally to have been the first to arrange a glossary by the order of the initial letters. His successor as librarian was the epic poet Apollonius Rhodius (born c.295 BC), whose older contemporary Callimachus (c.305–c.240 BC), also a leading poet, worked in the library, compiling an extensive catalogue of Greek literature. In the next generation Eratosthenes (c.275–194 BC), though he wrote poetry and contributed to literary scholarship, was more important as a geographer and mathematician. But his successor as head of the library, Aristophanes of Byzantium (c.257–180 BC), was another major textual scholar and lexicographer, and was succeeded in the former field by Aristarchus (c.217–145 BC), whose work embraced the whole of what might now be termed philology. Aristarchus was in turn the teacher of, among others, Dionysius Thrax (c.170–90 BC). A period of approximately 150 years, from the beginning of the third to the middle of the second century, had seen the foundation of textual scholarship, and great progress in the academic study of literature generally.[149]

The term *grammatikós* 'student of letters' is used from early in the
third century to describe the scholarly activity of Zenodotus and his
followers. Aristarchus, in particular, is described as the student of
letters par excellence (*ho grammatikótatos*, 'the grammaticalest').[150]
According to the early definition of Eratosthenes, the discipline
called *grammatikḗ* is 'a comprehensive expertise in letters' (*héxis
pante* *ēs en grámmasi*); as our source explains, the word 'letters' is to
be taken in the sense of 'literary compositions' (*suggrámmata*). A
century or so later we have the definition of Dionysius Thrax which,
unlike most of the grammar attached to his name, we can confidently
accept as genuine. According to this, *grammatikḗ* is a 'practical
knowledge' (*empeiría*) of 'the forms used for the most part in poets
and prose writers' (*tôn parà poiētaîs te kaì suggrapheûsin hōs epì tò
polù legoménōn*). It is said to have six parts. The first is reading with a
skilled rendering of prosody (*anágnōsis entribḗs katà prosōidían*).
The second is the explanation of figurative usages in poetry (*exḗgēsis
katà toùs enupárkhontas poiētikoùs trópous*). The third is an
accessible account of rare words and points of information (*glōssôn
te kaì historiôn prókheiros apódosis*). The fourth is the finding of
etymologies (*etumologías heúresis*). The fifth is the calculation of
analogy (*analogías eklogismós*). The sixth part, which is the finest of
all, is the critical assessment of poems (*krísis poiēmátōn*).[151]

The picture of grammar which is given by Dionysius is consistent
with Roman sources in the following century. A definition ascribed
to Varro employs an almost identical formula: 'grammar' or, in
Latin, *litteratura* is 'the knowledge of the forms used for the most
part by poets, historians and orators' (*scientia . . . (eorum) quae a
poetis historicis oratoribusque dicuntur ex parte maiore*). The discipline is said to have four tasks: these are given differently by
different sources, but according to one they are reading, exposition,
correction and judgment (*lectio, enarratio, emendatio, iudicium*).[152]
According to Cicero, the discipline of 'grammar' unites four things
which had previously been separate. The first is the detailed examination of the poets (*poetarum pertractatio*). The second and third
are the study of points of information (*historiarum cognitio*) and
the explanation of words (*verborum interpretatio*); these correspond
directly to the third part of Dionysius' definition. The fourth is a
particular sound in pronunciation (*pronuntiandi quidam sonus*).[153]

We have already noted that the reading and expounding of
literature (*lectio, enarratio*) forms the second part of Quintilian's
definition of grammar,[154] and the point by point examination of
literary texts, including endless points of information on the characters and so on, was to remain the backbone of the grammarian's
teaching in the classroom.

But the definitions of scholarly disciplines tend to lag behind their substance; and it seems clear that, in the course of the Hellenistic period, the notion of grammar evolved in two respects. First, its scope was enlarged to include not just the older literary texts but the use of language generally. Dionysius' definition is still restricted, and was criticised on that score (some three centuries later) by Sextus Empiricus. But Sextus also cites other definitions. According to another pupil of Aristarchus, grammar in its developed form (*teleía grammatiké*) is 'an expertise on scientific principles which distinguishes in the most precise way the things said and things thought among the Greeks, except those falling under other sciences' ([*phēsì*] *héxin eînai apò tékhnēs diagnōstikēn tôn par' Héllēsi lektôn kaì noētôn epì tò akribéstaton, plēn tôn hup'állais tékhnais*). As Sextus' critique makes clear, this is intended to cover not just literature, but every Greek vocal expression and everything signified. Another definition says that the science of grammar is 'the study of forms of speech in the poets and according to common usage'. This extension of the discipline involves the grammarian not just in the editing of texts, but in the whole problem of 'Greekness' or correct Greek (*hellēnismós*) which we discussed in the last section, 1.5.2.[155]

Second, there is evidence that the conception of grammar changed from that of a practical discipline (*empeiría* in the definition of Dionysius Thrax) to that of a *tékhnē* 'science' or, in the words of one of the definitions which we have just cited, a discipline which proceeds *apò tékhnēs* 'on scientific principles'. The term *empeiría* relates grammar to, in particular, the empirical approach to medicine. So too does Dionysius' qualification 'for the most part': in treating a patient empirically a doctor proceeds according to the weight of experience in other relevant cases, but does not invoke absolute laws. However, this aspect of Dionysius' definition soon attracted criticism. One grammarian of the first century BC is said to have objected both to the classification of grammar as an *empeiría* and to the phrase 'for the most part'. These are appropriate, he says, to sciences like navigation and medicine which are matters of guesswork and are subject to chance; grammar is not guesswork, but is comparable to music and philosophy. Our source is again Sextus Empiricus, according to whom at least one other scholar had already objected that practical knowledge is without rule (*álogos*) and based on mere observation and experience.[156] In another passage Sextus cites the assessment of Alexandrian grammar by the Stoic Crates of Mallos. Crates became the first head of a rival library in Pergamum, and described his own work as that of a *kritikós* or interpreter of literature on philosophical principles.

According to him, the *grammatikós* is merely someone who expounds rare words, explains prosody and is knowledgeable in other matters of that sort; the relation of the *kritikós* to the *grammatikós* is like that of a master builder to his underling.[157] Crates' comments are from the first part of the second century and imply that at this stage grammar was indeed the form of practical scholarship that Dionysius Thrax describes.

In Dionysius' account grammar, as we have seen, has six parts. But according to one of the first century writers whom we have cited it has three. The last is called the 'grammatical' part ([*méros*] *grammatikón*) or, in the apparently parallel division that Sextus takes as the framework for his own critique, the 'more peculiar' part (*idiaíteron*). This is concerned specifically with the study of poets and prose writers, and is said to rest on both the parts which precede it. Of these, the first is a 'scientific' part ([*méros*] *tekhnikón*), whose subject matter, again following the contents of Sextus' own exposition, comprises the classification of elementary sounds (*stoikheîa*), syllables, parts of speech and inflections, and the principles of correct Greek (*hellēnismós*). The second part is called *historikón*, which is an adjective derived from *historía*, earlier translated 'point of information'. This dealt with background information, including true 'history', false 'history' (legend) and things purporting to be true (as in plays).[158] Now the 'historical' and 'grammatical' parts are evidently a rethinking of grammar as Dionysius had conceived it. But the 'scientific' or 'technical' part is, on the face of it, new.

For its sources it seems that we must look in particular to Stoic work on language, both on semantic categories (subsection 1.5.1) and on the parts of speech (subsection 1.4.2) and Hellenism (subsection 1.5.2). But for the treatment of inflections, which will particularly occupy us in the remainder of this subsection, there is an Alexandrian source in the fifth part of Dionysius' division of grammar, 'the calculation of analogy'. In establishing the text of Homer and other poets, one of the principles that Aristarchus, in particular, had used was that of conformity to an inflectional proportion. For example, in *Iliad* 24.8

*andrôn te ptolémous alegeiná te kúmata peírōn*

'cleaving through wars of men and bitter waves'

he is cited as establishing the accentuation of the participle *peírōn* (literally 'piercing') by analogy with that of *keírōn*, 'cutting'. As *keírei*, 'he cuts' is to *keírōn*, so *peírei*, 'he pierces' must be to *peirōn*; therefore the last is correct and an alternative reading, *peirôn*, must be rejected. It seems that the notion of analogy, which was in origin mathematical, was first used simply as a tool in philology. But a wider contemporary issue, as we have seen, was that of *hellēnismós* or 'Greekness' in ordinary speech and writing. Although the assumption that language should follow analogical patterns is not in itself obvious, it seems entirely natural that, once it had been applied in the literary context, it should be extended to the other. Another natural development associates proportions with rules. In establishing an analogy a grammarian implied a framework of semantic categories: as the meaning of *keírei* is to that of *keírōn*, so that of *peírei* is to that of *peírōn*. Such categories may be named: in support of the acute accent in *peírōn*, Aristarchus also says that if the correct form were *peirôn* the imperfect (*paratatikós*) would be *epeíra*. From there it is a short step to a covering formula: if a word of category *X* has form *a* then the corresponding word of category *Y* will always (or 'for the most part') have form *b*.[159]

Although analogy enters into Dionysius' definition of grammar, there is no illustration or further mention of it in the summary text that bears his name. Nor is it a central topic in grammars that are indisputably of the third century AD and later. Donatus, for example, does not refer to it and another Roman grammarian says that the notion of a rule is more general.[160] But from the first century BC we may cite, in particular, the fragments of a work on analogy by Julius Caesar (100–44 BC). According to later sources Caesar argued, for example, that the nominative *turbo* (either the word for 'whirlwind' or the personal name *Turbo*) ought to form an accusative in *-onem* and not *-inem*. In that way it would follow the pattern of *Carbo*, accusative *Carbonem* (another personal name) instead of *homo* 'man', accusative *hominem*. Another prescription is that the word for 'sand' (*harena*) should not be used in the plural; in that respect it is analogous to the words for 'sky' (*caelum*) and 'wheat' (*triticum*). Our sources also indicate that Caesar formulated covering rules. Thus every neuter noun which ends in *-e* (for example, *mare*, 'sea') should have final *-i* (*mari*) in both the dative and the ablative singular; likewise neuter nouns in *-ar*, with the exception of *iubar* 'first light', which should follow the analogy of *far*, 'emmer wheat' (ablatives *farre, iubare*). A rule of a different kind, which is also standard among later grammarians, is invoked against a proposal by his contemporary Varro. According to Varro, whose contributions we will turn to later, the nominative and accusative of the word for 'milk' should be not *lac* but *lact*; compare genitive *lactis*. But Caesar pointed out that no Latin word ends in two 'mute' consonants.[161]

Caesar is also credited with one version of a set of conditions under which a proportion involving nouns can be accepted as valid. Five involve semantic categories: for the words to be compared they have to be of the same semantic type (*qualitas*), the same grade of comparison, the same gender, the same number and the same case. Another condition is that they must be identical in respect of derivational complexity (*figura*). Finally, they must have the same syllabic ending (for example, if one ends in *-us* the other must also end in *-us*), and the same consonant or vowel must precede it. Such conditions seem to date from the earliest Greek development of the concept. Aristophanes of Byzantium is said to have developed either five or six such parameters, and we are told that Aristarchus added the requirement that simple nouns should not be compared to compound. The same sources link these conditions to a Greek definition of analogy in general: 'a complex of parallel relations' (*sumplokḕ lógōn akoloúthōn*).[162]

So much for the concept of analogy in itself. It was not, however, the only criterion for 'Greekness' or 'Latinity', and there was therefore a problem in ranking it against other factors. In Quintilian's account, which we can take as representative of the Roman tradition, discourse (*sermo*) rests on four principles. The first is that of *ratio* or 'regularity', under which heading both analogy and etymology, which had formed the fourth of Dionysius Thrax' six divisions of grammar, are included. But the others all invoke usage, either that of an earlier period (*vetustas* or 'archaism'), or the 'authority' (*auctoritas*) especially of good prose writers, or the common usage (*consuetudo*) of educated people.[163] All four principles are in potential conflict. But, in particular, the principle of regularity (*ratio*) conflicts with that of common usage (*consuetudo*). For in Greek and Latin, as in other languages, many normal forms are irregular.

According to Quintilian, analogy (or, in Latin, *proportio*, 'proportionality') is the resolution of a point that is uncertain by reference to something similar that is undisputed. For example, one may be unsure whether *funis*, 'rope', is masculine or feminine (both genders are found in earlier writers); this doubt can be removed by comparison with *panis*, 'bread', which ends in the same way and is masculine. Alternatively, it is masculine because the diminutive *funiculus*, 'cord, thin rope', is masculine. For 'to boil' some ancient writers have *fervĕre*, with a short *e*. But it would be wrong to follow them: the form for 'I boil' is *ferveo* not *fervo*, and verbs which end in *-eo* (such as *prandeo*, 'I dine' or *pendeo*, 'I hang') have infinitives with long *e* (*prandēre*, *pendēre*). By analogy with these 'to boil' must be *fervēre*. Quintilian says that analogy is the main constituent of regularity. But it is clear that etymological arguments could also be used, to determine either the correct form of a word or its meaning. As a jocular example Quintilian cites a Republican orator who argued that he was *frugi*, 'thrifty' on the grounds that *frugalitas* 'thriftiness' comes from *fructuosus*, 'fruitful' and he was indeed useful, or fruitful, to many.[164]

In the instances which we have cited, the appeal to analogy resolves a genuine uncertainty. But once the principle of a rule is admitted, there is a natural temptation to insist on its application even in cases where usage is unambiguous. For Quintilian himself, this was to be resisted. Analogy, he argues, was itself created by usage; it was not sent down from heaven to tell people how to speak, but was discovered after they had begun to do so. It is not a law (*lex*), but a practice that is generally observed (*observatio*). Usage is, accordingly, the 'surest guide to speaking' (*certissima loquendi magistra*). But the examples which he rejects imply that the tendency was real. For example, it is an 'irritating pedantry' to replace *audacter*, 'boldly', which is used by all the orators, with a regularized form *audaciter* (compare *pertinaciter*, 'stubbornly'). Regularisers would also change *frugi*, 'thrifty', which is one of a handful of indeclinable adjectives, into *frugalis*, on the grounds that the noun *frugalitas*, 'thriftiness' must derive from it. 'Nothing distresses me more', Quintilian says, than the way nominatives are altered by analogy with the oblique cases: for example, by replacing the *u* in *ebur*, 'ivory' and *robur*, 'oak', 'forms spoken and written by the highest authorities', with the *o* of the genitives *eboris* and *roboris*. He specifically cites Antonius Gnipho (early first century BC) for a converse attempt to replace the plurals *ebora*, 'ivories' and *robora*, 'oaks' with *ebura* and *robura* (also to change both *marmor*, 'marble' and its plural *marmora* to *marmur* and *marmura*). In some instances it might not always be easy to distinguish conscious prescription from the ordinary workings of language change. But a remark at the end of this section brings out the special connection between regularization and 'grammar'. The point is made not inappropriately, Quintilian says, that 'it is one thing to speak correct Latin, and another to speak according to grammar' (*aliud esse Latine, aliud grammatice loqui*).[165]

A century earlier, Cicero had also objected to regularizations based both on analogy and on etymology. An example of the latter is an attempt to replace the *r* of *meridies*, 'midday' with the etymological *d* of *medius*, 'middle'.[166] For Greek, our main source is the systematic attack on the grammarians by Sextus Empiricus. After arguing first that the *grammatikoí* could not give a coherent definition of their subject (it is from this chapter that we have taken the definitions cited earlier), Sextus works through its entire 'scientific part' (*tekhnikòn méros*), including the treatment of Hellenism. There are two concepts, he says, of 'correct Greek'. One respects usage (*sunétheia*) and is derived from observation (*paratérēsis*) in ordinary conversation. The other 'is dissociated from our common usage and seems to proceed by grammatical analogy'. An example of the latter would be the replacement of the oblique forms of the name of Zeus (genitive *Zēnós*) with regularized forms such as a genitive *Zeós*) based on the nominative *Zeús*. Another would be the formation of a genitive *kúōnos* from the nominative *kúōn*, 'dog', or of nominative *kûs* from the actual genitive *kunós*. Sextus argues that the grammarians' concept of good Greek is without scientific foundation. One part of his case is that analogy is itself no more than an extrapolation from usage. A grammarian says, for example, that 'to use' should be *khrâsthai* and not *khrêsthai*, because that brings it into line with *ktâsthai*, 'to acquire'. But if we ask why *ktâsthai* is in turn to be preferred to *ktêsthai*, the only answer is that it is in fact the form which is used. At another point, he objects to the generalization of a rule at the expense of potential exceptions. A grammarian will say that the genitive of *eumenés* 'fortunate' should be *eumenoûs* and not *eumenoû*, because by rule every simple noun which ends in -*ēs* and has an acute on its final syllable must have a genitive in -*s*. But that begs the question: the rule may not be universal precisely because the form *eumenoû* does not follow it.[167]

For an earlier, fuller, but unfortunately much more problematical treatment we must return to the *De Lingua Latina* of Varro. In the third of three surviving books devoted to what would now be called inflection and word formation, Varro says that two pairs of things are analogous if their *ratio* or *lógos*, which in this context can be translated as 'relationship', is the same. For example, the bronze coin called an *as* stands in the same relationship to the half-*as* as the silver *libella* to the half-*libella*; there is therefore an analogy which links each pair to the other. Similarly, in language, there is an analogy between the accusative and dative singular of the word for 'love' (*amorem, amori*) and the corresponding cases of the word for 'pain' (*dolorem, dolori*). In speech, Varro says, analogies have been used with particular care by grammarians of the school of Aristarchus. He then points out that one relationship can intersect with another. For example, *albus*, 'white' (nominative singular masculine) is related on one dimension to the dative *albo* and the genitive *albi*, and on another dimension to the feminine *alba* and neuter *album*. These relations establish a system of three rows, defined by the genders, and three columns, defined by the three cases; the same holds analogously for other forms that, in our terms, share the same paradigm.[168]

Varro also speaks of analogies in which *a* is to *b* as *b* is to *c*. For example, of the three 'non-perfect' tenses, *legebam*, 'I was reading', has the same time relationship to *lego*, 'I am reading', as *lego* has to *legam*, 'I will read' (past to present as present to future).[169] But in general the term is again used in cases where there is both a semantic and an inflectional similarity. According to Varro, both Greek and Latin scholars had written many works for and against this principle. One side took the view that 'in speaking one ought to follow those words which are derived from like sources in like fashion' (*ea verba ... quae ab similibus similiter essent derivata*). These they called 'analogies'. Others took the view that 'this should be ignored and one should rather follow the unlikeness that is found in usage' (*dissimilitudinem quae in consuetudine est*). This unlikeness they call 'anomaly' (Gk. *anōmalía* 'unevenness'). As supporters of the first view, Varro refers to Aristarchus and his followers. In the surviving text they are mentioned on seven occasions (three times for the same point about noun inflection). There are also two references to Aristarchus' teacher Aristophanes of Byzantium, one saying that in certain things he followed 'truth rather than usage'. As a supporter of the opposite view Varro refers to Crates of Mallos. He is said to have written 'against analogy and Aristarchus'; on at least one point Varro says that Aristarchus had replied.[170]

Varro's account is dramatized by Aulus Gellius (mid-second century AD), and has been widely taken as evidence of a major dispute about the nature of language, between the grammarians of the Alexandrian school, dubbed 'analogists', and the 'anomalists' of a rival school in Pergamum.[171] But it is not necessary, or even natural, to read it in that sense. In the first place, the dispute as he describes it is not primarily about the nature of language. It is about how far, as a matter of policy, speech should be regularized. The view explicitly ascribed to Aristarchus is that, in inflecting words, one ought to 'follow a certain likeness, as far as usage allows'. This is a remark that fits easily into the context of competing criteria for correctness, as we find it in the later accounts of Quintilian and Sextus Empiricus. The same qualification ('as far as usage allows') appears at the end of a section setting out, in general terms, the arguments for following analogies. Not every word (the 'analogist' says) should be regularized, since in some cases an irregular form is established in usage and to change it would offend many speakers.[172] The opposite ('anomalist') view is that usage should be followed regardless of whether it is regular or irregular.

In a section purporting to set out this side of the argument, Varro says that the principle of regularity was rejected even when, as in some of Quintilian's examples, usage fluctuates. The aim of speech is to be brief and clear. Brevity is ensured by restraint, and clarity by conformity with usage; if two forms are in use (as Quintilian's *fervĕre* and *fervēre* or *funis*, masculine and *funis*, feminine), there is no need to disturb them since either meets these requirements.[173]

In neither of Varro's opposed camps is it denied that language as it stands is partly regular and partly irregular. Those who argue 'against similarity of inflections' – or 'against those who follow similarity'[174] are made to stress that like is not always derived from like. For example, the dative of *lupus*, 'wolf' is *lupo* but that of *lepus*, 'hare', which also ends in *-us*, is *lepori*. Like can also be derived from unlike: for example, the similar datives *Jovi* and *ovi* are from the dissimilar nominatives *Jupiter* (the name of the god) and *ovis*, 'sheep'. But these are set alongside other instances where like does yield like (*bonus*, 'good' and *malus*, 'bad' have datives *bono* and *malo*) and unlike does yield unlike (*Priamus* 'Priam' and *Paris* 'Paris' have datives *Priamo* and *Pari*). Their opponents, as we have seen, accept not just that there are irregularities but that some are irremediable. One imagines that they too would have recoiled from an attempt to replace *Jovi* with *Juppitri*, which Varro gives as an example of a 'crazy' regularization. Insofar as he presents the issue as one of factual disagreement, it is a matter of degree and interpretation. Those who say that in speech 'analogy does not exist' are made to argue that if it did there would have to be regularity in every part: it is not reasonable to say that a negro is white because he has white teeth. The preceding paragraph presupposes that there are more irregular words than regular. The opposite side is made to argue that the anomalies which are cited are a few rarely used forms 'picked out from the sea of speech'. To say on their account that 'analogies do not exist' is like saying that there is no regularity in men or cattle or horses, because one occasionally sees a man with only one eye, or a cow with only one horn, or a horse that is lame.[175]

The other arguments that Varro retails bear quite naturally on the positions stated. Those who want to regularize speech say that speakers do this anyway: when errors are made they are corrected by reference not just to usage, but to regularities in usage. Similarly, if the couches in a dining room are not set out properly, we correct them 'at once according to general usage and to the analogies of other dining rooms'. The rest of their argument, as Varro presents it, consists mainly of further appeals to spheres other than language. A doctor is not to be criticized if he improves the health of someone whom bad habits have made ill. Why then is it wrong to improve speech when it too suffers from bad habits? If someone habitually misbehaves in public we may punish him. Why should we not correct him, since it can be done without punishment, if he is in the habit of misbehaving verbally? If new and regular forms are rejected in the marketplace, poets and especially dramatists ought to din them into the public's ears. Usage has often shifted under their influence, for better and for worse; we should follow it, where possible, only when it is for the better. In other fields old usage does not obstruct the introduction of new: old laws, for example, are repealed. Why should a word that is new and in accordance with analogy be avoided? On the point of fact, those who support regularization say that there is regularity in every other sphere, in astronomy and geography, in the tides and seasons, in the way each species reproduces its kind. The human mind also has parts which are analogous to one another; one part gives rise to vocal sound and vocal sound constitutes speech; therefore 'by nature it is necessary that speech should have analogies'. Some might object to biological and other parallels that there is a difference between regularity in nature and regularity that is the product of will. But in Varro's own view, which we will return to in a moment, nature as well as will operate in the forms of words.[176]

Those who oppose regularization are also said to appeal to other spheres. In our houses the bedroom and the stable are not alike and we do not try to make them so. On grounds of utility 'we follow dissimilarities rather than similarities'. Likewise in furniture, clothing, food and so on; in speech, which is also for use, anomaly should also be accepted. It is the same if we consider elegance as well as utility: in the design of crockery or the decoration of furniture 'pleasure is often obtained more from dissimilarity than from similarity'. Accordingly where words are dissimilar in usage, that is not something to be avoided. As to regularity, it is either there in usage anyway or (as in the case of *Juppitri*) one would be mad to follow it. A final argument on this side is that the notion of analogy is not well founded. Does similarity reside simply in the sound of a word? According to the advocates of regularization it does not: it makes a difference whether, for example, a word refers to something male or female, or is a proper noun or common noun. But then, if we are talking about what the words refer to, names such as *Dion* and *Theon*, which they say are almost twins, are dissimilar if, for example, one refers to a boy and the other to an old man or one to someone who is white and the other to someone who is black. It is impudent to say that there are analogies if the nature of similarity cannot be clarified. Nor is it clear how

likeness is to be recognized. The regularizers want to say that
nominatives which appear to be similar are different if their vocatives are different. (We are told elsewhere that this is what Aristarchus said about cases such as *lupus* and *lepus*.) But that is like
saying that identical twins cannot be recognized as identical unless
one also looks at their children.[177]

So much for the sections in which Varro sets out his opposing
arguments. On this reading, any discussion of the actual nature of
speech (as to whether speakers do follow analogies or simply
respect usage) is incidental to the main controversy, which is about
how people ought to speak. But, in addition, it is uncertain how far
Varro's testimony can be trusted. We can accept that, for the
Romans at least, the attractions of regularity were seen as conflicting with usage. But for the controversy as Varro presents it there is
no other evidence. In particular, no independent source opposes
*anōmalía* to *analogía*, or applies the former to inflectional irregularities. Nor is there any other source for the specific arguments
which we have cited, which in Varro's exposition are set out with
artificial symmetry: first, those favouring anomaly (Book 8); then
a point by point reply in favour of analogy (Book 9). Nor are these
ascribed by name to Varro's protagonists: we are simply told that
'they' (the followers of anomaly) say this and 'they' (the followers
of analogy) say that. In interpreting such an account, one cannot
but suspect that arguments have been magnified or distorted. At
the very least they have been manipulated to fit Varro's rhetorical
scheme; and it is probable that, in raking points together and
arranging them in opposed camps, he has himself manufactured
most of the polemic.[178]

It is accordingly safer to look at his account of word-derivation
on its own merits. The theory which Varro himself presents
(whether his own in part or based entirely on his understanding of
Greek sources) is founded on a distinction between words created
by the will of individual speakers and those that result from
processes established in the community. In the former case, a
speaker takes the name for one thing and assigns a name to
something else (*a nomine aliae rei imponit nomen*). For example,
someone might call a slave after the city in which he was bought
(thus *Ephesius*, 'the Ephesian' from *Ephesus*); similarly *Romulus*, the
name of the legendary founder of Rome, was derived from *Roma*.
As we have seen in section 1.3, the process of 'assigning' names
(*impositio*, or in Greek *thésis*) was conceived as the means by
which words in general were originally invented. In the latter case,
the forms arise not by the will of individuals but by shared custom
(*a communi consensu*). Given that the name *Romulus* exists, we all

know how to form from it the dative or ablative *Romulo*, the genitive *Romuli* and the accusative *Romulum*. Given the verb *dico*, 'I say', we do not need to ask how to form *dicebam*, 'I was saying' or *dixeram*, 'I had said'. At the beginning of these three books, Varro speaks of the assigning of words as a source and their modification as a stream that flows from it. Assigned words (*imposiicia*) are designedly as few as possible, so that they can be learned more quickly. But modified words (*declinata*) are as many as possible, so that people may more easily say whatever they need to.

In the passage I have just cited creation (*impositio*) is opposed to modification (*declinatio*). But in later passages in all three books the term *declinatio* is applied to derivations of both the types which we have illustrated: derivation by will (*declinatio voluntaria* or *a voluntate*) and what Varro then calls 'natural' modification (*declinatio naturalis* or *a natura*). In the first type, naming is done by unskilled speakers; the forms are then accepted and, however muddled they may be, one has to use them. Neither the followers of Aristarchus nor anyone else have sought to introduce regularity into a part of language that is plainly unhealthy. But in natural modification regularity is dominant and necessary. Once one has learned the pattern in one word one can employ it in countless others, and the number of modified forms is itself countless. In this way Varro seeks to argue that both the followers of anomaly and the followers of analogy are, in their respective fields, right.[179]

The rest of Varro's treatment cannot easily be reconstructed, since the three books that partly survive are only half of those devoted to this aspect of language. But the details that they give confirm that morphological analysis was by then an intensive field of study. In his critical discussion of modification Varro deals equally with both inflectional and what we would now call derivational formations. Thus nouns can be modified in accordance with distinctions in the things they name (for example, the man's name *Terentius* is modified to the woman's name *Terentia*) or to show distinctions between what they name and something else (for example, *equiso*, 'stable lad' from *equus*, 'horse'). Under the first heading, one sub-type is according to the nature of the thing itself: examples are the modification of *homo*, 'man' to the diminutive *homunculus* (modification because of smallness) or the plural *homines* (modification because of numerousness). Both these involve the thing as a whole; others only a part (for example, *mammosae* 'women with large breasts' from *mamma*, 'breast' or *prudentes*, 'prudent people' from *prudentia*, 'prudence'). Another subtype is according to the speaker's use of the noun; this distinguishes the six cases. Elsewhere he employs a four-fold classification into naming (*equile*, 'stable' from *equus*, 'horse'), case, increase (*albius*, 'whiter' from *albus*, 'white') and diminution (*cistula*, 'little box' from *cista*, 'box'). In the case of verbs he speaks of modification according to time (present, past, future) and person (speaker, hearer, subject of discourse); also, among others, of distinctions between incomplete and complete (*emo*, 'I am buying' and *emi*, 'I have bought'), between once and many times (*lego*, 'I read' and *lectito*, 'I read again and again'), between doing and experiencing (active *uro*, 'I burn' and passive *uror*, 'I am being burnt'), and again of number.[180]

There are also glimpses of semantic insight, especially in the way that gaps within this framework of categories are explained. The genders contrast in, for example, *equus*, 'horse, stallion' and *equa*, 'mare'; however, there is no feminine *corva* alongside the masculine *corvus*, 'crow'. The reason offered is that, in the case of crows, we have no need to draw such a distinction. The word *mane*, 'in the morning', has neither a comparative *manius* nor a superlative *manissime*; similarly *vesperi*, 'in the evening'. Varro explains that time does not admit degrees, but only distinctions of before and after. There are no perfect imperatives; this is because one does not order someone to do something that has already been done. In Varro's account these are arguments by which a proponent of regularity can counter the assertion that such gaps are anomalous. But we might compare an argument by Tryphon which was mentioned in subsection 1.4.2, giving the semantic reason why a common noun, such as *ánthrōpos*, 'man', does not form a patronymic. Whatever its context, this form of reasoning attests an interest in language which transcends those of prescriptive Hellenism or of literary scholarship.[181]

The Stoics and the Alexandrian *grammatikoí* are the main contributors to the early development of grammar. But the relation between them remains problematic. A natural temptation is to see them as opposed schools: this is particularly seductive if we accept Varro's presentation of the arguments about regularity, in which the Stoic Crates of Mallos and the Alexandrian Aristarchus are protagonists in a major controversy. But other evidence would suggest an historical development in which a way of studying language, first developed within the structure of Stoic philosophy, was taken over by the grammarians and extended in a different direction. In the course of this some notions were suppressed, notably the Stoic division between the two parts of dialectic. Others were added: in particular, those relating to inflections. But the 'scientific part' of grammar – the *tekhnikòn méros* which is the forerunner of the grammatical texts which survive from later centuries – carried the marks of its Stoic origin, in the common concern with Hellenism, in the parts of speech system, in other basic semantic categories.

There is also a problem of dating. If the body of the text ascribed to Dionysius Thrax is genuine, then, despite the absence from his division of grammar of anything corresponding to its 'scientific part', the system of categories must have existed, in its definitive form, by the end of the second century BC. However, this text is plainly a compendium of results that have already been achieved. Therefore the decisive contribution must be earlier, and we naturally look to Aristarchus, who was Dionysius' teacher. If the work is not authentic, other evidence would suggest that the development was not complete until perhaps the middle of the first century. In that case the definitive contribution would be that of scholars such as Tryphon, who has already been mentioned in connection with the parts of speech, and others who are also shadowy. If this interpretation is correct, a Roman writer such as Caesar was applying to Latin methods and findings whose beginnings may indeed be earlier, but which were only then solidifying in the work of his Greek contemporaries.[182]

There is, in short, a great deal that we do not know, and for the Hellenistic period as a whole it is as well that we should acknowledge this. But whatever the details, as to dating, or the relations between schools, or the issue of regularity in particular, the main historical factors are sufficiently clear. All three – the dialectical origin of many basic categories, the concern with correctness, and the beginnings of grammar in philology – leave their traces in the discipline which emerged.

## 1.6 Grammars under the Empire

Grammar is a technical subject and the texts which are most likely to survive are those which had the greatest practical value. We therefore know little about the pioneers who first worked out the categories of the Greek language. Only when we reflect that it was the first analysis of its kind, and is itself the model for the description first of Latin, then indirectly of the modern European languages, and finally of many others throughout the world, do we appreciate the merit and the solidity of their achievement. The grammars that we do possess belong to the final stages of synthesis. In one case at least, in the surviving books of Apollonius Dyscolus, we find original arguments. But it is an originality that builds on and corrects the work of others who are lost to us. In others we find bald statements of alternative views; these are particularly

common in the fourth century Latin grammars of Charisius and
Diomedes. Other texts are simple epitomes, which at their best, in
the hands of Donatus for Latin or (pseudo-) Dionysius Thrax for
Greek, are neat and skilful. The teaching transmitted is not entirely
uniform, as we have seen already in the treatment of the parts of
speech. But it is uniform to a considerable degree, with the same
detailed sub-classes and the same illustrative examples repeated by
one grammarian after another. Before we examine this tradition we
must pay homage to the original minds whose discoveries lie
behind it. Similarly, the history of art must pay homage to Apelles,
whose paintings were ravaged in antiquity, or to the sculptors
Phidias, Praxiteles or Lysippus. But their greatest work is often
known from Roman copies, and the fortunes of grammars are not
dissimilar.

Of the subsections which follow, the first surveys the scope and
content of selected texts that have survived from the Imperial
period. It begins with short grammars that are representative of the
pedagogic tradition. But at the end we will pay particular attention
to the *Syntax* of Apollonius Dyscolus. This is a long work and its
genius lies above all in its discussion of individual problems. It will
therefore be surveyed book by book, and much of it in detail.
Finally, the second subsection, which ends our chapter, will comment on the general model of linguistic description which underlies
the grammarians' statements.

### 1.6.1 Analysis of texts

Let us begin our survey with the *Ars Minor* or 'Shorter Manual' of
Donatus, which is indeed one of the shortest grammars to have
survived (18 pages in the latest edition). Donatus also wrote a
fuller manual (the *Ars Maior*), which we will come to later. The *Ars
Minor* is the earliest of a handful of grammatical texts which is
designed as a catechism; another, which we will sample in a
moment, is a minor work by Priscian which scans and parses the
first line of each book of Virgil's Aeneid.[183] In Donatus' manual,
the teacher begins by asking his pupil how many parts of speech
there are. The answer is 'eight'. 'What are they?' Answer: 'noun,
pronoun, verb, adverb, participle, conjunction, preposition, interjection'. The teacher then takes each part in turn, asking first for a
definition. He then asks for a list of variable properties; for the
noun these are 'quality' or class comparison (of adjectives), gender,
number, 'form' (simple or compound) and case.[184] For each property he asks how many values it has. Thus: 'how many qualities of
noun are there?' Answer: two, either proper or common (*appellativum*). Under the heading of case the pupil recites the paradigms of

five words, which are chosen to illustrate different genders: *magister*, 'teacher' (masculine), *Musa*, 'Muse' (feminine), *scamnum*, 'bench' (neuter), *sacerdos*, 'priest' or 'priestess' (either masculine or feminine), *felix*, 'lucky' (all three genders). It will be noted that these are not chosen for the diversity of their inflectional paradigms: *magister* and *scamnum* are of the same declension, as are *sacerdos* and *felix*. But the questions which follow elicit rules for forming different endings of the genitive and dative/ablative plurals. They start from the ablative singular: if it ends in -*a* or -*o* (*Musa, magistro*), the genitive plural adds -*rum* (*Musarum, magistrorum*) and the dative/ablative plural is in -*is* (*Musis, magistris*); if it ends in -*e*, -*i* or -*u* the dative/ablative plural is in -*bus*; if it is a short -*e* the genitive plural is in -*um*, and so on.

The section on pronouns again begins with a definition and a list of variable properties; the pupil then gives the paradigms of thirteen individual pronouns (*ego*, 'I'; *tu*, 'you'; *ille*, 'he'; and so on) and at the end is asked what compounds are formed from them. In the case of verbs, the variable properties include not only quality, form, tense and so on, but also conjugation. For the Roman grammarians Latin had three conjugations. The first, as Donatus' pupil defines it, has a long *a* in the second singular of the present indicative (*amās*, 'you love', *amāris*, 'you are loved'); such verbs form a future in -*bo* or -*bor* (*amabo*, 'I will love'; *amabor*, 'I will be loved'). The second has a long *e* (*docēs*, 'you teach'; *docēris*, 'you are taught') with futures in -*bo* and -*bor*. The third has either a long or a short *i*; the difference can be seen immediately in the imperatives and infinitives, where the short *i* changes to *e* (*legĭs*, 'you read', with imperative *legĕ* and infinitive *legĕre*) while the long *i* remains (*audīs*, 'you hear'; imperative *audi*, infinitive *audire*). For these verbs the future is generally in -*am* and -*ar*, but the teacher also asks for exceptions (as *is*, 'you go'; *ibo*, with -*bo*, 'I will go'). In this way some inflectional rules are given, but not all; and the section ends with the recital of just one paradigm (of *lego*, 'I read'). That is also the only verb referred to in the section on participles, again with a complete paradigm.

In the section which deals with adverbs the pupil is required to distinguish different semantic types: adverbs of place, time, number (*semel*, 'once' or *bis*, 'twice'), of negation, and so on. There are 24, with adverbs of place further divided, at the end of the section, into 'in a place' (*in loco*), 'from a place' (*de loco*) and 'to a place' (*ad locum*). For each type the pupil gives one or two examples. The briefer section on conjunctions distinguishes five 'forces' (*potestates*): copulative, as *et*, 'and'; disjunctive, as *vel*, 'or' or *neque*, 'neither', 'and not'; and so on. Since their number is small, a

complete list can be given under each head. The even briefer
section on interjections distinguishes expressions of happiness, pain,
admiration and fear. For prepositions the only variable property is
the case of the noun that they govern. The pupil enumerates those
that take the accusative, the ablative, or either, listing them first
and giving brief illustrations of their construction afterwards. For
the prepositions that govern either case (*in*, 'in' or 'into'; *sub*,
'under'; *super*, 'over, about'), Donatus uses more interesting examples, from Virgil, to illustrate differences in meaning.

Of all the grammars, the *Ars minor* brings us closest to the basic
problems of the grammarian as a school master. It is clear that his
primary concern was to teach a system of classification; so that,
faced with a line of Virgil or some other poet, his pupil might
identify the first word as perhaps a noun, more specifically a
common noun, which is simple, plural and in the accusative, then
the second as an active verb in such and such a mood, tense, and
so on. This is indeed the kind of detailed and exhaustive parsing
exemplified in Priscian's catechism on the initial lines of the
*Aeneid*. Taking, for example, the first word of the poem (*arma*,
'weapons'), the teacher asks what part of speech it is. Answer:
'noun'. 'What sort?' Answer: 'common noun'. A subsequent question asks for its gender. Answer: 'neuter'. 'Why neuter?' 'Because',
the pupil replies, 'all nouns which end in -*a* in the plural are
without exception neuter.' 'Why is its singular not used?' Because,
the answer runs, the noun refers to many different things, not just
to military weapons (quotations from other passages of Virgil
where it is used of agricultural implements or nautical tackle); and,
since it is polysemous (in the ancient terminology it is *homonymon*,
'a homonym'), one uses a more particular term, such as *scutum*
'shield' or *galea* 'helmet', of any individual piece. 'Of what form
(*figura*) is it?' Answer 'simple'; but the pupil is then asked to form
compounds from it, such as *armiger* (literally, 'arm-bearer') or
*semermis*, 'half-armed'. 'What case is it in this context?' Answer:
'accusative', but since in neuters the nominative and the accusative
are identical the pupil has to explain how this is known. 'From the
construction', he replies; 'that is, the ordering and linking of what
follows'. In Virgil's line *arma* is linked by coordination to the next
word *virum*, 'man', which is unambiguously accusative, and the
two together are the objects of *cano*, 'I sing of', which governs this
case. 'What declension is *arma*?' 'Second.' 'Why?' 'Because it forms
the genitive *armorum*'; the pupil explains that all second declension
neuters follow the same rule. He is then asked to form derived
nouns (as *armarium*, 'cupboard'); then the denominative verb (*armo*,
'I arm'); then various inflected forms, participles and further nouns

which are in turn derived from that. Finally, Priscian launches into an appendix on nouns and participles which are identical either in the nominative singular or throughout their paradigms (the two meanings being distinguished by Greek translations).[185]

Although both texts are basically taxonomic, they also give sporadic rules for inflection. In part these are introduced as a criterion for identifying categories: in the *Ars Minor*, as we have seen, the basic test for assigning a verb to its conjugation is the quality and length of the vowel in the termination of the second singular. Similarly, in Priscian's catechism, the rule by which all neuter plurals end in -*a* is the criterion for identifying the gender of *arma*. But this does not explain why, for example, Donatus should have added the rules by which verbs form the future (first and second conjugations in -*bo*[*r*], third and fourth, with exceptions, in -*am* and -*ar*). A possible motive is that his pupils may already have had difficulty in forming them. In late Latin, even on the evidence of written texts, simple futures (such as *legam*, 'I will read') were increasingly replaced by periphrastic formations (*legere habeo*, literally, 'to read I have'), and these alone have reflexes in the Romance languages.[186] In his section on nouns, Donatus gives rules for the genitive and dative/ablative plural. They are very simple rules which schoolchildren who learn Latin are still taught. But it is noteworthy that, in a grammar as short and elementary as this, there was already a pedagogical reason for including them. Another distinction that Donatus takes pains to reinforce is between the cases governed by different classes of preposition. In the singulars of most nouns the spoken forms were probably the same: with the loss of vowel length and the disappearance of final -*m*, neither of which has any general reflex in the Romance languages, pairs such as *puellam* and *puellā, dominum* and *dominō*, or *patrem* and *patre* (accusative and ablative singular of the words for 'girl', 'master' and 'father') phonologically collapse. By the fourth century, the contrast which the grammarians taught may have existed only in writing. A century and a half later, in another minor work by Priscian, we have the first extant Latin text whose sole topic is the endings of nouns and verbs in the traditional declensions and conjugations.[187]

Let us now turn to Donatus' second grammar, the *Ars Maior* or 'Larger Manual', which is three times as long as the *Ars Minor* and fuller in scope. It can be divided into three parts. The first (10 pages out of 72 in the most recent edition) deals successively with vocal sound, letters, syllables, feet, accent and *positurae* (boundaries marked by punctuation). The second (40 pages) deals with the parts of speech and their variable properties, covering broadly the

same ground as the *Ars Minor*. The third (22 pages) begins with
sections on barbarisms, solecisms and other faults; the remainder
classify forms of deviation permitted for metrical or aesthetic
reasons, and figures of speech involving either syntax or word
meaning. Other grammars in this tradition have a greater or lesser
scope. That of Charisius, which we will also glance at, began with a
definition of grammar (now lost), followed by a relatively brief
treatment of vocal sound, letters and syllables (opening sections of
Book 1). It then plunges into a much more detailed account of
grammatical categories and word endings: first a general definition
of the word; then an exhaustive analysis of noun endings (remainder
of Book 1); then a systematic study of the parts of speech (Book 2),
the treatment of verbs having an extensive supplement, starting
with the forms of the perfect, in Book 3. Book 4 is largely
concerned with the faults and virtues of speech; its final topic is
reading (including sections on verse prosody).[188] A grammar with
a more restricted scope is the brief compendium of (pseudo-) Dionysius Thrax: its contents correspond to the first two parts of the *Ars
Maior* (letters, etc. and parts of speech) alone. It is clear from these
and other texts that might be summarized that the core of the
discipline is the classification and forms of the eight parts of
speech. As we have seen, that is the sole topic of Donatus' *Ars
Minor*. But it is also clear that grammar still included many topics
that modern writers have more firmly assigned to other subjects,
either to rhetoric or to the technical study of literature. In this it
reflects its Hellenistic origin, both Stoic and Alexandrian.

Let us now look in more detail at the *Ars Maior*. In the first
part, the opening section defines vocal sound and divides it into
articulate (representable by letters) and inarticulate. The next defines
the letter, with the standard division into vowels, half-vowels and
mutes and, at the end, a brief listing of the three properties of
name, shape and power (*nomen, figura, potestas*). The next defines
the syllable as 'a grouping of letters or the utterance of a single
vowel which is capable of a time value': the values are short, long
(either 'by nature' or 'by position') and variable (optionally either
short or long). The subject matter of these sections has been discussed earlier and is common to all grammarians. The section on
feet defines the unit as 'a fixed reckoning of syllables and time
values', and assigns the appropriate name to every combination of
two, three and four syllables. The last are 'double' feet (each being
analysable into sequences of feet of two syllables), and Donatus
adds that feet of three syllables can be combined similarly. The next
is on tones or accent: with other Latin grammarians, Donatus
distinguishes acute, circumflex and grave on the Greek model, and

gives individual rules for the accentuation of monosyllables (acute if the vowel is short, circumflex if it is long), of disyllables (acute on the first syllable if, for example, both are short) and of words with three syllables or more. He adds that compounds have a single accent, that there are uncertainties in interjections and foreign words, and that the rules are sometimes disturbed, for example to resolve an ambiguity. Finally in this part, the section on *positurae* defines the rhetorical units which in delivery were called the period, *colon* (a subordinate clausular unit less than the complete *sententia* or 'thought') and *comma*.[189]

The central part of the *Ars Maior* has the same plan as the *Ars Minor*, except that it is not a catechism and the classifications are fuller. For example, the *Ars Minor* says that there are eight parts of speech and lists them; the *Ars Maior* adds that the noun and verb are 'principal' parts of speech, that the Romans do not count the article nor the Greeks the interjection, that other scholars have recognized either more parts or fewer, and that three (noun, pronoun and participle) all distinguish six cases. In sub-classifying nouns, the *Ars Minor* distinguished the two basic 'qualities' (proper and common); the *Ars Maior* adds that the Romans had four types of personal name (compare our first names and surnames) and illustrates many different types of common noun. For example, some are concrete (*corporalia*) and others abstract (*incorporalia*); some have Greek inflections throughout; some are 'of intermediate meaning and are attributed (*adiecta*) to nouns' (this is the class that we call adjectives); some are 'said in relation to something' (one is a father, for instance, in relation to one's child); some are general and others specific; some have forms which look like those of verbs or participles. On the other hand, the section on nouns does not give paradigms for different genders, and the treatment of pronouns is shorter in the *Ars Maior* since it omits those of *ego*, *tu*, and so on. Similarly, the sections on verbs and participles do not take the reader through the paradigm of *lego*, 'I read'. On the other hand, they give more, in particular, about defective or other irregular patterns. Inchoatives, which are simply distinguished as a class in the *Ars Minor*, are said sometimes to have simple verbs as sources (*horresco*, 'I begin to shudder' from *horreo*, 'I shudder') and sometimes not (*quiesco*, 'I am or become still'; but no *quieo*); they also have no distinct past tense ( = perfect) and form a participle only in the present.[190]

The central part of the *Ars Maior* is a remarkably clear and economical presentation of the detailed word taxonomy that the Imperial grammarians evidently saw as the heart of their subject. In this respect, both it and the *Ars Minor* can be grouped with the

even sparser text of (pseudo-) Dionysius Thrax. This deals with the
participle in just two sentences, the first defining it and the second
deriving its variable properties from those of the noun and the
verb. The sections on the article and preposition are scarcely fuller:
the latter merely gives a definition and a list of individual prepositions, first monosyllables and then disyllables. But the section on
nouns distinguishes seven types of derived noun (patronymics,
adjectives indicating an owner, and so on) and 20 other classes,
including proper and common, adjectives (*epitheta*), numerals, and
generic and specific. In common with Donatus, (pseudo-) Dionysius
also has an extensive sub-classification of adverbs.[191] Whatever its
date and authorship, and whatever its relationship, direct or indirect, to its Latin counterparts, this grammar has the same efficient
style and in later centuries enjoyed the same success in the Greek
world that Donatus enjoyed in the West.

By contrast, a grammar such as that of Charisius is less efficient
and has long quasi-lexicographical episodes. In the sections covering noun forms, Charisius first introduces the categories of case,
gender and number. He then divides nouns into either four or five
declensions (*declinationes* or *ordines*); his authorities differ as to the
precise number. The first has a nominative singular in -*as*, -*a* or -*es*,
genitive and dative in -*ae*, accusative in -*am*, -*an* or -*en*, vocatives in
-*a* or -*e*. These are illustrated with various partial paradigms, both
masculine and feminine; Charisius adds that some authorities also
give archaic genitives in -*as* and datives in -*ai*. An excursus follows
on the adaptation to Latin declensions of Greek names in -*as* and
-*es*; following that, he illustrates complete sets of endings, including
the plurals and, at the end, the rare cases of dative/ablative plural in
-*bus*. The second declension has -*i* in the genitive; it includes nouns
of all genders (it is a great error, Charisius argues, to deny that it
includes feminines), with nominatives ending in -*us*, -*er*, -*ir* or -*eus*
in the masculine, -*us* in the feminine, and either -*um* or -*us* in the
neuter. A partial paradigm is given for a masculine in -*us* (similar
pattern for feminines and neuters; also no difference if -*us* is
preceded by -*i*); then a nearly complete paradigm (the only one in
this section) for a Greek name in -*eus*, and so on. The third
declension has a genitive in -*is*; Charisius has notes on 32 possible
endings of the nominative singular, usually illustrating just the
nominative and the genitive.[192]

After dealing briefly with the fourth and fifth declensions, Charisius continues with extended lists of nouns found only in the
singular or only in the plural; then of nouns which have only one
case form or are otherwise defective. The only general statement is
that the names of letters and the numerals from four to 100 are all

indeclinable. He then gives a long series of rules based on the form of the nominative singular. Thus 'all nouns which end in *-en* in the nominative singular are pronounced with *-nis* in the genitive, the preceding syllable being changed to *-i-*' (for example, *nomen*, 'name', genitive *nominis*). They are neuter except for nine which are masculine; all are listed, the neuters alphabetically. 'Names which end in the letter *-l* are neuter' (again certain exceptions), and similarly those in *-ar*. 'Nouns which end in *-o* are either masculine or feminine' (the only exceptions are indeclinable). They form a genitive in *-nis*, with the *-o-* sometimes changed to *-i-* (*Apollo*, genitive *Apollinis*) and sometimes not (*Cicero*, *Ciceronis*). The feminines alone are amenable to rule. Next, 'all nouns of the third declension form the accusative in *-em*' (exceptions *puppim*, 'stern of a ship' and others); nouns ending in *-es* either have *-ei* in the genitive (alphabetical list of those following this pattern), or they have *-is* (again an alphabetical list), and so on. The next section ('On the endings of nouns and various questions') is longer than the preceding sections of Book I put together: it too is organized by the ending of the nominative, but consists principally of remarks on individual forms. For example, regularity demands that *vectigal*, 'tax revenue' should have a final *-e* (*vectigale*); this is because the nominative plural (*vectigalia*) should not be more than one syllable longer. But usage is resistant and we do say *vectigal* (similarly, *animal*, 'animal' and others). Grammarians say that *oliva* should mean 'olive tree' and *olea*, 'olive fruit'; but older writers did not observe this (three quotations from Virgil in illustration). The word for 'lioness' is *leaena*, but at one point Ovid uses *lea*, and so on. Of the remaining sections of Book I, three are general and systematic: on comparatives and superlatives; on endings of the ablative singular and rules for deriving the plural cases from them (compare the *Ars Minor* on the genitive and dative/ablative plural); on the number of distinct case forms in the singular (six if there is no syncretism, and so on). But another section also gathers together notes on single forms, this time arranged alphabetically.[193]

The next book takes the individual parts of speech in turn. It is fuller than the corresponding part of Donatus, and often identifies alternative treatments. For example, the sections on the verb deal systematically with the four regular conjugations, giving both skeleton paradigms (present indicative complete, first singulars of other tenses, and so on) and rules. The latter include some which are not in Donatus. Thus the first conjugation forms the future optative and conjunctive (what we call the present subjunctive and future perfect indicative) in *-em* and *-ro*; it forms the imperative by removing the final *-s* of the second singular (*amas*, *ama*), and the infinitive by adding -re to that (*ama, amare*). The next sections deal with abbreviated forms in each conjugation (for example, first conjugation *parasti, parare*, 'you, they prepared' for *paravisti, paravere*); after further notes Charisius reproduces an alternative treatment (by Cominianus, largely known from this and other citations from him), which divides verbs initially into three classes (second singular in -*as*, in -*es* or in either short or long -*is*). The longest section in Book 3 is on adverbs, which among other things gives details of their formal derivation from other parts of speech (for example, there are four ways in which adverbs are formed from nouns ending in -*r*); also another alphabetical list, of forms and uses attested in literary sources. For example, Plautus has the form *ampliter*, 'fully'; by rule, Charisius says, it should be *ample* but the rule was not observed by older writers. In another note Charisius says that Terence uses the adverb *perdite*, 'desperately' in the sense of *valde*, 'greatly' ('to be desperately in love').[194]

Book 3, as we remarked earlier, deals in detail with additional aspects of the verb. It begins with a taxonomy of forms of the perfect. For example, in the third conjugation there are nine formations: in one the first syllable is repeated (*cucurri*, 'I ran'), another ends in -*xi* (*dixi*, 'I said'), and so on. Among later sections, one deals with the verbs that Charisius classes as 'defective'. These are basically those that we now call 'semideponent' – verbs whose forms are active in the non-perfect tenses (active *soleo*, 'I am in the habit of'), but passive in the perfect (*solitus sum*, with the periphrastic formation of the passive *monitus sum*, 'I have been advised'). Charisius gives skeleton paradigms for each of them; under the same heading he includes *fio*, 'I become', with perfect *factus sum* (literally 'I am made') and also has a note on verbs whose perfects, as he describes them, are borrowed from the paradigms of other verbs which have the same meaning. For example, *fero*, 'I carry' has a perfect, *tuli*, which is taken from that of *tollo*.[195]

Charisius' text is diffuse and derivative and, to a modern reader at least, indifferently organized; one should add that there are gaps in its transmission. But it is the longest extant grammar in this tradition, and in glancing through these first three books we can form a broader impression of the scholarly interests of a fourth-century Roman grammarian than from much sharper and pedagogically more useful texts such as those of Donatus. As we noted earlier, the same tradition also dealt with the faults of speech (barbarism, solecism) and with further topics overlapping those of rhetoric. For this we may return to the *Ars Maior*, of which the relevant sections occupy between a quarter and a third of the whole. The first defines a barbarism as 'a single element of the sentence uttered incorrectly (*vitiosa*) in normal discourse'. If a similar licence is employed in poetry it is called *metaplasmus*, and Donatus devotes a separate section to this. But here and throughout this third part his examples are predominantly from Virgil. For example, the second line of the *Aeneid* begins with the word *Italiam* 'Italy', where the metre requires the first vowel to be read long; but this is a barbarism, since it ought to be short. As this and other examples make clear, what the grammarians were concerned with was an error in the spelling or phonological form of a word. In their detailed classification, some errors involve addition (in this instance of a time value); others subtraction; others substitution (*immutatio*); others transposition.[196]

The next section defines a solecism as 'an error in the construction of elements of the sentence contrary to grammatical rule'. This may involve an error in the part of speech itself (for instance, if an adjective is used in place of an adverb), or in any one of its variable properties. These include the 'qualities' of nouns (for instance, the use of a proper noun instead of a common one), their genders (thus a wrong agreement, according to the grammarians, in Virgil's *amarae corticis* 'of bitter bark') or their cases, the mood or tense of verbs, or simply the choice of individual words (for instance, of the preposition *sub*, with the basic meaning 'under', in the sense of *ante* 'before'). A standard question, which we will meet again in Apollonius Dyscolus, is whether a solecism, like a barbarism, could involve an isolated word. What if, for example, one were to use the plural *salvete* ('Hullo', literally a plural imperative) in greeting a single person? According to Donatus, it is wrong to see the word as isolated, since the act of greeting supplies 'the force of a constructed sentence' (*vim contextae orationis*). When the error truly involves a single word it falls under the definition of barbarism: thus it is a barbarism, not a solecism, to use the singular *scala* instead of the plural *scalae*, 'ladder' (compare English *scissor*).[197]

The remaining sections deal summarily with other faults; with *metaplasmus*, which, as we have seen, is a licence which would otherwise be a barbarism; with figures (*schemata*), which are the licences which would otherwise be solecisms; and with tropes. Under 'other faults', of which there are 10, Donatus defines terms such as pleonasm (the addition of a word that adds nothing to the sense) and *amphibolia* 'ambiguity'. Under metaplasm he defines and illustrates fourteen species: for example, *ectasis* or 'drawing out', where his illustration is again *Italiam* in the first line of the *Aeneid*, or metathesis (as *Evandre* for vocative *Evander*). According to the general definition, *metaplasmus* is 'an alteration of correct running speech into some other form for metrical reasons or for

embellishment'. In the section on figures Donatus begins by noting
that there are figures both 'of speech' (*schemata lexeos*), which
belong to grammar, and 'of thought' (*schemata dianoeas*), which
belong to rhetoric; unlike Charisius, who includes both, he restricts
himself to the former. He gives no general definition; if he had he
would have said, as others say, that a *schema lexeos* is an anomalous
arrangement of words for metrical reasons or for literary effect. He
distinguishes 17 basic types: for example, *anadiplosis* (the terms
throughout this third part of the *Ars Grammatica* are direct translit-
erations from Greek) is the repetition of a word at the end of one
line and the beginning of the next. Finally, a trope (*tropus*) is a
word transferred from its strict sense. Thirteen species are defined.
For example, synecdoche involves reference to the whole when we
mean a part (thus when Virgil writes of a great 'sea' hitting a ship)
or to a part when we mean the whole.[198]

It is only in some sections of this third part of the *Ars Grammatica*, and then in part incidentally, that writers in this tradition
had a framework within which they could have dealt with syntax.
As we have seen, a standard example of solecism was the incorrect
agreement of an adjective with a noun, and in the same section, as
one example of solecism in conjunctions, Donatus cites an incorrect
word order (*autem fieri non debet*, 'however it should not become
so', instead of *fieri autem non debet*, with *autem*, 'however', in
second place). In the section on figures, *sylle[m]psis* ('taking together') is illustrated with an example from Virgil in which plural
*arma*, 'arms', and singular *currus*, 'chariot', both collocate as subject
with the singular verb *fuit*, 'was'.[199] But these are scattered instances, and the ancient term for syntax (Gk. *súntaksis*, 'setting out
together'; Lat. *constructio*, 'construction') is nowhere used. For a
systematic treatment of this topic, and a treatment of grammar
generally which shows greater intellectual engagement, we must
turn to the fuller works of Apollonius Dyscolus, in the second
century, and his follower Priscian, at the beginning of the sixth.

Of Apollonius' originally voluminous writings, the four books
on syntax have survived in large part; also his treatment of the
pronoun, and lesser books on adverbs and conjunctions. Various
fragments can also be attributed to him. But Priscian's *Institutiones
Grammaticae* ('Principles of Grammar') has survived complete.
Though derivative, it remains a major work, whose influence in the
Middle Ages, and on the subsequent development of grammar in
Western Europe generally, is comparable only to that of Donatus.
Like the earlier Roman grammars, it begins with vocal sound,
letters and syllables (no specific sections, however, on accents or
metrical units). Its central part (most of Book 2 and the whole of

Books 3–16) is devoted to the individual parts of speech, with very detailed treatment of formational processes. For example, there are three books (just under 80 pages in the standard edition) on the verb. The first (Book 8) defines it and deals in general with its variable properties: this includes the semantics of the tenses, moods, and so on (topics often omitted in shorter grammars) and, on the formal side, a more comprehensive treatment of derived verbs. The next two (Books 9 and 10) deal with inflections and are dominated by a very detailed treatment of the perfect. This begins with a general section, which among other things distinguishes eight perfect formations (first singular in -*vi*, in -*ii*, in -*ui*, and so on); Priscian then takes each conjugation in turn, and tries to give an exhaustive account of both the perfect and the nominal form (the supine) which is traditionally learned with it. In the case of the first conjugation, he begins with the regular perfect in -*avi*, excepts those with perfects in -*ui*, and then excepts four others, before dealing with the supines, which he derives from the perfects, in a similar way. In the third conjugation, whose treatment takes up most of Book 10, he works systematically through the possible endings of the present form. For example, presents ending in -*go* have perfects in -*si* if *r* precedes (*tersi*, 'I wiped' from *tergo*, 'I wipe'); otherwise in -*xi* (*rexi* from *rego*, 'I rule'); but then there are exceptions (such as *fregi* from *frango*, 'I break').[200]

These and other books contain a profusion of literary examples far greater than in any earlier or shorter Latin grammars. For example, *facio*, 'I make' is a 'neuter' verb (one with active inflections but no passive inflections corresponding to them); however, Priscian points out that a passive is used by Varro and another older author. Many neuter verbs have an absolute sense (one that does not need to be construed with an object). But, among other more straightforward instances in which such verbs do take an object, Priscian cites a line in Virgil's *Eclogues*, in which *ardeo* ('I burn', intransitive) is construed figuratively with an accusative: *ardebat Alexin* 'was burning (with love of) Alexis'. Older forms are repeatedly cited as exceptions to inflectional rules. For example, a compound such as *applico*, 'I attach', is among the verbs of the first conjugation which generally form a perfect in -*ui* (*applicui*). But Priscian cites Cicero, Varro and Pacuvius (born 220 BC) for alternative forms in -*avi*. On the same page of Keil's edition he gives an example from Virgil in which *nexo*, 'I bind' is inflected in the first conjugation, followed by others from Livy and Accius (born 170 BC) in which it is inflected in the third. He then argues that Virgil's usage is more regular. The accumulation of scholarship that lies behind such a grammar is one of its most striking features.[201]

The sections on syntax form the last two books of Priscian's grammar (the point at which, in the earlier Roman tradition, one would have expected the 'faults and virtues of speech'). They are very long (some 270 pages in Keil's edition), and their intellectual dependence on Apollonius is immediately evident. Both grammarians begin with a comparison between the ordering of letters and the ordering of words: both in sequence (for example, prepositions stand at the beginning of their constructions, just as, in diphthongs, there are vowels that appear only as the first member) and in description. Apollonius and Priscian sought a rationale behind the ordering of letters in the alphabet; likewise reasons were given, as we have seen in subsection 1.4.3, for the order in which they list the parts of speech. The introductory material ends (again in both grammarians) with a discussion of interrogative words. Why are these found only in two parts of speech, noun – recall that the words for 'who' and the like are nouns in Priscian's classification – and adverb?[202]

They then turn to the syntax of individual elements. In Apollonius' work, on which we will concentrate from here onwards, the arrangement of topics follows no explicit system, and their treatment, at least by modern priorities, is uneven. But for convenience we will divide it into five parts. The first deals with the article (remainder of Book 1), and the second with the pronoun (whole of Book 2). The third part is a general discussion of the nature of solecism or – as we can now safely call it – ungrammaticality. This occupies the first third of Book 3, and is introduced at this point on the pretext of a further problem involving pronouns. The next part, which is of equal theoretical importance, deals with the syntax of the verb. It completes Book 3, which for the historian of grammatical theory is the most concentratedly interesting testimony to Apollonius' linguistic insight. It will therefore be surveyed more thoroughly than any of the others. Finally, the last part (Book 4) turns to the remaining elements.[203]

## The Article

Ancient Greek had a definite article (*ho ánthrōpos*, 'the man' as opposed to *ánthrōpos*, 'a man'), normally construed, as in this example, with a noun. But Apollonius points out that it is also compatible with an infinitive (*tò philosopheîn* [*ōphélimon*], 'Philosophising (literally 'the to-philosophise') [is useful]'), and can further mark a word of any class which is mentioned rather than used (*tò lége*, 'the word *read!*').[204] In construal with nouns its characteristic function is anaphoric ('referring back'). This covers the simple case in, for example, *ho grammatikós se ezétei*, 'The grammarian was looking for you' (some grammarian already mentioned). But Apollonius distinguishes three others. *Ho grammatikós* might also mean 'the grammarian who stands above all others'; similarly *ho poiētḗs*, 'the poet', meaning Homer. With possessives an article indicates unique possession: compare *ho doûlós sou*, 'your slave' (the one slave you possess) with *doûlós sou*, 'a slave of yours, one of your slaves'. Anaphora can also involve an anticipated participant: for example, if we say 'May the tyrannicide be honoured' (*ho turannoktonḗsas timásthō*) with reference not to someone specific who has killed a tyrant, but to someone as yet unknown who might do so. There may finally be an implication of plurality. Thus Apollonius points out later that *ho deipnḗsas paîs koimásthō* (literally 'the having-dined boy let-him-go-to-bed') could, among other things, mean 'Any boys who have dined must go to bed'.[205]

Detailed sections deal with constructions in which the article either must be used, or cannot be used, or may or may not be used according to the needs of the utterance. For example, it must be used with a partitive genitive: 'Of the men (genitive plural *tôn anthrṓpōn*) some are Greeks and some barbarians.' The reason, Apollonius explains, is that divisions imply a whole; the whole must be known; and when something is known the article is used in referring to it. On the other hand, the article is not used with *amphóteroi*, 'both'; the word in itself refers to a pair already known, and therefore the expression *hoi amphóteroi*, 'the both' would be redundant. At various points there are polemic digressions. For example, Tryphon had argued that infinitives were verbs when they appeared without an article, but in phrases like *tò philosopheîn* ('the to-philosophise') they were 'in some sense names of the verbs' (*pêi ... onómata ... tôn rhēmátōn*). Apollonius rejects this, saying that they are always 'names of verbs'. He argues that the infinitive is the basic mood into which all other moods can be turned back. Thus the utterance *peripateî Trúphōn*, 'Tryphon is walking', with indicative *peripateî*, is reported in the form *hōrísato peripateîn Trúphōna*, 'He indicated that Tryphon was walking' (literally 'He-indicated to-walk Tryphon'); similarly the imperative *peripateítō Trúphōn*, 'Let Trypho walk' as *prosétaxe peripateîn Trúphōna* ('He-commanded to-walk Tryphon').[206] The book ends with a discussion of the 'postpositive article' (what we call the relative pronoun). Apollonius distinguishes its syntax from that of the 'prepositive': for example, he points out that while its reference is determined by the antecedent noun (in 'A grammarian came to whom Tryphon spoke', the referent of the word for 'to whom' is that of *grammatikós* 'grammarian'), its case is determined by the verb which follows ('to whom' is dative as required by *hōmílēse*, 'spoke').[207]

**Pronouns**

Apollonius first explains that, whereas the basic function of the article is to accompany a noun, that of a pronoun (as its name already indicates) is to stand in place of it. In his treatise on the pronoun it is described as having one of two roles. If it is a third person pronoun it may be anaphoric ('used in place of that which is named previously'): Apollonius gives an example from Homer's *Iliad* in which *autós*, with the meaning 'he himself', is substituted for the proper name *Zeûs*, linking the sentence to one in which Zeus has already been mentioned. He makes clear that, since an anaphoric pronoun refers, it has the force not of a single common noun (as English 'man'), but of a noun preceded by an article ('the man'). Alternatively, a pronoun may be deictic or 'identifying' (Gk. *deiktikós*, literally 'showing, pointing out'; Lat. *demonstrativus*). If it is first or second person it is always so: in the ancient classification, the term 'demonstrative' covers personal pronouns such as *me* in *épaisé me*, 'He hit me' or *se* in *étimēsé se*, 'He honoured you', as well as the third person *hoûtos*, 'this, this one' or *ekeînos*, 'that, that one'. In none of these uses can a pronoun be accompanied by an article. In general, therefore, the element can be characterized as 'that which is used instead of a noun (*tò* . . . *antonomazómenon*) with deixis or anaphora, and which the article does not accompany'.[208]

These preliminary sections are fairly lengthy and also deal, among other things, with cases where the word which in classical prose is generally the article (masculine singular *ho*) is itself pronominal. This is characteristic of Homeric Greek; as Apollonius explains it, a word which in form (*têi phōnêi*) remains an article becomes a pronoun by a process of transference (*metálepsis*).[209] The remainder of this part can then be divided into two main sections, of which the first covers the construction of pronouns with verbs. It begins with the nominatives and in particular with collocations such as *egṑ égrapsa* (literally 'I I-wrote'). According to many authorities, of whom the first century grammarian Habron is specifically referred to, the syntax of this sentence is more complete than if, as normally in Greek, one were to use the verb alone (*égrapsa*, 'I-wrote'). For supporting evidence they point out that a pronoun cannot be deleted in sentences connected by the particles *mén* and *dé* ('on the one hand', 'on the other hand'). Compare, for example, *egṑ mèn [paregenómēn] sù d(é) [oû]* ('I on-the-one-hand [I-was-there], you on-the-other-hand [not]'). But Apollonius distinguishes deixis which is contrastive (*antidiastaltikḗ*) from absolute or non-contrastive. It is only when there is contrast, as in the example with *mén* and *dé*, that the inclusion of the nominative

pronoun is correct. In the simple *égrapsa* its meaning is inherent in
the verb. Therefore the form does not require a pronoun, any more
than, as a singular verb, it requires the numeral 'one'.[210]

Apollonius then turns to the oblique cases, where the main
problem is that of accentuation. Since nominative pronouns are
contrastive, they are basically accented (*egó*, with acute accent on
the last syllable). But in oblique cases there is a distinction between,
for example, accented *emé* 'me', which is phonologically a word on
its own, and unaccented *me*, which must form a phonological unit
with a word preceding. In general the accented forms are contrastive
and the unaccented non-contrastive; but there are several special
cases which, as Apollonius sees it, all reduce to this same principle.
The first is when accented pronouns are joined by a conjunction to
a preceding noun: *Dionúsion timâi kaì emé* ('Dionysius he-honours
and me'). Another is when they accompany a preposition: *par[à]
emoí*, 'at my house' (preposition *pará* and accented dative *emoí*).
At this point Apollonius proposes a rule by which contrastive or
accented pronouns, including those which accompany a preposition, should come before the verb, and an unaccented pronoun,
since it forms a phonological unit with a preceding word, should
come after. It is not difficult to find examples to the contrary:
*sḗmerón elálēsa katà soû* ('Today I-talked about you'), with a
preposition and accented pronoun *soû* following the verb *elálēsa*,
or *sḗmerón se etheasámēn*, 'Today I watched you', where unaccented *se* forms a phonological unit with *sḗmerón*, 'today' instead
of the verb *etheasámēn*. But these are seen as transpositions from
the correct order (the technical term for this figure is *huperbatón*,
'hyperbaton'. Another case in which the pronoun is accented is
when it 'attests a disposition that is the opposite of earlier good
will': for example, in *emoì etólmēsen taûta poiêsai* 'He dared to
do these things to *me*!' (literally 'to-me he-dared . . .'). Another is
when the personal pronoun is followed by *autós*, in the sense of
'self'. Hence the accented dative in a line from Homer: *soì d(è)
autôi melétō* [. . . *phaídimos Héktōr*], 'But to you yourself (*soì* . . .
*autôi*) let [glorious Hector] be of concern'. The final sections of this
part deal, in particular, with third person reflexives. Apollonius
would be pleased if accented pronouns always marked no change
of participant, while the simple case, where there is transitivity to a
different participant, was unaccented. But he acknowledges that
the facts are not so.[211]

The last extended section of our second part deals with pronouns
standing in a possessive construction. For single oblique pronouns,
which Apollonius sees as primitive, there is a two-way distinction,
which he has examined in the preceding sections, between reflexive

and simple. But with possessive pronouns there is an additional participant, whatever it is that is possessed. Accordingly, Apollonius distinguishes three relationships. One possibility is that the verb takes its person from the thing possessed: for example, in *ho emòs híppos trékhei*, 'My horse is galloping' (literally 'the my horse it-gallops'), what gallops (third person) is the horse. In such a case, the primitive into which the possessive pronoun can be resolved can only be non-reflexive. Thus, in the example cited, *emós*, 'my', has the meaning of the simple genitive *emoû*, 'of me'. Another possibility is that the verb takes its person from the possessor: for example, in *tòn emòn agròn éskapsa*, 'I dug my field' the thing possessed is the object and the person of the verb corresponds to the possessive *emón*. In such a case the possessive pronoun may be contrastive; if so, a change of construction must involve the reflexive (in this example, the compound *emautoû*, 'of myself'). Otherwise it must be simple and unaccented (*tòn agrón mou*, 'the field of-me'). The third possibility is that the verb may take its person from neither the possessor nor the thing possessed. For example, in *tòn emòn huiòn edídaxen*, 'He taught my son', the teacher is neither the speaker, who is the possessor, nor his son.[212]

The ancient grammarians had no terms for subject or object, and the way in which these last patterns are described, with possessor and possessed related equally to the verb, may seem awkward. So, to a lesser degree, may the passages which we will cite from Book 3 in which Apollonius discusses verbal valencies. But from this necessarily hurried survey of Books 1 and 2 it will be clear that by the second century AD several familiar problems in syntax had been raised and had been handled with a genuine linguistic insight. Let us return, for example, to the collocation of a verb with a subject pronoun. If the verb is in the third person either a pronoun or a noun must always be supplied. That is not because we need a nominative as such: the case itself again subsists in the verb. It is because the meaning of a third person verb is necessarily indefinite. Therefore it must be circumscribed: with *gráphei*, 'writes' we must say *gráphei hóde*, 'This man writes' or *gráphei ekeînos*, 'That man writes', and so on. But that of a first person verb, such as *gráphō*, 'I write', is already circumscribed. Therefore, in Apollonius' view, the pronoun is required only for emphasis. Similarly, for a second person verb, such as *grápheis*, 'You write'. Whatever the philosophical origins of the criterion by which a definite subject is required, the arguments here are strictly linguistic. This is true both of the argument which Apollonius ascribes to his opponents (non-deletability of the pronoun when it is combined with a correlative conjunction) and of his own account of the semantic contrast.[213]

**Ungrammaticality**

The problem which leads Apollonius into his next topic concerns the use of what is normally a third person reflexive (*heautoús*, accusative plural, 'themselves') in the sense of either a first or a second ('ourselves', 'yourselves'). Thus, for the first person, *heautoùs hubrízomen*, 'We injure ourselves'. In the singular this pronoun can only be third person; Apollonius cannot therefore understand why in the plural it should 'cross over' in this fashion. One answer is that the usage might be thought to be ungrammatical. However, there is no way to correct it: one cannot say, for example, *hēmâs hubrízomen* (literally 'us we-injure'), since only the nominative of a non-reflexive pronoun (in this case *hēmeîs*, 'we') can be joined with a verb in the same person. The argument is then widened. One error, which Apollonius clears up in preliminary discussion, is the view that a solecism, or fault in syntax, can be found in just one word. Suppose that *hoûtos* (masculine singular of the word for 'this') is said of something either female or plural. According to some writers (unnamed) this would be a solecism. But Apollonius disagrees for two reasons. First, *hoûtos* alone is not a complete sentence. Suppose it is said in answer, for example, to the question *tís se étupse?* 'Who hit you?'; in that case the same verb is taken in common (*hoûtos* [understood *se étupse*], 'This man [hit you]'). Second, the error lies not in the word itself, but in a confusion of deixis. If such confusion were a fault in syntax we would have to say that there was no error if, say, it was dark and the speaker could not see who he was referring to. That would be ridiculous. So, if someone is hit by a woman and says *hoûtos me étupsen*, 'This man hit me' there is no solecism, since the words themselves agree. But there would be a solecism if he said *haútē me étupsan* (literally 'this-woman me they-hit') since, although the deixis of *haútē* is correct, *étupsan*, being plural, is not congruent with it.[214]

The 'most essential cause' of non-congruence, as Apollonius explains a few paragraphs later, involves the variable properties of case, number, person and gender. Some words, such as nouns, vary in respect of case and number; others, such as verbs and pronouns, in respect of number and person. Another class, which again includes nouns, varies in respect of gender. Finally, there is a fourth class whose members have no relevant property: this includes conjunctions, prepositions and 'almost all adverbs'. Words which belong to the first three classes must be distinguished in respect of their relationship to others with which they are construed. For example, plural agrees with plural when the implied participants are identical: *gráphomen hēmeîs*, 'We are writing' (plural *gráphomen*, 'we-write'; plural *hēmeîs*, 'we'); *gráphousin hoi ánthrōpoi*,

'The men are writing'. But Apollonius makes clear that there need
be no agreement when there is a change of participant. In *túptousi
tòn ánthrōpon*, 'They are hitting the man', the construction involves a 'crossing over' (*diábasis*) to a new participant (in the
corresponding Latin terminology it is 'transitive'). Therefore the
singular *tòn ánthrōpon* is grammatically as correct as the plural
*toùs anthrṓpous* (*túptousi toùs anthrṓpous*, 'They are hitting the
men'). The same rule applies to words that are linked to others in
respect of gender and case. For example, in *hēmôn autôn akoúousin*, 'They are listening to ourselves' the phrase translated 'ourselves' consists of the genitive *hēmôn*, 'us' and the corresponding
genitive *autôn*, 'selves', and in *hoûtoi hoi ándres*, 'these men'
(literally 'these the men'), all three words are nominative. But it
would again be perfectly correct to say, for example, *hēmôn autòs
akoúei*, 'He himself is listening to us', with a change of participant
from *autós* 'he, he himself' (masculine singular) to *hēmôn* 'us'
(genitive plural). Apollonius adds that when words in the same
case come together their referents will generally be taken to be
identical. An exception is when a conjunction intervenes: for example, in *hēmôn kaì autôn akoúousin*, 'They are listening to us and
them', *kaì*, 'and', distinguishes two participants referred to in the
same case (genitive *hēmôn*, 'us'; genitive *autôn*, 'them').[215]

Words which belong to the fourth class do not have to agree.
For example, the adverb *kalôs*, 'well' can be construed with verbs
of any person or any number: *kalôs gráphō*, 'I write well'; *kalôs
gráphete*, 'You (plural) write well'. It can also be construed with
any tense ('I write well', 'I wrote well'); however, that is not true of
a temporal adverb such as *aúrion*, 'tomorrow' (*aúrion gráphō* or
*aúrion grápsō*, 'I write tomorrow, I will write tomorrow', where
the tenses are non-past, but not *aúrion égrapsa*, 'I wrote tomorrow'). Later paragraphs make explicit certain further principles.
First, Apollonius argues that even with inflected words there is no
solecism unless there is a correct form that would eliminate the
putative error. Hence there is no error in collocations such as *emè
autón*, 'me myself' or *hemas autoús*, 'us ourselves' (where *autón*
and *autoús* could in other contexts mean 'him' and 'them'). Nor,
again, is there an error in the case with which this discussion began
(*heautoús* in the sense of 'ourselves' or 'yourselves'). Another
qualification is that words with different properties may formally
coincide. One cannot say, for example, *ekhthès gráphō*, 'I am
writing yesterday'. But there is no error in the collocation *ekhthès
gráphōn*, 'writing yesterday', even though *gráphōn*, 'writing', is
the participle corresponding to the present *gráphō*. This is because
it also corresponds to the imperfect *égraphon*, 'I was writing'; thus

one can turn the coordinate construction *égraphon kaì ēniṓmēn*, 'I was writing and I was having difficulty' into the participial *gráphōn ēniṓmēn*, '(while) writing I was having difficulty'. Apollonius gives several other examples of morphological syncretism, the last of which concerns the pronoun *sú* ('you', second singular). Tryphon had argued that this form was vocative only. But Apollonius shows that it must also be nominative: for example, in *egṑ kaì sù kaì Trúphōn*, 'I and you and Tryphon' it must have the same case as *egṓ* and *Trúphōn*. He then digresses into the vocatives of pronouns generally. Finally, in these sections on solecism Apollonius addresses the apparent non-agreement of singular verbs and neuter plural subjects. This is a regular pattern in Ancient Greek: one cannot say, for example, *hai gunaîkes légei*, 'The women speaks' (where the noun *gunaîkes* is a feminine plural), but if we put the subject into the diminutive we must say *tà gúnaia légei* (literally, 'the little-women speaks'), with neuter plural *gúnaia* but singular *légei*. Now verbs do not, of course, agree with their objects; and another feature of neuter nouns is that their nominative and accusative are always identical. Therefore, Apollonius suggests, the non-agreement 'escapes notice'. A sentence such as *gráphei tà paidía* is grammatical if the singular verb *gráphei* is construed with *paidía*, 'children' as accusative ('He is drawing the children'). It is not congruent if *paidía* is construed as nominative ('The children are writing'), but the error does not stick out as it would if the inflections were formally distinct.[216]

## Verbs

Apollonius' account of the verb can be divided into two main sections: the first on mood, and the second on voice and, as we would now say, valency. In the section on moods, he begins by demonstrating that infinitives are verbs, and not (as unnamed predecessors had claimed) adverbs. One argument they had used is that an infinitive, like an adverb, presupposes a verb: *Hellenistí* ('Greekly') is not complete without, for example, *légō*, 'I speak' (*Hellenistí légō*, 'I speak Greek'), and similarly *gráphein*, 'to write', is incomplete without, for example, *thélō*, 'I want' (*gráphein thélō*, 'I want to write'). One point which he makes in reply is that verbs such as *thélō*, which refer to dispositions of mind and not to actions, themselves require the infinitive to fill out their meaning. He then argues that the infinitive is the most general and most basic mood. It is marked for all the inherent properties of the verb (in Apollonius' analysis these are voice and tense); but not for person and number (which discriminates not the verbs themselves but different subject participants), nor for specific moods, which are also said to be those of the participants. Apollonius again relates the other moods to collocations of an infinitive with the corresponding main verb: thus indicative *peripatô*, 'I am walking' to *hōrisámēn peripateîn* ('I-indicated to-walk'), and so on. The paragraphs which follow deal with specific constructions: of an infinitive without a finite verb (which Apollonius sees as incomplete), and with the impersonals *deî* or *khrê* ('it is needful that', 'one ought'). In the latter case he rejects an analysis by which such verbs had been misclassed as adverbs. Finally, he turns to the accompanying case forms. These include both the cases governed by the infinitive itself, which will be accusative, genitive or dative as with the corresponding finite forms, and its subject, which is accusative and, for Apollonius, is governed by the main verb. Where both are accusative there will be ambiguities: for example, in *légousi Théōna hubrísai Díōna*, meaning either 'They say that Theon injured Dion' or 'They say that Dion injured Theon'.[217]

Of the remaining moods, the indicative (or 'declarative') is the most basic. Apollonius points out that it loses its 'indicating' force when it is used in an interrogative (*grápheis?*, 'Are you writing?'); however, the same mood would then be used in reply (*gráphō*, 'I am writing'). He also explains the types of conjunction (e.g. causal) and the form of negative (Greek had two negative particles, *ou*[k] and *mḗ*) that occur with it. The next mood is the optative: under this heading Apollonius deals with wishes generally (including those marked, for example, by the particle *eíthe*, 'would that!' and the aorist indicative). A problem in this last case is why, for something that cannot yet be, the tense is one that usually has past reference. He is faced with a similar problem in the case of perfect – which for him are again past – imperatives (*kekleísthō*, 'Let it have been closed!'). Under imperatives in general he addresses three main issues. One is whether they can be in the first person: according to Apollonius they cannot (one cannot command oneself, and more than, as he sees it, one can address oneself with a vocative). Forms expressing a proposal (*légōmen*, 'Let's speak') must therefore form a separate, complementary mood. Another concerns third person imperatives, which are said to be both third person and second person (*legétō*, 'Let him speak', meaning 'I command you (second) that he (third) should speak'). The third problem is a widespread morphological homonymy between second plural imperatives and indicatives (*légete*, 'Speak!' or 'You are speaking'). According to Apollonius, one way to distinguish them is by the case of an accompanying noun: if vocative, the verb is imperative (the implication is that vocatives do not construe with 'indications'); if nominative, it is indicative. The last mood is the subjunctive. The term (*hupotaktikós*) means 'subordinative', and for Apollonius the only subjunctives are forms in subordinate position. They are derived from the corresponding indicatives, their mood and tense (Apollonius discusses specific restrictions on tense) being determined by the semantic character of the subordinating conjunction.[218]

It will be seen that throughout this discussion the emphasis lies not on inflections but on semantic functions. For example, the verbs which express proposals ('Let's speak') are formally identical to subjunctives ('[in order that] we may speak'); but, because their role is non-subordinative, they have to be classed separately. The discussion which follows, of verbal voice and valency, brings out still more clearly Apollonius' concern for notional explanation. He begins by pointing out that not all verbs can have an active force. This term refers to an action that crosses over to some other entity (for example, *túptei*, 'he-hits'), and it is from this prior active force that the passive derives (*túptetai*, 'he-is-hit'). But verbs such as *zô*, 'I live' do not have that force. Therefore they do not have passive forms; since, in the forms which have an active inflection, there is no participant that is acted on, so there is nothing that, with respect to a passive form, could be the undergoer. The absence of a formal modification (*égklisis*) is thus explained by the absence of a semantic force (*diáthesis*). A grammarian could make up a passive inflection; but it would be a purely formal exercise, like making up, for example, a masculine adjective *husterikós*, 'having an illness of the womb', where only the feminine can make sense.[219]

Another set of verbs which do not take passive inflections are those in which the sense of 'undergoing' is already present: for example, *ophthalmiô*, 'I have eye trouble'. Such 'self-undergoing' may be desirable or undesirable (*khairō*, 'I am rejoicing' versus *thnéiskō*, 'I die'). Forming a passive from these verbs, Apollonius remarks, would be like trying to form a masculine from a noun that is already masculine. For another set a passive will ordinarily make sense only in the third person. For example, the first and second persons *peripatô*, 'I am walking' and *peripateîs*, 'you are walking' have no corresponding forms 'I am being walked' and 'you are being walked', since inanimates, which are the only things that can be walked, are not ordinarily speakers or those spoken to. But one can say *peripateîtai hē hodós*, 'The road is being walked'. Apollonius remarks later that these are all verbs which, in construction with a nominative, express a complete thought: for example, 'Tryphon is walking' (*peripateî Trúphōn*). This is true even though, with the 'self-undergoing' class, the cause of what is experienced may be added (for example, *páskhei Théōn* [*hupò toû gunaíou*]

'Theon is suffering [at the hands of his wife]'). Conversely, it is natural that certain verbs which have a transitive force should not always require a noun in an oblique case. For example, one may want to indicate the experience of being in love (*erâi hoûtos*, 'This man is in love') without referring to the specific object. In general, verbs which do not require an oblique case do not form passives; those which do always form them, with the addition of a genitive and *hupò*, 'by' ([*déromai*] *hupò Trúphōnos*, '[I am being thrashed] by Tryphon').[220]

The next problem concerns the rules for the oblique cases. In Ancient Greek, some verbs take an accusative (*túptō se*, 'I am hitting you'); others a genitive (*akoúō sou*, 'I am listening to you'); others a dative (*akolouthô soi*, 'I am following you'). If we wish to make, 'a thorough inquiry into the principles of syntax', we have to know which take which and also the reasons behind it. Apollonius begins with various classes of verbs that take the accusative: those of physical influence (several examples, including *túptō*, 'I hit'), of mental influence (for example, *loidorô*, 'I abuse', *humnô*, 'I praise'), of deception (*apatô*, 'I cheat' or *kléptō*, 'I steal'), of 'separation from objects' (*zētô*, 'I look for' or *heurískō*, 'I find'), and so on. A few are treated as more problematic or more interesting. In *boúlomai se gráphein*, 'I want you to write', a verb of purpose (*boúlomai*, 'I want') takes the accusative *se*. But in *boúlomai gráphein*, 'I want to write', the intention does not cross over from one participant to another; the syntax is that of 'self-undergoing', and therefore no pronoun is needed. However, according to Apollonius, there is the fuller form *boúlomai emautòn gráphein*, 'I want myself to write' – that is, 'I am disposed to writing' (*diatíthemai eis tò gráphein*). He again argues that such accusatives should be construed with the main verb and not with the infinitive. Another problem concerns verbs such as *trémō*, 'I tremble, am afraid' or *pheúgō*, 'I run away'. These take an accusative (*trémō se*, 'I am afraid of you'; *pheúgō se*, 'I run away from you'), even though, as Apollonius points out, they have no active force. Instead they are 'self-undergoing'; and, correspondingly, they form no passives. His explanation is that their construction is elliptical. Ellipsis is possible in normal speech, just as in literature; and in this case the full forms are *trémō dià sé*, 'I am afraid because of you' and *pheúgo dià sé*, 'I run away because of you', but *dià* is (by implication always) omitted.[221]

The discussion of the genitive begins with another problem. Why is it that verbs of seeing take an accusative (*horô se*, 'I see you'), while other verbs of perception, such as *akoúō*, 'I hear', and indeed the verb for 'to perceive' in general (*aisthánesthai*) take genitives? Apollonius' answer is that our senses are in general subject to external influence: we hear a voice, for example, even unwillingly. For this passive force the genitive construction is the nearest, though, since there is also an active aspect, it is not the genitive with *hupó*, 'by'. But seeing is the most active of the senses and the one which more clearly 'crosses over' (illustrated by a quotation from Homer in which the eyes 'see out' from the head). Nor is it under external control, since perception is blocked if we shut our eyes. Therefore it falls under a general pattern, stated a few paragraphs earlier, in which accusatives 'receive the active force originating from the nominative'. A similar explanation is proposed in the case of *phileîn* (with accusative) 'to love, to be friendly to' versus *erân* (with genitive) 'to be in love with'. Loving is active, like the love of a father bringing up his children, while sexual infatuation is under the additional influence of its object. According to Apollonius, there is also an external influence in verbs such as *kédesthai*, 'to care for', or verbs of domination, such as 'to rule'. In the latter case he relates a genitive governed by the verb to genitives construed with nouns. The clearest parallel is when a verb and noun are morphologically related ('I am ruling over you (genitive)', 'your (genitive) ruler').[222]

The dative (etymologically the 'giving' case) is said to be taken by all verbs indicating an acquisition. For example, *légō soi*, 'I am speaking to you' (dative *soi* 'to-you') means, according to Apollonius, 'I give a share of my speech to you'. He then compares a construction in which the same verb takes the accusative: *légo se kléptēn*, 'I say you are a thief'. This has the different meaning, 'By means of the speech which I am uttering I indicate of you that you have committed acts of theft'. Similarly, in a case of physical acquisition, *témnō soi*, 'I am cutting (something) for you' means that I am procuring your acquisition of part of whatever it is that I am cutting, whereas in *témnō se*, 'I am cutting you', with accusative *se*, the activity again bears on the object. Apollonius then remarks that passive verbs never refer to participants corresponding to a dative. Thus *áidomai*, 'I am being sung', could only correspond to the active *áidō se*, 'I am singing you'; it cannot have the meaning of, for example, English, 'I am being sung to'. The next paragraph recognizes one use of the dative that does not involve acquisition: in *aulô toîs auloîs* (literally 'I-play-the-flute the flutes'), the dative inflection of *toîs auloîs* marks not a beneficiary (as in *aulô soi*, 'I am playing the flute for you') but the means by which skill in music is exhibited ('I am playing on the flute'). But other uses are brought under the general rule. For example, in *douleúō soi*, 'I am a slave to you' or *akolouthô soi*, 'I am following you', the datives 'indicate the procuring of the activities inherent' in the verbs. This discussion also includes an unusually obscure paragraph on constructions with both an accusative and a dative: *phérō soi tòn oînon*, 'I am bringing you the wine'. In such sentences, 'the dative always encompasses in itself the accusative, which it takes in even from outside'. Since the dative thus includes the accusative, Apollonius thinks it not inappropriate that in Homeric usage, as too in this colloquial example, it should come first.[223]

Finally, in the very last paragraph of Book 3, Apollonius deals briefly with the valency of participles. By ancient criteria these were a separate element of the sentence; but, despite their different variable properties, they take the same oblique cases as the verbs corresponding to them. This distinguishes them from other deverbal elements: Apollonius points out that, whereas *gumnázōn toûton* (with accusative) is like *gumnázei toûton*, 'He trains this man', the form *gumnastḕs toûton* (literally 'a trainer this man') would be ungrammatical. One must say, with the genitive, *gumnastḕs toútou*, 'a trainer of this man'.[224]

## Other elements

So far Apollonius has addressed all the elements whose variable properties were described as having a bearing on grammaticality: with articles (inflected for case, number and gender) in their syntactic relationship to nouns, with pronouns (similar inflections with the addition of person), with verbs (inflected for tense, number and person) and their relationship to case-inflected elements. Book 4, which presumably dealt with all the remaining elements of the sentence, is unfortunately incomplete. It begins, however, with the syntax of prepositions, where Apollonius' main problem is that of distinguishing between prepositions as independent words (for example, in *katà tòn potamón*, 'down the river') and as the first members of compounds (for example, in the verb *katagráphō*, 'I write down'). For compounds in general the test is phonological: separate words carry separate accents, whereas a compound carries only one. But for a form such as *katagráphō* this is not decisive, since the sequence *katà gráphō* (where the grave of *katà* marks the suppression, in context, of a basic acute) would be phonetically identical. Apollonius points out that this is a very common ambiguity. So, what other criteria will be more reliable?

His first test is that independent prepositions do not collocate with nominatives or vocatives. Hence, for example, the nominative *súnoikos* 'fellow inhabitant' cannot, even regardless of its accentuation, be the two-word sequence *sún*, 'with' plus *oîkos*, 'house'. A form which is in an oblique case will then be resolved if we try to decline it systematically. If it is a compound we will be able to do so. But if it is a preposition governing a noun we will not: for example, *katà Ktesiphôntos*, 'against Ctesiphon' cannot be turned into *katà Ktesiphôn*, with the second word nominative instead of genitive. Another test is to add an article. If we are dealing with two words it will be inserted between them: *katà toû Ktesiphôntos* (literally 'against the Ctesiphon'). But if we add it to a compound it must come before the whole (*ho súnoikos*, 'the fellow inhabitant'). By these means we can distinguish cases where the accentuation is identical: for example, *parà [toû] phérontos*, 'from (the) one carrying' but *[toû] paraphérontos*, 'of (the) one serving'.[225]

Such distributions are a matter of simple observation. But Apollonius then embarks on a deeper inquiry into the elements that prepositions can and cannot combine with. In a sentence such as *Plátōn baínei*, 'Plato is coming', the nominative noun (*Plátōn*) refers to the same participant as the verb; in that light, he explains, any preposition which is added to the construction cannot be juxtaposed syntactically to the noun, since the meaning which is manifested by the preposition satisfies the relation subsisting from the verb.[226] Hence, if *en* 'in(to)' is added to this sentence it must form a compound with the verb *baínei* (*embaínei*, 'is coming in'). The only other possibility is that the sense assigned to the noun can also contract the same relation with the preposition: in that respect, Apollonius says, a compound noun such as *métoikos*, 'foreign resident' (*oîkos* compounded with the preposition *metá*) is not very different from the corresponding verb *metoikeîn*, 'to move or reside abroad'. He then turns to elements in oblique cases ('those, that is, which do not refer to the same participant'). These follow the opposite rule: whereas nominatives, as we have seen, behave correspondingly to verbs, oblique forms enter only into syntactic relationships. Now oblique compounds do exist. But according to Apollonius they are not formed directly, but are subsequent inflections of a compound already formed in the nominative. For example, the genitive *peribólou*, 'of an enclosure' is derived from a compound formed in the nominative or 'direct' case from *perí*, 'round about' and the simple *bólos*, 'cast of a net'; it is not formed in itself by the compounding of *perí* and the simple genitive *bólou*. He promises to justify this in a later passage (evidently lost).[227]

In the paragraphs which follow Apollonius defends this series of rules against various objections. In the case of oblique nouns, another view is that an independent preposition is derived by transposing the members of a verbal compound. For example, in *pròs Trúphōna eîpon* ('to Tryphon I-spoke'), *prós* would not combine directly with the accusative *Trúphōna*; instead this would be seen as a reordered version of *proseîpon Trúphōna*, 'I accosted

Tryphon', where the proposition forms a compound with the verb
*eîpon*. Apollonius rejects this analysis on the grounds that the
putative reordering cannot be made consistently. In some collocations the case of the noun does not correspond: for example, in
*pròs Apollōnion érkhomai*, 'I am coming to Apollonius' it is
accusative, but in *prosérkhomai Apollōníōi*, 'I am approaching
Apollonius' it is dative. For other collocations one construction or
the other is impossible. He then considers objections to the rule
that prepositions and nominatives can only form compounds, and,
in a later section, counters a whole series of objections to the
corresponding rule for verbs. For example, in collocations such as
*katagráphō*, 'I write down' (*katá* combined with *gráphō*), we can
insert a form between the preposition and the verb: *katagégrapha*,
'I have written down' (with insertion of a prefix *ge-*). Does not this
show that we are dealing with independent words, just as the
insertion of the article shows this in examples such as *parà* [*toû*]
*nómou*, 'according to (the) law'? Part of Apollonius' reply involves
an appeal to the corresponding participle. In *ho katagráphōn*, 'the
one writing down', the article (*ho*) precedes the participle *katagráphōn*; therefore that must be a compound and, since participles
are in this respect the same as the verbs from which they are
derived, the verb must be a compound too.[228]

As to the other elements of the sentence, Apollonius points out
that prepositions never form compounds with either a pronoun or
an article. But one preposition can combine with another: for
example, *parà* and *katà* combine in the compound noun *para-
katathḗkē*, 'deposit'.[229] He then turns to the syntax of adverbs.
After discussing the derivation of various particular forms, he
argues that this element too cannot combine with independent
prepositions. His basic reason is that they can only be construed
with their appropriate case, and adverbs are not inflected for case.
In addition, adverbs modify verbs; accordingly they contract the
same relationship, 'bringing the preposition (i.e. the preposition
with which they are compounded) into the verbal construction'.
But there are apparent counter-examples, such as *apò toû nûn*,
'from now' or *apò tês sḗmeron*, 'from today' (literally, 'from the
now', 'from the today'). Surely the position of the article shows
that *apò* does not form a compound with the adverbs *nûn* and
*sḗmeron*. But Apollonius explains that certain adverbs embody a
nominal concept. The concept of day is thus implicit in 'today' (in
Greek, too, the words are formally related), and in the (formally
unrelated) *khthés*, 'yesterday' and *aúrion*, 'tomorrow'; similarly,
the word for 'now' embodies the concept of time in general. It is
with this implicit concept that the relation is contracted. Accord-

ingly the preposition has to be independent, like any other which is construed with an oblique noun. Moreover, the article has to be added, so that the understood nominal can be perceived. It is characteristic of articles that they are construed with nominals; in Apollonius' examples they also agree appropriately (feminine *tês* with the case of the understood feminine *hēméra*, 'day', masculine *toû* with that of the understood masculine *khrónos*, 'time'). Apollonius points out that combinations such as *en sēmeron* (literally 'in today'), where *sēmeron* is without an article, are impossible.[230]

A few paragraphs later our continuous text ends, and of the remainder all we have is a substantial fragment on adverbs of time. But although we cannot form a complete picture of his work, it is clearly very different from the grammars surveyed earlier. The statements that they make were in an ancient context uncontroversial; they do not try to justify their classifications, and where there are indications of a differing opinion these too have been taken over, evidently at some remove, from more innovative predecessors. They have all the banality and usefulness of classroom grammars, and it is through their pedagogic value that they have survived. Apollonius' virtues and defects are the opposite. He is often obscure and elliptical; the organization of his work is not transparent; and various topics of a sort that might have seemed to him to be important (for example, why the prepositions govern one case rather than another) are not covered, at least where we might expect them. He also says things that reflection might have shown to be wrong (for example, that one cannot address oneself in the vocative), nor are all his arguments convincing – even, one might surmise, to his contemporaries. But these are the failings of an original academic mind, whose work belongs to a pioneering phase of grammatical theory. Apollonius is often right where some of his predecessors were, on his account of their opinions, wrong; moreover, he is right for reasons of the sort that modern grammarians would still consider valid. Clear examples are his rejection of the view that infinitives are adverbs, or that impersonal verbs are adverbs (in constructions of the type 'It-oughts me to'). In other cases he expounds points that have long been familiar: for example, the distinction between anaphoric and deictic pronouns, or between definite and potential referents for phrases such as 'the tyrannicide'. But his is the first work in which these distinctions are attested. Above all, he asks interesting questions. Thus it is not enough to say that a certain verb governs the accusative. We have to explain why it does so. What is there in the meaning of that verb that makes this case the correct one?

When a text is detached from its tradition we cannot safely say how far its basic concepts are original. Among Apollonius' predecessors, the Stoics are referred to six times and Aristarchus eight times, the latter more for philological comments than for general arguments. Tryphon is identified by name on ten occasions (also 30-odd times in Apollonius' other extant treatises). His views are usually criticized; but from their nature it seems clear that both grammarians were trying to answer the same kind of question. Although Tryphon is a shadowy figure, one is again tempted to ascribe to him a large role in the development of grammar as a linguistic discipline. Only two other predecessors are named in the *Syntax*: Comanus once (also twice in other treatises) and Habron seven times (apparently for the same work on pronouns). But others are criticized anonymously, and from the proposals that Apollonius rejects it seems likely that the theoretical devices which he relies on (for example, the concept of *metálepsis* as a change of wording, or his use of the rhetorical figure of *huperbatón* or transposition) were already current. We really know very little of those on whose shoulders Apollonius may have rested.

At the same time we should beware of magnifying their contribution. Three centuries later, Priscian saw the work of Apollonius and his son Herodian as a landmark in the history of grammar. 'What can be more penetrating', he asks, 'than Apollonius' meticulous investigations?' He therefore took these investigations as a model throughout his own grammar.[231] Our sampling of Apollonius' text will perhaps have shown the justice of Priscian's assessment. It is without doubt one of the great works in the history of our discipline.

### 1.6.2 The theoretical model of the grammarians

What, in general, was an ancient grammarian's model of the structure of language? The question is, of course, anachronistic. The grammarians themselves did not address such matters connectedly, and the terms in which it is framed cannot be rendered easily into contemporary Greek or Latin. But answers are implicit in their work, and, to counter what might otherwise seem an over-concern with detail, we will try to draw them out.

The backbone of the ancient conception of language is a hierarchy of four units. The smallest is the letter (*grámma, littera*), defined as 'the smallest part of articulate vocal sound'. For 'smallest part' read 'element'; as we saw in an earlier section, the terms 'letter' and 'element' are often interchangeable. The next unit is the syllable (*sullabḗ, syllaba*), defined by Priscian, for example, as 'a continuous combination of letters uttered with a single accent and

a single breath'. The notion of combination inherent in the term
(literally 'a taking together') was stretched to cover syllables with
one letter only. The third member of the hierarchy is the word
(*léxis, dictio* in the grammarians' terminology). This was defined –
again we will cite Priscian – as 'the smallest part of a connected
sentence'. Like the letter and the syllable, it too is a unit of vocal
sound (*phōnē, vox*); but, as Aristotle and the Stoics had made
clear, it is also a unit of meaning. Finally, the sentence (*lógos,
oratio*) is defined by Priscian as 'a congruent arrangement of words
expressing a complete idea'. In Stoic terms, this was not merely
meaningful, but independently meaningful.[232]

The relation between these units is basically one of size. A
syllable is formed by an appropriate combination of letters; similarly, a word is a combination of syllables and a sentence, in turn,
a combination of words. In the terminology of the twentieth-century linguist Leonard Bloomfield, they are all 'phonetic forms'. In
terms of the ancient definition of the *phōnē* or vocal sound, they
are successively larger divisions of the movements of air that pass
between a speaker and a hearer. But the two largest units, the word
and the sentence, also have meaning. In Bloomfield's theory, which
in this respect is following a tradition that begins with the Stoics,
they are not just phonetic forms but also 'linguistic forms'.[233]
There is therefore a specific parallel between the letter, as the
'smallest part' of vocal sound in general, and the word, as the
'smallest part' of meaningful vocal sound. Each is, on its respective
plane, an 'element'; and just as the smallest units of all combine in
specific ways to form syllables and then words, so the smallest
meaningful units – the *mérē toû lógou* or *partes orationis* –
combine in specific ways to form sentences. This parallel is brought
out at the beginning of the books on syntax by Apollonius Dyscolus
and Priscian. To cite Priscian once more, 'just as letters combining
appropriately form syllables and syllables words, so also words
form a sentence'.[234] There is thus some understanding, within the
single overall hierarchy, of what other twentieth-century linguists
have called 'duality of patterning' or 'double articulation'. There
are also some isomorphisms between the two planes. The syntactic
position of prepositions was compared to that of a vowel which
can appear in a diphthong only as the first member; similarly, both
letters and words can be redundant, can be found in transposed
orders, and so on.

The description of a language starts from the smallest unit and
proceeds upwards. Letters, as we have seen, were classified according to both their distributional and their phonetic properties. Thus
vowels were distinguished from consonants as letters that 'can

form a syllable on their own'; this refers to their function in the
higher unit. Among the consonants, 'half-vowels' were distinguished
from 'mutes' as letters that can be pronounced in isolation; this refers
to the sounds as such, the half-vowels, in particular, having few
distributional peculiarities in common. These broad classes were not
invented by the grammarians, but had been usual since at least the
fifth century BC. But Priscian's account has further details of both
kinds. On the phonetic side, he gives the standard classification of
mutes into aspirated, unaspirated and 'middle', with the three series
(bilabial, dental and velar in modern terminology) set out in parallel.
On the distributional side, he distinguishes the 'liquids' *l* and *r*: in
ancient terms, these were liquid (or more accurately 'variable') in
that metrical practice allowed the sequence of short vowel, stop and
liquid to be scanned either short or long. In a separate section on the
ordering of letters he distinguishes, for example, the positions of
vowels in diphthongs and of consonants in various types of cluster.
Priscian also includes some information that we might now see as
morphophonemic. For example, the double letter *x* (phonetically
[ks]) stands sometimes for *cs* (as in the nominative *apex* 'top',
genitive *apicis*) and sometimes for *gs* (as in *grex*, 'flock', genitive
*gregis*). Specific alternations are found in morphological derivations:
for instance, *s* can be changed to *n*, as in the genitive *sanguinis* 'of
blood', derived from nominative *sanguis*.[235] But the grammarians
had no separate heading under which such matters could be brought,
and it is clear that the ancient theory of the 'power' of letters did not
provide a sufficiently differentiated model.

We have already considered the ancient theory of the syllable. Its
main distributional role was in accentuation: in Greek the position
of the accent was subject to some limitations (for example, there
could be no word of three syllables with a circumflex or falling
pitch on the first), and in Latin it was fixed. From a linguistic
standpoint, a grammarian did not need to say much else about the
patterning of syllables within the word. But they were also important as the basis of verse metre, so that a grammarian such as
Donatus virtually treats them as a unit in another hierarchy, of
which the next term is the metrical foot. In Priscian's account,
where the following section proceeds directly to the next unit in the
main hierarchy, a syllable is said to have four variable properties:
its accent, its breathing (whether or not it begins with *h*), its time
value (long or short), and the numbers of letters that are in it. But
before this topic is introduced he devotes several pages to a list of
consonants that can begin and end syllables.[236] This is simply a
further aspect of the distribution of letters, of which most other
aspects have been covered in the preceding section.

So much for the second articulation. At this level, ancient models were not wholly coherent, and the relatively slight attention that the grammarians pay to it (in Priscian's case, some 50 pages in a modern edition of nearly a thousand) is the inverse of the role that it has often played in twentieth-century linguistics. It is when we turn to the 'first articulation' – to 'grammar' proper as many modern writers would conceive it – that their theory deserves more detailed elucidation. As we have seen, the units are just two: the word and the sentence. There is no concept of a unit comparable to Bloomfield's 'morpheme', which is smaller than the word and also has meaning.[237] Nor did the ancient grammarians talk of intermediate units such as the modern 'phrase' or 'clause'. In effect, there is no notion of what we now call 'constituency', other than that of words or elements of the sentence as constituents of the sentence as a whole. But within the sentence some elements were naturally more closely related than others. In Apollonius Dyscolus' account, the article relates to a noun. By definition adverbs relate to verbs, which are in turn related to nouns in various cases, both 'straight' (nominative or vocative) and oblique. The characteristic role of pronouns is to stand in place of nouns (in Apollonius' account for a noun preceded by the article); accordingly, they too bear relationships to verbs. From the definition of a preposition it follows that prepositions are construed with the element that follows: for example, a noun which might (in Greek) be accompanied by the article. In some of these relations there are clear indications of what we would now call dependency. Thus an adverb presupposes a verb: without the verb its meaning cannot be complete. In general, the noun and the verb are the 'principal' elements of the sentence, they alone being necessary if a thought is to be expressed completely.

Since there is no primitive notion of constituency, there is no independent formulation of what we would now call a constituency or 'phrase structure' rule. The ability of word *a* to enter into a relationship with word *b* simply follows from the semantic aspect of the words themselves. In the Latin phrase *in Italia*, 'in Italy', the first element (*in*) is a preposition and the second (*Italia*) is a noun. It is a property of prepositions in general that they enter into syntactic relationships with nouns (and, as Apollonius argues in Book 4 of his *Syntax*, only with nouns). Another general property of prepositions is that of preceding the elements they are related to; in Priscian's terms, this too is among the semantic characteristics (*proprietates significationum*) of the element. Among the *accidentia* or variable properties of prepositions is the ability to relate to nouns in one or more oblique cases: *in* relates to either an accusative or an ablative. *Italia*, for its part, is ablative. From all this it follows that *in Italia* is a congruent arrangement of words (whereas, for example, *Italia in*, with the preposition following, or *in Italiae*, where the noun is genitive, or *in venit*, where *in* is a separate word and *venit* 'is coming' is a verb, would not be). It is not a sentence, but could be part of a larger arrangement which also met the conditions of completeness.

For the grammarians and their pupils, the first preoccupation was that of parsing, and the information which we have cited is part of what is needed to construe a sentence with the sequence *in Italia* in it. But a model of sentence construction is merely the other side of the coin. In ancient accounts, a common metaphor is that of one word having a potential relationship which 'receives' that of another. A verb, for example, has an implicit relation which can receive the meaning of a preposition; the elements then form a compound. But the preposition cannot be received into a syntactic relationship with the accompanying nominative.[238] Similarly, the inherent potential of a verb receives the senses of the nouns to which it is linked: in modern usage, we still talk of a verb 'taking an object' or 'taking the accusative'. As we saw from Apollonius Dyscolus' explanations of the valencies of various classes of verbs, the particular relationships which can be contracted are seen as determined by the meanings of the words and categories involved. Thus a verb takes the accusative if it has the appropriate 'active' meaning, and can take a genitive, which is also the case of what we would call the agent in the passive, if its meaning implies external influence. A complementary metaphor is that of 'demanding': thus a particular element may be demanded if the sentence is to be complete.[239] Now, if an element with the semantic properties $x$ demands or can receive another element with the semantic properties $y$, it follows that there will be sentences in which such elements are related. In that sense there are phrases (as we would now call them) of which words with properties $x$ and $y$ are constituents. But these are not primitive concepts. In the ancient concept, constructions are a function of the meanings of the individual words.[240]

In some cases, an element has the property not only of receiving another element, but of receiving it in a fixed sequence. Thus a preposition not only seeks a relationship with a case-form, but also precedes it. Naturally, there may be exceptions: for example, Priscian notes that *cum*, 'with' follows certain pronouns (*mecum*, 'with me'). If so, they must be referred to the properties of the individual word. There may also be attested sentences in which the rule is not obeyed. If so, they may be handled as instances of hyperbaton or 'transposition': for example, Apollonius acknowledges that there are transpositions which run contrary to his rules for the ordering of accented and unaccented pronouns. But for other relationships no sequence is laid down. A transitive verb receives an oblique case-form, but so far as the grammarian is concerned their order may be equally Oblique (X) Verb (X being any intervening sequence) or Verb (X) Oblique. The reason lies partly in the character of the classical languages. In both Latin and Greek the order of words was variable, and in this case none of the implied orders (related elements adjacent or non-adjacent, verb before the case-form or following) would be a solecism. But another factor is the division between ancient grammar and rhetoric. Given that the words were congruent – that they fit together appropriately in respect of valency and agreement – their ordering could be exploited, and was indeed exploited sometimes in very artificial ways, for the sake of clarity, persuasion or ornament. A grammarian was concerned with congruence, or (to turn it the other way round) with the avoidance of solecism. He was not concerned with the putting together of words into periods or other smaller units of literary composition. Such 'putting together' (Gk. *súnthesis*, Lat. *compositio*) belonged to classical rhetoric.[241]

In such a model there is little to be said about the largest unit. A sentence must meet the requirements of congruence. It must also meet a condition of completeness; this too is part of Priscian's and other ancient definitions. But the grammarians do not classify sentences into types, or give a list of their variable properties. Instead they proceed directly to their parts or elements. Now for a modern grammarian these include such elements as subject and object, which are functions that words may fulfil in given structural patterns. But for an ancient writer they are simply the eight classes of words that have come down to us under the name of 'parts of speech'. We have remarked already that Apollonius has no terms by which the modern 'subject' and 'object' can be translated. In his analysis of sentences such as *Apollónios Trúphōna étupse*, 'Apollonius hit Tryphon', the subject (*Apollónios*) and the object (*Trúphōna*) are both nouns. In ancient terms they are the same 'element of the sentence' (*méros toû lógou, pars orationis*). The difference between them lies in their case and their consequential relation to the verb. *Apollónios* is nominative, and the entity that is said to be 'underlying' (*hupokeímenon*) is the same as that referred to by the verb (*étupse*, 'he-(Apollonius)-hit'). *Trúphōna* is accusative: the underlying entity is accordingly that to which the action of the verb 'crosses over'. Other concepts are basically cover terms. The term 'case form' (*ptōtikón*, 'having the property of case') is commonly used for 'either a noun or a pronoun or a participle'. The term 'oblique' covers any case other than the nominative and the vocative. In this way one could speak simply of an oblique form (Lat. *obliquum*, Gk. *plagíon*), meaning any of these elements in any of the 'non-straight' cases.

It is therefore on the elements of the sentence that the burden of description falls. Each of these has a definition, which in principle sets out the essential characteristics that distinguish it from other elements. Thus in Apollonius' account of the verb the essential features are those that are present in both the finite moods and the infinitive. The main purpose of these definitions is to define syntactic roles. The adverb is defined by its relationship to the verb, and the article (in the Greek system) by its relationship to the noun. The preposition is defined by its position, and the conjunction is a connecting element. Of the two principal elements, verbs signify the things that entities do or have done to them. They are therefore syntactically related to nouns, which signify the entities themselves and, in addition, assume varying case roles. Pronouns, in turn, are said to have the same roles as nouns. A participle, which is the only remaining element in the Greek system, shares the character of both principal elements. As Apollonius points out, it takes the same oblique form as the verb from which it derives. But it also has the syntax which is appropriate to its own case inflection. By contrast, an infinitive is not itself inflected for case; therefore the view which prevailed, (though from our sources it is clear that there were dissentients) did not see it as an element on its own. It is doubtful whether any system of this kind can be above criticism. But when it is seen in its ancient context it is more consistent than a modern reader might at first allow, and the changes which various grammarians made in it (in particular, the recognition of one class of nouns in place of two or three) were clear improvements.

Each element of the sentence is then assigned a set of variable properties (Gk. *parepómena*, 'accompanying'; Lat. *accidentia*). In principle, these cover any variation that is semantically relevant. Some variation is not: although Priscian classified syllables by the number of letters they contain, he did not classify words by the number of syllables. But the *parepómena* include variables that bear directly on syntactic congruence, in particular, the properties of case, person, number, gender and tense which Apollonius Dyscolus refers to in his theory of solecisms. They also include properties whose relevance to syntax is indirect: for example, the *ordines* or declensions of nouns, which distinguish different formal derivations of nouns with the same syntactic potentials, or the conjugations (Gk. *suzugíai*, 'correlated sets') of verbs. They include variables that can be associated with a pattern of formal derivation: for example, the case of nouns, where the oblique forms are derived systematically from the nominatives. But they also include properties with no formal mark, such as the case of prepositions (the property of governing nouns in one case or another) or the *potestas* or 'force' of a conjunction (copulative, disjunctive, and so on). In the description of nouns, the same category of *qualitas* or 'quality' embraces distinctions between simple forms (general, like *animal*, 'animal' as against specific, like *homo*, 'man') and between simple and derived (basic *mons*, 'mountain'; diminutive *monticulus*, 'little mountain'). In the ancient model, these are all dimensions on which the classification of a word may vary, and are therefore treated equally.

The terms for semantic properties are of varying transparency. 'Case' is one of the more specialized: its original sense was that of 'falling', and although this metaphor was kept alive by the grammarians' distinction between 'straight' and oblique cases, its precise import had become obscure. The Greek term for mood, *égklisis*, had a similar sense of 'slope' or 'leaning' and could still be used, in a linguistic context, for inflection or derivation in general. It is in that sense that the calque *declinatio* (later 'declension') was first introduced into Latin. The Latin grammarians' term for 'mood' (*modus*) derives from the ordinary sense of 'manner' or 'way', and was again relatively infelicitous. It was accordingly necessary for a grammarian such as Priscian to define the semantic character of the moods, as 'different leanings of the mind'.[242] But one scarcely had to explain the meaning of, for example 'tense'. As in Italian and other modern Romance languages, the term was simply the ordinary word for 'time' (Gk. *khrónos*, Lat. *tempus*) and the nature of time as a category or dimension of reality was taken for granted. The grammarians could then proceed immediately to the distinction of three times, past, present and future. The term for gender is the one that in other contexts we translate as 'genus' (Gk. *génos*, Lat. *genus*, originally 'race, lineage' or, more generally, 'kind'). The voice of a verb is, in Greek, its function or 'disposition' (*diáthesis*); in Latin its *significatio* or 'meaning' (it will be remembered that the distinction between acting and undergoing is part of the definition of the element) or, again and more usually, its *genus*. The term for person (Gk. *prósopon*, Lat. *persona*) is, in particular, the word for a character in a play; when a modern grammarian such as Lucien Tesnière talks of a verbal construction as describing 'tout un petit drame' he employs a very old metaphor.[243] The term for number, as in all the modern languages, is again the ordinary word (*arithmós, numerus*).

In the ideal case, or what one senses a grammarian might have seen as the ideal case, there is no conceptual distinction between a linguistic and an extra-linguistic category. A modern writer might say, for example, that a verb in the past tense indicates an action in past time. We thus assume a distinction, and with it the possibility of a discrepancy, between tense in language and time in the real world. But for the ancient grammarians a verb simply had a time value, just as, among other things, it had a mood value. So, in Priscian's definition, moods are not said to 'signify leanings of the mind' (in the way that, in the definition of the element itself, a verb signifies an action performed or undergone). They simply are such. Similarly, persons do not refer to, but are, the participants in the event. In Priscian's account, the first person is defined as 'the one who speaks about himself either alone or with others'. The second person is in turn 'the one to whom he speaks about that person himself either alone or with others', and the third person 'the one about whom the first person speaks who is external to himself and to the person to whom he addresses his speech'.[244] In many contexts 'participant' is an apter translation. According to Apollonius Dyscolus, the difference between the finite *peripatô*, 'I walk' and *peripatoûmen*, 'we walk', is that in the latter case the action of walking (*to peripateîn*, 'the to-walk') is seen as involving participants (*prósōpa*). In *peripatô*, 'I walk' versus *peripateîs*, 'you walk' and *peripateî*, '(he) walks', Apollonius says that the *prósōpa* who take part are divided into the *prósōpa* first, second and third. He uses the same term of participants other than the subject. In intransitives such as *zô*, 'I live' no participant (*prósōpon*) is acted on. In *boúlomai se gráphein* ('I-want you to-write'), *boúlomai* must take an object pronoun because there is a transfer of *prósōpa*. Here either 'participant' or 'person' would be a feasible translation.[245]

To a modern reader such formulations may seem clumsy and perhaps pernicious. But if we leave the conceptual status of the categories aside, the main problem with the ancient cross-classifications of words is simply that they were incomplete. All grammarians deal systematically with variables that we would call inflectional (case, number, tense, and so on). But their treatment of other categories tends to be uneven. On the one hand, even summary grammars include many non-inflectional sub-classes of nouns. Some are marked by processes of word formation: in the tradition followed by (pseudo-) Dionysius or Priscian, these are different 'species' (Gk. *eidē*, Lat. *species*) of derived nouns, which are themselves a 'species' of the element in general. Others have no formal mark: standard examples are relational nouns – a grammatical relic of a scheme of categories in Stoic philosophy – or generic and specific. The grammarians had also worked out a semantic classification of adverbs, which Donatus includes even in the *Ars Minor*. On the other hand, the variable properties of the verb do not include a number of important features. One is the case that they govern: since prepositions were so classified, Latin *ad* being in ancient terms an accusative preposition and *ab* an ablative, logic might have suggested that verbs which take an object should be treated similarly. In seeking to explain the valency of verbs, Apollonius distinguishes several notional classes, some very general, such as the class of 'active' verbs in which an action 'crosses over', some more particular, such as verbs of perception or, within these, verbs of seeing. If the model had been applied consistently, these could surely have been meanings or 'qualities' of verbs (*significationes*, *qualitates*) set out and in detail, as are those of adverbs, in the basic description of the element. In fact, the tradition merely distinguished voices, for which there is a formal criterion.

Given the inflectional properties of an element, a final task is to specify their formal realization. We remarked earlier that the ancient grammarians had no concept of the morpheme as an element of meaning. Neither did they have our modern concept of an inflectional affix. A twentieth-century account will say that in, for example, the Latin imperfect *amābam*, 'I loved, used to love', a stem *amā-* is followed by the suffix *-bā-*, marking the imperfect indicative, and a further suffix *-m*, marking the first singular. The process may be seen as one in which the word is built up gradually from a root (*am-*), first by forming the 'present' or non-perfect stem (*am-* → *amā-*), then adding *-bā-* to form the stem of the imperfect (*amā-* → *amābā-*), before finally adding the termination (*amābā-* → *amābam*). But in the ancient model words as wholes are derived from other words, also as wholes. In Priscian's account, *amābam* is derived from *amās* (second singular present indicative) by removing *-s* and putting *-bam* in its place. *Amās* is in turn derived from *amō* (first singular) by replacing *-ō* with *-ās*. Such changes are said to affect the end of the word, as in these examples, or the beginning or the middle. Some involve all three: for example, in the derivation of past perfect *cecidī*, 'I fell' from present *cadō*, 'I fall' the initial consonant is geminated (*ce-*), medial *a* is changed to *i*, and final *-ō* to *-ī*. They may increase the number of syllables (*amās* → *amābam*), or leave it unchanged (*amō* → *amās*), or decrease it (first singular *doceō*, 'I teach' → second singular *docēs*, 'you teach'). Finally, a change may be partly determined by 'euphony'. In the third conjugation, a present in *-bō* will typically form a past perfect in *-psi*: *scrībō*, 'I write' → *scrīpsī*, 'I wrote'. Analogy, as Priscian explains, would require that the form should be *scrībsī*; but *bs* cannot begin a syllable (the ancient syllabic division is between *scrī-* and *-psī*) and so the euphonic principle prevails.[246]

Here, too, we have a model which, whether or not the most attractive to a modern scholar, was certainly capable of refinement. Starting from the basic form of each inflected word (nominative singular of nouns, or first singular present indicative of verbs), one could in principle derive all other forms by sequences of rules applying to the part of speech in general, or to specific declensions or conjugations, or to words of certain phonological shapes, or exceptionally to particular items. But its actual development seems again to have been uneven. In Priscian's account of nominal inflections, the lines of derivation are set out clearly: the genitive and vocative singular are derived from the nominative (second declension *dominus* 'master' → *dominī*, *domine*); the nominative/vocative plural and the remaining cases of the singular are in turn related to the genitive (*dominī* without change, *dominō* with *-ī* changed to *-ō*, *dominum* with *-ī* changed to *-um*); finally, the other plural cases are derived from the ablative singular (*dominō* → *dominōrum* and *dominōs* by the addition of *-rum* or *-s*). Although one can point to what we would now see as deficiencies (in particular, the same rule is repeated for different declensions), and also to the occasional lacuna (for example, the rule for the vocative *domine* is not stated explicitly), the description is detailed and systematic.[247]

But the corresponding treatment of the verb is not. Where there are irregularities Priscian deals with them exhaustively: thus, in particular, the perfects and supines, which occupy the best part of his two books, and the present forms of the irregular verbs *ferō*, 'I carry', *volō*, 'I want' or *edō*, 'I eat'.[248] He also gives systematic rules for the two forms which we have cited in illustration (second singular of the present indicative and first singular of the imperfect). But in the remainder of the paradigm it is generally unclear what should be derived from what, and many forms, notably the tenses of the subjunctive and the other person and number terminations, are not mentioned. For a more consistent application we must turn to the 'Introductory Rules' (*eisagōgikoì kanónes*) of the Greek grammarian Theodosius of Alexandria (fourth to fifth century AD). These are works dealing only with inflections, which in the case of the verb distinguish every theoretically possible derivation from *túptō* 'I hit' 'and *títhēmi* 'I put'. But the directions that they take will often give a modern scholar cause for thought. In the present indicative the second singular *túpteis* is derived from *túptō* by the change of *-ō* to *-eis*, and third singular *túptei* from *túpteis* by the deletion of *-s*. This follows the order in which the forms are conventionally listed. But first plural *túptomen* is derived not from any of these, but from the genitive singular of the present participle (*túptontos*): first delete the final syllable *-tos*, then change *-n* to *-men*. This allows a generalization, saving the accent, to verbs such as *tithēmi* (*tithéntos* → *tithemen*). Similarly, third plural *túptousi* is related to the identical dative plural of the participle, and in the next paragraph the first singular of the imperfect indicative, *étupton*, is also derived from the genitive: remove the last syllable and augment the first. Other endings of the imperfect are derived in one or more stages from that, in the case of the third singular, for example, one simply applies the rule given earlier for the present (*étuptes* → *étupte*). In the section on the participle, *túptontos* is also the source for the feminine singular *túptoūsa*: change the ending to *-sa* and lengthen (sic) the preceding vowel. This rule is said to hold for all participles 'inflected by means of *-nt-*'. There is no other text from this period which treats the regular inflections with the same depth and generality.[249]

But in the end we must remind ourselves of the anachronistic nature of this inquiry. The ancient grammarians were not theoretical linguists in the twentieth-century sense: their concern was with the description and the maintenance, through teaching, of the standard forms of Greek and Latin, not with the structure of language in the abstract. On the Greek side, a grammarian such as Apollonius could write with sublime ignorance even of Latin. Their guiding principles must therefore be deduced very largely from the ways in which they dealt with concrete problems. However, both at the formal level and in their treatment of semantics, the grammatical works of the middle to late empire make a contribution to the development of linguistics as important as any that preceded them.

## Postscript, February 1992

This chapter was completed in the summer of 1986, and my responsibility for it ended with its publication in Italian by Il Mulino. I am therefore grateful to the editor and the publisher of the English edition for an opportunity to update the bibliography.

Most of the references that follow deal with the early and later history of grammatical notions. See, in particular, Ax (1986) on the theory of vocal sound and related matters; Baratin (1989) on syntax; Sluiter (1990), which among other things deals extensively with Apollonius Dyscolus. The authenticity of the grammar ascribed to Dionysius Thrax is a continuing problem: see further Di Benedetto (1990); also Law (1990b) which shows how one part of its doctrine fits into the chronology of Latin grammars in the Imperial period. Note now Robins's more non-committal treatment in the newest edition of his *Short History of Linguistics* (1990, 34). Meanwhile annotated translations of this grammar have appeared in both French (Lallot 1989) and English (Kemp 1986). For a general essay on Hellenistic grammar, written at the same time as my section, see Taylor's introductory chapter in Taylor (1987); the collection as a whole is reviewed by House-holder (1989). I list Bécares Botas (1985), unfortunately without having seen it.

For the primary sources see, in particular, Hülser's new and comprehensive edition of the fragments of Stoic dialectic (1987–8). The minor works of Priscian are being re-edited by Passalacqua (1987), but the one I cite will be in the second volume. I also list two earlier re-editions of parts of Keil's *Grammatici latini* which I missed. Law (1987) has identified an as yet unpublished grammar as possibly by the relatively early Roman grammarian Scaurus.

## Notes

1. *Crat.* 431e, *Soph.* 253a.
2. See Liddell and Scott, s.v. (1940) for references from Xenophon onwards.
3. Scholia in D. T. 160.10f.H, cited and discussed by Pfeiffer (1968, 162). See Pfeiffer (1968, 157f.) for the development of this sense in general.
4. D. T. 5f.U; also, for the main definition, S.E., *Math.* 1.57.
5. Quint., *Inst.* 1.4.2, 1.9.1; also 1.7.1 (for writing).
6. For later definitions of grammar see Barwick (1922, 215ff.); on the educational system Marrou (1965, part 2, chs 6–7; part 3, chs 4ff.). Donatus' work on Terence survives in altered form; his work on Virgil is largely lost, but was used extensively in the extant commentaries of Servius (see entries in *OCD*). On the selection of authors in the schoolroom see Marrou (1965, 404–6).
7. August., *Dial.*: on the problem of authenticity see Jackson (1975, 1ff.); Pépin (1976, ch. 2). On the grammars see Law (1984). For specific references to the *De Dialectica* see s. 1.5, n. 129 (for sign theory); s. 1.3, n. 62 (on etymology); s. 1.6, n. 213.
8. The system of seven 'arts' is in Martianus Capella (probably early to mid-fifth century AD).
9. Recent discussion, with references, by Gambarara (1984). For Varro's etymologies see the end of s. 1.3 below.
10. Pl., *Rep.* 475b,e. The term had apparently been invented by Pythagoras (Guthrie, 1962–81, 1, 204f.); see references in Guthrie (1962–81, 4, *passim*) for Plato's conception.
11. See Kerferd (1981, ch. 4 'On the meaning of the term sophist').
12. D.L., 7.39 (*SVF* 1, 15).
13. See Barwick (1922) for the relations between the Roman grammarians. For this tradition our terminal date has little significance; the reader is referred to recent studies by Holtz (1981) and Law (1982) for its continuation into the early Middle Ages.

14. '. . . the idiotic and scandalous Diogenes Laertius' (*OCD*, s.v. 'Sextus Empiricus'). For the early Stoics generally the main collection of sources is that of Von Arnim (*SVF*); the linguistic material was first collected by Schmidt (1839), in a work of which there is a recent German translation (1979).

15. For the arguments against the authenticity of this text see Di Benedetto (1958–9) and the summary of his case by Pinborg (1975, 104ff.): also Di Benedetto (1973); Siebenborn (1976, 71, n. 2). For a more optimistic view see Pfeiffer (1968, 267ff.); Erbse (1980, s. 2).

16. For a relatively short account see Robins (1967, chs 2–3), which rework the relevant parts of Robins (1951); two related articles (Robins, 1957; 1966) are reprinted in Robins (1970). But both Robins and more recently Hovdhaugen (1982, chs 3–4) make a division between Greece and Rome, which is surely anti-historical. For a genuinely historical sketch, which also takes pains to avoid anachronism, see Baratin and Desbordes (1981, 9–67). For the classical and Hellenistic periods Pinborg's bibliographical survey (1975) is particularly valuable; see also Leszl (1985) for a recent essay concentrating on the philosophical aspect. Siebenborn (1976, 4ff.) gives a useful historical account of modern scholarship on the origin of grammar. There is no twentieth-century contribution on the scale of that of Steinthal (1890–91) in the nineteenth; this has had an immense influence on most later work. For a useful collection of texts see again Baratin and Desbordes (1981).

17. See Marrou (1965, part 3, ch. 3) for the status of the two languages under the empire.

18. See discussion by Law (1985).

19. For the origins of alphabetic writing see Cohen (1958, ch. 8; Text, 144ff. on Greek specifically); Diringer (1968, ch. 12 and, for Greek, ch. 19). Diringer's volume of plates has a useful table comparing a North Semitic and various early Greek scripts (306, plate 19.5). For further assessment see Allen (1981) which is an excellent short account of Greek phonetics generally. Diringer (1968, 1, 357) speaks justly of 'the wonderful achievement of the invention of the Greek alphabet'.

20. Koller (1955; 1958).

21. Pl., *Theaet.* 202e–203c.

22. One might compare the ancient Indian concept of zero (Allen, 1955). For *stoikheîon* see Chantraine (1968–80, s.v.) and Liddell and Scott (1940); the etymology of *elementum* is more problematic but proposed alternatives link it to writing (Walde, 1965, s.v.).

23. Pl., *Crat.* 393d, 424c ('speechless' and non-speechless); *Theaet.* 203b (*s* a 'noise', but *b* not a noise). Ar., *Poet.* 29, 1456*β*25. For the grammarians see, for example, D.T. 9ff.U; Don. K IV, 367–8; Prisc. K II, 9. The ancient sense of *semivocalis* persists in the early modern period (*OED*, s.v. 'semivowel').

24. Diogenes of Babylon in D.L. 7.55; also Scholia in D.T. (Heliodorus), 482H. Democritus in Aul. Gell., 5.15; similarly Epicurus (D.L., 10.52–3). Aulus Gellius mentions other definitions which refer to the

actual act of setting air in motion. For the grammarians see Charis.
K I, 7; Diomedes K I, 420; Prisc. K II, 5f. For the sounds of animals
as *agrámmatoi psóphoi* compare Ar., *Int.* 16¹⁶29 (equivalently *Poet.*
1456β24)

25. Diogenes of Babylon again in D.L. 7.55; Lat. *figura* = Gk. *khar-
    aktḗr, nomen* 'name' = *ónoma, potestas* = *dúnamis.* Prisc. K II, 7,
    9; section on order 37ff. Priscian refers to a tradition which treated
    *ordo* (Gk. *táxis*) as a separate property: thus Schol. in D.T.
    (Melampus/Diomedes), 31H; Asper, K V, 548.3f.

26. For the letter as 'pars minima vocis articulatae', e.g. Don. K IV, 367;
    as 'elementum' Charis. K I, 7; as 'nota elementi', with example of *rp*,
    Prisc. K II, 6f. For discussion and modern senses of the 'letter' as a
    phonetic unit see Abercrombie (1949).

27. D. T. 9U.

28. Diomedes K I, 421.

29. D. H., *Comp.* 14. See Allen (1974) for the interpretation of these and
    other passages as evidence for the pronunciation of Greek; his Appen-
    dix B (145–51) is a useful anthology.

30. Vowel in *optimus*, Quint., *Inst.* 1.4.8; see discussion by Allen (1978,
    56ff.), who proposes a value of [ɨ] for this period. Values of
    *m*, Quint. 1.4.8.; Pliny on values of *l* in Prisc. K II, 29 (discussed by
    Allen, 33f). Anthology of passages, including these, in Allen's Appen-
    dix A (95–101).

31. 'Roughness' and 'smoothness' appear as terms in the text of Ar.,
    *Poet.* 1456G 32; earliest (?) definitions in Pseudo-Aristotle, *Aud.* 804β;
    for the 'addition of breath' in the 'rough' series see again D. H.,
    *Comp.* 14; 'intermediate' is explained in D. T. 13U. For the phonetic
    interpretation of the Greek evidence see Allen (1974, 12ff.). The
    Latin grammarians generally say nothing, but according to Priscian
    (K II, 20.9ff.) *b, d* and *g* have again more aspiration than *p, t* and *k*,
    but less than *ph* or *f* (Gk. φ, θ, χ were by his time voiceless fricatives),
    *th* and *ch*. Terentianus Maurus K VI, 331.

32. Don. K IV, 368f. Of the vowel letters in Greek, η and ω were
    described as 'long' (ē, ō) and ε and o as 'short' (e, o), with the same
    terms that are applied to syllables; the others again as variably
    'drawn out' or 'abbreviated' (D. T. 10U). It is instructive to compare
    Sanskrit accounts, which according to Allen (1953, 85) also involved
    confusions. In medieval and later treatments a short vowel in a long
    syllable is itself said to be 'long by position': this 'nonsensical doctrine'
    (Allen, 1978, 92) is perhaps foreshadowed by Priscian's description of
    the *a* in *amo* as a vowel 'short in itself' (*brevis per se*, K II, 51.26).

33. Charis. K I, 11; compare (for Greek) D.T. 17ff. U, also the awkward
    formulation of Quintilian (*Inst.* 9.4.85–6). On ancient syllable divi-
    sions as the basis for dividing words in writing see Allen (1974, 98f.,
    esp. n. 2). For disagreements between grammarians see S.E., *Math.*
    1.169, where these and other disputes are dismissed as pointless.

34. Prisc. K II, 7. For the change in Greek from a pitch to a stress accent
    see Allen (1974, 119f.).

35. For the dating of the *Cratylus* see Guthrie (1962–81, 5, 1f.). I will rely heavily on Guthrie's reading of the dialogue (summary *ibid.* 5–15, commentary 16–31) and on his coverage of the earlier literature. Among the studies he refers to, that of Anagnostopoulos (1973/74) is a lucid demolition of the traditional assessment of the dialogue; Kretzmann (1971) has a similar interpretation of Plato's own view on the naturalness of language. See also the brief account by Kerferd (1981, 75–7). For the centrality of the problem of language in ancient Greek philosophy, before and after Plato, see in particular Graeser (1977).
36. *Crat.* 383a–4d. For *nómos* and *phúsis* in general see Guthrie (1962–81, 3, ch. 4).
37. *Crat.* 385e–386a. On Protagoras' dictum see Kerferd (1981, 85ff.); Guthrie (1962–81, 181ff.).
38. *Crat.* 397c–d (*theós*), 399c (*ánthrōpos*), 402e–403a (Poseidon), 412c–e (*dikaiosúnē, díkaion*), 414b–d (*tékhnē*), 421b–c (*ón*). On the Heraclitean theory of flux see Guthrie (1962–81, 1, 449ff.).
39. 'and the goddess' name rightly begins from folly' (*Tro.* 990). See also the discussion in Kirk (1954), of the linguistic views of Heraclitus, which gives references (119) for etymologies in Aeschylus.
40. *Phaedrus* 238c, 244b–c.
41. See *Crat.* 396d, 399a, 407e. For Euthyphro compare the early dialogue which bears his name; summary and comments in Guthrie (1962–81, 4, 103ff.).
42. *Crat.* 409d–410a (*pûr*), 416a (*kakón*).
43. But this term is not used. Liddell and Scott's earliest citation is from Strabo (born 64/3 BC); in Ar. (*Cat.* 7a5 and elsewhere) the verb *onomatopoiéō* has the literal sense of 'to coin names'.
44. Comparison with painter 424d–425b; *r*, *i* and other specific letters 426d–427c.
45. *Crat.* 430a. Discussion, with reference to other dialogues, s.1.4.1 below.
46. *Crat.* 432e.
47. *Crat.* 434e (example of *sklerótēs* 434b-d).
48. Examples in *Crat.* 437a-c.
49. See Anagnostopoulos (1973/74, s.I) for a particularly thorough and convincing refutation of this reading.
50. Among the gods Hermes is particularly associated with speech: 'interpreter of *lógos* to mortals' (*Orphic Hymns* 28.4); 'leader of speech, ruler of wise *phōnḗ*' (Nonnus, *Dionysiaca* 26.284). The notion that Hermes instituted language is the first to be dismissed by Diogenes of Oenoanda. Allen (1948) compares Greek theories of the evolution of language with those of India and other ancient cultures.
51. Pl., *Prot.* 322a. The account is presented in a mythical dress, but I follow Guthrie (1962–81, 3, 63ff.) in assuming that this is for decoration only.
52. Diodorus 1.8.3–4. See too Manilius, *Astronomica* 1.82ff. (conventions of language, with agriculture and commerce, diffused in the commu-

nity after individual experiment). Diodorus' assumption of the plurality of languages can be set against Herodotus' story (2.2) of the
attempt by Psammetichus to discover which was original.

53. D.L. 10.75–6. Commentary in Bailey's edition of Lucretius (1947, 3,
1486–96).

54. 5.1028–90. See again Bailey's commentary.

55. Fr. 10; the context is again that of human evolution in general.
Diogenes is known only from the inscription of which this is part, an
Epicurean manifesto which he erected before his death for the enlight-
enment of his fellow citizens.

56. Thus Aulus Gellius (second century AD) 10.4.

57. *Crat.* 390d, where Socrates also describes the coining of a word as *hē
toû onómatos thésis.*

58. In *Crat.* 16. On the topic of this paragraph see Fehling (1965, s.2)
who argues convincingly that Aulus Gellius (n. 56) confused two
separate oppositions in which *phúsis* 'nature' was a term.

59. Ar., *Sense* 437α15; *Int.* 16α19, 27; McKeon (1946, 201ff.) usefully
assembles the passages in which Aristotle compares the communication
of man and animals. For Aristotle as a conventionalist one may add
the ancient testimony of Origen, *Cels.* 701–4 (Ch. 341), 1249–50 (Ch.
611); Proclus, *loc. cit.* (n. 56). I have followed the traditional interpretation of *katà sunthḗkēn*; an alternative view, in which it is equivalent
to [*phōnḕ*] *sunthetḗ* 'composite [vocal sound]' in *Poet.* 1457α, is put
forward by Engels (1963, s.1) and accepted by Pinborg (1975, 75).

60. On Boethius see Engels, (1963, s.2); *ad placitum* in, for example,
Dante, *De Vulgari Eloquentia* 1.3.3 (the reference to the Comedy is to
*Paradiso* 26.132.). The. opposition *naturalis/arbitraria* is in Aulus
Gellius (see below) and the formulae 'à plaisir', 'par institutions
arbitraires' are used in parallel by Rabelais (3.19). For the medieval
and later tradition generally see Engels (1963, s.3); Coseriu (1967).

61. Pinborg (1975, 95f.) retreats from the reconstruction of Barwick
(1957, 8ff.) and from his own early study (1962).

62. *Caelum*, etc. *L.L.* 5.18–20 (Varro also derives *caelum* from *caelatura,
Men.* 420, ed. Funaioli, fr. 91.); *terra L.L.* 5.21; *actus, via L.L.* 5.22, 34–
5; [*Ju*]*piter L.L.* 5.65; *Juno L.L.* 5.65; *testudo, lolligo, lutra L.L.* 5.79. Such
methods are strongly criticized by Augustine, *Dial.* 6; note also
Quintilian: 'Who, after Varro, may not be pardoned?' (*Inst.* 1.6.39).
For a general discussion of Varro's etymological work see Cavazza
(1981); for the overall scheme of place and time, with subdivisions,
Taylor (1975, 68ff.) and his references.

63. *L.L.* 5.2.

64. *L.L.* 6.2 (reference to the Stoics Chrysippus and Antipater and the
Alexandrians Aristophanes and Apollodorus, the former being said
to have more insight).

65. Aul. Gell. 10.4 (*loc. cit.*); compare Chrysippus' explanation of Gk.
*egṓ* 'I', pilloried by Galen, *De Placitis Hippocratis et Platonis* 214ff.

66. *Crat.* 430a (impossible to speak falsely); 385c (truth or falsity of
individual elements).

67. Ar., *Met.* 1024β32; also *Top.* 104β21. Compare *Met.* 1043β23–6 on the impossibility of definition.
68. *Euthyd.* 286c; *Crat.* 429d.
69. For the argument and its context see Guthrie (1962–81, 3, 209ff). Nuchelmans (1973, 9ff.); Kerferd (1981, 88f.); Leszl (1985, 19ff.).
70. *Euthyd.* 283c-d; discussion and summary of the dialogue generally in Guthrie (1962–81, 4, 266f.). The syntax of the verb 'to be' is the subject of an excellent philological study by Kahn (1973).
71. For the early senses of *lógos* see, in particular, Guthrie (1962–81, 1, 420ff.) (in the chapter on Heraclitus); Kerferd (1981, 83).
72. *Theaet.* 203a-b.
73. Argument that one cannot speak falsely *Euthyd.* 283e–284c; that one cannot contradict 285d–286b.
74. Thus especially *Soph.* 256b; for the context see Guthrie's running commentary (1962–81, 5, 151f.).
75. For the episode as a whole see *Soph.* 261c–263d; the same argument is then applied to thoughts, beliefs and sense impressions (*diánoiai, dóxai, phantasíai*). For useful running commentaries see Nuchelmans (1973, ch. 2); Guthrie (1962–81, 154ff.)
76. *Soph.* 262a.
77. Ar., *Poet.* 1456$^b$ 20 (for the term *mérē tês léxeōs*), 22–38 (for *stoikheîa* and syllables); according to the text, a syllable consists of a mute and a 'vocal sound' (*phōné*). On the passage which follows (1456$^b$ 38–1457$^b$ 10) see Pinborg, 1975, 72ff., and his references.
78. *Rhet.* 1413$^b$ 32. On the problem of the *árthron*, note that in later rhetorical sources (n. 90 below) the element is said to be introduced by the Stoics.
79. Nouns and verbs *Poet.* 1457$^a$ 10–23; *Int.* 16$^a$ 19–16$^b$ 25. In the grammarians *ptôsis* is the term for case (Lat. *casus*); for brief discussion of its origin and early senses, Aristotelian and Stoic, see Pinborg (1975, 76f., 82ff.).
80. Sentences briefly in *Poet.* 1457$^a$ 23–30; more fully *Int.* 16$^b$ 26ff. For the aims and context of this part of the *De Interpretatione* see, for example, the short account by Nuchelmans (1973, ch. 3).
81. A.D. *Fr.* 31ff. S = Sch. in D. T. 515ff.H; compare Sch. in D. T. 356f.H, where Tryphon is referred to three times. Brief version in Latin Prisc. K II, 54; parallel with the ship (below) also in Prisc. K II, 551f.
82. *Fr.* 32.25ff. S. For *gráphō* as a complete sentence see ss. 1.6.1 (references in n. 213).
83. Don. K IV, 372.26f.; Consentius K V, 338.6f.
84. Noun and Verb 'principales et egregiae' K II, 552.13 (egregiae = *tímia* in A.D., *Fr.* 32.34S); as non-deletable K III, 116, following A.D., *Synt.* 1.14.
85. For the divisions of dialectic see S. E., *Math.* 8.11–12; D. L. 7.43–4. We will return to the scheme, with references, in ss. 1.5.1. Details of the branch *peri phōnês* in D. L. 7.55ff.
86. D. L. 7.57–8; A.D., *Fr.* 33ff. S.

87. Counter-arguments specifically ascribed to Tryphon, Sch. in D. T. 356.29, 357.5H.
88. See also A. D., *Synt.* 4.5. (implying that other subclasses were distinguished by functional criteria).
89. The terminology is that of A. D., *Pron.* 5.13f. and, for the article, *Synt.* 1.111. The justification for grouping pronouns and articles together (still according to Apollonius) is that the forms of the article are also found in a pronominal role.
90. D. H., *Comp.* 2; for Dionysius as a source for contemporary grammar see Schenkeveld, 1983 (parts of speech 70–3). D. H., *loc. cit.* and Quint., *Inst.* 1.4.19 give slightly different accounts of the order in which the Stoics, especially (Quintilian), distinguished the elements.
91. D. L. 7.57 (loc. cit.). Robins (1966, 13) identifies this with the deadjectival adverbs in -ōs (*kalôs*, 'beautifully' or *sophôs*, 'wisely') that D. T. 74U calls 'of middleness' (*mesótētos*); but the sense of this term, which has no equivalent in Latin, was already lost to later Greek commentators (D. T., ed. Uhlig, index s.v.). In the account of Apollonius or Tryphon, adverbs have no place in the Stoic system; they are likened to 'side shoots' or 'leftovers' (Sch. in D. T. 356.16H). We are also told that the class of adverbs was called *pandéktēs*, 'catch-all' (Charis. K I., 247.15, 252.29). I do not think that any safe conclusions can be drawn.
92. They are listed in a later chapter of Diogenes Laertius (7.189ff; see 192–3 for *stoikheîa toû lógou*). On their tiresomeness see, for example, Galen in a passage cited earlier s.1.3, n. 65.
93. Quint., *Inst.* 1.4.20; on Dionysius of Halicarnassus see again Schenkeveld (1983).
94. Wouters (1979, 49) (papyrus dated to the first century AD); also Wouters, 176 (papyrus dated by him to the third century AD and restored in this sense).
95. Thus Quint., *Inst.* 1.4.20. According to Diomedes, K I, 320, the same terms were applied by Scaurus (third century AD) to a distinction between animate and inanimate.
96. *Skhetliastiká* are a subclass of adverbs in D.T. 77; the examples given are the exclamations *papaî, ioú, pheû*, and according to the commentators they are expressions of pain or misery (Sch. in D.T. 279.21ff., 100.10ff., 60.15H). But, as Priscian remarks elsewhere, interjections do not only express *skhetliasmós* (K III, 90.13f.). For a Greek grammarians' class of interjections see Prisc. K II, 54.26f.; the term was presumably *parénthesis* (as gloss in Dositheus K VII, 424.12).
97. On Varro see the opposed views of Taylor (1975), who,    .mmon with linguists writing on the history of their subject  !ooins (1967, 47ff); Mounin (1967, 99f.)), lauds his originality, and Fehling ('956–57: part 2; 51–60), who argues that his work is an incompetent mishmash of known sources. I have more sympathy with Fehling's estimate of Varro's intellectual capacity.
98. *L.L.* 8.9, 10.14.

99. *L.L.* 8.11; Ar., *Int.* 16ᵇ6.

100. *L.L.* 8.44. For *adminiculandi* and *iungendi* compare Prisc. KII, 551.19f., where, in Priscian's account of the Peripatetic system, elements other than the noun and verb are not parts of speech but *adminicula* or *iuncturae*; the application of such terms to adverbs and participles is surely a blunder (Fehling (1956–57, part 2, 54f.); forced interpretation in Robins (1967, 51)). Elsewhere Varro generally calls the second part the *verbum*, or (since this is also the term for 'word' as such) the *verbum temporale* 'word with time'; in *L.L.* 10.18 the first part is simply *casualis* 'with case'; for the fourth part *participium* is introduced in *L.L.* 8.58.

101. *L.L.* 6.36; *partes orationis* in *L.L.* 8.11, 44. A further variation is that in *L.L.* 8.11 the classes are subdivisions of modifiable words in general, whereas in *L.L.* 10. 14–16 they are specifically of words modified 'by nature' (see below, ss. 1.5.3). How beautiful the Varronian scheme appears (diagram in Taylor (1975, 83f.)) if one is willing to abstract away from obscurity and inconsistency!

102. *L.L.* 8.45; also 10.18. Commentary by Fehling (1956–57, part 2, 55–7). See above for the Stoic distinction between 'indefinite' and 'definite', *árthra* (references n. 23).

103. *L.L.* 9.31.

104. *L.L.* 8.11.

105. D.T. 23U; A.D., *Synt.* 1.14–29. On my reading Apollonius is arguing for a logical hierarchy of elements: for discussion see Pinborg (1975, 119f.); Schenkeveld (1983, 87f.) (apropos of the parts of speech in Dionysius of Halicarnassus); also Lambert (1984). Another order is found in a papyrus edited by Wouters (1979, 49ff.) and dated to the first century AD; this lists all the case-inflected elements before the verb, and also has the pronoun before the article and the preposition before the adverbs. See also the partial list in Wouters, 190.

106. Don. K IV, 372.25f. Prisc. K II, 3f. (in list of contents) and (with reasons following Apollonius) K III, 115f.

107. Prisc. K III, 119.28f.; earlier (K III, 11) the vocative *o* is the last candidate to be dismissed.

108. Don. K IV, 391.29f.; (earlier Diomedes K I, 419.20f.); Prisc. K III, 90.6ff. For exclamations (*epiphōnéseis*) as subordinate to an unrealized verb see A.D., *Adv.* 121.14ff.S. Charisius, following Romanus, makes clear that the interjection was separated for substantive reasons, not simply to supply an eighth part in place of the article (K I, 190.15f.).

109. K II, 55. In Greek, we must look at what is *ídion* and not at accidents (Sch. in D.T. 357.17ff.H).

110. A.D., *Pron.* 27.11f.S (also 9.7ff.).

111. Prisc. K II, 55.14ff. A.D., *Pron.* 26f.S argues the point in detail for *tís* interrogative, also enclitic *tis*, and so on.

112. Prisc. K II, 56.29f.; Greek original in Sch. in D.T. 524.7ff.H. Don. K IV, 373.1f.; D.T. 24U; Charis. K I, 152.17ff. *Sôma ê prâgma* is apparently Stoic (Nuchelmans 1973, 65f.)

113. A.D., *Pron.* 9.11f.S; for the wording ascribed to Dionysius, D.T. 63U.
     But Apollonius also reports the view of the real Dionysius Thrax and
     his contemporary Apollodorus of Athens who called the pronouns
     'deictic articles' *Pron.* 5.18 f.). This is linked to their Stoic classifica-
     tion as 'definite articles' (see above, n. 23); and Apollonius' testimony
     is supported by Schenkeveld's study of grammatical doctrine in
     Dionysius of Halicarnassus (1983, 76).
114. A.D., *Synt.* 1.25, 2.9. For Priscian see K II, 55.13f. (*loc. cit.*), 577.2f.;
     Stephanus in Sch. in D.T. 260.21ff.H; compare Heliodorus *ibid.*
     77.24ff.H.
115. Charis. K I, 157.24f.; likewise Dositheus K VII, 401.9f. and compare
     Diomedes K I, 329.2f. Don. K IV, 359.23f.
116. Diomedes K I, 334.2.
117. Charis. K I, 164.13f. According to another variant, a verb signifies
     either a deed (*factum*) or a state (*habitus*); the deed may have the force
     either of acting or of experiencing (Consentius, K V, 365.29ff.).
     Priscian's definitions K II, 55.20ff., 369.2f.; D.T. 46.4f.U; Apollonius
     Dyscolus as cited by Heliodorus Sch. in D.T. 71.24ff.H (partly, with
     equivalent terms, in A.D., *Synt.* 3.60).
118. K II, 552.18ff. For the ordering of the participle see A.D., *Synt.* 1.21;
     Prisc. K III, 119.12ff. (compare K II, 548.2ff.).
119. D. T. 60U; compare Don. K IV, 387.18ff. ('participium . . . quod
     partem capiat . . .'). Charis. K I, 180.
120. D. T. 61U (taking the text as Uhlig prints it).
121. Prisc. K II, 56.3f.; K III, 60.2f.; A.D., *Adv.* 119.5f.S, with explanation
     following (especially 120.20ff.). For the alternative Latin formula see
     Diomedes K I, 403.17f.; Charisius, K I, 180.2f.; Don. K IV, 385.11f.
122. Prisc. K II, 56.12ff.; K III, 25.13f.; Don. K IV, 389.19f. Greek
     definition, equivalent to Priscian's, in D.T. 70U.
123. Ascribed by Diomedes (K I, 415, 16f.) to Remmius Palaemon;
     compare Charis. K I, 224.24f., excerpted from Cominianus; Don. K
     IV, 388.28f. Other formulae in D. T. 86U; Diomedes, K I, 415.13f.;
     Prisc. K III, 93.2f.
124. Don., *Ars Minor* 366.13f. (praised on this point by Priscian K III,
     91.20); Diomedes K I, 419.2f. Priscian's discussion of interjections
     begins K III, 90; for Charisius see K I, 238f. (citing Cominianus,
     Remmius Palaemon, Iulius Romanus).
125. D. L. 9.53.
126. Ar., *S. E.* 173$^b$17; also *Rhet.* 1407$^b$6 in discussion of Hellenism.
     Aristophanes, *Nub.* 622ff. represents the character Socrates as arguing
     that the masculine *alektruón* should not be used for both a cock and
     a hen; the latter should be called an *alektrúaina* (feminine) instead.
     Siebenborn (1976, 15f.) briefly discusses Protagoras' remarks on
     correctness; see also, for a different conclusion, Fehling (1965, Part
     1).
127. D. L. 9.52; but it does not follow that Protagoras had a linguistic
     category in mind. For Aristotle see again *Int.* 16$^b$6.
128. The conventional history of this period has been based on two

assumptions. One is that the *tékhnē* traditionally ascribed to Dionysius Thrax is genuine; but this is disputed, as we remarked in s. 1.1.,
by Di Benedetto (1958–9). The other is that the testimony of Varro
can be trusted; this is denied, as we have seen already in the case of
parts of speech, by Fehling (1956–7). The arguments of both Di
Benedetto and Fehling are shrugged off by Robins (1967, 30; 1976),
but this is a position which it is hard to maintain. If the text of D. T.
is accepted, then grammar as we know it under the Empire was well
established by the mid first century BC, and, if that is what Varro is
supposed to be representing, no faith can be placed in him. On the
other hand, the best reply to Fehling is that the text of D. T. is
spurious; therefore we do not know what grammar was like in the
mid first century, and, however muddled Varro may be, his reports
may have some value. If both assumptions are rejected, then, as
Pinborg (1975, 111) remarks, 'the whole history of grammatical
theory in Hellenistic times will have to be rewritten'. This rewriting is
not yet complete.

129. For the notions of signifier, signified and *tugkhánon* the standard
reference is to S. E., *Math.* 8.11–13; for the division of dialectic see
again D. L. 7.43–44 (also 7.190ff., for the catalogue of Chrysippus'
writings). For a brief and general account of the Stoic theory of
language see Baratin (1982). For the *lektón* see, in particular, Nuchelmans (1973, Ch. 4); Long (1971a, 77ff., postscript 104ff.); Graeser
(1978, 87ff.); also Pinborg (1975, 8off.), who argues, contrary to
them, that a subject was also an incomplete *lektón*. It is worth
stressing that this is not a sign theory based on the word. For its
development in that direction see August., *Dial.* 5 (discussion by
Baratin and Desbordes (1981, 55ff.)); for an account in Latin of the
Stoic doctrine itself compare Seneca, *Ep. Mor.* 117.13 (aptly cited
and discussed by Long, 1971a, 77f.). On the *tugkhánon* and the
question of denotation see Graeser (1978, 81ff.); also Graeser (1977,
370ff.) for an account of Stoic theories of meaning in the context of
Greek philosophy in general. For the isomorphism of *sēmaínōn* and
*sēmainómenon* see the suggestive discussion by Lloyd (1971, 65ff.) of
possible correspondences between the parts of speech (s.1.4.2 above)
and Stoic categories. For the different types of complete *lektá* see
variant lists in D. L. 7.66; S. E., *Math.* 8.71 (conflated with the
evidence of other sources by Nuchelmans (1973, 63f.). For the individual grammatical categories Pinborg (1975) is invaluable; but, once
again, we have to note the meagreness and lateness of our sources
(comprehensive list in Pinborg (1975, 77f.). The importance of the
Stoics in the creation of the grammatical tradition is argued by, in
particular, Frede (1977); see also his general essay (1978). The parallels between Stoic dialectic and the Roman grammars especially were
long ago established by Barwick (1922).

130. In the sense of the term *ptôsis* see Pinborg (1975, 8off.); Nuchelmans
(1973, 72ff.); since it is used of the subject which completes a
proposition the problem is bound up with that of the *lektón* (n. 5).

For a novel and speculative account see Frede (1977, 62ff.). On the individual cases see varying interpretations in Pinborg (1975, 85–7). The genitive, dative and accusative are in D. L. 7.65; for five cases see D. L. 7.192 (title of work by Chrysippus). The Latin translations are in Varro, *L. L.* 8.16.

131. D. T. 53U; Prisc. K II, 405f. and, for the first two kinships, 414.9ff. It is perhaps worth noting at this point that the ancient grammarians did not recognize the Latin future perfect indicative; a form such as *amavero* 'I will have loved' was for them subjunctive (Prisc. K II, 416.25; reasons why there is no subdivision of the future 405.14ff.). For its identification in the Renaissance see Scaglione (1970, 90ff.).

132. Stephanus, Sch. in D. T. 250f. H. The same tradition is followed in the more fragmentary account by Priscian (K II, 414.21ff.).

133. The latter term is given by Priscian K II, 415.24.

134. Stephanus, *loc. cit.* Priscian (K II, 415f.) cites the same examples with adverbs in introducing his own distinction between the two uses of the Latin perfect, as an aorist (we would now say simple past) and to refer to something just completed.

135. Pinborg (1975, 92ff.) summarises and assesses three interpretations, and then adds a fourth of his own. See also Collinge (1986, 17ff.), in an interesting essay on binary and other schemes of opposition in Greek linguistics.

136. *L.L.* 9.96ff.; 10.48.

137. D.T. 48f.U. The distinction of active, passive and 'neutral' is general in the Roman grammarians, where, with deponent and variable (*communis*), they form five 'genera' of the verb. See, for example, Don. K IV, 383: corresponding Greek system in Sch. in D.T. 246.7ff.H.

138. Types of *súmbama* D.L. 7.64f.; according to Apollonius Dyscolus (*Synt.* 3.155), a verb such as 'harms' or 'loves' was explicitly called 'less than a predicate', since an oblique noun was required for completeness. For the *parasúmbama* as an impersonal predicate see A.D., *Synt.* 3.187 (also *Pron.* 115.11f.S); Priscian, an account which is in other respects erroneous. (K III, 211.20ff.), calls this an *asúmbama* (non-*súmbama*). Pinborg (1975, 89f.) has a useful synthetic discussion of these categories; on the *parasúmbama* see also Le Bourdelles (1984).

139. K V, 611.36f.

140. See Frede (1978, 33ff.) for one interpretation. Caujolle-Zaslawsky (1985) further questions the reliability with which the Stoic doctrine was transmitted.

141. Meillet (1935, part 3, ch. 2) gives an admirable account of the historical circumstances of the koine; more recent summary, with references, by Browning (1983, 19ff.).

142. D.L. 7.183.

143. Ar., *Rhet.* 1407[a]19; the examples of bad Greek which follow include syntactic errors such as the wrong use of the correlative conjunctions *mén* and *dé*, and non-agreement in number and gender. Theophrastus in Cic., *Orat.* 79.

144. D.L. 7.59; the wording might imply that there were additional vices. Barbarism earlier in Ar., *Poet.* 1458ᵃ26, solecism Ar., *S.E.* 173ᵇ17; there are also the verbs *barbarízein, soloikízein.* For the etymology of 'solecism' (speaking like someone from Soli in Cilicia) see Chantraine, (1968–80).

145. For the genre in general see Siebenborn (1976, 33f.). For the work by Varro see fragments, ed. Funaioli 199ff.; for Antonius Gnipho *ibid.*, 98f.; Philoxenus, ed. Theodoridis, *Fr.* 288–9; Tryphon, ed. De Velsen, *Fr.* 105–8. First reference to *Latinitas* in the *Rhetorica ad Herennium* 4.17.

146. For Atticism see Browning (1983, 44ff.). In the case of Latin, Wright (1982) argues that by the seventh century morphological endings existed only in writing; other discrepancies between speech and spelling are clearly implied by the contemporary 'Appendix Probi' (K IV, 193ff.).

147. Quint., *Inst.* 1.4; inflection, etc. 1.4.22ff.

148. *Ibid.* 1.5; examples from Virgil 1.5.35; formal classification of solecisms 1.5.38ff.; of barbarisms 1.5.10.

149. Details from Pfeiffer, (1968, part 2), who gives an invaluable account of the scope and development of the Alexandrian school.

150. See Athenaeus 15.671f.

151. D.T. 5f.U; S.E., *Math.* 1.57 gives the main definition with an immaterial change of wording. For an English translation see also Robins (1957, 77; 1967, 31). On Eratosthenes see again s.1.1, n. 3.

152. Fragments, ed. Funaioli, 234 (Marius Victorinus); 236 (Diomedes). The four tasks are otherwise said to be writing, reading, understanding and 'testing' (*probare*). In *Fr.* 235 (Augustine), *litteratura* ( = *grammatiké*) is distinguished from *litteratio*, the task of the *litterator* or elementary teacher (Gk. *grammatistés*).

153. Cic., *De Orat.* 1.42.

154. *Inst.* 1.4.2, 1.9.1; *lectio* 1.8.1.

155. For the first definition, by Chares or Chaeris, see S.E., *Math.* 1.76 and discussion, especially 1.81; shorter version Sch in D.T. 118, 11f.H. The second is ascribed to Demetrius Chlorus and others (S.E. 1.84). In gathering together the references to Aristarchus in the later grammarians Ax (1982) confirms that these too show broader interests.

156. S.E., *Math.* 1.60f., 72 for Asclepiades of Myrlea and, before him, Ptolemy the Peripatetic; for Ptolemy see also Sch. in D.T. 165.16ff.H. The word *empeiría* stuck in the throat of late commentators, one of whom (Sch. in D.T. 166.25H) says that Dionysius 'degraded the science' by so characterizing it. On the parallel with medicine and the interpretation of these passages generally see, in particular, Siebenborn (1976, 116ff.).

157. S.E., *Math.* 1.79, in discussion of the definition by Chaeris (above, n. 155). For Crates' scholarship see Pfeiffer (1968, 238ff.).

158. Following Siebenborn (1976, 32f.), I am taking together the classification in S.E., *Math.* 1.252 (Asclepiades) and Sextus' own introductory

classification (*ibid.* 1.91ff. details of the 'technical part' 1.97–247). In
the two-part scheme followed by Quintilian and the Roman grammarians, the first part is called *methodikḗ* and the second *historikḗ* (thus
Quint., *Inst.* 1.9.1).

159. The scholium is cited by Erbse (1980, 238), who remarks that this is
one of a few cases in which Aristarchus is quoted verbatim. For the
history of the concept see Siebenborn (1976, ch. 4) (beginning with a
summary of mathematical and other non-linguistic uses). Erbse (1980,
239ff.) argues, against Siebenborn, that there could have been no
stage at which proportions were invoked without an underlying
concept of rules; similarly Fehling (1956–57, Part 1, 264f.). But in
principle I do not find Siebenborn's account implausible. In earlier,
non-linguistic uses a proportion does not imply a rule; the method
could then have been developed by grammarians before its foundation
in their own discipline had been made explicit.

160. Consentius K V, 353.19ff; 363.25ff. The references to analogy in later
Roman writers are discussed in detail by Fehling (1956–7, part 1,
s.2), who traces them all to the lost work by Varro, *De Sermone
Latino*. For the later format of inflectional rules see s.1.6, especially
ss.1.6.2 for Theodosius and Priscian.

161. For the composition of this work, which dates from the intervals of
Caesar's Gallic campaigns, see Fragments, ed. Funaioli, 147. The
fragments cited are 3, 3a (*harena*); 7 (*turbonem*); 14 (*lac*); 23, 24, 24a
(neuters in -*e* and -*ar*).

162. Caesar as cited by Pompeius, K V, 197f. (ed. Funaioli, *Fr.* 11).
Compare Charisius (citing Romanus) K I, 116f.; Donatianus K VI,
275; also a précis of Herodian on noun inflection, 634.6ff.L.

163. Quint., *Inst.* 1.6.1–3. Compare Varro's list (*natura, analogia, consuetudo, auctoritas*) in Diomedes K I, 439 (also, without the source,
Charisius, K I, 50f.). Siebenborn (1976, ch. 3) points out that Roman
formulations of the criteria for *Latinitas* antedate any Greek equivalent.

164. Quint., *Inst.* 1.6.4 (definition of analogy), 5–6 (*funis*), 7–8 (*fervere*), 29
(etymology). For the use of etymological arguments see Siebenborn
(1976, 140–6).

165. *Inst.* 1.6.16–27 *passim.*

166. For the whole passage see Cic., *Orat.* 155–62. *Medidies* also in
Quintilian (*Inst.* 1.6.30).

167. S.E., *Math.* 1.176–240: concepts of Hellenism, with example of Zeus,
176f.; other examples (including word for 'dog') 198; *khrâsthai* and
*ktâsthai* 196–9; *eumenoû[s]* 222f. Sextus also argues that no rule can
claim universality, since the number of words is boundless (224ff.).

168. *L.L.* 10.37f. (definition of analogy), 42 (*amor, dolor*), 44 (forms of
*albus*); the last had apparently been discussed in more detail in the
passage beginning 9.23, where there is a lacuna in the MS.

169. *L.L.* 10.47. See again Siebenborn (1976, 57f.) on the mathematical
proportions that the grammarians were imitating. For example, 3 is
to 6 (3 × 2) as 6 is to 12.

170. References to Aristarchus and Aristarcheans *L.L.* 8.63, 68; 9.1, 43, 91; 10.16, 42. To Aristophanes 9.12; 10.68. To Crates 8.64, 68; 9.1.

171. Aul. Gell. 2.25. The interpretation dates back to the work of Lersch in the 1830s; for a brief and able version see Robins (1967, 19ff.).

172. *L. L.* 9.1; 9.35.

173. *L. L.* 8.26; the example is that of *Herculi* and *Herculis* as alternative genitives of *Hercules*.

174. *L. L.* 8.24–5. The expressions are plainly equivalent.

175. For the first side see *L. L.* 8.34ff.; for the second 9.32f. (and compare 9.107). *Lupus* and *lepus* are a stock pair that cannot be compared under Caesar's conditions (above, n. 38 and Pompeius, *loc. cit.*). *Juppitri* parallels *Zēnós* (S. E. *loc. cit.* n. 43.).

176. *L. L.* 9.8–35 *passim*. For the rejection of poets' usage if not regular compare 10.35.

177. *L. L.* 8.26–43 *passim*. For Aristarchus see 8.68 (and other passages cited n. 46).

178. For most of this (and worse) see Fehling (1956–7); note also Siebenborn's finding (n. 163 above) that the criteria for correctness first appear in Roman writers. *Anōmalía* was used in reference to language by the early Stoics: thus the books listed in the inventory of Chrysippus' writings (D. L. 7.192). But Varro himself makes clear that this did not refer to inflections, but to an inappropriate relation between words and things (*L. L.* 9.1). For interpretation see Fehling (1956–7, part 1, 267); Siebenborn (1976, 97ff.). The existence of the controversy is defended, in a more restricted form, by Cavazza (1981, 106ff.), who also gives full references to the secondary literature; earlier Calboli (1962, 176ff.).

179. The terminology evidently seeks to conflate the issue of regularization with the question as to whether language historically arose *thései* or *phúsei*. For the parallel of the source and the stream see *L. L.* 8.5; for voluntary and natural *declinatio* 8.21–22 (leading into introductory paragraphs on analogy and anomaly), 9.34–35, 10.15–16; for modifications as countless 8.3, 8.6, 9.35 (also, with fanciful but finite arithmetic, 6.36–38). Commentators have tended to identify voluntary and natural with the modern categories of word-formation and inflection: thus, for example, Taylor (1975, 22). But the examples of voluntary *declinatio* are all namings in the strict sense. Derivational and inflectional formations also fall together in the division reconstructed by Barwick (1957, 43ff.).

180. For nouns see *L. L.* 8.14ff., 52; for verbs 8.20 and 10.33.

181. *L. L.* 9.56 (*corva*), 73 (*mane*), 101 (perfect imperatives). In a context of regularization the first might just as well be argued against the analogical introduction of forms such as *corva*, or Aristophanes' *alektrúaina* (n. 126 above), with no basis in usage. For Tryphon's argument see s. 1.4, n. 87.

182. The current state of the question is neatly summarized by Ax (1982, 96–100). With Ax and Fehling (1956–7, Part 1, 260), I am unable to see the work of (pseudo-) Dionysius Thrax as the initiator of a

tradition. In a review of Siebenborn's monograph, Fehling (1976, 489) endorses the claim of Tryphon, to whom he suggests a floruit of c. 55 B.C.

183. Other catechisms in the *Grammatici Latini* are those of Audax (K VII, 320ff.) and Marius Victorinus (K VI, 187ff); an early example in Greek is the papyrus edited by Wouters (1979, 135ff.) and dated by him to c. 100 AD. On the form in general see Wouters, (1979, 87ff.); Holtz (1981, 99ff.). See Holtz, part 1, for a detailed re-evaluation of the place of Donatus in the grammatical tradition.

184. 'Form' = Lat. *figura*. 'Quality' (*qualitas*) is in origin a noun derived from *qualis*, 'of what kind?'; the term was invented by Cicero as a calque on Gk. *poiótēs*, itself invented by Plato.

185. Analysis of *arma* K III, 461ff.

186. For the periphrasis with *habeo* in Late Latin see Hofmann Szantyr (1965, 314f. and references).

187. The *Institutio de Nomine, Pronomine et Verbo* (K III, 443–56). Greek examples in ss.1.6.2 (n.249).

188. Table of contents in K I, 3–6.

189. Sections *De voce* to *De posituris* K IV, 367–72.

190. Parts of speech K IV, 372.26ff.; *qualitates* of nouns 373.7–374.14; inchoatives 359.11 (*Ars Minor*), 381.28–382.2, 382.8f., 388.2f. (*Ars Maior*).

191. Classification of nouns D. T. 25–29, 33–45U; of adverbs 73–86U.

192. *Ordines* of nouns Charisius, K I, 18ff.

193. Numerals and letters indeclinable K I, 37.6f.; nouns in *-en*, etc. 38ff.; *vectigal* 62.9ff.; *oliva*/*olea* 99.8ff.; *leæna*/*lea* 103.24f.; grades of comparison 112ff.; derivation of plurals and numbers of case forms 147–51; list in section *De analogia* (collected from Romanus) 117–47.

194. Conjugational paradigms K I, 169–73; abbreviated forms 173–5; conjugations according to Cominianus 175ff. Adverbs 180ff.: derivation from other parts 181–6; *ampliter*/*ample* 195.12ff.; *perdite* 213.16f. (citation from Terence).

195. K I, 243ff.: perfects in third conjugation 244–6; defectives 248ff.

196. K IV, 392f. For the formal classification of barbarisms see again Quintilian, *Inst.* 1.5.10. Donatus' examples of barbarism and solecism are discussed exhaustively by Holtz (1981, 150ff.). See also Holtz, 147ff. on the relation between faults in ordinary speech and writing (*barbarismus, soloecismus*) and licence as a form of literary elegance (*metaplasmus* and *schemata* 'figures').

197. K IV, 393f. For *amarae corticis* see ss. 1.5.2 and reference to Quintilian, *Inst.* 1.5.35.

198. Pleonasm K IV, 395.2f.; *amphibolia* 395.20ff. Definition and types of metaplasm 395ff. *Schemata lexeos*/*dianoeas* 397.5f.; *anadiplosis* 398.1f.; *schemata dianoeas* in Charisius K I, 283ff. Tropes K IV, 399ff. Full discussion of all these topics in Holtz (1981, 163–216).

199. Example with *autem* K IV, 394.21f. *Sylle[m]psis* (Gk. *súllēpsis*) 397.23ff.

200. Semantic definitions of tenses K II, 406f.; of mood 421ff. Derived

verbs 427ff. Perfect formations in general 463f.; in first conjugation 468ff.; in third conjugation 494–538 (verbs in -*go* 523ff.).

201. Passive forms of *facio* K II, 376f.; *ardeo* + accusative 378.15ff.; *applicui/applicavi* 469.1–10; *nexo* 469f.

202. Ordering of letters and parts of speech A.D., *Synt.* 1.2ff.; Prisc. K III, 108ff. Interrogatives A.D. 1.30ff.; Prisc. 121ff.

203. In interpreting Apollonius I have found Householder's translation (1981) invaluable; but it should perhaps be read without the commentary in double square brackets, which relates Apollonius' work to theories of transformational grammar in the early 1970s. A recent study is that of Blank (1982).

204. *Synt.* 1.37. In the case of mention the element is said to 'signify no more than merely the name itself of the vocal sound'.

205. *Synt.* 1.43–4, 111. See n. 208 for anaphora versus deixis.

206. *Synt.* 1.57–8 (partitive genitives), 71 (*amphóteroi*); 50f. (infinitives). Elsewhere the infinitive is called the 'name of an action' (*Adv.* 129. 16S); it signifies the action alone and the properties inherent in it (see below under Verbs) without additional reference to a participant who performs it. In the present passage Apollonius cites the Stoics as having said that the infinitive alone was a verb as opposed to a predicate.

207. Postpositive articles *Synt.* 1.142ff.: case determined by the verb 148ff. Apollonius does not refer to counter-examples, which in Ancient Greek are unusually common.

208. Distinction of pronoun and article *Synt.* 2.1; pronouns anaphoric or deictic *Pron.* 9f.S; equivalent to article + noun *Synt.* 2.9; summary definition of element *Synt.* 2.16.

209. *Synt.* 2.28.

210. *Synt.* 2.49ff. Similarly, Apollonius says, the meaning of *heîs*, 'one' subsists in *Aías*, 'Ajax'; those of *huiós*, 'son' and of the genitive singular of the base noun in the patronym *Kronídēs*, 'son of Cronus'; that of *éx*, 'from' in *Lesbóthen*, 'from Lesbos', and so on. For discussion of these and similar passages see Blank (1982, 32f.); but the 'things subsisting' (*paruphistámena*) are meanings of other elements, not accidents. Contrastive and non-contrastive deixis have already been distinguished in oblique pronouns (*Synt.* 2.6).

211. Accentuation of nominatives *Synt.* 2.54f.; of obliques 57ff. Obliques with a coordinating conjunction 59ff.; with prepositions 69; before or after verb 72ff. (examples of hyperbaton 77). 'Dared to do this to *me*' 78; construal with *autós* 86ff. Third person reflexives 100ff. especially. For the use of 'hyperbaton' compare *Adv.* 125f.S (discussed by Blank (1982, 48f.)).

212. *Synt.* 2.103ff. The next episode in Book 2 (117ff.) can be selected as representative of the remainder. In it Apollonius considers the form *emoû*, homonymously either a personal pronoun (genitive of *egó*, 'I') or a possessive (genitive of *emós*, 'my'). He propounds a general rule for the use of possessives, which allows us to tell which word it is in particular cases.

213. See again *Synt.* 2.49ff.; the third persons are discussed in 2.56. For a derivative discussion in Latin see Prisc. K III, 156f.; see too Augustine, *Dial.* 1.

214. *Heautoús* as first or second plural *Synt.* 3.3–5; against solecisms in single words 8–10.

215. For the *sunektikótátē aitía toû akatallélou* see *Synt.* 3.13; in passing, I cannot follow Blank (1982, 27 *et passim*) in translating *katallēlótēs*, 'congruence' as 'regularity'. In the corresponding account by Priscian (K III, 182f.) the first three classes are (1) elements inflected for number, case and gender (noun, pronoun, participle); (2) those inflected for person and number (verb, pronoun); (3) those inflected for tense (verb, participle). Note that tense also enters into Apollonius' discussion of verbs and temporal adverbs. For agreement among Apollonius' first three classes see *Synt.* 3.14–16.

216. *Synt.* 3.18 (*kalôs*); 19 (adverbs of time); 22–3 (*emè autón*, etc.); 29 (*gráphōn*); 35ff. (*sú*); 53 (singular verb with neuter plurals). For the last see discussion by both Householder (1981, *ad loc.*) and Blank (1982, 46f.).

217. Infinitives *Synt.* 3.55ff.; as verbs not adverbs 56–8. Infinitives the most general mood 59ff.; Apollonius rejects an earlier view of his own that the basic form of a verb is the indicative (62). Infinitive as main verb 63ff.; with impersonals 67ff. (on the latter see also *Adv.* 128f.S); cases construed with infinitive 78ff.

218. Indicatives *Synt.* 3.88–93; optatives 94–100; imperatives 101–22; subjunctives 123–46. For the rejection of imperatives in the first person see 104–11; for third person imperatives 112–15; for the homonymy of imperatives and indicatives 103, 116ff.

219. *Synt.* 3.148f.

220. *Synt.* 3.150–57.

221. Verbs taking accusatives *Synt.* 3.159ff.: construction with *boúlomai* etc. 161ff.; with *trémō* or *pheúgō* 166. See Blank's discussion (1982, 45f.) of this last passage.

222. *Synt.* 3. 169–76.

223. Construal of verbs with dative *Synt.* 3.177f. Householder (1981) also has difficulty with the last passage (183), which is the only section in which a construction with two oblique forms is discussed.

224. *Synt.* 3.190. A similar remark brings to an end the corresponding treatment by Priscian (K III, 278); it is followed by a list comparing individual points of usage in the two languages.

225. *Synt.* 4.12f.

226. *tó ek tôn prothéseōn sundēloúmenon epidékhetai hē ek toû rhématos paruphistaménē skhésis* (*Synt.* 4.15, 448.5f.U). See s. 1.6.2 for the model of linkages between word meanings.

227. Relations contracted with verbs and nominatives *Synt.* 4.15–17; with oblique nouns 18–19.

228. On the notion that prepositions are derived by transposition see *Synt.* 4.20f. Status of preposition plus verb 33ff. (35, 45 for the arguments cited).

229. *Synt.* 4.53–5.
230. Adverbs *Synt.* 4.56ff.
231. K II, 1.9f.; III, 107f.
232. For the definition of the letter see s. 1.2, n. 26; for those of the syllable, word and sentence K II, 44.1ff., 53.8, 28f. Diomedes (K I, 436.10f.) gives alternative definitions of the word, one referring to its function in the sentence and the other to its composition from syllables. For the Stoic *lógos* see ss.1.4.2 and references in s.1.5, n. 129.
233. Bloomfield (1933, 138).
234. K III, 108.9f.
235. K II, 10 (liquids); 32.14 (change of *s* to *n*); 33.14f. ($x = cs$ or $gs$); 37ff. (ordering of letters in diphthongs and clusters).
236. K II, 45ff.; properties of syllable 51.21.
237. Bloomfield (1933, 161f.).
238. A.D., *Synt.* 4.15 (above, n. 44).
239. *Ibid.* 1.4 (5.14U), 1.14 (17.14f.U).
240. For the meaning versus the form of a word see, in particular, A.D., *Adv.* 119.1 (the first sentence of the treatise). As Blank (1982, 35) correctly explains, its syntax falls under its meaning (*ennoía*).
241. On the theory of composition see, for example, Scaglione, (1972, ch. 2). On the centrality of the notion of congruence see, in particular, Apollonius' description of his work on syntax: *hē prokeiménē zḗtēsis tês katallēlótētos* (*Synt.* 1.60 (51.11U)). Baratin (1984) reads into Priscian (K III, 201.11ff. especially) a further requirement that the sentence should not only be congruent, but also intelligible.
242. K II, 421.17.
243. Tesnière (1959, 102).
244. K II, 448.11ff.
245. A.D., *Synt.* 3.59 (325.1–7U), 149 (396.3f.U), 161 (408.6–8U).
246. K II, 43.15ff., 506.16ff. For the general rules see the beginning of Book 9 (K II, 452f.).
247. Nominative and genitive Book 6, declensions in general Book 7. For the second declension see K II, 294ff.
248. K II, 454ff.
249. Theodosius, *Can.* 43H (*túptō→túpteis→túptei*); 44, 45H (*túptomen, túptousi, étupton*); 77.5ff.H (*túptousa*). For *étupte* see 46.2H: *eíretai*, 'The rule has been given'. This ingenious and penetrating work has sometimes been criticized on the grounds that not every form is attested. But its virtues are precisely those of systematic theoretical extrapolation.

## Abbreviations

Funaioli = *Grammaticae Romanae Fragmenta*, ed. by H. Funaioli, *T*, 1907.
*GG* = *Grammatici Graeci*, Teubner, Leipzig, 1867–1901.

*GL* = *Grammatici Latini*, ed. by Keil, H. [K], Teubner, Leipzig, 1857–80.
K = H. Keil's edition of *Grammatici Latini* (see *GL*, above).
L & S = Liddell and Scott, 1940.
*OCD* = *Oxford Classical Dictionary* (Hammond and Scullard, 1970).
*OCT* = *Oxford Classical Texts*.
*SVF* = *Stoicorum Veterum Fragmenta*, ed. by J. Von Arnim, Teubner, Leipzig, 1921–24.
*T* = *Bibliotheca Teubneriana*.

## References

### Ancient

For the dates of authors, here and in the text, see the *OCD* and *Der kleine Pauly* (Ziegler and Sontheimer, 1979).

*Abbreviations used in the Notes are given in square brackets.*

APOLLONIUS DYSCOLUS [A.D.] (second century AD) *De Pronomine* [*Pron.*], *De Adverbiis* [*Adv.*], *De Coniunctionibus* [*Conj.*], ed. by R. Schneider [S], *GG*2,1.
APOLLONIUS DYSCOLUS *De Constructione* [*Synt.*], ed. by G. Uhlig, [U], *GG*2,2.
APOLLONIUS DYSCOLUS *Fragments*, ed. by R. Schneider [S], *GG*2,3.
ARISTOTLE [Ar.] (384–322 BC) *Categoriae* [*Cat.*], *De Interpretatione* [*Int.*], ed. by Minio-Paluello, *OCT*, 1949.
ARISTOTLE *Metaphysica* [*Met.*], ed. by W. Jaeger, *OCT*, 1957.
ARISTOTLE *Poetica* [*Poet.*], ed. by R. Kassel, *OCT*, 1965.
ARISTOTLE *Rhetorica* [*Rhet.*], ed. by R. Kassel, De Gruyter, Berlin, 1976.
ARISTOTLE *De Sensu* [*Sens.*], in *Parva Naturalia*, ed. by D. Ross, Clarendon Press, Oxford, 1955.
ARISTOTLE *Sophistici Elenchi* [*S.E.*], *Topica* [*Top.*], ed. by W. D. Ross, *OCT*, 1970
(Pseudo-)ARISTOTLE, *De Audibilibus* [*Aud.*], ed. by C. Prantl, Teubner, Leipzig, 1881.
ASPER *Ars Grammatica*, ed. by H. Keil, *GL* 5.
ATHENAEUS *Deipnosophistae*, ed. by G. T. Kaibel, 1887–90.
AUGUSTINE [August.] (354–430 AD) *De Dialectica* [*Dial.*], ed. by J. Pinborg, in Jackson (1975).
AULUS GELLIUS [Aul. Gell.] (c. 130–180 AD) *Noctes Atticae*, ed. by C. Hosius, *T*, 1903.
CHARISIUS [Charis.] (fourth century AD) *Ars Grammatica*, ed. by K. Barwick, *T*, 1925.
CICERO [Cic.] (106–43 BC) *De Oratore* [*De Orat.*], ed. by A. S. Wilkins, *OCT*, 1902.
CICERO *Orator* [*Orat.*], ed. by A. S. Wilkins, *OCT*, 1903.
CONSENTIUS (fifth century AD), ed. by H. Keil, *GL* 5.
DIODORUS SICULUS (first century BC), ed. by F. Vogel and C. T. Fischer, *T*, 1888–1906.

DIOGENES LAERTIUS [D. L.] (third century AD) *Vitae Philosophorum*, ed. by H. S. Long, *OCT*, 1964.

DIOGENES OF OENOANDA (second century AD) *Fragments*, ed. by C. W. Chilton, *T*, 1967.

DIOMEDES (fourth century AD) *Ars Grammatica*, ed. by H. Keil, *GL* 1.

DIONYSIUS OF HALICARNASSUS [D. H.] (first century BC) *De Compositione Verborum* [*Comp.*], *Opuscula*, 2, ed. by H. Usener and L. Radermacher, *T*, 1929.

DIONYSIUS THRAX (c.170–c.90 BC) *Fragments*, ed. by K. Linke, De Gruyter, Berlin, 1977.

(Pseudo-)DIONYSIUS THRAX [D. T.] *Ars Grammatica*, ed. by G. Uhlig [U], *GG*1,1. Scholia [Sch. in D. T.], ed. by A. Hilgard [H], *GG*1,3.

DONATUS [Don.] (fourth century AD) *Ars Minor, Ars Maior*, ed. by L. Holtz, 1981.

DOSITHEUS (fourth century AD?) *Ars Grammatica*, ed by H. Keil, *GL* 7

GALEN (129–199 AD) *De Placitis Hippocratis et Platonis*, ed. by I. Müller, Teubner, Leipzig, 1874.

HERODIAN (second century AD), ed. by A. Lentz, [L], *GG* 3.

LUCRETIUS (94–55 BC) *De Rerum Natura*, ed. by C. Bailey, *OCT*, 1922.

MANILIUS (first century BC AD) *Astronomica*, ed by G. P. Goold, *T*, 1985.

NONNUS (fifth century AD?) *Dionysiaca*, ed. by R. Keydell, Weidmann, Berlin, 1959.

ORIGEN (c. 185–c. 254 AD) *Contra Celsum* [*Cels.*], in *Patrologia Graeca*, ed. by J. P. Migne, 11, 637–1632, Migne, Paris, 1857.

ORPHICA, ed. by E. Abel, Freytag, Leipzig, 1885.

PHILOXENUS (first century BC) *Fragments*, ed. by C. Theodoridis, De Gruyter, Berlin, 1976.

PLATO [Pl.] (c. 429–347 BC), ed. by I. Burnet, *OCT*:

PLATO *Cratylus* [*Crat.*]

PLATO *Euthydemus* [*Euthyd.*]

PLATO *Protagoras* [*Prot.*]

PLATO *Respublica* [*Rep.*]

PLATO *Sophista* [*Soph.*]

PLATO *Theaetetus* [*Theaet.*]

PRISCIAN [Prisc.] (fifth/sixth century AD) *Institutiones Grammaticae*, ed. by M. Hertz, *GL* 2–3.

PRISCIAN *Institutio de Nomine et Pronomine et Verbo, Partitiones Duodecim Versuum Aeneidos Principalium*, ed. by H. Keil, *GL* 3.

PROCLUS (412–485 AD) *In Platonis Cratylum Commentaria*, ed. by G. Pasquali, *T*, 1908.

QUINTILIAN [Quint.] (first century AD) *Institutio Oratoria* [*Inst.*], ed. by M. Winterbottom, *OCT*, 1970.

*Rhetorica ad Herennium* (first century BC), ed. by F. Marx, *T*, 1923.

SEXTUS EMPIRICUS [S.E.] (second/third century AD) *Adversus Mathematicos* [*Math.*], ed. by J. Mau and K. Janáček, *T*, 1954.

TERENTIANUS MAURUS (second century AD) *De Litteris, Syllabis et Metris*, ed. by H. Keil, *GL* 6.

THEODOSIUS OF ALEXANDRIA (fourth/fifth century AD) *Canones* [*Can.*], ed. by A. Hilgard [H], *GG* 4,1.

TRYPHON (first century BC) *Fragments*, ed. by A. De Velsen, Nicolai, Berlin, 1853.

VARRO (116–27 BC) *De Lingua Latina* [*L.L.*], ed. by G. Goetz and F. Schoell, *T*, 1910.

VARRO *Menippeae* [*Men.*], *Fragm.*, in Funaioli.

## Modern

ABERCROMBIE, D. (1949) What is a 'letter'?, *Lingua*, 2, 54–63. Reprinted Id., *Studies in Phonetics and Linguistics*, Oxford University Press, London, 1965, 76–85.

ALLEN, W. S. (1948) Ancient Ideas on the Origin and Development of Language, *Transaction of the Philological Society*, 35–60.

ALLEN, W. S. (1953) *Phonetics in Ancient India*, Oxford University Press, London.

ALLEN, W. S. (1955) Zero and Pāṇini, *Indian Linguistics*, 16, 106–13.

ALLEN, W. S. (1974) *Vox Graeca*, 2nd edn, Cambridge University Press, Cambridge.

ALLEN, W. S. (1978) *Vox Latina*, 2nd edn, Cambridge University Press, Cambridge.

ALLEN, W. S. (1981) The Greek Contribution to the History of Phonetics, *Towards a History of Phonetics*, ed. by R. E. Asher and E. J. A. Henderson, Edinburgh University Press, Edinburgh, 115–22.

ANAGNOSTOPOULOS, G. (1973/4) The Significance of Plato's Cratylus, *Review of Metaphysics*, 27, 318–45.

AUROUX, S., GLATIGNY, M., JOLY, A., NICOLAS, A. AND ROSIER, I., (eds) (1984) *Matériaux pour une histoire des théories linguistiques*, Université de Lille III, Lille.

AX, W. (1982) Aristarch und die 'Grammatik', *Glotta*, 60, 96–109.

BAILEY, C. (ed.) (1947) *Lucretius*, 3 vols, Clarendon Press, Oxford.

BARATIN, M. (1982) L'identité de la pensée et de la parole dans l'ancien stoïcisme, *Signification et référence dans l'antiquité et au moyen âge*, ed. by M. Baratin and F. Desbordes, *Langages*, 65, 9–21.

BARATIN, M. (1984) Grammaticalité et intelligibilité chez Priscien, in Auroux et al. (1984), 155–62.

BARATIN, M. and DESBORDES, F. (1981) *L'analyse linguistique dans l'antiquité classique*, 1. *Les théories*, Klincksieck, Paris.

BARWICK, K. (1922) *Remmius Palaemon und die römische Ars Grammatica*, Dieterich, Leipzig.

BARWICK, K. (1957) *Probleme der stoischen Sprachlehre und Rhetorik*, Akademie Verlag, Berlin.

BLANK, D. L. (1982) *Ancient Philosophy and Grammar: the Syntax of Apollonius Dyscolus*, Scholars Press, Chico, Calif.

BLOOMFIELD, L. (1933) *Language*, Holt, New York.

BROWNING, R. (1983) *Mediaeval and Modern Greek*, 2nd edn, Cambridge University Press, Cambridge.

CALBOLI, G. (1962) *Studi grammaticali*, Zanichelli, Bologna.

CAUJOLLE-ZASLAWSKY, F. (1985) La scholie de Stephanos: Quelques remarques sur la théorie des temps du verbe attribuée aux Stoïciens, *Histoire épistémologie langage*, 7, 13–46.

CAVAZZA, F. (1981) *Studio su Varrone etimologo e grammatico*, La Nuova Italia, Florence.

CHANTRAINE, P. (1968–80) *Dictionnaire étymologique de la langue grecque*, Klincksieck, Paris.

COHEN, M. (1958) *La grande invention de l'écriture et son évolution*, 3 vols, Imprimerie Nationale, Paris.

COLLINGE, N. E. (1986) Greek (and some Roman) Preferences in Language Categories, *Studies in the History of Western Linguistics in Honour of R. H. Robins*, ed. by T. BYNON and F. R. PALMER, Cambridge University Press, Cambridge, 11–22.

COSERIU, E. (1967) L'arbitraire du signe: zur Spätgeschichte eines aristotelischen Begriffes, *Archiv für das Studium der neueren Sprachen*, 204, 81–112.

DI BENEDETTO, V. (1958–59) Dionisio Trace e la *techne* a lui attribuita, *Annali della Scuola Normale Superiore di Pisa*, Ser. 2, 27, 169–210; 28, 87–118.

DI BENEDETTO, V. (1973) La *techne* spuria, *Annali della Scuola Normale Superiore di Pisa*, Ser. 3, 3, 797–814.

DIRINGER, D. (1968) *The Alphabet*, 3rd edn in collaboration with P. Regensburger, 2 vols, Hutchinson, London.

ENGELS, J. (1963) Origine, sens et survie du terme boécien *secundum placitum*, *Vivarium*, 1, 87–114.

ERBSE, H. (1980) Zur normativen Grammatik der Alexandriner, *Glotta*, 58, 236–58.

FEHLING, D. (1956–7) Varro und die grammatische Lehre von der Analogie und Flexion, *Glotta*, 35, 214–70; 36, 48–100.

FEHLING, D. (1965) Zwei Untersuchungen zur griechischen Sprachphilosophie, *Rheinisches Museum für Philologie*, 108, 212–30.

FEHLING, D. (1979) Review of Siebenborn, 1976, *Gnomon*, 51, 488–90.

FREDE, M. (1977) The Origins of Traditional Grammar, *Historical and Philosophical Dimensions of Logic, Methodology and Philosophy of Science*, ed. by R. E. Butts and J. Hintikka, Reidel, Dordrecht, 51–79.

FREDE, M. (1978) Principles of Stoic Grammar, in Rist (1978), 27–75.

GAMBARARA, D. (1984) Réflexion religieuse et réflexion linguistique aux origines de la philosophie du langage, in Auroux et al. (1984), 105–14.

GRAESER, A. (1977) On Language, Thought and Reality in Ancient Greek Philosophy, *Dialectica*, 31, 360–88.

GRAESER, A. (1978) The Stoic Theory of Meaning, in Rist (1978), 77–100.

GUTHRIE, W. K. C. (1962–81). *A History of Greek Philosophy*, Cambridge University Press, Cambridge.

HAMMOND, N. G. L. and SCULLARD, H. H. (eds) (1970) *The Oxford Classical Dictionary*, 2nd edn, Clarendon Press, Oxford.

HOFMANN, J. B. (1965) *Lateinische Syntax und Stilistik*, new edn by Szantyr, A., Beck, München.

HOLTZ, L. (1981) *Donat et la tradition de l'enseignement grammatical*, CNRS, Paris.

HOUSEHOLDER, F. W. (1981) *The Syntax of Apollonius Dyscolus*, translation and commentary, Benjamins, Amsterdam.

HOVDHAUGEN, E. (1982) *Foundations of Western Linguistics; from the Beginning of the End of the First Millennium AD*, Universiteitsforlaget, Oslo.

JACKSON, B. D. (1975) *Augustine, De Dialectica*, translated with introduction and notes, Reidel, Dordrecht.

KAHN, C. H. (1973) *The Verb 'Be' in Ancient Greek*, Reidel, Dordrecht.

KERFERD, G. B. (1981) *The Sophistic Movement*, Cambridge University Press, Cambridge.

KIRK, G. S. (1954) *Heraclitus, The Cosmic Fragments*, Cambridge University Press, Cambridge.

KOLLER, H. (1955) Stoicheion, *Glotta*, 34, 161–89.

KOLLER, H. (1958) Die Anfänge der griechischen Grammatik, *Glotta*, 37, 5–40.

KRETZMANN, N. (1971) Plato on the Correctness of Names, *American Philosophical Quarterly*, 8, 126–38.

LAMBERT, F. (1984) Naissance des fonctions grammaticales: les 'bricolages' d'Apollonius Dyscole, in Auroux et al. (1984), 141–6.

LAW, V. A. (1982) *The Insular Latin Grammarians*, Boydell Press, Woodbridge.

LAW, V. A. (1984) St Augustine's 'De Grammatica': Lost or Found?, *Recherches Augustiniennes*, 19, 155–83.

LAW, V. A. (1985) Linguistics in the Earlier Middle Ages: the Insular and Carolingian Grammarians, *Transactions of the Philological Society* 171–93.

LE BOURDELLES, H. (1984) La doctrine des impersonnels dans l'antiquité classique, in Auroux et al. (1984), 137–40.

LESZL, W. (1985) Linguaggio e discorso, *Introduzione alle culture antiche*, 2. *Il sapere degli antichi*, ed. by M. Vegetti, Boringhieri, Turin, 13–44.

LIDDELL, H. G. and SCOTT, R. (1940) *A Greek-English Lexicon*, new edn by H. S. Jones, with the assistance of R. McKenzie, Clarendon Press, Oxford.

LLOYD, A. C. (1971) Grammar and Metaphysics in the Stoa, in Long (1971b), 58–74.

LONG, A. A. (1971a) Language and Thought in Stoicism, in Long (1971b), 74–113.

LONG, A. A. (ed.) (1971b) *Problems in Stoicism*, Athlone Press, London.

MARROU, H. I. (1965) *Histoire de l'éducation dans l'antiquité*, 6th edn, Seuil, Paris.

MCKEON, R. (1946–7) Aristotle's Conception of Language and the Arts of Language, *Classical Philology*, 41, 193–206; 42, 21–50.

MEILLET, A. (1935) *Aperçu d'une histoire de la langue grecque*, 4th edn, Klincksieck, Paris.

MOUNIN, G. (1967) *Histoire de la linguistique des origines au XX^e siècle*, Presses Universitaires de France, Paris.

NUCHELMANS, G. (1973) *Theories of the Proposition: Ancient and Mediaeval Conceptions of the Bearers of Truth and Falsity*, North-Holland, Amsterdam.

PÉPIN, J. (1976) *Saint Augustin et la dialectique*, Villanova University Press, Villanova, Pa.

PFEIFFER, R. (1968) *History of Classical Scholarship from the Beginnings to the End of the Hellenistic Age*, Clarendon Press, Oxford.

PINBORG, J. (1962) Das Sprachdenken der Stoa und Augustins Dialektik, *Classica et Mediaevalia*, 23, 148–77.

PINBORG, J. (1975) Classical Antiquity: Greece, *Historiography of Linguistics*, ed. by T. A. Sebeok (Current Trends in Linguistics, 13), Mouton, The Hague, 69–126.

RIST, J. M. (ed.) (1978) *The Stoics*, University of California Press, Berkeley.

ROBINS, R. H. (1951) *Ancient and Mediaeval Grammatical Theory in Europe*, Bell, London.

ROBINS, R. H. (1957) Dionysius Thrax and the Western Grammatical Tradition, *Transactions of the Philological Society*, 67–106.

ROBINS, R. H. (1966) The Development of the Word Class System of the European Grammatical System, *Foundations of Language*, 2, 3–19.

ROBINS, R. H. (1967) *A Short History of Linguistics*, Longman, London.

ROBINS, R. H. (1970) *Diversions of Bloomsbury: Selected Writings on Linguistics*, North-Holland, Amsterdam.

ROBINS, R. H. (1976) Varro and the Tactics of Analogist Grammarians, *Studies in Greek, Italic and Indoeuropean Linguistics Offered to L. R. Palmer*, ed. by A. Morpurgo Davies and W. Meid, Innsbrücker Beiträge zur Sprachwissenschaft, Innsbruck.

SCAGLIONE, A. D. (1970) *Ars Grammatica*, Mouton, The Hague.

SCAGLIONE, A. D. (1972) *The Classical Theory of Composition*, University of North Carolina Press, Chapel Hill.

SCHENKEVELD, D. M. (1983) Linguistic Theories in the Rhetorical Works of Dionysius of Halicarnassus, *Glotta*, 61, 67–94.

SCHMIDT, R. (1839) *Stoicorum Grammatica*, apud Eduardum Anton, Halis (German translation *Die Grammatik der Stoiker*, Vieweg, Braunschweig, 1979).

SIEBENBORN, E. (1976) *Die Lehre von der Sprachrichtigkeit und ihren Kriterien: Studien zur antiken normativen Grammatik*, Grüner, Amsterdam.

STEINTHAL, H. (1890–91) *Geschichte der Sprachwissenschaft bei den Griechen und Römern*, 2nd edn, 2 vols, Dümmler, Berlin.

TAYLOR, D. J. (1975) *Declinatio: a Study of the Linguistic Theory of Marcus Terentius Varro*, Benjamins, Amsterdam.

TESNIÈRE, L. (1959) *Eléments de syntaxe structurale*, 2nd edn, Klincksieck, Paris.

WALDE, A. (1965) *Lateinisches etymologisches Wörterbuch*, 4th edn revised by J. B. Hofmann, Winter, Heidelberg.

WOUTERS, A. (1979) *The Grammatical Papyri from Graeco-Roman Egypt: Contributions to the Study of the 'Ars Grammatica' in Antiquity*, Royal Academy of Sciences, Brussels.

WRIGHT, R. (1982) *Late Latin and Early Romance*, Francis Cairns, Liverpool.

ZIEGLER, K. and SONTHEIMER, W. (eds) (1979) *Der kleine Pauly*, 5 vols, Deutscher Taschenbuch Verlag, München.

## Additional References

AMACKER, R. (1990) L'argumentation pragmatique chez Priscien: 'personne' et 'deixis', *Historiographia Linguistica*, 17, 269–91.

AX, W. (1986) *Laut, Stimme und Sprache: Studien zu drei Grundbegriffen der antiken Sprachtheorie*, Vandenhoeck and Ruprecht, Göttingen.

AX, W. (1990) Aristophanes von Byzanz als Analogist: zu Fragment 374 Slater (= Varro, de lingua latina 9, 12), *Glotta*, 68, 4–18.

BARATIN, M. (1989) *La naissance de la syntaxe à Rome*, Editions de Minuit, Paris.

BÉCARES BOTAS, V. (1985) *Diccionario de terminología gramatical griega* (Acta Salmanticensia. Artes Dicendi, 3), Universidad, Salamanca.

BELARDI, W (1985) *Filosofia, grammatica e retorica nel pensiero antico*, Ateneo, Roma.

CAVAZZA, F. (ed.) (1985– ) Aulo Gellio, *Le Notti Attiche*, Introduzione, testo latino, traduzione e note di Franco Cavazza, Zanichelli, Bologna.

DE NONNO, M. (ed.) (1982) *La grammatica dell' Anonymus Bobiensis (GL I. 533–565 Keil)*, Edizioni di Storia e Letteratura, Roma.

DESBORDES, F. (1988) La fonction du grec chez les grammairiens latins, in Rosier (ed.) (1988), 15–26.

DI BENEDETTO, V. (1990) At the origins of Greek Grammar, *Glotta*, 68, 19–39.

FREDE, M. (1987) *Essays in Ancient Philosophy*, University of Minnesota Press, Minneapolis.

GUTIÉRREZ, M. A. (1990) L'interprétation des théories des grammairiens latins sur les conjonctions selon le structuralisme fonctionnel, *Glotta*, 68, 105–18.

HOUSEHOLDER, F. W. (1989) History of Linguistics in the Classical Period (review article on Taylor (ed.) (1987)), *Historiographia Linguistica*, 16, 131–48.

HÜLSER, K- H. (ed.) (1987–8) *Die Fragmente zur Dialektik der Stoiker*, 4 vols, Frommann-Holzboog, Stuttgart.

KEMP, A. (1986) The Tekhne Grammatike of Dionysius Thrax: English translation with introduction and notes, in Taylor (ed.) (1987) ( = *Historiographia Linguistica*, 13, 343–63).

LALLOT, F. (1988) Origines et développement de la théorie des parties du discours en Grèce, in Colombat, B., (ed.) (1988), *Les parties du discours (Langages 92)*, 11–23.

LALLOT, F. (1989) *La grammaire de Denys le Thrace*, traduite et annotée par Jean Lallot, CNRS, Paris.

LAMBERT, F. (1986) Aspects de l'énonciation chez Apollonius Dyscole, *Histoire épistémologie langage*, 8: 2, 39–52.

LAW, V. A. (1987) An Unnoticed Late Latin Grammar: the *Ars minor* of Scaurus?, *Rheinisches Museum für Philologie*, 130, 67–89.

LAW, V. A. (1990a) *Auctoritas, consuetudo* and *ratio* in St. Augustine's Ars grammatica, in G. L. BURSILL-HALL, S. EBBESEN and K. KOERNER (eds) (1990), *De Ortu Grammaticae: Studies in Mediaeval Grammar and Linguistic Theory*, Benjamins, Amsterdam.

LAW, V. A. (1990b) Roman Evidence on the Authenticity of the Grammar Attributed to Dionysius Thrax, in H.-J. NIEDEREHE and K. KOERNER (eds) (1990), *History and Historiography of Linguistics*, vol. I, Benjamins, Amsterdam, 89–96.

PASSALACQUA, M. (ed.) (1984) *Tre testi grammaticali Bobbiesi (GL V 555.566; 634–654; IV 207–216 Keil)*, edizione critica con un'appendice Carisiana, Edizioni di Storia e Letteratura, Roma

PASSALACQUA, M. (ed.) (1987). *Prisciani Caesariensis Opuscula*, vol. I, Edizioni di Storia e Letteratura, Roma

ROBINS, R. H. (1990) *A Short History of Linguistics*, third edn (Longman Linguistics Library), Longman, London.

ROSIER, I. (ed.) (1988) *L'héritage des grammairiens latins de l'antiquité aux lumières*, Peeters, Louvain.

SLUITER, I. (1990) *Ancient Grammar in Context: Contributions to the Study of Ancient Linguistic Thought*, VU University Press, Amsterdam.

TAYLOR, D. J. (ed.) (1987) *The History of Linguistics in the Classical Period* ( = *Historiographia Linguistica* 13:2–3 (1986)), Benjamins, Amsterdam.

TAYLOR, D. J. (1988) Varro and the Origins of Latin Linguistic Theory, in Rosier (ed.) (1988), 37–48.

**Chapter 2**

# Medieval Linguistics

*Edoardo Vineis and Alfonso Maierù*

## 2.1 Introduction *by Edoardo Vineis*

The interest of contemporary scholars for medieval linguistic thought has been directed principally towards the analysis of *grammatica speculativa*, understood as a fundamental, not to say an essential element in the development of modern philosophy of grammar. This viewpoint has gradually established itself, often accompanied by facile, naive and indeed excessive enthusiasm for such rediscovery – an enthusiasm which is not justifiable on the basis of rigorous historiographical analysis on the part of the followers of generative-transformational grammar on the Chomskian model, who have appeared to be more interested in the cult of their *praedecessores* (or rather their *praecursores*) than in the varied epistemic context into which the many *disputationes* elaborately set out by the *magistri artium* ought to be arranged.

Second, much time and space have been dedicated to the study of Dante's doctrines (which are dealt with separately from the planned contents of this chapter), as if to recognize in them, on the one hand, the distant dawn of the rising – even if only as an isolated intuition, not open to immediate development – of a historical-comparative model (if not of geolinguistics or even of sociolinguistics), and on the other hand, especially in recent studies, an at least partial dependence on certain modist theories.

But medieval linguistic thought cannot be limited to only these two aspects (and not in our judgement alone), as if they were its fundamental characteristics: this is said, of course, with all due recognition for the importance that can certainly be attributed to them in the general framework of its historical development, or, if one prefers, of the conceptual heredity which the Middle Ages left to later investigation, especially in modern and contemporary thought. To make a comparison with the Classical age, a similar assumption would, by analogy, force the historian of Greek and Latin linguistics to pause extensively – and principally – on Plato and Aristotle, ignoring – or neglecting almost completely – someone like Dionysus Thrax, Varro, Donatus or Priscian.

In fact, the history of medieval linguistics is for a large part the history of grammar, in its double meaning of descriptive-normative grammar and of interpretative grammar. The former deals almost exclusively with Latin, but also introduces, as we shall see, some examples aimed at other languages. The latter gradually takes shape as a speculative re-interpretation of grammar itself – of its power of interpreting the signifying modalities of the object language – whether it depended on theology, and whether, on the other hand, it depended on logic, both of these disciplines being part of twelfth–fourteenth century episteme.

This development is therefore far from linear, nor can it be reduced to an arbitrary focusing on single significant moments, to be judged *sub specie novitatis* according to the parameters of those who, simplistically, like to relate the past – while making it relevant in terms of value judgement – to the concepts developed by contemporary linguistics. A preferable alternative is to enquire on how – in the complex interaction of many cultural factors – the specific approaches have come to be established that characterize medieval linguistics compared to the theoretical assumption inherited from late Antiquity.

These approaches, for example, even while granting Aristotelianism a privileged position, did not at all neglect the Platonic tradition (which will be widely revisited here), and, while contemplating a systematic and exact re-exploration of Donatus and/or Priscian, restructured the very codifications and categorizations of late Latin manuals on the basis of dogmatic principles and of *extra normam* linguistic usages drawn from the Bible, which was an obligatory reference point for the new Christian culture in the field of reading and interpretation of texts. These approaches, in the last analysis, seem to be closely linked to the demands of the schools, in every order and degree, which, according to their curricular needs, tackle the study of language at times from an elementary perspective, at other times at a higher level of enquiry. At this higher level of enquiry the teachers of dialectics *altius de praedicatione perscrutantur* (delved deeper into predication), and so began that difficult process of mutual permeation between logic and grammar which, having manifested itself almost subliminally in the Carolingian age, in the late Middle Ages was to bring about an intellectual challenge of European proportions.

Finally, one should not forget doctrinal speculation in the field of etymology – which was also conditioned by theology in several cases – in the context of the compilation of lexica intended to represent the *summa* of scientific knowledge, or the mental efforts aimed at discovering adequate descriptive and interpretative parameters for linguistic systems other than Latin, which had emerged long before in European cultural history, or, lastly, the need for a precise and detailed description of the specific modes of expression which characterized Latin, the universal language of learned communication, in the different ethnic and linguistic areas.

## 2.2  Linguistics and grammar *by Edoardo Vineis*

### 2.2.1  Schools and centres of culture from Late Antiquity to the Carolingian Renaissance

No consideration of the development of medieval reflection on language can be made, in our opinion, without a careful analysis of the schools, the centres of culture and the various methods of teaching the *artes* – particularly grammar, rhetoric and dialectics – inherited from the scholastic tradition of late antiquity.[1] A detailed examination of medieval *paideia* is outside our aim; the extensive studies that already exist[2] allow us, however, to make several observations centering more specifically on the reconstruction of the linguistic thought of an age whose chronological limits we set, for the purposes of this study, approximately between the fifth and the fourteenth century.

In drawing the picture of the way culture was organized in the period of change between late antiquity and the early Middle Ages people often use improperly the concept of decadence, in clear contrast with the Carolingian Renaissance, and above all in contrast with the undoubted intellectual fervour which characterized the twelfth century. In actual fact the classical school was never completely lost. Let us remember that sophisticated education which not only continued to be promoted at the heart of the senatorial class of the great landowners,[3] but which was also advocated by the emperors of lower social extraction[4] and even by the barbarian leaders who from the end of the fourth century onwards held the office of palace officials.[5]

The establishment of Christianity was not a serious obstacle, at least until the fifth century,[6] to the continuation of the traditional educational patterns which were established in the classical school, and did not modify these patterns in any significant way.[7] With the exception of the very first monastic schools which were completely organized for religious life, we have no evidence of any real

Christian school in the primary and secondary stages of teaching.[8] This differs from what occurred in higher education, which saw the appearance, especially in the East, of schools of theology and scriptural exegesis.[9]

There is also plenty of evidence for the survival of the ancient Roman school in the period of cultural decline which characterized the Romano-barbarian kingdoms: the fairly widespread use of writing, which continues to play an important part in public life, indirectly bears witness to the preservation of some primary level education even, presumably, among the middle classes;[10] the aristocratic classes kept the privilege of higher education, mainly of a rhetorical kind. Even a cursory list of the main centres of study and culture cannot ignore, during this period, Milan, Ravenna, Rome, Arles, Narbonne, Lyon, Bordeaux, Cordoba and Carthage;[11] the teaching there was mainly addressing a literary and oratorical type of education: this started using mainly the text of Donatus[12] – from grammar, 'mater gloriosa facundiae quae cogitare novit ad laudem, loqui sine vitio' ('glorious mother of eloquence which knows how to think laudably and to speak without fault'), or 'peritia pulchre loquendi ex poetis illustribus auctoribusque collecta' ('the skill of speaking beautifully drawn from the illustrious poets and *auctores*'[13]), continued by reading the classics[14] and reached its summit with the rhetorical exercises of *suasoriae* and *controversiae*.[15]

There was a decided cultural impoverishment in the West with the gradual disappearance of knowledge of Greek, which dates from the end of the fifth century: Claudianus Mamertus in Gaul and Boethius in Italy were the last representatives of a Hellenistic culture which was approaching extinction,[16] and during the sixth century there was a proliferation of Latin translations.[17]

From the sixth century onwards the monastic, episcopal and presbyterial schools assumed a growing importance. As centres of religious education whose origins date back to the Eastern world, the monastic schools imparted the education that was necessary to the study and interpretation of scriptures, and at the same time took on the task of organizing *scriptoria* and, consequently, of setting up libraries:[18] we need only think of Arles, Montecassino, Vivarium, as well as the constellation of minor centres scattered throughout Europe, but especially in Italy and Gaul (but some examples of these existed also in Africa and Spain), among which it is worth noting at least Lérins, the island that was the site of a monastery with a celebrated school of asceticism. The episcopal schools were not unlike the monastic schools, the seeds of the future medieval universities,[19] while the presbyterial schools had the principal task of educating the rural clergy.[20]

A decisive element in the reorganization of the ancient Roman school was Emperor Justinian's cultural policy, expressed, as is well known, by the Pragmatic Sanction of 554 AD, which set down a salary for teachers of grammar and rhetoric (as well as medicine and law), 'quatenus iuvenes liberalibus studiis eruditi per nostram rempublicam floreant' ('so that young people educated in liberal studies should flourish in our republic').[21] Italy in particular, with Rome and Ravenna, could then continue the tradition of secular teaching in parallel with the increasing spread of Christian schools; the importance of studying the liberal arts was all the more recognized the more they were considered suitable for in-depth scriptural exegesis.[22]

The seventh century saw a gradual consolidation of the Christian schools, which were destined to become the only heirs of classical culture throughout the western territory, particularly in Italy, Ireland and Britain.[23] In Italy, the fact that the secular tradition of teaching gave way almost entirely to religious education was due for the most part to the consequences of the Longobard invasion. The Church, being the only organized power, succeeded at least in part in limiting the effects of a disastrous cultural impoverishment. As for Ireland, unlike the rest of the West it had known no other tradition apart from its Christian schools, and although it remained outside the Roman Empire and consequently distant from classical culture, it quickly recovered this culture precisely through those monastic institutions which were to make it famous throughout Europe. In Britain, Christian schools were started at the time when Roman missionaries and Irish monks were becoming established. The new intellectual fervour which Ireland, in particular, radiated,[24] made a decisive contribution to the establishment of a true medieval culture. We can date from this period a renewed impulse for the circulation of ideas, for exchanging cultural experiences between the various Western countries, and all this takes place mostly through the complex network of relations between the various monastic communities, so that what some people study in York and Canterbury is not too unlike what others learn in Luxeuil, Bobbio or Sankt Gallen.[25]

The activity of the monastic and episcopal schools became more intense in the last decades of the seventh century and the first half of the eighth, ideally preparing the later Carolingian Renaissance; the intense work in the *scriptoria*, the wealth of the libraries, the reappearance – no longer as an isolated phenomenon – of the knowledge of Greek witness the first great pre-humanistic movement we can find in the development of medieval culture.[26] An interest in studying and teaching grammar was a constant in this period, especially in the Irish and Anglo-Saxon environments, where it was closely linked to the problem of learning Latin as a foreign language. Therefore, in monastic and episcopal libraries there was a strong presence of works by ancient and modern grammarians,[27] and at the same time we find a substantial new production of treatises on grammar: Aldhelm, Tatuinus, Bede and Boniface wrote on grammar and orthography, on prosody, metrics and tropes;[28] the *scriptorium* at Bobbio came into possession of books on grammar and metrics,[29] and at the court in Pavia, under Cunipert – towards the end of the seventh century – a grammarian called Felix symbolically received from the king a baton decorated with gold and silver;[30] the work of Virgilius Grammaticus was known as far as Bavaria.[31] A simple look at the educational practice of the time shows that primary teaching involved, apart from singing and calculation, the pupils memorizing most of the Psalter, both orally and in written form,[32] according to the kind of 'direct' teaching method which is not too dissimilar from the practice rightly or wrongly established in today's foreign language teaching. The student could learn a sacred text without any previous knowledge of the basics of Latin grammar, the language in which the text was written,[33] a language which by this time had become to all intents and purposes a foreign tongue even in Romance territories. The levels we could define as middle to higher involved the teaching of Latin grammar, which was done mainly on Donatus' *Ars minor*, but did not neglect more recent texts like the *Cunabula grammaticae artis Donati*,[34] or scholastic compilations of different grammarians, like the *Glosa de partibus orationis*.[35] An increased and more in-depth knowledge of Latin vocabulary was obtained by using bilingual or monolingual glossaries. The latter were particularly useful in explaining rare or obscure terms and if necessary, Graecisms.[36] Learning prosody was ensured by resorting to largely expositive manuals, such as Bede's *De arte metrica* and especially Aldhelm' *De metris*, which contained a wide range of examples.[37] Once the pupil had reached an optimum knowledge of Latin, so that he could read easily above all (or almost exclusively) the texts of the scriptures, higher teaching continued with the interpretation of the Bible according to those criteria of three-or more often fourfold exegesis which were destined to become canonical in the scholastic method: the sacred text could and/or had to und... literal, allegorical, moral and anagogic interpretation. In this way a system of education was taking shape, in its essential outline, which was to have a profound influence on the history of Western culture up to the twelfth century and beyond: the classical tradition leaves the Middle Ages and the Christian school the priceless legacy of an *ars grammatica*, of a complete metalanguage which was destined to be accepted as the most lucid and incisive instrument of intellectual penetration, the indispensable paradigmatic reference point for solving the most varied cultural *quaestiones* which clerics and lay scholars tirelessly pursued.

An initial and quite considerable contribution to the establishment of the type of educational practice that was developed by the Christian West came from the particular formulation of studies that was typical of the Eastern monastic schools. Beside the secular teaching provided by the schools of the classical tradition,[38] which continued without a break into Byzantine education,[39] Christian schools already existed in the East from the fourth century; the teaching there consisted mainly of the study of the Bible, where the Psalter and the New Testament were memorized, and which was in any case the basic text, and was even used for the most elementary grammatical exercises, starting from learning how to read and write.[40] Another important institution which was probably already in existence in the seventh century and was certainly perfectly organized in the eleventh, was in the East, and still within the confines of religious education, the patriarchal school. It was dedicated to higher education, with teachers who specialized in scriptural exegesis, and initially took shape as a sort of counterattraction to the imperial University, which was a centre of purely secular culture. However, the patriarchal school was not unaffected by the numerous and various influences of a traditional and decidedly secular humanism since, even as part of general preliminary preparation to the study of theology, it encouraged the teaching of grammar and mathematics.[41] Therefore the methods of the patriarchal school could also have supplied more than one element to the establishment of the *paideia* as it is found in the European Middle Ages.

The so-called Carolingian Renaissance[42] had important effects on the way education – and therefore culture – was organized, from the end of the eighth to the whole of the eleventh century: the extension (and the restructuring) of the episcopal and presbyterial schools in particular, which took place according to the laws of Charlemagne and of his successors guaranteed an undoubted increase in the general level of education, and not only in primary and secondary education.[43] The great monastic abbeys of Tours, Fulda, Reichenau, Sankt Gallen, Lorsch, Fleury, Saint-Riquier and Corbie would no longer be the only protagonists of an undisputed intellectual flowering, but beside them the centres of higher culture formed by the cathedral schools of Laon, Orléans, Paris, Metz, Cambrai, Reims, Auxerre and Chartres[44] would become ever more important. Rather than the pursuit of new methods and models, the cultural and literary movement of the eleventh century essentially aimed at the conservation of the ancient ones, as is borne out unequivocally by the importance given to the teaching of grammar,[45] by the renewed interest in the study of Greek,[46] the spread of the passion for libraries, even the reform of writing or the exemplary precise accuracy shown in the assiduous exercise of *emendatio textuum* – and not only within the learned surroundings of the Palatine court. However, one cannot deny the value of all these elements as indispensable premises to the great renaissance of the twelfth century, to the establishment of values, attitudes or modes of behaviour which could be defined, not improperly, as pre-humanist, even within a culture that can only be described as typically medieval for the way it profoundly aspired to transcendence, and consistently made use of the *artes* as tools for the ultimate purpose of biblical exegesis.

The cult of grammar and rhetoric overtook the interest shown for the study of dialectics with its tasks and functions in the Carolingian age. Dialectics was meant more as a mnemonic exercise than as an intellectual discipline, and despite being promoted by Alcuin[47] himself it had to wait until the eleventh century to acquire a place of decisive importance within the education of medieval man.[48] The subsequent rediscovery of Aristotle's so-called *Logica nova* through the translations made in the course of the twelfth and thirteenth century would ensure dialectics a position of absolute pre-eminence within the system of *artes*, which formed the basis for the development of theology and scholastic philosophy, and for the raising of grammar itself to the rank of an eminently speculative discipline.[49]

A glance at the range of books which formed the principal libraries with reference to the ninth and tenth century shows the almost constant presence of some texts which became canonical for the early medieval *Bildung* such as Martianus Capella, Donatus and/or Priscian, Boethius, Isidore and Bede; the Bible and the *auctores* of Christian patristics can be found beside them, while the classics are represented particularly by Cicero, Virgil, Horace, Ovid, Lucan and Statius.[50] Throughout the different geographical areas of Europe the fundamental unity of the basic preparation underlying the most diverse kinds of cultural production becomes clear. From hagiographic to poetic writing, from historical to juridic writing, it is clear that the preliminary procedure that underlies them is tendentially the same everywhere, and that it cannot ignore an accurate knowledge of exemplary texts which were considered indispensable to scientific knowledge.

### 2.2.2 Schools and centres of culture from the Carolingian Renaissance to the threshold of Humanism. The rediscovery of the Aristotelian corpus

The renewal of studies which Charlemagne made his aim especially with the help of Alcuin, survived in Europe until the end of the ninth century, thanks to great intellectuals such as Rabanus Maurus, Lupus of Ferrières, Johannes Scotus Erigena, Heiricus and Remigius of Auxerre,[51] and the tenth century, after a brief interval of true cultural decadence,[52] saw the so-called Ottonian renaissance, the ideal continuation, or, more precisely, the resumption of the Carolingian programme, which was put into action by means of, among other things, the intensification of cultural exchanges between the Germanic, Italian and French world.[53]

From the Ottonian renaissance to that of the twelfth century there is no longer a lack of continuity in the intellectual geography of Europe: the *magistri artium* develop a homogeneous knowledge which was destined to last up to the threshold of Humanism, beyond the diverging cultural directions which the great Cathedral schools, and particularly the universities, would follow. As Knowles pertinently observes (1962, 80),

> from 1050 to 1350, and above all in the century between 1070 and 1170, the whole of educated Western Europe formed a single undifferentiated cultural unit. In the lands between Edinburgh and Palermo, Mainz or Lund and Toledo, a man of any city or village might go for education to any school, and become a prelate or an official in any church, court or university (when these existed) from north to south, from east to west

and that is how Lanfranc of Pavia – like Anselm of Aosta – was abbot of Bec and then bishop of Canterbury, John of Salisbury went from Paris to Benevento, Canterbury and Chartres, Thomas Aquinas was able to teach in Cologne, Paris and Naples, Johannes Duns Scotus taught at Oxford, Paris and Cologne, William of Ockham lived in Oxford, Avignon and Munich.

Among the principal elements contributing to the construction of that prodigious cultural edifice that came to dominate the late Middle Ages, at least two are of fundamental importance for our purposes: the rediscovery of Aristotle and the birth of the universities. The knowledge of the so-called *Logica nova*[54] had a decisive effect on the traditional direction of the study of grammar, with the result of subjecting grammar to the rigid discipline of dialectics. On the other hand, precisely within higher education, although it was almost everywhere permeated by the new methodological models following the rediscovery of Aristotle, educational theory in universities in some cases upgraded the teaching of grammar and rhetoric in a traditional sense, directing it towards an increasingly sophisticated and subtle interpretation of the *auctores*.[55]

The consolidation of the great cathedral schools during the twelfth century is paralleled by a certain decline of the abbeys and monasteries as centres of culture and education: the splendours of Bec and Montecassino, whose importance decreases only from the second half of the century, represent the exception rather than the rule.[56] One should add to this the presence, especially in northern Italy, of a growing number of urban schools of grammar, where the teaching was mainly literary,[57] and lastly the growing popularity of individual teachers, who were true professional, mainly itinerant,[58] teachers.

An outline of scholastic educational theory as it gradually became established from the end of the eleventh century must take into account first of all the growing importance given to the study of dialectics.[59] At the very beginning of Radulphus Ardens' *Speculum universale*, that is in one of the first *partitiones scientiarum* that introduce the construction of the epistemological paradigm subtended to scholastic philosophy, dialectics, together with grammar and rhetoric, is considered to be one of the divisions of logic, which in turn is one of the four general divisions of science.[60] Higher teaching was based mainly on *lectio* and *disputatio*, the latter becoming established in consequence to the widespread exercise of dialectics. As for the way the *lectio* took place, the *magister artium*, as Grabmann (1909–11, II, 25) points out, 'would analyze and explain the relevant text book of grammar, dialectics, etc, first of all expounding, in an introduction, the title of the book, when and why it was written, the author's intentions, the reader's advantages, the text's position in the overall context of sciences, and would then explain the text itself sentence by sentence, word for word'. In the point-by-point exegesis of the *auctores* and especially of the *divina scriptura*, textual analysis was generally graded according to the tripartite canon of *littera*, or grammatical meaning, *sensus*, or elementary meaning, and *sententia*, or allegorical meaning of the work that was being studied. On this subject, Gilbert of Poitiers divided *lectores* into *recitatores*, if they did no more than paraphrase the words of an author without interpreting them, and *interpretes*, if on the other hand they tried to clear up the obscure and difficult parts of the text they were analysing.[61] As for the technique of *disputatio*, promoted by the rediscovery of Aristotle's *Analytica, Topica* and *Sophistici Elenchi*, it is thus defined by John of Salisbury:

Est autem disputare aliquod eorum, quae dubia sunt, aut in contradictione posita, aut quae sic vel sic proponuntur, ratione supposita, probare

vel improbare; quod quidem quisquis ex arte probabiliter facit, ad
dialectici pertingit metam.

So disputation is to prove and disprove certain things that are in doubt
or are placed in opposition, or are presented thus or thus, by introducing
reason; since whoever proceeds laudably according to art reaches the
goal of the dialectician.

A man identified only as *magister* Radulphus explains the procedure even more:

Disputatio est rationis inductio ad aliquid probandum vel contradicen-
dum. In omni autem disputatione legitima convenit esse interrogationem, responsionem, propositionem, affirmationem, negationem, argumenta, argumentationem et conclusiones. Quae omnia Deo annuente
loco suo secundum doctrinam Aristotelis explicabimus.

Disputation is the induction of reason to prove or contradict something.
So in every regular disputation it is right that there should be question,
answer, proposition, affirmation, negation, arguments, argumentation
and conclusions. Which, God willing, we shall explain in its place
according to the doctrine of Aristotle.[62]

The old method of *quaestio*,[63] widely used from late Latin grammatical treatise-writing, especially as an explanation of linguistic
behaviour that was considered anomalous, came together with
*disputatio*: this being another proof of the multiple connections
between grammar and dialectics in the process of elaborating a
structure of debate that would be equally and validly usable by
both disciplines.

An examination of the many reflections set out by the twefth-
century *magistri* on the various divisions of science makes a major
contribution to the understanding of the values and the organization of the disciplines in this study, and, as a consequence, clarifies
the reasons why they were taught.[64] It is worthwhile, in our
opinion, to quote first of all an anonymous introduction to philosophy and theology, found in a twelfth-century codex from the abbey
of St Michael of Bamberg, explained at length by Grabmann (1909–
11, II, 31ff.). The author makes a distinction, in the field of science,
between *sapientia*, (later subdivided into Theory, Praxis and Mechanics) and *eloquentia* – or Logic – later subdivided into Dialectics
(which includes rational and sophistic argumentation), Rhetoric and
Grammar. As for the teaching – which concerns us most here – of
*eloquentia*, it begins with Grammar, continues with Dialectics and
concludes with Rhetoric.[65] In a manuscript in Munich's Staatsbiblio-
thek, dating from the twelfth–fifteenth century and containing
an anonymous *divisio philosophiae*, there is a preliminary division

of philosophy into Theory, Practice and Logic: for our purposes it will be enough to note that within the successive subdivisions of Practice we find *spiritualis intelligentia*, including Tropology, Allegory and Anagogy, while Logic is divided into Dialectics, Apodictics and Sophistics.[66] But the most important scientific methodology of the twelfth century, undeniably crucial from a pedagogical view point, is offered by Hugh of St Victor's *Didascalicon*. The field of secular sciences is divided into four parts, Theory, Praxis, Mechanics and Logic, according to a widening of the Aristotelian pattern that was already present in Radulphus Ardens' *Speculum universale*, and which will form the basis not only for the work of Richard of Saint Victor, but also for the methodology of Albertus Magnus and Robert Kilwardby. As for Logic, whose subjects are the *species* and *genera*, and which sets itself the task of transmitting the *scientia recte loquendi et acute disputandi* (the science of speaking correctly and disputing acutely), it is divided into *grammatica* (grammar) and *ratio disserendi* (ability of discussing). The latter is in turn subdivided into the demonstration of certainty, the demonstration of probability – which belongs to Dialectics and Rhetoric – and sophistic: Grammar puts itself forward as *scientia loquendi sine vitio* (the science of speaking without defects), Dialectics as *disputatio acuta* (acute disputation) and Rhetoric as *disciplina ad persuadendum quoque idonea* (discipline suitable also for persuading). Though it is the last from a point of view of simple classification, Logic is the first in scientific teaching as regards the order of learning the different disciplines. It gives information on the various *modi* of *disputatio*, by means of which one can tell truth from falsehood, and moreover it deals with the nature of words and concepts. Finally, in the exposition of the various texts that are the object of the *lectio*, we find codified the succession of *littera*, understood as *congrua ordinatio dictionum* (coherent ordering of words), *sensus*, in other words *facilis quaedam et aperta significatio* (an easy and open signification), and *sententia*, described as *profundior intelligentia, quae nisi expositione vel interpretatione non invenitur* (deeper understanding, which is only obtained through the exposition and interpretation of the text).[67] One last mention must be made of the classification Radulphus de Longo Campo made at the beginning of the thirteenth century, according to which science, *rerum scibilium agnitio* (apprehending of the things which can be known), is divided into four parts: Philosophy, Eloquence, Poetry and Mechanics. Eloquence is divided into Grammar, Logic – whose main functions are definition, classification and deduction, and which is further subdivided into *Dialectica, Temptativa, Demonstrativa* and *Sophistica* – and Rhetoric, while *Poesis*, which is the *scientia claudens in metro vel prosa orationem gravem et illustrem* (the science that encloses grave and illustrious discourse in metre or in prose) is subdivided into the categories of *historia, fabula, ars* or *comoedia.*[68]

The summary of the character of late medieval culture within the concerns of the *artes Trivii* cannot be concluded without a mention of *dictamen*, that particular stylistic technique that used to be taught for the purposes of epistolary composition and later the writing of official acts: a kind of connection between the literary and legal disciplines, the *ars dictaminis*, which was codified from the eleventh century thanks mainly to Alberic of Montecassino and which soon spread through the Roman curia, reached its greatest splendour in thirteenth century Bologna, and also developed in France, especially in Orléans and Tours.[69]

By the thirteenth and fourteenth century the knowledge of the entire Aristotelian *corpus* can be said to be part of the accepted culture of Western Europe, as was the knowledge of Arab and Jewish thought, the latter principally transmitted through the works of Dominicus Gundissalinus. If one adds to this a more thorough penetration of Platonic and neo-Platonic philosophy – mainly the prerogative of the School of Chartres, in opposition to the overwhelming Aristotelianism of Paris and Oxford – one will have an overall picture of the cultural vastness within which the European intellectuals on the threshold of Humanism were operating. The compactness and at the same time the incomparable articulation of the scholastic edifice interest us here especially in order to remind the reader of the place that the study of grammar and logic continued to hold within that edifice. The study of logic was strengthened by the rediscovery, which by now had taken place, of all Aristotle's works relevant to it. Logic in particular, thanks especially to William of Ockham, through a slow process whereby its specific terms of investigation became autonomous of the instrumental ties it had contracted at various times with philosophy and theology, was becoming, as it is today, a purely formal field of research, or rather, to quote a definition by Pinborg, 'doctrine of the sign as sign, i.e. of the metalanguage elaborated by the intellect to be able to talk of the structure of knowledge and of language'.[70]

The linguistic instrument called upon to perform this task was Latin, *grammatica* by definition above the vulgar tongues, a markedly supranational communicative and interpretative structure. The inevitable process of formulaic standardization Latin underwent – together with a certain fixity and artificiality – as a consequence of being used as the language of learned conversation, was not the least of the causes of its taking shape and becoming enshrined as the ideal metalanguage any scholar could use to enlighten adequately and organically the very foundations of his knowledge.[71]

### 2.2.3 Knowledge of the Latin grammarians in the various areas of Europe

The complex edifice of late Latin grammar was received and communicated unequally in the different areas of Europe: while the works of Donatus were universally known, other authors, such as Cledonius, were known, in a very limited way, only within specific areas whose boundaries were extremely narrow. An exemplary picture of the Latin grammatical tradition of the early Middle Ages is presented to us by Law (1982, 11–29), with particular attention on the insular area: the brief summary outline that follows is based in great part on her work.

One must first of all mention Donatus, whose fame was no doubt increased by the fact that he had been Saint Jerome's *praeceptor*, and whose name soon came to be indissolubly linked to grammar par excellence, simply a synonym of grammar.[72] The enormous success enjoyed by both the *Ars minor* and the *Ars maior*[73] is probably justified by the elementary level of treatment and the absolute linearity of exposition which characterize both works, but especially the first one, a brief outline which synthesizes the essential features which characterize each part of speech; moreover, the numerous references to Donatus to be found in St Jerome, Cassiodorus and Isidore of Seville contributed to his being approved of in the Christian schools. He was mentioned in most of the library catalogues of the eighth and ninth century, and was the almost obligatory starting point in the writing of many grammars – especially the ones written in the British isles – and his dominant position was shaken only by the Carolingian rediscovery of Priscian's *Institutiones*, even if he continued to be used in school teaching up to the Renaissance.[74]

Among Donatus' commentators, Pompeius was widely known in various cultural centres of Europe: his work is present in the ninth century catalogues of Saint-Riquier, Reichenau, Freising, Sankt Gallen and Cologne, and is also mentioned by the tenth-century catalogues of Bobbio and Lorsch, as well as by the twelve-century ones from Saint-Bertin and Corbie. It was widely used by the authors of the *Ars Ambianensis* and the *Ars Bernensis*, by the Anonymus ad Cuimnanum, by Bede and Tatuinus, as well as by Boniface and Aldhelm in their own treatises on metrics; its fortunes, still flourishing in the Carolingian era, waned from the second half of the ninth century, at the same time as Priscian's increased popularity following his rediscovery.[75]

As for Consentius' grammatical work, it was known both in Irish and Anglo-Saxon circles: it was used by the *Ars Ambianensis*,[76] by the *Ars Bernensis*, by the *Ars Malsachani*, by the Anonymus ad Cuimnanum and by Tatuinus. It was also present in the *Donatus ortigraphus* and it is well represented in ninth and tenth century manuscripts, as well as being mentioned in the catalogues of Lorsch, Regensburg, Bobbio and Toul.[77]

Of the commentaries on the works of Donatus we have under the name of Sergius, the *De littera* was known in the British Isles, and was used by the *Ars Bernensis*, by Bede and by Aldhelm.[78] As for the *Explanationes in artem Donati*, Law (1982, 17) has found with certainty at least one case of correspondence to a passage from the *Ars Bernensis*. In the works of the grammarians of the British Isles we find numerous quotations of passages attributed to Sergius, which, however, do not appear in the *De littera* or in the *Explanationes*, but rather in Pseudo-Cassiodorus' commentary to Donatus *Ars maior*.[79] This work is used by Boniface, by the author of *Quae sunt quae* and perhaps by Tatuinus – who nevertheless do not mention its author – and by the *Ars Bernensis*, the *Ars Ambianensis*, by the *Donatus ortigraphus* and by the *Ars Ambrosiana*, all of which know it as the work of Sergius; the problem of its attribution is still open, and subject to further research[80]

As for Charisius' grammar, it is listed by the catalogue of the abbey of Saint-Riquier in 831 and by that of the monastery of Bobbio dating from the tenth century. It was known by the insular grammarians – who, however, list it under the name of Flavius, or Flavianus, and Cominianus (one of its sources) – and was used by the *Ars Ambianensis* and the *Ars Bernensis*, by Boniface, Bede and Malsachanus.[81]

Diomedes also enjoyed a certain popularity in the British Isles: in particular, the sections of the *Ars grammatica* concerning the verb and preposition are often used by Boniface, by the Anonymus ad Cuimnanum and by the common source used by Malsachanus and Clemens Scottus. The latter two, however, judging from their quotations, knew a more complete version of Diomedes' work than the one that has reached us, which dates from the Carolingian era.[82] A copy of Diomedes is mentioned in the ninth century catalogues of Sankt Gallen and Saint-Riquier, as well as appearing in Regensburg in the tenth century and in Corbie in the twelfth.

As far as Priscian is concerned, the *Institutiones grammaticae* did not become widely known before the ninth century, while from Alcuin onwards they became commonly used by every writer on grammar. In the British Isles they were used by the *Ars Ambianensis*, the *Ars Bernensis*, the *Sapientia ex sapore*, by Aldhelm and by

Virgilius Grammaticus, as well as by one of Malsachanus' sources. On the other hand, the *Institutio de nomine et pronomine et verbo*, like the works of Donatus, was widely known in the seventh and eighth century, and it can certainly be classed among the basic works that formed the *Bildung* of the insular grammarians: it was used by, among others, Tatuinus, Boniface, Malsachanus, the *Ars Ambianensis*, the *Ars Bernensis* and by the *Declinationes nominum*.[83]

The *Ars de verbo* by Eutyches, disciple of Priscian, is known and used by the *Ars Ambianensis*, the *Ars Bernensis*, by Tatuinus and Malsachanus, as well as being mentioned at least once by the Anonymus ad Cuimnanum and by Boniface, without, however, being used directly by these last two authors. It was most widely known during the ninth century, when Sedulius Scottus and Remigius of Auxerre wrote commentaries on it, and it continued in the three centuries that followed. The work is mentioned, among others, in Alcuin's list of the library at York, in the ninth century catalogue of Freising, in the tenth century catalogues of Bobbio, Lorsch and Regensburg, and in the tenth century catalogues of Toul.[84]

As far as Phocas's *Ars de nomine et verbo* is concerned, its use is not particularly widespread in the British Isles, being limited to Aldhelm and Boniface, while it was very widespread in Carolingian France, as proved by numerous copies from the French area dating from the end of the eighth and the beginning of the ninth century.[85] The fame of this brief grammatical treatise continued without interruption until the threshold of the Renaissance: it is mentioned in the tenth century in the catalogues of Bobbio and Lorsch, it is found in Toul in the eleventh century, and in the twelfth it can be found in Corbie, Salzburg and Durham.

The work of Martianus Capella had little effect on grammatical treatise writing before the ninth century, being used only by Tatuinus and the Anonymus ad Cuimnanum; it enjoyed greater popularity in the centuries that immediately followed starting already from Theodulf of Orléans but more for its encyclopedic character than for the specific section (made up by the third book) dedicated to a brief exposition of grammar.[86]

As for the grammars by Audax and Maximus Victorinus, they were used by Aldhelm, Bede, Boniface and the Anonymus ad Cuimnanum, especially for dealing with problems about metrics; both works appear to be widespread in continental Europe during the eighth and ninth century.[87] There are no certain examples of Augustine's grammatical works, which were relatively widespread around the ninth century,[88] being used by the grammarians of the British Isles.

The work of Sacerdos, which was barely known even by late Latin grammarians, is quoted with any certainty only by the *Ars Ambrosiana* and by the *Ars Bernensis*. The first of these was presumably drawn up in Bobbio, where the only manuscript of Sacerdos – now owned by the Biblioteca Nazionale in Naples – was found. In this manuscript we find the first two books of the *Ars grammatica* attributed to M. [Claudius] Sacerdos.[89]

As for Probus, whose name was very well known to the classical grammarians, none of the authors in the British Isles draws directly on him: the spread of his works beyond the Alps presumably dates only from the end of the eighth century,[90] and was never very wide anyway. During the late Middle Ages until the beginning of the Renaissance, Probus' circulation will continue to decrease: one can find isolated mentions of his work in the catalogues from Reichenau in 822, Bobbio in the tenth century, Toul in the eleventh and Corbie in the thirteenth century.

The *Appendix Probi*, part of which might have originated in Britain,[91] is known and used only by the Anonymus ad Cuimnanum. There was no direct knowledge of the works of Remmius Palaemon: any quotations of his work by the insular grammarians normally go back to Charisius and Diomedes, who explicitly mention it several time.[92] One can say the same thing about Asper, whose name was known mainly through Charisius[93] and whose *Ars* can be reasonably supposed, on the basis of the data of the manuscript tradition, to circulate only in France, at least up to the eleventh century: it is used only by the *Aggressus quidam*, a brief treatise which is preserved in four ninth-century manuscripts, all of them of French origin. The author of this treatise was perhaps an insular grammarian who lived in France.[94]

Finally, Cledonius' grammar seems totally unknown in pre-Carolingian British circles,[95] and Marius Victorinus, Servius, Dositheus and Macrobius seem to have been equally unknown, or at least unused before the ninth century.

### 2.2.4 Boethius, Cassiodorus and Isidore of Seville

To conclude, one needs to mention separately those authors who have traditionally been considered to mark the transition point between the classic age and the Middle Ages, as if they were interpreters who summarized the knowledge of late antiquity. By this time, this knowledge was condensed into an increasingly encyclopedic formulation aimed at religious instruction and, on a more specifically grammatical and rhetorical plane, as an instrument of scriptural exegesis. The writers who marked this transition are, first, Boethius and Cassiodorus – whose names are closely associated by a centuries-long tradition that places them ideally at the end of the ancient world – secondly, Isidore of Seville – also ideally seen as the initiator of true medieval culture. These were writers whose works were widespread and widely used in schools and scientific treatises even outside a purely linguistic context.

Among the works by Anicius Manlius Severinus Boethius (480–524), the famous philosopher with a neoplatonic background and last exponent of an in-depth, sophisticated knowledge of Greek, we shall list the already mentioned translations from Aristotle and the commentaries to Porphyry's *Isagoge*, as well as the original works about problems of logic, such as the *Introductio ad syllogismos categoricos*, the two books *De syllogismo categorico* (both based on Aristotle and Porphyry), the two books *De syllogismo hypothetico* (which use the peripatetic Eudemus), and finally the four books *De differentiis topicis*, dealing with matters of dialectics and rhetoric (based on works by Themistius and Cicero).[96] It is also right to point out that we owe to Boethius the origin of the term *quadrivium* to designate the *artes* dealing with more technical and scientific subjects (arithmetic, geometry, astronomy and music),[97] but above all we owe to him the use of a technical terminology in the context of logico-linguistic analysis, which was destined to be particularly successful especially in the scholastic age, and later to be a part of the European intellectual lexicon: one need only think, among the many examples, about the definitions of 'subject' and 'predicate', whose importance is indisputably of fundamental importance for any further progress of many disciplines other than the grammatical ones.[98]

Flavius Magnus Aurelius Cassiodorus' (c.480-c.575) great cultural personality is well known to be connected to the founding of the famous monastery of *Vivarium* – a kind of real theological university, a centre of teaching and assiduous translation of Greek texts, endowed with a vast library of sacred and secular texts. The work destined to enjoy enormous popularity and to play a fundamental role during the following centuries, especially for monastic studies, consists of the two books of *Institutiones quemadmodum divinae et humanae debeant intellegi lectiones* (551–562). The first book, concentrating on the sacred disciplines, indicates the literary tools necessary for the study of the Bible, while the second, dealing with the secular disciplines, gives a brief illustration in seven chapters of the seven liberal arts.[99] Another popular work was the *De orthographia*, written when Cassiodorus was 93, which also aimed primarily at monastic instruction.[100]

The value of Isidore, bishop of Seville (560–636), is quite different and much more significant for our purposes. His *Etymologiarum sive originum libri XX* were enormously popular in the medieval world,[101] and became the *summa* of an encyclopedic knowledge to whose *auctoritas* it was indispensable to refer in the daily practice of teaching and even of scientific research. Isidore's work starts by presenting the foundations of the seven liberal arts, and proceeds to survey the whole of human knowledge. The first book deals with grammar, in the classical – and mainly Donatian – sense of the word, the second is devoted to rhetoric and dialectics, while the third is about the disciplines of the *Quadrivium*, that is arithmetic, geometry, music and astronomy. Out of the other books, the ninth is of particular interest to us, since it is about the organization, mainly the linguistic organization, of the whole of human society. Among the most important elements in the first book one must point out particularly the general observations on the problem of etymology, where the contrast between the motivated and the arbitrary nature of the linguistic sign re-emerges, a contrast which was inherited from the classical world and will continue to be put forward until the present:

> Etymologia est origo vocabulorum, cum vis verbi vel nominis per interpretationem colligitur. Hanç Aristoteles *symbolon*, Cicero adnotationem nominavit, quia nomina et verba rerum nota facit exemplo posito; utputa 'flumen', quia fluendo crevit, a fluendo dictum. Cuius cognitio saepe usum necessarium habet in interpretatione sua. Nam dum videris unde ortum est nomen, citius vim eius intellegis. Omnis enim rei inspectio etymologia cognita planior est. Non autem omnia nomina a veteribus secundum naturam inposita sunt, sed quaedam et secundum placitum, sicut et nos servis et possessionibus interdum secundum quod placet nostrae voluntati nomina damus. Hinc est quod omnium nominum etymologiae non reperiuntur, quia quaedam non secundum qualitatem, qua genita sunt, sed iuxta arbitrium humanae voluntatis vocabula acceperunt (1, 29, 1–3);

> Etymology is the origin of words, in which the force of the verb or the noun is derived through interpretation. Aristotle called this symbol, Cicero called it annotation, because it makes known (*nota*) the nouns and verbs of things by giving an example; that is *flumen* (river) is named from flowing (*fluendo*), because it was formed by flowing. Whose cognition often has a necessary use in its interpretation. In fact, if you see from where the name originates, you better understand its meaning. Indeed, the examination of anything is clearer once the etymology is known. Not all names were imposed on things by the ancients according to nature, but some according to their will, as we sometimes name our servants and our possessions according to our will. And that is why one cannot find the etymologies for all names, because some things received their name not according to the quality according to which they were generated, but according to the choice of human will;

and note, secondarily, the implicit arbitrariness of the interjections, 'quae voces quarumcumque linguarum propriae sunt, nec in aliam linguam facile transferuntur' ('which *voces* are typical of individual languages and are not easily translated into other languages') (1, 14). Etymological research in the strict sense of the word invests, as is well known, the whole of Isidore's work, which aims constantly at the origin of every notion. Each one is generally made explicit both in its more remote and in its closer meanings, but above all according to that double direction of enquiry which examines its value both on the grammatical-atemporal plane and on the historical-chronological plane, in a kind of alleged linguistic and cultural reconstruction which still forms the basis of modern etymology;[102] see, for example, 9, 4, 18:

> Tribuni dicti quod plebi vel iura vel opem tribuunt. Constituti sunt autem sexto anno post reges exactos. Dum enim plebs a senatu et consulibus premeretur, tunc ipsa sibi tribunos quasi proprios iudices et defensores creavit qui eorum libertatem tuerentur et eos adversus iniuriam nobilitatis defenderent.

> They are called tribunes because they give (*tribuunt*) laws and power to the plebeians. They were established from the sixth year after the kings were banished. Indeed, while the plebeians were oppressed by the senate and the consuls, then they created these tribunes for themselves, almost as their own judges and defenders who would protect their freedom and defend them from the hostility of the nobles.

Acceptable etymologies, confirmed by the most recent scientific research, are found together with improbable, imaginative or absurd definitions that are, however, most interesting to us if they are understood and studied as attempts at synchronic motivation of the sign in the linguistic consciousness of the speaker, on the plane of the mental processes of paronomastic association and verbal puzzles. As a brief but significant set of samples, mostly taken by Isidore from the late Latin grammatical tradition, and taken up in various ways in the course of medieval speculation, we can consider at least 1, 1, 1: 'Disciplina a discendo nomen accepit: unde et scientia dici potest. Nam scire dictum a discere, quia nemo nostrum scit, nisi qui discit. Aliter dicta disciplina, quia discitur plena' ('Discipline takes its name from learning (*discendo*): hence it can also be called science. So to know (*scire*) is so called from to learn (*discere*), because none of us knows, unless he learns. Otherwise it is called discipline, because it is learnt fully (*discitur plena*)'); 1, 3, 3: 'Litterae autem dictae quasi legiterae, quod iter legentibus praestent, vel quod in legendo iterentur' ('They are called letters almost like *legiterae*, because they offer a path (*iter*) to the readers (*legentibus*), or because they are repeated in reading (*in legendo iterentur*)'); 1, 3, 8: 'Et dicitur Theta *apò toû thanátou*, id est a morte' ('And it is called *theta* from *thánatos*, that is from death'); 1, 5, 3: 'Oratio dicta quasi oris ratio. Nam orare est loqui et dicere. Est autem oratio contextus verborum cum sensu. Contextus autem sine sensu non est oratio, quia non est oris ratio. Oratio autem plena est sensu, voce et littera' ('It is called *oratio* almost like *oris ratio*, reason of the mouth. Indeed oration is speaking and saying. Oration is a texture of words with sense. The texture without sense is not an oration, because it is not a reason of the mouth. But oration is full of sense, voice and letter'); 1, 7, 1: 'Nomen dictum quasi notamen, quod nobis vocabulo suo res notas efficiat. Nisi enim nomen scieris, cognitio rerum perit' ('A name is so called almost like *notamen*, which makes things known (*notas*) to us with its words. In fact if you do not know the name, the knowledge of things is lost'); 1, 8, 4: 'Articuli autem dicti, quod nominibus artantur, id est conligantur, cum dicimus "hic orator"' ('Then articles are so called, because they are attached (*artantur*), that is connected, to nouns, when we say "hic orator"'); 1, 9, 1: 'Verbum dictum eo, quod verberato aere sonat, vel quod haec pars frequenter in oratione versetur' ('A verb is so called, because the struck (*verberato*) air resounds, or because this part is used (*versetur*) frequently in speech'); 2, 9, 1, where *argumentatio* is defined as 'quasi argutae mentis oratio' ('almost like oration (*oratio*) of a witty (*argutae*) mind (*mentis*)'); 9, 2, 95: 'Languebardos vulgo fertur nominasse prolixa barba et numquam tonsa' ('It is popularly believed that the Longobards were so named from their full un-shaven beards'); 9, 3, 4: 'Reges a regendo vocati ... Recte igitur faciendo regis nomen tenetur' ('Kings are named from ruling (*regendo*) ... One obtains the name king by acting justly (*recte*)'), where the association with *recte*, in the second proposition specifying the given etymology, underlines that frequent characteristic of Isidorian knowledge which is moralizing interpretation, a characteristic typology of the medieval world which was destined to continue until the beginnings of Humanism; and lastly 9, 3, 21: 'Dictus autem princeps a capiendi significatione, quod primus capiat, sicut municeps ab eo quod munia capiat' ('It is also called prince (*princeps*) from the meaning to take (*capiendi*), because he takes first (*primus capiat*), like *municeps* (citizen) is one who takes on (*capiat*) public duties (*munia*)').[103]

To return to the specific contents of the first book, it would be useful to examine them further to enucleate more than one observation of undoubted interest for the linguist. We can see first of all the acknowledgement of the presuppositional relation which exists between antonyms: 'Dici enim dexter non potest, nisi sinister fuerit' ('You could not say right, if left did not exist') (1, 7, 17); then, in the chapter *de orthographia*, the observation of the presence of a dental affricate in the written sequence intervocalic -*ti*-: 'Y et Z litteris sola Graeca nomina scribuntur. Nam cum "iustitia" sonum Z littera exprimat, tamen, quia Latinum est, per T scribendum est. Sic "militia", "malitia", "nequitia", et cetera similia' ('Only Greek words are written with Y and Z; indeed, even if *iustitia* expresses the sound Z, nevertheless, because it is Latin, it is written with a T. Thus *militia, malitia, nequitia* and other similar ones') (1, 27, 28), or, finally, in the chapter *de tropis*, the suggestion of an explanation of the proverbial structure *lupus in fabula*: 'Aiunt enim rustici vocem hominem perdere, si eum lupus prior viderit. Unde et subito tacenti dicitur istud proverbium: "Lupus in fabula"' ('Some country people say that a man will lose his voice if a wolf sees him first. Hence one says this proverb, "Lupus in fabula", to someone who is suddenly quiet') (1, 37, 28).[104]

Going on to consider the second book of Isidore's work, one will notice its clear division into two distinct parts. While chapters 1–21 deal broadly with rhetoric, tracing its history, presenting its subdivisions and illustrating the technical terminology of its complex theoretic apparatus, concluding with an exposition *de figuris verborum et sententiarum*, chapters 22–31 deal specifically with dialectics – whose history of development is also investigated. They go on to discuss philosophy in general, to conclude in an increasingly technical manner by dealing with Porphyry's *Isagoge*, with Aristotle's categories and *Perihermeneias*, with syllogisms, definitions, topics and opposites, in a sort of *encheiridion* that summarizes classical logic.[105]

On this subject, one cannot stress enough the fact that a vast part of ancient conceptualization about rhetoric, dialectics and actual logic was passed on to the medieval world almost exclusively through the synthesis of this agile manual, which was as lacking in originality as it was widely and thoroughly studied.[106] Even the explanation in Latin of the Greek terms that were widely used in a specific technical sense, especially by rhetoric and dialectics, owes largely to Isidore the reasons for its survival, especially within early medieval culture. However limited the bishop of Seville's direct knowledge of Greek may seem, correct interpretations are far from rare, and we can take as an example 2, 24, 7: '*Lógos* enim apud Graecos et sermonem significat et rationem' ('Among the Greeks *lógos* means discourse (*sermo*) and reason (*ratio*)').[107] Finally, a look at the ninth book easily shows its interest not only for linguists, but also for ethnologists, historians, sociologists and jurists, since Isidore writes about the origin of languages and nations, the vocabulary of political and military institutions and degrees of kinship. The first chapter, *de linguis gentium*, is a methodological introduction to the problem of the linguistic organization of human society. In it Isidore states first that originally Hebrew was the universal language – an idea that was by now generally accepted, and which was destined to be perpetuated among the key concepts of medieval culture[108] – and therefore that the different nations were born from the division of languages, not the other way round. One can see that the *incipit* of the first chapter mentions, with detached scientific objectivity, a *linguarum diversitas* – which came about 'in aedificatione turris post diluvium' ('in the building of the tower after the flood') (9, 1, 1) – rather than the *confusio linguarum* – which is, however, present elsewhere[109] – of the Bible, moralistically understood as a punishment for the act of pride represented by the building of the Tower of Babel, before which people spoke only Hebrew. Given, as we have seen, that 'ex una lingua multae sunt gentes exortae' ('from one language there arose many peoples') – and that 'ex linguis gentes, non ex gentibus linguae exortae sunt' ('peoples arose from languages, not languages from peoples') (9, 1, 14) – only three languages enjoy the privilege of being defined as *sacrae*, that is Hebrew, Greek and Latin, 'quae toto orbe maxime excellunt. His enim tribus linguis super crucem Domini a Pilato fuit causa eius scripta' ('which excel most throughout the world. In these three languages the cause of the Lord's death was written by Pilate on the cross') (9, 1, 3), not to mention that 'Graeca autem lingua inter ceteras gentium clarior habetur. Est enim et Latinis et omnibus linguis sonantior' ('The Greek language is held to be the most illustrious among other peoples. It is in fact more musical than Latin and all other languages') (9, 1, 4). Considerations such as the last one, about the acoustic perception of certain phonetic and prosodic elements that were felt to be characteristic traits of specific linguistic groups, are another reason for scientific interest in the first chapter; see also 9, 1, 8:

> Omnes autem Orientis gentes in gutture linguam et verba conlidunt sicut Hebraei et Siri. Omnes mediterraneae gentes in palato sermones feriunt sicut Graeci et Asiani. Omnes Occidentis gentes verba in dentibus frangunt sicut Itali et Spani

> All the Oriental peoples beat together their tongue and words in the throat, like the Hebrews and Syrians. All the Mediterranean peoples strike speech on the palate, like the Greeks and Asians. All the Western peoples break their words against their teeth, like the Italians and Spaniards[110].

The second chapter, *de gentium vocabulis*, lists the various nations descended from Shem, Ham and Japhet, as well as listing other peoples whose name has a different origin from the name of one of Noah's descendants. We can see that etymology plays a fundamental role, since the greater or lesser degree of 'etymological transparency' of the various peoples' names becomes the discriminating criterion leading to their being placed in a hierarchy and consequently evaluated in terms of a moral judgement. The further a nation is found to be from its *prima origo*, that is, the more difficult it is to reconstruct the original meaning of its name, the more that nation is corrupt and subject to barbarism: and therefore, in significant contrast to Goths, Vandals, Burgundians and Franks, founders of the Romano-barbarian kingdoms, some nations seem to Isidore 'linguis dissonae et origine vocabulorum incertae, ut Tolosates, Amsivari ... quorum immanitas barbariae etiam in ipsis vocabulis horrorem quemdam significat' ('dissonant in language and uncertain as to the origin of their names, like the Tolosates, the Amsivari ... whose savageness shows some barbaric horror even in the names themselves') (9, 2, 97). And even the observations which reveal Isidore's undoubted awareness of linguistic change – at times in apparently general and objective terms, for example 9, 2, 38–9:

> multarum gentium vocabula partim manserunt ita ut hodieque appareat unde fuerant dirivata ... Partim vero temporis vetustate ... mutata sunt ... Et si omnia considerentur, plura tamen gentium mutata quam manentia vocabula apparent. Quibus postea nomina diversa dedit ratio

> the names of many peoples remained in part, so that nowadays where they derived from is apparent. In part they have changed ... with the passing of time ... And all things considered, the names of peoples which have changed seem to be more numerous than those which have remained. To which reason later gave different names

– do not escape, in several instances, the conceptual pattern which moralistically interprets change itself as corruption, a separation from the original uncontaminated purity, an obscuration of a presumed ancient 'etymological transparency'. The judgement on the evolution of Latin, which in the Imperial days became increasingly corrupt because of the influx of foreign elements that disrupted its linguistic heritage (the *integritatem verbi*)[111], is a typical example of Isidore's opinion on the matter.

The third and fourth chapter, respectively *de regnis militiaeque vocabulis* and *de civibus*, but especially the last three in the third book, respectively *de adfinitatibus et gradibus*, *de agnatis et cognatis* and *de coniugiis*, form – like the rest of Isidore's work – a veritable terminological repertoire of the technical lexicon used in the ancient world, particularly by the Latin civilization, in the individual sectors of its complex cultural organization. They were indispensable to the compilation of glossaries, *derivationes* and *libri definitionum*, and were able to offer the Middle Ages a complete image of lost classical antiquity.

The *Etymologiae* were very widely known, and were destined to become one of the cornerstones of medieval culture, on a par with the works of Donatus and Priscian's *Institutio*. The first book, which was used by Boniface and Tatuinus, the Anonymus ad Cuimnanum and the *Ars Bernensis*[112], was particularly well known in the British Isles.

### 2.2.5 Iulianus Toletanus and the beginnings of the early medieval grammatical tradition up to the works of Virgil the grammarian

A constant presence of Isidore's work is immediately noticeable in the *Ars grammatica* attributed to Iulianus Toletanus, archbishop of Toledo in the years between 680 and 690[113], a work we shall consider here, before going on to examine early medieval treatises, for its characteristics as a full and correct, and not quite elementary, compilation, a florilegium summarizing the grammar of late antiquity and, together with the latter, a probable source of many later *artes*[114]. In principle the *Ars Iuliani* can be divided into three basic sections: a) a commentary to Donatus' two *Artes* (although it is incomplete as regards the *Ars maior*), drawing mainly on the works of Servius, Pompeius and Sergius as well as on Isidore; b) a treatise on final syllables, whose original source could be Maximus Victorinus; c) a treatise on meter, which can be traced back mainly to the teachings of Mallius Theodorus. One will find a wide use of classical authors, the Bible and Christian writers, from Ennius and Plautus to Dracontius and Eugenius of Toledo, with a decided prevalence of Virgilian passages. It was an eclectic *collatio*, not without organic unity and essentially marked by a conservative classicism, and it was widely present in monastic and episcopal libraries. The work of Iulianus Toletanus contains elements of undoubted interest in the field of linguistic reflection, even if it repeats – but sometimes it amplifies and/or varies in an original way – observations and definitions already found in the earlier tradition, most of which were gathered and almost sanctioned in Isidore's *Etymologiae*. Let us examine some examples. Consider to begin with, in the first part, the initial chapter *de nomine*, 11. 15–22, where the segmentation process applied to the linguistic units refers to an acquired awareness of double articulation:

Quare inchoavit Donatus a nomine et non a littera, cum alii a littera
inchoassent? sciens Donatus quia et ipsa littera nomen erat, ideo
inchoavit a nomine et non a littera. Quomodo? puta, si adsumam unum
nomen, dividam illum per syllabas, ultima syllaba quae remanserit
dividam illam per litteras, ultima littera quae remanserit dividi non
potest et nomen est; ideo a nomine inchoavit et non a littera;

Why did Donatus start from the name and not from the letter, while
others started from the letter? Because Donatus knew that the letter
was itself a name, therefore he started from the name and not from the
letter. How? say, if I take a name, and divide it into syllables, and
divide the last remaining syllable into letters, I cannot divide the last
remaining letter, and it is a name; therefore he started from the name
and not from the letter;

The argument is expressed even more forcefully and clearly at
11. 18–23 of the *de littera*, first chapter of the second part of the
treatise:

Littera quid est? pars minima vocis articulatae. Quomodo pars minima?
quia minor est, omnium partium minima est. Quomodo? si adsumas
unum nomen, ut puta 'Honorius', dividas illud per syllabas, ultima
syllaba quae remanserit dividas illam per litteras, littera quae remanserit
dividi non potest et est pars minima.[115]

What is a letter? the smallest part of the articulated *vox*. In what way
the smallest part? because it is smaller, it is the smallest of all parts. In
what way? if you take a name, for example 'Honorius', divide it into
syllables, divide the last remaining syllable into letters, you cannot
divide the remaining letter and it is the smallest part.

In the same context can be placed the important distinction
between *vox articulata* and *vox confusa*, the latter not being able to
be represented graphically by means of discrete elements (11. 23–
7):

Quomodo vocis articulatae? duae sunt voces, una articulata et altera
confusa. Quae est confusa? quae scribi non potest, ut puta ovium
balatus, equi hinnitus, mugitus bovis, et cetera. Item quare dicta confusa? quia ex aere verberato, nullo modo sono exiliente, vis sermonis exprimitur.[116]

In what way 'of the articulated *vox*'? there are two *voces*, one is
articulated and one confused. Which one is confused? The one you
cannot write, for example the bleating of sheep, the whinnying of
horses, the lowing of cattle, et cetera. Why is it called confused?
Because the force of discourse is expressed by striking the air without
making any sound emerge.

Returning to the first part, in the third chapter, *de verbo*, one must consider at least the observations on the frequency of the use of the verb itself, 'word' par excellence precisely because it is used more than the other *partes orationis* (ll. 26–35):

> Verbum quare dictum est? eo quod aerem verberet, et aere verberato ictu linguae sonus exiliet. Non quia et omnes partes aerem non verberantur, sed quia istud plus utimur in locutione, ideo istud sibi nomen generale adsumpsit. Da ubi plus utamur, in locutione: 'volo ire ad forum, videre et salutare amicum meum', 'volo' verbum est, 'ire' verbum est, 'ad' praepositio est, 'forum' nomen est, 'videre' verbum est, 'et' coniunctio est, 'salutare' verbum est, 'amicum' nomen est, 'meum' pronomen est. Ecce quattuor verba, duo nomina, unum pronomen, una coniunctio et una praepositio.[117]

> Why is it called verb (*verbum*)? because it strikes (*verberet*) the air, and sound emerges from the air that is struck by the beat of the tongue. It is not that all parts of speech do not beat the air, but because we use this one most in speaking, therefore it takes the general name. Say where we use it most in speech: 'volo ire ad forum, videre et salutare amicum meum' (I want to go to the square, to see and greet my friend), 'volo' is a verb, 'ire' is a verb, 'ad' is a preposition, 'forum' is a noun, 'videre' is a verb, 'et' is a conjunction, 'salutare' is a verb, 'amicum' is a noun, 'meum' is a pronoun. Here are four verbs, two nouns, one pronoun, one conjunction and one preposition.

As for the eighth and last chapter of the first part, *de interiectionibus*, we must mention the precious evidence of *totto*, an allocutive element of baby talk without precedent in the whole of Latin grammatical tradition (ll. 19–25):

> Significatio interiectionis in quo est? quia aut laetitiam significamus ... aut dolorem ... aut admirationem ... aut metum, ut attat, sicut solitum est parvulo dici 'totto' quando prohibetur comedere terram.[118]

> What is the meaning of an interjection? Because we indicate happiness ... or sorrow ... or surprise ... or fear, like *attat* (ah! oh!) as it is usual to say to a small child 'totto' when he is forbidden to eat earth.

Finally, phonetic analysis deserves a brief mention; in the sixth chapter of the first part, *de coniunctione*, the orthographical rules given (ll. 39–76) start from the explicit realization of the numerous cases of homonymy deriving, as we know, from the processes of neutralization of some phonologic oppositions:

> Quae sunt ex his communes cum aliis partibus? ...'Quae' est pronomen, est et coniunctio ... 'At' est coniunctio, est et praepositio ... 'Ac' est coniunctio, est et pronomen ... 'aut' est coniunctio, 'haud' est adverbium ... 'Ve' est coniunctio, est et interiectio.[119]

> Which are the parts of speech that are the same as others? 'Quae' is a pronoun, and is a conjunction ... 'At' is a conjunction, and is a preposition ... 'Ac' is a conjunction, and is a pronoun ... 'aut' is a conjunction, 'haud' is an adverb ... 'Ve' is a conjunction and an interjection.

Some observations of undoubted importance to the history of phonetic changes that took place in Latin as it was transformed into the Romance languages are present in the above mentioned chapter *de littera*, concerning both the change [j] > [dʒ] and [b] > [v] (or at least [ß]/[w]), with the obvious inverse phenomena of hypercorrectness (11. 70–72):

> Harum [*scil.* vocalium], duae, 'i' et 'u', transeunt in consonantium potestatem. Quomodo? quia et pro 'i' ponitur 'g' et pro 'g' ponitur 'i', pro 'u' et 'b' ponitur 'b' et 'u'.'[120]

> Of these [i.e. vowels], two, 'i' and 'u', pass into the consonants' power. How? Because 'g' is used instead of 'i' and 'i' is used instead of 'g', 'b' and 'u' are used instead of 'u' and 'b',

and also concerning the articulation of dental affricates (11. 248–50):

> Quarum 'y' inter vocales habemus, 'z' inter consonantes et est duplex, ut 'Mezentius', quia si 'z' non fuisset per 'd' et 's' scribi deberetur[121]

> Of which we have 'y' among vowels, 'z' among consonants and it is double, as in 'Mezentius', which, if 'z' did not exist would have to be written with 'd' and 's',

without counting the fact that phonetic description takes place at times by giving as examples actual phonological oppositions (11. 80–81):

> Da ubi cum aliis vocalibus iungantur [*scil.* 'i' et 'u']: 'Ianus', 'vanus'.[122]

> Say where ['i' and 'u'] are joined with other vowels: 'Ianus', 'vanus'.

Finally, we must mention, within the *de syllaba*, second chapter of the second part, the extensive and reasoned discussion on syllabic quantity, and especially a correct presentation of the problem of the *positio debilis* (particularly 11. 70–83).[123] There is also an awareness of the distinctive function of the accent's position in words like *pone* and *ergo* (so that one could have *póne* [imperative] vs. *poné* [adverb/preposition] and, respectively, *érgo* [conjunction] vs. *ergó* [with prepositional value, evidently in syntagms such as *legis, victoriae ergo*]), on which see, still in the second part, the twelfth chapter *de accentibus* (11. 74–88).[124] This, then, is the picture that would present itself overall to the later, more mature treatise-writing of the early Middle Ages, especially within the British Isles.

We have already seen the interest directed prevalently at Donatus and his commentators by the writers on grammar up to the end of the eighth century. Only from the following century is there an ever-increasing reliance on the wider and more articulate treatises that the surviving Latin grammatical tradition could offer, a fact that certainly received a decisive contribution from the new impulse given to the study of the classics by the so-called Carolingian Renaissance.[125]

As we approach an examination of treatise-writing specific to the early Middle Ages, we shall mention first that the changed aims of the traditional Roman school, which by this time was increasingly devoted to the teaching of Christian contents, favoured in the first instance a kind of Christianization of grammar itself: Law (1982, 30–41) has good reasons to believe that one can hypothesize the existence of a re-elaboration of Donatus, a 'Christian' *Ars minor* – dating back perhaps to the fifth-sixth century – which was lost, but can be reconstructed as underlying works in the seventh and eighth century through texts such as the *Ars Asporii*, the treatise on nouns and pronouns associated with the *Congregatio Salcani filii de verbo*,[126] the two main versions of the *Ars Ambianensis*, the *Ars Bernensis* and perhaps also the grammar by Clemens Scottus.[127] From the linguistic material found in these texts one can infer that in the 'Christian' *Ars minor* there was a systematic revision of classical examples in favour of the insertion, in its place, of religious lexis.[128] However, what remains problematic is discovering the causes of its disappearance, the reasons why no direct evidence of it has been preserved, unlike the case of the above-mentioned texts.

A review of the numerous grammatical texts which can be attributed to the early Middle Ages – and which originate almost exclusively from the British Isles – may start by considering the *Ars Asporii*.[129] Nothing is known for certain about its author,[130] who seems to date from before the middle of the seventh century, as one could deduce from the fact that he is quoted by Virgilius Grammaticus, who was supposedly active in the years around 650, or the second half of the seventh century. Based on the presumed Christianized version of Donatus *Ars Minor*, the *Ars Asporii* also uses different material – attributable to sources we cannot easily identify[131] – using an expositive procedure that occasionally reminds one of the *Regulae Augustini*; an interesting item is the reformulation in wider terms of Donatus' definition about the accusative governed by Latin prepositions that take two cases, this definition being no longer limited to physical motion only, and being exemplified by verses from the Psalms where the 'bad' qualities of the accusative are contrasted with the 'good' qualities of the ablative.[132] The *Ars Asporii* quickly became widespread in the British Isles, was known to Virgilius Grammaticus and was used by Boniface,[133] Tatuinus[134] and the Anonymus ad Cuimnanum; it was accepted by the Continental schools from the eighth century, and was forgotten towards the end of the ninth.[135]

Dealing with Virgilius Maro Grammaticus, the famous author of the two grammatical treatises *Epitomae* and *Epistolae*,[136] is a much more complex matter. His historical and geographical placing is far from certain: he may have lived in fifth century Gaul or in seventh century Spain or Ireland, or even in ninth century France, even if – as we have just mentioned and will make clearer shortly – today people tend to place his activity in the area of the British Isles towards the second half of the seventh century.[137] Equally doubtful is the meaning of his work, which is full of inexplicably modern ideas and suggestions for analysis, and at the same time is a disorganized and incoherent accumulation of strangeness and absurdity, not just in a linguistic context, where the recurrent taste for a kind of *fictio* accompanied by irony and paradox seems to want to build a kind of parody of the metalanguage used by official grammarians, searching for a *Latinitas inussitata* which is for the most part merely amused luxuriant invention, born out of an undoubted predilection for verbal puzzles. The *Epitomae* and the *Epistolae* approximately correspond, respectively, to Donatus' *Ars maior* and *Ars minor*.

At the beginning of the first *epitoma*, entitled *De sapientia*, after a brief analysis of knowledge Virgilius reviews the 12 *Latinitatis genera*, exemplified by the 12 different words allegedly used in Latin to indicate fire.[138] In the second, *De littera*, the different levels of combination of the elements of the second and first articulation – from syllabic units to sentence structure – are curiously compared to the successive phases of human growth, supporting this parallel with a simile between the general human condition and the intrinsic qualities of linguistic *stoikheîa*.[139]

In the third, *De syllabis*, one seems to be able to determine the identification – even if expressed in partial terms, since the examples are limited to single phonemes – of an important phonological principle that was destined to become the general rule, as we are able to see today, of syllabic structure as this structure was gradually changing in the passage from the Latin system to a large part of the proto-Romance systems: that is the principle of complementary distribution of vowel length relative to consonant length. Using a wider formulation we could say that a closed syllable presents a tendentially short vowel, while an open syllable presents a tendentially long vowel.[140]

In the fourth *epitoma, De metrorum conpossitione*, Virgilius analyses, in a rather incoherent way, some poetic structures of a
decidedly medieval kind,[141] relying on criteria of rhythmic-accen-
tual evaluation rather than on the traditional quantitative patterns:
this is important evidence of a different relevance of accentual
values, which leads Virgilius to formulate an improbable phonological opposition between verb and noun elements based, other things
being equal, precisely on different stress positions;[142] the fourth
*epitoma* closes with a brief description of the *filosophiae artes*, only
approximately equivalent to the seven liberal arts: *poema*,[143] *rehtoria*,[144] *gramma*,[145] *leporia*,[146] *dialecta*,[147] *geometria* and *astrono-
mia*.

In the fifth to the ninth *epitoma* the *partes orationis* are widely
examined, in the same order in which they appear in Donatus' *Ars
maior*.[148] The tenth, *De scinderatione fonorum*, deals with the most
sophisticated and unusual techniques of word segmentation, and
reveals Virgilius' strong preference for the most unscrupulous ma-
nipulations of the signifier, a perversely sophisticated taste for
every kind of tinkering up to the most daring verbal puzzles.[149]
The eleventh, *De cognationibus etymologiae aliorum nominum*, deals
with etymology, explaining the origin and meaning of various
words by relying on an unspecified *Latinitas filosophica* which re-
discovers certain base values in syllabic structures shared by several
signifiers, with no concern about the position where these structures
are found within the signifiers.[150] *Epitomae* 12–14 have been lost,
and the fifteenth and last, *De catalogo grammaticorum*, presents a
curious list of characters, from the mythical Donatus of Troy who
was supposed to have lived a thousand years, to Virgilius Assianus,
teacher of Virgilius Grammaticus and author of a *Liber nobilis de
duodecim Latinitatibus*. As for the eight *Epistolae*, each one deals
with a specific *pars orationis*, from noun to interjection, and here,
too, elements of traditional doctrine are mixed with fanciful observations and unreliable quotations from a *Latinitas inussitata*;[151]
explicit references to sources that are wholly imaginary, or at any
rate unknown to us, support this curious mixture, which, however,
seems to presuppose knowledge of the main commentaries on
Donatus, as well as of Priscian and perhaps of Isidore of Seville.[152]
An evaluation of Virgilius' work which leaves aside his more
specious fancies, fruit of his undoubted personal expressive abilities
– he was himself an *actor* rather than a *grammaticus* – might
recognize within it the attempt to present a synchronic image of
written and spoken Latin such as Virgilius himself and his contemporaries spoke, rather than the wish to present a prescriptive code,
fixed and inherited from tradition in forms that tended to be

immutable; however, on the basis of what is known at present, the problem remains open.[153]

## 2.2.6 'Elementary grammarians' and 'exegetic grammars' up to the Carolingian Renaissance

We shall now mention the so-called 'elementary grammarians', prevalently found within the British Isles (Law 1982, 53–80), who, as one may easily notice, have a whole series of characteristics in common, such as the preferential treatment of the variable parts of speech, giving examples of these by means of paradigms and long lists of words mostly drawn from the Christian vocabulary, the almost total absence of theoretical comment to accompany the presentation of data and the consequent purely didactic aspect that generally pervades their exposition.[154] The first text to consider is the *Declinationes nominum*, a brief grammatical treatise consisting solely of the presentation of nominal paradigms, including lists of examples and very limited comments; it is attested in various versions, though it is very difficult to reconstruct the original text from them, and it seems to date between the end of the seventh century and the end of the eighth century and, because it contains material derived from Aldhelm it might presumably be traced back to an Anglo-Saxon rather than Irish background.[155] Tatuinus, who was archbishop of Canterbury in 731 and died in 734, wrote an *Ars*[156] towards the end of the seventh century: it is an elementary grammar along the lines of Donatus' *Ars maior*,[157] which has Consentius as its primary source and also makes wide use of Eutyches, Pompeius, Asporius and Priscian's *Institutio de nomine et pronomine et verbo*, while Isidore's *Etymologiae* are used only sporadically; it is similar to the *Ars Bonifacii* in its adaptation of material drawn from the classical grammarians, and it was fairly popular in continental Europe from the end of the eighth century to the early ninth, as one may deduce from an examination of the manuscript tradition.[158] Similar to the *Ars Tatuini* is the *Ars Ambianensis*, an anonymous unpublished work, probably dating from the eighth century and perhaps by an Irish author: it uses mainly Charisius, as well as Eutyches, Pompeius and the so-called Christianized version of Donatus' *Ars minor*,[159] and basically consists of an elementary grammatical exposition. In its treatment of noun and pronoun the *Ars Ambianensis* shows close correspondences with part of the text printed by Löfstedt in his edition of the so-called *Ars Malsachani*.[160] Another elementary grammar, which is anonymous and incomplete, but was originally longer than the ones we have just mentioned, is the *Ars Bernensis*,[161] whose time and place of writing still present many problems:[162] it is one of the most widely studied in the late Middle Ages, and makes great use of Priscian, Donatus, Consentius, Pompeius, Eutyches, Charisius, Isidore, Virgilius Grammaticus, and to a lesser extent Sergius and Asporius; it classifies nouns according to their formative suffixes, a system that makes it resemble the *Ars Tatuini*, the *Declinationes nominum* and the *Ars Ambianensis*, which use similar procedures.[163] Finally, one can place the *Ars Bonifacii*, a detailed presentation of the eight parts of speech modelled on Donatus' *Ars maior*, at the beginning of the eighth century.[164] Vynfreth-Boniface's cultural isolation as he wrote his grammar seems to be reflected in the fact that he did not take the contemporary tradition of studies into account, although it did not prevent his reliance on numerous classical sources, among them Donatus, Charisius, Diomedes, Priscian's *Institutio*, Audax, Phocas, Isidore's first book of the *Etymologiae*, perhaps the *Regulae Augustini* and the Pseudo-Cassiodorus, as well as more recent texts like Asporius, Virgilius Grammaticus and Aldhelm's *De pedum regulis*. Precisely because of its distance from contemporary models – and despite the fact that it can be considered superior to them as a synthesis of classical grammar – the *Ars Bonifacii* did not become very popular within scholastic teaching.[165]

The 'exegetic grammars' (Law 1982, 81–97), so called because they applied some of the techniques of scriptural exegesis, especially to Donatus' *Ars maior*, deserve a separate mention. They date from the pre-Carolingian period, were written in the British Isles, and were very popular among the learned men of the ninth century; one of their specific characteristics is frequently the way the commentary on every single grammatical phenomenon is presented in the form of question and answer,[166] which will later become so popular in the development of dialectics. They are an ideal – though indirect – anticipation of the multiple interconnections between grammar, logic and theology that formed in the late Middle Ages, and at times they set up parallelisms between grammatical phenomena and religious concepts, explaining the former in the light of the latter.[167] Among the traits shared by this type of grammar one must mention the frequent references to Greek and Hebrew,[168] the interest for the compilation of lists of synonyms and the review of *loci* as a preliminary to the exposition of the concepts. This last trait was destined to become customary, and as a consequence was codified in rhetorical treatise writing from the twelfth century onwards.[169] The first 'exegetic grammar' in chronological order is an anonymous treatise whose incipit is *Quae sunt quae omnem veritatem scripturae commendant*,[170] dating from the end of the seventh century or the first decades of the eighth;[171] it is patterned on Donatus' *Ars minor* as far as the examination of the *partes orationis* is concerned – and is therefore an exception compared to other similar works, which follow the *Ars maior* on this subject – and it gives ample space to quotations from the Bible and the Fathers of the Church, often attempting to give a religious explanation for the grammatical phenomena that are being analysed, and showing an interest in several instances for Greek, Hebrew and etymological research.[172] Another grammar belonging to the same trend is the one by the Anonymus ad Cuimnanum, who worked in Ireland, presumably in the period from the end of the seventh century to the first half of the eighth:[173] it, too, applies interpretative criteria mediated by scriptural exegesis to linguistic analysis, showing an interest for Greek – which is owed more to the late Latin grammatical tradition rather than to Christian patristics – and developing in the form of a commentary to Donatus' *Ars maior*, preceded by an introduction to the *partes philosophiae*; Pompeius and Consentius are its principal sources, though they are used very freely, and other sources are Diomedes, Martianus Capella's third book, Maximus Victorinus or Audax, Isidore, Asporius, Eutyches and the Bible itself, a text from which many examples are drawn.[174] Then we have the *Congregatio Salcani filii de verbo*, commonly known as *Ars Malsachani*,[175] which makes a detailed analysis of verb and participle. It is the work of an Irishman, whose activity may have taken place either in the insular or continental area, and it can be placed within the eighth century,[176] very probably drawing much classical material from various intermediate sources, one of which was supposedly used by Clemens Scottus as well,[177] while another is shared by the anonymous compilation *Sapientia ex sapore*. Despite its abundance of materials, which mostly make up an exegesis of the Donatian definition of the verb, the *Congregatio* was not very popular, and shared in the decline of the other insular grammars after the middle of the ninth century. Another, very brief, text, known from the incipit as *Aggressus quidam*, consists of a partial re-elaboration of the section in Donatus' *Ars maior* that deals with the noun.[178] Its author seems to have been an Irishman who lived in France in the seventh or eighth century, and he seems curiously insistent in applying triadic patterns, based on the *auctoritas scripturarum*, to grammatical analysis: he claims that there are three tenses, three *modi* (*locus, tempus, persona*), three persons of the verb, and so on.[179] Finally, the *Ars Ambrosiana* presents itself as a commentary on the section in Donatus' *Ars maior* concerning the parts of speech. It can be placed, with much uncertainty, somewhere between the middle of the sixth century and the ninth – the latter being the time when the only codex where it can be found was presumably written[180] – and it seems unlikely that it was the work of an Irishman.[181] The sources it uses, basically of late Latin provenance,[182] include Pompeius, Consentius, Charisius, Diomedes, Maximus Victorinus, Priscian, Sacerdos, Sergius and the Pseudo-Cassiodorus, including many authors who were completely unknown in the British Isles, and who, on the other hand, are almost all present in the tenth century catalogue of the library in the monastery at Bobbio. This is another reason in favour of placing the *Ars Ambrosiana* in a Mediterranean rather than a northern environment.

The insular grammatical tradition continued mainly in the Carolingian era, when the conspicuous interest in the study of the classics prepared particularly favourable ground for the development of linguistic and exegetic treatise writing. In this context we have first of all the *Ars Donati quam Paulus Diaconus exposuit*,[183] based mostly on Donatus' *Ars minor*, with some reference to the *Ars maior* and especially with lists of examples accompanying the paradigms of nominal declensions, lists that, although they follow insular models, could be of continental origin.[184] Pietro da Pisa's *Ars* combines the characteristics of an elementary grammar with those of a more properly exegetic grammar,[185] and is presented as a detailed commentary on the Donatian text, with etymological observations on grammatical terms. In it, reminiscences of the late Latin commentaries on Donatus and of Iulianus Toletanus are found side by side with materials of clearly insular origin.[186] The *Ars grammatica* attributed to Clemens Scottus[187] has very similar characteristics. It is partly written in question and answer form on the model of the two we have just mentioned; it employs insular sources,[188] the usual late Latin material and Alcuin's grammar, joining some traits of elementary exposition with etymological explanations and comments typical of the purest exegetic tradition. Among the most interesting elements of the *Ars Clementis* we must mention first of all the definition of dialectics – which together with rhetoric is a part of logic, the latter being one of the three divisions of *Philosophia* – especially for what concerns the summary formulation of its procedures. This formulation was destined to be particularly successful in the often anonymous scholastic manuals of the period immediately following:

> dialectica vero est disciplina ad disserendas rerum causas inventa et per disputandi regulam intellectum mentis acuit et per hanc rationem a falsis vera distinguit. et in conquirendo ita sententiam eloquio armat, ut obiecta sine ulla dilatione et difficultate reiciat. et in disputando efficacia quattuor haec agit: proponit, assumit, confirmat testimoniis atque concludit

dialectics is the discipline found in order to discuss the causes of things, and through the rule of disputation it sharpens the intellect of the mind, and for this reason it distinguishes true things from false. And by this procedure it arms discourse with eloquence in such a way that it rejects objections without delay or difficulty. And in disputation it effectively achieves these four things: it proposes, assumes, confirms with proof and concludes (XIV, 5–7, Tolkiehn 1928, 9, 11. 23–8).

Another important element is the clear and well-argued presentation of the subjects studied by grammar, especially in what concerns the proposition and its minor and minimal parts, resulting from the process of segmentation of the linguistic chain into ever smaller successive units:

> vox, a qua grammaticorum ars incohat, aer est tenuissimus sonus videlicet sensibilis, qui proprie auribus accidit. Littera vero pars est minima vocis articulatae, quae iter ad legendum discentibus praebet. syllaba est comprehensio litterarum vel unius vocalis enuntiatio et temporum capax, dictio pars minima est vocis constructae plenumque sensum habentis. oratio est ordinatio dictionum congruam sententiam perfectamque demonstrans et est oratio dicta quasi oris ratio. definitio est brevis oratio unamquamque rem propria significatione concludens, ut 'homo animal est mortale, rationale, risus capax'. sed hoc intuendum est, quod definitio ad omnes disciplinas et res pertinet ... per vocem enim, ut praediximus, efficiuntur litterae; de litteris efficiuntur syllabae; de syllabis partes orationis octo nascuntur; de ipsis vero octo partibus omnis metrica prosalisque oratio efficitur

> the *vox*, from which the art of the grammarian begins, is very faint air, that is perceptible sound, which strikes the ear. A letter is the smallest part of the articulated *vox*, which offers the way of reading to the learner. A syllable is the taking together of letters, or the enunciation of a single vowel, and is able to take quantity, word (*dictio*) is the smallest part of a constructed *vox* which has full sense. Speech (*oratio*) is the ordering of words into a coherent and perfect sentence, and it is called *oratio* as if *oris ratio*. A definition is a brief speech which describes each thing with its meaning, like 'man is a mortal rational animal able to laugh'. But one must consider this, that a definition should be relevant to all disciplines and things ... with those *voces* we mentioned earlier, letters are made; syllables are made from letters; from syllables are born the eight parts of speech; indeed from these eight parts is made every speech in prose and verses (XX, 5–11 and XXI, 4, Tolkiehn 1928, 12, 11. 9–19 and 13, 11. 25–8).

But the *Ars Clementis* can be assigned an important place in the history of the evolution of grammatical theory for two points in particular, we believe: first of all the definition of the linguistic act in terms that are a concrete prelude to its interpretation as it can be found in the late speculative grammar of the *Modistae*, and secondly the recognition of the different aspectual values inherent in the single forms of the verbal preterite. Although both points are already found – as we shall see shortly – in Alcuin's work (the first one is influenced by Boethius, the second one by Priscian), the merit for having guessed their theoretical importance belongs undoubtedly to Clemens Scottus, who, as a consequence, contributed to their spread, or at least to their confirmation within the scientific community, subsuming them among the decidedly less repetitive elements of his own grammatical treatise; on this, see XXII, 8–9 (Tolkiehn 1928, 14, 11. 14–17): 'nec minus et hoc intuendum, quod omnis collocutio vel disputatio tribus modis constat: rebus, intellectu et vocibus. res vero sunt, quas animi ratione percipimus; intellectus, quibus res ipsas addiscimus; voces, quibus res intellectas proferimus' ('nor should one pay less attention to the fact that every speech or disputation consists of three modes: things, intellect and *voces*. Things are those which we perceive with the reason of the soul; the intellections are those with which we learn these things; *voces* are those with which we utter the things we have understood'), and also CXVI, 3–6 (Tolkiehn 1928, 71, 11. 8–18):

> universa, quae agimus, in tres dividuntur partes; ideo tria tempora esse dicimus. Tempora verborum quot sunt? Quinque secundum naturam: praesens, quod alio nomine instans vocatur, ut 'lego', praeteritum, ut 'legi', futurum, ut 'legam'. sed praeteritum tempus quadam necessitate in tres dividitur distantias; una imperfecta appellatur, quasi inchoativa sed nondum perfecta, ut 'legebam', alia proxima huic, sed tamen actum perfectum et consummatum ostendit, ut 'legi heri', quaedam vero, quae multo ante dicimus transacta, ut 'legeram', et ideo quinque tempora in declinatione verbi numerantur

> all ways in which we act are divided into three parts; therefore we say there are three tenses. Which are the tenses of verbs? Five according to nature: the present, which is called instant by another name, like *lego*, the preterite, like *legi*, the future, like *legam*. But the preterite tense is divided by necessity into three distances; one is called imperfect, as if inchoative but not yet perfect, like *legebam*, the next one is near to this, but it shows a perfected and completed act, like *legi heri*, and the one which we consider to have been completed much earlier, like *legeram*, and therefore we count five tenses in the declination of verbs.

As for the *Dialogus Franconis et Saxonis de octo partibus orationis* by Alcuin[189], it is decidedly outside the insular tradition, despite Alcuin's own origins, since he had taught in the school in York before officially joining the Carolingian court from 781; the structure of the exposition following a question and answer pattern, such as was followed in part, as we have just mentioned, by Paulus Diaconus and Pietro da Pisa, is much less stereotyped in Alcuin's work, where we find a real narrative dimension unfolding within the structure of a dialogue whose exchanges are not merely repetitive. Among the most interesting and undoubtedly new elements characterizing Alcuin's *Dialogus* – later repeated, as we have just seen, in the *Ars Clementis* – we must mention first of all the specific illustration of the linguistic act, influenced by Boethius, where it is already possible to discern the procedural basis that will lead to the later formulation of the theory of the *modi significandi*; on this, see PLM CI, 854 C-D:

> a voce, cuius causa litterae sunt inventae, inchoandam disputationem constat: vel magis primo omnium interrogandum est, quibus modis constet disputatio? ... Tria sunt quibus omnis collocutio disputatioque perficitur, res, intellectus, voces. Res sunt, quae animi ratione percipimus. Intellectus, quibus res ipsas addiscimus. Voces, quibus res intellectas proferimus; cuius causa, ut diximus, litterae inventae sunt

> It results that one must start disputation from the *vox*, to express which letters were invented: or rather, first of all one must ask, of which modes does disputation consist? ... There are three things of which every discourse and disputation consists, things, intellections, *voces*. Things are the ones we perceive with the reason of the soul. The intellections are the ones with which we learn these things. *Voces* are the ones with which we utter the things we have understood; and for their sake, as we say, letters were invented.

It is no chance that this statement is made by the *magister*, to whom the two *discipuli* protagonists of the dialogue expressly appeal (*ibid.* 854 B): 'si quid altius sit interrogandum, vel ex philosophica disciplina proferendum' ('if something deeper is to be asked, or uttered from philosophical discipline'), and therefore acquires special importance compared to the rest of the exposition. The clear repetition can be observed of the classical four-part division of the *vox* into *articulata, inarticulata, litterata* and *illitterata* (*ibid.* 854 D), and of the traditional four levels of successive segmentation of linguistic units, *sententia*, single *partes orationis*, *syllaba* and *littera* (ibid. 855 A), the repetition of the definition of *grammatica* as 'litteralis scientia, et ... custos recte loquendi et scribendi; quae constat natura, ratione, auctoritate, consuetudine' ('science of letters, and ... protector of correct speech and writing; which consists of nature, reason, *auctoritas*, usage') (*ibid.* 857 D), and of the presentation respectively of *dictio* and *oratio* as 'pars minima vocis constructae, plenumque sensum habentis' ('smallest part of the construed *vox*, which has complete sense') and as 'ordinatio dictionum, congruam sententiam perfectamque demonstrans' ('ordering of words, which offers a coherent and perfect sentence') (*ibid.* 856 A) – which is all stated by the *magister*. One

will also notice the re-statement (which is also influenced by
Boethius) of the principle of arbitrariness of the linguistic sign –
still attributed to the *magister* – which is exemplified by the simple
comparison of the different denominations of gold in Latin and in
Greek: '*Secundum placitum*, id est compositionem singularum gentium sunt nomina composita, ut quod Latine dicis aurum, hoc
Graece dicitur χρυσός. Una est substantia, sed diversa nomina'
('Names are formed by convention, that is according to the agreement of individual peoples, so where the Latins say *aurum*, the
Greeks say *khrusós*. The substance is one, but the names are
different') (*ibid*. 859 B-C). Although they are descended from
Priscian, no less deserving of consideration are the recognition of
the 'aspectual' diversity inherent in the different forms of the
preterite, or the classification of the three persons of the verb
which is effected by opposing the first two to the third in terms of
*determinate* vs. *indeterminate*, as well as the functional interpretation of the apocope that characterizes the four imperatives *dic*, *duc*,
*fac*, *fer*; see *ibid*. 875 D:

> *Fr.* Tempora quot sunt? – *Saxo.* Tria secundum naturam: praeteritum,
> ut legi; praesens, ut lego; et futurum, ut legam. Quadam tamen necessi-
> tate praeteritum tempus in tres dividitur distantias; quia quaedam sunt
> quae multo ante dicimus transacta, ut legeram. Aliquando quaedam
> quae paulo ante, ut legi heri. Quaedam inchoata sunt, sed nondum
> perfecta, ut legebam

> *Fr.* How many are the tenses? *Saxo.* Three according to nature: the
> preterite, like *legi*; the present, like *lego*; and the future, like *legam*. The
> preterite tense is divided by necessity into three distances; in fact some
> things which we say took place a long time earlier, like *legeram*.
> Sometimes some took place a short time earlier, like *legi heri*. Some are
> begun, but not yet completed, like *legebam*,

then 881 D: 'Personae verborum tres sunt . . . Et primae quidem et
secundae verborum personae finitae sunt; praesentes enim demon-
strant. Tertia vero infinita est, itaque eget plerumque praenomine,
ut definiatur' ('there are three persons in verbs . . . And the first
and second persons of the verb are finite; in fact they indicate those
who are present. But the third person is indefinite, indeed most of
the time it needs a pronoun in order to be defined'), and finally 882
D: 'Sic fac, duc, dic, fer, placuit auctoribus per apocopam proferri
differentiae causa, ne si face, duce, dice, fere, diceremus, aliud
significare putaremus' ('Thus authors liked to express *fac*, *duc*, *dic*,
*fer* with an apocope in order to differentiate them, because if we
said *face*, *duce*, *dice*, *fere*, we would seem to be saying something
else').

Alcuin draws heavily on Donatus, but mostly on Priscian and other late Latin grammarians, following the tendency to return to the classics that was typical of the Carolingian Renaissance, and starting a trend that will become increasingly well-established in the course of the ninth century. This trend was a consequence of the rediscovery of Priscian's *Institutiones grammaticae*, which earlier were almost unknown.[190] We can place Rabanus Maurus along the same lines, with his *Excerptio de arte grammatica Prisciani*,[191] a collection of prosodic matters based on Priscian's *Institutiones* which was destined to enjoy a certain amount of success in the almost total absence of any kind of manual-writing specifically aimed at illustrating the study of prosodic and metric facts; a disciple of Rabanus Maurus, Walahfrid Strabo seems to have been responsible for a series of adaptations of Donatus' and Priscian's work, the latter in an extremely abbreviated form.[192] So there is an increasing number of extracts and summaries from the late Latin grammarians, like the *Excerptum Prisciani grammatici de V declinationibus*, or similar compilations of materials drawn from Pompeius, Diomedes and Charisius.[193] We must also mention an anonymous *Donatus ortigraphus* among the works that use mainly late Latin grammar; its author could be a ninth century Irishman working in France.[194] But the insular model of exegetic grammars did not disappear altogether: examples of it are the *Commentum in Donati Artem maiorem* by the Irishman Murethach,[195] who was working in France around 840, the *Tractatus super Donatum* by Erchanbert,[196] the grammar by Ursus of Benevento,[197] and above all the *Liber in partibus Donati* by Smaragdus, abbot of Saint-Mihiel-sur-Meuse.[198] For an exemplification of the co-existence, in the *Liber* by the abbot of Saint-Mihiel, of grammatical explanation and theological interpretation of the linguistic categories, see the following passages, which are paradigmatic of an obstinate application of the *auctoritas Scripturarum* to the exegesis of linguistic facts:

> Multi plures, multi vero pauciores partes esse dixerunt. Modo autem octo universalis tenet ecclesia, quod divinitus inspiratum esse non dubito. Quia enim per notitiam Latinitatis maxime ad cognitionem electi veniunt Trinitatis et ea duce regia gradientes itinera festinant ad supernam tenduntque beatitudinis patriam, necesse fuit, ut tali calculo Latinitatis compleretur oratio. Octavus et enim numerus frequenter in Divinis Scripturis sacratus invenitur

> It is said that there are many more or many fewer parts of speech. The church believes that there are only eight, which I do not doubt to have been divinely inspired. Indeed, because through the study of Latinity the elect mostly reach knowledge of the Trinity, and with its guide,

moving along royal paths, they hurry and tend towards the higher
realm of beatitude, it was necessary that Latin speech should correspond
to this calculation. In fact the number eight frequently appears as a
sacred number in the Scripture. (*Liber* cit., 1986, 1 T, 17–24),

Sunt item nomina incerti generis inter masculinum et femininum, ut
cortex radix silex finis stirps dies pinus pampinus. In his omnibus
Donatum non sequimur, quia fortiorem in Divinis Scripturis auctori-
tatem tenemus. Corticem enim, silicem, stirpem et diem communis
generis esse non negamus: radicem vero et finem et pinum feminini
generis esse Scripturarum auctoritate docemur.

There are also nouns of gender that is uncertain between masculine and
feminine, like *cortex radix silex finis stirps dies pinus pampinus*. In all
this we do not follow Donatus, because we consider the authority of
Divine Scripture to be stronger. Indeed, we do not deny that *cortex,
silex, stirps* and *dies* belong to a common gender; however, the authority
of Divine Scriptures teaches that *radix finis* and *pinus* are of feminine
gender (*ibid.*, 4 T, 119–25)

'de scala et scopa et quadriga Donatum et eos, qui semper illa
dixerunt pluralia, non sequimur, quia singularia ea ab Spiritu
sancto cognoscimus dictata' ('as for *scala* and *scopa* and *quadriga*
we do not follow Donatus and those who said they are always
plurals, because we know that they were set down as singular by
the Holy Spirit') (*ibid.*, 5 T, 62–4),

Aliqui etiam hoc ipsud scribentes dixerunt, quod 'ipse' pronomen sit
dignitatis, 'iste' vero abiectionis, sed falluntur. Falsum enim est. Invenimus enim 'ipse' et pro dignitate et pro abiectione, similiter 'iste' et pro
dignitate et pro abiectione. Nullam enim hinc differentiam scriptores
Divinarum fecerunt Scripturarum, sed indifferenter istis particulis usi sunt

Others have also written the same thing, that *ipse* is an honorific
pronoun, and *iste* on the other hand a pejorative pronoun, but they are
wrong. This is false. We find *ipse* used as an honorific and a pejorative,
and in the same way *iste* used as an honorific and a pejorative. The
writers of Divine Scriptures made no difference between them, but used
these particles indifferently (*ibid.*, 8 T, 115–20)

'multi dicunt: Opus non est dicere "ego lego" aut "ego legi" aut
"ego legam", quia "lego" cum dicit aliquis aut "legi" aut "legam",
personam pariter absolute demonstrat et tempus. Sed nos, quos
Divinarum Scripturarum plura instruunt testimonia, haec dicere
non formidamus' ('many people say: there is no need to say *ego
lego* or *ego legi* or *ego legam*, because by saying *lego, legi* or *legam*
the person and the tense are clearly indicated. But we, who are
taught by the many testimonies of Divine Scripture, do not fear to
say this') (*ibid.*, 9 T, 52–7), 'Sunt . . . quaedam verba, quae infinitiva

dicuntur, quibus sicut et nominibus casum habentibus sic alia verba praeponuntur, ut proferantur, veluti dicas "da mihi bibere", "da mihi manducare" . . . Quam figuram locutionis multi Graecam esse magis volunt quam Latinam. Nos vere Latinam eam tenemus, quia in Divinis Scripturis eam invenimus' ('There are certain verbs, called infinitives, which are placed after other verbs just like nouns that have a case; as when you say *da mihi bibere, da mihi manducare* . . . Many believe that these figures of speech are more Greek than Latin. But we believe them to be Latin, because we find them in Divine Scripture') (*ibid.*, 9 T, 64–72), 'Quod vero dicit Donatus, quia clam praepositio casibus servit ambobus, quaerat lector. Ego autem non memoror, ubi accusativo in Divinis Scripturis serviat casui' ('Let the reader seek what Donatus says, that the preposition *clam* serves both cases. I do not remember where it is used with the accusative in Divine Scripture') (*ibid.*, 14 T, 217–9). The importance of the Bible is such that, starting from some of the linguistic usage in it, Smaragdus can recognize a new use for the imperative compared to those that were attributed to it by the classical grammatical tradition, that is the possibility of its being used in prophetic utterance:

> Qui modus aliquando solummodo imperandi, aliquando precandi, aliquando inridendi, aliquando, ut videtur, maledicendi affectu profertur. Sed si diligenter adtendas, non maledicentis voto, sed prophetandi dicitur mysterio . . . Aliquando maledicentis sono, sed prophetantis mysterio dicitur, ut in Psalmo: *Effunde super eos iram tuam* et *Effunde iram tuam super gentes, quae te non noverunt* et *Da illis, Domine, secundum opera illorum*; et plura talia

> This mood at times is used with the value of an imperative, at times of a prayer, at times for mocking, at times, as it seems, is used to curse. If you pay careful attention, it is not used in the expression of a curse, but of the mystery of prophecy . . . At times it has the sound of a curse, but it partakes of the mystery of prophecy, like in the Psalm: *Effunde super eos iram tuam* and *Effunde iram tuam super gentes, quae te non noverunt* and *Da illis, Domine, secundum opera illorum*; and several such others (*ibid.*, 9 T, 146–64).

On this subject, it will be useful to mention that examples of dependence on the Biblical text, or at least of acceptance of the linguistic rules drawn from it, are also found in anonymous treatises and grammatical commentaries from the ninth and tenth century, for which see, respectively, Thurot (1869, 65): 'Personae autem verbis accidunt III. Quod credo divinitus esse inspiratum, ut quod in Trinitatis fide credimus in eloquiis inesse videatur' ('Three persons are found in verbs. Which I believe to have been divinely inspired, so that what we believe by faith in the Trinity should be evident in discourse') and Thurot (1869, 81–2):

> Priscianus dicit quia communia in *er*, quae non exeunt in *is*, proferunt
> ablativum per *e* tantum, ut *hic* et *haec* et hoc pauper a paupere ... Ista
> est regula certa Prisciani, quamvis inveniantur in divina Scriptura etiam
> per *i* ablativum proferre. Auctores enim divinae Scripturae non timent
> ferulas grammaticorum, sicut Sanctus Silvester

> Priscian says that common nouns in *er*, which do not end in *is*, show
> the ablative only in *e*, like *hic pauper*, *haec pauper*, *hoc pauper*, *a*
> *paupere* ... This is Priscian's certain rule, although in divine Scripture
> one can also find the ablative in *i*. The authors of divine Scripture do
> not fear the rod of the grammarians, as St Sylvester

(where, incidentally, the *ferulas grammaticorum* is a clear reminis-
cence of Augustine). But as early as the end of the ninth century
one can notice a first break from this kind of exegetic tradition.
The numerous commentaries by Sedulius Scottus[199] and Remigius
of Auxerre[200] belong to a movement returning to the classics, since
they tend to be distant from insular models; this is the case even
more for the grammatical writings by Godescalc d'Orbais[201] or
Ermanrich of Ellwangen[202]

### 2.2.7 The tenth–twelfth century commentaries on Donatus and Priscian: first indications of the appearance of a speculative grammar. Petrus Helias, Ralph of Beauvais and Petrus Hispanus.

The commentaries on Donatus and especially on Priscian increase
in the course of the tenth–twelfth centuries:[203] grammar, the foundation and root of every discipline according to a famous definition
by John of Salisbury,[204] takes first place in the study of logic and
even of theology, particularly during the twelfth century.[205] On the
basis of Hunt's important studies on this matter,[206] we shall try to
trace a synthesis of the most relevant aspects of this wide linguistic
production.

One can consider first of all the *Glosule super Priscianum*
*maiorem*,[207] mentioned in three manuscripts dating from the
eleventh-twelfth centuries,[208] although neither its author nor its
approximate date of composition are known; among the most
significant elements characterizing it we must mention, on the one
hand, the hypothesis of a *primus inventor* or *impositor* of language
– an idea that will continue to be expounded up to the *Modistae*'s
speculative grammars[209] – and on the other hand, the observation
according to which every word must be judged not so much for the
way it is used in a certain construction, but on the basis of the
nature and purpose for which it was created, as an 'appropriate'
designation imposed by the *primus inventor* on a specific reality.[210]
These same problems are developed, in connection with the distinc-

tion between what is substantial and what, on the other hand, is accidental in each part of speech, by the so-called *Note Dunelmenses*, glosses to Priscian found in a Durham manuscript from the end of the twelfth century.[211] As one can easily deduce, we are now some way from the treatises dealing with basic learning of Latin grammar: in several cases the definitions given are consciously recognized as being different from those taught at the lower levels of primary instruction. On this subject one should consider the following passage from the *Glosule*, where the difference is clearly pointed out:

> Nota quod adiectiva proprie non possunt dici omnia mobilia, nisi comparationem sortiantur. Unde 'Grecus', 'Romanus' non sunt adiectiva, nisi large accipiantur adiectivum, licet puerilis instructio hoc habeat;[212]

> Note that not all movable nouns can be properly called adjectives, unless they receive a comparison. Therefore 'Greek', 'Roman' are not adjectives, unless one takes adjective in a wider sense, although children's teaching does so;

from the point of view of grammatical description pure and simple, discussion often slides towards the logic of language, encouraged to do so by the terminology, which is, for the most part, shared by the two disciplines. The distinction between these continues to be reinforced, even if often in conventional terms and more from a theoretical point of view rather than having specific effects on actual teaching practice.[213] Another very important element found in the *Glosule* is the definition of the verb, which is given by means of the concept of inherence:

> Et ideo dicimus quod nec actionem simpliciter nec personam agentem, sed actionem inesse persone agenti significat, ut currit. Nomen vero, ut cursus, quamvis significet actionem, simpliciter eam tamen significat, nec dicit eam inesse. Nec hoc negandum est quin verbum, cum inherentiam utriusque actionis et substantie significet, ipsam substantiam et actionem quodammodo significare dicatur, sed alio modo quam nomen, quia nomen significat eas per se simpliciter consideratas, verbum significat eas in hoc quod coherent.[214]

> And therefore we say that it does not mean either the action alone or the person who acts, but it means that the action is inherent in the person who acts, like *currit* (he runs). The noun however, like *cursus* (running), although it indicates action, indicates it simply as such, not as inherent in someone. One cannot deny that, because the verb indicates the inherence of some action and substance, the verb could also be said to indicate this substance and action, but in a different way from the noun, because the noun indicates them simply as considered in themselves, the verb indicates them inasmuch as they cohere.

Finally, in the *Note Dunelmenses*, we cannot neglect the discussion on the relationships that exist between nouns, verbs and co-radical derivatives, where distinctive divergent traits are present together with an underlying identity of meaning:

> Cum lectio, legit, lector idem significent, diverso modo hoc faciunt. Nam, ut per simile dicam, lectio significat lectionem quasi extra domum positam, legit significat eandem intrare domum, id est secundum hoc quod est in motu, lector de eadem agit ut de manente et quiescente in domo et hoc sine respectu omnino temporis. Eodem ⟨modo⟩ albedo albet album idem significant et alia huiusmodi.[215]

> Although *lectio, legit, lector* mean the same thing, they do so in a different way. Indeed, if we say it through a comparison, *lectio* means a lesson almost placed outside the house, *legit* means going into that house, i.e. it concerns a movement, *lector* deals with the same, with reference to a man who remains and rests in the house, without taking any account of tenses. In the same way *albedo albet album* (whiteness, it grows white, white) mean the same thing, and others as above.

The abovementioned *Glosule* can clearly be considered among the most important sources of that much more organic work, which became very soon a constant reference point for the *magistri* authors of speculative grammars, the *Summa super Priscianum*[216] by Petrus Helias, who taught in Paris around the middle of the twelfth century.[217] Although he starts from a traditional definition of grammar, seen as 'scientia gnara recte scribendi et recte loquendi' ('the science which knows how to write correctly and speak correctly'), whose *officium* is 'litteras congrue in sillabas, sillabas in dictiones, dictiones in orationes ordinare et easdem competenter pronunciare ad evitationem soloecismi et barbarismi' ('to order letters appropriately into syllables, syllables into words, words into sentences and to pronounce them competently, avoiding solecisms and barbarisms'),[218] Petrus Helias operates by this time in the context of complex theoretical reflection on linguistic categories: so 'the language of Priscian becomes a sort of metalanguage used to explain the categories themselves, in the sense of Latin as an idealized language, the object and instrument of study'.[219]

In every language there is an underlying *inventio* of categories whose task is to represent in a suitable way the referents' properties, as one can deduce from the following passage about the invention of genders: 'Videntes itaque auctores alterum de his sexibus in quibusdam rerum esse, in quibusdam neutrum, tales invenerunt voces, quibus sic substantias notarent, ut secundario significarent an aliquis sexuum inesset eis, an neuter' ('As the authors saw that one of the sexes was present in some things, and none in others, they found words, with which to note substances, and secondarily

indicate one sex, or none, inherent in it'.[220] We find a certain
tendency towards etymological analysis as opposed to the lack of
interest shown for phonetic analysis,[221] but decidedly the newest
aspect in Petrus Helias' work concerns the deepening, in a speculative sense, of Priscian's definitions of the parts of speech,[222] as well
as of the problems concerning syntax.[223]

The span of little more than 50 years separating the works of
Petrus Helias from Alexander de Villa Dei's *Doctrinale*[224] brings
another series of commentaries, especially on Priscian, which are
also amply illustrated by Hunt's research (1980): they are the so-
called *Promisimus* Gloss, mentioned in a manuscript from the
second half of the twelfth century, other glosses on Priscian –
among them the *Tria sunt* Gloss – mentioned in manuscripts that
can be dated from the end of the twelfth century to the whole of
the thirteenth, and the *Summa super Donatum*, which, with the
*Liber Titan*, is by Ralph of Beauvais.[225] Among the characteristics
typical of these closely interrelated texts, one must number first of
all the interest for classification of the various nominal derivation
suffixes on a semantic basis,[226] and second, the use of illustrative
quotations from the classics, especially from poetic texts like Virgil,
Horace, Ovid, Lucan, Statius, Persius and Juvenal,[227] but also, to
a lesser extent, from prose texts like Cicero's *De inventione*, the
*Rhetorica ad Herennium*, Porphyry's *Isagoge*, Aristotle's *Categoriae*,
*De interpretatione* and *Sophistici Elenchi*, Boethius' commentaries
on Aristotle together with the *De consolatione philosophiae*, and the
*De arithmetica* and the *De musica*, as well as Macrobius' commentary on the *Somnium Scipionis*, Servius' commentary on the *Aeneid*,
Isidore's *Etymologiae* and Bede's *De arte metrica*.[228] From a more
strictly theoretical point of view, we must take note of the importance of the following statement in the *Promisimus* Gloss:

> Sciendum quod in omni collocutione id est unius ad alterum locutione,
> tria sunt necessaria, res supposita, intellectus, vox; res ut de ea sermo
> fiat, intellectus ut per ipsum rem cognoscamus, vox ut per ipsam
> representemus intellectum. Et quia multi modi sunt intellectus oportuit
> multimodas esse voces, et ideo invente sunt minutissime particule vocis
> que soni elementares dicuntur, ut ex illis diversis modis variatis diverse
> voces constituerentur.[229]

> It must be known that in every dialogue, that is one person speaking to
> another, three things are necessary, the thing that is spoken about, the
> intellect, and the *vox*; the thing, so that one may speak about it, the
> intellect because through it we may know the thing, the *vox* so that
> through it we may represent the intellect. And since there are many
> kinds of intellect, it was necessary that there should be *voces* of many
> kinds, and therefore the very minute particles of *vox* were found, which

> are called elementary sounds, so that different *voces* could be made up
> from them in different ways

This is a lucid representation of the act of speech in that it
presupposes that, in order for communication to take place between
a speaker and a listener, there must be an objectual referent, a
concept by means of which one can know it (or rather, the intellect
inasmuch as it is able to know it, to gain conceptual knowledge of
it), and a verbal signifier through which to represent this concept.
It is not difficult to recognize here the beginnings of the doctrine of
the *modi essendi, intelligendi* and *significandi*, which will become
one of the theoretical foundations of speculative grammar. Finally,
we must mention the special attention paid by the School of Ralph
of Beauvais to the examination of syntactic phenomena,[230] which,
among other things, is deliberately confirmed by the *Promisimus*
Gloss in the definition of the principal duties of the student of
grammar: 'Hec duo, certa regularum assignatio et subtilis circa
iudicium constructionum inquisitio et solutio perfectum faciunt
gramaticum' ('These two things make a perfect grammarian, the
certain assignment of rules and subtle enquiry into the judgement
of construction and its solution').[231] Interest in syntax also fore-
shadows the developments of logical analysis of language, which will
be a prerogative of speculative grammar.

Between 1150 and 1175 we can place Petrus Hispanus' *Summa
super Priscianum*, a work generally known in the schools of the late
Middle Ages as *Absoluta*, from the incipit 'Absoluta cuiuslibet
discipline perfectio', mentioned in about 15 manuscripts dating
from the twelfth-fourteen centuries, some of which attribute it to
Petrus Helias.[232] The author should not be confused with his more
famous namesake Petrus Hispanus – who wrote, among other
things, the *Summulae logicales*, became Pope under the name of John
XXI, and died in 1277.[233] The treatise, which often uses whole
definitions and/or statements from Petrus Helias without quoting
its sources,[234] shows traces of the influence of dialectics, even if
this is kept separate from grammar, compared to which it pursues
other aims, such as the judgement on the truth or falsity of a
proposition.[235] As was characteristic of treatises of logic, the
*Summa super Priscianum* contains a very limited number of illustrative quotations from the Bible or from classical authors; the term
*modus significandi* recurs a little more frequently than in Petrus
Helias, even if it does not seem to be used in a technical sense.[236]
Petrus Hispanus could also be considered the author of another
work, whose incipit is *Strenuum negotiator*;[237] this presents, among
other things, an interesting discussion on the three terms *res,*

*intellectus* and *vox*, already mentioned, as we have just seen, in the *Promisimus* Gloss, as well as in William of Conches[238] and in other anonymous commentaries on Priscian.[239]

> Vide ergo quod in omni locutione, id est in unius ad alium locutione, tria sunt necessaria, scilecet res supposita locutioni, intellectus, et vox. Res autem necessaria est ut de ea loquamur, intellectus ut eo mediante rem intelligamus, vox vero ut per eam intellectus nostros representemus. Est igitur causa inventionis tam vocum omnium quam literarum significatarum manifestatio intellectuum. Cum enim oporteat nos plerumque intellectus nostros absentibus insinuare et hoc viva voce facere non possumus, necesse fuit vocem significativam inveniri ut ea mediante hoc faceremus. Ideoque invente sunt minime particule vocis que soni elementares dicuntur quas oportuit in compositione dictionum multis modis variari ut ex eis tam infinita vocum construeretur multitudo.[240]

> See therefore that in every dialogue, that is one person speaking to another, three things are necessary, that is the thing underlying the speech, the intellect, and the *vox*. The thing is necessary so that we may speak about it, the intellect because through it we understand the thing, the *vox* so that we may represent our understandings through it. The manifestation of the intellects is the cause of invention as much of all the *voces* as of the letters signified. Since we mostly need to make our intellects reach those who are absent and we cannot do so in person, it was necessary to discover the signifying *vox* by means of which we could do so. Therefore the smallest parts of the *vox*, called elementary sounds, were discovered, and it was necessary to vary them in many ways when composing words, so that with them one could create such infinite multitude of *voces*.

The *Liber derivationum* by Osbern of Gloucester also dates from the same period, more precisely from the third quarter of the twelfth century. It is a method for the teaching of Latin that was very widespread not only in Britain, but in the whole European continent up to the beginning of the Renaissance.[241] It was used by Hugutio of Pisa in his *Derivationes*,[242] it shows the effects of the discussions about the different areas of relevance of the etymological research which had spread in the second half of the twelfth century and were also reflected in the *Promisimus* Gloss.[243]

## 2.2.8 Normative treatise writing typical of the *Doctrinale* and the *Grecismus*. The Oxford grammatical school of the Late Middle Ages

In the course of the thirteenth century the most widespread manuals for the teaching of Latin were Alexander de Villa Dei's *Doctrinale*[244] and Eberhard of Béthune's *Grecismus*,[245] two grammatical expositions which were easy to memorize because they were written in verses,[246] respectively of hexameters only and hexameters and pentameters. They showed traces of deliberately classical construction, but with frequent errors of prosody that show an imperfect knowledge of vowel and syllable length, and were destined to become, in the course of the fourteenth century, the official texts prescribed by the statutes of the Universities of Toulouse, Paris, Heidelberg and Vienna,[247] besides being widely glossed as early as the second half of the thirteenth century.[248] Despite having its grammatical base in Priscian, the Latin described and commented by these two works presents, beside strictly classical elements, others that are specific to contemporary use, and particularly to ecclesiastical Latin,[249] considering them normative in the same way as the traditional Horatian, Virgilian or Ovidian *exempla*, and referring also to the terminology that had become consolidated in the field of logic. The *Doctrinale* was not aimed at an exclusively elementary public, even if it did contemplate the possibility of being explained in *lingua laica*, i.e. in the 'vernacular', by the *magister* whose task it was to teach it: 'si pueri primo nequeant attendere plene, / hic tamen attendet, qui doctoris vice fungens, / atque legens pueris laica lingua reserabit; / et pueris etiam pars maxima plana patebit' ('if at first the children cannot fully understand, / he will understand, who playing the part of the doctor / and reading to the children will open [the sense] in the vernacular; / and the greatest part will be clear also to the children'), nor did it claim to be original: 'pluraque doctorum sociabo scripta meorum'[250] ('I shall put together several works of my teachers'). A very similar case also holds true for the *Grecismus*, whose name derives from its tenth chapter, crammed with Greek etymologies, which in actual fact reveal how poor, with few exceptions, and how completely vague was Eberhard of Béthune's knowledge of this language.[251] We must mention that the glosses to the *Doctrinale* exemplify the use of *appositio* to indicate the construction of a noun qualifying another noun.[252] Moreover, the normal structure of the Romance sentence, where the constituent parts are arranged according to the SVO (Subject-Verb-Object) pattern, is clearly reflected in the 'debita et communis forma constructionis' ('due and common form of construction') in the 'communis modus in contextu partium orationis' ('common mode in joining together the parts of speech') – that is to say the *ordo naturalis*, so defined in contrast to the inversion of the constituent parts, or *ordo artificialis*[253] – as they appear in the so-called *Admirantes* Gloss.[254]

From the end of the thirteenth century to the whole of the fourteenth, speculative grammar will dominate the course of linguistic research, by this time heavily influenced by the rediscovery of the lost works of Aristotle: the systematic application of logic to

the study of language will leave the interest for exclusively normative, more traditionally descriptive treatises in second place; even
where it will survive longer, as in the case of the grammatical
production that flowered in Oxford up to the beginning of the
fifteenth century, this kind of treatise will feel the effects of the new
conceptual framework determined by the scientific change effected
by the *Modistae*. To the Oxford school, whose characteristic was
the study of grammar based in practice on the use of the *auctores*,
belonged Richard of Hambury, who died in 1293 or 1294, author
of a *Tractatus de octo partibus orationis secundum ordinem Presciani
et earum accidentibus* and of a *Summa*, also called *Questiuncule de
quatuor partibus principalibus gramatice et de octo partibus orationis
et earum accidentibus*, as well as – probably – of a work entitled
*Questiones difficiles de constructione partium et earum accidentibus*;
John of Cornwall (Johannes Brian de Cornubia), author of a
*Speculum gramaticale* dating from 1346; and finally John Leland,
who died in 1433, who wrote a certain number of grammatical
pamphlets about the main aspects of morphology and syntax.[255]
Among the classical texts most used by the so-called Oxford
grammarians we can include Donatus and Priscian;[256] as for the
medieval texts, the most widely used, especially by Richard of
Hambury and John of Cornwall, were Remigius of Auxerre, Papias,
Petrus Hispanus, the *Doctrinale*, the *Grecismus*, Uguccione's *Derivationes*, the works of John of Garland and, as far as John Leland is
specifically concerned, Joannes Balbus of Genoa's *Catholicon*.

For further information about that wide body of minor treatises
that developed especially in the twelfth–fourteenth centuries,
which was hardly original and prevalently repeated the most customary scholastic precepts about the 'correct' teaching of Latin, we
refer the reader to Thurot (1869, 11–54). These treatises are often
anonymous works, glosses, compendia and commentaries on Priscian, concerning the pronunciation and spelling of Latin, problems
of prosody, metrics and occasionally of syntax, but in some cases
interesting individual authors emerge, at least because at times they
provide, as we shall see, cues for synchronic analysis that are
important for us. We shall mention here the monk Paul of Camal-
doli in the twelfth century, then Peter Riga in the following century,
known for the poem *Aurora* (the Bible in verse), Boncompagno, a
teacher at the University of Bologna, Poncius of Provence, Parisius
de Altedo, all in the thirteenth century, and finally Bartolomeo da
S. Concordio, in the fourteenth century. Some of these authors
affect more directly and specifically the developments of that *ars
dictandi* (or *dictaminis*) that enjoyed such popularity especially in
Italy, but also had wide implications in French territories, at the

same time as the complex theoretical structure of speculative grammar was rising and becoming established north of the Alps.

## 2.2.9 Lexicographic activity

A detailed examination of Latin lexicographic activity as it became established in the Middle Ages would require separate treatment, because of the size and complexity of the subject; therefore we shall simply set down the essential points, following the outline offered by Bertini (1981), to whom we also refer the reader for a first, general bibliographic guide.

The Latin models that were supposedly followed by medieval lexicography can certainly be identified as a series of texts including first the *De verborum significationibus* by Sextus Pompeius Festus,[257] the works attributed to the grammarian Flavius Caper,[258] the *Saturnalia* by Macrobius,[259] the *De compendiosa doctrina* by Nonius Marcellus,[260] the *Expositio sermonum antiquorum* by Fulgentius[261] and above all the *Etymologiae* by Isidore of Seville, particularly book X of this work, which is wholly dedicated to illustrating, both in meaning and etymology, a series of words in alphabetical order, mostly according to their initial only.[262] We have already mentioned Virgilius Grammaticus' lexicographic activity – as it is expressed specifically in the XI *Epitoma*, entitled *De cognationibus etymologiae aliorum nominum*, which is full of impossible explanations, as an amused parody of the traditional procedures of etymological investigation, re-interpreting them with a provocative taste for paradoxical paronomastic associations[263] – and we have also mentioned Paulus Diaconus's epitomizing effort, practised towards the end of the eighth century on the above-mentioned work by Festus.[264] As well as these texts, one must mention at least the *Glossarium Ansileubi* or *Liber glossarum*,[265] compiled around the end of the eighth century, which formed the basis for the subsequent *Glossarium Salomonis*,[266] compiled in Sankt Gallen between the ninth and tenth century, then the *Elementarium doctrine rudimentum* by Papias, which can be placed about the middle of the eleventh century,[267] the already mentioned *Liber derivationum* by Osbern of Gloucester, written soon after the middle of the twelfth century,[268] but above all the *Derivationes* by Hugutio of Pisa,[269] probably dating from the years around 1160. To these we must add William the Breton's *Summa*, from the early thirteenth century,[270] and Joannes Balbus of Genoa's *Catholicon*, dating from 1286.[271]

The cultural importance of these latter lexicographical repertoires – one need only think of the importance Dante attributed to Hugutio – cannot be doubted, even if a scientifically appropriate evaluation seems totally premature at the moment, considering both the current state of research on the subject, and especially the lack, in many cases, of modern and reliable critical editions.

### 2.2.10 Grammars for the teaching of Latin written in other languages: the example of Aelfric

Among the normative grammars for the teaching of Latin, as well as the ones written in Latin that have been considered up to now, but outside their domain, particular attention must be paid to Aelfric's *Grammar* written in Anglo-Saxon but with the same basic pedagogic purpose.[272] Dating from 994–995, it fits into the background of a precise cultural programme promoted by the Benedictine monks and principally aimed at the clergy's education; Aelfric followed the *Grammar* with a Latin-Anglo-Saxon *Glossary* containing about 1300 words,[273] and a *Colloquium*, a kind of little manual on how to start a conversation in Latin,[274] works dating respectively from the years 997–999 and about 1002.[275] As for what expressly concerns the *Glossary* we must mention at least the ordering of the words, which were not in alphabetical order, but grouped, for evident didactic reasons, according to lexical fields of varying breadth (including designations of elements of the universe, of the human body, of society, of the family, names of birds, fish, terrestrial animals, plants and trees, parts of the house, tools and various objects), in a hierarchic taxonomic classification. This classification moved from the more general to the more specific categories, and was based on the succession of extensive terms which organize single sets of co-hyponyms subordinated to them.[276] Returning to the *Grammar*, one can first of all identify its sources in Priscian and Pompeius, as Aelfric himself explicitly states in the Latin preface;[277] each Latin definition is followed by its translation into Old English, but as the treatise continues there appear increasingly often some Anglo-Saxon phrases as explanatory notes that have no Latin correspondent at all. The Benedictine monk made a very interesting attempt at creating a tendentially homogeneous grammatical terminology in his own language, and he succeeded in this, not without difficulty, by means of opportune, though often complex and artificial borrowings and semantic calques: in any case the patterning of the morphology and at times even of the semantics of English on the model of Latin, if on the one hand it ideally corresponds to the tradition established by the Latin grammarians – who framed their own metalanguage on the basis of Greek grammar – on the other hand sets down the premises for a real 'synchronic grammar' of Anglo-Saxon, and in the last analysis the work of Aelfric can implicitly be read in this sense also.[278]

## 2.2.11 The grammatical description of languages other than Latin: the *Auraicept na n-Éces*, the *First Grammatical Treatise* and the *Donatz Proensals*

The grammatical description of languages other than Latin – which was destined to develop in the Humanist and Renaissance periods, hastened at the same time by the need to codify the vernaculars, which by now had risen to the rank of languages of culture – is not without significant examples in the span of the Middle Ages. One must mention first of all the *Auraicept na n-Éces*,[279] a didactic work that testifies that the elaboration of Irish grammatical thought had taken place, following the encounter of the indigenous culture with the essential theoretical models of the late Latin linguistic and cultural tradition. It is a variously stratified work, with prevalently rhetorical aims,[280] whose composition seems to have lasted for at least four centuries, starting from the middle of the seventh, and whose oldest portion is attributed to Cend Faelad. The *Auraicept* transfers the reflections of Latin grammar onto the Ogham alphabet and the structures of Old Irish, drawing mainly from Donatus, Pompeius, Consentius, Priscian, Isidore and Virgilius, while keeping its own autonomy and interpretative originality. On this subject one must remember the recognition of the phenomenon of lenition and the specific answers given by the Irish grammatical culture to the Latin theories of 'accents', which are known to include the questions concerning vowel length and aspiration: unlike the Latin grammarians, who followed more closely the teaching of the Greeks on the subject of prosody, the Irish tried to adapt the theoretical model they had acquired to the reality of their own language, recognizing one type of accent (an intensive stress) and the opposition of length as relevant to the analysis of their own prosodic system. Another element deserving consideration is the recognition, by the *Auraicept*, of five stylistic registers, which can be characterized on the basis of the different distribution of the lexical elements according to progressive deviations from the colloquial level.[281]

The four so-called *Icelandic Grammatical Treatises*, dealing with phonetic, orthographic and rhetorical subjects[282] are particularly important in the description of languages other than Latin; the first and most famous of them, already known to Rask in the early nineteenth century, has come to the attention of modern scholars of phonetics and phonology especially thanks to the 1950 edition by Haugen,[283] with translation and commentary: as Albano Leoni

(1975, 10) rightly points out, the interest which the *First Icelandic Grammatical Treatise* continues to attract 'does not lie so much in the strictly graphic aspect (the letters and the diacritic signs proposed are largely already known to the Anglo-Saxons and Scandinavian *scriptoria*), as in the complexity of analysis, especially for the vowel system, underlying the proposals about writing: in this short treatise new vowel segments are identified when compared to Latin, quantitative differences, for both vowels and consonants, are recognized, as well as the presence of nasalized vowels. Moreover, and this is perhaps the most interesting aspect, the text does not stop at introducing the innovations by listing and prescribing them, but shows that they are necessary, arguing in an explicit way what is implicit in any adaptation of an alphabet'. The brief treatise, which seems to date from the second half of the twelfth century,[284] on the one hand gives precious indications to enable scholars to reconstruct an archaic stage of Icelandic phonology, and on the other hand it would appear to anticipate interpretative instruments and analytical techniques, like the commutation test, distinctive opposition and even the concept of phoneme,[285] that will develop fully only in the twentieth century, by an understanding of the phenomena as apparently brilliant as it was destined to remain isolated. As for the sources of the anonymous *First Treatise*, precise identification appears to be totally unlikely; the terminology used, even where it is possible to recognize the presence of corresponding Latin elements, cannot be attributed to any one specific author, either late Latin or early medieval. Names have been pointlessly suggested, such as those of Donatus, Priscian, Diomedes, Isidore of Seville, Remigius of Auxerre, the *Anecdota Helvetica*, Sedulius Scottus and Clemens Scottus, whereas one must remember that 'the values of terms such as *vox, sonus, littera, consonans, potestas*, to mention just a few, are not the result of one author's reflection, but rather form the common property of a cultural context that stretches very far in time and space'.[286] The brief treatise basically consists of a proposal of orthographic reform: the Latin alphabet, insufficient for giving an adequate representation of the sounds of Old Norse, especially the vowel sounds, needs suitable amplification and adjustment, following the example of what had been done by Anglo-Saxon scholars. So, first of all, the anonymous author adds to the five Latin vowels *a, e, i, o, u*, the vowels *ǫ, ę, ø, y*, briefly describing how they are to be pronounced and written;[287] the need for these new signs is justified by the fact that the sounds for which they were proposed are important because they produce differences in meaning, as is clear from some minimal pairs used as examples.[288] In the same way the need to distinguish nasalized vowels from oral vowels,[289] and short from long vowels,[290] through 36 possible distinctions,[291] is then demonstrated; a brief digression on the problem of diphthongs concludes the section devoted to vowels. The treatment of consonants, as well as presenting a series of comments on individual letters,[292] dwells on the relationship between simple and geminate consonants: to indicate the latter it intends to use the corresponding capital letters, arguing the need to distinguish the two different types of consonants by resorting to examples of oppositional minimal pairs in a way that parallels exactly the procedure it adopted when describing vowels.[293] Compared to traditional grammars, which generally show little interest, if not actual inability, to adapt their formulations which are often repetitive stereotypes of Donatus and/or Priscian to the changed phonic reality of Latin or to realize the existence of Romance or Germanic vernacular languages, the anonymous Icelandic *First Treatise* undoubtedly has a very important place in the history of Western phonetics. This shows that it has reached awareness 'of the fact that the type of segmentation of phonic material put forward by the Latin alphabet was not the only possible one, or that, at least, it was not exhaustive' to give an adequate representation of the phonic reality of Icelandic.[294] In the last analysis, this is precisely the newest and most interesting aspect of the text, beyond any possible comparison with the modern acquisitions of structural phonology.

The second, and equally anonymous, Icelandic grammatical treatise knows and partially makes use of the first one, even if in several cases it is noticeably different compared to the earlier one: it centres on orthographical problems, but uses a technical vocabulary that seems for the most part to belong to the indigenous tradition, rather than being an adaptation or a specific, individual and original reformulation of classical or early medieval terminology. It is a list of rules without a precise purpose of reform, and unlike the first treatise, the second one also has a rather more heterogeneous structure, incorporating elements outside phonetic description in a strict sense, like the classification of natural sounds and the comparison of the sounds of human language with the notes of musical instruments, particularly, it seems, the notes of the hurdy-gurdy.[295] An attempt at distributional classification of phonetic elements – in some cases only of graphic elements – is certainly the most interesting characteristic of this text,[296] whose sources cannot be identified with absolute certainty: the different sections of the treatise seem to be traceable to a fairly composite background, whose hypothetical reconstruction does not exclude, among other things, the possibility that some definitions occurring in the *Modistae*'s speculative grammar may have influenced the anonymous author.[297]

Finally, the last two Icelandic grammatical treatises deserve at least a mention: the third one includes elements of orthography and phonetics, but also, unlike the first two and conforming with classical tradition, a brief exposition of the parts of speech, as well as a compendium of rhetoric and stylistics; the fourth treatise deals exclusively with elements of stylistics, almost as if it were a kind of continuation of the earlier one.[298]

Within Romance culture, the first description of a neo-Latin linguistic system is the *Donatz Proensals*[299] by Uc Faidit, a brief treatise which was almost certainly written in Italy – and principally for Italians to use[300] – around 1240, whose Provençal version has reached us together with a Latin translation which in many ways seems attributable to the same author.[301] It is characterized by an elementary exposition, basically following the model of Donatus, and has no specific theoretical interests; the brief work concentrates on morphology and lexicon – with long lists of words in rhyme, a real poetic dictionary that makes one suppose it was intended for those who expressly meant to compose in Provençal – and completely neglects phonetics and syntax. Its absolute faithfulness to the Latin interpretative model causes inevitable incongruities in synchronic description, even though there are examples of correct linguistic analysis, as when Faidit pertinently identifies the two-case system typical of a specific class of Provençal nouns.[302] A precise definition, both in terms of level of usage and of regional variation, of the linguistic register studied by the *Donatz Proensals* presents many problems:[303] the treatise does not seem to present itself as a grammar of the Troubadours' language, nor, on the other hand, as a grammar of the spoken language to be found in a geographical area with well-defined boundaries. Uc Faidit's work enjoyed a certain popularity, though only in Italy, was translated twice into Italian, and aroused a certain interest especially in the Humanist and Renaissance periods, in the context of antiquarian taste and curiosity in respect of Provençal, the prestigious linguistic instrument of the refined and elegant Troubadour culture.[304]

### 2.2.12 Elements of synchronic description of the different local pronunciations of Latin inferable from medieval Latin grammars

In the matter of phonetic description, even while they exploit in principle the notions and precepts typical of late Latin tradition, medieval grammars in several cases present general definitions and/or actual realizations that decidedly deviate from the classical

norm, and that cast light in various ways on the local pronunciations of Latin, particularly within the Romance territories, where it
is necessarily liable to the most noticeable interference with vernacular languages, both in the period when the latter were being formed
and during the centuries after they had become established.

One may observe first of all, in the context of general definitions,
the loss of distinction between vowel and syllable length, and the
consequent overlap of the two different notions; the fact is very
well attested in an anonymous comment to Donatus' *Ars maior*
dating from the ninth century: 'Positio quare dicta? A ponendo, eo
quod poete abstrahant duo dimidia tempora in metro a sequentibus
consonantibus, ut vocalis correpta queat esse producta habens ex
se unum tempus et ex sequentibus consonantibus alterum' ('Why is
it called position? From *ponendo* (to put), because the poets derive
two half lengths (*tempora*) in the metre from following consonants,
so that the short vowel may become lengthened taking one length
(*tempus*) from itself and another from the consonants that
follow').[305] The confusion remains in Petrus Helias: '[Vocalis]
longa positione est, quando propter duas consonantes sequentes
vel propter unam dupplicem producitur' ('A vowel is long by
position, when it is lengthened because of two following consonants
or because of a double consonant'),[306] and we can find it again in
Alexander de Villa Dei's *Doctrinale*: 'quando vocalem duo consona
iuncta sequuntur / aut unum duplex, producit eam positura' ('when
two joined consonants or a double consonant follow a vowel, it is
lengthened by position'),[307] it is confirmed by the *Admirantes*
Gloss: 'Dicit actor quod, quando due consonantes sequuntur unam
vocalem, ita tamen quod prior ex illis consonantibus se teneat cum
vocali, vocalis dicta debet produci per positionem' ('The author
says that, when two consonants follow a vowel, so that, however,
the first of these consonants is linked to the vowel, such a vowel
must be lengthened by position')[308] and is destined subsequently to
be perpetuated in school manuals to the present day.[309]

As for the phonetic analysis inferable from the indications on the
pronunciation of Latin, an anonymous *Ars lectoria* probably dating
from the tenth century already gives us a series of very interesting
observations on the subject:

> Sunt litterae quarum pronunciacio posicione litteratoria variatur. Sunt
> autem hae C G R S P T U X. C soni proprietatem, E vel I subsequenti-
> bus, exprimit, ut *cecitas*. Aliis enim adiuncta quasi Q profertur, ut
> *cadit, codex, culpa.* G isdem adnexa vocalibus enunciacionis suae idioma
> retinet, ut *Georgius*. Reliquis aeque et sequentibus debilitatur, ut *Garga-
> nus, Gotthus, gula*. R et S, cum vocalem utrimque admiserint, expressum
> sonum non habent, ut *esurit, deserit, visurus, adheserunt, scelerosus,*

*disertus, exosus*. Si vero ab ipsis dictiones ceperint aut in dictionum medio consonantem intrinsecus habuerint, expresse denuntiantur, ut *dispersit, subruit, res, sus*. In compositis quoque idem et agitur, exceptis dumtaxat ipsis ubi euphoniae causa prevalens videtur exposcere, ut *malesanus, presensit, resolvit, desolata, prosequitur, Iherusalem*, quod compositum esse ipsius interpretatio monstrat, et similia ... P, si aspiretur, sonum F obtinet, ut *Phaeton, Phineus, Phoceu*. T quoque, si aspiretur, ut C enuntiatur, ut *aether, nothus, Parthi, cathedra, catholicus, ethicus, Matheus*. Eiusdem necnon obtinet sonum, si duae subsequantur vocales, id est post ipsam, priore non tamen S precedente, ut *prophetia, silentium, etiam, quatio*. Sed providendum lectori ne errore implicitus T in similibus, ubi non est, ponere velit. Nam *amicicia, pudicicia, avaricia, duricia, malicia, iusticia, leticia* et similia denominativa, quae duabus sillabis primitivi genitivum superant, in penultimis C habere debent. Numquam enim T ante duas vocales, I post ipsam, priore non tamen S precedente, venire potest, ut *species, glacies, porcio, concio, nuncius, socius, ocium, spacium, propicius, tercius*, nisi sint primitiva a quibus T retineant, ut *scientia* a sciente, *sapientia* a sapiente, *prudentia* a prudente, *militia* a milite, *astutia* ab astuto, *peritia* a perito ... T ergo, S precedente, sonum non immutat, ut *modestia, ustio, questio* ... Non ergo I subsequente, T pronuntiationis suae proprietatem servat, ut *fateor, fatuus* ... In fine quoque dictionum D ipsius enuntiationem videtur habere, ut *et, it, aut, sonat, tenet* et similia. Excipiuntur *at* et *quot* ob differentiam, ne videlicet ab audiente *ad* et *quod* dici autumaretur, et *tot* et *attat* euphoniae tantum gratia: ita tamen ut non precedant N et S; nisi enim has duas ante se, cum finalis est, non recipit consonantes, ut *ast, est, post, constant*, tacent, dicunt ... U quoque sonum Y greci videtur habere, cum inter Q et E, ut *que* coniunctio, vel I vel A, necnon inter G et easdem ponitur vocales, ut *quisque, linguis, linguae, anguis, angue, inguen, unguentum*, licet ipsorum verba U non habeant, ut *lingis lingebam, angis angebam, ungis ungebam, ingeris ingerebam*. Nonnulli tamen imperiti per U scribi debere putant, decepti in verbis propter nomina et in nominibus propter verba ... X in simplicibus sonat dictionibus duplex, ut *exorcizo, exodus, uxor*. In compositis vero duplex non profertur, ut *exaro, exortor, exoro, exanimis, exacerbat, exarsit, exordiri, exordium, exosus* ...[310]

There are letters whose pronunciation varies according to the position of the letters. They are C G R S P T U X. The property of the sound C is expressed when E or I follow, like *cecitas*. When others are added, it sounds like Q, like *cadit, codex, culpa*. G connected to the same vowels maintains its proper sound, like *Georgius*. In the same way it becomes weaker when the others follow, like *Garganus, Gotthus, gula*. R and S, when they have received a vowel on both sides, have no distinct sound, like *esurit, deserit, visurus, adheserunt, scelerosus, disertus, exosus*. However, if words begin with such consonants, or have an adjacent consonant in the middle of a word, they are pronounced distinctly, like *dispersit, subruit, res, sus*. In compounds the same thing also happens, except only for the ones in which the cause of euphony seems to prevail, like *malesanus, presensit, resolvit, desolata, prosequitur, Iherusalem*, which is shown to be a compound by its interpretation, and other similar ones ... P, if it is aspirate, takes the sound of F, like *Phaeton, Phineus, Phoceu*. T also, if it is aspirate, is pronounced like C, like *aether, nothus, Parthi, cathedra, catholicus, ethicus, Matheus*. The same sound results, if two vowels follow, i.e. after it, but there is no S before it, like *prophetia, silentium, etiam, quatio*. But one must warn the reader not to let himself be put in error by wanting to put T where it should not be. *Amicicia, pudicicia, avaricia, duricia, malicia, iusticia, leticia* and similar nouns, which are longer by two syllables than the original genitive, must have C in the penultimate. In fact T followed by I can never come before two vowels, unless an S precedes it, like *species, glacies, porcio, concio, nuncius, socius, ocium, spacium, propicius, tercius,* unless their primitive terms maintain the T, like *scientia* from *sciente* (one who knows), *sapientia* from *sapiente* (wise), *prudentia* from *prudente* (prudent), *militia* from *milite* (soldier), *astutia* from *astuto* (cunning), *peritia* from *perito* (skilled) ... therefore T does not change sound if S precedes it, like *molestia, modestia, ustio, questio* ... Therefore if I does not follow, T keeps the property of its pronunciation, like *fateor, fatuus* ... Also at the end of the word it is seen to have the same pronunciation as D, like *et, it, aut, sonat, tenet*, and similar others. *At* and *quot* are the exception in order to differentiate, so that those who hear do not think that one says *ad* and *quod*, and *tot* and *attat* only for euphony: always as long as N and S do not precede it; indeed, when T is final, it cannot be preceded by any other consonant apart from these two, like *ast, est, post, constant, tacent, dicunt* ... one also sees that U has the sound of Greek Y, when it is placed between Q and E, as in the conjunction *que*, or I or A, and between G and the same vowels, like *quisque, linguis, linguae, anguis, angue, inguen, unguentum*, although the verbs of these words do not have U, like *lingis lingebam, angis angebam, ungis ungebam, ingeris ingerebam*. Some who are inexperienced think they must be written with U, deceived in the verbs because of the nouns and in the nouns because of the verbs ... X in simple words sounds with a double pronunciation, like *exorcizo, exodus, uxor*. However, in compound words it is not pronounced double, like *exaro, exortor, exoro, exanimis, exacerbat, exarsit, exordiri, exordium, exosus* ...

Despite some uncertainties in interpretation, one can deduce the following: a) the voiceless, bilabial aspirated stop [p'], typical of borrowings from Greek, is systematically realized as [f], that is as a voiceless labiodental fricative, at the end of an evolutionary process that has its roots in late Latin;[311] b) the voiceless dental stop [t] positioned at the end of a word, undergoes sonorization – except in the cases where it is preceded by [n] or [s] and as long as any possible opposition with an original voiced consonant is not neutralized – a phenomenon seen here in the context of syntactic phonetics, but having a much broader application and in any case going back to the formation of Romance vernaculars;[312] c) the voiceless velar stop [k] followed by palatal vowels and by the semivowel [j] advances its point of articulation presumably being realized as the palatal affricate [tʃ] or the dental/alveolar [ts], if not even as a simple sibilant – respectively [ʃ] or [s] – with a progressive weakening of the occlusive component, which in certain areas can lead, as is known, to the latter's disappearance, therefore risking confusion with the results of T + J;[313] d) the voiceless dental sibilant [s] tends to be realized as a voiced [z] when in an intervocalic position, as long as – one could add – it is not immediately preceded by a potential pause;[314] e) the rolled [r] has a tense articulation at the beginning of a word, while in an intervocalic position it has a lax articulation; f) one can infer the presence of a rounded front semivowel [ɥ] in the sequences *que/qui* and *gue/gui*;[315] the Latin sequence [ks], graphically represented by *x*, when in an intervocalic position is subject to a regressive assimilation phenomenon, and appears as [s:]/[s] or is reduced to the simple voiced sibilant [z].[316] Other interesting indications about consonantism concern the pronunciation of stop consonants placed at the beginning of a word and the lenition of the same stops in an intervocalic position; on this subject, see the following evidence from the *Tractatus orthographie* by Parisius de Altedo, written in 1297:

> *B* litera magnum habet sonum in principio posita, ut *bibo, bibi*, maiorem in fine, ut *Iacob, Achab*, mediocrem, si intercipiatur, ut *ambesus, ambigo* ... *C* litera muta suaviter sonat, *e* vel *i* sequentibus, ut *cecitas*, nisi interponitur *r*, ut *cremium* [?]. Aliis iuncta vocalibus grande sonat, ut *cadit, codex, culpat*. Magis quoque sonat in principio quam in medio, ut *occidit* ... Hec litera [scil. *D*] plus sonat in principio, ut *dominus*, in medio et in fine debilius, ut *adheret, id, istud* et *quod* ... *T* muta litera est que in principio dictionis posita magnum sonum habet, ut *tibi*, in medio [mediocrem], ut *retuli*, nisi geminetur, quia tunc bene sonat, in fine vero debiliter sonat, ut *legit, docet*.[317]

> The letter *B* has a loud sound when placed at the beginning, like *bibo, bibi*, louder at the end, like *Iacob, Achab*, and middling if it is placed in the middle, like *ambesus, ambigo* ... The mute letter *C* sounds more gently when *e* or *i* follow, like *cecitas*, unless an *r* comes between them, like *cremium* [?]. When joined to other vowels it has a loud sound, like *cadit, codex, culpat*. It sounds louder at the beginning than in the middle, like *occidit* ... This letter [i.e. *D*] sounds more at the beginning, like *dominus*, weaker in the middle and at the end, like *adheret, id, istud* and *quod* ... *T* is a mute letter that has a loud sound when placed at the beginning of a word, like *tibi*, [a middling sound] in the middle, like *retuli*, unless it is double, because then it sounds clearly, but at the end it sounds weakly, like *legit, docet*.

It is clear that there is a contrast between a strong articulation –

we could call it tense – typical of the occlusive at the beginning of a
word (whether the latter is voiced or unvoiced) and a weak – or lax
– articulation of the same occlusive when it is found instead in the
middle of a word in an intervocalic position, and is then liable to
lenition. Precisely on the subject of this phenomenon, some significant signs emerge from multiple orthographic recommendations
like the following, which can be drawn from the anonymous tenth
century treatise we have already quoted several times in the earlier
notes: '*Faber* per *b* ... nam per *v favi* scribitur' ('one writes *faber*
(smith) with a *b* ... but *favi* (honeycombs) with a *v*').[318] More
important indications come from the *Gramaticale*, an anonymous
fourteenth century treatise in hexameters – dating perhaps from
1337 – both for what concerns the pronunciation of the semivowel
[j] at the beginning of a word, presumably by this time a voiced
palatal affricate [ʤ], as one could deduce from the verse 'Non
amat ille Ihesum, qui fert ad prelia gesum' ('The man who takes a
*gesum* (javelin) to war does not love Jesus'),[319] and for what, on the
other hand, concerns the realization of the voiceless labiovelar
[kʷ], which comes close to being confused with the simple voiceless
velar occlusive [k] due to the weakening – if not the total disappearance – of its labial appendix: 'Si clames, quantum poteris, dices
male cantum; / Incipitur primum per *q*, sed per *c* secundum' ('If
you shout as much as (*quantum*) you can, you will say *cantum*
wrongly; / the first begins with *q*, but the second with *c*'.[320] It
seems superfluous to point out that all these phenomena relating to
the pronunciation of Latin in the late Middle Ages, as they appear
in the direct or indirect evidence of medieval treatises, are paralleled
in the historically provable changes that led to the formation of
Romance languages.[321] We have no particularly decisive evidence
regarding Latin on the pronunciation of the aspirate at the beginning of a word.[322] In the first half of the thirteenth century,
however, Boncompagno gives us very interesting indications about
Germanic aspiration, whether this is the true aspirate [h], the
glottal stop or the aspiration that accompanies the production of
the voiceless stops at the beginning of a word:

> Item nota quod omnia propria nomina virorum et mulierum in quorum
> principio est vocalis prima sillaba, secundum Teotonicorum consuetu-
> dinem aspirantur. Sane Teotonici ex natura ydiomatis proprii aspere
> verba proferunt. Quare frequenter dictiones aspirant et asperius pronun-
> ciant aspiratas. Aspirantur etiam apud eos *Henricus* et *Hermannus* et
> similia, et illos in aspiratione tali aliquando imitamur ... Teotonici de
> tribus vocalibus aspiratis faciunt unam interiectionem dolentis vel
> plorantis, videlicet *hahuhe* ... Aspiratur etiam *phi*, quod Francigene
> cum narium corrugatione pronunciant, quando abhorrent aliquid vel
> derident.[323]

Note that all proper names of men and women whose first syllable begins with a vowel, are aspirate according to the Teutonic custom. Indeed the Teutons pronounce words harshly because of the nature of their language. Therefore often they aspirate words and pronounce aspirates more harshly. Among them, *Henricus* and *Hermannus* and similar words are pronounced as aspirates, and at times we imitate them in this aspiration ... The Teutons make one interjection of three aspirate vowels, that is *hahuhe*, to indicate sorrow or weeping ... *Phi* is also aspirate, which the French pronounce with a wrinkling of the nostrils, when they abhor something or mock it.

As for the tendencies that showed in vowel production, the most interesting indications are about the phenomena of oscillation *i/e* and *o/u*, reflected in the well-known phonetic evolutions from Latin to Romance vocalism;[324] see on this subject the following examples, concerning specific orthographic recommendations that do not always conform to the classical norm, found in an anonymous orthography treatise dating from the tenth century: '*Abscondet, recondet, gaudet, ardet, dormet*, per *e* litteram ... *Crux, nux* per *u*. *Mox, vox*, per *o* ... *Dilectum, diligam, dilectio, diligit*, si de dilectione fuerit, per *i* scribitur, si de peccato fuerit, ut est *delicta*, per *e*. *Delectatio, delectat* per *e* litteram scribendum est' ('*Abscondet, recondet, gaudet, ardet, dormet* are written with *e* ... *Crux, nux* with *u*. *Mox, vox* with *o* ... *Dilectum, diligam, dilectio, diligit*, if it concerns love (*dilectio*), are written with *i*, if it concerns sin, like crimes (*delicta*) with *e*. *Delectatio, delectat* must be written with *e*'.[325] Also in an anonymous twelfth century orthographic treatise: '*Tempora*, non *timpora*. *Extemplo*, non *extimplo*. *Saltem*, non *saltim*' ('*Tempora*, not *timpora*. *Extemplo*, not *extimplo*. *Saltem*, not *saltim*'),[326] and finally in the *De dubio accentu* by Hugutio:

De *quatenus* dicimus quod scribi debet per *e* et nunquam per *i* ... De *protinus* dicimus quod potest dici per *i* ... et potest dici *protenus* per *e* ... *Saltim* et *saltem* dicitur sed in diversis significationibus ... *Tempus* semper debet dici per *e* et nunquam per *i* ... *Extemplo*, id est statim, per *e* debet scribi et nunquam per *i*

As for *quatenus* we say that it must be written with *e* and never with *i* ... About *protinus* we say that one can say it with *i* ... and one can say *protenus* with *e* ... One says *saltim* and *saltem* but with different meanings ... *Tempus* must always be said with *e* and never with *i* ... *Extemplo*, that is straightaway, must be written with *e* and never with *i*.[327]

We shall remember also the widespread prescription, from the twelfth century onwards, according to which one should write *dii, diis, hii, hiis* and pronounce *di, dis, hi, his*; as is found in the

anonymous *Opusculum de accentibus*: 'Qui in *dii* et *diis* ad differentiam *dis*, *hii* et *hiis* ad differentiam *is*, alterum *i* dampnant vel
utrumque pronuntiant ..., omnes qui sic emendant corruptores
sunt librorum, non correctores' ('Those who in *dii* and *diis*, as
against *dis*, *hii* and *hiis*, as against *is*, condemn the other *i* or
pronounce both ... all who make these changes are corruptors and
not correctors of books'), and likewise in Alexander de Villa Dei:
'*Hi* profers et *di*; debet tamen *i* dupla scribi' ('Pronounce *hi* and *di*;
but you must write a double *i*') and in the anonymous fourteenth
century poem *Gramaticale*:

> *Is* vult plurali recto sextoque dativo/ *I* duplex scribi simplexque legendo
> referri, / Ne par dicatur *eo* verbi vel videatur. / Sic quoque vult *idem*. Sed
> non dabat *hic* ita pridem./ *I* duc, sed simplex; tamen usus dat tibi
> duplex

> *Is* in the plural of the direct case, in the ablative and in the dative,
> needs to be written with a double *I* and pronounced with one when
> reading,/ so that it should not be said as if seeming the same as a part of
> the verb *eo*./ *Idem* also wants the same. But *hic* does not give the same
> rule./ Pronounce *I*, but simple; however custom gives you a double *i*[328]

On the uncertainties about *y*, see the following statements from an
anonymous thirteenth century treatise: 'Nos ... non utimur hac
figura *y*, nisi in dictionibus grecis vel barbaris, et non ubique. Unde
in multis dictionibus grecis vel barbaris dubium est an debeat scribi
apud nos per *i* latinum an per *y* grecum, cum nesciamus illas ex
toto latinas vel grecas vel barbaras, quia apud Grecos et barbaros
in quibusdam locis scribitur *iotha*' ('We do not use the letter *y*
except in Greek or barbarian words, and not in all of them. Hence
in many Greek or barbarian words it is doubtful whether they
should be written among us with a Latin *i* or with a Greek *y*, if we
do not know whether they are completely Latin or Greek or
barbarian, because among the Greeks and barbarians in certain
passages people write *iotha*'); and in Boncompagno: 'Quandocunque
post has litteras *p* et *t* aspirationis nota ponitur et dictio post
aspirationem *i* requirit, illud *i* debet sicut *y* grecum scribi vertice
duplicato cum puncto superius posito, quoniam pronunciatio ipsius
greci elementi ad sonum talium aspirationum accedit' ('Whenever
one places an aspirate after the letters *p* and *t* and the word
requires *i* after the aspirate, this *i* must be written like Greek *y* with
a double vertex with a dot placed above it, since the pronunciation
of this Greek element approaches the sound of such aspirates'.[329]
Finally, as for remarks about diphthongs, we can observe that: a)
*ae* and *oe* normally come together into *e*, although there are no
convincing elements to determine whether it was an open or closed

vowel – as is well known this is instead attested by the late Latin grammarians, by the Romance developments, respectively [ɛ] and [e] and later outcomes[330] – even if in some cases the first element of the diphthongs in question seems to have been pronounced, however weakly, and in other cases we are faced with what appear to be, at least on the level of orthographic prescription, over-correct restorations of the diphthong *ae* where classical norm envisaged a brief, or even a long, vowel *e*;[331] b) the diphthongs *au* and *eu* appear to be stable.[332]

## Notes

1. The importance of the seven liberal arts is well known – to the just mentioned *Trivium* one must add the *Quadrivium* made up by geometry, arithmetic, astronomy and musical culture – within late Latin education, which in turn is the direct heir of classical pedagogy: the almost definitive formation of the list of *artes* can be placed as early as the middle of the first century BC, between Dionysius Thrax and Varro; on this subject see Marrou (1948, 177), keeping in mind, within the vast bibliography on the subject, Norden (1898, II, 670–87), Appuhn (1900), Abelson (1906), Paetow (1910), Marrou (1937, 211–35), Koch (1959), Gibson (1969), Mathon (1969), O'Donnell (1969), Giacone (1974). It may be opportune to state at this point that we intend to give this analysis of medieval linguistic thought a fundamentally historical and philological slant, and that we intend to avoid – as much as possible – any arbitrary re-readings of the past conducted exclusively according to modern and/or contemporary interpretative methods, since we are convinced that filtering medieval linguistic thought (and, of course any other that is not contemporary) through the scientific models that predominate today means selectively discriminating between its acquisitions by undesirable value judgements, with the obvious danger of attributing inappropriately to it – and too early, in any case – theoretical intuitions and operative procedures which emerged and became established among scholars only in later periods. The same criteria are followed, in general, by the bibliographical indications provided, which can easily be increased according to the reader's specific direction of research, given the impressive number of works about medieval linguistics: the comprehensive and articulate surveys by Bursill-Hall (1975, 219–30; 1980b, XXVII–XXXVI) and by Koerner (1980, 265–99) remain an indispensable starting point on the subject.

2. On the different types of school – from primary education to the Universities – of which we have evidence in the various geographical areas of Europe, and on the culture that was at the same time the foundation and the object of teaching there, especially in the subjects relevant to linguistic, literary, philosophical and religious exegesis, see – apart from Norden (1898; II, 659–731), Marrou (1937; 1948)

and the other works mentioned in the note above – the contributions by Kaufmann (1869), Denifle (1885), Specht (1885), Denifle-Chatelain (1889–97), Fournier (1890–94), Clerval (1895), Salvioli (1898), Sandys (1903–8), Roger (1905), Watson (1908), Grabmann (1909–11), Manacorda (1913–14), Haarhoff (1920), Mengozzi (1924), Paré et al. (1933), D'Irsay (1933–5), Chenu (1935), Rashdall (1936), Lesne (1938; 1940), Courcelle (1943), Lorcin (1945), Quain (1945), Curtius (1947), Delhaye (1947), Hunt (1948), Smalley (1952), Bardy (1953), Delhaye (1958), de Lubac (1959–64), Riché (1962, 1979), Salmon (1962), Glorieux (1968), Delhaye (1969), Verger (1973), Arnaldi (1974), Contreni (1981); for other specific studies see the *Bibliography* of this chapter.

3. Among possible examples we may take that of the fifth century Gallo-Roman nobility described by Sidonius Apollinaris, whose culture resembles that of the aristocracy in the time of Pliny the Younger; see on this subject Marrou (1948, 346) and Riché (1962, 74).

4. As one may judge from the actions of Valentinian I, who called Ausonius to educate his son Gratianus and was not averse to interests in the problems of instruction, cf. Marrou (1948, 309).

5. See on this respect Marrou (1948, 309), who mentions such behaviour by Stilicho, Alaric and Theodoric II.

6. Manifest oppositions to pagan tradition concern not so much the system and methods of classical education, but rather the whole of the specific contents whose vehicle classical education was: see on this regard the evidence quoted by Marrou (1948, 318–23). For more extensive and detailed information it is indispensable to refer to Marrou (1937, 339–56), Ellspermann (1949) and especially Hagendahl (1958).

7. Cf. Marrou (1948, 324–6), Riché (1962, 48–9).

8. Cf. Marrou (1948, 326).

9. Cf. Marrou (1948, 326–8).

10. Cf. Riché (1962, 60–1).

11. In the early sixth century classical schooling could still ideally be reflected in the teaching of a certain Felix, in Rome, who was a teacher of eloquence and worked on the text of Martianus Capella, and, in Milan, in the teaching of the grammarian and rhetorician Deuterius, who is quoted several times by Ennodius, the famous bishop of Pavia; see Marrou (1948, 346) and Riché (1962, 62–78).

12. We must remember what Cassiodorus said of it, *Inst.* 2, i, 1 (Mynors 1937, 94, 9–11), which was destined to become *communis opinio* throughout the early Middle Ages: 'nobis tamen placet in medium Donatum deducere, qui et pueris specialiter aptus et tyronibus probatur accommodus' ('we, however, like to quote Donatus, who is to be approved as especially suitable for children and useful for beginners').

13. Both quotations are from Cassiodorus, respectively *Var.* 9, 21, 3 (*MGH* AA XII, Mommsen 1894, 286), which continues (*ibid.*, 3–4):

'haec in cursu orationis sic errorem cognoscit absonum, quemadmodum boni mores crimen detestantur externum. Nam sicut musicus
consonantibus choris efficit dulcissimum melos, ita dispositis congru-
enter accentibus metrum novit decantare grammaticus. Grammatica
magistra verborum, ornatrix humani generis, quae per exercitationem
pulcherrimae lectionis antiquorum nos cognoscitur iuvare consiliis'
('it [grammar] in the course of speech recognizes a discordant mistake
in the same way that good morals detest a crime displayed. Indeed,
as musicians produce sweet melody with harmonious choirs, so the
grammarian knows how to speak with accents congruously arranged
in the metre. Grammar is the mistress of words, the ornament of
humankind, which, as is known, is useful to us in its counsel through
the practice of the most beautiful readings of the ancients'), and *Inst.*
2, i, 1 (Mynors 1937, 94, 3–4), which continues (*ibid.*, 4–5): 'officium
eius est sine vitio dictionem prosalem metricamque componere' ('its
purpose is to compose without fault utterances in prose and in
metre').

14. Among the poets, the most quoted are Virgil and Silius Italicus, then
Terence, Horace, Ovid, Tibullus, Lucan and Statius; among the prose
writers, Cicero, Sallust, Caesar and Valerius Maximus, cf. Riché
(1962, 79).

15. Cf. Marrou, (1948, 346).

16. Cf. Marrou (1948, 261; note that the English translation mistakenly
mentions Claudius Mamertinus instead of Claudianus Mamertus)
and Riché (1962, 83–4). Only in Africa did some isolated knowledge
of Greek survive.

17. Cf. Steinacker (1954) and, more generally, Courcelle (1943) and
Siegmund (1949). Even a cultural figure as important as Gregory the
Great resorts to translations, and confesses explicitly on several
occasions that he knows no Greek; for evidence on this subject see
Riché (1962, 189).

18. Cf. Marrou (1948, 333–4), Riché (1962, 140–63). It may be interesting
to point out that the practice of personal silent reading, in contrast to
the ancient custom of *recitatio*, begins precisely within monastic
schools.

19. Cf. Marrou (1948, 334–6), Riché (1962, 163–9), Verger (1982).

20. Cf. Marrou (1948, 336), Riché (1962, 169–71).

21. The evidence is found in *Novell. Iust.* app. 7, 22 (CIC III, Schoell-
Kroll 1968, 802, 18–9).

22. On this subject, we have the example of a famous piece of evidence
from Gregory the Great in his commentary on the First Book of
Kings, cf. *in I Reg. expos.* 5, 3, 30 (*PLM* LXXIX, 355 D): 'Quae
profecto saecularium librorum eruditio, et si per semetipsam ad
spiritualem sanctorum conflictum non prodest, si divinae Scripturae
coniungitur, eiusdem Scripturae scientia subtilius eruditur. Ad hoc
quidem tantum liberales artes discendae sunt, ut per instructionem
illarum divina eloquia subtilius intelligantur' ('Certainly this learning
of secular books, even if in itself it does not help the spiritual

discussion of holy books, if it is joined with the divine Scriptures, a more subtle knowledge of these Scriptures is acquired. Therefore these liberal arts should be studied with this aim only, so that through their teaching divine discourse may be more subtly understood'); for further evidence, conceptually similar, found in the same text, see Riché (1962, 198).

23. Cf. Marrou (1948, 340–9), Riché (1962, 353–409).

24. One need only think of the tireless efforts on the part of Saint Columba and his followers, particularly in Gaul and Northern Italy, for which see Riché (1962, 357–80, 389–92) and Bischoff (1966–81, I, 195–205).

25. Compared to the unification process taking place in large areas of Western Europe concerning new religious culture, Rome, Sicily and Spain – where the famous Toledo School became established – remained more closely anchored to their intellectual traditions, cf. Riché (1962, 392–409).

26. During the seventh century knowledge of Greek is sporadic in Rome and Ravenna, despite contacts with the East and the presence of Byzantine officials; there is more certain evidence, at least judging from the considerable number of Greek inscriptions which can be dated to that time, about Sicily, particularly Agrigento, Siracusa and Palermo: see Riché (1962, 395–7). As for Britain, the arrival in Canterbury in 669 of the new bishop appointed by the Pope, the monk Theodore, who came originally from Tarsus and escaped to Rome, also means the first official appearance of the teaching of Greek in an ecclesiastic school. Bede was able to say enthusiastically of Theodore's disciples – and probably of the African monk Hadrian, who accompanied Theodore into the Anglo-Saxon territories, also by papal decree – that 'Latinam Graecamque linguam aeque ut propriam in qua nati sunt norunt' ('they know the Greek and Latin language equally as their own native one') (*Hist. Eccl.* IV, 2, Colgrave and Mynors 1969, 334). Bede himself, and also St. Boniface, seem to have known some Greek; we learn from the *Liber pontificalis* that many of the Popes also had a good knowledge of Greek: they were Leo II (682–83), Gregory III (731–41), Zachary (741–52) and Paul I, who in 761 offered asylum to the monks banished from Constantinople – building a monastery for them so that they could hold services in Greek – and sent Pepin the Short Greek works of grammar and geometry. On the problem of the knowledge of Greek in the West in the early Middle Ages, see, as well as Riché (1962, 415, 420, 425, 437, 468, 471), Steinacker (1954), Roger (1905), Siegmund (1949) and especially Bischoff (1966–81, II, 246–75).

27. Particularly the works of Donatus, Dositheus, Charisius, Phocas, Audax, Isidore of Seville, Iulianus Toletanus, and Virgilius Grammaticus, cf. Roger (1905, 328–9); on the importance of *scriptoria* and libraries as centres of cultural mediation and elaboration, see Bischoff (1966–81, I, 122–33; II, 312–27).

28. Interest in the study and investigation of grammatical questions is

also motivated by the interpretative and exegetic needs of the Bible, which by this time had become the fundamental text of medieval culture: Aldhelm, Bede and Boniface all express this concern, cf. Riché (1962, 442). The study of rhetoric and dialectics was less widespread at this time, if not even rejected. The low esteem in which particularly dialectics was held is justified by the temporary abandoning of the study of philosophy, an integral part of the culture which had characterized the more comprehensively humanistic attitude of someone like Boethius, Cassiodorus or Isidore of Seville.

29. Among them Charisius, Servius and Probus, as well as glossaries and extracts from Macrobius, cf. Riché (1962, 454); at times, manuscripts of Biblical texts were actually erased in order to copy grammatical texts.

30. As we read in Paulus Diaconus, for which see Marrou (1948, 349) and Riché (1962, 460).

31. Cf. Riché (1962, 491).

32. Cf. Riché (1962, 515–16) and, for further details, Lesne (1938; 1940) and Lorcin (1945).

33. As for the specific linguistic character of the Latin Biblical text, it must be remembered that both the so-called *Vetus Latina* and Jerome's *Vulgata* were in circulation, with frequent reciprocal contamination; on this problem and, more generally, on the transmission of Biblical versions in the early Middle Ages, including the considerable role they played on the more strictly linguistic level, see the important contributions by Franceschini (1963, 13–37), Devoto (1963, 55–66), Manselli (1963, 67–101), Salmon (1963, 491–517), Fischer (1963, 519–600), Gribomont (1963, 601–30).

34. A work attributed to Bede; see the edition in PLM, XC, 613–32 and the brief mentions given by Law (1982, 103, n. 22).

35. The manuscript that mentions it originates from Bobbio.

36. On the glossaries of the early Middle Ages, reference to the works by Hessels (1890; 1906), Loewe and Goetz (CGL 1888–1923), Lindsay (1921a; 1921b), Lindsay et al. (1926–31) is still indispensable.

37. Cf. Riché (1962, 523). Bede's *De arte metrica*, together with the *De schematibus et tropis*, is edited by Kendall in *Bedae Venerabilis Opera didascalica*, I, 81–171 (CCSL, CXXIII A, Jones et al.ii, 1975), while for the *De metris et enigmatibus ac pedum regulis* by Aldhelm see Ehwald's edition in *Aldhelmi Opera*, 59–204 (MGH, Auctores Antiquissimi XV, 1913–19).

38. The schools of the classical tradition were distinguished in the Eastern world especially because of the high standard of their higher level teaching, which is also, and not by chance, the best documented. One need only think of the importance that centres of culture such as Athens, Alexandria, Antioch and Constantinople had until the beginning of the sixth century, nor should one forget the policy of active intervention followed by the imperial power towards public instruction: a famous example of this is the constitution of 27 of February 425, 'by means of which Theodosius II organizes a State University

in Constantinople, which has a real monopoly of higher teaching in the capital (only private teaching remains free). The teachers are forbidden to give individual teaching ... The teaching body includes three rhetoricians and ten grammarians to teach Latin letters, five rhetoricians and ten grammarians for Greek letters; finally, for the other studies, a teacher of philosophy and two of law' [Marrou (1948, 215 and, for the quotation, 307–8)].

39. Compared to what happened in the West, one cannot say that there occurred a real break between the civilization of the late Roman Empire and that of the Byzantine early Middle Ages: the University of Constantinople from 425 to 1453 – the year the city was captured by the Turks – kept the same type of teaching set down by classical norms, which had the liberal arts at its base, and rhetoric, philosophy and law at its apex; secondary teaching continued to be founded on grammar and commentary on the classics, which were learned from Hellenistic manuals and commentaries or from texts that imitated them closely. On this subject, see Marrou (1948, 340) and, more specifically, the works of Fuchs (1926), Hussey (1937), Buckler (1948) and Bréhier (1950).

40. As the *Rules* of St Pacomius and St Basilius show, the pupil initially learned to read and write the names of Biblical characters and verses from the Book of Proverbs and from the holy stories: an Egyptian papyrus from the fourth or fifth century confirms this educational organization in general, since it is the exercise book of a pupil containing, among other writing exercises, verses from the Psalms; it is also confirmed by some Egyptian *ostraka* dating from the seventh or eighth century, where one can find lists of words containing many Christian terms and fragments of psalms, also used for writing exercises, cf. Marrou (1948, 330–3).

41. Thus we see 'Nicephoros Basilakes, who was going to become a teacher of Gospel exegesis, writing a manual of *Progymnasmata* towards the middle of the twelfth century, which conforms to the purest Hellenistic tradition; at the most, in the chapter on character portrayal he adds a certain number of themes taken from sacred history to the usual topics of Atalanta, Danae or Xerxes ... Eustathius of Thessalonica, the great commentator on Homer and the other classics, is one of the most representative figures of Byzantine humanism for modern readers; nevertheless he had been educated in a monastery and was "master of the rhetoricians" of the patriarchal school' [Marrou (1948, 342)]; it is possible to compare a good proportion of Western intellectuals with the figure of Eustathius, who takes on an almost emblematic value.

42. For an overall evaluation of the various historical and cultural aspects inherent in this definition, see particularly Lehmann (1954, 309–58) and Monteverdi (1954, 359–72), as well as the brief syntheses by Haskins (1958, 16ff.) and Knowles (1962, 71–8).

43. The teaching programme initially concerned the monasteries and episcopal schools, where the teaching of psalms, musical notation,

singing, counting the years and seasons, and of grammar, was supposed to take place, all by making use of books specifically adapted for that purpose; the episcopal schools also had the task of providing literary teaching and the study of the Bible. Very soon, however, especially thanks to Theodulf, bishop of Orléans and abbot of Fleury, friend and successor of Alcuin, the aim of some kind of cultural education, even to a minimum level, reached the presbyterial schools as well, considering their spread in urban centres as well as in rural communities; see Knowles (1962, 72–3).

44. The prestige and importance of episcopal schools annexed to cathedrals reached their height in the period from the end of the tenth century to the beginning of the thirteenth, when the role of cultural guide was taken over by the Universities; it is to these schools, as is well known, that great intellectual figures such as Gerbert of Aurillac and Bernard of Chartres would be indissolubly tied.

45. The reader will be aware of the promotion work carried out especially by Alcuin for this purpose. Priscian and Donatus were the texts most used for the study of grammar, which was the preliminary base for approaching the *auctores* and at the same time the instrument needed to acquire the technique of Latin composition, both in prose and in verse: in this context it will be useful to note that at this time the distance between the spoken and written language (or at least the language that should be written) was being felt in a way that showed decided self-awareness for the first time in the Romance world, as can be deduced from the well-known prescriptions of the Council of Tours of 813. For the study of rhetoric the texts used were Cicero's *De oratore* and Quintilian's *Institutio oratoria*, while for the teaching of dialectics Porphyry's *Isagoge* and Aristotle's *Categoriae* and *De interpretatione* in Boethius' translation with his commentary were used. Finally, an encyclopedic information on literary authors, aimed at the interpretation of the Bible and the major representatives of Latin patristics, was guaranteed by reading Isidore of Seville, studied in the most recent editions provided especially by Bede and Alcuin, cf. Knowles (1962, 74).

46. The imperial greeting – written by Pietro da Pisa – addressed to Paulus Diaconus celebrates his knowledge of Greek, although within the canons of rhetorical *amplificatio*, as well as conferring on him the task of teaching Greek to the palatine clerics who had been appointed to accompany Rothrude, daughter of the king, to Constantinople, where she was to be the bride of the Byzantine emperor's son: so we can presume that at least some elementary teaching of this language took place in the palatine school in Pavia – perhaps under the rule of the grammarian Flavian, Felix's heir and follower – attended by Paulus Diaconus when he was young. There is evidence of some knowledge of Greek in Milan from the eighth to the eleventh century, cf. Viscardi (1957, 94–5); nor should one forget the uninterrupted tradition of Greek culture that existed in Central and Southern Italy: a famous example in the ninth century is the assiduous translation

work carried out by Anastasius the Librarian in the Roman Curia. The information we have on the search for texts in Rome and in the East – which was done in a very similar spirit to the one that was later to characterize Humanism – is further proof of the intention to recover Greek within the palatine court, as is also the philological reconstruction of the Biblical texts carried out by Alcuin, by resorting also to advice from Greek and Syrian scholars: on this subject, we refer the reader to the important work by Fischer (1957). One must mention, finally, the work of Johannes Scotus Erigena as a translator from Greek; the celebrated philosopher was at Charles the Bald's court and was the author, among other works, of a commentary on Martianus Capella, on which see Mathon (1969) and Contreni (1981).

47. Among whose works is a *De dialectica* (edited by Forster (Frobenius), PLM,CI, 947 ff.), where the main points of the subject are set out didactically in the form of a dialogue between Alcuin himself and Charlemagne; the treatment is not original, being based on Cassiodorus and Isidore of Seville, on the pseudo-Augustinian *Categoriae decem* and on the first commentary by Boethius on Aristotle's *Perihermeneias*, cf. Grabmann (1909–11, I, 234). Among Aristotle's known works were the so-called *Logica vetus*, that is the *Categoriae* (or *Praedicamenta*) and the *De interpretatione* (or *Peri(h)ermeneias*) translated by and with a commentary by Boethius; also available for the teaching and study of dialectics were Porphyry's *Isagoge*, also in Boethius' translation, and Augustine's *Principia dialecticae*, as well as the above-mentioned pseudo-Augustinian *Categoriae decem*. However, knowledge had been lost of the so-called Aristotelian *Logica nova*, which included the two *Analytica*, the *Topica* and the *Sophistici Elenchi*, and which was recovered only later, with the twelfth and thirteenth centuries' translations; among the vast bibliography concerning the various phases of medieval knowledge of Aristotle, see at least Grabmann (1916; 1939; 1950), Franceschini (1976) and Minio-Paluello (1952a; 1952b; 1954; 1962; 1965b; 1966).

48. However, didactic texts with ample notes, which could be used for the teaching of dialectics, are to be found in the ninth and tenth centuries' miscellanies, cf. Grabmann (1909–11, I, 189); in an anonymous *Tractatus de Trivio* dating from the twelfth century and written as a dialogue, the principal characteristics and duties of dialectics are defined thus: 'Dyalectica vero est disciplina ad disserendas rerum causas inventa et per disputandi regulam intellectum mentis acuit et per hanc ratio a falsis vera distribuit et in conquirendo ita sententiam eloquio armat, ut obiecta sine ulla dilatione et difficultate eiiciat et in disputandi efficacia quattuor hec agit: Proponit, adsumit, confirmat testimoniis atque concludit' ('So dialectics is the discipline that was found in order to discuss the causes of things, and through the rule of disputation it sharpens the intellect of the mind, and through it reason separates what is false from what is true, and in proceeding with the search it so arms meaning with eloquence, that it may reject

objections without delay and difficulty, and in the efficacy of argument it does these four things: it proposes, it assumes, it confirms
with evidence and it concludes') cf. Grabmann (1909–11, I, 191).
There is plenty of evidence for the rapid spread of dialectics, and its
degeneration into the most subtle and quibbling formalism in the
eleventh century, in the *Rhetorimachia* by Anselm of Besate called the
Peripatetic, on which see Manitius (1958); and from this same period
we have an intimate connection between dialectics and rhetoric,
which with all probability is to be related to the contemporaneous
development of juridical studies (one should remember the importance the law schools in Pavia and Ravenna were gaining), cf.
Grabmann (1909–11, I, 217).

49. Starting from the twelth century up to 1450 the monumental edifice
of scholastic logic took shape, and for more information on this we
refer the reader to Rijk (1962–7), Pinborg (1972) and Maierù (1972).
On the translations of Aristotle, see specifically Minio-Paluello (1943;
1945; 1952a; 1957; 1965b; 1966; 1972).

50. Thus, for example, the library of Theodulf of Orléans included
Donatus and Isidore, Virgil and Ovid, beside numerous Christian
authors, such as Hilarius and Ambrose, Cyprianus, Jerome and
Augustine, Prudentius, Sedulius and Gregory the Great; the library
at York described by Alcuin included Probus, Phocas, Servius, Eutyches, Pompeius, Donatus and Priscian, as well as Cicero, Virgil,
Statius, Pliny, Christian poets and prose writers, Cassiodorus, Bede
and Aldhelm. The library in the Augiensis monastery of Reichenau
also included, according to the *Brevis librorum* of 822, secular and
patristic texts, beside the works of Donatus, Sergius, Priscian, Bede
and Isidore. As we can see from the catalogue drawn up after 831,
the fund owned by the library at Saint-Riquier was very similar, and
it also contained – for the subject that concerns us most – Martianus
Capella, Victorinus, Velius Longus and the *Rhetorica ad Herennium*;
finally, very similar lists can be collated both from the catalogue of
the Chartres library and from those of the libraries at Sankt Gallen,
Toul, Bobbio or Cremona. The texts that were being taught and
studied seem therefore to be part of a tendentially organic and
unified programme, cf. Viscardi (1957, 477–84).

51. It seems appropriate to mention here, apart from Rabanus Maurus'
numerous commentaries on the Bible, his didactic work in three
volumes *De institutione clericorum*, a true Christian educational work
inspired mostly by Augustine. The most learned among Rabanus
Maurus' disciples, the abbot Lupus Servatus of Ferrières became
famous above all for his tireless philological work; as for Scotus
Erigena, with his Latin translation of the works of the pseudo-Areop-
agite, he made neo-Platonic speculation available to the Western
world: the author, as we have seen, of glosses on Martianus Capella,
and even more on Boethius, expert on dialectics and famous theologian, he set out in the *De divina praedestinatione* a classification of
the denominations of God that recurred in written and oral theologi-

cal language. Among the works by Heiricus of Auxerre, disciple of
Lupus of Ferrières and perhaps also of Erigena, we can mention the
commentary on the pseudo-Augustinian *Categoriae decem* and the
glosses on Boethius' translation of Porphyry's *Isagoge*; Remigius of
Auxerre, disciple of Heiricus, as part of his very intensive activity as a
glossator, wrote commentaries on Martianus Capella and above all,
as we shall see, on Donatus' grammar. For a detailed analysis of
these authors' contribution to the establishment of scholastic method,
see Grabmann (1909–11, I, 178 ff.).

52.  With the exception of Britain – where the effects of the intellectual
activity promoted by King Alfred and his immediate successors were
still being felt – and the monastic communities in general, but in
particular the ones belonging to the reformed Benedictine congrega-
tion, among which we must number the Abbey of Cluny, a very
important cultural centre whose name is connected to the famous
figure of Oddo; see Leclercq (1947).

53.  Following the example of Charlemagne, Otto I the Great also loved
to surround himself with a good number of intellectuals, for the most
part coming from Italy, among whom it may be appropriate to
mention especially Liutprand of Cremona, who had some knowledge
of Greek. The activity of Notker of Sankt Gallen can be placed
during the reign of the House of Saxony: he translated the Aristotelian
*Logica vetus* in the version by Boethius into German, as well as
Boethius' *De consolatione philosophiae* and Martianus Capella's *De
nuptiis Philologiae et Mercurii*; another Notker, bishop of Liège,
made his cathedral school into an important centre of culture, developing the study of the disciplines of the Trivium and the Quadrivium.
To the same period belong Gunzo Novariensis and Abbon of Fleury,
teachers of grammar, but above all Gerbert of Aurillac, teacher of
grammar, dialectics and rhetoric in the cathedral school in Reims,
and his disciple Fulbert, who was first in the series of great teachers
in the cathedral school in Chartres and had a very significant place in
the teaching of the Arts of the Trivium. Fulbert's school trained
teachers of rhetoric like Lambert of Paris and Engelbert of Orléans,
as well as Regimbald, teacher of grammar at Tours; on this subject,
see Haskins (1958, 25–9). For the recurring concept of renaissance,
applied both to the Carolingian and the Ottonian period – as well as
to the wide cultural movement that characterized the twelfth century,
as we shall see – see Anagnine (1958).

54.  Brought about by the rediscovery of the ancient Boethian version, to
which were added Giacomo Veneto's translations from Greek; on
this, as well as the essential outline by Maierù (1972, 9–22), see
Minio-Paluello (1952a; 1957; 1965b; 1966; 1972).

55.  One could think of the opposition that came about between Chartres
and Paris, respectively the strongholds of literary teaching – together
with a certain predilection for Platonism – and of the study of
Aristotelian logic. In the thirteenth century, the analogous contrast
between Orléans and Paris is mirrored in the famous poem *La*

*bataille des sept arts*, on which see Paetow (1914). As for the approach to the study and interpretation of classical and early medieval authors in the context of higher teaching, we shall mention at least the *Dialogus super auctores* by Conrad of Hirschau and the *Summa super rhetoricam* by Thierry of Chartres, both from the first half of the twelfth century, on which see, respectively, Huygens (1954) and Hunt (1980, 117–44). On the school at Chartres, Paris and the Universities, with particular emphasis on the study of the liberal arts, see, beside the classic works by Clerval (1895), Denifle-Chatelain (1889–97) and Paetow (1910), the contributions by Paré et al. (1933), Delhaye (1947) and Verger (1973).

56. To keep to a few significant examples, we shall mention that in the preceding century figures of undoubted cultural importance, such as Lanfranc of Pavia and Anselm of Aosta had worked in Bec, while in Montecassino the monk Alberic was setting down the first *ars dictaminis* manual.

57. The cultural importance of these institutions can be measured by the fact that intellectual figures of the stature of Bernard of Clairvaux, Anselm of Aosta and Peter Damian completed their early studies there, cf. Knowles (1962, 86).

58. To this category belonged the above-mentioned Anselm of Besate, who took the nickname of Peripatetic, and who was an itinerant teacher from Burgundy to Germany.

59. Evidence of the value – either extreme and absolute or more relaxed and instrumental – given to dialectics within theological speculation is given respectively by Berengarius of Tours, disciple of Fulbert of Chartres, and his adversary Lanfranc of Pavia, a monk from Bec and later archbishop of Canterbury; Anselm of Aosta, disciple of Lanfranc, believed his own dialogue *De grammatico* to be a useful introduction to dialectics; on this cf. Grabmann (1909–11, I, 215, 258 ff., 311–22) and Henry (1974).

60. In Radulphus' classification dialectics *docet discernere ad probandum vel improbandum* (teaches to distinguish in order to prove or disprove), while grammar *docet recte scribere et loqui ad intelligendum* (teaches to write and speak correctly in order to understand), and rhetoric *docet loqui ad persuadendum* (teaches to speak in order to persuade); as for the other definitions and classifications that concern us here, it must be borne in mind that 'scientia est vera perceptio mentis infinita finite comprehendens. Dicitur quippe scientia collective. Unde et ars nuncupatur ea videlicet ratione, quum infinitatis confusionem sub certorum locorum et regularum artat et concludit brevitate. Scientia vero sive ars quadrifariam recipit partitionem. Dividitur siquidem in *theoricam, ethicam, logicam* et *mechanicam* ... Logica est eloquendi ratiocinandique scientia. Unde et logica dicitur id est sermocinalis sive ratiocinativa. Logos enim grece sermo sive ratio dicitur latine' ('science is the true perception of the mind which understands infinite things in a finite way. Indeed, it is called science in the collective sense. Hence one also says art for this reason, because art compels

(*artat*) and restricts the confusion of the infinite within the brevity of certain *loci* and rules. Indeed science or art has a fourfold partition. It is divided into *theoretical, ethical, logical,* and *mechanical* . . . Logic is the science of speaking and reasoning. Therefore it is called logic, that is involved in speaking and reasoning. In fact, *lógos* in Greek is rendered as *sermo* or *ratio* in Latin') cf. Grabmann (1909–11, I, 252).

61. See Grabmann (1909–11, II, 15).

62. Cf. Grabmann (1909–11, II, 18, 20).

63. Frequent examples of the procedure of *quaestio* as applied to scriptural exegesis are found in Abelard and Peter Lombard; the method of *disputatio* became particularly well-established within theological teaching, and became increasingly important in the course of the thirteenth century.

64. For a systematic survey of the scientific classifications and methodologies typical of scholastic philosophy, see the classic works by Mariétan (1901) and Baur (1903); Grabmann (1909–11, II, 28 ff.), provides precious information by analysing for the first time unpublished anonymous material of great cultural importance.

65. It states, in particular, that 'scientie species due sunt sapientia et eloquentia. Sapientia est vera cognitio rerum. Eloquentia est scientia proferendi cognita cum ornatu verborum . . . Eloquentia ipsa eadem est, que dicitur loyca. Hec dividitur in dyalecticam, rhetoricam, grammaticam. Dyalectica in dissertivam sive rationalem et in sophisticam dividitur . . . In eloquentia sive in loyca, quia ipsa est que de vocibus tractat, primo addiscenda est grammatica, quia principium eloquentie scire recte scribere et recte pronuntiare scripta. Deinde dyalectica quasi augmenta et verum sal eloquentie i. scientia disserendi rationabiliter vel' sophistice. Deinde rhetorica quasi perfectio eloquentie, que in ornatu verborum et sententiarum consistit. Hec ergo due species sapientia et eloquentia sicut diximus distribute perfectam conficiunt scientiam' ('there are two species of science: knowledge (*sapientia*) and eloquence. *Sapientia* is the true knowledge of things. Eloquence is the science of expressing known things in ornate words . . . Eloquence is the same thing which is called logic. It is divided into dialectics, rhetoric, grammar. Dialectics is divided into discussional or rational and sophistical . . . In eloquence, that is in logic, since it is the one that is concerned with *voces*, first one must learn grammar, because the beginning of eloquence is to know how to write correctly and how to correctly pronounce what is written. Then dialectics is almost the development and true salt of eloquence, that is the science of discussing rationally · or sophistically. Then rhetoric is almost the perfection of eloquence, which consists of ornate words and sentences. Therefore these two species, knowledge and eloquence, distinguished as we have said, produce perfect science') cf. Grabmann (1909–11, II, 36–7).

66. See Grabmann (1909–11, II, 43): 'Philosophia trifarie primo dividitur in Theoricam, Practicam et Logicam . . . Item practica spiritualis intelligentie in has tres subdividitur scilicet in Tropologiam, que est

de morum compositione, in Allegoriam, que est de figurata dictione, et in Anagogen, que est de superiorum ductu et intellectione; ducit enim intellectum hominis ad superiora. Logica rationalis trifario modo subdividitur in tres: in Dyalecticam, que est disputatoria, in Apodicticam i. demonstrativam, in Sophisticam i. fraudulentam et fictam' ('Philosophy is first divided into three parts, Theoretical, Practical, and Logical . . . Also, the practice of spiritual intelligence is subdivided into these three: Tropology, which deals with the composition of behaviour, Allegory, which deals with figurative diction, and Anagogy, which concerns the leading and understanding of higher things; indeed it leads the intellect of men to higher things. Rational logic is subdivided into three in a threefold way: Dialectics, which is concerned with arguments, Apodictical, i.e. demonstrative, Sophistical, i.e. deceptive and fictitious').

67. Cf. Grabmann (1909–11, II, 235–49). The fact that the *sententia*, understood as the true *intelligentia textus*, is the ultimate purpose of the *lectio*, is established by Robert of Melun, Hugh of St Victor's companion of studies in Paris and later a prestigious university teacher who had John of Salisbury among his disciples. A confirmation of the importance of logic, defined, according to the double meaning of the Greek *lógos* (*sermo* and *ratio*), *loquendi et disserendi ars* – where in any case the close ties that connect it to grammar appear very clearly – is present precisely in John of Salisbury; it will be remembered that another of his greatest teachers, Gilbert of Poitiers, an eminent representative of the school of Chartres, had worked out a very strict theory and technique of the *quaestio*, which had become a true literary genre starting from William of Champeaux and Anselm of Laon, for which see Grabmann (1909–11, II, 386, 413, 424 ff.). The unquestionable value of logic, whose application in the theological field is supposedly justified according to its own etymology (*lógos* as an equivalent not only of *sermo* and *ratio*, but also of *verbum*, with the multiple religious implications this term has in the language of Biblical Revelation), is also pointed out by Peter Abelard; finally, one should remember how widespread were the *sophismata logicalia*, especially in the thirteenth century. These were dialectic exercises, mostly carried out with a taste for paradox: there are examples, among others, in the work of John Garland, dealing with some sophisms of verbal logic that consisted mostly 'of grammatically singular or unsuitable sentences, requiring judgement', cf. Grabmann (1909–11, II, 116). As for Hugh of St Victor's *Didascalicon*, see its critical edition by Buttimer (1939), keeping in mind, on the problem of the classification of the sciences inherent in it, the work of Calonghi (1956).

68. Cf. Grabmann (1909–11, II, 48–54).

69. Cf. Haskins (1958, 139–46). The teaching of the *ars dictaminis* (or *dictandi*) is closely connected to that of rhetoric, which is also linked to the copious production of *artes poeticae*, a conspicuous characteristic of late medieval culture; for *artes poeticae* see, as well as Faral

(1924), the works by Baldwin (1928), Bagni (1968) and Gallo (1974). For Alberic of Montecassino see Hagendahl (1956), and the studies by Lindholm (1963), which are very informative on the *artes* (or *summae*) *dictaminis* in general.

70. Cf. Pinborg (1972, 12); see also, for a broad overview, Knowles (1962, chs 15, 18, 24). We must mention that among the most prestigious teachers of this period, the number of Englishmen was greater than any other nationality: even keeping to the most representative figures alone, there were Alexander of Hales, Robert Grosseteste, Robert Kilwardby, Roger Bacon, John Duns Scotus and William of Ockham; interest in the study of Greek was present in several exponents of British philosophical and theological culture, as in the case of Robert Grosseteste, who encouraged the teaching of Greek and was himself an indefatigable translator from it. On the spread of philosophical thought of a Platonic and neo-Platonic type, see particularly Klibansky (1937), Garin (1958), Gregory (1958), and, for the important place attributable to Dominicus Gundissalinus within grammar and rhetoric, see Hunt (1980, 118–25, 129–31).

71. Precisely this kind of rigidity and artificiality of wording, of repetitive modularity, which constrained Latin in so many of the medieval treatises – and not only the grammatical, poetical or rhetorical treatises – can be considered one of the main reasons for the very negative judgements expressed by the Humanists on these writings: let the example of Erasmus stand for all, when he defines the medieval *auctores* 'barbariei duces vel praecipuos ... indignos etiam qui nominentur' ('principal leaders of barbarity ... unworthy even to be named'), and also remarks that 'mirum vero si his authoribus quis quid Latine dicat, cum ipsi nihil non barbare locuti sint' ('we should wonder that with authors like these, one should manage to say anything in Latin, because they spoke only barbarically'), for which see Cremascoli (1969, 53–4).

72. By the end of the sixth century the *regulae Donati* already are for Gregory the Great, in the dedication letter of the *Moralia* to bishop Leander, the grammar par excellence.

73. We have evidence for the immediate spread of these two works – unlike Donatus' other two works, the commentaries on Terence and Virgil – from the commentaries on them written by the grammarians Servius, Sergius, Cledonius and Pompeius in the span of little more than a century after their appearance.

74. On Donatus' success see the fundamental study by Holtz (1981a), and consider also Chase (1926) and Bursill-Hall (1981).

75. On the tradition and spread of Pompeius, see Holtz (1971).

76. In the *recensio* associated with the *Congregatio Salcani filii de verbo* in ms. IV.A.34 in Naples Biblioteca Nazionale, coming from Luxeuil and datable from the beginning of the ninth century, for which see Jeudy (1974a, 114–16).

77. The most ancient manuscript where we can find Consentius's grammatical work, although only in an incomplete state, is believed to be

from Ireland. For the problems about the role played by Ireland in the transmission of Latin grammar see Holtz (1977b); in any case, reference to Lowe's monumental work (1934–71) and to Becker's classic repertoire (1885) is still indispensable.

78. It is also mentioned in the library catalogues at Bobbio and Lorsch in the tenth century.

79. The attribution of this grammatical commentary – precisely, *Commentarium de oratione et de octo partibus orationis* – to Cassiodorus seems totally improbable, since it is founded on a debatable conjecture of its first editor, Garet (in PLM LXX, 1219–40); the attribution had already been questioned by Keil.

80. On this subject see Holtz (1975).

81. On Charisius' circulation, refer particularly to Holtz (1978).

82. On the problem of its transmission, see the remarks by Barwick (1922, 31), Beeson (1947, 76) and Bischoff (1966–81, III, 153).

83. Cf. Gibson (1972), Jeudy (1972), O'Donnell (1976) and Passalacqua (1978).

84. For the hypothesis of its possible circulation in Southern Gaul around the seventh century, see Riché (1962, 241).

85. There are also copies from the Germanic area, and one from Montecassino, cf. Jeudy (1974a); the presence of Phocas is also mentioned by Alcuin in the verse description of the books owned by York library.

86. A book of general culture, it is often present in the library catalogues written in the ninth–twelfth centuries, and a *Quellenforschung* relating to the materials used by medieval Latin poets can definitely prove that they knew it: the example of Alan of Lille, who used it as one of the models for his *Anticlaudianus*, will suffice for all. On the fortunes and transmission of Martianus Capella see Leonardi (1955; 1962).

87. Cf. Roger (1905, 319–29), Gebauer (1942).

88. As we can see, among others, from the catalogues of Würzburg and Saint-Riquier, respectively from the end of the eighth century and from 831.

89. It is well known that the manuscripts of the *De metris*, which Keil edited as a third book of the grammar in question, attribute this work to M. *Plotius* Sacerdos.

90. A manuscript, possibly from Fleury, dates from this time; it is kept in the Bibliothèque Nationale in Paris, and contains the *De ultimis syllabis*; another Paris manuscript from North-Eastern France, containing the *Instituta artium*, also dates from the first half of the ninth century. It does not seem improbable to suppose that a rediscovery of Probus might have happened in Carolingian circles.

91. Cf. Robson (1963).

92. Unlike the isolated references found in Consentius, Priscian and Cassiodorus.

93. And, though in isolated instances, through Consentius, Pompeius and Priscian.

94. There is no cogent proof that the *Ars Asperi* was known in the British Isles in the eighth century.

95. The only manuscript where it can be found dates from the sixth or seventh century, and comes from Southern France or Italy.
96. For the editions of Boethius' works and their value as mediators of Aristotelian thought, the premise of the development of medieval logic of modality, see Maierù (1972, 11–13, 327–32).
97. This promoted the later creation of the analogous term *trivium*, which was used to indicate the more decidedly 'humanistic' disciplines such as grammar, rhetoric and dialectics; both terms enjoyed an immediate and lasting success throughout medieval culture.
98. On this subject, see the passage from Boethius' first commentary on Aristotle's *Perihermeneias*, quoted by Maierù (1972, 55, n. 22): 'Termini autem sunt nomina et verba, quae in simplici propositione praedicamus, ut in eo quod est Socrates disputat, Socrates et disputat termini sunt. Et qui minor terminus in enuntiatione proponitur, ut Socrates, subiectus dicitur et ponitur prior; qui vero maior, praedicatur et locatur posterior, ut disputat' ('Terms are nouns and verbs, which we predicate in simple propositions, as in *Socrates disputat*, *Socrates* and *disputat* are terms. And the minor term which is proposed in the enunciation, like *Socrates*, is called the subject and is put first; the one which is major is predicated and is placed after, as *disputat*').
99. The work is edited by Mynors (1937); for more information on the cultural milieu of Cassiodorus and his time, see Momigliano (1955).
100. See the edition in Keil GLK, VII, 127–210).
101. Edited in two volumes by Lindsay (1911); for the second and ninth books see the more recent editions – with an exhaustive historical, philological and linguistic commentary – by Marshall (1983) and Reydellet (1984), which also provide, respectively, a translation into English and into French of the books in question. Compared to the text provided by Lindsay, which follows the orthographical norms of classical tradition, Marshall and Reydellet present Isidore's work in a linguistic form that follows much more closely the different rules of medieval writings, especially where quotations of Greek lexical elements, which are normally transliterated, are concerned. As for the huge influence that Isidore had on medieval thought, Marshall (1983, 3, n. 6) rightly points out that it has not yet been exhaustively analysed in all its aspects; on this, see Anspach (1936), Fontaine (1959) and Bischoff (1966–81, I, 171–94).
102. For a clear statement of the problem, the reader is referred to the introductory pages of Reydellet (1984); on Isidore's etymology see Engels (1962) and Fontaine (1978), as well as Klinck's vast work (1970), concerning medieval etymology in general, which is analysed specifically keeping in mind the concepts of *derivatio* and *compositio*, which are closely connected to etymology for the explanation of the make-up of the lexicon and its semantic transformations.
103. Many of Isidore's definitions are lifted, often quite literally, from the earlier tradition of grammatical, philological-antiquarian or technical-scientific treatises: as an example, the definition of *argumentatio* is an exact copy of Cassiod. *Inst.* 2, 2, 11 (Mynors 1937, 105, 1).

104. See also, in 1, 4, 7, the choice, taken up from late Latin tradition, of a minimal pair to exemplify the value of [j] and [w] at the beginning of a word, in front of a vowel element: 'coniunctae aliis pinguius sonant, ut "Ianus", "vanus"' 'joined with others they have a fatter sound, as *Ianus, vanus*'; then, in 1, 18, 6, the observations (probably obtained through Pompeius, cf. GLK V, 130, 34–131, 15) on the distinctive function of the position of the accent: 'Accentus autem reperti sunt vel propter distinctionem, ut (Virg. *Aen.* 8, 83): "Viridique in litore conspicitur sus", ne dicas "ursus" ... vel discernendae ambiguitatis causa, ut "ergo". Nam cum producitur "go", causam significat; cum corripitur, coniunctionem' ('As for accents, they were found either in order to differentiate, as [Virgil, *Aeneid*, 8, 83] *Viridique in litore conspicitur sus* (on a green shore a pig is seen), so that one does not say *ursus* ... or in order to distinguish ambiguity, as *ergo*. In fact, when it is long *go*, it indicates cause; when it is shortened, it indicates conjunction'). The latter is a statement that, under a terminology that is traditionally relevant to vowel quantity, in actual fact hides reflections of a suprasegmental nature, as one can note by its close repetition by Iulianus Toletanus in terms, as we shall see, (cf. p. 161 and n. 124) of a difference in the position of the accent (*ergó* ~ *érgo*); and finally, in 1, 27, the evidence for the loss of the aspirate at the beginning of a word and for the neutralization of the opposition [t] ~ [d] at the end of a word and for *ae/oe* ~ *e* – as well as for some isolated cases of *l/d* exchange – can be drawn, even indirectly, from the reaffirmation of the distinctions (evidently not just graphic distinctions): '"ad", cum est praepositio, D litteram; cum est coniunctio, T litteram accipit. "Haud", quando adverbium est negandi, D littera terminatur et aspiratur in capite; quando autem coniunctio est, per T litteram sine aspiratione scribitur ... "Deus" per E solam: "daemon" per AE dipthonga est notandus. "Equus", quod est animal, per E solam scribendum. "Aequus", quod est iustus, per AE dipthonga scribendum ... L autem litteram interdum pro D littera utimur, ut "latum" pro "datum" et "calamitatem" pro "cadamitatem"; a cadendo enim nomen sumpsit calamitas ... "Pene" vero, quod est coniunctio, per E; "poena", quod est supplicium, per OE' ('*ad*, when it is a preposition, receives a letter D; when it is a conjunction, a letter T. *Haud*, when it is an adverb of negation, ends in D and begins with an aspiration; when it is a conjunction, is written with a T without aspiration ... *Deus* is written with E alone: *daemon* with the diphthong AE. *Equus*, the animal, is written with an E alone. *Aequus*, i.e. just, is written with the diphthong AE ... Sometimes we use the letter L for the letter D, as in *latum* for *datum* and *calamitatem* for *cadamitatem*; *calamitas* has taken its name from *cadere* ... *Pene*, which is a conjunction, is written with E; *poena*, which is a torment, with OE'). The same goes for other oppositions such as *it* ~ *id*, *quit* ~ *quid*, *hos* ~ *os*, *hora* ~ *ora*, *quae* ~ *-que*, *vae* ~ *-ve*, etc.

105. Among the numerous sources for the second book we can count Augustine, the two Boethian commentaries on Porphyry's *Isagoge*,

the *Ars grammatica* by Diomedes, Jerome, Lactantius, the *Liber de definitionibus* by Marius Victorinus, the *De nuptiis Philologiae et Mercurii* by Martianus Capella, Servius and Tertullian – and not, as one would expect for rhetoric at least, Cicero or Quintilian – as well as Cassiodorus: from the latter in particular, Isidore draws the classical definitions of the *orator* as *vir bonus dicendi peritus* (2, 3, 1) (a good man expert in speaking), of the five canonic parts of rhetorical speech, *inventio, dispositio, elocutio, memoria, pronuntiatio* (*ibid.*), of the three *genera causarum, deliberativum, demonstrativum, iudiciale* (2, 4, 1), of the difference between dialectics and rhetoric (2, 23, 1), as well as single summary sketches of Aristotle's *Categoriae* (2, 26, 15), of the *Perihermeneias* (2, 27, 1), of dialectic syllogisms (2, 28, 1 ff.) and of the *Topica* (2, 30, 1 ff.).

106. Many of Isidore's definitions, transmitted synthetically from earlier tradition, were going to be – in the absence of direct classical, especially Greek, sources – an indispensable reference point for the establishment of early medieval *Bildung*; one could take as an example the definition of the *artes Trivii* (1, 2, 1): 'Prima grammatica, id est loquendi peritia. Secunda rhetorica, quae propter nitorem et copiam eloquentiae suae maxime in civilibus quaestionibus necessaria existimatur. Tertia dialectica cognomento logica, quae disputationibus subtilissimis vera secernit a falsis' ('The first is grammar, i.e, mastery of speaking. The second is rhetoric, which is considered most necessary in civil law questions because of the brightness and abundance of its eloquence. The third is dialectics, also called logic, which with its most subtle disputations discerns truth from falsehood'). And Cassiodorus above all was going to play the analogous role of the ideal pedagogue in this sense.

107. Among the examples of correct interpretation of Greek, see, among others, the explanations of terminology concerning the syllable, metrical analysis, accent and the *notae sententiarum*, mentioned at 1, 16–21.

108. Cf. 9, 1, 1: 'priusquam superbia turris illius in diversos signorum sonos humanam divideret societatem, una omnium nationum lingua fuit quae hebrea vocatur, quam patriarchae et prophetae usi sunt non solum in sermonibus suis, verum etiam in litteris sacris' ('before the pride of that tower divided human society in different sounds of signs, there was one language for all nations, called Hebrew, which the patriarchs and prophets used not only in their speech, but also in holy writings'), remembering that on the origin of the alphabet Isidore had already stated in 1, 3, 4 'ut nosse possimus linguam Hebraicam omnium linguarum et litterarum esse matrem' ('so that we may know that the Hebrew language was mother of all languages and letters'); for the sources of Augustine and Jerome that are condensed here, see Reydellet's edition of Isidore, book IX (1984, 30). A further statement of the same idea is found in 12, 1, 2.

109. Isidore mentions the *confusio linguarum* in *Quaest. in Gen.* 2, 4 and 9, 1 (PLM LXXXIII, 213 B and 237 B), the latter being a passage that

reaffirms the diversification of languages as a consequence of the pride of Babel (9, 3, 237 D): 'per superbiam ab una lingua in multas divisi sunt' 'through pride they are divided from one language into many', in compliance with the Biblical story in *Gen.* 11, 7–9. The more neutral and detached *linguarum diversitas* probably echoes Jerome, *epist.* 18, 6 (PLM XXII, 365).

110. The observations on the articulatory typology of the *Occidentis gentes* could refer, among other things, to a conspicuous presence of dental and alveolar affricates, whose formation process at the time of Isidore can definitely be considered to have been concluded.

111. See 9, 1, 7, within the very brief outline of the history of the Latin language: 'Latinas autem linguas quattuor esse quidam dixerunt, id est priscam, latinam, romanam, mixtam ... Mixta quae post imperium latius promotum simul cum moribus et hominibus in Romanam civitatem inrupit, integritatem verbi per soloecismos et barbarismos corrumpens' ('It is said that there are four Latin languages, i.e. the ancient, the Latin, the Roman, and the mixed ... The mixed language is the one that after the wide spread of the empire, burst into the Roman city together with customs and men, corrupting the integrity of words with solecisms and barbarisms'), a passage that will be quoted word for word by Iulianus Toletanus (*Ars*, II, 1, 11.123–5). It will be remembered that Cicero, in *Brutus* 258, already attributed to the influx of immigrants into Athens and Rome the corruption of Greek and Latin respectively; the Roman idea of corruption is associated, in Isidore's *Weltanschauung*, to the specifically Christian idea of the fall from an ancient state of grace.

112. From the Irish area, which supposedly received it directly from Spain, Isidore's work spread into continental Europe; see on this subject, apart from the studies mentioned in note 101, Hillgarth (1961–2) and Mayr-Harting (1972). Finally, we must mention the success enjoyed by the other two works by Isidore with a mainly linguistic content, the *Differentiarum, sive de proprietate sermonum libri duo* – with its relative *Appendix* – and the *Synonymorum libri duo* (edited in PLM LXXXIII, 9–98, 1319–32 and 825–68 respectively): they both consist mainly of a lexicon of synonyms, but the second also adds an ascetic and moral tone, and is conceived in the form of a dialogue between man and his *ratio*, on the Christian theme – as one can deduce from the subtitle – *de lamentatione animae peccatricis* (on the lament of the sinful soul). On the possible influence of other, lost works by Isidore concerning grammatical questions, we refer the reader to Anspach (1936, 347–8).

113. See the edition, amply commented and annotated, by Maestre Yenes (1973); among the studies we must mention at least Funaioli (1911), Lindsay (1922) and Beeson (1924). The possibility that Iulianus Toletanus' grammatical treatise may actually be a collective work by a group of his disciples is not to be totally discounted, although there is no decisive and cogent proof to show that he was definitely not the author: on this problem, see the edition by Maestre Yenes (1973, XXVI–XXVII).

114. It is found in many monastic and episcopal libraries, and was probably known to Aldhelm; however, it is often difficult to determine
whether the insular grammarians drew directly from it or from
common sources.

115. There are many possible comparisons with the earlier grammatical
tradition, which had already started this segmentation procedure of
the linguistic chain into four successive units, from sentences (or
*partes orationis*), divisible into words (or *dictiones*), to the further,
progressive divisions of words into *syllabae* and *litterae*; on this
subject, see especially Pompeius (GLK V, 99, 21–27): 'nam vox est
quicquid loquimur, ut puta si dicas "orator venit et docuit". Potest
tamen et solvi, orator, venit, et, docuit: ecce solvisti orationem in
verba. potes ipsa verba solvere in syllabas o et ra; potes ipsam
syllabam solvere in litteras. Numquid potes ipsam litteram solvere
ulterius? nequaquam potes. Ergo propter has res quas dixi omnes
vide et definitionem Donati, "littera quid est? pars minima vocis
articulatae"' ('in fact *vox* is whatever we speak, e.g. if you say *orator
venit et docuit* (the orator came and taught). You can also divide it,
*orator, venit, et, docuit*: here you have divided the speech into words.
You can divide these words into syllables *o* and *ra*; you can divide
these syllables into letters. Can you divide these letters further? You
cannot. Therefore for all these things I have said see Donatus'
definition, "what is a letter? the smallest part of the articulated
*vox*"'). On the *loci paralleli* illustrating this kind of *ante litteram*
structural analysis, it is still indispensable to refer to Jeep (1893, 108–
15), but compare also Abercrombie (1949, 58) and, lastly, the further
investigation of the problem in Tavoni (1984, 85–7).

116. The texts that can be recalled here too go from Diomedes to Probus,
Dositheus and Audax, on which see, respectively (GLK I, 420, 11–18,
IV, 47, 4–13, VII, 381, 2–4, VII, 323, 1–9). See also the bibliographical
references in the preceding note.

117. Here, too, it is possible to see many references to the earlier tradition,
especially to Pompeius (GLK V, 212, 7–15).

118. The *varia lectio* offered by codex F (*Floriacensis*, Bern 207) is significant
in this context: 'quomodo sic solitum est infantum nutrices minare
totto' ('as the infants' nurses are accustomed to threaten *totto*'). A full
historical analysis of any evidence of the use of this expression up to its
present-day Tuscan survival documented in the spoken language of
the area of Pisa and Lucca – assuming that these are actual continua-
tions of it rather than mere coincidence – has yet to be undertaken.

119. The most immediate comparison, without excluding the preceding
ones, is here with Isidore, *Etym.* 1, 27.

120. In the absence of explicit *loci paralleli* within the earlier tradition, one
could think about a direct, specific observation by Iulianus on the
effective linguistic use that was contemporary to him, even if, at least
as far as the 'correct' graphic distinction between *b* and *v* is concerned,
there is no lack of specific normative indications that can be inferred
from long lists of words among the late Latin grammarians (one

could mention the *Appendix Probi*): however, the way the archbishop of Toledo presents both phenomena remains new.

121. The fact that the alphabet letter *z* had the value of a complex consonant, i.e. of a dental affricate, can be deduced, among others, from Isidore, *Etym.* I, 27, 28, as mentioned earlier, to which it will be worth adding *ibid.* 20,9,4, where Isidore attributes specifically to Italians the pronunciation *oze* for *hodie* (to be found in CIL VIII, 8424, from the middle of the second century AD).

122. The immediate antecedent is definitely Isidore, *Etym.* 1,4,7, quoted in note no. 104.

123. For the many possible parallels with the late Latin grammatical tradition see the edition by Maestre Yenes (1973, 127–35 *ad 11.*).

124. The most direct comparison in this case is with Isidore, *Etym.* 1,18,6, for which see note no.104, but the source for both could be Pompeius (GLK V, 131, 1–15).

125. One should keep in mind that from the fifth to the eighth century the success of Donatus – and, consequently, of his commentators – is mostly due to their being principally clear and often elementary expositions, which were very suitable in scholastic education in order to teach the first rudiments of a language, Latin, whose knowledge, due to the increasing spread of Christianity, was required even among people who originally spoke a different language, and which was also becoming a foreign language even in the territories where it had enjoyed uninterrupted linguistic and cultural supremacy without too much conflict up to the late imperial period.

126. In the codex from Luxeuil, dating from the early ninth century and now kept in the Biblioteca Nazionale in Naples, IV.A.34.

127. It is difficult to say whether this revision of Donatus took place in the British Isles or elsewhere, since one can identify its beginnings in Isidore of Seville himself, who in the first book of the *Etymologiae* shows that he draws on sacred texts as well as the classical pagan authors for the relevant examples for the traditional discussion of *schemata* and *tropi*; on this subject, for the hypothesis that Isidore in turn was drawing on a source that has been lost to us, see Schindel (1975). The fact that the 'Christianization' of grammar was undertaken on Donatus rather than on other authors must be attributable as much to the particular clarity, simplicity and concise exposition that are especially typical of the *Ars minor*, as to the fact that Donatus was St Jerome's celebrated teacher; on this, see notes 12 and 72.

128. We have, for example, *ecclesia* and *ieiunium* instead of *musa* and *scamnum*, and similarly *Hierusalem, Iordanis, civitas, fluvius* instead of *Roma, Tiberis, urbs, flumen*, cf. Law (1982, 33).

129. Published in GLK VIII (*Anecdota Helvetica*, ed. Hagen), 39–61.

130. Variously known as *Asporius, Asperius* or *Asper*; the name *Asper minor* suggested by Löfstedt (1976, 132) is not found in any of the manuscripts in our possession, cf. Law (1982, 35, n. 27).

131. On this matter see Holtz's hypotheses (1981b, 143), about which Law (1982, 35, note 29) expresses well-founded reservations.

132. Donatus' 'tunc accusativi casus sunt cum ad locum vel nos vel
     quoslibet ire isse ituros esse significamus' ('then the accusative case is
     used when we want to say that we, or other people, go, went or will
     go somewhere') (GLK IV, 390, 24–5) becomes 'tunc accusativo casui
     serviunt, quando aut gressu aut verbo aut iniuria aut lapsu aut labore
     aut ira motus adsignatur' ('then the accusative case is used, when
     movement is assigned because of walking, or verb, or insult, or slip,
     or labour, or wrath') (GLK VIII, 59, 6–8); for the examples, see ibid.,
     60, 6–10: 'et illud denique in ablativo: "et induxisti nos in refrigerio",
     "induxisti" motus esse videtur, sed quod in refrigerio, merito in
     ablativo conplicatur. Si enim dixisset: "induxisti nos in incendium",
     quod ad poenam pertinebat, accusativum posuisset' ('and this finally
     takes the ablative: *et induxisti nos in refrigerio* (and you brought us
     into solace, *induxisti* seems to indicate movement, but because it is to
     solace, it must rightly be put into the ablative. If one said: *induxisti
     nos in incendium* (you brought us into a fire), which is concerned with
     suffering, it would be put into the accusative').
133. Cf. Gebauer (1942, 91–5) and Law (1978, XXIV–XXV).
134. Cf. Cobbs (1937, 49–53) and Löfstedt (1972a; 1972b).
135. An examination of the manuscript tradition allows us to recognize
     two different versions of the text; for a detailed analysis of the
     philological problems inherent in its reconstruction see Law (1982,
     37–41). Remarks like the following: 'Murus fornus focus hortus
     gladius masculini generis sunt et dicis pluraliter muri forni foci horti
     gladii' ('*Murus fornus focus hortus gladius* are of masculine gender,
     and in the plural you say *muri forni foci horti gladii*') (GLK VIII, 46,
     23 ff.), 'hic armus generis masculini et hii armi de armo non de arma'
     ('*armus* is of masculine gender and *armi* comes from *armus* not from
     *arma*') (*ibid.*, 47, 2 ff.), 'Cavendum est, ne quis dicat grada curra
     aquaeducta' ('One should avoid saying *grada curra aquaeducta*')
     (*ibid.*, 47, 11 ff.) are supposedly evidence of close relations with the
     Romance world, as well as the British Isles environment; remarks of
     this kind, together with the warning not to abbreviate the *e* in *ridere,
     torquere, fervere, mordere, tergere*, (*ibid.*, 53, 11–16), show the desire
     to correct the specific tendencies that were developing within spoken
     Latin in the context of its evolution into the Romance languages:
     metaplasms of gender and declination or changes in verb conjugation
     are all well-attested phenomena, as is well known, in the varied
     picture of the origins of neo-Latin languages, cf. Väänänen (1967).
136. Edited by Huemer (1886) and then by Polara (1979), with a transla-
     tion into Italian; see also Poli (1982–4b).
137. For a synthesis of critical contributions about possible dating, general
     interpretative problems and even the purpose of Virgilius' work see
     Herren (1979) and the *Introduction* to Polara's above-mentioned
     edition (1979, XIX–XXXIV, followed, XXV–XLII, by a *Nota sui
     codici di Virgilio Marone grammatico* by M. Ferrari).
138. Cf. *Epitomae* I, 4, 1–4 (Polara 1979, 6, ll.57–78): 'Latinitatis autem
     genera sunt XII, quorum unum ussitatum fitur, quo scripturas Latini

omnes atramentantur. Ut autem duodecim generum experimentum habeas, unius licet nominis monstrabimus exemplo. In ussitata enim Latinitate *ignis* primo habetur, qui sua omnia ignit natura; II *quoquihabin*, qui sic declinatur ... *quoquihabin* dicimus, quod incocta coquendi habet dicionem; III *ardon* dicitur, quod ardeat; IIII *calax calacis*, ex calore; V *spiridon*, ex spiramine; VI *rusin*, de rubore; VII *fragon*, ex fragore flammae; VIII *fumaton*, de fumo; VIIII *ustrax*, de urendo; X *vitius*, qui pene mortua membra suo vigore vivificat; XI *siluleus*, eo quod de silice sileat, unde et *silex* non recte dicitur, nisi ex qua scintilla silet; XII *aeneon*, de Aenea deo, qui in eo habitat, sive a quo elimentis flatus fertur. Sic per omnia pene oracula Latina haec summa generum supputatur' ('There are twelve kinds of Latin language, of which one is in normal use, and all Latins write their texts in it. But so that you may have proof of the twelve kinds, we shall show them, with the example of one name. In usual Latin one has, for the first form, *ignis*, which by its nature burns (*ignit*) everything; II *quoquihabin*, which is declined in this way ... we say *quoquihabin* because it has (*habet*) the power of cooking (*coquendi*) what is raw; III one says *ardon* because it burns (*ardeat*); IIII *calax calacis*, from heat (*ex calore*); V *spiridon* from breath (*ex spiramine*); VI *rusin*, from the colour red (*de rubore*); VII *fragon* from the crackling (*ex fragore*) of the flame; VIII *fumaton* from smoke (*de fumo*); VIIII *ustrax* from the fact that it flares (*de urendo*); X *vitius* because with its strength it gives life (*vivificat*) to almost dead limbs; XI *siluleus* because it springs out of the flint (*de silice sileat*), therefore it is not precise to call *silex* (flint) any other stone than the one from which the spark springs out (*silet*); XII *aeneon*, from Aeneas the god who lives in it, or from which breath is given to the elements. So for almost all Latin words one can suppose this total of twelve kinds').

139. Cf. *ibid.* II, 1, 2–3 (Polara 1979, 8 and 10, ll. 4–27): 'Ut enim infans dicitur qui loqui nescit, et parvulus ... et puer ... adulescens ... iuvenis ... vir ... ita etiam littera ab ipsis cerae caracteribus usque ad quassorum conpossitionem hosce ordines directat: siquidem infans appellatur, cum artem non sonet, hiis dumtaxat, qui caraxandis per ceras grammulis eisdem indigent, parvula vero est cum syllabarum conglutine paulatim gradiatur, puerula cum pedum mensuris crescat, adulescentula cum poetica metra per versuum carminula soffat, at iuvencula cum cassuum verborumque quandam intellegentiam capissat, virgo autem cum quassorum, ut dixi, conpossitionem plenissime perdoceat. Et ut aliquid intimatius aperiam, littera mihi videtur humanae condicionis esse similis: sicut enim homo plasto et affla et quodam caelesti igne consistit, ita et littera suo corpore – hoc est figura arte ac dicione velut quisdam conpaginibus arctubusque – suffunta est, animam habens in sensu, spiridonem in superiore contemplatione' ('Indeed the one who is unable to speak is called infant (*infans*), and little one (*parvulus*) ... and child (*puer*) ... adolescent (*adulescens*) ... youth (*iuvenis*) ... man (*vir*), in the same way a letter, from characters in wax to the composition of sentences, goes

through these levels: because it is called infant (*infans*) when it does not reproduce the required sound, at least for those who are unable to trace characters in wax, it is a little one (*parvula*) when it proceeds gradually gathering into syllables, a little girl (*puerula*) when it grows with the measure of feet, an adolescent (*adulescentula*) when it expresses poetical metres in poems composed in verses, then a young maiden (*iuvencula*) when it begins to have a certain significance of cases and words, finally a woman (*virgo*) when, as I said, it explains completely the composition of sentences. And, to illustrate a deeper thought, a letter seems to me similar to the human condition: for as man is made up of body, soul and a certain celestial fire, so a letter is also made up of its body – i.e. the graphic, grammatical and phonetic aspect, which are almost its organs and its limbs – and has its soul in its meaning, its spirit in higher contemplation'. It is not difficult to notice an echo of the classical attributes normally conferred on *littera*, i.e. *nomen, figura* and *potestas*, in the definition of its constitutive properties.

140. Cf. *ibid.* III, 1, 3–5 (Polara 1979, 14, ll. 9–18): 'Sciendum sane est quod ubicumque vocalem quamlibet in media arte possitam *s* duplicata secuta fuerit, eandem vocalem corripiemus, ut *vassa fossa clussit vissit vessit*; at si una *s*, vocalis producetur, ut *gloriosus visus*; omnis superlativus gradus *s* duplicatam semper habebit, ut *altissimus*. Sic et *m* duplicata antesitam corripit vocalem, ut *summus gammus*; sin alias, producetur, ut *sumus ramus*. Una littera quae opus syllabae facit, sicut *i* fortis, ita et longa erit ut *a e i o*' ('one must keep in mind that whenever a double *s* follows any vowel placed in the middle of a word, this vowel will be brief, as *vassa fossa clussit vissit vessit*; but if it is one *s*, the vowel will be long, like *gloriosus visus*; every superlative will always have a double *s*, like *altissimus*. In the same way the double *m* shortens the preceding vowel, like *summus gammus*; otherwise, the vowel is long, like *sumus ramus*. When a single letter acts as a syllable, like a strong *i*, it is also long, as *a e i o*'). The principle of vowel length in a free syllable appears clearly explicit especially in the last statement.

141. The examples discussed are drawn from supposed poets such as *Aeneas, Varro, Cato, Lupus Christianus, Don, Gergesus, Sagillius Germanus* and *Vitellius*; see especially the verses *Catonis eligantissimi rehtoris*, with a rhyming structure and some alliteration (*ibid.* IV, 2, 7; Polara 1979, 20, ll. 39–42): 'bella consurgunt poli praesentis sub fine, / precae temnuntur senum suetae doctrinae, / regis dolosi fovent dolosos tyrannos, / dium cultura molos neglecta per annos' ('wars break out at the end of this world, / the usual prayers according to the teachings of the old people are neglected, / treacherous kings support treacherous tyrants, / the worship of the gods has been neglected for many years'), and the one by Lupus Christianus, dense with alliteration and etymological figures (*ibid.* IV, 2, 9; Polara 1979, 22, ll. 48–49): 'veritas vera, aequitas aequa, largitas lauta, fiditas fida diurnos dies tranquilla tenent tempora' ('true truth, just justice,

generous generosity, faithful faithfulness daily occupy the days and this quiet time'), the ones by Gergesus, echoing Christian hymns (*ibid.* IV, 3, 3; Polara 1979, 24, ll. 70–71): 'sol maximus mundi lucifer / omnia aera inlustrat pariter' ('the sun, greatest light of the world, / lights up all the air equally'), and finally, the verses, with internal rhyme and/or assonance, by Sagillius Germanus (*ibid.* IV, 5, 2, Polara 1979, 26, ll. 101–2): 'mare et luna concurrunt una / vice altante temporum gande' ('the sea and the moon correspond to each other / in the alternating of their rising in a length of time'), and by Vitellius (*ibid.* IV, 5, 2; Polara 1979, 26, ll. 105–6): 'mea, mea Matrona, tuum amplector soma, / nobis anima una heret atque arctura' ('My, my Matrona, I embrace your body, / and our souls are joined in a single knot').

142. Cf. *ibid.* IV, 4, 1–4 (Polara 1979, 24, ll. 77–93): 'Nonnulli aiunt quod in unoquoque gresu duum pedum primus elevetur et secundus inclinetur vel, ut proprius dicam, solvatur, ut *légit ágit núbit vádit*. Sed nos dicimus, quod rectum esse sentimus, quia non minus secundos pedes repperimus elevari quam primos, ut *egó amá docé audí*. Maxime autem haec diversitas ob similium fonorum discretionem repperta est, ne confussibilitas aliqua nascatur. Dicimus enim nominativo cassu *sédes* elevato primo pede, at, si verbum sit, versa vice secundum levantes pedem dicimus *sedés*. Sic cum dicuntur *réges* primus erigitur, at cum verbum *regés* secundus pes elevatur; quod tamen non secundum rationem metrorum, sed secundum discretionis aptitudinem facere solemus; sicut etiam *póne* imperativo modo primam acuimus syllabulam et novissimam calcamus, atque e diverso ubi adverbium fit aut praepossitio, prima calcata novissima acuitur' ('Some say that in each grouping of two feet the first is stressed (raised) and the second lowered, or, more properly, is weakened, like *légit ágit núbit vádit*. But we say, as we think is right, that we found the second feet to be as stressed as the first, like *egó amá docé audí*. And this difference was invented above all to distinguish between similar words, so that no confusion should arise from them. In fact we say *sédes* in the nominative with the stress on the first foot, but if it is a verb on the contrary we stress the second foot and say *sedés*. Thus when one speaks of *réges* (kings) one stresses the first foot, but when it is the verb *regés* one stresses the second one; but one does not do this according to a metrical rule, but according to the convenience of the distinction; and in the same way in *póne* in the imperative we stress the first syllable and lower the second, and on the contrary where it is an adverb or preposition the first is lowered and the second stressed'. For the last example there is a possibility of parallels within the earlier grammatical tradition: one can think of Pompeius (GLK V, 131, 2–3) and Iulianus Toletanus (*Ars*, II, 12, 11. 75–84).

143. One cannot overlook an acute observation on the intrinsic obscurity of poetry (a remark to be connected to Virgilius' knowledge of hermetic compositions like the *Hisperica famina*?), cf. *ibid.* IV, 7, 1 (Polara 1979, 26, ll. 119–20):

'Inter poemam et rehtoriam hoc distat, quod poema sui varietate contenta angusta atque obscura est' ('Poetry differs from rhetoric because poetry, satisfied by its variety, is closed and obscure').

144. Cf. *ibid.* IV, 7, 1 (Polara 1979, 26, ll. 121–4): 'rehtoria autem sui amoenitate gaudens latitudinem ac pulchritudinem cum quadam metrorum pedum accentuum tonorum syllabarumque magnifica annumeratione praepalat' ('rhetoric on the other hand, delighting in its pleasantness, displays breadth and beauty with a magnificent calculation of metres, feet, accents, tones and syllables').

145. Cf. *ibid.* IV, 9 (Polara 1979, 30, ll. 160–64): 'Gramma est litteraturae pervidatio, quae quasi quaedam totius lectionis semitula est; unde et a plerisque *littera* interpretatur legitera, quod est legendi itinerarium, cuius praeconizo et laudo utilitatem, quam omnis pene participat mundus' ('Grammar is the deepening of literature, and it is like a path for any reading, so that most people understand *littera* (letter) as *legitera*, which means itinerary of reading (*legendi itinerarium*), and I praise its usefulness and proclaim it, in which almost the whole world shares'; the emphasis on the guiding function attributed to grammar is significant. For the etymology of *littera* see [Serg.] *Expl.*, GLK IV, 518, 31; Isidore, *Etym.* I, 3, 3; Iulianus Toletanus, *Ars* II, I, II. 31–3.

146. Cf. *ibid.* IV, 8, 1 (Polara 1979, 28, ll. 142–6): 'leporia est ars quaedam locuplex atque amoenitatem mordacitatemque in sua facia praeferens, mendacitatem tamen in sua internitate non devitat; non enim formidat maiorum metas excedere, nulla reprehensione confunditur' ('elegance is a certain rich art, which on the outside shows pleasantness and wit, but on the inside does not escape falsehood; indeed it does not hesitate to go beyond the limits imposed by the ancients, and is not disturbed by any disapproval'), an important recognition of fiction as an intrinsic characteristic of the linguistic message as it condenses in the specific elegance of poetic writing.

147. Cf. *ibid.* IV, 10, 1 (Polara 1979, 30, ll. 165–70): 'Dialecta est mordatrix omnium verborum quae legi dici ac scribi ab omnibus solent, exinterans quodammodo atque effibrans viscera sententiarum, medullas sensuum, venas fonorum, cuius auctores in omni pictura crocitant acriterque in reprehensionem omnium scribtorum rictu hiante avidant' ('Dialectics bites all the words which everyone usually reads, says and writes, it disembowels – so to say – and dismembers the guts of sentences, the marrow of meanings, the veins of words. Its authors crow on every description, and stand avidly with their mouths open, ready to bite all writers with their disapproval'); notice the rich meanings of the metaphors used here, by no means the least example of a kind of prose that, because of its strongly·expressionistic character, is far from the colourless scientific uniformity of the more traditional grammatical writings.

148. However, the matter treated in it widely transcends Donatus' linear organization, as also happens in the eight *Epistolae*, which also correspond in general to the *Ars minor*; on the peculiar characteristics of Virgilius' presentation of the *partes orationis* see Meredith (1916).

149. Cf. *ibid.* X, 1, 2–8 (Polara 1979, 128 and 130, ll. 14–44): 'Scinderationis autem triplex effectus est ordo: primus quo versus scindimus, Catone dicente: mare oceanum / classes quod longae / sepe turbatur / simul navigant; hoc enim dicere debuit: mare oceanum / sepe turbatur,/classes quod longae / simul navigant; secundus quo ipsa scindimus fona vel syllabas, sicut Lucanus edidit: *ge ves ro trum quando tum affec omni libet aevo*, et sic solvitur: *quandolibet vestrum gero omni aevo affectum*; tertium genus, quo litteras scindimus. Scinderatio autem litterarum superflua est, sed tamen a glifosis sensuque subtilibus recipitur; unde et fona brevia scindi magis commodum est quam longa, ut Cicero dicit: RRR SS PP MM N T EE OO A V I, quod sic solvendum est: *spes Romanorum perit*. Virgilius quoque Assianus: GGGG L B FF RR S NNN TT EEE I VVV AE, quod sic solvitur: *glebae gignunt, fruges ferunt*. Emilius quoque rehtor eliganter ait: SSSSSSSSSSS PP NNNNNNNN GGGG RR MM TTT D CC AAAAAAA IIIII VVVVVVVV O AE EEEEEEE, cuius haec solvitio: *sapiens sapientiae sanguinem sugens sanguissuga venarum recte vocandus est*. Galbungus quoque in laudibus defunctorum longas lineas texens in prohemio sui talia factus est Fausti: PPPPPPP RRRRRR L MM SSSS NN TT C IIII AAA OO EEEEEE, quod taliter solvitur: *primi patres proceres pares pleni pompis erant*' ('Division can be effected in three ways: the first is the one according to which we divide verses, as when Cato says: *mare oceanum / classes quod longae / sepe turbatur / simul navigant*; in fact he should have said: *mare oceanum / sepe turbatur, / classes quod longae / simul navigant* (the ocean is often enraged because long fleets sail together); the second is the one according to which we also divide words and syllables, as Lucan wrote: *ge ves ro trum quando tum affect omni libet aevo*, and is explained thus: *quandolibet vestrum gero omni aevo affectum* (because in every moment I feel affection for you); the third kind is the one according to which we divide letters. The division of letters is actually useless, but is accepted by enigmatic writers of subtle wit; it is more convenient to divide short words than long ones, as Cicero says: RRR SS PP MM N T EE OO A V I, which is explained like this: *spes Romanorum perit* (the hope of the Romans dies). Also, Virgilius Assianus: GGGG L B FF RR S NNN TT EEE I VVV AE, which is explained like this: *glebae gignunt, fruges ferunt* (the earth gives birth and produces fruit). Emilius the rhetorician also elegantly said: SSSSSSSSSSS PP NNNNNNNN GGGG RR MM TTT D CC AAAAAAA IIIII VVVVVVVV O AE EEEEEEE, and this is the solution: *sapiens sapientiae sanguinem sugens sanguissuga venarum recte vocandus est* (the learned man who sucks the blood of learning must rightly be called leech of the veins). Galbungus also, writing long lines in the praises of the dead, wrote this in the proem to the praise for his Faustus: PPPPPPP RRRRRR L MM SSSS NN TT C IIII AAA OO EEEEEE, which is explained like this: *primi patres proceres pares pleni pompis erant* (the first fathers, noble and optimate, were full of greatness').

150. See, among numerous examples, *ibid.* XI, 1, 6–7 (Polara 1979, 148,
ll. 33–44): '*Terra* ob hoc dicitur quia hominum pedibus teritur, sed
aliter si separetur, quia *ra* portatrix vel genitrix in Latinitate filosophica interpretatur, unde et naves quae portant *rates* dicuntur; ter
igitur *ra* dicitur, primo quia ex ea nascimur, unde et ex humo *homo*
dicitur, secundo quod eius fructibus alimur ac recreamur, tertio quia
in ea loeto soluti velut in matris vulva recondimur. *Mare* a Latinis ex
amaritudine dirivari putatur, ab Hebreis aquarum collectus dicitur; a
filosophis ex duobus conponitur vocabulis velut magna res, quae
nulli mortalium ut est patere potest' ('*Terra* (the earth) is so called
because *teritur* (it is trodden down) by the feet of men, but if the
word is divided its origin is different, because *ra* in philosophical Latin
means carrier or bearer, so that cargo ships are also called *rates*;
therefore the earth is called *ter* (three times) *ra*, the first because we
are born from it, so that *homo* (man) takes its name *ex humo* (from
the soil), the second because we are nourished and restored by its
fruit, the third because, once we are dissolved in death, we are placed
in it as in a mother's womb. The Latins think that *mare* (the sea)
derives *ex amaritudine* (from bitterness), for the Hebrews it means
"gathering of water"; for the philosopher it consists of two words,
i.e. *magna res* (great thing), which no mortal can see as it is').

151. On this subject Virgilius repeats, as a justification of his work and
almost as an answer to unnamed *detractores*, that 'Latinity is so vast
and so deep that it is necessary to explain it in many ways, with many
words and by means of different forms and interpretations', cf. *Epist.*
III, 1, 1–6 (Polara 1979, 228 and 230, ll. 3–43): 'respondendum reor
hiis qui nos profano et canino ore latrant ac lacerant dicentes nos in
omnibus artibus contradicos videri nobis invicem, cum id quod alius
adfirmat alius distruere videatur, nescientes quod Latinitas tanta sit
et tam profunda, ut multis modis fonis fariis sensibus explicare
necesse sit. Quis enim Latinitatem sensatus putet tam angustam
haberi tamque artatam, ut unumquodque verbum uno tantum fario
unoque sensu contentum esse videatur, praesertim cum Latinitatis
ipsius genera duodecim numero habeantur, et unumquodque genus
multas in sese conplectatur artes? Unusquisque igitur legentium sa-
noque scrutantium sensu (si tamen livoris nullo torquetur morbo;
nihil enim livens sanum sentire potest, qui dum aliis invideat, semet
ipsum aperto quidem veritatis lumine fraudat), omnis inquam lector
subtili studens animo multimodis Latini sermonis vias intentare con-
sideret in primis ipsius orationis vim atque naturam, si tamen pro
subtilitate atque habundantia considerari a quoquam recte queat;
deinde multas esse sciat causas, ob quas singulorum inmotatio verborum fieri soleat: nunc enim necessitatibus, nunc discretionibus personarum, nunc metrorum conpossitionibus, nunc eloquutionum orna-
tibus omnis oratio serviat necesse est ... haec de qua tractamus
Latinitas, una quidem lingua in proprietate sua consistit, multas
tamen immo pene tam innumerabiles sententias et orationes habet,
quibus diverso quidem sermonis tramite, unius tamen linguae veritas

approbatur' ('I think I must answer those who with irreverent and canine mouth bark against us and insult us, saying that in all the treatises it seems that we contradict each other, because what one upholds seems to be demolished by another, and they do not know that Latinity is so vast and so deep that it is necessary to explain it in many ways, with many words and by means of different forms and interpretations. Indeed, what person of any sense would think that Latinity is so restricted and compressed that for every word one form and one meaning alone would be sufficient, especially because the forms of Latin itself are counted in the number of twelve, and every form includes many arts within it? Therefore each of those who read and examine with a sensible mind (as long as they are not wholly afflicted by the evil of envy, because the envious man cannot think of anything sensible, since, envying others, he deprives himself of the clear light of truth), every reader who commits himself with zeal and perception to following the many roads of the Latin language should consider first the strength and nature of discourse itself, if these can be considered by anyone because of their complexity and richness. Then he should know that there are many causes for change to take place in individual words: as it is necessary for every discourse to adapt itself now to necessity, now to the distinction of persons, now to the composition of metres, now to the embellishment of expression . . . this Latinity we are dealing with proves to be a single language in its property, but it has many, indeed almost countless, expressions and discourses, by means of which the truth of a single language is shown, even through the different path of language').

152. Cf. Law (1982, 48).

153. On Virgilius' historical setting, the most probable hypothesis is the second half of the seventh century, keeping in mind, on the one hand, his use of Isidore's *Etymologiae*, published in 636, and, on the other hand, the fact that his work seems to be already known to Aldhelm between 675 and 690, and is certainly known to Boniface – whose grammar dates from the early eighth century – and to Bede, who uses it in the *De orthographia*, a work that was completed in 731, but whose editing continued for some decades. His geographical setting presents greater problems: having discarded the old hypothesis that he came from southern Gaul, today one tends to think rather of the insular area, the same area as the grammarians who use Virgilius' work before the ninth century. On this complex question see Herren (1979) and Law (1982, 49). The possible evidence of his Irish ascendency seems to be counterbalanced by a series of considerations aimed rather at emphasizing his probable connections with Britain. What is certain is that Virgilius does not offer any clues within his work that might prove at all useful to solve the controversies about his place of origin: only an accurate examination of the text's transmission allows some reasonably valid inferences. Finally, as for his success, the eighth century already brings its progressive decline: in Law's opinion (1982, 51-2), the only text to follow Virgilius' methods is the very

brief, unpublished *Ars Sergi(li)i*, which is preserved in two versions by two manuscripts, one in Leiden and one in Paris. On the first of these, see also Bischoff (1966–81, II, 251).

154. Among the nouns belonging to the first declension are inserted numerous Graecisms relevant to religious language, like *propheta, anchorita, heremita, evangelista, pascha* and *manna*, the last two being classified as neuter, a category which generally is not envisaged for the original themes ending in *-a* in Latin, which previously were only masculine and feminine.

155. Some versions draw part of the material from the *Ars Asporii*; finally, two of them also present a description of the *coniugationes verborum*. On the complex problems about the transmission of the text, see Law (1982, 56–64), who is preparing its critical edition.

156. Edited by De Marco in De Marco and Glorie (1968, I, 1–93); on this, see Löfstedt's observations (1972a; 1972b).

157. Who, however, is barely quoted.

158. Cf. Cobbs (1937), Law (1977; 1979; 1982, 64–7). Bede, although he quotes Tatuinus (*Hist. Eccl.* V, 23 and 24, Colgrave-Mynors 1969, 558 and 566), does not mention his grammar.

159. The presence of elements drawn from Priscian's *Institutio de nomine* and *Institutiones grammaticae* does not seem to be drawn directly, but can rather be attributed to an intermediate source, which is used by the *Ars Ambianensis* and other grammarians like Paulus Diaconus and Pietro da Pisa. Two of the three versions of the text that have come down to us independently quote Virgilius Grammaticus, which is probably attributable to different interpolations in the original text. This cannot be reconstructed easily from the manuscripts in our possession, which differ between each other in various ways. A further version of the *Ars Ambianensis* is found in the ninth century in the grammar attributed to the Irishman Clemens Scottus, cf. Law (1982, 67–74).

160. Cf. Löfstedt (1965); the text in question is preserved in the manuscript from the early ninth century, frequently mentioned above, which comes from Luxeuil and is now kept in Naples (Biblioteca Nazionale, IV.A.34), folios 235v–41v.

161. Edited by Hagen in GLK VIII (*Anecdota Helvetica*), 62–142; on this, see Law (1982, 74–7).

162. The reference to a certain *Flaccus* (GLK VIII, 134, 10), interpreted as Alcuin, who was known by this nickname in Charlemagne's court, induced Manitius (1911–31, I, 469) to date the text from just before or soon after the death of Alcuin himself (who lived from 735 to 804); on the subject however, Law points out (1982, 74) that the passage in question derives directly from Virgilius Maro Grammaticus (cf. *Epit.* VI, 2, 1, Polara 1979, 68, ll. 21–2) and therefore simply proves that the unknown author of the *Ars Bernensis* is to be placed later than Virgilius. As for the Irish origin of the treatise, as put forward by Löfstedt (1965, 20), it appears to be far from certain: many clues seem rather to place him in the Anglo-Saxon area.

163. The *Ars Ambianensis* presents many more parallels with the *Ars Bernensis*, so much that it may lead one to infer a common source; finally, a more extended version of the *Ars Bernensis* can be surmised as a common source of the edition we presently have and of Clemens Scottus' grammar.

164. It is certainly earlier than 719, the year in which Boniface (who lived from 675 to 754), having received this name from the Pope, would no longer be called Vynfreth, the name that still appears as an acrostic in the verses that accompany the letter of dedication of his own grammar, the *Epistola ad Sigeberhtum*. The *Ars Bonifacii* is edited by Gebauer and Löfstedt (Boniface 1980, 15–99; here, 9–12, is also the above-mentioned *Epistola*), whose text supersedes the one in the still notable 1835 edition by Cardinal A. Mai; among more recent studies, see Gebauer (1942) and especially Law (1978; 1979; 1982, 77–80).

165. For a detailed discussion on the techniques of compilation used by Boniface in the editing of his grammar, see Law (1978, XXVIII–XXXVII).

166. So, after every general definition, a debate begins, introduced by *cur*, *quare*, *interrogandum est*, *requirendum est*, *quaeritur*, followed by a series of arguments designed to give the best solution to the grammatical problem under examination in each case; it will be remembered that a similar procedure was not unknown to the classical commentators on Donatus, even if here it is enlivened by the polemic tones of *disputatio*.

167. A particularly significant example of this is provided by the anonymous *Quae sunt quae*, folio 56ra, quoted by Law (1982, 83): 'tres persona<e> sunt in verbo, quia res divina amplius non sinet nisi tres personas esse: sicut in trinitate tres persona<e> sunt, ita et genus humanum' 'there are three persons in a verb, because divine law does not allow that there should be more than three persons: as there are three persons in the trinity, so also in human kind'.

168. For the Greek see Bischoff (1966–81, II, 246–75, particularly 249–51); for the Hebrew, Thiel (1973). On the history and examples of the use of the *tres linguae sacrae* in the scriptural exegesis of Irish scholarship, see McNally (1958).

169. Cf. Bischoff (1966–81, I, 205–73), Faral (1924, 150); in the late Middle Ages, as is well known, the *locus a persona*, the *locus a re*, the *locus a loco*, the *locus ab instrumento*, the *locus a causa*, the *locus a modo* and the *locus a tempore* were commonly used, and were memorized by means of the questions formally set down in the famous hexametre *quis, quid, ubi, quibus auxiliis, cur, quomodo, quando?* – as well as the *locus a simili*, the *locus a contrario*, the two *loci a simili impari*, i.e. the *locus a maiore ad minus* – or deduction – and the *locus a minore ad maius* – or induction.

170. Cf. Law (1982, 85–7); the work is still unpublished, with the exception of some *excerpta* edited by Hagen (GLK VIII (*Anecdota Helvetica*), XLI–XLIII).

171. A *terminus post quem* is given by the use made in the work of

Isidore's *Etymologiae* and the *Ars Asporii*; the *terminus ante quem* could be deduced by the use the Anonymus ad Cuimnanum makes of it, if we knew the exact historical placing of the Anonymus, about whom we know only – on the basis of the presumed dating of the only manuscript we have of his work – that he could be placed before the middle of the eighth century.

172. Among the most noteworthy remarks, one could mention the discussion on the terms *vox*, *littera* and *syllaba*, and, on this last term, the digression on the origin of *bannita*, its synonym in the British Isles, on which see Bischoff (1966–1981, III, 243–7); the last part of the treatise consists of *excerpta* from the first book of Isidore's *Etymologiae*.

173. Cf. Law (1982, 87–90) and Bischoff (1966–1981, I, 273–88, especially 282).

174. As for the preceding one, this grammar too, which is still one of the most interesting ones of the time, contains plenty of etymological digressions of Isidorian descent.

175. The name *Malsachanus* is added in a later hand in one of the two manuscripts where we can find the treatise, while the same manuscript's explicit bears the caption *Congregatio Salcani filii de verbo*, in the same hand that transcribed the whole text: this second title therefore is the one to be preferred; the original form of the author's name was presumably Mac Salcháin. The work has been edited by Roger (1905) and Löfstedt (1965) with a full linguistic commentary; see also Law (1981; 1982, 90–92).

176. The beginning of the ninth century, the date of the two manuscripts where we are to find the treatise, is its obvious *terminus ante quem*, while the *terminus post quem* is the beginning of the eighth century, the time where we can place the Old Irish glosses used by one of the sources used by the *Congregatio*.

177. The source in question, which has been lost, must have been based on Consentius, Diomedes and Eutyches, but must also have incorporated material from Donatus and Virgilius Grammaticus. For a systematic review of the linguistic features that characterize the so-called *Ars Malsachani*, especially in the matter of the controversial problem of the interpretation of some of them as 'Hibernisms', see the very detailed analysis by Löfstedt (1965, 81–156).

178. Cf. Law (1982, 92–3); the text is edited by Hagen (GLK VIII (*Anecdota Helvetica*), XXXIX–XLI).

179. Apart from Donatus, among possible sources we can point out Asper and Asporius; two brief texts are associated to the *Aggressus quidam* in the codices; one of these texts, about noun declension, is edited in part by Hagen (GLK VIII (*Anecdota Helvetica*), XLI, 4–12), while the other, concerning the pronoun, is still unpublished. On this, see Law (1982, 93).

180. This could date from the early tenth century: for the two different suggested dates for the manuscript, see, respectively, Beeson (1946, 179) and Sabbadini (1903, 166).

181. An attribution to this effect has been widely supported by Sabbadini (1903, 168), Beeson (1946, 179), Bischoff (1966–81, I, 198). Löfstedt (1965, 21) and Holtz (1977a, 70; 1977b, 61); only Manitius (1911–31, I, 519–21) had expressed any doubts on this matter, though without offering alternative solutions. On this subject, we refer the reader to the detailed discussion by Law (1982, 93–7) and to Löfstedt's critical edition (1982) in the *CCSL*.

182. Neither Isidore nor Virgilius Grammaticus are used, even if the latter might appear to be subsumed in several places in the *Ars Ambrosiana* for some etymologies that are actually to be found in the eleventh epitome; see the following passages collected by Law (1982, 95, n. 79): 'homo ab humo sive ab humore dicitur' ('*homo* (man) is so called *ab humo* (from the earth) or *ab humore* (from humour)'), 'terra autem ter portatrix sive quod teritur' ('*terra* (the earth) *ter* (three times) bearer or *quod teritur* (because it can be treaded)'), 'mare magna res sive amaritudine dicitur' ('*mare* (the sea) is named from *magna res* (great thing) or from *amaritudine* (bitterness)'), 'caelum ... celsitate dictum est vel celando arcana vel quod celat sidera in se apparentia, nam dicuntur caelata quia cernuntur in qualitate structure cum in superficie non appareant' ('*caelum* (the sky) ... takes its name from its *celsitate* (height) or from *celando* (hiding) mysteries, or because *celat* (it hides) the stars as they appear, indeed those things are called *caelata* (hidden) that are discerned in the quality of structure and do not appear on the surface') – the first drawn from folio 9v, the last from the folio 33rv of the manuscript kept in the Biblioteca Ambrosiana in Milan, L. 22 sup. – comparable to Virgilius Maro Grammaticus, *Epit.* XI, 1, 4–7 (Polara 1979, 146 and 148, ll. 17–44). In actual fact the etymological material contained in the eleventh epitome probably dates from a time before it was used by Virgilius, and must have circulated independently from his work: the etymologies of the *Ars Ambrosiana*, which also appear to be formulated in a more restricted way compared to the corresponding passages in the eleventh epitome, cannot, therefore, be defined certainly as being of direct Virgilian descent.

183. Edited by Amelli: see Paulus Diaconus (1899).

184. Cf. Law (1982, 101). Among the works by Paulus Diaconus (720–99), who was born into a noble Longobard family from Friuli and educated in Pavia at Rachis' court, we should also mention his famous epitome – presumably written during his stay in France, between the years 782 and 786 – of Sextus Pompeius Festus' *De verborum significatu*, which concentrated mainly on etymological and grammatical problems, a work that was meant especially for schools and consisted mainly of a lexicon whose task was to aid the teaching of grammar. For the edition, see Lindsay (1913), while among the numerous studies on the subject we must mention at least Neff (1891) and Engels (1961), but especially Cervani (1978) and Moscadi (1979), and refer the reader to Bertini (1981, I, 407) for further bibliographical information.

185. Some *excerpta* are edited by Hagen, GLK VIII (*Anecdota Helvetica*), 159–71; on the latter, however, Bischoff (1966–81, III, 218, n. 31) believes, with good grounds, that the text of pp. 159, 21–161, 7 does not belong to Pietro da Pisa's *Ars*. Pietro, it must be remembered, was called to teach in the Palatine School after the fall of Pavia and the end of the Longobard kingdom in 774 – at whose court school he had already taught – and died in 799.

186. Cf. Law (1982, 102).

187. Edited by Tolkiehn (1928) for which cf. Law (1982, 102–3); on the problems of its actual attribution to Clemens Scottus – about whose life, between the eighth and the ninth century, despite the fame the grammarian came to have not only among his contemporaries, 'perpauca atque partim ficta et commenticia traduntur' ('very few and partly fictitious and imaginary things are known') (Tolkiehn 1928, V) – see the review by Barwick (1930, 394 ff.) of the edition quoted.

188. Among these we should mention Virgilius Grammaticus (but only for the *Epitomae*), the *Ars Ambianensis*, an anonymous treatise on the verb also used by Malsachanus, and the description of the partitions of *philosophia* that was widespread not only in the British Isles (although presumably it originated there), and that might have reached Clemens Scottus from the Anonymus ad Cuimnanum or from a common source. Another important source consists of the first two books of Isidore's *Etymologiae*.

189. Edited in PLM CI, 849–902; cf. Law (1982, 103).

190. On Alcuin's re-introduction of Priscian's *Institutiones* see O'Donnell (1976). Among other works by Alcuin that might interest the historian of medieval linguistics we shall mention the *De orthographia* (edited in PLM CI, 901–20, then in GLK VII, 295–312), the *Dialogus de rhetorica et virtutibus* (edited in PLM CI, 919–46, then in Halm 1863, and, with a translation, introduction and notes, in Howell 1965) and especially the *De dialectica* (edited in PLM CI, 949–76). There is no lack of interesting elements in the latter, particularly from the didactic point of view, such as the definition – on the model of Varro and Cassiodorus – of the fields of pertinence of dialectics and rhetoric, traditionally understood as the two subdivisions of logic: 'Dialectica est disciplina rationalis quaerendi, diffiniendi et disserendi, etiam et vera a falsis discernendi potens . . . Dialectica et rhetorica est, quod in manu hominis pugnus astrictus et palma distenta. Illa brevi oratione argumenta concludit; ista per facundiae campos copioso sermone discurrit. Illa verba contrahit; ista distendit. Dialectica siquidem ad inveniendas res acutior; rhetorica ad inventas dicendas facundior' ('Dialectics is the rational discipline of seeking, defining and discussing, able to discern truth from falsehood . . . Dialectics and rhetoric are like the closed fist and the open palm in the hands of men. The first encloses arguments within a brief speech; the latter goes over the fields of eloquence with copious discourse. The first contracts words; the second opens them up. If dialectics on the other hand is sharper for finding things, rhetoric is more eloquent to say the things that

have been found') (PLM CI, 952 D-953 A), and the definitions –
influenced by Aristotle and Boethius – of *nomen, verbum, oratio* and
*enuntiatio*, on which see, respectively, PLM CI, 973 A–B: 'Vox
significativa secundum placitum, sine tempore, diffinitum aliquid
significans, in nominativo casu, cum *est* et *non est*, in obliquis casibus
nihil, cuius nulla pars est significativa separata. Ut: Socrates' ('A *vox*
signifying according to agreement, without tense, indicating something definite in the nominative, with *est* and *non est*, in the oblique
cases it does not signify anything definite; no separate part of it is
signifying'), *ibid.* 974 A: 'Vox significativa secundum placitum, cum
tempore diffinitum aliquid significans, et accidens' ('A *vox* signifying
according to agreement, with tense, signifying something definite,
and an accident'), *ibid.* 974 C: 'Congrua partium ordinatio, perfectam
sententiam demonstrans, cuius partium aliquid separatum significativum est' ('Coherent ordering of parts offering a perfect sentence, of
whose parts something separate is signifying') and *ibid.* 974 C–D:
'Enuntiatio est oratio veri vel falsi significativa ... Principales sunt
species orationis, secundum dialecticos, quinque; sed haec sola, id est,
enuntiativa verum aliquid vel falsum significat; ut, *homo est,* vel *homo
non est*; *Socrates disputat, Socrates non disputat.* Horum enim unum
verum esse necesse est, id est, aut Socratem disputare, aut Socratem
non disputare. Et in hac sola specie philosophi, qui de veritate rerum
vel de falsitate disputaverunt, omnes suas posuerunt controversias
... et illae aliae species quatuor (*scil.* interrogativa, imperativa,
deprecativa et vocativa) ... non pertinent ad dialecticos, sed ad
grammaticos' ('*Enuntiatio* is a speech that indicates truth or falsehood ... According to the dialecticians, the principal kinds of speech
are five; but only this one, i.e. the enuntiative kind, indicates something true or false, like *homo est* or *homo non est, Socrates disputat* or
*Socrates non disputat.* Only one of these things can be true, i.e. either
that Socrates disputes or that Socrates does not dispute. And the
philosophers, who have disputed on the truth or falsehood of things
have placed all their controversies within this only kind ... and all
the other four kinds (i.e. interrogative, imperative, deprecatory and
vocative) ... do not pertain to dialecticians, but to grammarians').
For Alcuin's *recensio* of the Bible, see Fischer (1957).

191. Edited in PLM CXI, 613–70, followed by the *Glossae verborum in
Donatum maiorem,* ibid. 670–8; cf. Law (1982, 103–4). Compared to
Alcuin's grammar, the brief treatise by the *praeceptor Germaniae* is
more strongly marked by scholastic compilation, though conducted
with precision and intelligence; among the most interesting observations we shall mention, within the usual fourfold division of linguistic
units, the repetition of the traditional comparison – mostly derived
from Priscian – between *littera* and the natural prime elements that
are not divisible: 'littera quoque ipsa minime potest dividi, unde haec
a philosophis *atomos* dicitur, id est, indivisibilis ... Elementum est
enim minima vis, est indivisibilis materia vocis articulatae ... Veteres
etiam litteras elementa dixerunt, ad similitudinem mundi elemento-

rum; eo quod sicut illa coeuntia omne perficiunt corpus, sic etiam ista coniuncta orationem conservant et disiuncta dissolvunt' ('the letter itself cannot be divided, hence it is called *atomos*, i:e. indivisible, by philosophers ... The element is in fact the minimal essence, the indivisible matter of articulated *vox* ... The ancients also called letters elements, similarly to the world's elements; because, as elements by joining together form all individual bodies, so letters by joining together preserve discourse, and dissolve it if they are separate') (PLM CXI, 614 C–D).

192. See Bischoff (1966–81, II, 34–51).

193. Cf. Law (1982, 104) and, particularly for the extracts from Charisius, Holtz (1978).

194. Cf. Law (1982, 104–5); the ample, typically scholastic treatise, is edited by Chittenden (1982) in CCCM. Among the grammatical works from the Carolingian period with the clearest characteristics of manuals we must also mention the *Ars Laureshamensis*, an *expositio in Donatum maiorem* edited by Löfstedt (1977), also in the CCCM.

195. Edited by Holtz (1977) in the CCCM. Murethach, a contemporary of Iohannes Scotus Erigena and of Sedulius Scottus, taught in Metz and, earlier, in Auxerre, where among his pupils was the founder of the famous School, Haimo of Auxerre, the theologian among whose disciples is Heiricus, teacher of Remigius. *Doctissimus populi* – as he defined himself – *vel doctissimus plebis* (cf. Murethach 1977, 79, 44), the Irish grammarian must be remembered mainly for the pedagogic approach that characterizes his treatise, which concentrates specifically on the method of *quaestio*, which was widely tested in the field of scriptural exegesis and was frequent even in late Latin grammar of the fourth and fifth century; when they are considered from a more general point of view, Murethach's materials are mainly analogous to those found in the *Ars Laureshamensis* and in the commentary on the Donatian *Ars maior* by Sedulius Scottus, so that one may easily suppose that they both derive from a common source. A certain banality and repetitive scholasticism seem to predominate in Murethach's work compared to the instances of original exposition, within which one can place both the theory of the *officia partium orationis* (for which see the above-mentioned edition by Holtz: Murethach 1977, 50, 26 ff.) and the introductory paragraphs to each chapter of the treatise. A definite taste for etymology and sophisticated discussion remains, however, the most interesting element in Murethach's text, which moreover is written very clearly in a Latin which basically follows classical rules. Discussion is used to explain the Donatian text of the *partes orationis* according to precise exegetic systems, which aim to define what is appropriate to each *pars* and what it has in common with others, so that, through grammatical teaching, the principles of dialectic teaching are set out. This text soon spread into France – but not into Germany, Italy or Spain – and for some generations remained as the manual used by the Auxerre School. After the eleventh century it started a slow decline, when it was

supplanted by Remigius' treatises, which by this time were closer to the new educational organization that would relegate Donatus (and particularly the *Ars minor*) to elementary teaching, preferring Priscian, Phocas and Martianus Capella for teaching at a higher level. See the introduction to the above-mentioned edition by Holtz (Murethach 1977, XXI–XXXV, LXII–LXXVIII).

196. Edited by Clausen (1948). It rightfully takes its place along a line which is mostly analogous to Murethach's and the insular models, although it presents, in the long and diffused commentary to the definitions of the *Ars minor*, some expositive characteristics that already take into account the new tendencies that matured in the field of scholastic pedagogy, as we have just illustrated in the preceding note.

197. Some extracts from it were edited by Morelli (1910).

198. It seems that Smaragdus could be placed in the first decade of the ninth century, and more precisely around 805; the provenance of the abbot of Saint-Mihiel is stil uncertain, although by this time one is led to believe that he was of southern origin, perhaps specifically Spanish, by a whole series of clues – not least the stylistic clues – among which we must consider the use of the grammar by Iulianus Toletanus and a good knowledge of Visigoth names. However, it seems clear that Smaragdus was deeply influenced by the cultural climate of the Carolingian court, as is proved, among other things, by the numerous connections between his grammar and the grammars of Alcuin and Clemens Scottus. Edited – after the data and the *excerpta* collected in Thurot (1869, 4–5, 65, 68–9, 81, 85–6, 118) – by Löfstedt et al. (1986) in CCCM, the *Liber in partibus Donati* shows a true theological vision of language on the part of its author, which brings to an ideal completion the already present or at least identifiable instances in the 'Christian' revision of Donatus' *Ars minor*, and also reflects in several cases the contemporary linguistic *consuetudo*, especially noting the cases of convergence with the Latin of Biblical scriptures, the greatest *auctoritas* to which the norm which is the object of grammatical teaching should conform, all the more so when the usage found in the scriptures diverges from that found in the classical authors. An exegetical purpose and a solid doctrinal preparation are interwoven in Smaragdus' work, whose basic postulations are thus expressed by Holtz in the introduction to his edition (1986, LI–LII): 'les lois du langage supposent une conception globale de l'univers ... la grammaire des hommes est aussi celle de Dieu, puisqu'il a emprunté leur langage pour leur parler dans l'Ecriture ... les règles de grammaire jadis établies par les païens reflètent un ordre de réalité transcendant: elles trouvent leur justification et leur signification dans la conception chrétienne d'un univers créé et racheté ... étudier la grammaire n'est donc pas se détourner de Dieu, mais tout au contraire entrer plus avant dans la lecture et dans la compréhension des Saintes Ecritures (*Diuinae Scripturae*): ainsi, le nombre huit des parties du discours est en correspondance avec la vie future (1 T, 40 sqq.). A travers les

réalités du langage, l'élève est invité à découvrir les signes de la
présence de Dieu au monde' ('the laws of language presuppose a
global conception of the universe ... men's grammar is also God's
grammar, since he has borrowed their language in order to speak to
them in the Scriptures ... the rules of grammar that had been set
down by the pagans reflect a transcendental order of reality: they
have their justification and their significance in the Christian concept
of a created and redeemed universe ... therefore studying grammar
does not mean turning away from God, but on the contrary going
further into reading and understanding the Holy Scriptures (*Diuinae
Scripturae*): so, the number eight of the parts of speech corresponds
to the future life (1T, 40 ff.). Through the realities of language, the
pupil is invited to discover the signs of God's presence in the world').
Smaragdus' work, which was widespread throughout the ninth century, suffered a gradual decline from the end of the following century,
in the context of a scholastic education which by this time was aimed
more at the study of the classics and less disposed to an unconditional
acceptance of the Bible's and the classical authors' *auctoritas*.

199. The *Commentum in Maiorem Donatum Grammaticum* is edited by
     Brearley (1975) and by Löfstedt (1977) in CCCM, XL B; the other
     commentaries by Sedulius Scottus, *In Donati Artem minorem*, *In
     Priscianum* and *In Eutychem*, are edited by Löfstedt (1977) in the
     CCCM, XL C. A first edition of the commentary on Eutyches had
     been done by Hagen in GLK VIII (*Anecdota Helvetica*), 1–38.
200. The commentary *In Artem Donati minorem* is edited by Fox (1902),
     while the *In Artem maiorem Donati* was published by Hagen as
     *Commentum Einsidlense* in GLK VIII (*Anecdota Helvetica*), 219–74,
     an edition to be completed with Elder's supplements (1947). For a
     preliminary outline on the many other commentaries attributed to
     Remigius of Auxerre, see Brunhölzl (1975, 486–9 and 572–4).
201. Edited by Lambot (1945, 353–496).
202. This author produced mainly scattered grammatical observations to
     be found in his letters, most of which have been collected in Lambot
     (1945, 504–8).
203. See the full survey done by Thurot (1869, 11–26): apart from authors
     of great cultural importance, such as Abelard, Hugh of St Victor,
     William of Conches and Petrus Helias, they are mostly anonymous
     works, consisting of glosses, precepts and commentaries on the most
     varied grammatical questions – more rarely on those specifically
     pertinent to prosody and metre – often in a confused, disorganized
     and fragmentary form.
204. Cf. *Metalogicon* I, 23, Webb 1929, 53.
205. See especially Chenu (1935).
206. Collected in Hunt (1980).
207. It may be useful to mention that the *Priscianus maior* included books
     I–XVI of the *Institutiones grammaticae*, while books XVII–XVIII
     were known by the name of *Priscianus minor*; the term *Orthographia
     Prisciani* referred to the material in books I, 3–II, 13.

208. See a detailed description in Hunt (1980, 2–3).
209. Cf. the passage discussed by Hunt (1980, 19, n. 2): 'Non debet mirum videri si iuniores gramatice artis dicuntur perspicaciores in inventione, quia, cum primus inventor per totam vitam suam in quatuor forsitan litteris elaborasset inveniendis, iunior in solo die potuit eas addiscere, et post ex sua parte alias invenire, et ita per additionem successorum ad perfectionem ista ars increvit' ('It must not seem strange if the younger students of the grammatical art seem more acute in invention, because where the first inventor worked to find perhaps four letters in all his life, the younger was able to learn them in just one day, and later discover more for himself, and so through the addition of each successor this art reached perfection'); as for the general problem of the attribution of names to things, a possible source of the *Glosule* can be discerned in the treatise *De eodem et diverso* by Adelard of Bath, a famous translator of Greek and Arab texts, who was educated in the theological milieu of the Schools of Laon and Tours in the twelfth century, and this treatise in turn can be considered to have been influenced by Boethius.
210. See the following statements, quoted by Hunt (1980, 19, n. 3, 4 and 20): 'Nomina vero non dicuntur alique voces simpliciter quia designant substantiam cum qualitate, sed quia ad hoc officium explendum proprie sunt invente' ('Some words (*voces*) are not called nouns simply because they indicate a substance with quality, but because they were discovered in order to fulfil this function'); 'Non enim sunt iudicande voces secundum actum constructionis, sed secundum propriam naturam inventionis' ('Therefore *voces* should not be judged according to the act of construction, but according to its own nature of invention'); 'Proprium est nominis substantiam cum qualitate significare tantum secundum hoc quod est nomen, id est secundum suam inventionem' ('It is proper of the noun to signify a substance with quality only according to the fact that it is a noun, i.e. according to its invention').
211. Cf. Hunt (1980, 3–5).
212. Cf. Hunt (1980, 21, n. 5).
213. See the passage in the *Note Dunelmenses* quoted by Hunt (1980, 22, n. 1): 'Gramatica . . . tantum considerat rectam coniunctionem vocum secundum regulas et usus actorum; dialectica vero veritatem et falsitatem investigat . . . Unde conicimus in eadem oratione secundum gramaticos et dialecticos diversos esse sensus, ut cum dicitur "Homo est albus", gramaticus simplicem sensum attendit, ut exponitur pueris; dialecticus vero altius de predicatione et subiectione considerat' ('Grammar . . . considers only the correct joining of words according to the rules and customs of the authors; on the other hand, dialectics examines truth and falsehood . . . Hence we assume that in the same discourse there will be different senses according to the grammarians and the dialecticians, as when one says *Homo est albus*, the grammarian is concerned with the simple meaning, as it is explained to children; but the dialectician considers more deeply the use of predi-

cate and subject'). Very suitably Hunt mentions, in the same context, Abelard's developments of such a methodological perspective.

214. Cf. Hunt (1980, 25, n. 1)
215. Cf. Hunt (1980, 26, n. 4).
216. Edited by Tolson (1978) for the part concerning the *Priscianus minor*; several *excerpta* of varying length can be found in Thurot (1869), Pinborg (1961), de Rijk (1962–7), Fredborg (1973) and Hunt (1980).
217. In particular, it seems, between 1135 and 1160; Petrus Helias, a disciple of Thierry of Chartres in Paris in 1130, is mentioned among his rhetoric teachers by John of Salisbury. For other news on the life and works of the *Pictavensis* (according to a statement by William of Tyr who studied in Paris between 1145 and 1165) see the Introduction by Margaret T. Gibson to Tolson's above-mentioned edition (1978, 159–66).
218. Cf. Thurot (1869, 121–2); it will be noticed that the definition does not include the interpretation of the *auctores*, a task that was still carried out in the practice of grammatical teaching.
219. Cf. Cucchi (1983, 65). It could be pointed out that the immediate antecedent to Petrus Helias' work is certainly traceable in the *Glose super Priscianum* by William of Conches; on the close connections whereby the *Summa* depends on the *Glose* see Fredborg (1973) and Hunt (1980, 104–6).
220. Cf. Thurot (1869, 122); being still far from the hypothesis that, underlying the accidental variations typical of each idiom, there is a single general grammar, which alone can be the object of scientific speculation, Petrus Helias believes that every language has its own specific grammar that can be treated differently: 'Species cuiuslibet artis qualitates sunt quas artifex per artem attribuit materie. Cum enim species pluribus modis accipiatur, hic pro forma vel pro qualitate ponitur. Sunt ergo species artis gramatice genera linguarum in quibus ars gramatica tractata est et composita. Vocem enim format artifex in diversa linguarum genera secundum artem gramaticam. Est autem gramatica composita in lingua greca, latina, ebrea, et caldea. Et possunt huius artis species crescere, hoc est plures esse, ut si gramatica tractaretur in gallica lingua (quod posset fieri facile, si tantum nomina et figure proprie illius secundum illam linguam invenirentur), sive in alia aliqua in qua nondum tractata est' ('The species of any art are the qualities which the *artifex* attributes to matter by his art. Since *species* can be understood in various ways, it is taken here for form or quality. Therefore the (different) kinds of languages in which the grammatical art is discussed and composed are species of the grammatical art. Indeed the *artifex* forms the *vox* in different kinds of languages according to the grammatical art. Indeed grammar is composed in the Greek, Latin, Hebrew and Chaldean languages. And the species of this art can grow, that is be more, if, for example, one discussed grammar in the Gallic language (which may happen easily, if only one could find its own nouns and figures according to that language) or in another language in which it has not yet been

discussed') (Thurot 1869, 126–7). In the following century, as we shall see, Robert Kilwardby will be able to recognize grammar, as a speculative science, as having the main task of investigating the constitutive principles of *oratio congrua*, irrespective of any special language.

221. Defined and carried out according to the traditional Isidorian method: 'Ethimologia ... est expositio alicuis vocabuli per aliud vocabulum, sive unum sive plura magis nota, secundum rei proprietatem et litterarum similitudinem, ut *lapis* quasi ledens pedem, *fenestra* quasi ferens nos extra; hic enim rei proprietas attenditur et litterarum similitudo observatur ... ut dicatur ethimologia quasi veriloquium, quoniam qui ethimologizat veram, id est primam, vocabuli originem assignat. Differt autem ab interpretatione, que est translatio de una loquela in aliam; ethimologia vero fit sepius in eadem loquela' ('Etymology ... is the explanation of a word by another word, either by one or by several better known words, according to the property of the thing and the similarity of letters, like *lapis* as if *ledens pedem* (hitting the foot), *fenestra* as if *ferens nos extra* (taking us out); in this way one pays attention to the properties of the thing and observes the similarity of letters ... so etymology can be called almost a speaking the truth (*veriloquium*), because whoever seeks an etymology assigns the true, i.e. the first, origin of the word. But it differs from interpretation, which is the translation from one language into another; whereas etymology is carried out more often in the same language') (Thurot 1869, 146–7). As well as being different from *interpretatio*, as we have just seen, etymology is also different from *compositio*, as is clear from the following examples, which are fairly representative of the explanatory procedures adopted by Petrus Helias: '*Mancus* dicitur quasi manu carens; et videtur ethimologia esse, non compositio' ('One says *mancus* (maimed) almost like *manu carens* (missing a hand); and it is seen to be etymology, not composition'), '*Gladius* dicitur quasi gulam dividens per ethimologiam' ('One says *gladius* (sword) almost like *gulam dividens* (dividing the throat) by etymology'), '*Cadaver* dicitur quasi caro data vermibus, et est ethimologia. Vel a carendo dicitur, eo quod careat debito honore sepulchri' ('One says *cadaver* (corpse) almost like *caro data vermibus* (meat given to the worms), and it is an etymology. Or it is so called from *carere* (to lack), because he lacks the due honour of the grave') (Thurot 1869, 147); ' "Persona" ' ... a personando dicitur. Unde debuit dici penultima correpta, sed ad differentiam imperativi "persona" dicitur penultima producta. Quod enim persona quasi pars una, id est per se una, dicitur, non est compositio immo ethimologia' ('*Persona* is so called from *personando* (resounding). Therefore one should say it with a short penultimate syllable but to distinguish it from the imperative *persona* is said with a long penultimate syllable. And because *persona* is said almost like *pars una* (one part), i.e. *per se una* (one for itself), it is not composition but etymology') (Tolson 1978, 20, 99–3). It should be kept in mind that in the following

century the term *ethimologia* will also include the study of declensions, conjugations and word formation: as we can read at the beginning of the *Catholicon* by Joannes Balbus of Genoa, 'sub ista [*scil.* ethimologia] comprehenduntur octo partes orationis et earum accidentia' ('under this [etymology] are included the eight parts of speech and their accidents') (Thurot 1869, 147).

222. See especially the application of the notion of *modus significandi*, later destined to play an essential role in the theoretical development of speculative grammar: 'Scis quare omnia nomina dicantur esse una pars et eadem orationis, ita quod unumquodque illorum est illa pars: ideo scilicet quia hec pars orationis distinguitur ab aliis secundum suum modum significandi. Hic enim modus significandi qui est significare substantiam cum qualitate, facit quod nomen sit et dicatur una pars orationis ... Esse namque eandem partem orationis non est idem esse, sed potius eundem modum significandi habere. Secundum hoc ergo exponenda est descriptio illa: pars orationis est vox indicans mentis conceptum, id est vox reperta ad significandum aliquid vel consignificandum' ('You know why all nouns are said to be one and the same part of speech, so that each of them is this part: therefore also because this part of speech is distinguished from the others according to its *modus significandi*. This *modus significandi*, which is to indicate a substance with quality, makes it be a noun, and be called one part of speech ... Indeed being the same part of speech is not being the same thing, but rather having the same *modus significandi*. Therefore this description can be accordingly explained like this: a part of speech is a *vox* indicating a concept of the mind, i.e. it is a *vox* found in order to signify something or to consignify') (Thurot 1869, 153); this notion is expressly used to determine and at the same time to justify the number of parts of speech: 'Queritur autem quare magis dicantur esse septem partes quam octo vel novem. Ad quod dicendum est quod non sunt nisi septem modi significandi vel consignificandi in locutione et propter unumquemque modum significandi reperta est pars orationis ut unus est modus significandi in locutione significare substantiam cum qualitate, propter quem modum significandi reperta est hec pars orationis nomen, quia omne nomen significat substantiam cum qualitate, sicut expositum est. Est autem alius modus significandi significare actionem vel passionem, propter quem modum significandi reperta est hec pars orationis verbum. Est autem alius modus significandi significare agentem vel pacientem quid, propter quem modum significandi repertum est participium ... Est autem alius modus significandi significare substantiam sine qualitate, propter quem repertum est pronomen ... Est alius modus significandi vel consignificandi determinare qualitatem actionis vel passionis que per verbum significatur, propter quem repertum est adverbium. Est alius modus significandi vel consignificandi significare circumstantias rerum, propter quem reperta est prepositio ... Est autem alius modus significandi significare coniunctionem vel disiunctionem rerum, propter quem reperta est coniunctio.

Secundum Priscianum vero non est unus modus significandi per se, propter quem reperta sit interiectio; ideoque non sunt nisi septem partes orationis' ('One asks why it is said that there are seven parts of speech rather than eight or nine. To this one must say that there are only seven *modi significandi* or *consignificandi* in speech and for each *modus significandi* one part of speech has been discovered, as one *modus significandi* in speaking is to signify a substance with quality, and for this *modus significandi* the part of speech called noun has been found, because each noun signifies a substance with quality, as has been explained. There is another *modus significandi*, which is to signify an action or a passive condition, for which *modus significandi* the part of speech called verb has been found. There is another *modus significandi* that signifies the agent or patient of something, and for this *modus significandi* the participle was found . . . There is another *modus significandi* which signifies a substance without quality, for which the pronoun was found . . . There is another *modus significandi* or *consignificandi* which determines the quality of an action or a passive condition which is signified by a verb, for which the verb was found. There is another *modus significandi* or *consignificandi* that signifies the circumstances of things, for which the preposition was found . . . There is another *modus significandi* that signifies the conjunction or disjunction of things, for which the conjunction was found. According to Priscian there is no single *modus significandi* per se, for which the interjection might be found; therefore there are no more than seven parts of speech') (Tolson 1978, 31, 95–32, 37). We could also mention the frequent use of the term *nomen substantivum*, already found in Abelard (and present in isolated instances, in the guise of *nomen substantiale*, in an anonymous ninth century commentary on Donatus' *Ars maior*, possibly belonging to the School of Auxerre, cf. Thurot 1869, 80–1), although the corresponding notion of *nomen adiectivum* – which was also used by Abelard – does not appear consistently to be attributed a precise status of its own. On the subject, see Thurot (1869, 165–6, including notes). The Priscianean notion of *verbum substantivum* caused Petrus Helias many difficulties in interpretation; it was an incorrect translation, as we know, of *huparktikòn rhêma*, derived from the confusion between the ideas of *húparxis* 'existence', and *ousía* 'substance': for a detailed discussion of the problem, see Thurot (1869, 177–9) and Hunt (1980, 27–9)

223. See, among other things, the definition of *oratio* and the linked definition of *constructio*: 'non quelibet dictionum coniunctio debet dici oratio, sed illa tantum que aliquam inherentiam, id est rerum coniunctionem, significat, quoniam *in domo*, licet ibi sit dictionum coniunctio, quia tamen nullam illa rerum inherentiam significat, ideo non est oratio. Sed *homo albus*, quamvis sit imperfecta oratio, tamen, quia significat quandam accidentis et substantie coniunctionem, debet oratio appellari' ('not any conjunction of words should be called a sentence (*oratio*), but only the one that signifies some kind of inherence, i.e. a joining of things, since *in domo*, although there is a joining

of words, because it does not signify any inherence of things, therefore it is not a sentence. But *homo albus*, although it is an imperfect sentence, still, because it signifies some kind of joining of accident and substance, must be called a sentence') (Thurot 1869, 214–5); 'Constructio itaque est congrua dictionum ordinatio. "Congrua" intelligendum est tam voce quam sensu. Tunc est ordinatio dictionum congrua voce quando sua accidentia sibi congrue coniunguntur . . . ut "homo albus currit"; ibi masculinum masculino et singulare singulari coniungitur. Congrua vero sensu est ordinatio dictionum quando ex dictionibus predicto modo ordinatis habet auditor quid rationabiliter intelligat sive verum sit sive falsum, ut cum dicitur "homo currit", vel "Socrates est lapis". Quamvis enim hec propositio falsa sit, tamen ea auditor aliquid rationabiliter intelligit' ('Construction is a congruous ordering of words. "Congruous" should be understood as both in *vox* and meaning. Then the ordering of words is congruous regarding *vox*, when its accidents are joined together congruously . . . as in *homo albus currit* (the white man runs); here masculine is joined with masculine and singular with singular. But the ordering of words is congruous in meaning when from the words ordered in such a way the listener has something which he may rationally understand, whether true or false, as when one says *homo currit* (the man runs), or *Socrates est lapis* (Socrates is a stone). Although this proposition is false, nevertheless through it the hearer understands something rationally') (Tolson 1978, 1, 4–15). Semantic and grammatical/syntactical congruence do not presuppose each other in *constructio*, since, for example, *turba ruunt* (the crowd run) is a 'dictionum ordinatio' which, though it is incongruous regarding *vox*, is still congruous for its meaning, and, on the contrary, *Socrates habet ypoteticos sotulares cum cathegoricis corrigiis* (Socrates has hypothetical shoes with categorical laces) is a result of a joining of 'dictiones' which is certainly correct from the grammatical point of view, but is meaningless for a possible listener. A sentence that is judged false by reason, such as the above-mentioned *Socrates est lapis* (Socrates is a stone), or *propositio est alba* (the proposition is white), is still 'Latin' – and therefore 'correct' or, if preferred, 'congruous' and 'adequate' in every way – insofar as it generates 'aliquem intellectum . . . in auditore' ('some understanding . . . in the hearer'). If this condition does not apply, a sentence cannot be said to be properly 'Latin', even if it is made up 'ex Latinis dictionibus' 'of Latin words' in its individual elements. See Tolson 1978, 1, 16–2, 67 and particularly 2, 53–9: 'Aliter enim non erit constructio, nisi aliquem intellectum constituat in auditore. Et queritur si sit Latina locutio habens "cappam negativam". Quod est dividendum; Latina locutio est, id est ex Latinis dictionibus, verum est; Latina locutio est, id est qui ita loquitur Latine loquitur, falsum est. Non enim dicitur Latine loqui nisi ille cuius locutio aliquem intellectum generat in auditore' ('There is no construction unless it creates understanding in the hearer. And one asks if an expression including *cappa negativa* (negative cloak) is

Latin. This should be distinguished: it is true that it is a Latin expression, i.e. made from Latin words; it is false that it is a Latin expression, i.e. that whoever utters it speaks Latin. One cannot be said to speak Latin, unless with his speech he generates some understanding in the hearer'). One should also note the appearance of the terms *supponi* and *apponi* (the first of these, however, had already been used by Boethius in the *De differentiis topicis*), the immediate antecedents of the use of *suppositum* and *appositum* to indicate, respectively, the subject and predicate. This use would not be supplanted by the corresponding terms *subiectum* and *praedicatum*, which are usually present in treatises on logic: 'Sicut enim nomen repertum est ad significandum de quo dicitur, ita et verbum ad significandum quid de aliquo dicitur. Unde . . . quodlibet nomen per se supponitur, et verbum per se apponitur' ('In fact as the noun was found in order to signify what one speaks about, the verb was found in order to signify what is said about something. Hence . . . any noun per se is used as a subject (*supponitur*: lit. is placed under), and a verb per se is used as a predicate (*apponitur*: lit. is placed alongside)' (Thurot 1869, 217, and see Maierù 1972, *s. vv.*). We should also mention the explanation given by Petrus Helias on the use of *regere*: 'Ubi grammatici huius temporis dicunt quod dictio regit dictionem, ibi dicit Priscianus quod dictio exigit dictionem, et quod alii dicunt "regimen" ipse dicit "exigentiam" magis aperta utens locutione. Non tamen culpo nostrorum grammaticorum locutionem, quia metaphorice dictum est quod regat dictio dictionem, et est metaphora satis congrua. Sicut enim dux regit exercitum sic verbum regit nominativum in constructione positum' ('Where the grammarians of the present time say that a word governs (*regit*) another word, there Priscian says that a word requires (*exigit*) another word, and what others call "government" (*regimen*) he calls "requirement" (*exigentia*) using a clearer expression. However, I do not blame our grammarians' expression, because it is said metaphorically that a word governs another word, and it is a fairly suitable metaphor. As the ruler commands or governs the army, so a verb governs the nominative, placed in a construction') (Tolson 1978, 153, 13–9, and see the following, detailed discussion on whether the verb 'governs' the nominative or vice versa, *ibid.*, 153, 20–155, 93); *regere*, which was commonly used by Abelard and Hugh of St Victor, and gradually replaced the classical *coniungi / adiungi / construi / desiderare / exigere / sequi / trahere / servire*, is already present in isolated cases in the eighth and ninth centuries, and is found in Baudry de Bourgueil at the beginning of the twelfth century (cf. Thurot 1869, 82–4, 239–46, 523; Pinborg 1967, 51, 74–5, 130). Finally, we cannot neglect the use of the term *absolutus* applied to the particular ablative construction which is still defined thus: 'Illud quoque addit quod quando Greci volunt ostendere consequentiam aliquarum rerum utuntur genitivo casu ubi nos ponimus ablativum. Diceret enim Grecus "solis ascendentis dies fit" ubi nos dicimus "sole ascendente dies fit" et notatur ibi consequentia dici ad solem. Si

vero queratur a quo regitur "sole" vel "ascendente" dico quod
ablativi absoluti sunt nec ideo induxi de hiis, ut regantur ab aliqua
dictione, sed ut ostenderem quod ubi Greci ponunt genitivum ibi nos
ponimus ablativum' ('He also adds·that when the Greeks want to
show the consequence of something they use the genitive where we
put the ablative. The Greeks would say *solis ascendentis dies fit* (the
day comes of sunrise), where we say *sole ascendente dies fit* (the day
comes with sunrise) and here the consequence is attributed to the
sun. If one asks by what is *sole* or *ascendente* governed, I say that
they are absolute ablatives, and that, concerning them, I have not
suggested that they are governed by another word, but I wanted to
show that the Greeks use the genitive where we use the ablative'
(Tolson 1978, 134, 13–9, but see also Thurot 1869, 246–7). For
further comments the reader is referred to section 2.3, The Philosophy
of Language.

224. Probably datable from 1199, cf. Thurot (1869, 28) and especially
     Reichling (1893, XXXVI–XXXVII).

225. See a detailed description in Hunt (1980, 39–41 and 50–3).

226. Cf. Hunt (1980, 64): 'Hec est differentia inter nomina in -eus desinen-
     tia et illa que in -osus, quod illa ad materiam pertinent, ut ferreus de
     ferro, ista plenitudinem rerum notant per primitivum significatarum,
     ut saxosus plenus saxis' ('This is the difference between nouns ending
     in *-eus* and those ending in *-osus*, that the first concern matter, as
     *ferreus* (ferrous), "made of iron" from *ferrum* (iron), the second
     indicate the abundance of the things signified by the original word, as
     *saxosus* (stony) "full of stones" from *saxum* (stone)'); 'Item invenitur
     quod dictio, que deberet significare plenitudinem rei significate a qua
     sumitur dictio, non notat nisi plenitudinem rei illius quod est inferius,
     ut formosus dicitur non qui habet formam, sed qui bonam habet
     formam, et morosus non qui mores habet, sed qui malos habet
     mores' ('One also finds that the word which ought to indicate the
     abundance of the thing signified by the term from which the word is
     taken, only denotes the abundance of a lower thing, as one calls
     *formosus* (shapely) not someone who has a shape (*forma*), but some-
     one who has a good shape, and *morosus* not one who has habits
     (*mores*), but one who has bad habits'); 'Nomina verbalia in -io
     desinentia, ut visio, notant actum videntis vel passionem rei vise vel
     ipsum visum vel aptitudinem videndi' ('Verbal nouns ending in *-io*,
     like *visio* (vision), denote the act of seeing or the passive condition of
     the thing that is seen, or seeing itself, or the capacity of seeing'); 'Et
     nota quod huiusmodi verbalia visio, discretio, sepe aptitudinem signifi-
     cant, ut cum dicitur discretio sexus aptitudo discernendi sexum'
     ('And note that this kind of verbal nouns like *visio, discretio*, often
     indicate aptitude, like when the ability of distinguishing (*discernendi*)
     gender is called distinction (*discretio*) between the genders'). On the
     subject of these last two examples one should note, following Hunt
     (1980, 64–7), the use of the term *aptitudo*: this was found for the first
     time in Boethius' translation of the *Isagoge* by Porphyry, then in

Anselm, Peter Abelard and in the School of Chartres, and from then on the term acquires, in the context of grammatical speculation, those same technical characteristics found in the term *qualitas*, which had already been consolidated in the terminology of teachers of logic.

227. This is one of the most noticeable novelties in the School of Ralph of Beauvais compared to the tradition of earlier commentators and of Petrus Helias himself, in whose work the number of quotations from the classics is almost insignificant, cf. Hunt (1980, 67–8); references to Christian poetry, on the other hand, are still scarce.

228. They are the same texts, as can be easily verified, as those used in the curriculum of the contemporary *studia artium*; another set of quotations concerns the Bible, especially the Psalms and the Gospels. One should remember that, according to the exegetic stance taken by late Latin patristic writing and by a large proportion – as we have seen – of early medieval grammar, in cases where the language of the scriptural text diverges from classical usage, the principle according to which 'Divina pagina non subiacet regulis gramatice' ('The divine page is not subject to the rules of grammar') is restated, see Hunt (1980, 69–70).

229. Cf. Hunt (1980, 48), and see also de Rijk (1962–7, II, 1, 112). On this subject we cannot ignore the clear antecedents of Alcuin's and Clemens Scottus' above-mentioned observations, and the warning that, as we shall see, in all these cases it becomes indispensable to refer to Boethius' commentaries on Aristole's *De interpretatione*, which are, in the last analysis, the sources of a considerable part of the conceptual structure used and developed in various ways by medieval reflection on linguistics. See particularly Boethius, in *Comment in Arist. Periherm.*, II ed., Meiser 1880, 20: 'tribus his totus orandi ordo perficitur: rebus, intellectibus, vocibus. res enim ab intellectu concipitur, vox vero conceptiones animi intellectusque significat, ipsi vero intellectus et concipiunt subiectas res et significantur a vocibus' ('all the order of speech consists of these three aspects: things, intellections, words (*voces*). The thing is conceived by the intellect; the word (*vox*) signifies the conceptions of the soul and the intellections; the intellections themselves conceive the underlying things and are signified by words (*voces*)') cf. de Rijk (1962–67, II, 1, 179), Maierù (1972, 141–2), Hunt (1980, 70–1).

230. See, for example, the analysis on the ablative absolute. This is a denomination that became increasingly established in the grammatical tradition, cf. Hunt (1980, 74–5). On the development of the theory of syntax in the second half of the twelfth century see contributions by Kneepkens (1976; 1977; 1978).

231. Cf. Hunt (1980, 75).

232. For a systematic description of these, see Hunt (1980, 95–7), and especially Kneepkens (1987).

233. In the chronicle of the monastery of Saint-Martial in Limoges and in the catalogue of the monastery's library (written by Bernard Itier, who died in 1225) there are references to a Magister Petrus Hispanien-

sis: we know from the chronicle that he became a monk there in
1213, while from the catalogue we learn of the presence of a *Summa
magistri Petri Hispaniensis super librum Prisciani de constructione*,
and it seems fairly likely that they should be the same person, even if
we cannot be absolutely certain of it; however, an identification with
his namesake, the author of the *Summulae logicales*, can certainly be
rejected for chronological reasons. On this problem, see Hunt's
arguments (1980, 97–8).

234. This shows, in the last analysis, how widespread was Petrus Helias'
text, a kind of compulsory reference manual in schools of grammar;
among the many examples of literal repetition of this work in Petrus
Hispanus' *Summa* is the definition of *constructio* as *congrua dictionum
ordinatio*, cf. Hunt (1980, 100).

235. As for grammar, 'generaliter in omnibus huius artis rationibus non
necessitatem querimus sed probabilitatem' ('generally in all the explanations of this art we do not seek necessity but probability'), and it
should be kept in mind that 'aliter ... dicit grammaticus queri de
qualitate, aliter dialecticus' ('a grammarian says that quality is investigated in one way, and a dialectician in another') cf. Hunt (1980, 101).

236. As for its occurrences, the term is used at times in discussing those
parts of speech to which *substantia* (*cum* or *sine qualitate*) is attributed,
*substantia* as such being referable to *inventio dictionis*, cf. Hunt (1980,
105). We should also notice, still following Petrus Helias, the use of
*suppositum*, both in an ontological and a grammatical sense: in the
grammatical sense the term is a synonym of *subiectum* (as *appositum*
is a synonym of *praedicatum*); finally, we also find the use of *suppositio*, a term that is also destined to acquire technical values within the
conceptual apparatus of speculative grammar.

237. Cf. Hunt (1980, 108–11); on the problems of attribution see especially
Kneepkens (1987, 524–5).

238. Cf. de Rijk (1962–67, II, 1, 222); but we could go back to Alcuin and
Clemens Scottus, as we have seen, as well as referring to Boethius,
whether through them or not.

239. Cf. de Rijk (1962–67, II, 1, 111 and 239), Hunt (1980, 48 and 70).

240. Cf. Hunt (1980, 109).

241. Cf. Hunt (1980, 151–4).

242. On the hypothesis of a common source, on which both Osbern and
Hugutio might have drawn independently, see Hunt (1980, 151).

243. See, in this work – belonging, as we know, to the school of Ralph of
Beauvais and datable from the last quarter of the twelfth century –
the definitions of *ethimologia, interpretatio, derivatio* and *compositio*:
'Sunt qui assignent differentiam inter ethimologiam et interpretationem et derivationem hanc: Ethimologia est expositio unius vocabuli per aliud per vel alia magis notum vel magis nota secundum
rerum proprietatem et similitudinem litterarum, ut oratio quasi oris
ratio, lapis ledens pedem, fenestra ferens nos extra, cadaver caro data
vermibus, amicus animi custos, et hi dicunt quod amicus derivatur ab
hoc verbo 'amo' et ethimologiam ducit ab animo et custode. Interpre-

tatio est expositio unius lingue per aliam, ut antropos, i.e. homo. Derivatio est detorsio alicuius vocabuli ad similitudinem alicuius alterius prius inventi. Compositio est plurium dictionum ad unam dictionem faciendam adiunctio ... Et ethimologia quandoque fit per vocem non significativam, ut imago quasi imitago, quandoque per significativam' ('There are those who assign the difference between etymology and interpretation and derivation like this: Etymology is the explanation of one word by means of another that is better known or by means of others that are better known according to the property of things and the similarity of letters, like *oratio* (speech) as if it were *oris ratio* (reason of the mouth), *lapis* (stone): *ledens pedem* (hitting the foot), *fenestra* (window): *ferens nos extra* (leading us outside), *cadaver* (corpse): *caro data vermibus* (flesh given to the worms), *amicus* (friend): *animi custos* (guardian of the soul), and these say that *amicus* is derived from the verb *amo* (to love) and the etymology is drawn from *animus* (soul) and *custos* (guardian). Interpretation is the explanation of one language by means of another, like *antropos*, i.e. *homo* (man). Derivation is turning some word in the likeness of some other which has been found earlier. Composition is making an addition of several words to make one word ... And etymology sometimes has recourse to a *vox* that is not signifying, as *imago* (image) as if it were *imitago* (cf. *imitari* to imitate), sometimes with a signifying one') cf. Hunt (1980, 155–6); although there is a basic dependence on Petrus Helias, there is also evident progress compared to his definitions. Even the *Tria sunt* gloss, which we also saw earlier, has some interesting observations on this subject: 'hoc interest inter ethimologiam et interpretationem quod interpretatio est expositio alicuius vocabuli in alia lingua sive servetur vocum similitudo sive non. Ethimologia vero, ut quidam volunt, est simplex expositio vocabuli per aliam vocem vel per plures iuxta rei proprietatem et literarum similitudinem, ut per hoc nomen "simplex" removeatur compositio vel derivatio, ut fenestra ferens nos extra; sed largius ethimologia accipitur secundum Ysidorum ut amplectatur etiam expositionem que fit per compositionem vel per derivationem vel per aliam linguam iuxta litterarum similitudinem. Nam quandoque fit per compositionem, ut celebs celestium vitam ducens, cadaver caro data vermibus; quandoque per derivationem et hoc vel cum affinitate vocis et rei, vel cum affinitate vocis et non rei, sed similitudine contrarii, ut dux a ducendo, lux a lucendo, quandoque utroque, ut lapis ledens pedem, homo ab humo' ('this is the difference between etymology and interpretation, that interpretation is the explanation of some words in another language whether one keeps the similarity of the *voces* or not. Etymology however, according to some people, is the simple explanation of a word by means of another word or by means of several other words, according to the property of the thing and the similarity of letters, so that by the word "simple" (*simplex*) composition or derivation are excluded, as in *fenestra ferens nos extra* (window: leading us ouside); but etymology is taken in a wider sense according to Isidore, so as to embrace also the explanation which has recourse to composition or to derivation or to another language according to the similarity of letters. In fact at times it has recourse to composition, as *celebs: celestium vitam ducens* (celibate: leading the life of the celestians), *cadaver: caro data vermibus* (corpse: flesh given to the worms); at times to derivation, whether there is affinity between word (*vox*) and thing, or there is only affinity of word (*vox*) and not of the thing, but similarity to the opposite, as *dux* (leader) from *ducendo* (leading), *lux* (light) from *lucendo* (shining), at times both, as *lapis ledens pedem* (stone: hitting the foot), *homo* (man) from *humus* (soil)'), followed by the almost literal repetition of Isidore, *Etymol.* 1, 29, cf. Hunt (1980, 156–7).

244. Cf. Thurot (1869, 28–36, 98 ff.), who gives sizeable extracts as illustration; see also the critical edition in Reichling (1893), containing a very well-documented historical and exegetical introduction. As we have already seen, the *Doctrinale* is likely to have been written in 1199, cf. Reichling (1893, XXXVI–XXXVII). Its author, Alexander de Villa Dei, originated from Normandy and presumably was born towards the end of the 1160s, or, at the latest, in the early 1170s; he studied in Paris and, as well as the *Doctrinale*, which had been commissioned from him by the Bishop of Dol for his nephews' instruction – he wrote an *Alphabetum maius*, an *Alphabetum minus* and the *Ecclesiale*: for information on these works (and other minor works, beyond the interest of this study), see Reichling (1893, XXIX–XLIII). He probably died towards the middle of the thirteenth century, cf. Reichling (1893, XX–XXVI).

245. Cf. Thurot (1869, 27–8, 100 ff.); see the critical edition by Wrobel (1887). The publication date for the *Grecismus* seems to be 1212, cf. Reichling (1893, LXXIX–LXXXIII); *natione Flandrensis*, Eberhard of Béthune was a contemporary of Alexander de Villa Dei, although we are unable to give any more precise chronological detail.

246. See, on this subject, the reason given in the glosses on the *Doctrinale* recognizing it as superior to Priscian: 'Videtur quod superfluat liber iste, cum totam totaliter gramaticam tradiderit Priscianus. Ad hoc dicendum est quod non superfluit. Nam secudum philosophos eorum que sunt, quedam sunt ad esse, quedam ad bene esse, et neutrum horum superfluit ... Sermo metricus, quem sequitur actor iste, ad plura se habet quam prosaycus, quem sequitur Priscianus; et hoc ita probatur: sermo metricus utilis factus est ad faciliorem acceptionem, ad venustam et lucidam brevitatem, et ad memoriam firmiorem. Quod patet sequi ex diffinitione versus que sequitur: versus est metrica oratio, succincte et clausulatim progrediens, venusto verborum matrimonio et sententiarum flosculis picturata, nichil in se superfluum nichilque continens diminutum. Non est igitur mirum, si legitur liber iste, in quo compendiose traditur quod erat primitus dispendiosum et confusum, in quo ordinate traditur quod erat primitus inordinatum, in quo sub luce traditur quod erat primitus nubilosum, in quo potest capi de facili quod nonnulli capere desperabant'

('It seems that this book is superfluous, because Priscian handed down the whole of grammar completely. In this regard it must be said that it is not superfluous. According to the philosophers, out of the things that are, some are in order to be, some so that it is a good thing that they exist, and neither of them is superfluous ... Metrical speech, which this author follows, is used for more things than the speech in prose which Priscian follows; and here it is proved: metrical speech is useful for making acceptance easier, for its elegant and clear brevity, and for being remembered more strongly. Which follows clearly from the following definition of verse: verse is a metrical speech, which proceeds concisely by clauses, with an elegant marriage of words and adorned with flowers of sentences, containing nothing superfluous and nothing missing. One should not wonder, if one reads this book, in which what before was dispersed and confused is handed down in a compendious way, in which what was untidy is handed down tidily, in which what before was clouded is handed down in the light, in which one can easily understand what many despaired of understanding') cf. Thurot (1869, 101–2).

247. Respectively in the years 1328, 1366, 1386 and 1389, cf. Thurot (1869, 102) and Reichling (1893, XLIX); concerning the *Doctrinale* specifically, the presence of more than two hundred manuscripts and almost three hundred printed editions up to 1600 is unequivocal evidence of its success in Europe, especially in France and Germany, cf. Reichling (1893, XLIV–LXXI and, for the complete example of the *codices manu scripti et libri typis impressi*, CXXI–CCCIX). This success was certainly not hampered by the very negative criticism expressed on Alexander de Villa Dei by Roger Bacon in 1271, and later especially by Valla, at the height of Humanism: on this, see Thurot (1869, 28) and Reichling (1893, LXXXIII–LXXXV).

248. Among the most important commentaries on the *Doctrinale* we must mention especially the so-called *Admirantes* Gloss, that often suggests strained interpretations of the text, according to the practice of the *sophismata*, reducing normative examples drawn from the *auctores* to a minimum, but at times making interesting comparisons between Latin and French constructions, as in the case of the nominative absolute, of the *legitur Virgilium* syntagm, and the accumulation of prepositions such as *de ultra pontem*, cf. Thurot (1869, 28 ff., 119 ff.)

249. See, in the *Doctrinale*, statements like the following: 'Accentus normas legitur posuisse vetustas; / non tamen has credo servandas tempore nostro' ('One reads that the ancients set down the rules of the accent; / but I believe they are not to be kept in our time') (11. 2330–1, cf. Thurot 1869, 113; Reichling 1893, 155).

250. Cf. Thurot (1869, 99) and Reichling (1893, 7); they are, respectively, 11. 7–10 and 1. 2 of the proem.

251. On this subject, see explanations like the following: '*Armenis interpres, ut peryarmenias. / Bucolon* est *cultura boum*; *bucolica* monstrant. / Quod *sententia* sit *bole* probat *amphibolia*, / Quodque *fides broge* fit, hoc probat *Allobroga*. / *Materiamque baton* dicas; sit *yperbaton* inde.

/ Est quoque *dulce cymen*; inde *cymiterium*. / *Universale catha*; fit
*catholicus* inde. / Atque *fecem calcon auricalcon* probat esse. / *En
contra* signat; hinc et *elencus* erit. / Est *egle capra*; hinc *egloga* nomen
habet. / Est *lectos requies*; *allecto* dicitur inde. / Estque *melos dulcis* ac
inde *melodia* dicas. / Immutat *morphos*; hinc *metamorphoseos*. / *Orge
cultura* est; dic inde *georgica* nasci' ('*Armenis* (*hermeneus*) is interpreter,
as *peryarmenias*. / *Bucolon* is the care of oxen, as the *bucolica* show. /
*Amphibolia* proves that a *bole* is a *sententia*, / and *Allobroga* proves
that *broge* is *fides*. / You call *materiam baton*; hence *yperbaton*. /
*Cymen* is also *dulce*; hence *cymiterium*. / *Catha* is *universale*; hence
one says *catholicus*. / And *auricalon* proves that *calcon* is *fecem*. / *En*
indicates *contra*; hence there is *elencus*. / *Egle* is a *capra*; hence the
*egloga* takes its name. / *Lectos* is *requies*; hence one says *allecto*. /
*Melos* is *dulcis*, hence one says *melodia*. / *Morphos* changes; hence
*metamorphoseos*. / *Orge* is *cultura*; from which say that *georgica* is
born'), cf. Thurot (1869, 109–10).

252. See the commentary on 11. 1083–4 ('apponens duplices substantivos
sibi iunges / in casu simili, poteritque genus variari' 'when you
"appose" you join together two substantives / of similar case, but the
gender can vary', Reichling 1893, 71): 'Appositio est minus specifica-
tivi sive minus communis ad magis commune specificativa adiunctio'
('Apposition is the specifying addition of what is less specific or less
common to what is more common'); 'In appositiva ... constructione
illud cui alterum apponitur debet esse ut per se stans, et illud quod ei
apponitur, debet esse in ratione adiacentie et dependentie; ad ipsum
enim apponitur' ('In appositive ... construction, the element to
which another is appended must be independent, and the one that is
appended to it must be in a relationship of adjacency and dependency;
it is in fact appended to it'), cf. Thurot (1869, 255, and also 256–7).

253. According to the terminology that gradually becomes established in
the thirteenth century, cf. Thurot (1869, 342–3ff.).

254. Similar precepts are explicit in the *Doctrinale*'s ninth chapter,
11.1390–6: 'Construe sic: casum, si sit, praepone vocantem; / mox
rectum pones; hinc personale locabis / verbum, quod primo statues,
si cetera desint. / tertius hinc casus et quartus saepe sequuntur, / aut
verbo subdes adverbia. subde secundum / casum rectori. debet vox
praepositiva / praeiungi quarto vel sexto, quem regit illa' ('Construct
like this: if it is there, put the vocative first; / then put the direct case;
then put the personal verb, / which stands first, if the other elements
are missing. / Then the third and fourth cases often follow, / or make
the adverbs subordinate to the verb. Subordinate the second / case to
the one that governs it. The preposition / must be placed before the
fourth or the sixth case, which it governs'), cf. Thurot (1869, 342)
and Reichling (1893, 88–9); however, similar indications are already
present in an anonymous eleventh century manuscript: 'Omnis constructio ex substantia et actu fit. Que aut erit absoluta, ut *Iohannes
legit*, aut transitiva, hoc est ut agentis actus in pacientem transferatur,
ut *Iohannes legit librum*. In transitiva denique tria sunt constructionem

querentia, id est agentis et illius actus et in quo fit paciens, cum quibus etiam frequenter et qualitates et quantitates substancie vel actui adiecte positae inveniuntur, et ubi et quando et quare, ut ambiguitas pellatur et cercior ratio reddatur ... In omni namque constructione anteponitur agens, qui nominativo vel vocativo profertur, dehinc vero illius actus, postea autem in quo fit paciens, ut *Iohannes percussit Petrum.* Adiectiva vero si adfuerint, plerumque anteponuntur cui adiciuntur, ut *fortis Iohannes multum percussit debilem Petrum,* nisi vel figurate sint adiecta vel obliquos asciscentia; tunc enim postponuntur, ut *Iohannes magne virtutis* vel *Iohannes fortis brachium* vel *dignus laude percussit Petrum multe audacitatis* vel *fortem brachium* vel *dignum laude virga* vel *cum virga* ... Quare vero et ubi et quando, si adsunt frequentius, in constructione postponuntur, inter se autem quovis ordine poni possunt, ut *Iohannes magne virtutis multum percussit Petrum hodie in ecclesia ob furtum* vel *multum percussit Petrum ob furtum hodie in ecclesia.* Unde vero sepe postponitur, ut *Iohannes hodie venit de civitate'* ('Every construction consists of substance and act. Which will be either absolute, like *Iohannes legit* (Iohannes reads), or transitive, i.e. such that the act of the agent is transferred to the patient, like *Iohannes legit librum* (Iohannes reads a book). Finally, in a transitive one, there are three things requiring construction, i.e. concerning the agent, and his act, and the one who, in this act, becomes the patient; and with these one also frequently finds the quality and quantity are added to the substance, or to the act, and where and when and why, so that ambiguity should be rejected and understanding become clearer ... In every construction one places the agent first, which is given in the nominative or in the vocative, then its act, then again the one who, in this act, becomes the patient, like *Iohannes percussit Petrum* (Iohannes beat Petrus). The adjectives, if they are present, mostly are placed before the words to which they are added, like *fortis Iohannes multum percussit debilem Petrum* (strong Iohannes beat weak Petrus very much), unless used figuratively or requiring oblique cases; then they are placed after, like *Iohannes magne virtutis* (Iohannes of great virtue) or *Iohannes fortis brachium* (Iohannes of the strong arm) or *dignus laude percussit Petrum multe audacitatis* (the one who is worthy of praise beat Petrus who has great audacity) or *fortem brachium* (of the strong arm) or *dignum laude virga* (worthy of praise with a rod) or *cum virga* (with a rod) ... The why and where and when, if they are present more frequently, are placed after in the construction, but among themselves they can be placed in any order, like *Iohannes magne virtutis multum percussit Petrum hodie in ecclesia ob furtum* (Iohannes of great virtue beat Petrus very much today in the church because of a theft) or *multum percussit Petrum ob furtum hodie in ecclesia.* But the whence is often placed after, like *Iohannes hodie venit de civitate* (Iohannes came from the town today)') cf. Thurot (1869, 87–8).

255. Cf. Hunt (1980, 167ff., 172ff.). It is relevant to point out that Robert

Kilwardby appears among the sources or, at least, among the grammatical *auctoritates* quoted by Richard of Hambury and John of Cornwall. Robert Kilwardby was one of the exponents of speculative grammar; in particular, in John of Cornwall's *Speculum* presupposes the theory of the *modi significandi* in its most complete form, as can be deduced from the following examples: 'Item si queratur differentia inter adiectivum et substantivum, respondendum est quod adiectivum est istud quod significat rem ab alio dependentem vel alii adherentem per modum dependentis vel adherentis. Unde nota quod omnis dictio casualis significans rem ab alio dependentem sive alii adherentem per modum dependentis vel adherentis est adiectivum' ('Also if one enquires what is the difference between adjective and substantive, one must answer that the adjective is what signifies one thing that depends on another or adheres to another in the mode of the dependent or the adherent. Hence note that every word which has a case and signifies a thing that depends on another or adheres to another in the mode of the dependent or of the adherent, is an adjective'); 'Item modi significandi sunt cause constructionis, etc. Arguitur sic: ubicumque reperitur proporcio in modis significandi per quam aliquod nomen vel aliqua dictio quecumque sit potest construi cum genetivo, illud potest regere genetivum. Sed in nomine proprio est reperire modum significandi per quem potest construi cum genetivo' ('So the *modi significandi* are the causes of construction, etc. One argues thus: wherever one finds a possible relation in the *modi significandi* such that some noun or some word, whichever it is, can be constructed with the genitive, this noun can govern the genitive. But in a proper noun one has to find the *modus significandi* by means of which one may construct it with the genitive') cf. Hunt (1980, 181–2). It should also be remembered that Richard of Hambury's treatises are based on the fourfold division of grammar, used in the thirteenth century, into *orthographia, prosodia, ethimologia* and *diasentetica* and concentrate especially on problems concerning these last two parts, which correspond to morphology and syntax.

256. As well as the Donatian commentary by Pompeius, which, however, was used only by John of Cornwall.

257. See the edition in Lindsay (1913); we also refer the reader to the study by Moscadi (1979), while mentioning that in this work Festus summarized the *De verborum significatu* by Verrius Flaccus, on which cf. Bona (1964).

258. On the probable existence of two separate grammarians called Caper, of whom one lived in the second century AD and was the author of a *De Latinitate*, while the other lived in the fourth century AD, and wrote the *De orthographia* and the *De verbis dubiis*, see Rutella (1977). The edition of these two works is in GLK VII, 92–112.

259. See the edition by Willis (1963).

260. For this work we refer the reader to Lindsay's edition (1903), but also to the many philological and linguistic contributions by various authors collected in the ten volumes of *Studi Noniani* (1967–85). It

should be kept in mind that, in the 20 volumes of the African grammarian's work, ample space is devoted to etymology especially in book I, *De proprietate sermonum*, in book II, *De honestis et nove veterum dictis*, in book IV, *De varia significatione sermonum*, in book V, *De differentia similium significationum*, in book VI, *De inpropriis*, and in book XII, *De doctorum indagine*, while books XIII–XX (apart from XVI, which was lost) present some useful and interesting lists of technical terms concerning navigation, clothing, utensils, food and drink, weapons and kinship. As for what concerns one of the most classical aspects of late Latin and early Medieval lexicography, consisting of the so-called *differentiae verborum*, i.e. dealing with words showing close analogy on the level of signifier or signified, especially homophones or homographs and synonyms – as in the already mentioned book V of the Nonian *De compendiosa doctrina* – the reader is referred to Brugnoli's studies (1955).

261. The brief treatise by the fifth century African grammarian consists of 62 entries concerning the meaning of difficult or obsolete words, for which see Pizzani's edition (1968), accompanied by a full introduction, translation into Italian and commentary.

262. As a further illustration of Isidorian procedures as they are realized in the *De vocabulis*, the tenth book of the *Etymologiae*, let the following examples suffice: 'Amicus, per derivationem, quasi animi custos' ('Friend, (*amicus*) by derivation, as if it were guardian (*custos*) of the soul (*animi*)') (10, 4), 'Beatus dictus quasi bene auctus, scilicet ab habendo quod vellet et nihil patiendo quod nollet' ('One says blessed (*beatus*) as if it were well increased (*bene auctus*), i.e. from having what he wants and not suffering what he does not want') (10, 22), 'Fatigatus, quasi fatis agitatus' ('Tired, (*fatigatus*) as if it were troubled (*agitatus*) by the fates (*fatis*)') (10, 102), 'Gloriosus a frequentia claritatis dictus, pro C G littera conmutata' ('Glorious (*gloriosus*) is so called from the frequency of clarity (*claritatis*), with the letter C changed to G') (10, 112), 'Interpres, quod inter partes medius sit duarum linguarum, dum transferet' ('Interpreter (*interpres*), because he stands midway between the parties (*inter partes*) of the two languages while he translates') (10, 123), 'Inprobus dictus quod instat etiam prohibenti' ('One is called wicked (*inprobus*) because he is opposed (*instat*) even to one who forbids (*prohibenti*)') (10, 136), 'Luculentus, ab eo quod sit lingua clarus et sermone splendidus' ('Excellent (*luculentus*), because he is clear of language (*lingua clarus*) and splendid (*splendidus*) in speech') (10, 154), 'Piger, quasi pedibus aeger' ('Lazy (*piger*), as if it were ill in the feet (*pedibus aeger*)') (10, 212), 'Taciturnus, in tacendo diuturnus' ('Taciturn (*taciturnus*), constant (*diuturnus*) in being silent (*tacendo*)') (10, 267).

263. See the following examples, as well as the ones mentioned previously: '*Sol* dicitur quia solus per diem sui fulgoris vi totum orbem obtunsis una stellis cum luna inlustrat; vel certe sol ex sollemnitate, hoc est abundantia splendoris, nuncupatur' ('The sun (*sol*) is so called because during the day it illuminates the whole world by itself (*solus*) with the

strength of its splendour, obscuring the stars together with the moon; or the sun takes its name from the solemnity (*sollemnitate*), i.e. from the abundance of its splendour') (*Epit.* XI, 1, 8; Polara 1979, 148, 44–7), '*Avis* de aviditate carpendi dicenda est' (The bird (*avis*) takes its name from its greed (*aviditate*) in grasping') (*ibid.*, 2, 1; Polara 1979, 150, 61), '*Bestia* dicitur de bessu, hoc est more ferocitatis, *belua* marina erit, *bel* enim a filosophis mare vocatur' ('the beast (*bestia*) takes its name from *bessus*, i.e. from the habit of ferocity, a wild beast (*belua*) is a marine creature, since philosophers call the sea *bel*') (*ibid.*, 2, 3; Polara 1979, 150, 69–71), '*Caro* a caritate cognationis, *corpus* a corruptibilitate naturae dicendum' ('Flesh (*caro*) derives from the affection (*caritas*) of relations, body (*corpus*) from the corruptibility (*corruptibilitate*) of nature') (*ibid.*, 3, 1; Polara 1979, 150, 72–3), '*Caput* a capacitate sumendi dictum est' ('the head (*caput*) is so called from the ability (*capacitate*) to understand') (*ibid.*, 3, 3; Polara 1979, 152, 78–9), '*auris* eo quod auditus cordis sermones internos hauriat' ('the ear (*auris*) because hearing gathers (*hauriat*) the heart's intimate speech') (*ibid.*, 3, 4; Polara 1979, 152, 84–5), 'Filosophi virtutem et cursum *man* et *pen* vocaverunt, quorum nominum per omnes cassus numerosque et genera monoptota declinatio est; a man ergo, hoc est a virtute, *manus* appellatae sunt et a pen *pedes*, quod est a cursu' ('Philosophers called strength and running *man* and *pen*, and the declension of these nouns is invariable in all cases, numbers and genders; so from *man*, i.e. from strength, hands (*manus*) are named, and from *pen*, i.e. from running, feet (*pedes*) are named') (*ibid.*, 3, 9; Polara 1979, 152, 99–103), '*cor* vocatur a correctione sensuum' ('the heart (*cor*) is so called from its domination (*a correctione*) of the senses') (*ibid.*, 4, 1; Polara 1979, 154, 109–10), '*Labia* ex labore loquendi dicta intelleuntur; Aeneas meus in hoc nomine aliud intellexit: *ob hoc* inquit *labia vocantur quia cotidie per verba in vitium labuntur*' ('It is believed that the lips (*labia*) are so called from the labour (*labor*) of speaking; my Aeneas gave another interpretation on the subject of this name: "they are called lips (*labia*) because every day they fall (*labuntur*) into sin through words"') (*ibid.*, 4, 4; Polara 1979, 154, 115–8).

264. For the edition of Paulus' epitome see Lindsay (1913); we also refer the reader to the studies by Engels (1961), Cervani (1978) and Moscadi (1979).

265. Edited in Lindsay et al. (1926, I); on this work see the studies by Niedermann (1943–4) and Cazzaniga (1953).

266. In the absence of a modern critical edition, we refer the reader at least to the study by McGeachy (1938).

267. The two humanistic editions by Mombricius (1476; 1496) at the moment are the only complete reference for Papias' work, while we wait for the completion of the critical edition which Violetta De Angelis is carrying out, whose first three volumes on the letter A have been published up to now (1978–80). For all information about Papias' life and activity we definitely refer the reader to the full and

very well documented critical survey by Cremascoli (1969), mentioning in particular the contributions by Zonta (1960), Daly and Daly (1964), De Angelis (1970–71). We merely point out that 1045 remains the *terminus ante quem* to be able to fix the date of composition of the *Elementarium doctrine rudimentum*, this being the title that appears to be best documented; and that if Papias' work must undoubtedly be recognized to have an originality of its own in the way it 'adopts for the first time the derivatory method of cataloguing linguistic material, thus modifying the structure fixed by the lexicographic tradition leading to Ansileubus' (Cremascoli 1982, 244), it is also true that in general it shows certain features of a compilation, which is confirmed both by the author's own testimony, who in the Preface gives a detailed list of the sources he draws on, and by modern philological investigation, which has effectively shed light on its dependence especially on the *Liber glossarum* and on Priscian (on the subject see Cremascoli 1969, 41–2). Whether Papias knew Greek well is certainly not easy to prove: for what expressly concerns Greek words in grammatical and rhetorical terminology, as well as the etymological explanations of many words present in the *Elementarium*, they simply appear to be taken from Isidore or from the *Glossarium Ansileubi* and do not prove anything. Papias, whose name quickly became a common term to indicate, antonomastically, any type of lexicon, and which was often quoted as an authority up to the end of the fourteenth century – he is quoted and used in several instances even by Boccaccio – underwent a rapid decline in humanist circles, so much so that he was included among the *barbariei duces vel praecipuos* (main leaders of barbarism) in the severe judgement passed by Erasmus from Rotterdam on the rough language and style that was supposed to have characterized the writers of the Middle Ages in general (cf. Cremascoli 1969, 53).

268. Also known as *Panormia*, it was edited as an anonymous work by cardinal Angelo Mai in 1836 under the title *Thesaurus novus Latinitatis*; see on this subject the studies by Robustelli Della Cuna (1972; 1975) and Hunt (1980, 151–66).

269. While we wait for the critical edition which is being carefully prepared by Giancarlo Schizzerotto, we refer the reader for the moment to the *excerpta* in Riessner (1965, 193–233 and *passim*, on which, however, see Schizzerotto's critical review 1967). The contents of earlier lexica flow to a wide extent into Hugutio's work, particularly the contents of the *Liber glossarum*, of Papias' work, and of Osbern of Gloucester's *Liber derivationum*, as well as, obviously, the material drawn from Isidore's *Etymologiae*. For the date of composition of Hugutio's lexicon, see Cremascoli (1978, 95–6), who puts forward an argued chronology of Hugutio's writings, proving unequivocally that it is impossible to place the *Derivationes* in the years 1190–7, the time that earlier scholars generally accepted. In a way Hugutio's lexicon seems to take shape as the first real dictionary in the modern sense of the term, understood as a systematic inventory of the whole lexical

wealth of the language, whose make-up derives from the confluence
of the various techniques used in the glossaries – which often collected
only the most rare and obsolete terms – and in the so-called *disciplina
derivationis*, one of the fundamental components, as we have already
seen, of etymological research. Hugutio's work, which was continued
by Willelmus Noviomensis (or William of Noyon, on whom see
Haskins 1927), was widely used by Joannes Balbus of Genoa in
compiling the *Catholicon*; the latter improved the system of arranging
words in alphabetical order, and was imitated by Angelo Senisio at
the time of writing the *Declarus* (on which see Marinoni 1955). On
the alleged attribution to Hugutio of the Latin-Germanic dictionary
in ms. 314 in Mainz civic library, see the evidence decidedly to the
contrary brought forward by Cremascoli (1966); as for his knowledge
of Greek, it is more than legitimate to have doubts about it, to the
extent that the Greek words present in the *Derivationes* normally can
be traced to Isidore or other sources. For information on all questions
regarding the life of Hugutio and his activity as a student of language
and law, the reader is referred to Cremascoli's full and well organized
bibliographic essay (1968); and we must also mention at least the
works by Marigo (1927; 1936) and Hunt (1980, 145–9).

Among Hugutio of Pisa's works we should mention, apart from
the *Derivationes*, the *De dubio accentu*, a brief treatise presumably
dating from a little before the 1160s, which discusses the exact
position of the accent in approximately forty words, especially when
they are composite, or when their penultimate syllable is followed by
*muta cum liquida*, with the principal task of teaching clerics the
correct pronunciation of Latin in liturgical usage. Its principal source
is Priscianus, although with probable derivations from Petrus Helias;
for further information in this regard we refer the reader to Cremascoli's extremely accurate edition (1978, 11–90). We should also
mention the *Agiographia*, presumably dating from the years immediately after 1160, which intends to set out the *interpretatio* or the
*etymologia* of the names of festivities and calendar saints, and whose
sources can be traced mainly to St Jerome's *Liber interpretationis
Hebraicorum nominum* – as well as to the Bible and Isidore – including
some elements with specific parallels in Papias' lexicon; this brief
work was used, almost a century later, by Iacopo da Varazze in his
*Legenda aurea*, and thereafter Joannes Balbus drew on it for his
*Catholicon*. See the edition in Cremascoli (1978, 91–177), from which
we quote here some significant examples to illustrate the techniques
of etymological analysis employed in it: 'Marcellus dictus est quasi
mala arcens a se, vel Marcellus quasi maria percellens, id est mun-
danas adversitates percutiens et conculcans, vel Marcellus quasi
martia cella, quia fuit cella id est habitaculum virtutum et fuit
marti< u >s id est bellicosus contra vitia' ('Marcellus is so called as if
it were putting evils away from himself (*mala arcens*), or Marcellus as if
violently shaking the seas (*maria percellens*), i.e. beating and despising
the adversities of the world, or Marcellus as if a martial cell (*martia*

*cella*), because he was the cell (*cella*) i.e the home of virtues, and martial (*martius*), i.e. warlike against vices'), 'Sebastianus dictus est a sequens et beatitudo et astim quod est civitas et ana quod est sursum, inde Sebastianus quasi sequens beatitudinem superne civitatis' ('Sebastian is so called from following (*sequens*) and beatitude (*beatitudo*) and *astim* which is "city" and *ana* which is "upwards", hence Sebastian as if it were following the beatitude of the heavenly city'), 'Leonardus quasi odor populi, a leos quod est populus et < a > nardo que est arbor aromatica et redolens, quia odore virtutum ad se trahat populum' ('Leonardus as if it were odour of the people, from *leos* which is "people" and from *nardus* which is an aromatic scented tree, because with the odour of virtue he draws the people to himself'), 'Cecilia dicta est quasi cecans cilia, id est oculos volentium eam removere a proposito castitatis' ('Cecilia is so called as if it were blinding (*cecans*) the eyelashes (*cilia*), i.e. the eyes of those who want to remove her from the purpose of chastity'), 'Perpetua dicta est quasi perpetiens dea, quia amore Dei multa perpessa sit, vel quia perpetuam et eternam vitam sibi acquisivit, vel Perpetua quasi perfecte peccata tuens, id est prospiciens, et eis postpositis et mortificatis Christo ad < h > esit' ('Perpetua is so called as if it were a goddess (*dea*) who endures (*perpetiens*), because for the love of God she has endured many things, or because she acquired perpetual (*perpetuam*) and eternal (*eternam*) life for herself, or Perpetua as if it were perfectly (*perfecte*) *tuens*, i.e. contemplating, sins (*peccata*), and having put them behind her and repressed them, she followed Christ'), 'dian quod est claritas' ('*dian* which is clarity'). (This last explanation is already present in the *Derivationes*, and later is taken up – as we can find in many other similar cases – by Eberhard of Béthune's *Graecismus*, on which cf. Wrobel 1887, 35, 110: 'Est clarere dian, et dicitur inde Diana' ('To be clear is *dian*, and hence one says Diana'), 'ener quod est vis vel fortitudo' ('*ener* which is strength or fortitude') (another definition that had already appeared in the *Derivationes*; cf. pp. 149, 150, 173, 172, 154, 159, respectively II. 341–5, 355–8, 907–9, 903–4, 443–7, 563 and 571). Finally, concerning the mechanisms of *derivatio nominum*, interesting observations are to be found in the *Expositio de symbolo Apostolorum*, also edited by Cremascoli (1978, 179–257).

270. See the edition in Daly and Daly (1975); on the influence Bene da Firenze (a teacher of grammar and rhetoric in the Bologna Studio, who died in 1239, and wrote the *Candelabrum* and a *De accentu*) might have had on William the Breton, cf. Hunt (1980, 148).

271. Before the actual glossary, which takes the earlier tradition into account, there is a treatise on various grammatical subjects, where Hugutio's *De dubio accentu* is quoted literally and often explicitly. We have evidence of the success enjoyed by the *Catholicon* in the 24 editions at least which can be counted from the *princeps* Mainz 1460 edition, up to the 1520 Lyons edition. What we have already mentioned for William the Breton, i.e. the influence of Bene da

Firenze, also holds true for Joannes Balbus of Genoa; there is no modern critical edition, but see at least the contributions by Marigo (1936, 31–40) and Hunt (1980, 148, 185–8).

272. See the edition in Zupitza (1880); for information on the life and works of Aelfric the reader is referred to the studies by White (1898), Dubois (1943) and Hurt (1972). Bolognesi's work (1967) specifically addresses the search for the sources of the *Grammar*; on the way Aelfric used Latin treatises on grammar, see Paroli's precise examination (1967–68). For an index of Aelfric's grammatical terminology, cf. Pàroli (1968); a summary of the linguistic and cultural aspects of the Benedictine monk's work is offered by Pàroli (1969). Finally, one should keep in mind the full bibliography gathered in Lazzari and Mucciante (1984a, 9–18).

273. The most recent edition is Gillingham (1981), but it is still indispensable to refer to Zupitza's classic edition (1880); as for the studies, see the important contributions by Lazzari and Mucciante (1984a; 1984b), to which we refer the reader for exhaustive bibliographical information, which among other things includes numerous indications about the rich cultural heritage of the Latin-Old English glossaries, some of which are very important from a linguistic point of view. For the delicate and controversial problem of the sources of Aelfric's *Glossary*, see the the well-argued conclusions in Lazzari and Mucciante (1984a, 199–204), derived from an in-depth analysis of the parallels which exist between the Benedictine monk's glosses and the earlier and contemporary bilingual tradition: in this new perspective it will no longer be necessary to assume the direct use of texts such as the Isidorian *Etymologiae* or *Differentiae*, but rather the mediation of a very large part of ·the material through the sizeable and well-documented indigenous bilingual tradition.

274. On the *Colloquium*, which in a way is the practical application of the *Grammar* and the *Glossary*, see particularly Lendinara (1983); we have the Latin text of this work with an Anglo-Saxon interlinear translation which is present in its entirety in one codex only.

275. Cf. Lazzari and Mucciante (1984b, 5).

276. Cf. Lazzari and Mucciante (1984a, 21–5), a work that tackles the vast and complex problem of the parallels between Aelfric's *Glossary* and the earlier and contemporary bilingual texts; on this subject we cannot overlook the importance of the glossaries – dating from the eighth century and the beginning of the ninth century – in the mss. of Epinal, Erfurt and Cambridge, on which see Lindsay (1921a; 1921b).

277. This is accompanied by a longer Anglo-Saxon preface, which examines the cultural situation of the time and the problems arising from it.

278. Cf. Pàroli (1969, 779–81). For a general picture of linguistic education in Britain from King Alfred to Aelfric see Bullough (1972).

279. Edited by Calder (1917) with an English translation.

280. Even the title is significant, since it immediately refers to the use of language in literature: 'The precepts of the poets.'

281. Following a sequence ascending from the 'everyday' to the 'sublime', we have first the 'language of the Irish' – which is also the 'everyday language used by all' – then the language of the 'lawyers' maxims', the 'language of decomposition', the 'poet's obscure language' and finally the 'archaic language', cf. Poli (1981; 1982–4a, 96–7).

282. The first and the fourth are preserved only in the *Codex Wormianus*, the famous manuscript constituting one of the main sources for the tradition of the text of Snorri's *Edda*; the second and third are preserved, at least in part, in other codices also: of these, we must mention the *Codex Upsaliensis*, which contains a slightly different version of the second treatise from the one found in the *Wormianus*. For all textual problems we refer the reader to Albano Leoni (1975, 8–9, 33–42) and Raschellà (1982, 10–20).

283. This was followed by Haugen (1972) – an expanded edition compared to the earlier one – Benediktsson (1972) and Albano Leoni (1975). We refer the reader to this last edition for any further bibliographical information, as well as for the faultless Italian translation, accompanied by a full philological and linguistic commentary.

284. It seems that the second treatise, which is generally believed to be a little later, should rather be dated between 1270 and 1300, according to Raschellà's careful calculations (1982, 126–32). This puts it after the third treatise – which has been tentatively placed between 1245 and 1252 – and before the fourth, dating from about 1350; for the relative chronology of the first and second treatise, see also Albano Leoni (1975, 33 ff.)

285. Cf. Albano Leoni (1975, 10); in the course of the almost eight centuries between the writing of the anonymous Icelandic first grammatical treatise and the modern acquisitions of the Prague linguistics School, 'an embryonic awareness of the distinctive function of articulated sounds' and 'a certain systematic order presenting some opposition series which are very similar to those that can be defined on the basis of modern phonological analysis' will reappear – and once again it will be a fundamentally isolated case – in Beauzée's *Grammaire générale*, published in Paris in 1767, on which see Rosiello (1967, 160).

286. Cf. Albano Leoni (1975, 21); the most credible hypothesis is that the anonymous author knew some Latin text of elementary grammar, or even a simple collection of scholia. The actual Latin models do not appear to be followed slavishly: an example of this is the fact that the author of the brief treatise 'makes no distinction in terminology between *semivocales* and *mutae*, despite the fact that the two sound categories are clearly identified' (*ibid.*, 17).

287. Cf. Albano Leoni (1975, 82–3); they are elements whose metaphonetic origin can be identified today.

288. Cf. Albano Leoni (1975, 85); Benediktsson (1972, 215): 'I shall . . . give examples how each of them, with the support of the same letters, (and) placed in the same position, one after another, makes a discourse of its own, and in this way give examples, throughout this

booklet, of the most delicate distinctions that are made between the letters: *sár, sǫ́r; sér, sę́r; sór, sőr; súr, sýr.* A man has inflicted one *wound (sár)* on me; I inflicted many *wounds (sǫ́r)* on him. <...> The priest *swore (sór)* the *fair (sőr)* oaths only. *Sour (súr)* are the *sow's (sýr)* eyes ....'

289. The graphic device suggested to denote nasalized vowels is a dot over the alphabet sign of each letter, cf. Albano Leoni (1975, 85 and 87), Benediktsson (1972, 217 and 219): 'But now each of these nine letters will produce a new one if it is pronounced through the nose, and this distinction is in fact so clear that it can change the discourse, as I shall now show in what follows, and I shall place a dot above those that are pronounced through the nose: *hár, hằr; rǫ́; rǫ̇́; Þel, Þė́l; fę́r, fę̇́r; ísa, i̇́ sa; órar őrar; óra, őra; Þú at, Þ ủat; sýna, sẏ́na. Hair (hár)* grows on living creatures, but the *shark (hằr)* is a fish. The *yard (rǫ́)* is a wooden pole in the rigging, but *(rǫ̇́)* is the *corner* of the house. *Woollen nap (Þel)* is to be found on a bandaged fist or as part of a cloak, but a *file (Þė́l)* is an implement. It is one thing that the *sheep* is called *(fę́r)*, and quite another that it *conceives (fę̇́r)* a lamb. One could *look through (i̇́ sá)* the rift in the clouds, when we got into the *ice floes (ísa)*. *Madness (órar)* (that is what) *our (őrar)* neglect is. The oldest child should be gentle, for the older can *vex (óra)* the *younger (őra)*. *You* were *present (Þú at)* where the feather bed [was] *pressed down (Þủat)*. Bilgewater three *laps (sýna)* deep I shall *show (sẏ́na)* you.'

290. The graphic device suggested to denote long vowels is an acute accent above the alphabet sign for each vowel, cf. Albano Leoni (1975, 87 and 89); Benediktsson (1972, 219–23): 'This distinction, too, I wish to show because it changes the discourse just like the previous ones, and (I shall) mark the long ones with a stroke (to distinguish them) from the short: *far, fár; ràmr; rằmr; ǫl, ǫ́l; vǫn; vǫ́n; sé Þú, séÞu; framèr, frá mèr; vęr, vę́r; vęnisk, vę̀nisk; vil, víl; minna, mìnna; goð, góð; mòna, mőna; Goðrøði, góð røði; mǫnde, mǫ̀nde; dura, dúra; rùnar, rűnar; flytr, flýtr; brýnna, brẏnna.* A ship is called a *vessel (far)*, but *harm (fár)* is a kind of distress. A strong man is *mighty (ràmr)*, but the hoarse (man is) *harsh-voiced (rằmr)*. *Beer (ǫl)* is the name of a drink, but a *strap (ǫ́l)* is a cord. The tongue is *accustomed (vǫn)* to speaking, but from the teeth there is a *prospect (vǫ́n)* of a bite. *Look thou (sé Þú)* how well they *nailed (séÞú)* (the boards), those who were in charge of the nailing. Those men are very brazen *(framèr)* who are not ashamed to take my wife *from me (frá mèr)*. Of her husband *(vęr)* many a woman is so *fond (vę́r)*, that she hardly ever takes her eyes off him. A good man *should* not *get into* this *habit (vęnisk)*, even though an evil man *is confident of (vę̀nisk)* (being able to obtain the favors of good) women. Self-conceit and *wilfulness (vil)* expect that labor and *misery (víl)* will abate. I shall *remind (minna)* an attentive man of *my (mìnna)* cherished concerns. That woman honors *God (Goð)* who herself is *good (góð)*. My *mother (mőna)*, says a child, *will not (mòna)* treat me the worst of her

household. Well did *Godred* (*Goðrøði*) like *góð røði*, that is the *good oars*, as the scald said [Þioðolfr Arnórsson, from the middle of the eleventh century]: the chief's men can pull / straight *oars* (*røði*) out of the sea. The house *would* (*mønde*) leak, if the carpenter did not *ridge* (*mǿnde*) (the roof). If the guest knocks at the *door* (*dura*), the master (of the house) should not *doze* (*dúra*). Male pigs are called *boars* (*runar*), but letters (are called) *runes* (*rúnar*). Look how the raft *floats* (*flýtr*) that the raftsman *drives* (*flytr*). The captain needs a *sharper* (*brýnna*) breeze than he who is to *water* (*brynna*) the cattle.'

291. Cf. Albano Leoni (1975, 85); Benediktsson (1972, 215): 'I split thirty-six distinctions, each of which makes a discourse of its own if they are precisely distinguished.'

292. Some of these comments give synchronic indications which are very interesting not only for the pronunciation of Norse, but also for the pronunciation of the Latin spoken at the time of the anonymous author of the treatise; see, in Albano Leoni (1975, 95 and 97), Benediktsson (1972, 235 and 237), examples like the following: 'The letter that is here written *c* most Latins call *ce* and use for two letters, (viz.,) for *t* and *s*, when they join it with *e* or *i*, although they join it as *k* with *a* or *u* or *o*,; which is the way in which the Irish join this letter with all vowels in Latin and call (it) *che*; this (letter) I, too, shall call *che* in our alphabet, and I shall join it with all vowels in the same way as *k* or *q*, while these two (letters) I take out of the alphabet, and let the one, *c*, stand for either of the others as well as for itself, since they all previously had the same sound or value in [most] places. . . . The *n* which comes immediately before a *g* in one syllable is spoken less in the nose and more in the throat than other *n*'s, because it receives some slight admixture from the *g*. Now, for this (reason) I shall make their intercourse friendly, and I shall fashion one letter from the two, which I shall call *eng* and write in this manner: ǥ. This (letter) alone I give the same value as the other two, so that it will come to the same thing whether you write *hringr* or *hriǥr*.' In the same context it will be useful to note the description of the dental fricative, introduced, with the name of *Þorn*, into insular writing, whence it passed into the Icelandic and Scandinavian *scriptoria*, and called *tha* in the brief treatise.

293. See the following passages: 'except where I write a consonant – whichever (of them) I am writing, in the shape of a capital, provided also that it follows the vowel in a syllable; then I shall let this one (letter) represent as much as if two of one and the same kind were written instead . . . Now, here are the examples that were found in a hurry, and afterwards, with somewhat greater clarity, (they will be) put into meaningful context: *u be*, *uBe*; *secr*, *seKr*; *hǫ do*, *hǫDo*; *afarar*, *aFarar*; *Þagat*, *ÞaGat*; *ǫl*, *ǫL*; *frame*, *fraMe*; *vina*, *viNa*; *krapa*, *kraPa*; *hver*, *hveR*; *fus*, *fuS*; *skiót*, *skióT*. *U be* are the two names of two letters, but *UBe* is one name of one man; an outlaw is a *convict* (*secr*), but a *sack* (*seKr*) is a bag. A *tall* (woman) *died* (*hǫ do*) when Hǫlgatroll died, but (one could hear) the handle (*hǫDo*) (rattle)

when Tor carried the cauldron. . . . It is better for everyone to have *become silent* (*Þagat*) before someone else should have *silenced* (*ÞaGat*) (him). Not *all* (*ǫL*) *beers* (*ǫl*) are alike. The captain's *fame* (*frame*) is held to be greater than his who bunks on the deck *in front* (*fraMe*). He is the greatest of God's *friends* (*vina*) who is willing to *work* (*viNa*) the hardest to (deserve this). People often wade to church through *wet snow* (*crapa*), even though they have a *difficult* (*kraPa*) road (to go). *Every* (*hver*) woman and [*every* (*hveR*)] man should be *eager* (*fus*) for that which God is *eager* (*fuS*) for; then they will be *quick* (*sceót*) to (do) good deeds and *quickly* (skióT) gain the grace of God', cf. Albano Leoni (1975, 93 and 101), Benediktsson (1972, 231 and 245–7).

294. Cf. Albano Leoni (1975, 68).
295. Cf. Raschellà (1982, 2–3, 103–7), to whom we owe the most recent and reliable critical edition of the second Icelandic grammatical treatise, together with a translation and an accurate commentary on the text (both in English); for the earlier edition and other related studies, among which one should mention Albano Leoni's important contribution (1975, 35–43 and 57–64), cf. Raschellà (1982, 21-4).
296. One can identify the following subdivisions: a) sounds that can occur only at the beginning of a syllable, [þ, v, h, q]; b) consonant sounds [b, d, f, g, ⟨k⟩, l, m, n, p, r, s, t,]; c) vowel sounds, which are further divided into: 1) six 'simple' vocalic elements, either brief or long [a, e, i, o, u, y], 2) three 'ligatures' [ae, ao, au, of which the first two should correspond respectively to ę, ǫ of the first treatise, while for the third it is argued whether it should be similarly understood as ø or rather whether it represents the true diphthong aw], 3) two digraphs [ei, ey, which can be interpreted as diphthongs], 4) a 'variable' [i, 'which is a true vowel if it is preceded and followed by a consonant in the syllable, but if a vowel follows it it changes into a consonant and many whole words are made with it, such as: *já* (yes, also) or *jǫrð* (earth) or *jór* (horse). Its second variation occurs when it is a diphthong, like the ones written before, and it is so if a consonant precedes it and a vowel follows it immediately, such as: *bjǫrn* (bear) or *bjór* (beer) or *bjǫrg* (mountain)', cf. Albano Leoni (1975, 37) and see also Raschellà (1982, 62–3, with a plausible text restoration)]; d) double consonant sounds [B, D, F, G, K, L, M, N, P, R, S, T]; e) sounds that can occur only at the end of a syllable [ð, z, x, c], cf. Albano Leoni (1975, 39–40) and Raschellà (1982, 80–99). One should also mention the description, preceded by a rectangular figure, of the way in which the consonants and vowels combine with each other to form minimal phonic sequences, cf. Raschellà (1982, 70–5 and 103–7).
297. Martin of Dacia, John of Dacia and Roger Bacon's *Summulae dialectices* have been suggested – as well as technical and scientific treatises, particularly those concerning the making of musical instruments, cf. Raschellà (1982, 107–14); see also Melazzo (1985).
298. While the fourth treatise survives only in the *Codex Wormianus*, the third is also present in other manuscripts; for the editions, see Ólsen

(1884), with its rich historical and philological commentary, for both. The third treatise, attributed to Ólafr Þórðarson hvítaskáld, owes much to the *Institutiones* by Priscian – who, like Plato, is expressly mentioned – and to the third part of Donatus' *Ars maior*, cf. Albano Leoni (1985); the anonymous fourth treatise has Alexander de Villa Dei's *Doctrinale* and perhaps Eberhard of Béthune's *Grecismus* as its sources, cf. Albano Leoni (1975, 8–9) and Raschellà (1982, 2–5, 116, 129–32).

299. See the critical edition, complete with a full introduction, notes and appendices, by Marshall (1969).

300. In particular, at the instance of Giacomo di Mora and Corraduccio di Sterleto, noblemen from Frederick II's imperial court, cf. Marshall (1969, 62–4).

301. Cf. Marshall (1969, 18–9, 64–5).

302. See Marshall (1969, 92, 11. 51–4 and 93, 11. 51–4a): 'E no se pot conosser ni triar l'acusatius del nominatiu sino per zo que · l nominatius singulars, quan es masculis, vol − *s* en la fi e li autre cas no · l volen, e · l nominatiu plural no [lo] vol e tuit li altre cas volen lo enl plural', Latin text: 'Et non potest conossi neque descerni acusativus a nominativo nisi per hoc quod nominativus singularis, quando est masculini generis vel comunis vel omnis, vult − *s* in fine dictionis et alii casus singul[ar]i[s] nolunt − *s*, et nominativus pluralis e converso non vult − *s* in fine et omnes alii casus volunt − *s* in plurali' ('And one cannot know or discern the accusative from the nominative except for this: that the nominative singular, when it is of masculine, or common or overall gender, requires − *s* at the end of the word and the other cases of the singular do not want − *s*, and on the contrary the nominative plural does not want − *s* at the end and all the other cases want − *s* in the plural'); for a balanced judgement on the methods of grammatical analysis to be found in the *Donatz Proensals* we refer the reader to Marshall (1969, 66–78).

303. Cf. Marshall (1969, 71–7).

304. The brief treatise's fame lasted in Italy to the end of the eighteenth century: on this, see Marshall (1969, 79–80).

305. Cf. Thurot (1869, 86); in the same way, in an anonymous commentary on the *Donatus maior* probably dating from the tenth century, we find: 'Dicta ergo positio a ponendo, eo quod poetae artificialiter composuerunt ut brevis vocalis, quae per se unum tempus habet, ex duabus quae sequuntur consonantibus habeat alterum et ex correpta queat esse producta' ('Therefore it is called position from *ponendo* (to place), because the poets agreed in an artificial way that short vowels, which have one length (*tempus*) in themselves, take another from the two consonants which follow, and from short may become long') (Thurot 1869, 86, no. 2).

306. Cf. Thurot (1869, 419); on this subject, it is symptomatic that Petrus Helias should ask a question like the following:'Quomodo poterit sciri quod bis tantum teneatur longa littera, quam brevis? Quis hoc potuit dimetiri? Sed fortasse non ideo dicitur duum temporum. Sed

quia que correpta est dicitur unius temporis, ideo fortasse producta
dicitur duum temporum, eo quod multo plus teneatur quam brevis,
non quod bis tantum teneatur secundum rectam mensuram. Vel ideo,
quia due breves ponuntur sepe pro una longa, et e converso' ('In
what way can one know that a long letter is evaluated only as twice
as long as a short one? Who could measure this? But perhaps it is not
because of this that it is called of two lengths (*duum temporum*). But
because the one which is short is said to be of one length (*tempus*),
and therefore perhaps one says that a long letter is of two lengths
(*duum temporum*), because it is evaluated much more than a short
one, not because it is evaluated as only twice as long according to
correct measurement. Or else because two short ones are often placed
instead of a long one, and *vice versa*') (Thurot 1869, 419).

307. In 11. 1607–8, cf. Reichling (1893, 102) and Thurot (1969, 419).
Owing to the wide diffusion of this text, the error was perpetuated
systematically in teaching, and took on the characteristics of a generally accepted normative statement.

308. Cf. Thurot (1869, 420).

309. The same confusion remains in describing the facts concerning the
problem of *muta cum liquida*; on this subject see the *Doctrinale*,
11.1611–4: 'si faciat curta vocali syllaba finem / mutaque cum liquida
vocem subeant in eandem, / ex vi naturae propria licet hanc breviare,
/ et propter mutam liquidamque potes dare longam' ('if a syllable
ends in a short vowel, / and a *muta cum liquida* follows the vowel in
the same word, / because of its own nature it is allowable to shorten
it, / and because of the *muta cum liquida* one can also give it long'),
and 11.1699–1702: 'vocalem mediae breviant, si muta sequatur / cum
liquida; tamen hanc productam pone brevemque. / longa sit *adiutrix*,
*Octobris*, nomen in *atrix*. / cum *chiragra podagram* quidam breviant,
alii non' ('internally the group *muta cum liquida* shortens the vowels
which it follows; however you can consider it both long and short. It
is long in *Adiutrix, Octobris*, nouns in *atrix* are long. / Some shorten
*chiragra* together with *podagra*, others do not') (Reichling 1893, 102
and 106), and the respective commentary by the *Admirantes* Gloss:
'Dixerat actor . . . quod quando post vocalem naturaliter brevem
sequitur muta et liquida, illa vocalis indifferenter potest poni. Sed hic
ponit aliam regulam, dicens quod quotiescunque in mediis sillabis
muta et liquida sequuntur aliquam vocalem, illa vocalis corripitur,
quantum est de se, ut *aratrum*. Produci tamen potest per naturam
gemine consonantis, et sic potest ad indifferentiam se habere' ('The
author said . . . that when after a naturally short vowel a *muta cum
liquida* follows, that vowel can be considered (long or short). But here
he gives another rule, saying that any time *muta cum liquida* follows
some vowel in a middle syllable, this vowel is shortened, in as far as
one considers it in itself, like *aratrum*. But it may be lengthened by
nature of the double consonant, and thus it may behave indifferently')
cf. Thurot (1869, 421). In an anonymous twelfth century *Opusculum
de accentibus*, in the section dedicated to the *denotatio accentuum*

*secundum usum* Cistercensium, there are examples such as *árătrum, cómmătres, cónfrătres* and the like, which evidently were fairly wide-spread if Hugutio of Pisa, in his *De dubio accentu* (Cremascoli 1978, 80, 194–81, 207), could stigmatize them as errors of prosody, recognizing the precise value of the original vowel quantity: 'Sed aratrum, confratres, commatres procul dubio habent accentum acutum tantum in penultima et nunquam in antepenultima: est enim penultima earum producta naturaliter. Illam regulam que dicit: "liquida posita post mutam facit precedentem syllabam esse communem", nemo ita fatue intelligat quod qualemcumque syllabam precedentem faciat esse communem. Hoc enim est impossibile quod si antecedat syllaba naturaliter longa, brevietur propter sequentes consonantes. Est ergo sic intelligenda regula: liquida posita post mutam facit precedentem syllabam, si naturaliter fuerit brevis, communem, id est patitur eam quandoque corripi, quandoque produci. Ergo sine omni excusacione penitus male dicitur aratrum ut acuatur antepenultima. Similiter male dicitur cómmatres et cónfratres, in quibus penultima longa est naturaliter' ('But *aratrum, confratres, commatres* without doubt have the acute accent only on the penultimate syllable and never on the antepenultimate: indeed their penultimate syllable is long by nature. The rule that says: "a liquid placed after a mute makes the preceding syllable common", should not be understood fatuously as if it said that it makes any preceding syllable common. Because it is impossible that if a naturally long syllable precedes them, it should be shortened because of the following consonants. Therefore the rule must be understood like this: a *muta cum liquida* makes the preceding syllable common, if by its nature it would be short, i.e. it allows the syllable to be sometimes shortened and sometimes lengthened. Therefore there is no excuse for people to say in an utterly wrong fashion *aratrum* so that the stress falls on the antepenultimate. Similarly they say wrongly *cómmatres* and *cónfratres*, in which the penultimate syllable is long by nature') cf. Thurot (1869, 421 and, for a list of words used with a different quantity compared to the precepts of classical prosody, 428–40).

310. Cf. Thurot (1869, 77–9).
311. Cf. Väänänen (1971, 116). Compare also the *Admirantes* Gloss (Thurot 1869, 532): '*f* ponitur pro *ph*' '*f* is used instead of *ph*'.
312. Cf. Väänänen (1971, 136); an anonymous treatise on orthography dating from the tenth century insists (Thurot 1869, 520): '*Apud, illud, istud, aliquid* per *d. Caput, inquit, tot, quot*, si de numero fuerit, per *t*' '*Apud, illud, istud, aliquid* with *d. Caput, inquit, tot, quot*, if it is about number, with a *t*', which indirectly confirms the change [t] > [d] at the end of a word. Other, later evidence completes the picture with very interesting observations; see first of all the anonymous twelfth century *Opusculum de accentibus*: 'Sonus *t* in fine dictionis debilitatur, ut *amat, docet*, et in omnibus, preter *at, tot, quot, quotquot, aliquot* ad differentiam, et *sat* et *atat* propter euphoniam' ('The sound *t* at the end of words is weakened, like *amat, docet* and in all other words,

except *at, tot, quot, quotquot, aliquot* for the sake of distinction, and *sat* and *atat* because of euphony') (Thurot 1869, 144), but particularly Petrus Helias, *Summa s. Prisc. min.* (Tolson 1978, 76, 9–16): 'Nam "d" et "t" confundunt sonos suos ad invicem ut pro "d" ponatur "t" et econverso, quod faciunt barbari et maxime Theutonici, pro "deus" dicentes "teus". Similiter etiam et in Latina locutione, quia sicut profertur "d" in hoc pronomine "id", eodem modo pronunciatur "t" cum dicimus "legit", "capit", unde sunt quidam qui maxime nos reprehendunt, ut Hiberni. Volunt enim sic pronunciare "t" in "legit", sicut in "tibi", dicentes quod aliter nulla erit differentia inter "d" et "t", sed male reprehendunt cum iste due littere invicem confundant sonos suos' ('the sounds of "d" and "t" are confused one with the other, so that people put "t" instead of "d" and vice versa, which the barbarians do, most of all the Teutons, who say "teus" instead of "deus". Similarly also in the Latin language, because one pronounces "d" in the pronoun "id" in the same way as one pronounces "t" when we say "legit", "capit", hence there are some who reproach us strongly, like the Irish. They want to pronounce "t" in "legit" as in "tibi", saying that otherwise there is no difference between "d" and "t", but they reproach wrongly if the sounds of these two letters are confused one with the other'), and finally Parisius de Altedo, whose *Tractatus orthographie* dates from 1297 (Thurot 1869, 144): '*T* muta litera est que in principio dictionis posita magnum sonum habet, ut *tibi*, in medio mediocrem, ut *retuli*, nisi geminetur, quia tunc bene sonat, in fine vero debiliter sonat, ut *legit, docet* . . . Item si *h* sit post *t*, retinet sonum suum, ut *Sabaoth*. Et licet precedat *n, r, s* vel *l*, non amittit sonum suum, ut *stant, aufert, est, vult*' ('*T* is a mute letter which when placed at the beginning of a word has a strong sound, like *tibi*, a middle sound when placed in the middle, like *retuli*, unless it is doubled, because then it sounds clearly, but at the end it has a weak sound, like *legit, docet* . . . Also if there is an *h* after the *t*, it maintains its own sound, like *Sabaoth*. And even if *n, r, s* or *l* precede it, it does not lose its sound, like *stant, aufert, est, vult*'). Petrus Helias' evidence points out two very important facts: a) the tendency shown by speakers of Germanic languages to pronounce as [ḍ], a lax and redundantly unvoiced dental occlusive, the voiced and redundantly lax dental occlusive [d] of Latin, which justifies the French grammarian's perception of a voiceless consonant; b) the evolution of Latin pronunciation in the lands where Latin-derived languages were spoken, as a consequence of the constant interference due to these languages' phonetic evolution, in contrast with the rules strictly based on classical texts which prevailed in the teaching of Latin in the insular area, particularly among the Irish people, for whom Latin was a totally foreign language, and therefore much less liable to interference phenomena. On the weakness of the pronunciation of [d] in the middle and at the end of a word, compared to the beginning, see again Parisius de Altedo (Thurot 1869, 141): 'Hec litera plus sonat in principio, ut *dominus*, in medio et in fine debilius, ut *adheret, id, istud* et *quod'* ('This letter sounds stronger at the beginning of a word, like *dominus*, weaker in the middle and at the end, like *adheret, id, istud* and *quod'*).

313. Cf. Väänäneen (1971, 113–5). The possibility of the alveolar affricate (or simple sibilant) – as well as the palatal affricate – can certainly be deduced from the graphemic confusion *c*/*t* in front of the sequence [j + vowel], for which there is ample evidence as far back as late Latin texts; for further indications of this see the anonymous twelfth century *Opusculum de accentibus*: '*Vitium*, quod *culpam* significat, per *t* scribendum est, quoniam a *vitando* derivatur, ab *exitu, exitium*, a *potu, potio; porcio* et *concio* per *c*' ('*Vitium*, which means sin, is written with a *t*, because it is derived from *vitare* (avoid), from *exitus*, one has *exitium*, from *potus, potio; porcio* and *concio* are written with a *c*'), the spellings *spacium, vicium, ocium*, present in Alexander de Villa Dei's *Doctrinale*, Parisius de Altedo's *Tractatus orthographie*: 'Item *t* ante *i*, sequente alia vocali, assumit sonum *c*, ut *lectio, amatio*. Quod fallit quattuor modis: videlicet quando *s* vel *x* precedit, ut *Salustius, bestia, commixtio*; item quando aspiratur, ut *Emathia, Corinthios*; item causa differentie, ut *lis, litium*, ad differentiam de hoc *licium* pro instrumento tele, et *vitis, vitium*, ad differentiam de hoc *vicium, vicii*; item quando *i* cadit in junctura compositionis, ut *vigintiunus* . . . Sane propterea non credas quod hic sonus *ci*, sequente vocali, semper debeat per *t* scribi, quia plerumque debet scribi per *c*, ut *facio, cis, socius, socii*. Quandoque autem per *t* et quandoque per *c* huiusmodi sillaba sit scribenda circumspectio provida scriptoris advertat ex derivatione, compositione, vel condeclinio dictionis' ('Also *t* before *i*, when another vowel follows, takes the sound *c*, like *lectio, amatio*. This is not so in four cases: i.e. when *s* or *x* precedes it, like *Salustius, bestia, commixtio*; also when it is aspirate, like *Emathia, Corinthios*; also for the purpose of difference, like *lis, litium* (quarrel), to differentiate from *licium* the instrument of weaving, and *vitis, vitium* (vine) to differentiate from *vicium, vicii* (vice); also when the *i* falls in the junction of a compound, like *vigintiunus* . . . Also do not believe that this *ci* sound, if a vowel follows, must always be written with a *t*, because often it must be written with a *c*, like *facio, cis, socius, socii*. In what circumstances such a syllable has to be written with *t* and in what circumstances with *c*, will be decided by the prudent circumspection of the writer on the basis of derivation, composition, or the declension of the word') cf. Thurot (1869, 144–5). Finally, an anonymous twelfth century manuscript sets down the spelling *sce* instead of *ce* in *scementum, sceroma, scetra*, and, conversely, writes *lucinie* instead of *luscinie*, cf. Thurot (1869, 533). Similar observations can be made for the realizations of [g] before palatal vowels or the sequence [j + vowel], which become confused with the realizations of [d] followed by [j + vowel]; it may be useful to mention the spelling *zabulus*, allowed by an anonymous orthography treatise dating from the tenth century, cf. Thurot (1869, 522), which was already present in late Latin Christian texts, cf. Väänänen (1971, 111).

314. This restriction could be deduced from some examples of compound
words – in which *s* appears at the beginning of the second element of
the compound, and despite the position between vowels it is pronounced as voiceless – even if other quite similar examples show it
being realized as voiced, which perhaps is attributable to the fact that
the speaker is not always clearly aware of the compound. On this, see
the above-mentioned *Opusculum de accentibus*: 'Dictiones que ab *s*
incipiunt si componantur, ut vocalis ante *s* habeatur, aliquando,
prout euphonia permiserit, molliter sonat, ut *desidero, preses, presum,
desum* . . . Aliquando vero propter euphoniam expresse pronunciatur,
ut *desolata, designat, conservat, resisto, deservio, persequor, resurgo*'
('If words that begin with *s* enter into a compound, so that there is a
vowel before the *s*, at times, as much as euphony allows, it sounds
soft, like *desidero, preses, presum, desum* . . . At times, however,
because of euphony it is pronounced more distinctly, like *desolata,
designat, conservat, resisto, deservio, persequor, resurgo*'), and Parisius
de Altedo: '*S* litera semivocalis, si ponatur in principio dictionis,
expresse pronunciatur, ut *solus, semel*; similiter in medio, si alia
consonans sit iuxta eam, ut *considero*. Si vero consonans desit, non
expresse sonat, ut *vesanus*. Nam cum inter vocales est, non habet
sonum expressum, ut *esurit, deserit, rosa*. In aliquibus tamen ob
euphoniam sonum suum exprimit, ut *presensit*. Idem est in quibusdam
propriis, ut *Matusalem, Melchisedech*' ('The semivocalic letter *S*, if it
is placed at the beginning of a word, is pronounced more distinctly,
like *solus, semel*; similarly in the middle, if another consonant is next
to it, like *considero*. But if the consonant is missing, it does not sound
distinctly, like *vesanus*. When it is between vowels, it does not have a
distinct sound, like *esurit, deserit, rosa*. In some words, however, it
expresses its sound because of euphony, like *presensit*. The same in
proper nouns like *Matusalem, Melchisedech*') cf. Thurot (1869, 143–
4).

315. Probably due to regressive assimilation caused by the palatal vowels
*e* and *i*; however, this is already found in the late Latin grammatical
tradition.

316. It seems difficult to extrapolate a precise rule on the distribution of
the two variants; see also the anonymous twelfth century *Opusculum
de accentibus*: '*X* in simplicibus duplex sonat et ex utraque parte
exprimitur, ut *dixi, vexi, duxi, exemplum, exodus*. In compositis
autem ex parte *ex* prepositio sonat, manente vocali, ut *exaro, exhortor, exordior, exordium, exoro*. Quod si *ex* prepositio vocalem post se
mutaverit, tunc expresse, hoc est ex utraque parte, sonat in corruptis,
ut *eximius, exiguus, exhibeo, exigo, exerceo, eximo*. Et quod propter
corruptionem exprimatur *x* in ipsis ostendunt eorum quedam preterita
vel supina, que prepositio non corrumpit, et in quibus *x* duplex non
sonat, ut *exemi, exemplum, exegi, exactum*. In omnibus illis in quibus
alterum componentium ab *s* incipit, *x* expresse sonat, ut *exurgo,
exupero, exulto, exolvo, exuo* et cetera. Sciendum quoque quod si *ex*
prepositio et verbum simile ablativo componantur, propter differen-

tiam dupplex *x* sonat, ut *exalto, exeo, exacerbo, exanimo* . . . In hoc
nomine *examen*, quoniam vocalis non corrumpitur, sed de medio
consonans aufertur, *x* tamen ex parte prepositionis sonat et in verbo
suo similiter, ut *examino*' ('*X* in simple words sounds double and is
expressed from both parts, like *dixi, vexi, duxi, exemplum, exodus.*
However in composite words the preposition *ex* sounds only in part,
the vowel remaining, like *exaro, exhortor, exordior, exordium, exoro.*
But if the preposition *ex* changes the vowel that follows, then it
sounds distinctly in these corrupted words, i.e. it is expressed in both
its parts, like *eximius, exiguus, exhibeo, exigo, exerceo, eximo.* And
that *X* is expressed in those words because of corruption, is shown in
some preterite or supine forms, which the preposition does not
corrupt, and in which *x* does not sound double, like *exemi, exemplum,
exegi, exactum.* In all those in which the second component begins
with *s*, *x* sounds distinctly, like *exurgo, exupero, exulto, exolvo, exuo,*
etc. It must also be known that if the preposition *ex* and a verb
similar to the ablative are compound together, for the sake of
distinction *x* sounds double, like *exalto, exeo, exacerbo, exanimo* . . .
In the noun *examen*, because the vowel is not corrupted, but the
consonant is taken away from the middle, still *x* sounds like part of
the preposition, and similarly in its verb, like *examino*') cf. Thurot
(1869, 145). Note the justification of distinctions in otherwise identical
contexts, prompted by the need to keep the meanings distinct. Finally,
we can deduce from an anonymous tenth-century treatise on orthography, cf. Thurot (1869, 522), that the realization [ks] was recommended
in *externus* to distinguish this term from *hesternus*, which indirectly
reveals the tendency [ks] > [s] even before consonants other than [s].

317. Cf. Thurot (1869, 141–4).
318. Cf. Thurot (1869, 522); as well as true lenition processes, the possibility of a voiced realization of intervocalic or initial voiceless stops (in
the latter case when they are followed by a vibrant) is also recorded
in the same treatise: '*Negat* de negando per *g*, *necat* de occidendo per
*c* . . . *Grassator* per *g*, quod est latro. *Crassus*, quod est pinguis, per *c*'
('*Negat* is written with a *g* from *negare* (deny), *necat* is written with a
*c* from "to kill" (*necare*) . . . *Grassator* with a *g*, which is a thief.
*Crassus*, which is fat, with a *c*') cf. Thurot (1869, 520, 522).
319. Cf. Thurot (1869, 142). One should not exclude that a voiced palatal
affricate could also occur between vowels; however, on this subject, a
standard text like the *Doctrinale* by Alexander de Villa Dei seems to
mention only the gemination of [j]: 'dum teneant iotam vocales
undique clausam, / consona iota duplex' ('when vowels have the *iota*
closed on both sides, / the consonant *iota* is double') (ll.1599–1600,
Reichling 1893, 101), which seems to be reinforced by the commentary
on the passage to be found in the *Admirantes* Gloss, cf. Thurot (1869,
142). As for the value of [ʤ] which *g* has before the vowels *e* and *i*, the
affricate realization seems to parallel in every way what we saw
happen to the voiceless *c*; on this, see Parisius de Altedo: '*G* litera
muta est que, sequentibus *e* vel *i*, sonum suum servat, ut *georgica*,

*gemma, gigno*, sequentibus vero aliis vocalibus, mutat sonum, ut *gallus, gobio, gula*' ('*G* is a mute letter which, when *e* or *i* follow, keeps its sound, like *georgica, gemma, gigno*, but when other vowels follow, it changes sound, like *gallus, gobio, gula*'), cf. Thurot (1869, 141).

320. Cf. Thurot (1869, 143). On the different values taken in different contexts by [w], see the remarks by Petrus Helias: 'Nos vero dicimus quod *u* ibi [in *quis*] est littera et vocalis plane. Sed quod non retinet ibi vim littere propter metrum dicitur, quoniam in metro nichil operatur, nec sonum plenum habet, sed collisim, ita tamen ut non omnino debeat taceri, sed cum quodam sibilo proferri' ('However, we say that there [in *quis*] *u* is clearly a letter and a vowel. But it is said, because of the metre, that it does not maintain there the force of a letter because it does not operate in the metre, nor has a full sound, but a compressed one, such that it must not be completely silent, but should be pronounced with some kind of hiss') (Thurot 1869, 143), and in Alexander de Villa Dei's *Doctrinale*: 'vocali praeiungitur *u* non consona vimque / perdit, et hoc *suavis, queror* aut *aqua, lingua* probabit. / nam diphthongus ab *u* nostro non inchoat usu. / mosque modernus habet quandoque, quod *s* praeeunte / syllaba dividitur; tunc *u* vocalis habetur' ('in front of a vowel a non-consonantal *u* is added and it loses / its strength, and this is confirmed by *suavis, queror* or *aqua, lingua*. / In fact the diphthong does not start with *u* according to our usage. / At times, in modern fashion, when there is a preceding *s*, / the syllable is divided; then one has *u* as a vowel') (ll.1593–7, Reichling 1893, 101).

321. Cf. Väänänen (1971, 109 ff.).

322. Some indication of its realization could be drawn from Petrus Helias: 'De *h* queritur utrum sit vox. Nos vero dicimus quod non est vox, sed sonus. Neque enim plectro lingue formatur; sed ad modum tussis subripitur' ('Some ask if *h* is a *vox*. But we say that it is not a *vox*, but a sound. Indeed it is not formed with the plectrum of the tongue, but it jumps out like a cough'), cf. Thurot (1869, 141–2). Evidently there were plenty of uncertainties and variations, if even Petrus Helias could state elsewhere that 'constat quod *abundo* non habet aspirationem ante *a*, cum sit compositum ex *ab* et *undo*. Plerique tamen dicunt *habundo* per *h* aspirationem. Quod si dicitur, simplex est et derivatum ab *habeo*. Sed istud non ex auctoritate habetur, sed illud' ('it seems that *abundo* has no aspirate before the *a*, because it is composed from *ab* and *undo*. But many say *habundo* with an aspirate *h*. If one says this, it is a simple word and is derived from *habeo*. But this pronunciation does not come from authority, but the former does'); and Parisius de Altedo prescribed the use of *h* in *Haimericus, Habel, Henuerardus, Heremus, Hodericus, Hugo, Hieremias*, while the *De arte lectoria* by a certain Aimericus (whose chronological placing is uncertain) reproved both the spellings *Ihesus, Iherusalem*, and the forms *Hiesus, Hieremias, Hierusalem*, and Boncompagno, in the thirteenth century, could advise that people should write *Habraham*,

*Hisahac, Haymericus, Hubaldus, Hymelda, Heverardus, hidioma, Harmenia, habissus, hedifico, habundanter* and others, cf. Thurot (1869, 533–4); finally, Parisius de Altedo complained that 'circa dictiones aspirandas vel non multum solent tabelliones errare' ('concerning the words that should or should not be aspirated the notaries usually make many mistakes'), also mentioning the need to write an *h* after *c, p, t, r* in certain words 'quales sunt *prehendo, michi, nichil, Philippus, Rhenus, thorus* et similia' ('such as *prehendo, michi, nichil, Philippus, Rhenus, thorus* and similar ones'), cf. Thurot (1869, 142).

323. Cf. Thurot (1869, 534).

324. Cf. Väänänen (1971, 87ff.). The sliding of lax vowels towards a more open timbre, the possibility of a further closure of tense vowels and the specific tendency towards the passage [e] > [i] in pretonic position are well documented in the context of the formation of neo-Latin languages. Certain cases of hyper-correctism show a noticeable amount of uncertainty in the precise knowledge of classical norm.

325. Cf. Thurot (1869, 521); the same treatise contains some points that are equally relevant from our point of view, with implications on the morphological level of the distinction before singular and plural: '*Peccatores, patres, fratres, nepotes* ... per *e* litteram. Sic et de similibus, si de pluribus fuerint. *Apostolos, magistros, discipulos, filios* ... si de pluribus fuerint, per *o* scribendum est, si de singulari numero, per *u*' ('*Peccatores, patres, fratres, nepotes* ... with a letter *e*. And also similar words, if they are plural. *Apostolos, magistros, discipulos, filios* ... if they are plural, are written with an *o*, if they are singular, with a *u*') cf. Thurot (1869, 520).

326. Cf. Thurot (1869, 532).

327. Cf. Cremascoli (1978, 83, 229–85, 245).

328. Cf. Thurot (1869, 139–40). As far as the pronunciation of *hic* is concerned, which varied according to whether it was a pronoun or the adverb of place, it is worth mentioning the rules set down by Virgilius Grammaticus, who in turn attributes them to the *auctoritas* of a *Mitterius quidam Spaniensis vir, cui ut vati credidimus* (a Spaniard called Mitterius, whom we believed in as one believes in a prophet): 'Sunt etiam pronomina et adverbia quae litteris hisdem esse dicuntur, nisi sono discrepaverint, ut "hic" "hic"; sed si emendatius et melius scribere vis adverbium per duo i caraxabis, ut "hiic"' ('There are also pronouns and adverbs that are said to consist of the same letters, unless they are different in pronunciation, like *hic* and *hic*; but if you want to write better and more correctly you will trace the adverb with two *i*, i.e. *hiic*'), cf. *Epist.* I, 7, 1 and 6 (Polara 1979, 190, 148–9 and 192, 167–71).

329. Cf. Thurot (1869, 535). In the same way Parisius de Altedo: 'Hec figura *y* secundum Priscianum et Uguccionem solum in dictionibus ponitur peregrinis, id est grecis vel barbaris vel ab eis detortis. Quidam tamen dixerunt quod, ubicunque et aspiratio ponitur post *c, t, p* vel *r* et post aspirationem ponitur *i*, illud *i* debet scribi figura greci *y* cum puncto superius ducto, quia pronunciatio illius greci *y*

secundum eos ad sonum talium aspirationum accedit. Quam rationem forsan ex ingenii vel lingue grossitie intelligere nequeo. Nec *michy* pronomen ita scriptum recolo invenisse' ('This letter *y* according to Priscian and Hugutio should only be used in foreign words, i.e. Greek or barbarian, or words drawn from them. Some also said that, wherever an aspirate is placed after *c, t, p* or *r* and an *i* is placed after an aspirate, that *i* must be written with *y* with a dot above it, because the pronunciation of that *y* according to them approaches the sound of such an aspirate. Which reason I cannot understand, perhaps because of the thickness of my mind or tongue. Nor do I remember having found the pronoun *michy* written in this way'). A manuscript containing part of the *Admirantes* Gloss. states as follows on the phonetic value of *y*: '*Y* grecum habet sonum grossum, *i* latinum habet sonum exilem' ('Greek *Y* has a fat sound, Latin *i* has a thin sound'), cf. Thurot (1869, 146).

330. Cf. Väänänen (1971, 90–1); as is well known, Pompeian inscriptions already provide evidence of the spelling *e* for *ae, oe*, and conversely the spelling *ae* especially for *ĕ*, but in one case for *ē* also.

331. We find sure traces of a transformation of the monophthong *ae* into a vowel *e*, which in turn can be likened to the successors of both *ĕ* and *ē*, in the following etymological suggestion by Virgilius Maro Grammaticus: '*Celum* ob hoc dici putatur quia quaedam intra se grandia celat archana et ipsius aeris spatiis nubiumque obstaculis ab humanis celatur obtutibus; sed quod et litterae et statui magis conpetat dicamus: celum a celsitudine sua rectissime nomen accipit' ('It is believed that the sky (*celum*) is so called because it hides (*celat*) great mysteries inside, and is hidden (*celatur*) from human eyes by the spaces of the air and by the obstacles of clouds; but we give an explanation that better suits both the letter and the sense: the sky takes its name precisely from its height (*celsitudine*))' cf. *Epit.* XI, 1, 4 (Polara 1979, 146, 17–22). The same conclusions can be drawn from a similar etymological suggestion, though not directly connected to the one above, put forward by the *Ars Ambrosiana*, for which see Law (1982, 95, n. 79). An anonymous tenth century treatise on orthography prescribes: '*Praemium, praeceptum, praepositio, prae timore*, cum *a, preces, pretium*, sine *a* . . . *Celebrat, ceterum, cecitas, cesus, cecidit, cerulum*, et cetera similia, sine *a* in capite scribendum est. *Caelum, caelestia* et cetera ad caelum pertinentia per *a* scribenda sunt. Sciendum sane quia nullum *ce* per *a* scribendum, nisi *caelum* et cetera ad eum pertinentia' ('*Praemium, praeceptum, praepositio, prae timore* with *a, preces, pretium* without *a* . . . *Celebrat, ceterum, cecitas, cesus, cecidit, cerulum* and other similar words should be written without *a* at the beginning. *Caelum, caelestia* and others relating to the sky should be written with *a*. It should be known that no *ce* is to be written with *a*, except for *caelum* and other words relating to it'); in another tenth century treatise we can read: '*Aestatem* per *ae* scribendum . . . *Aesus*, quod est cibus, per *ae, aedis* per *ae* . . . *Aemtio*, quod vendicio est, per dyptongon scribendum, *cedo*, quod est condono,

sine *a, caedo*, quod est occido, per *ae, caleum, caesaries* per *ae* ...
*Haec* per *h* et dyptongon scribendum ... *Laeva*, quod est sinistra, per
*ae* ... *Moechus*, quod est adulter, per *o* et *e* ... *Raeda* per *a* et *e'*
('*Aestatem* should be written with *ae* ... *Aesus*, which is food, with
*ae, aedis* with *ae* ... *Aemtio*, which is a sale [this must be a mistake
for 'acquisition'], is written with the diphthong, *cedo*, which is to
grant, without *a, caedo*, which is to kill, with *ae, caelum, caesaries*
with *ae* ... *Haec* is written with *h* and the diphthong ... *Laeva*,
which is left, with *ae* ... *Moechus*, which is adulterer, with *o* and *e*
... *Raeda* with *a* and *e'*) cf. Thurot (1869, 521–2). An anonymous
twelfth-century verse treatise on the quantity of initial syllables prescribes that one should use the initial syllable of words beginning
with *pre* as long, as well as the first syllable of *cecus, demon, edes,
eger, Egiptus, Egoceron, emulus, eneus, enigma, Grecus, ledo, secula,
tedet, theda, celum, cenum, federa, fedo, fenix, fenum, mecus, clodus,
colem*; an anonymous fourteenth-century *Tractatus artis metrice*
points out that 'Secundum veteres utraque vocalis huius dyptongi *oe*
et *ae* scribebatur. Sed cum quidam minus periti proferrent quicquid
scriptum inveniebant, consultum est imperitie eorum, et instituerunt
minores ut tantum illa vocalis que erat proferenda, scriberetur, et in
loco illius que erat scribenda quedam virgula curva supponeretur'
('According to the ancients both vowels in the diphthongs *oe* and *ae*
were written down. But because some inexperienced people pronounced everything they found written down, one has addressed their
inexperience, and it has been decided that only the vowel that is to be
pronounced is to be written, and in place of the one that used to be
written one will place a curved comma underneath', cf. Thurot (1869,
532–3). Petrus Helias' *Summa* clearly seems to show the monophthong: on this, see Thurot (1869, 140) and the full discussion of the
alleged compounds with *pr[a]e –* in Tolson (1978, 10, 28–49), while
Parisius de Altedo's *Orthographia* points out:'Quando [scil. *e*] pre-
ponitur, tota diptongus scribitur et profertur, ut *eunucus*. Cum vero
postponitur, pro parte scribitur et profertur, ut *foenum musae*' ('When
[*e*] is placed first, diphthongs are written and pronounced in their
entirety, like *eunucus*. But when *e* is written after, it is written and
pronounced in part, like *foenum musae*'), and finally the anonymous
fourteenth century *Gramaticale* confirms the weakness in articulating
the first element of the diphthong, which is no longer reflected in
writing: 'Sed cum finit in *e* diptongus, more moderno / *a* vel *o* vix
resonat, nec scribitur, ut caveatur / *ae* de diptongo sic fiat sillaba
bina' ('But when a diphthong ends in *e*, according to modern custom
/ *a* or *o* are barely pronounced, nor written, to avoid that *ae* from a
diphthong should become a double syllable') cf. Thurot (1869, 140–
1). The diphthong *oe* seems to have remained stable in the technical
term *soloecismus*, cf. Thurot (1869, 141).

332. See the following evidence by Parisius de Altedo: 'Diptongus qui
terminatur in *u*, scribitur et profertur ex toto, [*au*], ut *audio, eu*, ut
*eunuchus*' ('A diphthong that ends in *u* is written and pronounced

entirely, [*au*], like *audio, eu,* like *eunuchus*'), cf. Thurot (1869, 140). It will be observed that the keeping of [aw] within medieval Latin conforms in some way to what can be traced in the development of many Romance languages, where the change from diphthong to monophthong comes late – unlike the reduction of *ae* – and it takes place independently and at different times in the various languages, cf. Väänänen (1971, 91–3).

## 2.3 The philosophy of language *by Alfonso Maierù*

### 2.3.1 Platonism in the early Middle Ages

Philosophical reflection on language in the Middle Ages is practised on certain texts which must be kept in mind constantly. First of all the text of the Bible, which works in two directions. One considers the origin, evolution and differentiation of languages (God names things, *Gen.* 1, 5; Adam 'Appellavit . . . nominibus suis cuncta animantia et universa volatilia caeli et omnes bestias terrae' ('gave names to all cattle, and to the birds of the air, and to every beast of the field'), *Gen.* 2, 20; the tower of Babel, the confusion of tongues as divine punishment and the consequent scattering of the peoples of the world, *Gen.* 11). The other direction considers how 'regular' was the text available to the Latins, which is a result of a transla-tion, but is the vehicle of divine revelation (Gregory the Great: 'indignum . . . ut verba celestis oraculi restringam sub regulis Donati' ('unfitting . . . that the words of the heavenly oracle should be constrained by the rules of Donatus')).[1] Beside the presence of the Bible we must place the grammatical tradition of late antiquity, which is known mostly through the writings of Donatus and above all Priscian. Finally, there was the Aristotelian tradition, particu-larly as represented by the *De interpretatione* and mediated through Boethius' work. These elements functioned and interacted in differ-ent ways in the course of the centuries.

For our purposes it is best to start from the grammatical tradition of late antiquity as received by Isidore of Seville. Together with the grammatical doctrines proper, Isidore adopts an idea of language in which we can find the echo of the Stoic, Platonic and Aristotelian reflections which have been present in the Latin tradition from Varro to Augustine, from Jerome to Cassiodorus and Gregory the Great.[2] According to Isidore, grammar is the first of the liberal arts and is the origin and foundation of all later acquisition of knowledge;[3] it makes use of four procedures (analogy, etymology, gloss and difference)[4] which define the all-pervasive character he finds in the discipline. If difference aims to identify the meaning of a word by distinguishing it from the opposite meaning of another word (king, tyrant),[5] etymology gives one access to the profound meaning of a word and to the essence of the signified things ('Nisi ... nomen scieris, cognitio rerum perit', 'if you do not know the name, the knowledge of things perishes'),[6] while analogy reassembles knowledge by a synthesis whose structure follows the thread of similarities, and gloss utilizes the knowledge that has already been acquired to explain a difficult term, proceeding from what is known to what is unknown. In Isidore's perspective homology and isomorphism exist between language and reality. As Jolivet pointed out,[7] it is a concept of the relationship between language and reality which tends towards Platonism. However, the world of forms is absent from this concept, and the role of forms is played here by the lexicon, the vocabulary, and the role of the dialectician is played by the grammarian.

A similar conception of the relationship between language and reality is exemplified in the time of Charlemagne by Fridugisus of Tours in the letter *De substantia nihili et tenebrarum*. In order to show that *nihil* and *tenebrae* are something, the author resorts to arguments of reason and authority. First, to show that nothingness is something. Every finite noun signifies something: this is the case for 'man', 'stone', 'wood'; so *nihil* is a signifying *vox* and every signification refers to what it signifies.[8] Finally, every signification is a signification of what is, that is of something that exists. By reasoning, *nihil* appears to be not only *aliquid*, but 'magnum quoddam', 'something great';[9] and if we keep in mind that the authority of the Church taught by God teaches that God created 'ex nihilo' earth, water, fire, light, angels and the human soul, it must be concluded that nothing is 'magnum quiddam ac praeclarum', 'something great and illustrious'.[10] The author follows a similar procedure to show that darkness is: arguments of reason (the existential value of the verb to be) and of authority (the Bible) allow one to conclude that darkness exists.[11] The course of the argument leads us to understand the profound meaning of Fridugisus' attitude: at the moment of creation, God called things into being, and named them; the universe of things and the universe of names both originate from divine initiative, which is the foundation of their correspondence to each other, and the necessity of both: because God does not do anything which is superfluous. If this is so, then the name God gave things is not superfluous in any way; and, if it is not superfluous, it is 'secundum modum'; and if it is so, it is also necessary, since it is used to recognize the thing it signifies. It follows that God has created 'secundum modum' things and names, which are necessary to each other.[12] In this way it is recognized that names have an ontological consistency which makes them equal to things.

Isidore and Fridugisus are good examples of that kind of 'grammatical Platonism' Jolivet has talked about since 1958,[13] a suggestion which Chenu received enthusiastically (1967). This idea examines closely the line followed by Guimet since 1948. Guimet was writing about a literary, or more precisely, linguistic Platonism in which language is recognized as having the value of metaphysical suggestion, since by means of etymology one discovers the essence behind every word,[14] However, as Jolivet also points out, 'it is a Platonism which is ignorant of Plato',[15] and he goes on to indicate how in the twelfth century the gap was filled by Thierry of Chartres as he recognized the presence of form beside name and thing. Thierry is of the opinion that nouns are connected to things and not only express their essence, but are actually its foundation ('Nomina quippe essentiant res', 'nouns in fact give essence to things').[16] He indicates the reason for this to be the fact that names and things are eternally joined in the mind of God (where the divine naming of things of *Gen.* 1, 5 takes place, which Fridugisus recalled for different purpose).[17] And if in one respect form gives being to the things that share it,[18] in another, but parallel, respect, Man (Adam), moved by the Holy Spirit, names all things:[19] shared form and name go together, so that a certain name suits something that has a certain form,[20] and vice versa a certain thing is such because it has a certain name.[21] Hence Thierry's formula: 'unio rerum et vocabulorum et comitantia forme et vocabuli', 'the union of things and words and the accompaniment of form and words',[22] which expresses the original unity of name and thing, and the concomitance of name and form as equal founders of the essence: it is because names are the foundation of the essence of things that they bring knowledge of things.[23]

This tendency towards Platonism in linguistic thought, which is realized into Platonic doctrine in the twelfth century, is not absent from the more strictly grammatical texts (Priscian and his early medieval commentators), and it is also active in the Aristotelian tradition of the commentaries to the first chapter of the *Categories*: in both cases the Boethian doctrine of participation comes to the fore to justify linguistic and grammatical considerations.

Let us first look at grammatical texts. Priscian (*Institutiones*, XVII, 35) states that the definition 'animal rationale mortale' manifests the species 'homo', which, 'quamvis videatur esse communis omnium hominum, tamen est propria ipsius speciei incorporalis', 'although it seems to be common to all men, it is however typical of his incorporeal species';[24] and later (para. 44) he points out that in definitions 'common nouns' (*appellativa nomina*) should be used, which can introduce a difference, although they could be considered 'proper nouns' when relating to those forms (general and special) of things which, in an intelligible way, existed in the divine mind before they descended into bodies ('propria . . . quibus genera et species naturae rerum demonstrantur', 'proper (nouns) . . . with which the genders and the species of natural things are demonstrated').[25] A tenth century commentator derives from the first passage the conviction that *homo* is a proper noun because it indicates the human species, distinct and separate from all others. He goes on to recall the Platonic doctrine of ideas and the origin of things from them by participation:

> Illa enim species propria est que individua est et semper manet, neque augeri neque minui potest. Nam ab illa specie propria incorporali homo est. Plato ideas appellat, id est species incorporales proprias individuas, quarum participatione discernuntur animalia, que etiam apparent in formis corporalibus. Et ipsa species in alias species dividi non potest, in multos autem homines multiplicari potest.

> A species is proper because it is individual and remains always as it is, and cannot be increased or diminished. Indeed man is from that proper incorporeal species. Plato calls them 'ideas', i.e. proper individual incorporeal species, through whose participation animals are distinguished, and which also appear in corporeal forms. And the same species cannot be divided into other species, but it can be multiplied in many men.[26]

But in the *Glosule* on Priscian (end of the eleventh century) the thesis which considers names of species as 'proper' nouns rather than 'common' or 'appellative' nouns is refuted, and at the same time there is a refusal of a realistic solution to the problem of universal questions: whoever imposed the name *homo* did not look at some 'species informis', 'formless species', but at the thing that strikes the senses ('res sensibus subiacens', 'a thing subject to the senses'), which he considered perceptible, rational, mortal, and he gave that name to it and to all other beings *convenientia* with it in the same nature; if then the rational soul, 'quadam similitudine aliarum rerum ductus', 'led by some similarity of other things' reaches the point of conceiving with the intellect alone, and not as something existing in nature, a 'res una' common to all men as if it were subsistent in itself, and calls it by the name *homo*, *homo* is not to be considered a proper noun because of that.[27] In fact, the criterion to evaluate a noun is not the way it is used, but the nature or cause of its invention.[28]

The other tradition involving the metaphysics of participation is the one of the doctrine of paronyms or denominatives. It deals with nouns in the tradition of Donatus[29] or Priscian,[30] where the concrete is primitive and the abstract is derived, but it concerns the things in the first chapter of Aristotle's *Categories* (1, 1a13–15, and cf. 8, 10a32–b9), according to which those entities which take their name from something else, with the suffix as the only difference, are called denominatives (and here the abstract is the original and the concrete is the denominative: *grammatica/grammaticus*; *fortitudo/fortis*). In his commentary Boethius clarifies that there are three conditions to having 'denominative things' and 'denominativa vocabula': first of all, that in reality there should be participation of the object to the *res* ('ut re participet', 'so that it should share in the thing': having grammar or force); second, that there should be participation in the noun; and finally, that there should be 'quaedam nominis transfiguratio', 'some kind of transfiguration of the noun', so that the denominative does not end in the same syllable as the noun from which it is derived.[31] In Boethian interpretation the doctrine of paronyms is rooted in the doctrine of participation, illustrated by Boethius mainly in theological treatises, and according to which perceptible matter is a compound ('id quod est', 'that which is'), which is constituted by virtue of participation in a form which makes it be what it is ('esse', later expounded as 'quo est' 'that through which something is what it is').[32] Participation in a form ultimately provides the foundation for participation in a form's name, with the paronym's name differing from it only in the final part.

But the grammatical and the Aristotelian-Boethian tradition meet in actual fact, and the circle is complete, with the interpretation in Boethian terms of the definition of the noun given by Priscian (*Institutiones*, II, 18): 'Proprium est nominis substantiam et qualitatem significare', 'It is typical of the noun to signify substance with quality'. According to a passage in the *Glosule*, each noun (e.g. *homo*) signifies a substance, that is whatever acts as a substratum (the *res* which is man) and is capable of receiving a form; moreover, it signifies a quality, that is the form (e.g. *humanitas*), which makes it possible for that thing to be what it is; Petrus Helias, who mentions this opinion, concludes: 'Hoc autem est illud quod plerique dicunt, scilicet quod omne nomen significat id quod est et id quo est, ut hoc nomen "homo" significat id quod est, idest rem que est homo, et illud quo est, scilicet humanitatem qua est homo, quoniam homo ab humanitate est homo' ('This is what most people say, that is that every noun signifies that which is and that through which it is, so that the noun *homo* signifies what it is, that is the thing that is a man, and that through which it is, that is the humanity by which it is a man, because a man is a man by his humanity').[33] Whereby it is recognized that all nouns, whether of substance or of accident, are entitled to the same status and consequently the same semantic analysis.

In the eleventh century the doctrine of paronyms was already one of the subjects most thoroughly examined by philosophical research, with Anselm of Canterbury's *De grammatico*. The distinction between a noun of substance (*homo*) and a noun of quality (*grammaticus*) is clear to St Anselm. The first noun 'per se et ut unum', 'in itself and as one', signifies what it implies, and, while it is capable of signifying, it is equally capable of naming what it signifies, i.e. the substance ('hoc nomen est significativum et appellativum substantiae', 'this noun is significative and appellative of substance').[34] The second, a noun of accident, does not signify grammar and the man who is informed by it 'ut unum', but signifies grammar directly and primarily ('per se'), and man indirectly and obliquely ('per aliud'). In other words, 'grammaticus' properly 'signifies' ('est significativum') grammar, but 'is a name of', or is used to name ('est appellativum'), the man who bears grammar.[35]

Abelard is of the same opinion on this problem. He recognizes a double signification for the paronym ('nomen sumptum'): the principal one is the signification of the quality or form from which the noun was found; the secondary one is the signification of the subject in which the quality is inherent, or which the form determines; this subject is named by the paronym.[36]

On the other hand, the interpretation by means of Boethian instruments of the definition of the noun given by Priscian, acquires renewed importance in the use made of it by Gilbert of Poitiers, according to whom every noun (even in the context of the Trinity: *deus/deitas*) has different meanings, corresponding to substance and quality.[37] Thus *homo* has two meanings: it signifies the human individual (in Boethian terms, the 'id quod est'), which the grammarians call 'substance'; and it signifies that thanks to which he must be a man ('id quo esse debet homo'), which is called 'quality'.[38] One or other of these two meanings comes to the forefront according to the context[39] in which the noun *homo* is placed. In the sentence 'homo est risibilis', the term *homo*, though it has both meanings, implies only the first of them, the substance of the noun, since 'risibilis', 'capable of laughter', is said of the one who is man. In the sentence 'homo est individuorum forma', 'man is the form of the individuals', the predicate ('forma individuorum') applies only to the 'id quo est homo', that is to the quality of the noun.[40] In such a way, although in the two sentences the subject is the same (*homo*), the term implies (or 'stands for') different meanings.[41]

The data that can be gathered from Anselm's reflections on paronyms (with the distinction between signifying and 'being the name of') and from Gilbert's ideas have been seen, if not as anticipations, certainly as discussions similar to those that will be developed later by terministic logic in the context of the doctrine of supposition, and particularly of the distinction between personal supposition and simple supposition.[42] Besides, one cannot understand a position like the one taken by William of Ockham on the subject of denominatives (or 'connotatives') – since he believes, reversing Anselm's tradition, that among the various meanings of such terms the principal meaning is the one indicating the subject which bears the form, about which one uses the term itself, and the secondary (or 'connoted') meaning is the one concerning inherent form[43] – if one leaves aside reflections such as Gilbert's, as well as an adequate reformulation of the doctrine in the overall rethinking of the function of parts of speech and of the theory of supposition. On the other hand, it is certain that the grammatical definition of the name, interpreted in the light of Boethian tradition, has contributed to the articulating of the logical doctrine of meaning, with the distinction of sense and reference. There is evidence of this in a passage by Albertus Magnus (thirteenth century) quoted by Chenu,[44] in which logical and philosophical language run beside grammatical language: 'Duo sunt attendenda in nomine, scilicet forma sive ratio a qua imponitur, et illud cui imponitur; et haec vocantur a quibusdam significatum et suppositum, a grammaticis autem vocantur qualitas et substantia' ('One must pay attention to two things in a noun, that is the form or ratio by which it is given, and that to which it is given; and these things are called by some signified and suppositum, but they are called by the grammarians quality and substance').

But the most well-known result of the realism influenced by Plato which was widespread until the middle of the twelfth century is the doctrine of semantic unity of the name as well as the verb, attributed to the so-called *nominales* grammarians, whose representative is Bernard of Chartres according to John of Salisbury (*Metalogicon*, III, 2). Once again paronyms, or denominatives, are on the scene. According to the *nominales*, these nouns mean principally the same thing ('idem significant') which is signified by the names from which they derive, with the only difference of consignification ('sed consignificatione diversa', 'but with different consignification'). Thus *albedo* (whiteness) indicates the quality, that is a kind of colour considered in itself ('simpliciter et sine omni participatione subiecti', 'simply and with no participation of the subject'); *albet* (it grows white) indicates principally the same thing, but allows the participation of the 'person' (which is a grammatical accident of the verb); *album* (white) means the same quality, 'sed infusam commixtamque substantie', 'but infused and mixed with the substance', so that the noun itself indicates the bearer of the whiteness as a substance, and the colour as a quality. In the end, according to Bernard, *albedo* is comparable to an uncorrupted virgin, *albet* to the same virgin getting into the nuptial bed, *album* means the same, but corrupted. This represents the process through which the quality signified, starting from the original condition, comes to be contaminated, delivering itself to the 'substance' that receives it and whose form it is.[45]

We find a similar position in the contemporary *Note Dunelmenses* on Priscian Maior: 'Cum lectio, legit, lector idem significent, diuerso tamen modo hoc faciunt', 'Although *lectio, legit, lector* mean the same thing, they do so in a different way'.[46] The statement of accidentality, or 'adjacency', of consignification (according to Bernard) – that is of the grammatical traits of the noun and verb (the tense is 'consignified' by the verb: Aristotle, *De interpretatione*, 3 16b6) – or of the 'different mode' in which the same meaning is expressed (according to the *Note Dunelmenses*) is made possible by the consideration that the fundamental identity of the meaning[47] is guaranteed by the identity of nature which, at an ontological level, remains in the process of participation of the form into perceptible reality. Such a viewpoint can be overcome by investigating further the role of the knowing subject (*intellectus*) who mediates between the things that are known (*res*) and language (*sermo*), according to Aristotelian teaching (*De interpretatione*, 1) handed down by Boethius. The reflection on the relationship between *res, intellectus* and *sermo* as elaborated by Boethius[48] is present here and there in the early Middle Ages,[49] and, once it is taken up again on a steady basis, allows a re-elaboration of linguistic doctrines which gives way to the centrality of the knowing subject and to the systematic influence of Aristotle.[50]

### 2.3.2 Aristotelianism in the eleventh and twelfth centuries
The grammatical reflection which occurs between the eleventh and the beginning of the twelfth century takes place in a cultural context which sees the full use of Aristotle's *Categories* and *De interpretatione*, of the commentaries by Boethius on these works, as well as the recovery of the corpus of Boethius' monographs on logic and the use of his theological works as text books. The more confident control of logical tools and the more acute perception of the problems set for theological reflection by using the human language to name God, stimulate the development of grammatical thought, whose results are used by logic and theology. The effects of this use, in turn, are felt in a grammatical context in terms of a greater awareness of the discipline's autonomy, which is thus driven further to investigate its doctrinal wealth.

We mention the three following problems out of the ones discussed in this period. The first is the discussion on the possibility of a universal grammar for all languages,[51] referring both to the fact that other languages apart from Latin (such as Greek, Hebrew, Chaldean) appear to the authors to be provided with a grammar, and to the experience of vernacular languages, which are not provided with a grammar but are the teachers' own mother tongue, so that the teachers live in constant bilingualism.[52] The second problem is an attempt at redefining the various parts of speech according to categories which, while preserving the properties of each, might highlight their formal and functional aspects rather than their material and semantic ones. The third problem is the working out of a syntactic theory which introduces the category of *regimen* and then uses the categories of 'construction', 'congruity' (or grammaticalness) and 'perfection' (or completeness).

The possibility of a universal grammar is first discussed in William of Conches' glosses on Priscian. William refuses to accept the statement made by his predecessors or contemporaries, according to which the grammar of the Latin language and that of the Greek language are supposedly 'species' of the art of grammar: in organizing knowledge according to the system of liberal arts, William, criticizing this opinion, wishes to preserve the art's unity, which is carried out by different words in different languages: 'sunt enim artes generales et eaedem apud omnes, quamvis diverse Graecus eas per diversas explicet voces', 'arts are therefore general and the same for everyone, although Greek explains them differently with different *voces*'.[53] William of Conches' attitude is not shared by Petrus Helias, according to whom the grammars of the various different languages are the 'species' of common grammar, which is their genus; there is a limited number of these species, but it could increase if one came to the treatment of the grammar of vernacular languages.[54] Petrus' position, however, does not deny the unity of the art, as is clear in another who holds the same opinion, Dominicus Gundissalinus: 'Species vero artis sunt ea in quorum unoquoque tota ars continetur, ad similitudinem specierum generis in quarum unaquaque totum genus inuenitur', 'the species of the art are those things in each of which the whole of the art is contained, in a similar way to the species of a genus in each of which the whole of the genus is found'; and, after listing some of the species (Latin, Greek, Hebrew and Arabic), Dominicus repeats: 'in unaquaque earum inuenitur tota grammatica cum omnibus partibus suis', 'in each of them the whole of grammar with all of its parts is to be found'.[55] So this position, like William's, maintains the unity of the art and the universality of grammar, which is common to all languages like a genus is shared by all species. This opinion, overcoming some dissent,[56] reaches thirteenth century authors and is adopted by the Pseudo-Kilwardby.[57]

Considerations such as these on the one hand shed light on the effort to define grammar, on a theoretical level, in relation to its concrete realizations, and on the other hand denote (in the version of Helias and Gundissalinus) a positive evaluation of the variety of languages, each of which is in itself capable of achieving the condition of a language with a grammar. The ghost of Babel and the related negative judgement of the varying of languages seem far away, while a more relaxed naturalistic attitude pervades linguistic thought. In political thought too, a positive value is attributed to the possession of one's own language, which is indeed included (together with country, customs and laws) among the distinctive characteristics of the new-born kingdoms, and, with a conviction that was not unknown even in patrology, it is stated that languages were distinct and diversified before the tower of Babel.[58] But the shadow of Babel remains active for a long time (we need only think of Dante in the *De vulgari eloquentia*, I, vi, 5–6, and vii, 4–8), or at least it remains in the background, as the answer 'secundum fidem', 'according to the faith', to the question 'unde processit diversitas ydiomatum', 'from where does the diversity of languages come', which 'secundum philosophiam', 'according to philosophy', is answered instead in a naturalistic way, saying that the diversity is 'ab aeterno' and therefore has never had a beginning, while its final cause is identified in the beauty of the universe; alternatively, one answers that the diversity comes from the influence of the heavens, from custom and from the diversity of human beings' natural constitution.[59]

For the second aspect we intend to consider, that of the redefining of the parts of speech, we also take William of Conches as a starting point, and in particular his *Philosophia mundi*, where he sets out his programme of grammatical studies and offers a negative judgement of Priscian, who gives obscure definitions and leaves out the causes of the invention of the various parts of speech and of the various accidents. The author believes that the work of the 'ancient glossators' should be integrated, and especially that the 'causae inventionis' should be illustrated and the exposition of Priscian's definitions should be provided.[60] The notion of 'causa inventionis', returning in the *Glosule* (but the idea is present in Priscian, *Institutiones*, X, 9: 'sicut igitur pronomen ideo est inventum, ut . . . sic participia inventa sunt, ut . . .', 'As the pronoun was found in order that . . . so the participles were found in order that . . .'),[61] is used systematically by William in the first version of his glosses on

Priscian, both in his accounting for the reason why the invention of
*vox* has taken place beside *res* and *intellectus* (which is the manifesta-
tion of the speaker's will), and in his accounting for the invention
of letters (the reason is, to teach those who were absent and to
preserve memory),[62] and also in determining why noun and verb
were found: since 'in omni oratione perfecta dicitur aliquid de
aliquo', 'in every perfect sentence something is said about something', a *vox* (the noun) is needed to indicate 'de quo est sermo',
'what the discourse is about', and another (the verb) to indicate
.'quid de altero dicitur', 'what is said of the other',[63] and so on for
the other parts of speech. In analysing the signifying function of
the noun (*significatio*), with reference to Priscian's well-known
definition, William introduces a fourfold distinction: some nouns
signify substances (common nouns, e.g. *homo*, and proper nouns,
e.g. *Socrates*); others signify what is inherent in the substance
(nouns of accidents: *albedo*); others are names of imaginary entities
(*yrcocervus*, *chimaera*); finally, others indicate *modi loquendi* (syncategoremata, e.g. quantificators). For each of these groups William
identifies what the nouns mean (the 'sense'), and what they name
(the 'referent'). In the first group, common nouns (e.g. *homo*)
indicate the substance in an indeterminate way ('non aliqua'), and
also the quality (*rationalis et mortalis*).[64] To those who object that
a substance cannot be anything but a certain substance, and
therefore one cannot signify anything except a determinate
('aliqua') substance, William replies with the clear statement of the
autonomy of the intellect in relation to things, and of the dependence of language on the intellect.[65] In actual fact common nouns
do not indicate the actual concrete substance, but the intelligible,
universal substance (the 'species', not the individual). On the other
hand, they 'name' (denote) concrete individuals, even if in a context
('ex adiuncto') they can name the species ('homo est species', later
an example of simple supposition), or themselves ('homo est
nomen', later an example of material supposition).[66] Proper nouns,
in turn, signify an individual substance ('substantia aliqua indi-
vidua') and its own quality (being Socrates, or *Socratitas*), and
name the same substance they signify, but do not name its quality;
but sometimes they have an autonomous function, and name
themselves ('Socrates est nomen').[67]

As for the second group, William distinguishes the nouns of
accidents (*albedo*) from adjectives (*album*); the first signify only the
quality and name its individuals (*haec albedo*), while the second
ones signify the same accident which is signified by the first ones
(the quality) but *aliter*, that is determining the inherence of the
accident and the subject. *Albedo* and *album* therefore do not differ

in the 'res significata', but 'in modo significandi'; and since *albedo* signifies the quality, *album* too will signify the quality, and the substance as well, but in a secondary way, making it understood ('secundario, idest innuendo'). However adjectives, unlike nouns of accidents, name the substances in which accidents are inherent. The nouns in the third group do not signify substance and quality, but signify and name a 'figmentum animi'. The nouns in the fourth group do not signify substance and quality either, nor do they name anything: they signify purely a 'modus loquendi'.[68]

Other classes of nouns considered by William are those of the technical language of grammar (*verbum, pronomen*) and logic (*genus, species*); Priscian's definition is applied to these, since in the first case the terms signify the substance (the *vox*) and the quality which is common to words of a certain class, and name them; and in the second case the terms, 'found' to signify substance and quality, have been transferred to name the universals and to signify their common properties. In conclusion, William believes that the Priscianean definition is characteristic of the noun, in the sense that it belongs exclusively to it, although it is not applied to all nouns, but only to those that can be predicated of substances (common nouns and adjectives).[69]

Petrus Helias, although he depends heavily on William of Conches in his *Summa*,[70] goes in a different direction. In examining the earlier opinions, he mentions the one put forward in the *Glosule* and adopted by Gilbert of Poitiers, according to which every noun signifies substance, i.e. a thing as substratum, and quality, i.e. the form that makes it be what it is,[71] he then reports William of Conches' opinion,[72] and finally he introduces a third opinion which he shares: every noun signifies substance and quality, not in the sense that it must signify a substance or a certain quality, but in the sense that it signifies in the manner of a substance.[73] In the beginning, when names were found 'propter substantias', nouns actually signified substances; but later 'dilatata est locutio', 'speech was widened', and men wanted to speak of other things as well.[74] Now, given this situation, a noun does not signify something because it is a substance, but as if it were a substance. To signify *modo substantiae* is 'significare aliquid sine tempore et in casuali inflexione communiter vel proprie vel quasi communiter vel proprie', 'to signify something without tense and with case inflection, in a common or proper manner, or almost common or proper'. 'To signify' is taken here in its broadest sense, and includes 'to con-signify', so that syncategoremata (like *omnis*) which consignify are also considered nouns that signify 'sine tempore in casuali inflexione et quasi communiter'.[75] In this sense all names signify substance and quality, since this is their *modus significandi*.[76] In the same way, verbs, which were found originally to designate only the action and passion of a substance, later came to designate other accidents as well, designating them in the same way as the first ones; thus *albet*, which indicates a quality, 'modo tamen actionis vel passionis significat, id est cum tempore in verbali terminatione et ut de altero dicitur', 'however, signifies in the manner of action or of passion, that is with the tense in the verb ending and as is said of another thing'.[77] The same can be said for the other parts of speech.[78] In this way Petrus Helias defines the parts of speech in terms of 'modes of signifying',[79] an idea that was already present in William of Conches,[80] who did not make much use of it, preferring, as we have seen, 'causae inventionis' (for every grammatical phenomenon, from parts of speech onwards), as well as *significatio* and *officium* (or function, for the parts of speech).[81] But Petrus himself does not use the notion of a mode of signifying to deal with grammatical accidents.[82] Both authors therefore appear to us as thinkers who, in different ways, brought to conclusion a process of elaboration and refinement of the grammatical tradition, rather than as innovators,[83] even though their contribution and their wide influence are undeniable.

The third theme is syntax and the introduction of the term *regere* (used sporadically in the eighth and ninth centuries, then with increasing frequency) as the equivalent of *exigere*,[84] and from it came *regimen*, to indicate a theory to explain construction. The elements are given by Priscian, in whose work we find the term *constructio*,[85] with the distinction of the four types: transitive (*transitio*), intransitive (*intransitio*), reflexive (*reciprocatio*) and re-transitive (*retransitio*);[86] we also find the origin of the distinction between *transitio actus* and *transitio personarum*, and above all the definition of *oratio* as 'ordinatio dictionum congrua perfectam sententiam demonstrans', 'congruous ordering of words that shows a perfect sentence' (*Institutiones*, II, 15), from which medieval scholars derive the notions of congruity and perfection and the definition of construction as 'congrua dictionum ordinatio', 'congruous ordering of words';[87] finally, we find the statement in XVII, 187: 'omnis constructio ... ad intellectum vocis est reddenda' (or 'referenda', as the medieval teachers often read), 'Every construction is to be referred to the intellect of the *vox*', which authorizes the distinction between the superficial level of expression, and the deep level of the intellect, which seems to be the only one that can guarantee construction. However, the medieval teachers find no systematic treatment in Priscian. A systematic treatment of syntax can be found in the twelfth century with the theory of *regimen*, according to which a word (*regens*) is said to 'govern' another word (*rectum*). The problem then becomes establishing which is the *regens* and which is the *rectum*, that is the problem of setting down the basic criterion of the construction consisting of two words.

One of the first known answers is provided at the beginning of the twelfth century in the context of the tradition of the *Glosule* by a certain Master Guido. He uses a semantic notion, employed by Boethius[88] for the division of *voces*: when a *vox* signifies many things, and therefore raises doubts in the intellect of the listener, it is necessary to have a *determinatio* to conclude (and define) the meaning of the discourse. Master Guido believes that a word governs another when one 'demands' another because of some *incertitudo* in its meaning.[89] Naturally, the more uncertain words have more need of *determinatio*. Consequently, he believes that *rectum* is the *dictio* which has *incertitudo* (the *determinatum*), while *regens* is the *determinans*.[90] On the basis of these elements the author establishes which word governs and which is governed, with reference to parts of speech and to the different cases, both direct and oblique: thus nominative and vocative are governed intransitively by the verb, and the oblique cases are governed by transitive verbs and their participles, by the nominative, by adverbs and prepositions; he considers 'absolute' cases, which are not subject to *regimen*, as well as the more complex constructions such as the one of accusative and infinitive.[91]

William of Conches on the other hand does not rely on purely semantic criteria to explain the *regimen*. Having distinguished *constructio* from *oratio*, since *oratio* is what results from a construction, he attributes to the *regens* a 'vis et natura', 'force and nature' such that it 'requires' that another word should be placed in the sentence. This initiates a more morphological consideration of the syntagmatic relation, which is defined as a binary relation, i.e. one that exists between two words. The words that govern or are governed are classified by William as follows: nominative, vocative, verb, adverb and preposition govern and are not governed; only the oblique cases do not govern but are governed (they, however, sometimes govern, that is, they govern the oblique which is governed by their nominative); only conjunctions do not govern and are not governed.[92]

Petrus Helias follows William in refusing the semantic criterion of determining signification as an explanation of the *regimen*, and introduces the criterion of the 'perfectio constructionis', or fullness of the sense of construction.[93] According to Petrus one word governs another when it brings the second with it ('trahere secum') into the construction in order to reach the perfection of the construction itself. So, the verb (which means 'sermonem fieri de alio', 'that a discourse is about something') requires the nominative (which means 'id de quo fit sermo', 'that which the discourse is about') without which one would not have the *perfecta constructio* and the sense would not be complete.[94] But the verb, as well as governing the nominative, also governs the oblique case when it indicates an act passing into something else; and although 'perfecta constructio' already exists in the case of 'Socrates legit', 'Socrates is reading', the oblique case can be added ('Socrates legit Virgilium', 'Socrates is reading Virgil') to take away any remaining suspense from the mind of the listener, that is 'ad maiorem constructionis perfectionem', 'to the greater perfection of the construction'. In a similar way the participle governs the oblique case: the construction 'intelligens delector', 'I delight in understanding', is perfect without the oblique, but 'intelligens Virgilium delector', 'I delight in understanding Virgil', is a more perfect construction.[95] Nouns ('pater filii', 'the son's father'), adverbs ('similiter illi', 'similarly to him') and prepositions also govern oblique cases.[96] The distinction between various levels of the construction's *perfectio* is barely introduced and not developed further,[97] and does not seem to have been widespread. However, another point of Petrus Helias' treatise on syntax, preceding and underlying the treatment of the *regimen*, has proved more interesting, in which the author, having defined construction as 'congrua dictionum ordinatio', continues by stating that congruity must concern both the *vox* and the sense ('"Congrua" intelligendum est tam voce quam sensu', '*Congrua* must be understood as regards both the *vox* and the sense').[98] A construction is 'congrua voce' when the correct combination of accidents (gender, number, case, etc.) of the construed words is given; it is 'congrua sensu' (*sensus* corresponds to *intellectus* in Priscian XVII, 187) when it has an adequate meaning (independently of its truth or falsehood). Naturally, there are constructions which are congruous in respect of accidents and not congruous in respect of sense, and vice versa. But while he accepts, following tradition, constructions 'according to sense', or figurative constructions, that is where there is no respect of the concordance of accidents, but in which an adequate sense is communicated ('turba ruunt', 'the crowd run'), Petrus Helias refuses constructions which are congruous in respect of concordance and incongruous in respect of content ('Socrates habet ypoteticos sotulares cum cathegoricis corrigiis', 'Socrates has hypothetical shoes with categorical laces'), since language is used to express intellect and in these cases nothing rational is communicated to the listener.[99] Construction can be perfect or imperfect; the definition given ('constructio est congrua dictionum ordinatio') also fits imperfect expressions; and indeed one has adequate (*competens*) construction when two terms are properly joined together (e.g. 'homo albus', 'white man'), even if they do not engender a perfect sense in the listener.[100] Clearly, Helias considers congruity and perfection as separate properties of construction.

The definition of *regimen* given by Petrus Helias did not survive long, and was supplanted by Ralph of Beauvais' definition,[101] according to which a word governs another when it causes it to be put into a certain case. But the distinction in Petrus of two types of congruity influenced later discussion. Towards the end of the twelfth century Robert Blund reconsiders the relationship between semantic level and syntactic level by distinguishing clearly between *regere* and *determinare*, and states that the syntactic *regimen* presupposes semantic *determinatio* and not vice versa; moreover, he states clearly that construction is the relation between terms and not sentences: hypothetical sentences are made up of two constructions that are not constructed in relation to each other[102] (this position was long held by grammarians, as we shall see).

In the thirteenth century, Robert Kilwardby, discussing figurative constructions in the commentary on Priscian Minor, and Roger Bacon in the *Summa grammatica*, which is a collection of grammatical sophisms and for the most part concerns constructions according to sense,[103] examine the notions of congruity and perfection and introduce the distinction of a two-fold intellect (also present in Master Jordanus)[104] to express levels of sense. Because, as we have seen, one can have congruity on the level of *vox* or on the level of sense (*intellectus*). Now, the intellect is two-fold for these two authors: there is an *intellectus primus*, given by the level of the modes of signifying (about which we shall talk later), and there is an *intellectus secundus*, corresponding to the meanings of words. The congruity or perfection of the first intellect cannot exist without congruity on the level of *vox*, while congruity or perfection of the second intellect can exist without congruity and perfection of the *vox*. The distinction to be made in discussing figurative expressions is properly the one between congruity and perfection of the *vox* (which bears with it that of the first intellect, or of the *modi significandi*) and congruity and perfection of the second intellect.[105] Since the dominion of grammar is that of the *modi significandi*, the discussion of figurative expressions leads the grammarian to cross into the realm of meanings, which is the province of the logician.[106] (It is in fact the logician who proceeds to examine the problems of semantic congruence and to frame the relevant rules; cf. Ebbesen (1981)). On this basis, around the middle of the thirteenth century a linguistic trend was established (as documented in a *corpus* of texts which includes, as well as Kilwardby and Bacon, various works attributed to Kilwardby, the *Admirantes* Gloss on Alexander de Villa Dei's *Doctrinale*, and other anonymous works) which on the one hand makes detailed use of the 'mode of signifying' category in order to account for linguistic phenomena (as the *Modistae* will do), while on the other hand (unlike the *Modistae*) this trend allows ample room for figurative expressions, formulating a kind of syntactic system with three values (congruous, incongruous, figurative), and, in evaluating constructions, it also pays attention to the realm of meanings and to the speaker's intention, as well as to the modes of signifying. This implies the recognition of the purely instrumental function of language compared to the intellect, and a heightened interest in the speaker's freedom. The presence of English authors and texts and the fact that in Oxford in 1277 grammatical propositions were censored indicate that the debate, which began in the years when Kilwardby and Bacon were teachers of the arts in Paris (1235–47), must also have continued in a heated manner in Oxford for some decades.[107] But the best known linguistic current is that of the *Modistae*.

### 2.3.3 The grammar of the *Modistae*

Between the twelfth and thirteenth century the reception of Aristotelianism promoted a thorough re-thinking of the conception of the traditional world of the Latin West, of the scientific system adopted and of the constitution of the various disciplines. As for what concerns us here, the influence of the *Posterior Analytics*, but also the influence of the *De anima*, of Aristotle's *Physics* and *Metaphysics*, of Arab doctrines (those of Alfarabi, Avicenna, Averroes) are felt in the new conception of grammar proposed by the *Modistae*, that is by the theoreticians of language who were so called from the expression *modi significandi* used by them to indicate the grammatical category they use systematically to account for linguistic phenomena.[108]

The *Modistae* teachers flowered between the first half of the thirteenth century and the first decades of the fourteenth century, first in Paris, then in Bologna and Erfurt. But the texts from the 1240s and 1250s put forward and discuss the question whether grammar is an art or a science. Master Jordanus introduces (in the objections) within the question whether grammar is an art, the Aristotelian paradigm according to which one can have a science of the universal and of what is necessary and permanent, and he goes so far as to state that, even if the object of grammar is what is sensible, in actual fact by abstracting from the single particular datum one can talk of 'common sensible' which is universal and of which one can have a science: although they are different among different people, the *voces* grammar deals with are the same for everybody if they are considered inasmuch as they are 'ordered' and in relation to the *intellectus* which they bring to the listener's knowledge; but not only the *intellectus* are common to all men (Aristotle, *De interpretatione*, 1, 16a 6–7), but also the *modus ordinandi* words according to the correspondence or the lack of it in their grammatical accidents is the same for all languages.[109] Pseudo-Kilwardby is more explicit both in organizing of the themes discussed (whether grammar is art or science; whether it is one or more; whether it is speculative or practical), and in resorting to Aristotelian elements (the necessity of principles and their mediate origin from the senses, *Posterior Analytics*, II, 19, 100a 3–7: science as 'habit' or dianoetic virtue; the need for science to have an object whose properties are demonstrated), and in defining grammar both as science (as a habit) and art (as a principle of operation: *Posterior Analytics*, II, 19, 100a 7–9) and in including among its principles – which are necessary and identical for all – the *modi significandi*, in affirming the unity of grammar starting from the unity of the object and its speculative character.[110] Therefore it will not be surprising to find in the masters in the second half of the thirteenth century, and particularly in Boethius of Dacia, a firm statement of the autonomy of the discipline and the acknowledgement that it is a science.

According to the *Modistae*, grammar deals with what is common to all languages, and not with what varies from one language to another (linguistic expression). What is common is permanent beyond the variety of idioms, which are to grammar as individuals are to the species. Grammar is essentially the same in the individual languages, which differ among themselves in expression as well as in partially dissimilar realizations of the same principles (the article, which is present in Greek, answers the same need for distinguishing *voces* according to gender, number and case which Latin fulfils by using declension).[111] But all this has to do with the accidental aspect of languages and with their numerical diversity, which makes them individuals; beyond this, their common essence or substance (the deep structure) guarantees their specific unity, which is the foundation of the universality of grammar.[112]

The object of grammar is necessary inasmuch as it is considered in relation to its causes, given which, the effect follows. According to Boethius of Dacia, for the object to be considered necessary, its immutable permanence of being is not required (because one also has knowledge of what is contingent, as long as one knows its causes), but the necessity of the object's relation to its causes is sufficient: therefore it is a hypothetical necessity (given the causes, the effect follows), and therefore a relative necessity.[113] In the same way, the principles of grammar, which are the *modi significandi*,[114] are not absolute principles, since they are effects, as we shall see: they are absolute only within the boundaries of grammar, and are capable of explaining all the phenomena that take place in language. The ancient grammarians did not produce science because they did not supply the causes of the phenomena they described.[115] Finally, grammar is a speculative, i.e. theoretical, science, even if it is not an essential part of philosophy, but is only an instrumental and introductory part to the superior sciences (metaphysics, mathematics, physics).[116] It has its own *corpus* of doctrines which make it a 'special' science next to other sciences, but it should be considered an art (Boethius of Dacia)[117] or a science (Simon)[118] which is 'common' because its object is discourse, which is used by all other sciences; it has its own discovery procedures of the *modi significandi*, arguing *a priori* (from causes to effects), *a posteriori* (from the linguistic phenomenon to the cause that brought it into being), or even proceeding from a *modus significandi* present in a word to the one that must correspond to it in the word that is constructed with the first.[119]

The *Modistae* have given us commentaries on Priscian in the form of questions (Boethius of Dacia, about 1270, on Priscianus Maior; Simon of Dacia, 1280, Radulphus Brito, about 1300, and the contemporary Gentile da Cingoli on Priscianus Minor), but they also wrote three treatises which were used as manuals and were commented several times (Martin of Dacia in the 1270s; Michael of Marbais,[120] 1280–85; Thomas of Erfurt in the early 1300s); finally, they left two incomplete *Summae* (a monumental one by John of Dacia, about 1280; another by Siger of Courtrai, 310–20).

The *Modistae*, after an introduction which sets out the general problems, essentially develop the treatment of parts of speech and the treatment of syntax, out of the traditional treatment of grammar, which was divided into four parts: orthography (the elements: sound, *vox*, letters, syllables), etymology (parts of speech), diasynthetica (syntax), and prosody. The *Modistae* generally dedicate little space to the other problems (only John of Dacia[121] gives ample room to dealing with elements), but they ask whether grammar is *sermocinalis* (as in the tradition of the *Glosule*[122]) or whether it should be referred back to rational philosophy (as Master Jordanus believes, according to whom 'ordering' a word with another is the effect not of nature or morality, but of reason.[123] By this method they define the relationship of grammar with the *vox*.

Man, who means to communicate his thought, uses signs and principally language. The purpose of language is therefore communication between people; in order to reach this end 'orationes congruae et perfectae' are used; therefore the object of grammar is the sentence with its properties, which are, as we have seen, construction, congruity and perfection. Thus, all of the *Modistae's* study of grammar tends towards syntax. This applies to the study of parts of speech, which, combining with each other, give rise to construction. It also applies to the study of what enters into the constitution of a part of speech, and particularly the sound (*vox*) which, though it is an object of the philosophy of nature, is also object of grammar inasmuch as it is a sign, i.e. a bearer of something other than itself, the meaning.[124] By this the *vox* is established as *sermo*[125] and is the most suitable sign to express human thought.[126] Therefore, to the question whether grammar is a *sermocinalis* science, John answers that it is so *per accidens* because the *vox* is considered *per accidens* by the grammarian;[127] while Boethius,[128] Simon[129] and Radulphus[130] believe that grammar is properly *sermocinalis* because it deals with *sermo significativus* and with its *passiones* or properties. On the contrary, Gentile da Cingoli, in the prologue of his commentary on Martin, believes that grammar belongs to rational philosophy because it concerns entities formed by our reason; therefore it is properly a 'rational science',[131] while in the commentary on Priscianus Minor, Gentile states that in itself grammar is not *sermocinalis*, since all that concerns the essence of grammar ('ratio essentialis grammaticae') can exist apart from the *sermo*; therefore the *sermo* does not come *per se* under the grammarian's consideration; rather, grammar is *sermocinalis per accidens*, not only because it expresses its concepts (as all sciences do, which are all *sermocinales* in this sense), or because it is, with logic and rhetoric, 'magis sermocinalis' than other sciences to which the sciences of the trivium are preparatory; but it is the most *sermocinalis* (even compared to the other arts of the trivium) because grammar is the first to be learned, and is 'transmitted' by means of signifying *vox*; this *sermocinalis* grammar is clearly the positive and usual one, not the scientific and speculative one.[132]

The *modi significandi* are drawn from the common properties of things. This is possible thanks to the intervention of the intellect. The intellect, which knows things and signifies them, is the mediator between reality and language. Here is the process as it is illustrated by the *Modistae*: things have an essence of their own, or essential traits that are proper to them, and have properties that are common to several types of things (such as genus, which is common to several species, or being male or female, which identifies subclasses of animals and men). The essence of the known thing (the concept) is associated by the intellect with a phonic sequence, which therefore becomes signifying. The result is called *dictio*, and is the fruit of the 'prima articulatio vocis'. The properties or modes of being of things (*modi essendi*), once known (*modi intelligendi*), are attributed to the *dictio* as *modi significandi* thanks to the 'secunda articulatio vocis',[133] and are signified by the same phonic sequence. The union of voice and meaning, or *dictio*, has been compared to the lexeme of contemporary linguistics.[134] The meaning, considered as corresponding to a word's lexical value, is called by the *Modistae* 'significatum speciale'[135] and corresponds to things (*res*) that fall into the ten categories or predicaments (*res praedicamentales*).[136] Things are the object of real sciences and grammar in itself does not deal with them; and besides, from the grammatical point of view it is accidental that a *vox* should mean one thing rather than another, or even that it should mean an extra-mental entity.[137] If with the 'prima articulatio' the *vox* receives its form, with the 'secunda articulatio' the *dictio* (lexeme) receives the *modi significandi* (morphemes) which make it a part of speech. One concept can be signified by various parts of speech, whose *modi significandi* are not repugnant to it.[138] As Boethius of Dacia shows,[139] *dictio* itself is a *nomen* if it falls under the *modi significandi* of the noun (*dolor*, 'ache'), a verb if it falls under the modes of the verb (*doleo*, 'I ache'), a participle if it receives the *modi significandi* of the participle (*dolens*, 'aching'), and in the same way it can be an adverb (*dolenter*, 'achingly') or an interjection (*heu*, 'ouch'). The *modi significandi* presuppose, in short, that *dictio* is established and therefore that *vox* has its (special) meaning. Grammar, as we have mentioned, does not concern itself with it, but proposes instead the semantic interpretation of parts of speech based on *modi significandi*, which define the 'significatum generale' (the grammatical meaning) of words.[140] Grammar as science has as its object the semantic side of parts of speech, that is the *modi significandi* that are bestowed on *dictio* by the second 'articulation' of the *vox*.

A part of speech is structured by several *modi significandi*. Essential modes constitute its being and define its properties, accidental modes regulate its inflection. Essential modes are further divided into general modes, common to several parts, and specific modes, which are added to the general mode to contract it to an individual part of speech.[141] In practice, there is a general mode common to noun and pronoun (and is called 'significare per modum habitus et quietis', 'signifying by the mode of habit and quietness': modality of stability and permanence), a general mode common to verb and participle ('significare per modum fluxus et fieri', 'signifying by the mode of flux and becoming': modality of movement and becoming), and, starting from the commentary of Simon to Martin,[142] a general mode common to indeclinable parts ('significare per modum disponentis', 'signifying by the mode of the disponent': modality of disposition or modification). The specific *modi significandi*, appropriate to each part of speech are: the 'modus determinatae apprehensionis', 'mode of determinate apprehension' or 'qualitatis', 'of quality' for the noun and 'modus indeterminatae apprehensionis', 'mode of indeterminate apprehension' for the pronoun (the first is the modality of qualification and definition of substance, the second is the modality of non-qualification and indefinition of substance). For the verb the 'modus distantis', 'mode of the distant', and for the participle the 'modus indistantis' (the verb does not combine directly with the noun and needs an accidental mode, the mode of *compositio*, in order to be able to enter into a relationship with substance, while the participle combines with substance with no need of an intermediary); the 'modus determinantis actum', 'mode of the determinant of the act' (modality of determination or qualification of the act expressed by the verb) for the adverb; the 'modus retorquentis casuale ad actum', 'mode of leading back the casual to the act' (modality of leading back the object, or oblique, to the act) for the preposition; the 'modus unitatis', 'mode of unity' (modality of joining) for the conjunction; the 'modus afficientis animam', 'mode of the affection of the soul' (modality of emotional affection of the soul) for the interjection.

In turn, accidental *modi significandi* correspond for the most part to the accidents of traditional grammar. They can be differentiated into *absoluti* and *respectivi*.[143] Those that set the possibility for each part to enter into construction (syntactic dimension)[144] are *respectivi*; those that do not determine construction, but set some grammatical traits typical of each part of speech in relation to the modes of being of the signified thing (semantic dimension) are absolute. When it is set out in this way, a part of speech is able to act as an element of a construction, and therefore it is called *constructibile*.

*Modi essendi*, *modi intelligendi* and *modi significandi* are isomorphous with each other, since the intellect considers things and their properties, and the constitution of language depends on this consideration. But the intellect is not purely passive in its knowledge and in the organization of *sermo*: once the *modi significandi* have been derived from the properties of things (but not all the properties have a corresponding mode),[145] the intellect can form words to which nothing corresponds in reality, and can attribute the *modi significandi* of substance to them, which are appropriate to the noun ('chimaera', 'nothing'), or can attribute the modes of being stable and permanent to realities which are not properly stable or permanent ('time', 'movement' are nouns and as such have the *modi significandi* of nouns, but they signify 'things' or accidents to which the modality of succession and becoming applies, rather than the one of permanence). Therefore the intellect depends on things on the one hand, and on the other it signifies them according to all the ways in which it can know them.

It has been said that the grammarian as such does not concern himself with the things that are signified. But the question has arisen whether he is concerned with them in some way, and whether he should consider the properties and modes of being of things. Moreover, one asks oneself what is the relationship between modes of being and modes of understanding, and modes of signifying. The masters do not maintain one position, which allows one to find different trends within the same doctrinal context.

When faced with the questions about how far consideration of things and their properties is the grammarian's province, Boethius of Dacia answers categorically that he, as a pure grammarian, does not concern himself, not even *per accidens*, with things or their properties, since the grammarian considers only what is necessary to his science, and this can be complete without a concern for these matters.[146] Boethius, then, is strongly aware not only of the completeness, but also of the autonomy of his science. John, on the contrary, though he is aware of the discipline's completeness, believes that the grammarian considers things *per accidens*, 'in quantum accidit constructibilia esse res predicamentales', 'inasmuch as predicamental things are constructible *per accidens*'[147] (which leads him to exclude the possibility of considering *per se* the 'res speciales'), while he considers the *modi essendi* of things insofar as they are principles of construction (which is threefold: real, whose principles are the modes of being; mental, whose principles are the modes of understanding; and vocal, whose principles are the modes of signifying).[148] Finally, Radulphus Brito proposes a more complex solution: having divided grammar into positive, usual and speculative, he believes that the positive grammarian must consider things, not in their real being, but as far as they are the meaning of *dictio* (since such grammar cannot be known if one does not have knowledge of the meanings entrusted to *dictio*); on the contrary, usual grammar does not need to know the 'res speciales', unless it is applied to some special science (such as natural philosophy); finally speculative grammar, which is founded on causes and principles, must consider things, 'quamvis non per se nec principaliter',

'although not *per se*, nor principally': the reason is that the grammarian must consider that without which there can be no knowledge of the modes of signifying, and these are not known if one has
no knowledge of the properties of things; hence the necessity for
the grammarian to consider 'proprietates rerum et res, non tamen
ex principali sed ex adiuncto' (or 'per accidens'), 'the properties of
the things and the things, not however principally, but additionally'.[149]

The examination of the positions concerning the relationships
between modes of being, modes of understanding and modes of
signifying allows us to perceive the differences between the various
authors even more clearly. For Martin, modes of being, understanding and signifying are the same thing (*idem*), accidentally diversified
by their taking place in reality, in thought and in language, just as
Socrates is the same even when he is in different places (and so the
modes of signifying are in the thing which is signified as in their
*subiectum* and in the *vox* 'sicut in signo', 'as in the sign'[150]);
consequently, modes of signifying are not signs of modes of understanding and of modes of being, since nothing can be a sign of
itself, but the *vox* is a sign for them, which signifies a thing and
together with it signifies (*consignificat*) its properties.[151] John follows Martin, pointing out that the modes of signifying are in the
thing which is signified as in the *subiectum*, in the soul as in the
efficient cause, and in the voice as in the sign.[152] Boethius criticizes
this formulation, and believes that modes of being, of understanding and of signifying are not the same thing, because, if they were,
if the mode of being of a thing were given, the mode of signifying
in the *dictio* which signifies that thing would also be given, which is
false; instead, they are similar: the mode of signifying has a resemblance to the mode of understanding and the latter to the mode of
being;[153] moreover, *dictio* is the mode of signifying's *subiectum*,
while the soul is its efficient cause;[154] finally, the modes of signifying are signs of the modes of being.[155]

Radulphus Brito's reflection on the relationship between the
three planes seems to mediate between the different positions of
Martin (and John) on one side and of Boethius on the other, which
is made possible for him by adopting the distinction of the *modus*
into active and passive, which is applied to the modes of understanding and of signifying.[156] Radulphus identifies the 'ratio consignificandi' (and 'ratio cointelligendi') with the active 'modi significandi'
(and 'intelligendi'), and he believes that the 'ratio', which is in the
*vox*, makes it possible for the *vox* to consignify the corresponding
mode of being. He identifies two components in the passive modes
of signifying (and of understanding), a material component, which

is the thing that is signified (or thought), and a formal component, which is the 'ratio consignificandi' (or 'cointelligendi') itself, and which makes it possible for the thing to be signified (and thought). Now, the passive modes of signifying and of understanding are identical *materialiter* with the mode of being (it is the same property of a thing), but are not identical to each other *formaliter*, because from the formal point of view the passive modes of signifying and of understanding are identical to the respective active modes, and the active modes of signifying and of understanding are not identified with the *modi essendi*.[157] Finally, the active modes of signifying and of understanding are different among themselves because the first are form and perfection of the parts of speech and the second are form and perfection of the intellect. They are, however, similar, in the same way in which the modes of understanding, forms of the intellect, are similar to the reality which is signified.[158] As we can see, Martin's identity of the three orders of modes reappears in the identity of the passive modes considered *materialiter*, while the similarity stated by Boethius applies to the active modes. But in explaining his position Radulphus is able to refute the thesis – which is also held by Siger of Courtrai[159] – according to which the active mode of signifying is supposed to be in the soul as in its *subiectum*, so that it could be identified with the active mode of understanding, differing from it only accidentally because it is related to the *vox*: it is difficult to understand, according to Radulphus, how the *vox* is a sign owing to something that is in the soul. Thus the author reaffirms the autonomy of language relative to thought. To quote Simon's commentary on Martin, the correctness of discourse is not to be justified by the correctness of the intellect, but by the intrinsic principles of construction.[160] Thomas of Erfurt follows the lines of thought drawn by Radulphus.[161]

The discussion on syntax includes the analysis of the three properties of the sentence: construction, congruity (grammaticality) and perfection. As we have seen, a part of speech, which is set up starting from the modes of signifying, is liable to enter into a construction. Now, every construction is made up of two elements, and therefore impersonal expressions (*fulminat*, 'it lightens'; *tonat*, 'it thunders') are considered in the same way as expressions like *currit*, 'he runs', *disputat*, 'he disputes', which are considered imperfect on the level of *vox*, but complete on a conceptual level ('secundum intellectum'), because they let the unexpressed *constructable* be understood. In the same way, the former, against Priscian's teaching, are considered imperfect on the expressive level, since from a grammatical point of view nothing differentiates them from the latter ones.[162]

The notion used by the *Modistae* to account for construction is the idea of dependency: an element is *dependens*, unsatisfied or 'unsaturated', and another element is *terminans* because it satisfies and 'saturates' dependence. The elements in a construction cannot be both of the same type, but one must be the dependent and the other the term. A construction is intransitive when a constructable has *dependentia* on the first constructable, which is intuitively held to be the subject; and it is transitive when a constructable has *dependentia* on an element other than the first constructable.[163]

A construction is qualified by the relationship that is established between the modes typical of the various constructibles. If there is agreement, or compatibility of the modes of signifying or morphemes, there is congruity, or grammatical correctness of the sentence. The agreement can be of two types, according to whether the elements of the construction have similar modes (i.e. the same type of mode: gender, number and case for adjective and substantive; person and number for noun and verb), or proportional modes (the mode of permanence and that of adjacence for substantive and adjective, the mode of 'passing into something else' in the transitive verb and the mode of 'term of passing' in the complement). Not every construction is congruous, but only one that is well-formed according to the correspondence of the modes of signifying owned by the constitutive elements is congruous, so that the modes of signifying limit the possibilities that a word has of being correctly construed with another.

Finally, the perfection of a sentence presupposes the congruity of the construction, and requires, moreover, that every dependence should terminate (that the sentence should be complete and independent) and that a noun (*suppositum*) and a verb (*appositum*) of finite mood should appear in the sentence. If the purpose of the communication is to generate a complete sense in the listener, the sentence's perfection does not coincide with simple grammatical correctness, on the level of modes of signifying (general or grammatical meaning) but also calls into question the first semantic level (special meaning). Among correct constructions, some make sense, and they are the ones whose constituent (constructable) elements are connected among themselves in an appropriate way. Now, only the presence of an intransitive construction of the noun-finite verb type guarantees this last condition.

Within this common syntactical doctrine too, one can identify different positions, which relate to two systems,[164] one proposed by Martin of Dacia (and further investigated by his commentators,[165] the other by Radulphus Brito followed by Thomas of Erfurt. These positions are compared in what follows, and related to three aspects of the discussion: the type of construction which is being examined; the number of elements in the construction; the constructability of the conjunction and of more than one sentence.

Given that the principles of construction are two, dependent and term, and that in every construction there is a first element (a construction is union and order, and order presupposes a first and a second element); and finally that every construction (e.g. *homo albus*, 'white man') is not necessarily a composition (a sentence of a finite type), according to Martin there are only two modes of signifying for the dependent: the one through which the dependent goes to the first constructable or to an element which in turn goes to the first; or the mode of signifying through which the dependent does not go to the first. The first mode of signifying, through which each element of construction goes immediately or mediately to the first, is the principle of an intransitive construction. The second (negatively defined) is the principle of a transitive construction. Every construction is therefore either intransitive or transitive. The two modes of signifying which have been mentioned are not identified, according to Martin, with modes of single parts of speech (morphology does not explain syntax completely), but are considered independently from them: they are the highest and the most general modes, and preside over construction.[166] On the other hand Martin, while he refers to a binary construction (*dependens-terminans*), explicitly admits that several elements can enter into a construction: 'homo currit', 'the man runs' is an intransitive construction in which a verb has an immediate dependence on the substantive which is the first constructable; in 'homo currit bene', 'the man runs well', the adverb is drawn back to the substantive through the verb (which is the adverb's 'proprium determinabile per se'); 'homo albus currit bene', 'the white man runs well', is an intransitive construction, in which adjective and verb are immediately dependent on the substantive and the adverb, as we have said, is dependent on it through the verb.[167] As an example of transitive construction we find 'percutio Socratem', 'I hit Socrates'.[168] But it must be said that Martin does not deal with the transitive construction, and analyses only the intransitive, of which he studies the appositive (a *determinatio* is added to its *determinabile*: for example, 'homo albus', 'omnis homo', 'every man'),[169] the construction between *suppositum* and *appositum* ('Socrates currit', 'Socrates runs', 'a me legitur', 'it is read by me', 'me legere', 'me read'),[170] and the intransitive construction *a parte post*, presented as a relation between determinable and determinant ('homo est animal', 'man is an animal' is treated like 'homo currit bene').[171] In Martin it seems that the distinction between 'constructio actuum' 'construction of acts' and 'constructio personarum', 'construction of persons', does not occur, and the construction of conjunction does not seem to present problems. As well as the case of conjunction in the noun phrase ('Socrates et Plato currunt', 'Socrates and Plato run': the two nouns are one *suppositum* and 'unum constructibile primum'),[172] one could mention the occurrence of the conjunction *si* in 'si Socrates currit', 'if Socrates runs', where the *perfectio* of the sentence is discussed: Martin states that *si* requires the consequent ('si currit, movetur', 'if he runs, he moves') in order to be closed and finished.[173] The example seems to be used to illustrate the need that in a phrase no dependence must remain open, but that is all.

The constructability of the conjunction is questioned by Boethius of Dacia, who answers negatively: a conjunction does not have the principles of construction that are present in the other parts of speech; it joins or disjoins, it is a sign of inference, but it does not construct. In the case where a conjunction joins several constructions or propositions, if it were constructable, with its modes of signifying it would require corresponding modes in the individual constructions or propositions, but if these had modes of signifying, they would be parts of speech; in fact modes of signifying are in *dictio*, not in *oratio*.[174]

Radulphus adopts the fundamental distinction between intransitive and transitive construction[175] and characterizes intransitive construction as the one in which an element is dependent on another which precedes it and which is the first, and transitive construction as the one in which an element is dependent on another which follows it and which is different from the first.[176] But Radulphus also adopts the distinction between verbal constructions which make up propositions ('constructio actuum') and nominal constructions, which do not form propositions ('constructio personarum'). And since each of these types of construction can be transitive or intransitive, there are four basic constructions: *constructio intransitiva actuum* (intransitive construction of acts) ('Socrates currit'), *constructio intransitiva personarum* (intransitive construction of persons) ('homo albus'), *constructio transitiva actuum* (transitive construction of acts) ('lego librum', 'I read a book'), *constructio transitiva personarum* (transitive construction of persons) ('cappa Socratis', 'Socrates' cloak').[177] The author denies that a third element could be constructed *mediate* with the first, and each construction, according to him, is made up of two main elements. If in a sentence there are several elements, they are to be traced back to one of the two principal elements, either as *medium* of their construction (in 'vado in ecclesiam', 'I go to church', the preposition is considered a *medium* of the construction of the verb with the complement and assigned to the complement), or as determination of one of the two main constructables (in 'homo albus currit' and in 'homo currit bene', the adjective *albus* and the adverb *bene* are determinants of one of the two principal elements of the sentences in which they are found. In the first example, the adjective determines the *terminans*, in the second example the adverb determines the *dependens*).[178] In such a way there are various constructions in a sentence, all of them hierarchically ordered in relation to the principal construction conceived as the result of a noun phrase (*suppositum*) plus a verb phrase (*appositum*). Finally, in a sentence like 'Socrates percutit Platonem', 'Socrates hits Plato', there should be two constructions, one intransitive (noun + verb), the other transitive (verb + oblique);[179] but, as far as I know, only Thomas of Erfurt[180] says explicitly that the *appositum* is the first constructable when it depends on a term (the oblique) which follows it (in a verb + oblique construction), and it is the second constructable in relation to the preceding *suppositum*, which confirms that in a subject + verb + oblique sentence there are two constructions.

As for the conjunction, Radulphus believes that it is constructed with the extremes which it joins ('Socrates et Plato'), and that it has an intransitive construction as determinant with the determinables.[181] Moreover, he recognizes that conjunctions can join *orationes* because they can join the terms present in them: in the case of the copulative 'Socrates currit et Plato currit', 'Socrates runs and Plato runs', the conjunction connects sentences that are different in themselves, but their difference comes from the difference of subject; in the inference 'Socrates currit, ergo homo currit', 'Socrates runs, therefore a man runs', the conjunction *ergo* joins antecedent and consequent because of the (logical) relation between *Socrates* and *homo*.[182] Thus accidental modes of signifying are recognized for propositions, and allow them to be joined (constructed) among themselves. To the objection that accidental modes presuppose at least an essential mode, Radulphus replies that the essential mode does not apply to a proposition as such (because it is not a part of speech), but that it is nothing more than the mode of one of its terms.[183] But another possibility seems to be put forward in this context by Radulphus and is adopted by one of his contemporaries, that is the possibility of recognizing accidental modes for propositions as such, without demanding that accidental modes should presuppose essential modes in propositions.[184] Such a view goes beyond mere consideration of the parts of speech and of the terms, as is prevalent among the *Modistae*, towards a more precise focusing on the relations between sentences and statements, but we do not know how much progress was made in this direction.

If the Aristotelian-Boethian triad – thing, intellect and language – is found at the base of the doctrine of the modes of signifying, and Aristotelian ideas and doctrines, such as those of matter and form and of substance and accident, operate at the base of the theory of parts of speech, we can also discern, against the background of the *Modistae's* syntax, the paradigm of the movement as passage from potentiality to actuality (the *dependens* is potential, the *terminans* is the actual that realizes the potential). We can discern, too, the distinction between an action which is immanent in the subject and an action which passes into an object. This paradigm and this distinction are used for the interpretation of intransitive and transitive constructions.[185] The Aristotelianism which pervades this linguistic theory places the *Modistae* among the partisans of moderate realism, for whom the intellect can know things by abstracting from individuating conditions, and can signify them according to the manner in which it can know them. Therefore language signifies thought in the first place, and things indirectly and mediately, according to traditional Aristotelian teaching,[186] which, however, begins to be criticized precisely in those years and in the environment in which the *Modistae* were working: Siger of Brabant[187] and Radulphus Brito[188] believe that *voces* signify things and not the concepts of things, which at the most are consignified.[189]

The semantics of the *Modistae* puts sense rather than reference at the centre of attention, with the corresponding distinction between formal meaning and material meaning.[190] The formal meaning is stable, fixed by *inventio*, which defines the nature of words both as to special meaning and as to general meaning,[191] and guarantees their use; and material meaning itself, to which reference applies, is defined and 'given' by the formal meaning, and cannot be properly determined by the context.[192] If the 'virtus locutionis' defines that which the *locutio* always signifies, its occurrence in a discourse (*acceptio*) determines that to which it refers in relation to the conditions of truth (*causae veritatis*) of the proposition, which remains outside the relation between a word and its sense. For this reason the *Modistae* have difficulty in articulating the material meaning; the concept of *acceptio* is not very productive, and they rarely have recourse to the terministic doctrine of supposition (or of the differentiation, according to the context, of the reference of a term, which keeps the same signification).[193] In order to understand the *Modistae's* position better, one can compare two authors who have opposite attitudes, Roger Bacon and William of Ockham.

The Franciscan Bacon, who is interested, as a grammarian, in the study of figurative locutions, which, as we have seen, respond better to the speaker's requirements, also exalts the speaker's freedom in his theses on the relation between *vox* and meaning: words directly and arbitrarily signify things; having been found to name present realities, they lose their meaning when these things are no longer, so that, when one uses the name 'Caesar' to speak of a man who lived two thousand years ago, one tacitly proceeds to a new imposition, thanks to which that name indicates the dead Caesar. The actual situation therefore becomes decisive for determining the meaning of words.[194] Also the attribution of a predicate does not modify the subject either, but offers the intellect the occasion for a new, tacit imposition.[195]

Ockham shares some of Bacon's requirements, but does not share his extreme theses. In discussing terministic doctrines, he redefines both sign and signification in relation to supposition, that is to the use of a term in discourse. A sign is what brings to mind something and can stand for it ('natum est pro illo supponere', 'was produced to stand for it'); a sign signifies something when it has supposition for it, that is when it stands for it in a proposition.[196] Thus one can glimpse the possibility of overcoming the conception of the signification of a word connected to imposition and permanently fixed outside and before a context, and, instead, of structuring signification depending on the contexts in which it occurs.

### 2.3.4 Critics of the *Modistae*

Criticism on the *Modistae's* linguistic theory takes a clear form in the years 1320–1330 and, although it comes from areas that are characterized by different speculative trends, it answers the same requirement for a more economical explanation of linguistic facts. Against the proliferation of modes of signifying one can place the precise conviction that they are useless in explaining grammatical phenomena. This is, at least, the 'scholastic' reaction we can find in William of Ockham, John Aurifaber and Peter of Ailly (I shall leave aside the polemic against modes of signifying coming from humanist circles).[197] William of Ockham thinks that the mode of signifying is not something added to *dictio*, but that it is a metaphor ('metaphorice locutio') to say that words signify in a different mode (*diversimode*) what they signify, so that some do not properly signify, but 'consignify' when added to others (syncategoremata, invariable parts of speech), while others (categoremata, variable parts of speech) signify things in a complete way.[198] But syncategoremata and categoremata are also found at a mental level,[199] and in fact it can be said that some concepts are nouns by their nature, others are verbs, as in the spoken language (and in the written one) there are nouns and verbs through human institution.[200] Grammatical traits are therefore transferred to the mental level,[201] starting from the articulation of parts of speech (perhaps excluding the participle, which, considered in relation to the need for signification, does not differ from the verb according to our author; and the same doubts according to him could occur for the pronoun, which, however, is explicitly counted among the parts of speech found in the soul),[202] and from the articulation of most of their accidents, that is of those that influence the truth or falsehood of the proposition (case and number for the name; mood, gender, number, tense and person for the verb); the other accidents, which refer to the simple congruity of discourse, do not occur on the mental level, and Ockham can state that all grammatical accidents found in mental language are also found in the spoken (and written) language, but not vice versa.[203] Mental language, which is the only important one from the scientific point of view, has grammatical categories which relate to truth or falsehood, while consideration of mere grammaticality or congruity of discourse seems to be left to the spoken language.[204] But for Ockham language is subordinated to thought, to the point that, if a concept changed meaning, the corresponding word would automatically change meaning without the intervention of a new imposition.[205] Now thought is articulated in words (*verba*) that do not belong to any language.[206] Therefore universality belongs to thought, not to language, and one cannot see how linguistic form can be saved in relation to logical form. Ockham' logic seems to be endowed with the kind of rules of transformation that allow one to resolve apparently categorical propositions into conjunctions of propositions equivalent to them,[207] rules that had never been attributed to grammar, and it attracts the philosopher's attention. But it must also be said that grammar, together with logic and rhetoric, is not acknowledged as a speculative science, and must be content to be recognized as a practical and 'ostensive' science, which can describe 'how something is done', but not prescribe rules of conduct.[208]

Ockham is not the only one to distance himself from the tradition of speculative grammar which was prevalent on the continent, though it was not widespread in Britain. Around 1330 John Aurifaber, in a disputation which took place in Erfurt, developed the critique on modes of signifying from a realistic point of view, similar to that found in the works of the Averroist John of Jandun.[209] Given that any possible thing is substance or accident, and that any accident is inherent in a substratum, the author argues 1) that the modes of signifying are not possible, because they are not substance and are not inherent in a subject (if they were inherent in a *vox*, the *vox* would be substance); moreover 2), that they are useless for the purpose for which they were found, that is to account for congruity and perfection of discourse: no grammarian has resorted to them in the past, either explicitly or implicitly; apart from the *vox* that signifies and consignifies it is not necessary to postulate something attributed to it by the intellect; also 3), that they are not products of nature, and therefore are not 'idem apud omnes', and are not even necessary, and therefore are not principles of science; nor are they produced by a free agent, because what is produced in such a way is contingent and not necessary, while grammar is concerned with what is necessary, like the other sciences, even if it presupposes something contingent (the 'impositio vocis'), which, however, is presupposed by all sciences. Another argument is 4): if there were modes of signifying, they should be 'form' of the *vox* and of parts of speech; this is absurd, and to postulate them would lead to postulating also the form of a form, or the mode of a mode, and so on ad infinitum: and indeed such a form of the *vox* would leave an effect in it which could only be a mode of signifying, and so on; in actual fact a *vox* is formed in its signifying and consignifying function only by the human will and by its use for that of which one speaks ('Relinquitur ergo, quod vox sola voluntate nostra et usu eius pro alio sit significativa et consignificativa', 'It remains therefore that the *vox* is signifying and consignifying of something only through our own will and through its use').[210] The following argument 5) starts from the statement that, if there were modes of signifying, they should be such as to form the parts of speech; but this is false, since the logician has parts of speech (noun, verb, and the syncategorematic ones) which he defines by referring only to the 'signifying', not to the 'mode of signifying'; neither does the logic tradition know these modes, nor does logic presuppose them in grammar, since this would make logic subordinate to grammar and would solve logic into the principles of grammar. Finally 6), the distinction of modes into active and passive is not possible: if it were, since the *vox* is a sign of a concept, one would need to introduce such a distinction on the conceptual level as well: thus a concept would not be the natural sign of things, but a sign *ad placitum*, because it would be sign of the thing not in itself, but thanks to a property of the thing added by the intellect, and therefore the intellect would add a property to the thing before knowing, and in the final analysis would know before knowing.[211]

Aurifaber's position can be outlined in the following terms:

establishing *voces* has been necessary for all sciences, because a *vox* is the most convenient sign to express the mind's concept; consequently two sciences were found which have vocal signs as their object, that is grammar, which deals with them from the point of view of congruity and incongruity, and logic, which deals with them from the point of view of truth and falsehood. But in any language *voces* are differentiated according to the differentiation of things and the concepts they express. Indeed, concepts, which are the same for everybody, are natural and primary signs of things. The intellect has the ability to signify and consignify and is the main agent of signification; the *vox* signifies and consignifies in a secondary way, as the means by which we communicate with others; it is a voluntary sign, and signifies 'ex solo usu et exercitio'. Finally, 'mode of signifying' does not indicate something attributed to the *vox* by the intellect, but only the way in which the intellect that signifies and consignifies acts.[212]

And we come to Peter of Ailly, author of the *Destructiones modorum significandi* (1377–88).[213] To put forward the *Modistae*'s doctrines in the first part[214] he uses materials and arguments which are very similar to those used by John Aurifaber;[215] in the second part he proposes a confutation of their foundations,[216] and finally presents his own opinion[217] before answering the arguments used in the first part to support the *Modistae*'s point of view.[218] The author's opinion is expressed in two premises, a declaration and twelve conclusions. In the two premises one can identify three types of signs: mental, vocal and written, which are divided into natural signs (concepts) and voluntary signs (*voces* and writing). The declaration states that *voces* were assigned the function of signifying to others outside us what cannot be shown in any way by means of concepts; that the need for communication between men is a consequence of human nature, since human beings are social animals; and finally that the system of written signs was found as a substitute of the vocal linguistic system, to communicate with absent and distant people.[219] The twelve conclusions express how the mental level, the one of natural signs, is assigned the grammatical properties (*congruitas, regimen, constructio*), by stating that they are naturally and 'per se et primo' appropriate to natural signs (conclusions 1–5)[220] and with no need of modes of signifying, but through their natural disposition and in themselves (conclusions 7–9).[221] The spoken language has grammatical properties insofar as it is subordinated to the mental level, and since it is an artificial system of signs, it has grammatical properties that are proper to it both artificially and *ad placitum* (conclusions 5–6).[222] The last three conclusions resolve the grammatical properties of language in the fact that it is subordinate to the mental level, showing that a part of speech, for example the noun, is such only because it is the sign (*nota*) of a concept that is noun, and would not be noun if it ceased to be the sign of a concept-noun, as it was not before it became a sign (this goes both for the spoken and for the written language: conclusion 10).[223] The same can be said for the *regimen*, which is referred to the intellective level, and is made to depend on the *regimen* which is realized between concepts thanks to their nature (conclusions 11–12).[224] To those who ask why the mental noun is that concept which is first required in order to obtain the 'oratio mentalis perfecta', while the verb is the concept required in the second place, the author answers referring to the experience everyone can have by reflecting on himself. The distinction of different grammatical functions is indeed learned from experience, in the same way in which one learns from experience which element is hot and dry and which is not.[225]

As we can see, the author transfers the whole grammatical system to the mental level, resolving it into the nature of concepts which are the natural signs of things; and although he develops the idea of dependence and subordination of voluntary signs compared to natural signs, an idea that was already in Ockham (and was energetically taken up by Buridan),[226] he seems here to keep grammar and logic separate (against Ockham's view), and therefore does not resort, in this discussion, to the criterion of the truth-value.[227]

It is doubtful that the transposition of grammar from language to the mind has produced a new linguistic theory. Rather, once the idea of the universality of grammar as a science has been abandoned, some obvious consequences seem to emerge, such as the revaluation of the 'positive' aspects of traditional grammatical teaching, and a return to the texts in which authors have set down the standards of use of different languages.

## Notes

1. *Moralia in Job*, epist. ad Leandrum 5, 7.
2. Fontaine (1959, vol. I, 27–51).
3. Isidore, *Etym.*, I, 2 and 5.
4. *Ibid.*, I, 28–31.
5. Fontaine (1959, vol. I, 37).
6. *Etym.* I, 7, 1.
7. Jolivet (1966, 94–5).
8. Fridugisus, *De substantia*, 126.
9. *Ibid.*, 127.

10. *Ibid.*, 128.
11. *Ibid.*, 131–2.
12. *Ibid.*, 134.
13. Jolivet (1958, 183, and see also 23–30, 47–52, 65–73).
14. Guimet (1948, 231 n. 6), also mentioned by Chenu (1967, 668 n. 12).
15. Jolivet (1966, 98).
16. Thierry of Chartres, *Lectiones*, II, s. 52, 172, *Glossa*, II, s. 42, 278; from Victorinus, *Expl. in Rhet. Ciceronis*, I, 24, quoted by Häring, 277–8.
17. Thierry of Chartres, *Lectiones*, II, s. 53, 172.
18. *Ibid.*, s. 50, 171.
19. *Ibid.*, s. 53, 172, and *Glossa*, II, s. 42, 277–8.
20. Thierry of Chartres, *Lectiones*, II, s. 53, 172.
21. *Ibid.*, s. 52, 172.
22. *Ibid.*, s 53, 172.
23. Jolivet (1966, 99).
24. Quoted in Curtotti (1985–6, 72)
25. *Ibid.*
26. Cf. Thurot (1869 and 1964, 75), and Curtotti (1985–6, 73).
27. Hunt (1980, 19 n. 4).
28. Cf. *ibid.*: 'Non enim iudicande sunt uoces secundum actum constructionis, sed secundum propriam naturam inuentionis', *'Voces* are not to be judged according to the act of construction but according to the proper nature of invention'.
29. *Ars gramm.*, GLK IV, 373: *appellativa nomina primae positionis / derivativa, mons / montanus* ('appellative nouns of first position / derivative, mountain / mountainous').
30. *Inst. gramm.*, IV, 1, GLK I, 117: *nomina primitiva / denominativa* ('primitive / denominative nouns'), and XI, 1, 549: *primitiva / derivativa* ('primitive / derivative').
31. *In Cat. Arist.*, PLM LXIV, 168 A–B.
32. *De hebdomadibus*, PLM LXIV, 1311 B–C (*id quod est / esse*); cf. de Rijk (1981); but see Schrimpf (1966, 127: *esse...quo est* in Gilbert of Poitiers).
33. Petrus Helias, *Summa*, ed. by Reilly, 1978, 116, and 493.
34. Anselm, *De grammatico*, 156.
35. *Ibid.*, 157.
36. Abelard, *Dialectica*, 113, and cf. 596. 'Sumptum' is already present in the *Glosule*: cf. Hunt (1980, 26 n. 1); on the closeness between *Glosule* and St Anselm's *De grammatico* and the probable influence of the grammatical doctrines on the debate that followed, cf. de Libera and Rosier (1992).
37. Gilbert, *Contra Euticen*, IV, s. 48, 297: 'Omne uero nomen diuersa significat, substantiam uidelicet et qualitatem: ut album id quod appellatur album – quod est substantia nominis – et id quo appellatur album – quod est eiusdem nominis qualitas', 'Every noun signifies different things, that is substance and quality: like *album* (white), that which is called white – which is the substance of the noun – and that

because of which it is called white – that is the quality of the same noun'.

38. *Ibid.*, s. 44, 296.
39. Cf. Nielsen (1982, 106).
40. Gilbert, *Contra Euticen*, IV, ss. 44–5, 296.
41. The function of the subject is called 'suppositio': cf. *ibid.* s. 46, 296.
42. For Anselm, cf. Henry (1967, 108–16); for Gilbert, cf. Pinborg (1968, 155–6) and Pinborg (1972, 47–9); on Gilbert's influence, cf. *Compendium logicae Porretanum* and *Grammatica Porretana*.
43. Cf. *Summa logicae*, I, 10, 36–7; *Quaestiones in Librum secundum Sent.*, q.1, 10; *Quaestiones in Librum tertium Sent.*, q.4, 145–6. Cf. Spade (1975 and 1988).
44. Albertus Magnus, *I Sent.*, d.2, a. 11, sol., cit. in Chenu (1966, 102).
45. Cf. John of Salisbury, *Metalogicon*, 124.13–125.14; and Chenu (1966, 95–6).
46. In Hunt (1980, 26, n. 4); and cf. Jolivet (1975, 232).
47. Cf. Pinborg (1967, 30–4). See below, n. 139, on the unity of 'dictio'.
48. Boethius, *Commentarii: De inter. ed. prima*, 37.5–10, and *editio secunda*, 20.15–25.
49. Cf. Alcuin, *Grammatica*, 854 C (from the *editio prima*); *Libri Carolini*, IV, 23, 217–8 (1st edn; I am grateful to G. d'Onofrio for pointing out this text); Minio-Paluello (1972, 747–53), and cf. Vineis (1988), and see Vineis, above p. 180.
50. Cf. Chenu (1966, 95–100).
51. Cf. Fredborg (1980).
52. Cf. Murphy (1980).
53. Cit. in Fredborg (1980, 71). Cf. the text of the second version in Jeauneau (1960, 246) reprinted in Jeauneau (1973, 369).
54. Petrus Helias, *Summa*, ed. by Reilly, 3. On the vernaculars, cf. Swiggers (1988) and also Lusignan (1986).
55. Gundissalinus, *De divisione*, 50.
56. Cf. Fredborg (1980, 74–5).
57. Pseudo-Kilwardby, *The Commentary*, 47–8.
58. Borst (1957–63, vol. II, 2, 828) and see Nardi (1949, 242–3).
59. Cf. Albert of Saxony, '*Quaestiones de sensu*', 69–71.
60. William of Conches, *Philosophia mundi*, IV, 41, col. 100 D-102 A; and see Jeauneau (1960, 218), reprinted in Jeauneau (1973, 341).
61. Cf. Hunt (1980, 18–20), Fredborg (1973, 14–5) and Fredborg (1987, 182); on Priscian, cf. Rosier (1988, 43).
62. Cf. the text of the first version in de Rijk (1962–7, vol. II, i, 222).
63. Cf. the text of the first version in Fredborg (1973, 13).
64. Cf. Fredborg (1981, 30–1).
65. Cf. *ibid.*, 31–2.
66. Cf. *ibid.*, 32.
67. Cf. *ibid.*
68. Cf. *ibid.*, 33–4.
69. Cf. *ibid.*, 34–5.
70. Cf. Fredborg (1973); on the autonomy of grammar according to Petrus, cf. Maierù (1986), 149.

71. Petrus Helias, *Summa*, ed. by Reilly, 116; cf. above, n. 33.

72. *Ibid.*, 117–20.

73. *Ibid.*, 121.

74. *Ibid.*, 120.

75. *Ibid.*, 121.

76. *Ibid.*, 122, and cf. 108.

77. *Ibid.*, 121–2.

78. Petrus Helias, *Summa*, ed. by Tolson, 31–2.

79. Cf. Pinborg (1967, 35); on the relationship between Petrus Helias and Thierry of Chartres on this matter, cf. Fredborg (1973, 52–4).

80. Cf. Fredborg (1973, 28).

81. Cf. *ibid.*, 22.

82. Cf. *ibid.*, 28 (and see 34 and 42–3).

83. Cf. *ibid.*, 44; on Petrus Helias, see Rosier (1987a).

84. Cf. Thurot (1869 and 1964, 82); for the awareness of breaking new ground on the part of teachers who find no 'authorities' in this field, cf. Kneepkens (1978, 123, 130, 132, 135).

85. On this and on what follows, cf. Kneepkens (1987, vol. I, 33–66).

86. According to Percival (forthcoming) the basic criterion for the classification of the four types of construction is coreferentiality.

87. Cf. Covington (1984, 5–8 and 42), and Rosier (1988a).

88. *Liber de divisionibus*, col. 888 D–889 C.

89. Cf. Kneepkens (1978, 124).

90. Cf. *ibid.*, 129; Abelard, *Dialectica*, 586–90, deals with similar problems, but reverses the relation between *determinatio* and *determinatum*: cf. Kneepkens (1978, 128–9).

91. Cf. *ibid.*, 124–6.

92. Cf. *ibid.*, 130–1 (the glosses on Priscian Minor are known only in the second version).

93. Petrus Helias, *Summa*, ed. by Tolson, 154.

94. *Ibid.*

95. *Ibid.*, 156.

96. *Ibid.*, 155 and 156–7.

97. Cf. Kneepkens (1978, 136).

98. Petrus Helias, *Summa*, ed. by Tolson, 1.

99. *Ibid.*

100. *Ibid.* 2–3.

101. *Glose*, 11, and cf. Kneepkens' introduction, XXII–XXIII, and Fredborg (1987, 193).

102. Cf. Kneepkens (1978, 139–40) for the distinction between *regere* and *determinare* and see Robert Blund, *Summa*, 12, for the statement that construction is between terms, not sentences; cf. Fredborg (1987, 194).

103. Cf. Kneepkens (1985, 119).

104. *Notulae*, 64–6.

105. Kilwardby is in Kneepkens (1985, 140–1); and see Roger Bacon, *Summa*, 19–20.

106. Cf. Kneepkens (1985, 123).

107. Cf. Rosier (1988b), and see also Rosier (1988d); on the three-value system, cf. Pseudo-Kilwardby, *The Commentary*, 31: grammar is speculative since 'docet ... speculari quid sit congruum, quid incongruum circa sermonem, et quid figurativum', 'teaches ... to speculate on what is congruous and on what is incongruous concerning language, and on what is figurative'. On the Oxonian condemnations, apart from Rosier (1988b, 40–6), cf. Lewry (1981). I am grateful to Irène Rosier for having read this text and provided me with many interesting insights, and above all for having brought to my attention this aspect of thirteenth century doctrines and for having supplied me with copies of her recent and forthcoming publications.

108. Cf. Kelly (1977a and 1977b), and Pinborg (1982, 255).

109. Master Jordanus, *Notulae*, 4–5.

110. Pseudo-Kilwardby, *The Commentary*, 27–32.

111. Cf. Boethius of Dacia, *Modi*, q. 114, 263.

112. *Ibid.*, q. 2, 10–4.

113. Cf. Pinborg (1974, 169–74).

114. Boethius of Dacia, *Modi*, q. 17, 62.

115. *Ibid.*, q. 9, 39, but cf. q. 133, 306: 'oppositum patet per Priscianum et Donatum, et alios *philosophos grammaticae*' (my Italics), 'the opposite appears from Priscian and Donatus and other *philosophers of grammar*'; see also Radulphus Brito, *Quaestiones*, I, q. 14, p. 137: 'Alia est grammatica regularis sive speculativa quae procedit per causas et principia et haec tradita est nobis a Prisciano et aliis grammaticis', 'Regular or speculative grammar is something else, proceeding through causes and principles, and this has been handed down to us by Priscian and other grammarians'.

116. Cf. Boethius of Dacia, *Modi*, q. 3, ad 3., 18; John of Dacia, *Summa*, 50; Simon of Dacia, *Quaestiones*, q. 1, 92–3 (speculative in purpose).

117. *Modi*, q. 8, 33–6.

118. *Quaestiones*, q. 3, 97.

119. Cf. Martin of Dacia, *Modi*, ss. 228–30, 99–100; John of Dacia, *Summa*, 82; Radulphus Brito, *Quaestiones*, I, q. 30, 197–8, and q. 42, 246.

120. On Michael of Marbais see Thurot (1869 and 1964).

121. Cf. *Summa*, 83 ff.

122. Cf. Gibson (1979, 249–50 and 254).

123. *Notulae*, 2.

124. Cf. Martin, *Quaestiones super librum Perihermeneias*, q. 8, 243: 'significare accipitur dupliciter, scilicet proprie et extensive. Primo modo significare est aliquid intellectum repraesentare ... et hoc modo oportet, quod significatum sit aliud a signo. Secundo modo significare est se ipsum repraesentare, et sic non differt significatum a signo', 'to signify is understood in two ways, i.e. in a proper or extensive mode. In the first mode, signifying is representing something that one has understood ... and in this way it is necessary that the signified should be different from the sign. In the second mode, signifying is representing oneself, and then the signified does not differ from the

sign'; John of Dacia, *Summa*, 89: 'vox per essentiam suam non est signum, sed accidit sibi ratio signi', 'the *vox* is not a sign in its essence, but it has as an accident the value of a sign'; 107–8: 'cum vox significat ad placitum, aliquid derelinquit intellectui sicut suum significatum, quod diuersum est ab ipsa voce', 'as the *vox* signifies arbitrarily, it leaves something to the intellect, like its signified, which is different from the *vox* itself'; 195–6: 'ratio significandi est illud, quo refertur vox significatiua ad significatum . . . Nam in signo sunt duo, scilicet illud, quod est signum, et ratio significandi. Quantum ad id, quod est signum, ipsum offert se sensui, quantum autem ad rationem significandi offert se intellectui', 'the value (*ratio*) of signifying is that by which the signifying *vox* is referred to the signified . . . In fact there are two elements in the sign, i.e. the one that is the sign itself, and the signifying value. As for what is the sign, this offers itself to the sense, and as for the signifying value (*ratio significandi*), it offers itself to the intellect', and also 196: 'significatum seu ratio significandi', 'signified, or signifying value'; 197: 'significatio seu ratio significandi', 'signification or signifying value', 198: 'ratio significandi seu significare', 'signifying value, or signifying'.

125. Cf. Radulphus Brito, *Quaestiones*, I, q. 4, ad 1., 104: '. . . ut est quidam sermo, qui includit vocem et significatum et ratio consignificandi . . .', '. . . like a *sermo*, which includes *vox*, signified and value of consignifying'.

126. Cf. Martin, *Modi*, s. 10, 7; John of Dacia, *Summa*, 178, 187; Radulphus Brito, *Quaestiones*, I, q. 13, 135.

127. *Summa*, 56–8 and 187, and see Martin, *Modi*, s. 10, 7.

128. Boethius of Dacia, *Modi*, q. 6, 27.

129. *Quaestiones*, q. 6, 99–103.

130. Radulphus Brito, *Quaestiones*, I, q. 2, 93–4.

131. Published in Grabmann (1941, 65, repr. 1979, 1701).

132. Gentile, *Quaestiones*, q. 2, 10–3 (the grammar 'quae habetur per modum fabularum' 'which one receives by way of storytelling', not the kind one has 'per rationem'), and cf. Pinborg (1967, 103–5).

133. On the two *articulationes* cf. Martin, *Modi*, s. 11, 8; Boethius of Dacia, *Modi*, q. 114, 262–3; John of Dacia, *Summa*, 105; Radulphus Brito, *Quaestiones*, I, q. 4, 101, and see Thomas of Erfurt, *Grammatica*, 136; Radulphus, I, q. 3, 99, believes that with the same imposition one has the two *articulationes*.

134. Cf. Pinborg (1982, 257).

135. Cf. Martin, *Modi*, s 11, 8; Simon, *Domus*, 21 (an author not to be confused with the Simon author of the *Quaestiones*); Radulphus, *Quaestiones* I, q. 14, 136 ff.

136. Cf. Boethius of Dacia, *Modi*, q. 11, 42–6; John of Dacia, *Summa*, 206–8.

137. Thus Boethius of Dacia, *Modi*, q. 11, ad 3., 48.

138. For Boethius of Dacia, *Modi*, q. 14, 55–6, the same concept can be signified by 'every part of speech, but in his work one can find already

the theme of *repugnantia*, which is more accentuated in John of Dacia, *Summa*, 218–19, for whom the same concept cannot be signified by all, but by several parts of speech, based on the *repugnantia* or lack of it between concept and modes of signifying of the parts; and cf. Radulphus Brito, *Quaestiones*, I, q. 21, 164, and ad 6., 167; Pinborg (1967, 80) believes that according to Boethius the 'concept' can be expressed in any part of speech because it is indeterminate and can be formed by the *modi intelligendi*; repugnance can arise from the determination of the concept; clearly, John of Dacia attributes some kind of determination to the concept; see also Pinborg (1967, 88 n. 54).

139. *Modi*, q. 14, 56; cf. above, n. 47, on the (platonically founded) identity of meaning of the various parts of speech.

140. Cf. Boethius of Dacia, *Modi*, q. 13, 51–3; Radulphus Brito, *Questiones*, I, q. 15, 138–9, and Pinborg (1967, 27, 66 and 124).

141. Thus, at least, for Siger of Courtrai, *Sophismata*, I, 43.

142. Cf. Pinborg (1967, 125–6), and see also Siger of Courtrai, *Sophismata*, III, 56–64.

143. Thus Radulphus Brito, *Questiones*, I, q. 17, 144–5, and Thomas of Erfurt, *Grammatica*, 150, while an addition to Radulphus, *loc. cit.*, and Siger of Courtrai, *Sophismata*, I, 43, attribute this distinction to all *modi significandi*, both essential and accidental.

144. Cf. Boethius of Dacia, *Modi*, q. 85, ad 2., 203: 'modus significandi respectivus per se est principium constructionis', 'the respective mode of signifying is by itself the principle of construction'.

145. Cf. *ibid.*, q. 19, 70–1, and see q. 14, 56; cf. Jolivet (1981, 152–3). On the role of the intellect, cf. Maierù (1986).

146. Boethius of Dacia, *Modi*, q. 11, 45–6; q. 21, 74–5.

147. John of Dacia, *Summa*, 208.

148. *Ibid.*, 248–9.

149. Radulphus Brito, *Quaestiones*, I, q. 14, 137; 'per accidens': q. 11, 129.

150. Martin, *Modi*, ss. 7–9; the idea that both existence and universality are accidental to essence as such, as according to the definition, and that essence is indifferent to accidental differences, is a doctrine of Avicenna, which seems to be here presupposed; cf. Martin, *Quaestiones super librum Porphyrii*, q. 8, 132; Pinborg (1967, 44–5), and see above, n. 138, on Boethius of Dacia.

151. Martin, *Modi*, s. 8, p. 6–7.

152. John of Dacia, *Summa*, 232–6.

153. Boethius of Dacia, *Modi*, q. 26, 81.

154. *Ibid.*, q. 28, 85.

155. *Ibid.*, q. 29, 88.

156. Cf. Pinborg (1975, p. 75, n. 46), and Incertorum auctorum *Quaestiones*, q. 54, 122.

157. Radulphus Brito, *Quaestiones*, I, q. 18, 153–5.

158. *Ibid.*, q. 19, 157–8.

159. *Ibid.*, 158 and Siger, *Summa*, 2; *Sophismata*, I, 42, and III, 56.

160. Quoted in Pinborg (1972, 111).

161. *Grammatica*, 142–6.

162. Boethius of Dacia, *Modi*, q. 11, ad 2., 46–8; and cf. John of Dacia, *Summa*, 209–10.
163. Cf. Pinborg (1973), Covington (1984), Rosier (1987b) and Benedini (1988).
164. Cf. Pinborg (1973).
165. Cf. Pinborg (1967, 127–31).
166. Cf. Martin, *Modi*, ss. 203–11, 90–4; Pinborg (1967, 54).
167. Martin, *Modi*, s. 207, 92.
168. *Ibid.*, s. 201, 90.
169. *Ibid.*, s. 215 ff., 95 ff.
170. *Ibid.*, ss. 224–6, 98–9; ss. 234–6, 100–2; 241, 103–4.
171. *Ibid.*, ss. 242–6, 104–6.
172. *Ibid.*, s. 221, 97.
173. *Ibid.*, s. 269, 114 (the terms *finitatio, finitari* are used).
174. Boethius of Dacia, *Modi*, q. 132, 302–5.
175. Radulphus Brito, *Quaestiones*, I, q. 24, 175–8.
176. *Ibid.*, q. 24, 176 (ad 3., 178).
177. *Ibid., ad indicem*, and see I, q. 24, ad 2., 178 ('cappa Sortis' 'Socrates' cloak'); q. 48, ad 3., 270; II, q. 16, 432.
178. *Ibid.*, I, q. 8, 115–6.
179. *Ibid.*, q. 24, 176; q. 48, 266–7, q. 65, 315–7; II, q. 4, 362–3; cf. Pinborg (1972, 124).
180. Thomas of Erfurt, *Grammatica*, 280; cf. Rosier (1983, 166). For the possible interpretations of transitivity (at the sentence level, or at the level of a construction with two elements), cf. Rosier (1984b, 182).
181. Radulphus Brito, *Quaestiones*, I, q. 24, ad 1., 177.
182. *Ibid.*, q. 70, 332–3.
183. *Ibid.*, q. 70, ad 1., 333–4.
184. Cf. Pinborg (1980, 204–6).
185. Cf. Kelly (1977a; 1977b), Rosier (1983, 145–50); Covington (1984, 76–82).
186. Cf. Martin, *Quaestiones super librum Perihermeneias*, q. 7, 242–3.
187. *Quaestiones logicales*, 63, 10–4.
188. Questions on the *De interp.*, q. 3, quoted in Pinborg (1971, 275): 'in nominibus prime impositionis voces significant res et non conceptus rerum', 'in the nouns of first imposition, *voces* signify things, and not the concepts of things'.
189. Cf. Radulphus Brito quoted in Pinborg (1971, 276): 'Et ex hoc sequitur quod ⟨con⟩significant istos conceptus', 'And from that it follows that they consignify these concepts'.
190. Cf. Pinborg (1982, 264).
191. Cf. Peter Abelard, *Logica 'Nostrorum'* 522:'Quid enim aliud est nativitas sermonum sive nominum, quam hominum institutio?', 'What else is the origin of discourses and of nouns, if not a human institution?', and Petrus Helias, *Summa*, ed. Reilly, 1978 22: 'Natura enim in vocabulis nihil aliud est quam inventio ipsorum. "Natura" enim a "nascor" dicitur. Nasci vero vocabula, quid aliud est quam invenire ea?', 'In fact the nature in words is nothing other than their finding

(*inventio*). Indeed one says *nature* from *nascor* (to be born). And for a word, what is to be born, if not to be found (*invenire ea*)?'

192. Rosier (1984a, 30), quotes Boethius of Dacia, *Topica*, ed. by J. Pinborg and N. G. Green-Pedersen, Hauniae 1976, 134: 'Omnes acceptiones possibiles in termino universali causam habent in ipso', 'All possible meanings in the universal term have their cause in it', and Petrus de Ybernia from Pinborg and Ebbesen, *Cahiers de l'institut du moyen âge grec et latin*, 3, 1970, 19: 'Quod est suppositum alicuius per se, semper est eius suppositum', 'What is *suppositum* of something for itself, is always its *suppositum*'; and cf. Pinborg (1975a 66, n. 92): 'Supposita accidunt significato', '*Supposita* are accidents of the signified' (Peter of Alvernia), and 'quamvis ita sit quod terminus supponat pro supposito, ipsum suppositum terminus non supponit de virtute sermonis', 'although a term is supposed for the *suppositum*, the term does not suppose the *suppositum* itself, by virtue of the discourse' (Siger of Brabant).

193. Cf. Pinborg (1975a, 66–9).

194. Roger Bacon, *De signis*, ss. 38–52, 94–100, and ss. 82–96, 109–14; see also Maierù (1972, 96–7); Rosier (1984a, 27–9); Pinborg (1981); Maloney (1983), and Roger Bacon, *Compendium*.

195. Roger Bacon, *De signis*, s. 97, 114, quoted in Rosier (1984a, 29).

196. William of Ockham, *Summa logicae*, I, 33, 87, and cf. Biard (1981 and 1989); Panaccio (1983) goes in a different direction.

197. For other authors see Pinborg (1967, 167–210).

198. William of Ockham, *Summa logicae*, III-4, ch. 10, 798.

199. William of Ockham, *Expositio*, I, *prooemium*, s.6, 357.

200. *Ibid.*, s.12, 374.

201. Cf. Jolivet (1981, 158–60).

202. William of Ockham, *Summa logicae*, I, ch. 3, 11 (on the pronoun cf. Panaccio [1980]); interjection is not mentioned in this chapter and occurs in chapter 2, 10, 'nec interiectio est terminus', 'and interjection is not a term', if *terminus* is taken in the third mode, 'praecise et magis stricte', 'precisely and more strictly' (but the case concerns the verb, syncategoremata, and the four indeclinable parts that were listed (9–10).

203. *Ibid.*, 11–13.

204. Cf. Covington (1984, 122–4).

205. William of Ockham, *Summa logicae*, I, ch. 1, 8.

206. *Ibid.*, 7.

207. Cf. Maierù (1972, 393–498) and Pinborg (1972, 103–11).

208. William of Ockham, *Scriptum*, I, prol. q. 11, 316–7.

209. Cf. Pinborg (1975b) and Pinborg (1982, 267–8).

210. The passage by John Aurifaber, *Determinatio* in Pinborg (1967, 218).

211. *Ibid.*, 216–9.

212. *Ibid.*, 225–7.

213. Cf. Kaczmarek et al. (1986, 608–12). Dr Kaczmarek informs me that the work's manuscript tradition makes its authorship questionable, and involves other authors.

214. Peter of Ailly, *Destructiones* in Kaczmarek (1980, 31–7).

215. Cf. Pinborg (1967, 202–3).
216. Peter of Ailly, *Destructiones* in Kaczmarek (1980, 38–50).
217. *Ibid.*, 51–63.
218. *Ibid.*, 64–70.
219. *Ibid.*, 51–2.
220. *Ibid.*, 52–3.
221. *Ibid.*, 54–5.
222. *Ibid.*, 53–4.
223. *Ibid.*, 55–9.
224. *Ibid.*, 59–63.
225. *Ibid.*, 63.24–38.
226. Cf. Reina (1959, 412–13).
227. Cf. Covington (1984, 124).

# Bibliographical references

## Editions

Aelfric, *Colloquy*: G. N. Garmonsway, *Aelfric's Colloquy*, London, 1939, 1947², reprinted Exeter, 1978.

Aelfric, *Glossary*: R. G. Gillingham, *An Edition of Abbot Aelfric's Old English-Latin Glossary with Commentary*, diss., Ann Arbor, 1981.

Aelfric, *Grammar* and *Glossary*: J. Zupitza, *Aelfrics Grammatik und Glossar*, Berlin, 1880, reprinted 1966 with introduction by H. Gneuss; a new edition of both works has been announced in the collection of the *Early English Texts Society*.

*Aggressus quidam*: GLK VIII (*Anecdota Helvetica*), XXXIX–XLI.

Albert of Saxony, *Le 'Quaestiones de sensu' attribuite a Oresme e Alberto di Sassonia*: J. Agrimi, Florence, 1983.

Alcuin, *De dialectica*: PLM CI, 951D–976B.

Alcuin, *De orthographia*: PLM CI, 902D–920A, then GLK VII, 295–312 and, with an analysis of the sources, A. Marsili, Pisa, 1962.

Alcuin, *Dialogus de rhetorica et virtutibus*: PLM CI, 919C–946D, then Car. Halm, *Rhetores Latini minores*, Lipsiae, 1863, 523–50 and, with English translation and notes, W. S. Howell, *The Rhetoric of Alcuin and Charlemagne*, New York, 1965.

Alcuin, *Grammatica*, or *Dialogus Franconis et Saxonis de octo partibus orationis*: PLM CI, 849C–902B.

Aldhelm, *De metris et enigmatibus ac pedum regulis*: R. Ehwald, *Aldhelmi Opera*, MGH, *Auctores Antiquissimi*, XV, Berolini, 1913–1919, 59–204.

Alexander de Villa Dei, *Doctrinale*: D. Reichling (Monumenta Germaniae Paedagogica, Bd. 12), Berlin, 1893, reprinted New York, 1974.

Anonymus ad Cuimnanum, *Commentum in Donati partes maiores*: GLK V, 326 (*excerpta*).

Anselm of Aosta, *De grammatico*, in *Opera Omnia*: F. S. Schmitt, 1946, Edinburgh: I, 145–68.

*Appendix Probi*: GLK IV, 193–204.

*Ars Ambrosiana*: B. Löfstedt, CCSL CXXXIII C, Turnhout, 1982.

*Ars Bernensis*: GLK VIII (*Anecdota Helvetica*), 62–142.

*Ars Laureshamensis*: B. Löfstedt, CCCM XL A, Turnhout, 1977.

*Ars Malsachani*: M. Roger, Paris, 1905, also B. Löfstedt, *Der hibernolateinische Grammatiker Malsachanus* (Acta Universitatis Upsaliensis. Studia Latina Upsaliensia, 3), Uppsala, 1965, with full historical, philological and linguistic exegesis.

Asper, *Ars*: GLK V, 547–54.

(ps.-) Asper (Asporius or Asper minor), *Ars*: GLK VIII (*Anecdota Helvetica*), 39–61.

Audax, *De Scauri et Palladii libris excerpta per interrogationem et responsionem*: GLK VII, 320–62.

Augustine, *Ars pro fratrum mediocritate breviata*: A. Mai, *Nova Patrum Bibliotheca*, I, Romae, 1852, 167–81, also C. F. Weber, Marburg, 1861, and GLK V, 494–6 (*excerpta*).

(ps.-) Augustine, *Principia dialecticae*: PLM XXXII, 1409–20, also J. Pinborg, Dordrecht and Boston, 1975.

Augustine, *Regulae*: GLK V, 496–524.

*Auraicept na n-Éces*: G. Calder, Edinburgh, 1917.

Bede, *De arte metrica*: GLK VII, 227–60, also C. B. Kendall, CCSL CXXIII A, Turnhout, 1975, 81–141.

Bede, *De orthographia*: GLK VII, 261–94, also Ch. W. Jones, CCSL CXXIII A, Turnhout, 1975, 7–57.

Bede, *De schematibus et tropis*: Car. Halm, *Rhetores Latini minores*, Lipsiae, 1863, 607–18, also C. B. Kendall, CCSL CXXIII A, Turnhout, 1975, 142–71.

Bede, *Historia ecclesiastica gentis Anglorum*: Ch. Plummer, 2 vols, 1896, Oxonii, also, with English translation, B. Colgrave and R. A. B. Mynors, Oxford, 1969.

(ps.-) Bede, *Cunabula grammaticae artis Donati a Beda restituta*: PLM XC, 613C–32C (followed by *De octo partibus orationis libellus*, up to 642 C).

Boethius, *Commentarii in librum Aristotelis perihermeneias*: Car. Meiser, Lipsiae, 1877 (Pars prior, versionem continuam et primam editionem continens), 29 ff., and Lipsiae, 1880 (Pars posterior, secundam editionem et indices continens).

Boethius, version of Aristotle's *Perihermeneias*: Car. Meiser, Lipsiae, 1877, 3–28, also L. Minio-Paluello, 'Aristoteles Latinus' II, 1–2, Bruges-Paris, 1965, 1–38.

Boethius, *In Categorias Aristotelis libri quatuor*: PLM LXIV, 159 A-294 C.

Boethius, *De hebdomadibus* (*Quomodo substantiae*): PLM LXIV, 1311 A-1314 C.

Boethius, *Liber de divisione*: PLM XLIV, 875 D-892 A.

Boethius of Dacia, *Modi significandi sive Quaestiones super Priscianum maiorem*: J. Pinborg, H. Roos, S. Skovgaard Jensen (CPhDMA, IV, 1–11), Hauniae, 1969.

Boethius of Dacia, *Compendium logicae Porretanum ex codice Oxoniensi Collegii Corporis Christi 250: a Manual of Porretan Doctrine by a Pupil of*

*Gilbert's*: S. Ebbesen, K. M. Fredborg, L. O. Nielsen, *Cahiers de l'institut du moyen âge grec et latin*, 46, 1983.

Boniface (Vynfreth), *Ars grammatica*: G. J. Gebauer, B. Löfstedt, CCSL CXXXIII B, Turnhout, 1980, 15–99.

Boniface (Vynfreth), *Epistola ad Sigeberhtum*: G. J. Gebauer, B. Löfstedt, CCSL CXXXIII B, Turnhout, 1980, 9–12.

Caper, *De orthographia*: GLK VII, 92–107, 2.

Caper, *De verbis dubiis*: GLK VII, 107, 3–112, 5.

Cassiodorus, *De orthographia*: GLK VII, 145–210.

Cassiodorus, *Institutiones*: R. A. B. Mynors, Oxford, 1937, 1961[2].

Cassiodorus, *Variae*: Th. Mommsen, MGH, *Auctores Antiquissimi*, XII, Berolini, 1894, repr. München, 1981.

(ps.-) Cassiodorus, *Commentarium de oratione et de octo partibus orationis*: v. Sergius (ps.-Cassiodorus).

*Categoriae X* (or *Paraphrasis Themistiana*): L. Minio-Paluello, 'Aristoteles Latinus' I, 1–5, Bruges-Paris, 1968, 129–75.

CCCM: *Corpus Christianorum. Continuatio Mediaevalis*, Turnhout, 1966 and ff.

CCSL: *Corpus Christianorum. Series Latina*, Turnhout, 1953 and ff.

CGL: *Corpus Glossariorum Latinorum*, ed. by G. Loewe, G. Goetz, 7 vols, Lipsiae et Berolini, 1888–1923, reprinted Amsterdam, 1965.

Charisius, *Ars grammatica*: K. Barwick, Leipzig, 1925, reprinted Leipzig, 1964, with additions and corrections by F. Kühnert.

CIC: *Corpus Iuris Civilis*, ed. by R. Schoell, W. Kroll, 3 vols, Frankfurt a.M., 1968[9].

Cledonius, *Ars*: GLK V, 9–79.

Clemens Scottus, *Ars grammatica*: J. Tolkiehn (*Philologus*, Supplementband XX, Heft III) Leipzig, 1928; a new edition, ed. by A.M. Puckett and F. Glorie in CCCM (XL E), is imminent.

*Congregatio Salcani filii de verbo*: B. Löfstedt, *Der hibernolateinische Grammatiker Malsachanus*, Uppsala, 1965, (v. *Ars Malsachani*) 194–260.

Consentius, *Ars de duabus partibus orationis nomine et verbo*: GLK V, 338–404.

CPhDMA: *Corpus philosophorum Danicorum medii aevi.*

Dante, *De vulgari eloquentia*: P. V. Mengaldo (Opere minori II) Milano-Napoli, 1979.

*Declinationes nominum*: V. Law is preparing the edition of its various versions, based on her Fellowship diss., *The* Declinationes nominum *in Cod. lat. monac. 6281*, Cambridge, 1976.

*De dubiis nominibus*: F. Glorie in *Tatuini opera omnia*, ed. by M. de Marco-F. Glorie, CCSL CXXXIII A, 2 vols, Turnhout, 1968, II, 743–820.

Diomedes, *Ars grammatica*: GLK I, 299–529.

Donatus, *Ars maior*: GLK IV, 367–402, also L. Holtz (see below, Studies), 1981a, 603–74.

Donatus, *Ars minor*: GLK IV, 355–6, also L. Holtz (see below, Studies), 1981a, 585–602.

Donatus Ortigraphus, *Ars grammatica*: J. Chittenden, CCCM XL D, Turnhout, 1982.
Dositheus, *Ars grammatica*: GLK VII, 376–436.

Eberhard of Béthune, *Grecismus*: J. Wrobel (Corpus Grammaticorum Medii Aevi, 1), Breslau, 1887.
Erchanbert, *Tractatus super Donatum*: W. V. Clausen, Chicago, 1948.
Ermanrich of Ellwangen: collection of grammatical observations in D. C. Lambot, *Oeuvres théologiques et grammaticales de Godescalc d'Orbais*, Louvain, 1945, 504–8.
Eutyches, *Ars de verbo*: GLK V, 447–89.

Festus, *De verborum significatione* (or *significatu*): C. O. Müller, Lipsiae, 1839, also W. M. Lindsay, Lipsiae, 1913, reprinted Hildesheim, 1965.
*First Icelandic Grammatical Treatise*: E. Haugen, *Language*, supplement to vol. XXVI, 4, 1950 (with English translation and commentary), re-edited with additions, London, 1972, also H. Benediktsson, Reykjavík, 1972, and F. Albano Leoni, Bologna, 1975 (with Italian translation and commentary).
*Fourth Icelandic Grammatical Treatise*: B. M. Ólsen, København, 1884.
Fridugisus of Tours, *De substantia nihili et tenebrarum*: C. Gennaro, Padova, 1963.
Fulgentius, *Expositio sermonum antiquorum*: L. Lersch, Bonn, 1844, also P. Wessner, *Commentationes Philologae Ienenses*, 6.2, 1898, 63–143; R. Helm, Lipsiae, 1898, reprinted Stuttgart, 1970, with bibliographical additions by J. Préaux; and U. Pizzani, Roma, 1968, with translation and commentary.

Gentile da Cingoli, *Quaestiones supra Prisciano minori*: R. Martorelli Vico (Centro di cultura medievale della Scuola Normale Superiore, I), Pisa, 1985.
Gilbert of Poitiers, *Contra Euticen et Nestorium*: N. M. Häring, *The Commentaries on Boethius by Gilbert of Poitiers* (Studies and Texts, 14), Toronto, 1966, 233–364.
GLK: *Grammatici Latini*, ed. by H. Keil, 8 vols (vol. VIII = *Anecdota Helvetica*, ed. by H. Hagen), Lipsiae, 1857–80, reprinted Hildesheim, 1961.
*Glossaria Latina*, ed. by W. M. Lindsay *et al.*, 5 vols, Paris, 1926–31, reprinted Hildesheim, 1965.
*Glossarium Ansileubi*: see *Liber glossarum Ansileubi*.
*Glossarium Salomonis*: see J. A. McGeachy (see below, Studies) 1938.
Godescalc d'Orbais: collection of grammatical observations in D. C. Lambot, *Oeuvres théologiques et grammaticales de Godescalc d'Orbais*, Louvain, 1945, 353–496.
*Grammatica Porretana* (*Glosule Porretane super Priscianum minorem*): K. M. Fredborg and C. H. Kneepkens, *Cahiers de l'institut du moyen âge grec et latin*, 57, 1988, 11–67.
Gregorius Magnus, *Moralia in Job* (books I and II): R. Gillet and A. de Gaudemaris, Paris, 1952.

Gregorius Magnus, *Moralia in Job*: M. Adriaen (CCSL, CXLIII-CX-LIIIB), 3 vols, Turnhout, 1979–85.
Gundissalinus, *De divisione philosophiae*: L. Baur (Beiträge zur Geschichte der Philosophie des Mittelalters, IV, 2–3), Münster, 1903.

Hildericus, *Ars grammatica*: A. Lentini, Montecassino, 1975.
Hugh of Saint Victor, *Didascalicon*: C. H. Buttimer, Washington, 1939.
Hugutio of Pisa, *De dubio accentu, Agiographia, Expositio de symbolo apostolorum*: G. Cremascoli, Spoleto, 1978.
Hugutio of Pisa, *Magnae Derivationes*: C. Riessner, *Die* Magnae Derivationes *des Uguccione da Pisa und ihre Bedeutung für die romanische Philologie*, Roma, 1965, 193–233 and *passim* (*excerpta*); the critical edition by G. Schizzerotto has been expected for years.

*Icelandic Grammatical Treatises*: see *First Icelandic Grammatical Treatise, Second Icelandic Grammatical Treatise*, . . . .
Incertorum Auctorum *Quaestiones super Sophisticos Elenchos*: S. Ebbesen (CPhDMA, VII), Hauniae, 1977.
Isidore, *Differentiarum sive de proprietate sermonum libri duo*: F. Arévalo, PLM LXXXIII, 9A–98A.
Isidore, *Etymologiarum sive originum libri XX*: W. M. Lindsay, 2 vols, Oxonii, 1911, reprinted 1957, also, for book II, P. K. Marshall, Paris, 1983 (with English translation and full commentary), and, for book IX, M. Reydellet, Paris, 1984 (with French translation and full commentary).
Isidore, *Quaestiones in Vetus Testamentum*: PLM LXXXIII, 207B–434A.
Isidore, *Synonymorum libri duo* (*sive de lamentatione animae peccatricis*): F. Arévalo, PLM LXXXIII, 825C–68C.
Iulianus Toletanus, *Ars*: M. A. H. Maestre Yenes, Toledo, 1973, also (for the section on the *de partibus orationis*) L. Munzi, *Annali Istituto Orientale di Napoli*. Sez. filol.-letter., II–III, 1980–1, 153–228.

Jerome, *Epistolae*: PLM XXII, 325–1224.
Jerome, *Interpretationes nominum Hebraicorum*: P. de Lagarde, CCSL LXXII, Turnhout, 1959, 57–161.
Johannes Aurifaber, *Determinatio de modis significandi*: J. Pinborg (1967, 215–32).
Joannes Balbus of Genoa, *Catholicon*: Mainz, 1460, reprinted 1971.
John of Dacia, *Summa gramatica*, in *Opera*: A. Otto (CPhDMA, I, i–ii), Hauniae, 1965.
John of Salisbury, *Metalogicon*: PLM CIC, 823 A–946 B, also C. C. I. Webb, Oxonii, 1929.

Pseudo-Kilwardby, *The Commentary on 'Priscianus Maior' Attributed to Robert Kilwardby*. Selected texts ed. by K. M. Fredborg, N. J. Green-Pedersen, L. Nielsen and J. Pinborg, *CIMAGL*, 15, 1975.

*Liber glossarum Ansileubi: Glossaria Latina*, ed. by W. M. Lindsay, Paris, 1926–31, vol. I.

*Libri Carolini*: H. Bastgen, MGH. Legum sectio. Concilia. Tomi II supplementum, Hannoverae et Lipsiae, 1924.

Macrobius, *Saturnalia*: I. Willis, Lipsiae, 1963.

Malsachanus, *Ars*: see *Ars Malsachani*.

Martianus Capella, *De nuptiis Philologiae et Mercurii*: A. Dick, Leipzig, 1925, reprinted Stuttgart, 1978, with additions and corrections by J. Préaux.

Martin of Dacia, *Modi significandi*, in *Opera*: H. Roos (CPhDMA, II), Hauniae, 1961, 1–118.

Martin of Dacia, *Quaestiones super librum Perihermeneias*, in *Opera*, 233–63.

Martin of Dacia, *Quaestiones super librum Porphyrii*, in *Opera*, 119–52.

Master Jordanus, *Notulae super Priscianum minorem*: M. Sirridge, *Cahiers de l'institut du moyen âge grec et latin*, 36, 1980.

MGH: *Monumenta Germaniae Historica*: Berolini, 1877–1919 (for the *Auctores Antiquissimi*), reprinted 1961.

Murethach (Muridac), *Commentum in Donati Artem maiorem*: L. Holtz, CCCM XL, Turnhout, 1977.

Nonius Marcellus, *De compendiosa doctrina*: L. Müller, Lipsiae, 1888, also W. M. Lindsay, Lipsiae, 1903, reprinted Hildesheim, 1964.

Oresmes, see Albert of Saxony.

Osbern of Gloucester, *Liber derivationum* (or *Panormia*): A. Mai (under the title of *Thesaurus Novus Latinitatis*) (Classicorum auctorum e Vaticanis codicibus editorum tomus VIII), Romae, 1836.

(ps.-) Palaemon, *Ars*: GLK V, 533–47.

Papias, *Elementarium doctrine rudimentum*: B. Mombricius, Mediolani, 1476, Venetiis, 1496, reprinted Torino, 1966, also, for the *Littera A*, V. De Angelis, Milano, 1977–80 (3 vols).

Paulus Diaconus, *Ars Donati quam Paulus Diaconus exposuit*: A. Amelli, Montecassino, 1899.

Paulus Diaconus, *Excerpta ex libro S. Pompeii Festi De verborum significatu*: see Festus.

Peter Abelard, *Dialectica*: L. M. de Rijk, Assen, 1970².

Peter Abelard, *Logica Nostrorum petitioni sociorum*: B. Geyer, *Peter Abaelards philosophische Schriften*, II (Beiträge zur Geschichte der Philosophie und Theologie des Mittelalters, XXI, 4), Münster 1973²

Peter of Ailly, *Destructiones modorum significandi*: L. Kaczmarek (1980, 31–70).

Petrus Helias, *Summa super Priscianum*: L. A. Reilly (for the part concerning the first three books of Priscian's *Institutiones*), diss., Toronto, 1975, also J. E. Tolson (for the part concerning the last two books), *Cahiers de l'institut du moyen âge grec et latin*, 27–8, 1978.

Phocas, *Ars de nomine et verbo*: GLK V, 410–39, also F. Casaceli, Napoli, 1974.

Pietro da Pisa, *Ars*: GLK VIII (*Anecdota Helvetica*), 161–71 (*excerpta*).
PLM: *Patrologiae Cursus Completus. Series Latina*, ed. by J. -P. Migne, 221 vols, Paris, 1844–64, reprinted 1879 and ff.
Pompeius, *Commentum Artis Donati*: GLK V, 95–312.
Priscian, *Institutio de nomine et pronomine et verbo*: GLK III, 443–56.
Priscian, *Institutiones grammaticae*: GLK II and III, 1–377.
Probus, *Catholica*: GLK IV, 3–43.
Probus, *Instituta artium*: GLK IV, 47–192.
(ps.-) Probus, *Appendix*: see *Appendix Probi*.

*Quae sunt quae*: GLK VIII (*Anecdota Helvetica*), XLI–XLIII (*excerpta*).

Radulphus Brito, *Quaestiones super Priscianum minorem*: H.W. Enders, J. Pinborg, (Grammatica speculativa, 3, 1–2), Stuttgart-Bad Cannstatt, 1980.
Ralph of Beauvais, *Glose super Donatum*: C.H. Kneepkens (Artistarium, 2), Nijmegen, 1982.
*Religio ideo dicitur*: GLK VIII (*Anecdota Helvetica*), 297–9 and 299–301.
Remi of Auxerre, *Commentum in Martianum Capellam*: Cora E. Lutz, 2 vols, Leiden, 1962 and 1965.
Remi of Auxerre, commentary on Phocas' *Ars*: M. Manitius, *Neues Archiv der Gesellschaft für ältere deutsche Geschichtskunde*, 36, 1911, 47–8 and *Didaskaleion*, 2, 1913, 73–8 (*excerpta*).
Remi of Auxerre, commentary on Bede's *De schematibus et tropis*: J.P. Elder, *Mediaeval studies*, 9, 1947, 141–50 (*excerpta*).
Remi of Auxerre, commentary on Priscian's *Institutio de nomine et pronomine et verbo*: M. de Marco, *Aevum*, 26, 1952, 495–517.
Remi of Auxerre, *In Artem Donati minorem commentum*: W. Fox, Leipzig, 1902.
Remi of Auxerre, *In Artem maiorem Donati commentarium*: GLK VIII (*Anecdota Helvetica*), 219–74 (ed. by H. Hagen as *Commentum Einsidlense in Donati Artem maiorem*), with supplements by J.P. Elder, *The missing portions of the* Commentum Einsidlense *on Donatus's* Ars grammatica, *Harvard Studies in Classical Philology*, 56–7, 1945–6 [but 1947], 129–60.
Remi of Auxerre, Scholia on Eutyches' *Ars*: M. Manitius, *Münchener Museum*, 2, 1913, 101–8 (*excerpta*).
Rhabanus Maurus, *Excerptio de Arte grammatica Prisciani*: PLM CXI, 613 C-70 D.
Robert Blund, *Summa in arte grammatica*: C.H. Kneepkens (1987, III).
Roger Bacon, *Compendium studii theologiae*: ed. by T.S. Maloney, *Compendium of the Study of Theology* (Studien und Texte zum Geistesgeschichte des Mittelalters, XX), Leiden, 1988.
Roger Bacon, *De signis*, ed. by K.M. Fredborg et al., *Traditio*, 34, 1978, 75–136.
Roger Bacon, *Summa gramatica*: R. Steele (Opera Hactenus inedita Rogeri Baconi, XV), Oxonii, 1940, 1–190.

Sacerdos, M. Claudius, *Ars grammatica*: GLK VI, 427–95.

Sacerdos, M. Plotius, *De metris*: GLK VI, 496–546.

*Second Icelandic Grammatical Treatise*: F.D. Raschellà, Florence, 1982 (with translation and commentary, both in English).

Sedulius Scottus, *Commentum in Maiorem Donatum Grammaticum*: D. Brearley, Toronto, 1975, also B. Löfstedt, CCCM XL B, Turnhout, 1977.

Sedulius Scottus, *Commentaria in Donati Artem minorem, in Priscianum, in Eutychem*: B. Löfstedt, CCCM XL C, Turnhout, 1977.

Sergius, *De littera*: GLK IV, 475–85.

[Sergius], *Explanationes in Artem Donati*, I and II: GLK IV, 486–565.

Sergius (ps. -Cassiodorus), *Commentarium de oratione et de octo partibus orationis*: PLM LXX, 1219 A–1240 B.

Servius, *Commentarius in Vergilii Aeneidos libros I-XII*: G. Thilo-H. Hagen, 2 vols, Lipsiae, 1881–4.

Servius, *Commentarius in Artem Donati*: GLK IV, 405–28 and 443–8.

Servius, *De finalibus*: GLK IV, 449–55.

Servius, [Sergius], *Commentarius in Artem Donati*: GLK IV, 428–43.

Siger of Brabant, *Quaestiones logicales*: B. Bazàn, *S.d.B. Ecrits de logique, de morale et de physique* (Philosophes médiévaux, XIV), Louvain et Paris, 1974.

Siger of Courtrai, *Summa modorum significandi*; *Sophismata*: J. Pinborg (Amsterdam Studies in Theory and History of Linguistic Science, III. Studies in the History of Linguistics, 14), Amsterdam, 1977.

Simon of Dacia, *Domus Grammatica*, in *Opera*: A. Otto (CPhDMA, III), Hauniae, 1963, 3–88.

Simon of Dacia, *Quaestiones super 2ᵉ minoris voluminis Prisciani*, in *Opera*, 89–178.

Smaragdus, *Liber in partibus Donati*: B. Löfstedt, L. Holtz and A. Kibre, CCCM LXVIII, Turnhout, 1986.

Tatuinus, *Ars*: M. de Marco, *Tatuini Opera omnia*, ed. by M. de Marco and F. Glorie, CCSL CXXXIII, 2 vols, Turnhout, 1968, I, 1–93.

Thierry of Chartres, *Glosa super Boethii librum de Trinitate*: N. M. Häring, *Commentaries on Boethius by Thierry of Chartres and his School* (Studies and Texts, 20), Toronto, 1971, 257–300.

Thierry of Chartres, *Lectiones in Boethii librum de trinitate*: N. M. Häring, *Commentaries*, 123–229.

*Third Icelandic Grammatical Treatise*: B. M. Ólsen, 1884, København.

Thomas of Erfurt, *Grammatica speculativa*: G. L. Bursill-Hall, 1972, London (with English translation on facing pages).

Uc Faidit, *Donatz Proensals*: J. H. Marshall, Oxford, 1969, also including the Latin version.

Ursus of Benevento: grammatical *excerpta* published in C. Morelli, I trattati di grammatica e retorica del cod. Casanatense 1086, *Rendiconti della Reale Accademia dei Lincei – Classe di scienze morali, storiche e filologiche*, 5ᵉ Serie, 19, 1910, 287–328.

Victorinus, Marius, *Ars grammatica*: GLK VI, 3–173, also I. Mariotti, Firenze, 1967.

Victorinus, [Maximus], *Ars*: GLK VI, 187–205.

Victorinus, (attr. to Palaemon), *De metris*: GLK VI, 206–15.

Virgilius Maro Grammaticus, *Epitomae* and *Epistolae*: J. Huemer, Leipzig, 1886, also G. Polara, Napoli, 1979, with Italian translation.

Vynfreth: see Boniface.


William the Breton, *Summa sive Expositiones vocabulorum Biblie*: L. W. Daly and B. A. Daly, 2 vols, Patavii, 1975.

William of Conches, *Glosule super Priscianum*: E. Jeauneau (Lectio Philosophorum) Amsterdam, 1973.

William of Conches, *Glosule super Priscianum*: extracts from the first version in De Rijk (1962–7, vol. II, i) and in Fredborg (1973, 1980 and 1981); extracts from the second version in Jeauneau (1960) and Kneepkens (1978).

William of Conches, *Philosophia mundi*: PLM, CLXXII, 39–102 A (under the name of Honorius Augustodunensis).

William of Ockham, *Expositio in librum Perihermeneias Aristotelis*: A. Gambatese, S. Brown (Opera philosophica et theologica. Opera Philosophica, II, 341–504), St Bonaventure, NY, 1978.

William of Ockham, *Quaestiones in librum secundum Sententiarum* (*Reportatio*): G. Gál, R. Wood (Opera theologica, V), St Bonaventure, NY, 1981.

William of Ockham, *Quaestiones in librum tertium Sententiarum* (*Reportatio*): F. E. Kelley, G. I. Etzkorn (Opera theologica, VI), St Bonaventure, NY, 1982.

William of Ockham, *Scriptum in librum primum Sententiarum. Ordinatio. Prologus et distinctio I*: G. Gál, S. Brown (Opera theologica, I), St Bonaventure, NY, 1967.

William of Ockham, *Summa logicae*: P. Boehner, G. Gál, S. Brown (Opera philosophica, I), St Bonaventure, NY, 1974.


## Studies

ABELSON, P. (1906) *The Seven Liberal Arts. A Study in Mediaeval Culture*, New York.

ABERCROMBIE, D. (1949) What is a 'Letter'?, *Lingua*, 2, 54–63 (then in Abercrombie, D., *Studies in Phonetics and Linguistics*, London, 1965).

ALBANO LEONI, F. (1975) *Il primo trattato grammaticale islandese*, Bologna (introduction, text, translation and commentary).

ALBANO LEONI, F. (1985) Donato in Thule. *Kenningar* e *tropi* nel terzo trattato grammaticale islandese, *Quaderni Linguistici e Filologici*, of the University of Macerata, 3. 385–97.

AMIROVA, T. A., B. A. OL'CHOVIKOV AND JU. V. ROŽDESTVENSKIJ (1980) *Abriss der Geschichte der Linguistik*. Ins Deutsche übersetzt von Barbara Meier, herausgegeben von Georg Friedrich Meier, Leipzig (Russian original Moskva, 1975).

ANAGNINE, E. (1958) *Il concetto di Rinascita attraverso il Medioevo* (*V-X sec.*), Milano e Napoli.

ANSPACH, E. (1936) Das Fortleben Isidors im VII. bis IX. Jahrhundert, *Miscellanea Isidoriana. Homenaje a S. Isidoro de Sevilla en el XIII centenario de su muerte, 636–1936*, Roma, 323–56.

APPUHN, A. (1900) *Das Trivium und Quadrivium in Theorie und Praxis. I. Das Trivium*, Erlangen.

ARENS, H. (1969) *Sprachwissenschaft. Der Gang ihrer Entwicklung von der Antike bis zur Gegenwart*, Freiburg and München (1st edn 1955).

ARNALDI, G. (1974) *Le origini dell'Università*, Bologna.

*Arts libéraux et philosophie au moyen âge* (1969) *Actes du IV$^{me}$ Congrès international de philosophie médiévale*, Montréal and Paris.

ASHWORTH, E. J. (1978) *The Tradition of Medieval Logic and Speculative Grammar. From Anselm to the End of the Seventeenth Century. A Bibliography from 1836 onwards* (Subsidia Mediaevalia, 9), Toronto.

BAEBLER, J. J. (1885) *Beiträge zu einer Geschichte der lateinischen Grammatik im Mittelalter*, Halle a.S. (reprinted Hildesheim, 1971).

BAGNI, P. (1968) *La costituzione della poesia nelle Artes del XII–XIII secolo*, Bologna.

BAGNI, P. (1984) Grammatica e retorica nella cultura medievale, *Rhetorica. A Journal of the History of Rhetoric*, 2, 3, 267–80.

BALDWIN, C. S. (1928) *Medieval Rhetoric and Poetic (to 1400)*, New York (reprinted Gloucester, Mass., 1959).

BARDY, G. (1953) Les origines des écoles monastiques en Occident, *Sacris Erudiri*, 5, 86–104.

BARWICK, K. (1922) *Remmius Palaemon und die römische Ars grammatica*, Leipzig (reprinted Hildesheim and New York, 1967).

BARWICK, K. (1930) Review of J. Tolkiehn, *Clementis Ars grammatica, Gnomon*, 6, 385–95.

BAUR, L. (1903) *Dominicus Gundissalinus, 'De divisione philosophiae'*, Münster.

BECKER, G. (1885) *Catalogi bibliothecarum antiqui*, Bonn.

BEESON, C. H. (1924) The ars grammatica of Julian of Toledo, *Miscellanea Francesco Ehrle*, I (Studi e Testi, 37), Roma, 50–70.

BEESON, C. H. (1946) The Palimpsests of Bobbio, *Miscellanea Giovanni Mercati*, VI (Studi e Testi, 126), Roma, 162–84.

BEESON, C. H. (1947) The Manuscripts of Bede, *Classical Philology*, 42, 73–87.

BENEDINI, P. (1988) La teoria sintattica dei Modisti: attualità dei concetti di reggenza e dipendenza, *Lingua e stile*, 23, 113–35.

BERTINI, F. (1981) La tradizione lessicografica latina fra tardo antico e alto medioevo, *La cultura in Italia fra tardo antico e alto medioevo*, I, 397–409.

BIARD, J. (1981) La redéfinition ockhamiste de la signification, *Sprache und Erkenntnis im Mittelalter, Miscellanea Mediaevalia*, 13/1, 451–8.

BIARD, J. (1989) *Logique et théorie du signe au XIV$^e$ siècle* (Études de philosophie médiévale, LXIV), Paris.

*La Bibbia nell'alto medioevo* (1963) Settimane di studio del Centro italiano di studi sull'alto medioevo, X, Spoleto.

BISCHOFF, B. (1966–81) *Mittelalterliche Studien*, 3 vols, Stuttgart. They include: Biblioteche, scuole e letteratura nelle città dell'alto medioevo, I, 122–33; Die europäische Verbreitung der Werke Isidors von Sevilla, I, 171–94; Il monachesimo irlandese nei suoi rapporti col continente, I, 195–205; Wendepunkte in der Geschichte der lateinischen Exegese im Frühmittelalter, I, 205–73; Eine verschollene Einteilung der Wissenschaften, I, 273–88; Ein Brief Julians von Toledo über Rhythmen, metrische Dichtung und Prosa, I, 288–98; Eine Sammelhandschrift Walahfrid Strabos (Cod. Sangall. 878), II, 34–51; Muridac doctissimus plebis, ein irischer Grammatiker des IX. Jahrhunderts, II, 51–6; The Study of Foreign Languages in the Middle Ages, II, 227–45; Das griechische Element in der abendländischen Bildung des Mittelalters, II, 246–75; Scriptoria e manoscritti mediatori di civiltà dal sesto secolo alla riforma di Carlo Magno, II, 312–27; Die Hofbibliothek Karls des Grossen, III, 149–69; Die Bibliothek im Dienste der Schule, III, 213–33; Bannita: 1. Syllaba, 2. Littera, III, 243–7.

BOLOGNESI, G. (1967) *La grammatica latina di Aelfric. Parte prima. Studio delle fonti*, Brescia.

BONA, F. (1964) *Contributo allo studio della composizione del De verborum significatu di Verrio Flacco*, Milano.

BORST, A. (1957–63) *Der Turmbau von Babel. Geschichte der Meinungen über Ursprung und Vielfalt der Sprache und Völker*, 4 vols, 6 tomes, Stuttgart.

BRÉHIER, L. (1950) *La civilisation byzantine*, Paris.

BROOKS, N. (1982) *Latin and the Vernacular Languages in Early Medieval Britain*, Leicester.

BRUGNOLI, G. (1955) *Studi sulle* Differentiae verborum, Roma.

BRÜLL, H. (1904) *Die altenglische Lateingrammatik des Aelfric. Sprachliche Untersuchung*, Berlin.

BRUNHÖLZL, F. (1975) *Geschichte der lateinischen Literatur des Mittelalters. Erster Band. Von Cassiodor bis zum Ausklang der karolingischen Erneuerung*, München.

BUCKLER, G. (1948) Byzantine Education, *Byzantium. An Introduction to East Roman Civilization*, ed. by N. H. Baynes and H. St L. B. Moss, Oxford, 200–20.

BULLOUGH, D. A. (1972) The Educational Tradition in England from Alfred to Aelfric: Teaching *utriusque linguae*, *La scuola nell'Occidente latino dell' alto medioevo*, II, 453–92.

BURSILL-HALL, G. L. (1963) Medieval Grammatical Theories, *Canadian Journal of Linguistics*, 9, 39–54.

BURSILL-HALL, G. L. (1971) *Speculative Grammars of the Middle Ages. The Doctrine of partes orationis of the Modistae* (Approaches to Semiotics, 11), The Hague.

BURSILL-HALL, G. L. (1974) Toward a History of Linguistics in the Middle Ages (1100–1450), *Studies in the History of Linguistics. Traditions and Paradigms*, ed. by D. Hymes, Bloomington-London, 77–92.

BURSILL-HALL, G. L. (1975) The Middle Ages, *Historiography of Linguistics* (Current Trends in Linguistics, 13, ed. by H. Aarsleff, R. Austerlitz, D. Hymes *et al.*), The Hague, 179–230.

BURSILL-HALL, G. L. (1977) Teaching Grammars of the Middle Ages: Notes on the Manuscript Tradition, *Historiographia Linguistica*, 4, 1–29.

BURSILL-HALL, G. L. (1978) A Check-list of Incipits of Medieval Latin Grammatical Treatises: A-G, *Traditio*, 34, 439–74.

BURSILL-HALL, G. L. (1980a) *A Census of Medieval Latin Grammatical Manuscripts* (Grammatica Speculativa, 4), Stuttgart-Bad Cannstatt.

BURSILL-HALL, G. L. (1980b) *Select Bibliography*, in Hunt (1980), XXVII–XXXVI.

BURSILL-HALL, G. L. (1981) Medieval Donatus Commentaries, *Historiographia Linguistica*, 8, 1–72.

CALONGHI, L. (1956) *Le scienze e la classificazione delle scienze in Ugo di San Vittore*, Torino.

*Caratteri del secolo VII in Occidente* (1958) Settimane di studio del Centro italiano di studi sull'alto medioevo, V, Spoleto.

CAZZANIGA, I. (1953) Osservazioni intorno alla tradizione del glossario di Ansileubo, *Acme*, 6, 343–7.

*Centri e vie di irradiazione della civiltà nell'alto medioevo* (1964) Settimane di studio del Centro italiano di studi sull'alto medioevo, XI, Spoleto.

CERVANI, R. (1978) *L'epitome di Paolo del 'De verborum significatu' di Pompeo Festo. Struttura e metodo*, Roma.

CHASE, C. (1981) Alcuin's Grammar Verse: Poetry and Truth in Carolingian Pedagogy, *Insular Latin Studies*, 135–52.

CHASE, W. J. (1926) *The Ars Minor of Donatus, for 1000 Years the Leading Textbook of Grammar*, Madison, Wisc.

CHENU, M.-D. (1935) Grammaire et théologie aux XIIᵉ et XIIIᵉ siècles, *Archives d'histoire doctrinale et littéraire du moyen âge*, 10, 5–28.

CHENU, M.-D. (1966) *La théologie au douzième siècle*, 2nd edn (Études de philosophie médiévale, XLV), Paris.

CHENU, M.-D. (1967) Un cas de platonisme grammatical au XIIᵉ siècle, *Revue des sciences philosophiques et théologiques*, 51, 666–8.

CLERVAL, J. (1895) *Les écoles de Chartres au moyen âge (du Vᵉ au XVIᵉ siècle)*, Paris (reprinted Frankfurt a.M., 1965).

COBBS, S. P. (1937) *Prolegomena to the* Ars grammatica Tatuini, PhD diss., Chicago.

CONTRENI, J. J. (1981) John Scottus, Martin Hiberniensis, the Liberal Arts, and Teaching, *Insular Latin Studies*, 23–44.

COURCELLE, P. (1943) *Les lettres grecques en Occident de Macrobe à Cassiodore*, Paris (re-ed. 1948).

COVINGTON, M. A. (1984) *Syntactical Theory in the High Middle Ages. Modistic Models of Sentence Structure*, Cambridge.

CREMASCOLI, G. (1966) Termini del diritto longobardo nelle 'Derivationes' e il presunto vocabolario latino-germanico di Uguccione da Pisa, *Aevum*, 40, 53–74.

CREMASCOLI, G. (1968) Uguccione da Pisa: saggio bibliografico, *Aevum*, 42, 123–68.

CREMASCOLI, G. (1969) Ricerche sul lessicografo Papia, *Aevum*, 43, 31–55.

CREMASCOLI, G. (1982) Review of Papiae *Elementarium. Littera A*, ed. by

V. de Angelis, 3 vols, Milano 1977–1980, *Studi Medievali*, 3ᵃ S., 23, I, 243–6.

CREMASCOLI, G. (1990) Note sur des problèmes de lexicographie médiévale, *Latin vulgaire-latin tardif II. Actes du IIᵉᵐᵉ Colloque International sur le latin vulgaire et tardif* (Bologne, 29 Août-2 Septembre 1988) édités par G. Calboli, Tübingen, 75–88.

CUCCHI, A. (1983) Concezioni grammaticali dell 'Alto Medioevo, *Lingua e stile*, 18, 1, 47–73.

*La cultura antica nell'Occidente dal VII all'XI secolo* (1975) Settimane di studio del Centro italiano di studi sull alto medioevo, XXII, Spoleto.

*La cultura in Italia fra tardo antico e alto medioevo* (1981) Atti del Convegno tenuto a Roma, Centro nazionale delle ricerche, dal 12 al 16 novembre 1979, 2 vols, Roma.

CURTIUS, E. R. (1947) Das mittelalterliche Bildungswesen und die Grammatik, *Romanische Forschungen*, 60, 1–26.

CURTIUS, E. R. (1948) *Europäische Literatur und lateinisches Mittelalter*, Bern (French trans. Paris, 1956; English trans. Princeton 1967).

CURTOTTI, D. (1985–86) La semantica grammaticale di Prisciano nello sviluppo della grammatica speculativa, *Annali Istituto Orientale di Napoli*, Sez. filos, 8–9, 51–87.

DALY, L. W. (1961) *The Medieval University 1200–1400*, New York.

DALY, L. W., DALY, B. A. (1964) Some techniques in Medieval Latin Lexicography, *Speculum*, 39, 229–39.

DE ANGELIS, V. (1970–1) Critica e tradizione glossografica del lemma *AR aries* nell'*Elementarium* di Papias, *Studi Classici e Orientali* 19–20, 99–105.

DE ANGELIS, V. (1977) Indagine sulle fonti dell'*Elementarium* di Papias, Lettera A, *Scripta Philologa*, I, Milano, 117–34.

DELARUELLE, E. (1946) La connaissance du grec en Occident du Vᵉ au IXᵉ siècle, *Mélanges de la Société Toulousaine des Études Classiques*, I, 207–26.

DELHAYE, PH. (1947) L'organisation scolaire au XIIᵉ siècle, *Traditio*, 5, 211–68.

DELHAYE, PH. (1958) 'Grammatica' et 'Ethica' au XIIᵉ siècle, *Recherches de théologie ancienne et médiévale*, 25, 59–110.

DELHAYE, PH. (1969) La place des arts libéraux dans les programmes scolaires du XIIIᵉ siècle, *Arts libéraux et philosophie au moyen âge*, 161–73.

DE MARCO, M. (1957) Letture grammaticali a Lorsch nel secolo X, *Aevum*, 31, 273–7.

DENIFLE, H. (1885) *Die Entstehung der Universitäten des Mittelalters bis 1400*, Berlin (reprinted Graz 1956).

DENIFLE, H., CHATELAIN, E. (1889–97) *Chartularium Universitatis Parisiensis*, 4 vols, Paris.

DEVOTO, G. (1963) La Bibbia e le forze di conservazione linguistica nell'alto medioevo, *La Bibbia nell 'alto medioevo*, 55–66.

DIAZ Y DIAZ, M. C. (1969) Les arts libéraux d'après les écrivains espagnols et insulaires aux VIIᵉ et VIIIᵉ siècles, *Arts libéraux et philosophie au moyen âge*, 37–47.

DINNEEN, F. P. (1967) *An Introduction to General Linguistics*, New York.

DIONISOTTI, C. (1982) On Bede, Grammars, and Greek, *Revue bénédictine*, 92, 111–42.

D'IRSAY, S. (1933–1935) *Histoire des universités françaises et étrangères des origines à nos jours*, 2 vols, Paris.

DUBOIS, M. M. (1943) *Aelfric sermonnaire, docteur et grammairien*, Paris.

EBBESEN, S. (1981) The Present King of France wears Hypothetical Shoes with Categorical Laces. Twelfth-century Writers on Well-Formedness, *Medioevo*, 7, 91–113.

ECKSTEIN, F. A. (1887) *Lateinischer und griechischer Unterricht im Mittelalter*, Leipzig.

ELLSPERMANN, C. L. (1949) *The Attitude of the Early Christian Latin Writers Toward Pagan Literature and Learning*, Washington.

ENGELS, L. J. (1961) *Observations sur le vocabulaire de Paul Diacre*, Nijmegen.

ENGELS, L. J. (1962) La portée de l'étymologie isidorienne, *Studi Medievali*, 3ᵃ S., 3, 99–128.

EVANS, G. (1978) The Borrowed Meaning: Grammar, Logic and the Problem of Theological Language in Twelfth-Century Schools, *The Downside Review*, 96, 165–75.

FARAL, E. (1924) *Les Arts Poétiques du XIIᵉ et du XIIIᵉ siècle*, Paris (reprinted 1962).

FERRARI, M. (1979) Nota sui codici di Virgilio Marone Grammatico, in *Virgilio Marone Grammatico, Epitomi ed Epistole*, ed. by G. Polara, Napoli, 1979, XXXV–XLII.

FISCHER, B. (1957) *Die Alkuin-Bibel*, Freiburg i.B.

FISCHER, B. (1963) Bibelausgaben des frühen Mittelalters, *La Bibbia nell'alto medioevo*, 519–600.

FLORESCU, V. (1971) *La retorica nel suo sviluppo storico*, Bologna (Romanian original Bucureşti, 1960).

FONTAINE, J. (1959) *Isidore de Séville et la culture classique dans l'Espagne wisigothique*, 2 vols, Paris.

FONTAINE, J. (1978) Cohérence et originalité de l'étymologie isidorienne, *Mélanges Elorduy*, Bilbao, 113–44.

FOURNIER, M. (1890–94) *Les Statuts et Privilèges des Universités françaises depuis leur fondation jusqu'en 1789*, 4 vols, Paris (reprinted Bologna, 1969).

FRANCESCHINI, E. (1963) La Bibbia nell'alto medioevo, *La Bibbia nell'alto medioevo*, 13–37.

FRANCESCHINI, E. (1976) Studi sull' 'Aristoteles Latinus', in *Scritti di filologia latina medievale*, by E. Franceschini, 2 vols, Padova 1976, *La Bibbia nell'alto medioevo*, 377–692.

FREDBORG, K. M. (1973) The dependence of Petrus Helias' *Summa super Priscianum* on William of Conches' *Glose super Priscianum*, *Cahiers de l'institut du moyen âge grec et latin*, 11, Copenhague, 1–57.

FREDBORG, K. M. (1980) Universal Grammar According to Some 12th-

Century Grammarians, *Studies in Medieval Linguistic Thought dedicated to G.L. Bursill-Hall*, ed. by K. Koerner, H.-J. Niederehe and R. H. Robins, Amsterdam, 69–84.

FREDBORG, K. M. (1981) Some Notes on the Grammar of William of Conches, *Cahiers de l'institut du moyen âge grec et latin*, 37, 21–39.

FREDBORG, K. M. (1987) Speculative Grammar in the 12th Century: in *The Cambridge History of Twelfth Century Philosophy*, ed. by P. Dronke, Cambridge, 177–95.

FUCHS, F. (1926) Die höheren Schulen von Konstantinopel im Mittelalter, (Byzantinischer Archiv, supplement of the *Byzantinische Zeitschrift*, VIII), Leipzig.

FUNAIOLI, G. (1911) Su Giuliano Toletano, *Rivista di Filologia e di Istruzione Classica*, 39, 42–79.

GALLO, E. (1974) *The Poetria Nova and Its Sources in Early Rhetorical Doctrine*, The Hague and Paris.

GARIN, E. (1957) *L'educazione in Europa*, Bari.

GARIN, E. (1958) *Studi sul platonismo medievale*, Firenze.

GEBAUER, G. J. (1942) *Prolegomena to the* Ars grammatica Bonifatii, Chicago.

DE GHELLINCK, J. (1939) *Littérature latine au moyen âge*, 2 vols, Paris.

DE GHELLINCK, J. (1946) *L'essor de la littérature latine au XIIe siècle*, Bruxelles (reprinted 1964).

GIACONE, R. (1974) Le arti liberali e la classificazione delle scienze. L'esempio di Boezio e Cassiodoro, *Aevum*, 48, 58–72.

GIBSON, M. T. (1969) The *Artes* in the Eleventh Century, in *Arts libéraux et philosophie au moyen âge*, 121–6.

GIBSON, M. T. (1972) Priscian, *Institutiones Grammaticae*: A Handlist of Manuscripts, *Scriptorium*, 26, 105–24.

GIBSON, M. T. (1978) Introduction to *The Summa of Petrus Helias on Priscianus Minor*, ed. by J. E. Tolson, *Cahiers de l'institut du moyen âge grec et latin*, 27–8, Copenhague, Part II, 159–66.

GIBSON, M. T. (1979) The Early Scholastic 'Glosule' to Priscian, Institutiones Grammaticae: the Text and its Influence, *Studi Medievali*, 20, 235–54.

GILSON, E. (1944) *La philosophie au moyen âge*, Paris (re-edited 1947, 1952).

GLORIEUX, P. (1968) L'enseignement au moyen âge. Techniques et méthodes en usage à la Faculté de Théologie de Paris au XIIIe siècle, *Archives d'histoire doctrinale et littéraire du moyen âge*, 35, 65–186.

GLORIEUX, P. (1971) *La Faculté des Arts et ses maîtres au XIIIe siècle*, Paris.

GODFREY, R. G. (1965) Late Medieval Linguistic Metatheory and Chomsky's Syntactical Structures, *Word*, 21, 251–6.

GODFREY, R. G. (1967) A Medieval Controversy concerning the Nature of General Grammar, *General Linguistics*, 7, 79–104.

GOTTLIEB, TH. (1890) *Ueber mittelalterliche Bibliotheken*, Leipzig.

GRABMANN, M. (1909–11) *Die Geschichte der scholastischen Methode*, 2 vols, Freiburg i.B.

GRABMANN, M. (1916) *Forschungen über die lateinischen Aristotelesübersetzungen des XIIIten Jahrhunderts* (Beiträge zur Geschichte der Philosophie und Theologie des Mittelalters, 17, Heft 5–6), Münster.

GRABMANN, M. (1922) Die Entwicklung der mittelalterlichen Sprachlogik (Tractatus de modis significandi), in Grabmann (1926–56), I, 104–46.

GRABMANN, M. (1926–56) *Mittelalterliches Geistesleben*, 3 vols, München.

GRABMANN, M. (1939) *Methoden und Hilfsmittel des Aristotelesstudium im Mittelalter* (Sitzungsberichte der Bayerischen Akademie der Wissenschaften, Philosophisch-historische Klasse, Heft 5), München.

GRABMANN, M. (1941) *Gentile da Cingoli, ein italienischer Aristoteleserklärer aus der Zeit Dantes*, München (Sitzungsberichte der Bayerischen Akademie der Wissenschaft. *Philosophische-historische Abteilung*, 1940, 9), now in M. Grabmann, *Gesammelte Akademieabhandlungen*, Herausgegeben vom Grabmann-Institut der Universität München, 2 vols, Padeborn-München-Wien-Zürich, 1979, 1639–724.

GRABMANN, M. (1950) Aristoteles im zwölften Jahrhundert, Grabmann (1926–56), III, 64–127.

GRABMANN, M. (1951) Die geschichtliche Entwicklung der mittelalterlichen Sprachphilosophie und Sprachlogik. Ein Ueberblick, in Grabmann (1926–56), III, 243–53.

GREGORY, T. (1955) *Anima mundi: la filosofia di Guglielmo di Conches e la Scuola di Chartres*, Firenze.

GREGORY, T. (1958) *Platonismo medievale. Studi e ricerche*, Roma.

GRIBOMONT, J. (1963) Conscience philologique chez les scribes du haut moyen âge, in *La Bibbia nell'alto medioevo*, 601–30.

GUALAZZINI, U. (1943) *Ricerche sulle scuole pre-universitarie del Medioevo*, Milano.

GUIMET, F. (1948) 'Caritas ordinata' et 'amor discretus' dans la théologie trinitaire de Richard de Saint-Victor, *Revue du moyen-âge latin*, 44, 225–36.

HAARHOFF, TH. (1920) *Schools of Gaul. A Study of Pagan and Christian Education in the Last Century of the Western Empire*, Oxford.

HAGENDAHL, H. (1956) Le manuel de rhétorique d'Albericus Casinensis, *Classica et Mediaevalia*, 27, 63–70.

HAGENDAHL, H. (1958) *Latin Fathers and the Classics*, Göteborg.

HALLER, R. (1962) Untersuchungen zum Bedeutungsproblem in der antiken und mittelalterlichen Philosophie, *Archiv für Begriffsgeschichte*, 7, 57–119.

HASKINS, CH. H. (1923) *The Rise of the Universities*, New York.

HASKINS, CH. H. (1927) Guillaume de Noyon, *Speculum*, 2, 477–8.

HASKINS, CH. H. (1958) *The Renaissance of the 12th Century*, Cleveland and New York (1st edition Cambridge, Mass., 1927).

HEINIMANN, S. (1963) Zur Geschichte der grammatischen Terminologie im Mittelalter, *Zeitschrift für romanische Philologie*, 79, 23–37.

HENRY, D. P. (1967) *The Logic of Saint Anselm*, Oxford.

HENRY, D. P. (1974) *Commentary on* De grammatico. *The Historical-Logical Dimension of a Dialogue of St Anselm's* (Synthese Historical Library, 8), Dordrecht and Boston.

HERREN, M. W. (1979) Some New Light on the Life of Virgilius Maro Grammaticus, *Proceedings of the Royal Irish Academy*, 79 C, 27–71.

HERREN, M. W. (1981) Hiberno-Latin Philology: The State of the Question, *Insular Latin Studies*, 1–22.

HESSELS, J. H. (1890) *An Eighth-Century Latin-Anglo-Saxon Glossary Preserved in the Library of the Corpus Christi College*, Cambridge.

HESSELS, J. H. (1906) *A Late Eighth-Century Latin-Anglo-Saxon Glossary Preserved in the Library of the Leiden University*, Cambridge.

HILLGARTH, J. N. (1961–2) Visigothic Spain and Early Christian Ireland, *Proceedings of the Royal Irish Academy*, 62 C, 167–94.

HOLTZ, L. (1971) Tradition et diffusion de l'oeuvre grammaticale de Pompée, commentateur de Donat, *Revue de Philologie, de Littérature et d'Histoire Anciennes*, 45, 48–83.

HOLTZ, L. (1972) Sur trois commentaires irlandais de l'*Art majeur* de Donat au IXᵉ siècle, *Revue d'histoire des textes*, 2, 45–72.

HOLTZ, L. (1975) Le Parisinus Latinus 7530, synthèse cassinienne des arts libéraux, *Studi Medievali*, 3ᵉ S., 16, 97–152.

HOLTZ, L. (1977a) Grammairiens irlandais au temps de Jean Scot. Quelques aspects de leur pédagogie, *Jean Scot Erigène et l'histoire de la philosophie* (Colloques internationaux du Centre national de la recherche scientifique, no. 561.), Paris, 69–78.

HOLTZ, L. (1977b) Le rôle des Irlandais dans la transmission des grammaires latines, *Influence de la Grèce et de Rome sur l'Occident moderne*, ed. by R. Chevallier, Paris, 55–65.

HOLTZ, L. (1977c) A l'école de Donat, de Saint Augustin à Bède, *Latomus*, 36, 532–8.

HOLTZ, L. (1978) Sur les traces de Charisius, *Varron, grammaire antique et stylistique latine. Recueil offert à Jean Collart*, Paris, 225–33.

HOLTZ, L. (1981a) *Donat et la tradition de l'enseignement grammatical. Etude sur l'*Ars Donati *et sa diffusion (IVᵉ-IXᵉ siècle) et édition critique*, Paris.

HOLTZ, L. (1981b) Irish Grammarians and the Continent in the Seventh Century, *Columbanus and Merovingian Monasticism*, ed. by H. B. Clarke, M. Brennan, Oxford, 135–52.

HORSFALL, N. (1979) Doctus sermones utriusque linguae?, *Echos du monde classique / Classical News and Views*, 23, 79–95.

HUNT, R. W. (1948) The Introductions to the *Artes* in the Twelfth Century, in Hunt (1980), 117–44.

HUNT, R. W. (1980) *Collected Papers on the History of Grammar in the Middle Ages*, ed. by G. L. Bursill-Hall (Amsterdam Studies in the Theory and History of Linguistic Science, Series III – Studies in the History of Linguistics, vol 5), Amsterdam. They include: Studies on Priscian in the Eleventh and Twelfth Centuries. I: Petrus Helias and His Predecessors, 1–38; Studies on Priscian in the Twelfth Century. II: The School of Ralph of Beauvais, 39–94; *Absoluta*: The *Summa* of Petrus Hispanus on Priscianus *Minor*, 95–116; The Introductions to the *Artes* in the Twelfth Century, 117–44; Hugutio and Petrus Helias, 145–9; The

'Lost' Preface to the *Liber Derivationum* of Osbern of Gloucester, 151–66; Oxford Grammar Masters in the Middle Ages, 167–97.

HURT, J. (1972) *Aelfric*, New York.

HUSSEY, J. M. (1937) *Church and Learning in the Byzantine Empire, 867–1185*, Oxford-London.

HUYGENS, R.B.C. (1954) *Accessus ad auctores* (Collection Latomus, 15), Bruxelles.

*Insular Latin Studies* (1981) *Papers on Latin Texts and Manuscripts of the British Isles: 550–1066*, ed. by M. W. Herren (Papers in Mediaeval Studies, 1), Toronto.

*Introduction to Medieval Latin Studies* (1977) *A Syllabus and Bibliographical Guide*, ed. by M. R. P. McGuire and H. Dressler, Washington D. C.

IRIGOIN, J. (1975) La culture grecque dans l'Occident latin du VII<sup>e</sup> au XI<sup>e</sup> siècle, *La cultura antica nell'Occidente dal VII all'XI secolo*, 425–46.

ISAAC, J. (1953) *Le Peri Hermeneias en Occident de Boèce à Saint Thomas. Histoire littéraire d'un traité d'Aristote* (Bibliothèque Thomiste, XXIX), Paris.

JEAUNEAU, E. (1960) Deux rédactions des gloses de Guillaume de Conches sur Priscien, *Recherches de théologie ancienne et médiévale*, 27, 212–47.

JEAUNEAU, E. (1964) Notes sur l'Ecole de Chartres, *Studi Medievali*, 3<sup>a</sup> S., 5, 2, 821–65.

JEAUNEAU, E. (1972) Les Écoles de Laon et d'Auxerre au IX<sup>e</sup> siècle, *La scuola nell'Occidente latino dell'alto medioevo*, II, 495–522.

JEAUNEAU, E. (1973) *'Lectio Philosophorum'. Recherches sur l'Ecole de Chartres*, Amsterdam.

JEAUNEAU, E. (1975) L'héritage de la philosophie antique durant le haut moyen âge, *La cultura antica nell'Occidente dal VII all'XI secolo*, 19–54.

JEAUNEAU, E. (1979) Jean Scot Erigène et le grec, *Archivum Latinitatis Medii Aevi*, 41, 5–50.

JEEP, L. (1893) *Zur Geschichte der Lehre von den Redetheilen bei den lateinischen Grammatikern*, Leipzig.

JEUDY, C. (1971) La tradition manuscrite des *Partitiones* de Priscien et la version longue du commentaire de Rémy d'Auxerre, *Revue d'histoire des textes*, 1, 123–43.

JEUDY, C. (1972) L'*Institutio de nomine, pronomine et verbo* de Priscien: manuscrits et commentaires médiévaux, *Revue d'histoire des textes*, 2, 73–144.

JEUDY, C. (1974a) L'*Ars de nomine et verbo* de Phocas: manuscrits et commentaires médiévaux, *Viator*, 5, 61–156.

JEUDY, C. (1974b) Les manuscrits de l'*Ars de verbo* d'Eutychès et le commentaire de Rémi d'Auxerre, *Mélanges E.-R. Labande. Etudes de civilisation médiévale (IX<sup>e</sup>–XII<sup>e</sup> siècles)*, Poitiers, 421–36.

JEUDY, C. (1978) Donat et commentateurs de Donat à l'abbaye de Ripoll au X<sup>e</sup> siècle (ms. Barcelone, Archivo de la Corona de Aragón, Ripoll 46), *Latomus*, 158, 56–75.

JOLIVET, J. (1958) *Godescalc d'Orbais et la Trinité. La méthode de théologie à l'époque carolingienne* (Études de philosophie médiévale, XLVII), Paris.

JOLIVET J. (1966) Quelques cas de 'platonisme' grammatical du VII<sup>e</sup> au XII<sup>e</sup> siècle, *Mélanges R. Crozet*, Poitiers, I, 93–9.

JOLIVET J. (1969) *Arts du langage et théologie chez Abélard*, Paris.

JOLIVET J. (1975) Vues médiévales sur les paronymes, *Revue internationale de philosophie*, 29, no. 113, 222–42.

JOLIVET J. (1977) L'enjeu de la grammaire pour Godescalc, *Jean Scot Erigène et l'histoire de la philosophie* (Colloques internationaux du Centre national de la recherche scientifique, no. 561), Paris, 79–87.

JOLIVET J. (1981) Éléments pour une étude des rapports entre la grammaire et l'ontologie au moyen âge, *Sprache und Erkenntnis im Mittelalter, Miscellanea Mediaevalia*, 13/1, 135–64.

JOLIVET, J. (1987) *Aspects de la pensée médiévale. Abélard. Doctrines du langage*, Paris (includes Jolivet (1966, 1975, 1977, 1981).

KACZMAREK, L. (1980) *Modi significandi und ihre Destruktionen: zwei Texte zur Scholastischen Sprachtheorie im 14. Jahrhundert* (Materialen zur Geschichte der Sprachwissenschaft und der Semiotik, 1), Münster.

KACZMAREK, L., CHAPPUIS, M., PLUTA, O. (1986) Die philosophischen Schriften des Peter von Ailly. Authentizität und Chronologie, *Freiburger Zeitschrift für Philosophie und Theologie*, 33, 593–615.

KAUFMANN, G. (1869) *Rhetorenschulen und Klosterschulen in Gallien während der 5. und 6. Jahrhunderte*, Leipzig.

KELLY, D. (1966) The Scope of the Treatment of Composition in the Twelfth and Thirteenth Century Arts of Poetry, *Speculum*, 41, 261–78.

KELLY, L.G. (1972) De modis generandi. Points of Contact between Noam Chomsky and Thomas of Erfurt, *Folia Linguistica* 5, 225–52.

KELLY, L.G. (1977a) 'Introduction' to Pseudo–Albertus Magnus, *Quaestiones Alberti De Modis Significandi* (Amsterdam Studies in the Theory and History of Linguistic Science. III. Studies in the History of Linguistics, 15), Amsterdam, xiii–xxxvii.

KELLY, L.G. (1977b) La Physique d'Aristote et la phrase simple dans les ouvrages de grammaire spéculative, in *Grammaire générale des Modistes aux Idéologues*, Lille, 107–24.

KLIBANSKY R. (1937) *The Continuity of the Platonic Tradition During the Middle Ages*, London.

KLINCK, R. (1970) *Die lateinische Etymologie des Mittelalters*, München.

KNEEPKENS, C.H. (1976) Mulier quae damnavit, salvavit. A Note on the Early Development of the *relatio simplex*, *Vivarium*, 14, 13–25.

KNEEPKENS, C.H. (1977) The *relatio simplex* in the Grammatical Tracts of the Late 12th and Early 13th Century, *Vivarium*, 15, 1–30.

KNEEPKENS, C. H. (1978) Master Guido and His View on Government. On 12th Century Linguistic Thought, *Vivarium*, 16, 108–41.

KNEEPKENS, C. H. (1985) Roger Bacon's Theory of the Double Intellectus. A Note on the Development of the Theory of Congruitas and Perfectio in the First Half of the Thirteenth Century, *The Rise of British Logic*, ed. by P. O. Lewry, O. P. (Papers in Medieval Studies, 7), Toronto, 115–43.

KNEEPKENS, C. H. (1987) *Het iudicium constructionis. Het leerstuk van de constructio in de 2de helft van de 12de eeuw*, I. *Een verkennende en inleidende studie*; II. *Uitgave van Robertus van Parijs*, Summa 'Breve sit'; III. *Uitgave van Robert Blund*, Summa in arte grammatica; IV. *Werkuitgave van Petrus Hispanus*, Summa 'Absoluta cuiuslibet', Nijmegen.

KNOWLES, D. (1962) *The Evolution of Medieval Thought*, London.

KOCH, J. (ed.) (1959) *Artes Liberales. Von der Bildung der Antike zur Wissenschaft des Mittelalters* (Studien und Texte zur Geistesgeschichte des Mittelalters, V), Leiden-Köln.

KOERNER, K. (1980) Medieval Linguistic Thought. A Comprehensive Bibliography, *Studies in Medieval Linguistic Thought*, 265–99.

LAISTNER, M. L. W. (1924) The Revival of Greek in Western Europe in the Carolingian Age, *History*, 9, 177–87.

LAISTNER, M. L. W. (1931) *Thought and Letters in Western Europe AD 500-900*, London-New York (reprinted London, 1957).

LAPIDGE, M. (1981) The Present State of Anglo-Latin Studies, *Insular Latin Studies*, 45–82.

Latin Script and Letters AD 400–900 (1976) *Festschrift Presented to Ludwig Bieler on the Occasion of His 70th Birthday*, ed. by J. J. O'Meera, B. Naumann, Leiden.

LAW, V. (1977) The Latin and Old English Glosses in the *Ars Tatuini, Anglo-Saxon England*, 6, 77–89.

LAW, V. (1978) *The* Ars Bonifacii. *A Critical Edition with Introduction, and Commentary on the Sources*, PhD diss., Cambridge.

LAW, V. (1979) The Transmission of the *Ars Bonifacii* and the *Ars Tatuini, Revue d'histoire des textes*, 9, 281–8.

LAW, V. (1981) Malsachanus Reconsidered: A Fresh Look at a Hiberno-Latin Grammarian, *Cambridge Medieval Celtic Studies*, 1, 83–93.

LAW, V. (1982) *The Insular Latin Grammarians* (Studies in Celtic History, III), Woodbridge.

LAW, V. (1983) The Study of Latin Grammar in Eighth-Century Southumbria, *Anglo-Saxon England*, 12, 43–71.

LAW, V. (1985) Linguistics in the Earlier Middle Ages: The Insular and Carolingian Grammarians, *Transactions of the Philological Society*, 171–93.

LAW, V. (1986a) Late Latin Grammarians in the Early Middle Ages: A Typological History, *Historiographia Linguistica*, 13, 365–80.

LAW, V. (1986b) Originality in the Medieval Normative Tradition, *Studies in the History of Western Linguistics. In Honour of R. H. Robins*, ed. by T. Bynon and F. R. Palmer, Cambridge-London, 43–55.

LAW, V. (1986c) Panorama della grammatica normativa nel tredicesimo secolo, *'Aspetti della letteratura latina nel secolo XIII'*, Atti del primo Convegno internazionale di studi dell' Associazione per il Medioevo e l'umanesimo latini (Perugia 3–5 ottobre 1983), ed. by C. Leonardi and G. Orlandi, Perugia-Firenze, 125–45.

LAZZARI, L. and MUCCIANTE, L. (1984a) *Il Glossario di Aelfric: studio sulle concordanze* (Quaderni di *Abruzzo*, 13), Roma.

LAZZARI, L. and MUCCIANTE, L. (1984b) Aspetti formali del *Glossario* di Aelfric e delle sue concordanze, *Abruzzo*, 22, 2–3 (Linguistica), 5–40.

LECLERCQ, J. (1947) *Les études universitaires dans l'ordre de Cluny*, Saint-Wandrille.

LECLERCQ, J. (1948) Smaragde et la grammaire chrétienne, *Revue du moyen âge latin*, 4, 15–22.

LECLERCQ, J. (1972) Pédagogie et formation spirituelle du VIᵉ au IXᵉ siècle, *La scuola nell 'Occidente latino dell 'alto medioevo*, I, 255–90.

LEFF, G. (1968) *Paris and Oxford Universities in the Thirteenth and Fourteenth Centuries*, New York.

LE GOFF, J. (1957) *Les intellectuels au moyen âge*, Paris.

LEHMANN, P. (1954) Das Problem der karolingischen Renaissance, *I problemi della civiltà carolingia*, 309–58.

LENDINARA, P. (1983) Il 'Colloquio' di Aelfric ed il Colloquio di Aelfric Bata, in *'feor ond neah'. Scritti di filologia germanica in memoria di Augusto Scaffidi Abbate* (Annali della Facoltà di Lettere e Filosofia dell'Università di Palermo, Studi e ricerche, 3), Palermo, 173–249.

LENTINI, A. (1932) Ilderico e la sua grammatica contenuta nel codice Cassinese 299, *Bullettino dell'Istituto storico italiano e Archivio Muratoriano*, 47, 167–72.

LENTINI, A. (1953a) Citazioni di grammatici e di classici nell''Ars' di Ilderico, *Aevum*, 27, 240–50.

LENTINI, A. (1953b) La grammatica d'Ilderico documento dell'attività letteraria di Paolo Diacono, *Atti del 2° Congresso internazionale di studi sull'alto medioevo*, Spoleto, 217–40.

LEONARDI, C. (1955) Nota introduttiva per un'indagine sulla fortuna di Marziano Capella nel Medioevo, *Bullettino dell'Istituto storico italiano per il medioevo*, 67, 265–88.

LEONARDI, C. (1962) *I codici di Marziano Capella*, Padova.

LEONARDI, C. (1972) La scuola nella civiltà altomedioevale, *La scuola nell'Occidente latino dell 'alto medioevo*, II, 861–71.

LEONARDI, C. (1973) Il venerabile Beda e la cultura del secolo VIII, *I problemi dell'Occidente nel secolo VIII*, 603–58.

LEONARDI, C. (1975a) I commenti altomedievali ai classici pagani, da Severino Boezio a Remigio d'Auxerre, *La cultura antica nell'Occidente dal VII all'XI secolo*, 459–504.

LEONARDI, C. (1975b) Remigio di Auxerre e l'eredità della scuola carolingia, *I classici nel Medioevo e nell'Umanesimo*, Genova, 271–88.

LESNE, E. (1938) *Les livres, scriptoria et bibliothèques du commencement du VIIIᵉ siècle à la fin du XIIᵉ siècle* (Histoire de la propriété ecclésiastique en France, 4), Lille.

LESNE, E. (1940) *Les écoles de la fin du VIIIᵉ siècle à la fin du XIIᵉ siècle* (Histoire de la propriété ecclésiastique en France, 5), Lille.

LEWRY, O. (1981) The Oxford Condemnations of 1277 in Grammar and Logic, *English Logic and Semantics from the End of the Twelfth Century to the Time of Ockham and Burleigh*, ed. by H. A. G. Braakhuis, C. H. Kneepkens, L. M. de Rijk (Artistarium. Supplementa, I), Nijmegen, 235–78.

DE LIBERA, A. and ROSIER, I. (1992) La penseé linguistique médiévale, section 3: l'analyse de la référence, *Histoires des idées linguistiques*, ed. by S. Auroux, t. II, Liège, 137–58.

LINDHOLM, G. (1963) *Studien zum mittellateinischen Prosarhythmus*, Stockholm.

LINDSAY, W. M. (1921a) *The Corpus, Epinal, Erfurt and Leyden Glossaries*, London.

LINDSAY, W. M. (1921b) *The Corpus Glossary*, Cambridge.

LINDSAY, W. M. (1922) *Julian of Toledo De vitiis et figuris*, Oxford.

LINDSAY, W. M., MOUNTFORD, J. F., WHATMOUGH, J. (1926–31) *Glossaria Latina*, 5 vols, Paris (reprinted Hildesheim, 1965).

LÖFSTEDT, B. (1965) *Der hibernolateinische Grammatiker Malsachanus* (Acta Universitatis Upsaliensis – Studia Latina Upsaliensia, 3), Uppsala.

LÖFSTEDT, B. (1972a) Zu Tatwines Grammatik, *Arctos. Acta Philologica Fennica*, N. S., 7, 47–65.

LÖFSTEDT, B. (1972b) Weitere Bemerkungen zu Tatwines Grammatik, *Acta classica*, 15, 85–94.

LÖFSTEDT, B. (1976) Zur Grammatik des Asper minor, *Latin Script and Letters AD 400–900*, 132–40.

LÓPEZ, R. S. (1948) Le problème des relations anglo-byzantines du VIIᵉ au Xᵉ siècle, *Byzantion*, 18, 147–54.

LORCIN, A. (1945) La vie scolaire dans les monastères irlandais aux Vᵉ-VIIᵉ siècles, *Revue du moyen âge latin*, 1, 221–36.

LOWE, E. A. (1934–71) *Codices Latini Antiquiores. A Palaeographical Guide to Latin Manuscripts Prior to the Ninth Century*, 11 vols and 1 supplement, Oxford.

DE LUBAC, H. (1959–64) *Exégèse médiévale. Les quatre sens de l'Écriture*, 4 vols, Paris.

DE LUBAC, H. (1960) Saint Grégoire et la grammaire, *Recherches de sciences religieuses*, 6, 185–226.

LUSIGNAN, S. (1986) *Parler vulgairement. Les intellectuels et la langue française au XIIIᵉ et XIVᵉ siècle*, Montréal/Paris.

LUTZ, CORA E. (1956) Remigius' Ideas on the Classification of the Seven Liberal Arts, *Traditio*, 21, 65–85.

LUTZ, CORA E. (1977) *Schoolmasters of the Tenth Century*, New York.

MAIERÙ, A. (1972) *Terminologia logica della tarda scolastica* (Lessico intellettuale europeo, 8), Roma.

MAIERÙ, A. (1986) La grammatica speculativa, *Aspetti della letteratura latina del secolo XIII*, ed. by C. Leonardi and G. Orlandi, Perugia-Firenze, 147–67.

MALONEY, T. S. (1983) The Semiotics of Roger Bacon, *Mediaeval Studies*, 45, 120–54.

MANACORDA, G. (n.d., but 1913–14) *Storia della scuola in Italia*, 2 vols, Milano-Palermo-Napoli (reprinted Firenze, 1980, with introduction by E. Garin).

MANGO, C. (1973) La culture grecque et l'Occident au VIIIᵉ siècle, *I problemi dell'Occidente nel secolo VIII*, II, 683–721.

MANITIUS, K. (1958) *Gunzo*, Epistula ad Augienses, *und Anselm von Besate*, Rhetorimachia, Weimar.

MANITIUS, M. (1911–31) *Geschichte der lateinischen Literatur des Mittelalters*, 3 vols, München (vol. 3 in collaboration with P. Lehmann; a new edition of vol. 1, 1959).

MANSELLI, R. (1963) Gregorio Magno e la Bibbia, *La Bibbia nell'alto medioevo*, 67–101.

MARIÉTAN, J. (1901) *Le problème de la classification des sciences d'Aristote à Saint Thomas*, Paris.

MARIGO, A. (1927) De Huguccionis Pisani 'Derivationum' Latinitate earumque prologo, *Archivum Romanicum*, 11, 98–107.

MARIGO, A. (1936) *I codici manoscritti delle 'Derivationes' di Uguccione Pisano. Saggio d'inventario bibliografico con appendice sui codici del 'Catholicon' di Giovanni da Genova*, Roma.

MARIGO, A. (1937) I trattatelli 'De accentu' e 'De orthographia' di fra Bartolomeo da S. Concordio nel testo e nelle fonti dottrinali, *Archivum Latinitatis Medii Aevi* 12, 1–26.

MARINONI, A. (1955) *Dal 'Declarus' di A. Senisio. I vocaboli siciliani*, Palermo.

MARROU, H. I. (1937) *Saint Augustin et la fin de la culture antique*, Paris (new edn and *Retractatio*, 1949).

MARROU, H. I. (1948) *Histoire de l'éducation dans l'antiquité*, Paris (sixth edition 1965; English transl. *A History of Education in Antiquity*, London and New York, 1956, to which citations refer).

MASTRELLI, C. A. (1963) La tecnica delle traduzioni della Bibbia nell'alto medioevo, *La Bibbia nell'alto medioevo*, 657–81.

MATHON, G. (1969) Les formes et la signification des arts libéraux au milieu du IX^e siècle. L'enseignement palatin de Jean Scot Erigène, *Arts libéraux et philosophie au moyen âge*, 47–65.

MAYR-HARTING, H. (1972) *The Coming of Christianity to Anglo-Saxon England*, London.

MCCAWLEY, J. D. (ed.) (1976) *Notes from the Linguistic Underground* (Syntax and Semantics, 7), New York.

MCGEACHY, J. A. (1938) The *Glossarium Salomonis* and its Relationship to the *Liber Glossarum*, *Speculum*, 13, 309–18.

MCKEON, R. P. (1942) Rhetoric in the Middle Ages, *Speculum*, 17, 1–32.

MCNALLY, R. E. (1958) The 'tres linguae sacrae' in Early Irish Bible Exegesis, *Theological Studies*, 19, 395–403.

MELAZZO, L. (1985) The Opening of the So-called Second Grammatical Treatise: in Search of the Sources, *Quaderni Linguistici e Filologici* of the University of Macerata, 3, 399–424.

MENGOZZI, G. (1924) *Ricerche sull'attività della scuola di Pavia nell'alto medio evo*, Pavia.

MEREDITH, C. O. (1916) *The* partes orationis *as Discussed by Virgilius Maro Grammaticus*, Guilford, NC.

MINIO-PALUELLO, L. (1943) The Genuine Text of Boethius' Translation of Aristotle's Categories, *Mediaeval and Renaissance Studies*, 1, 151–77.

MINIO-PALUELLO, L. (1945) The Text of the Categoriae: The Latin Tradition, *The Classical Quarterly* 39, 63–74.

MINIO-PALUELLO, L. (1952a) Jacobus Veneticus Grecus, Canonist and translator of Aristotle, *Traditio*, 8, 265–304.

MINIO-PALUELLO, L. (1952b) Note sull'Aristotele latino medievale, VI–VII, *Rivista di filosofia neoscolastica*, 44, 398–411 and 485–95.

MINIO-PALUELLO, L. (1954) Note sull'Aristotele latino medievale, IX, *Rivista di filosofia neoscolastica*, 46, 223–31.

MINIO-PALUELLO, L. (1957) Les traductions et les commentaires aristotéliciens de Boèce, *Studia Patristica*, II, 358–65 (republished in a German trans. in *Boethius*, hrsg. von M. Fuhrmann und J. Gruber [Wege der Forschung, Band CDLXXXIII], Darmstadt 1984, 146–54).

MINIO-PALUELLO, L. (1962) Note sull'Aristotele latino medievale, XIV–XV, *Rivista di filosofia neoscolastica*, 54, 131–7 and 137–47.

MINIO-PALUELLO, L. (1965a) 'Magister Sex Principiorum', *Studi Medievali*, 3ª S., 6, 2, 123–51.

MINIO-PALUELLO, L. (1965b) Aristotele dal mondo arabo a quello latino, *L'Occidente e l'Islam nell 'alto medioevo*, 603–37.

MINIO-PALUELLO, L. (1966) Giacomo Veneto e l'aristotelismo latino, *Venezia e l'Oriente fra tardo Medioevo e Rinascimento*, ed. by A. Pertusi, Firenze, 1966, 53–74.

MINIO-PALUELLO, L. (1972) Nuovi impulsi allo studio della logica. La seconda fase della riscoperta di Aristotele e di Boezio, *La scuola nell'Occidente latino dell'alto medioevo*, 743–66.

MOMIGLIANO, A. (1955) Cassiodorus and Italian Culture of His Time, *Proceedings of the British Academy*, 41, 207–45 (and in Id., *Secondo contributo alla storia degli studi classici*, Roma, 1960, 191–229; also in Id., *Studies in Historiography*, London, 1966, 181–210).

MONTEVERDI, A. (1954) Il problema del rinascimento carolino, *I problemi della civiltà carolingia*, 359–72.

MORELLI, C. (1910) I trattati di grammatica e retorica del cod. Casanatense 1086, in *Rendiconti della Reale Accademia dei Lincei* – Classe di scienze morali, storiche e filologiche, 5ª S., 19, 287–328.

MOSCADI, A. (1979) Verrio, Festo e Paolo, *Giornale Italiano di Filologia*, 31, 17–36.

MOUNIN, G. (1967) *Histoire de la linguistique des origines au XX^e siècle*, Paris.

MUCKLE, J. (1942–1943) Greek Works Translated Directly into Latin before 1350, *Mediaeval Studies*, 4, 33–43 and 5, 102–14.

MUNZI, L. (1979) Note testuali all'Ars grammatica di Giuliano di Toledo, *Annali Istituto Orientale di Napoli*, Sez. filol. -lett., 1, 171–3.

MUNZI, L. (1980–81) Ancora sul testo dell'Ars grammatica di Giuliano di Toledo, *Annali Istituto Orientale di Napoli*, Sez. filol. -lett., 2–3, 229–31.

MURPHY, J. J. (1961) The Arts of Discourse, 1050–1400, *Mediaeval Studies*, 23, 194–205.

MURPHY, J. J. (1962) The Medieval Arts of Discourse. An Introductory Bibliography, *Speech Monographs*, 29, 71 ff.

MURPHY, J. J. (1974) *Rhetoric in the Middle Ages*, Berkeley–Los Angeles–London.

MURPHY, J. J. (1980) The Teaching of Latin as a Second Language in the 12th Century, *Studies in Medieval Linguistic Thought*, 159–75.

NARDI, B. (1949), *Dante e la cultura medievale*, 2nd edn, Bari.

NEFF, K. (1891) *De Paulo Diacono Festi epitomatore*, Erlangae.

NIEDERMANN, M. (1943–4) Les Gloses médicales du *Liber Glossarum, Emerita*, 11, 257–96 and 12, 29–83 (reprinted in *Recueil Max Niedermann*, Neuchâtel, 1954, 65–136).

NIELSEN, L. O. (1982) *Theology and Philosophy in the Twelfth Century. A Study of Gilbert Porreta's Thinking and the Theological Expositions of the Doctrine of the Incarnation during the Period 1130–1180* (Acta theologica Danica, XV), Leiden.

NORDEN, E. (1898) *Die antike Kunstprosa vom VI. Jahrhundert v. Chr. bis in die Zeit der Renaissance*, 2 vols, Leipzig (Italian trans. Roma, 1986, with updated note by G. Calboli and foreword by S. Mariotti).

*L'Occidente e l'Islam nell'alto medioevo* (1965) Settimane di studio del Centro italiano di studi sull'alto medioevo, XII, Spoleto.

O'DONNELL, J. R. (1969) The Liberal Arts in the Twelfth Century with Special Reference to Alexander Nequam (1157–1217), *Arts libéraux et philosophie au moyen âge*, 127–35.

O'DONNELL, J. R. (1976) Alcuin's Priscian, *Latin Script and Letters A.D. 400–900*, 222–35.

OPELT, I. (1959) Zur Uebersetzungstechnik des Gerhard von Cremona, *Glotta*, 38, 135–70.

ORME, N. (1973) *English Schools in the Middle Ages*, London.

ORME, N. (1976) *Education in the West of England, 1066–1548*, Exeter.

PAETOW, L. J. (1910) *The Arts Course at Medieval Universities, with Special Reference to Grammar and Rhetoric* (The University of Illinois Studies, III, 7), Urbana, Ill.

PAETOW, L. J. (1914) *The Battle of the Seven Arts* (Memoirs of the University of California, 4, 1), Berkeley, Calif.

PAETOW, L. J. (1927) *Two Medieval Satires on the University of Paris: La Bataille des Sept Arts of Henri d'Andeli, and the Morale Scolarium of John of Garland*, 2 vols, Berkeley, Calif.

PANACCIO, C. (1980) Occam et les démonstratifs, *Studies in Medieval Linguistic Thought*, 189–200.

PANACCIO, C. (1983) Guillaume d'Occam: Signification et supposition, *Archéologie du signe*, ed. by L. Brind'amour and E. Vance, Toronto, 265–86.

PARÉ, G., BRUNET, A. and TREMBLAY, P. (1933) *La Renaissance du XII siècle. Les écoles et l'enseignement*, Paris–Ottawa.

PÀROLI, T. (1967–1968) Le opere grammaticali di Aelfric, *Annali Istituto Orientale di Napoli*, Sez. germ., 10, 5–44 and 11, 35–134.

PÀROLI, T. (1968) Indice della terminologia grammaticale di Aelfric, *Annali Istituto Orientale di Napoli*, Sez. ling., 8, 113–38.

PÀROLI, T. (1969) Rapporto preliminare sugli aspetti linguistici e culturali della grammatica latina in anglosassone di Aelfric, *Arts libéraux et philosophie au moyen âge*, 777–83.

PARRET, H. (ed.) (1976) *History of Linguistic Thought and Contemporary Linguistics*, Berlin-New York.

PASSALACQUA, M. (1978) *I codici di Prisciano*, Roma.

PERCIVAL, W. K. (1976a) Deep and Surface Structure Concepts in Renaissance and Medieval Syntactic Theory, in Parret (1976), 238–53.

PERCIVAL, W. K. (1976b) On the Historical Source of Immediate Constituent Analysis, in McCawley (1976), 229–42.

PERCIVAL, W. K. (forthcoming) *Syntax in the Middle Ages.*

PERTUSI, A. (1964) Bisanzio e l'irradiazione della sua civiltà in Occidente nell'alto medioevo, *Centri e vie di irradiazione della civiltà nell'alto medioevo*, 75–133.

PETRUCCI, A. (1972) Libro, scrittura e scuola, *La scuola nell'Occidente latino dell'alto medioevo*, I, 313–37.

PFISTER, R. (1976) Zur Geschichte der Begriffe Subjekt und Prädikat, *Münchener Studien zur Sprachwissenschaft*, 35, 105–19.

PINBORG, J. (1961) Interjektion und Naturlaute: Petrus Heliae und ein Problem der antiken und mittelalterlichen Sprachphilosophie, *Classica et Mediaevalia*, 22, 117–38.

PINBORG, J. (1964) Mittelalterliche Sprachtheorien: was heisst Modus Significandi? *Fides Quaerens Intellectum. Festskrift tilegnet Heinrich Roos*, København, 66–84.

PINBORG, J. (1967) *Die Entwicklung der Sprachtheorie im Mittelalter* (Beiträge zur Geschichte der Philosophie und Theologie des Mittelalters, 42, 2), Münster-Kopenhagen.

PINBORG, J. (1968) review of de Rijk (1967), *Vivarium*, 6, 155–8.

PINBORG, J. (1969a) Pour une interprétation moderne de la théorie linguistique du moyen âge, *Acta Linguistica*, 12, 238–43.

PINBORG, J. (1969b) Miszellen zur mittelalterlichen lateinischen Grammatik, *Cahiers de l'institut du moyen âge grec et latin*, 1, 13–20.

PINBORG, J. (1971) Bezeichnung in der Logik des XIII. Jahrhunderts, *Miscellanea Mediaevalia*, 8, 238–81.

PINBORG, J. (1972) *Logik und Semantik im Mittelalter. Ein Ueberblick* (Problemata, vol. 10), Stuttgart-Bad Cannstatt.

PINBORG, J. (1973) Some syntactical Concepts in Medieval Grammar, *Classica et Mediaevalia Francisco Blatt dedicata*, København, 496–509.

PINBORG, J. (1974) Zur Philosophie des Boethius de Dacia. Ein Ueberblick, *Studia Mediewistyczne*, 15, 165–85.

PINBORG, J. (1975b) A Note on Some Theoretical Concepts of Logic and Grammar, *Revue internationale de philosophie*, 29, no. 113, 286–96.

PINBORG, J. (1975a) Die Logik der Modistae, *Studia Mediewistyczne*, 16, 39–97.

PINBORG, J. (1976) Some Problems of Semantic Representations in Medieval Logic, in Parret (1976), 254–78.

PINBORG, J. (1980) Can Construction be Constructed? A Problem in Medieval Syntactical Theory, *Studies in Medieval Linguistic Thought dedicated to G. L. Bursill-Hall* ed. by K. Koerner et al., Amsterdam, 201–10.

PINBORG, J. (1981) Roger Bacon on Signs: A Newly Recovered Part of the Opus Maius, *Sprache und Erkenntnis im Mittlalter, Miscellanea Medievalia*, 13/1, 403–12.

PINBORG, J. (1982) Speculative grammar, *The Cambridge History of Later Medieval Philosophy*, ed. by N. Kretzmann, A. Kenny, J. Pinborg, Cambridge, 254–69.

PINBORG, J. (1984) *Medieval Semantics. Selected Studies on Medieval Logic and Grammar*, ed. by S. Ebbesen (Variorum Reprints), London.

POLARA, G. (1977) Gli studi su Virgilio Marone Grammatico, *Vichiana*, 6, 241–78.

POLI, D. (1981) Gli 'accenti' nella teoria grammaticale irlandese, *Quaderni Linguistici e Filologici* of the University of Macerata, 1, 71–86.

POLI, D. (1982–4a) I *praecepta* della retorica antica e l'*Auraicept na n-Éces* della cultura irlandese altomedioevale, *Quaderni Linguistici e Filologici* of the University of Macerata, 2, 107–138

POLI, D. (1982–4b) I frammenti di Virgilio Marone grammatico ser. n. 3762 dell'*Osterreichische Nationalbibliothek* di Vienna, *Quaderni Linguistici e Filologici* of the University of Macerata, 2, 107–138.

*I problemi della civiltà carolingia* (1954) Settimane di studio del Centro italiano di studi sull'alto medioevo, I, Spoleto.

*I problemi dell'Occidente nel secolo VIII* (1973) Settimane di studio del Centro italiano di studi sull'alto medioevo, XX, 2 vols, Spoleto.

QUADLBAUER, F. (1962) *Die antike Theorie der genera dicendi im lateinischen Mittelalter*, Wien.

QUAIN, E. A. (1945) The Medieval *Accessus ad Auctores, Traditio* 3, 215–64.

RASCHELLÀ F. D. (1982) *The So-Called Second Grammatical Treatise* (Filologia Germanica – Testi e Studi, II), Firenze.

RASHDALL, H. (1936) *The Universities of Europe in the Middle Ages*, Oxford (revised in three vols, ed. by F. M. Powicke and A. B. Emden, from the 1895 edition).

REINA, M. E. (1959) Il problema del linguaggio in Buridano, I. Voci e concetti, *Rivista critica di storia della filosofia*, 14, 367–417.

REYDELLET, M. (1966) La diffusion des *Origines* d'Isidore de Séville au haut moyen âge, *Mélanges d'archéologie et d'histoire de l'École française de Rome*, 78, 383–437.

RICHÉ, P. (1962) *Éducation et culture dans l'Occident barbare, VI^e VIII^e siècles*, Paris.

RICHÉ, P. (1979) *Les écoles et l'enseignement dans l'Occident chrétien de la fin du V^e siècle au milieu du XI^e siècle*, Paris.

RICHTER, M. (1980) Monolingualism and Multilingualism in the 14th Century, *Studies in Medieval Linguistic Thought*, 211–20.

RIESSNER, C. (1965) *Die* Magnae Derivationes *des* Uguccione da Pisa *und ihre Bedeutung für die romanische Philologie*, Roma.

RIESSNER, C. (1976) Quale codice delle *Etymologiae* di Isidoro di Siviglia fu usato da Uguccione da Pisa?, *Vetera Christianorum*, 13, 349–65.

DE RIJK, L. M. (1962–7) *Logica modernorum. A Contribution to the History of Early Terminist Logic*, 2 vols (the second in two parts), Assen.

DE RIJK, L. M. (1963) On the Curriculum of the Arts of the Trivium at St Gall (850–1000), *Vivarium*, 1, 33–86.

DE RIJK, L. M. (1981) Boèce logicien et philosophe: ses positions sémantiques et sa métaphysique de l'être, *Atti del Congresso internazionale di studi boeziani (Pavia, 5–8 ottobre 1980)*, ed. by L. Obertello, Roma, 141–56.

ROBINS, R. H. (1951) *Ancient and Medieval Grammatical Theory in Europe*, London.

ROBINS, R. H. (1967) *A Short History of Linguistics*, London (3rd edn, 1990).

ROBINS, R. H. (1980) Functional Syntax in Medieval Europe, *Studies in Medieval Linguistic Thought*, 231–40.

ROBSON, C. A. (1963) L'*Appendix Probi* et la philologie latine, *Le moyen âge*, 18, 37–54.

ROBUSTELLI DELLA CUNA, F. (1972) Osbern da Gloucester: vocaboli volgari, *Quadrivium*, 13, 2, 43–65.

ROBUSTELLI DELLA CUNA, F.. (1975) Sulla *Panormia* di Osbern da Gloucester, *Aevum*, 49, 127–36.

ROGER, M. (1905) *L'enseignement des lettres classique d'Ausone à Alcuin*, Paris (reprinted Hildesheim, 1968).

ROOS, H (1947) Sprachdenken im Mittelalter, *Classica et Mediaevalia*, 9, 200–15.

ROOS, H (1959) Die Stellung der Grammatik im Lehrbetrieb des XIIIten Jahrhunderts, in Koch (1959), 94–106.

ROSS, H. (1969) Le 'Trivium' à l'Université au XIIIᵉ siècle, *Arts libéraux et philosophie au moyen âge*, 193–7.

ROSIELLO, L. (1967) *Linguistica illuminista*, Bologna.

ROSIER, I. (1983) *La grammaire spéculative des Modistes*, Lille.

ROSIER, I. (1984a) Grammaire, logique, sémantique, deux positions opposées au XIIIᵉ siècle: Roger Bacon et les Modistes, *Histoire, épistémologie, langage*, 6, 21–34.

ROSIER, I. (1984b) Transitivité et ordre des mots chez les grammariens médiévaux, *Matériaux pour une Histoire des théories linguistiques/Essays toward a History of Linguistic Theories/Materialen zu einer Geschichte der sprachwissenschaftlichen Theorien*, Lille, 181–90.

ROSIER, I. (1987a) Les acceptions du terme 'substantia' chez Pierre Hélie, *Gilbert de Poitiers et ses contemporains. Aux origines de la* Logica modernorum, éd. par J. Jolivet et A. de Libera (History of Logic, V), Napoli, 299–324.

ROSIER, I. (1987b) La syntaxe des modistes. A propos d'un ouvrage récent, *Le moyen âge*, 93, 461–8.

ROSIER, I. (1988a) La définition de Priscien de l'énoncé. Les enjeux théoriques d'une variante, selon les commentateurs médiévaux, *Grammaire et histoire de la grammaire. Hommage à la mémoire de Jean Stéfanini*, Recueil d'études rassemblées par C. Blanche-Benveniste, A. Chervel et M. Gross, Aix/Marseille, 353–73.

ROSIER, I. (1988b) 'O Magister . . .'. Grammaticalité et intelligibilité selon un sophisme du XIIIᵉ siècle, *Cahiers de l'institut du moyen âge grec et latin*, 56, 1–102.

ROSIER, I. (1988c) Les parties du discours au confin du XIIᵉ siècle, *Langage*, 23, 37–49.

ROSIER, I. (1988d) Le traitement spéculatif des constructions figurées au XIIIᵉ siècle, *L'héritage des grammariens latins de l'Antiquité aux Lumières*, ed. par I. Rosier, Paris, 181–204.

ROTTA, P. (1909) *La filosofia del linguaggio nella Patristica e nella Scolastica*, Torino.

RUTELLA, F. (1977) Chi fu Flavio Capro, *Studi e ricerche dell'istituto di latino della Facoltà di Magistero di Genova*, I, 143–59.

SABBADINI, R. (1903) Spogli ambrosiani latini, *Studi italiani di filologia classica*, II, 165–388.

SALMON, P. (1962) Ueber den Beitrag des grammatischen Unterrichts zur Poetik des Mittelalters, *Archiv für das Studium der neueren Sprachen und Literaturen*, 199, 2, 65–84.

SALMON, P. (1963) Le texte biblique des lectionnaires mérovingiens, *La Bibbia nell'alto medioevo*, 491–517.

SALVIOLI, G. (1898) *L'istruzione pubblica in Italia nei secoli VIII-IX-X*, Firenze.

SANDYS, J. E. (1903–8) *A History of Classical Scholarship*, 3 vols, Cambridge (republished New York, 1958 and 1967).

SCAGLIONE, A. D. (1970) *Ars grammatica* (Janua Linguarum – Series minor, 77), The Hague–Paris.

SCHIAFFINI, A. (1943) *Tradizione e poesia nella prosa d'arte italiana dalla latinità medievale a G. Boccaccio*, Roma.

SCHINDEL, U. (1975) *Die lateinischen Figurenlehren des 5. bis 7. Jahrhunderts und Donats Vergilkommentar (mit zwei Editionen)* (Abhandlungen der Akademie der Wissenschaften in Göttingen, Philologisch-historische Klasse, Dritte Folge, Nr. 91), Göttingen.

SCHIZZEROTTO, G. (1967) Review of Riessner (1965), *Studi medievali*, 3ª S., 8, 219–33.

SCHMITT, W. O. (1969) Die Janua (Donatus). Ein Beitrag zur lateinischen Schulgrammatik des Mittelalters und der Renaissance, *Beiträge zur Inkunabelkunde*, 3. Folge, 4, 43–80.

SCHMITZ, W. (1908) *Alcuins Ars grammatica, die lateinische Schulgrammatik der Karolingischen Renaissance*, Diss. Greifswald.

SCHNEIDER, B. (1971) *Die mittelalterlichen griechisch-lateinischen Uebersetzungen der Aristotelischen Rhetorik*, Berlin.

SCHRIMPF, G. (1966) *Die Axiomenschrift des Boethius (De Hebdomadibus) als philosophisches Lehrbuch des Mittelalters* (Studien zur Problemgeschichte der antiken und mittelalterlichen Philosophie, II), Leiden.

SCHRIMPF, G. (1977a) Gelehrsamkeit und Philosophie im Bildungswesen des 9. und 10. Jahrhunderts. Ein Literaturbericht für die Jahre 1960 bis 1975, *Zeitschrift für philosophische Forschung*, 31, 123–37.

SCHRIMPF, G. (1977b) Wertung und Rezeption antiker Logik im Karolingerreich, *Logik, Ethik, Theorie der Geisteswissenschaften*, XI. Deutscher Kongress für Philosophie, Hamburg, 451–6.

*La scuola nell'Occidente latino dell'alto medioevo* (1972) Settimane di studio del Centro italiano di studi sull'alto medioevo, XIX, 2 vols, Spoleto.

SIEGMUND, A. (1949) *Die Ueberlieferung der griechischen christlichen Literatur in der lateinischen Kirche bis zum zwölften Jahrhundert,* München.

SMALLEY, B. (1952) *The Study of the Bible in the Middle Ages,* Oxford.

SOFER, J. (1930) *Lateinisches und Romanisches aus den* Etymologiae *des Isidorus von Sevilla,* Göttingen.

SPADE, P. V. (1975) Ockham's Distinction between Absolute and Connotative Terms, *Vivarium,* 13, 55–76.

SPADE, P. V. (1988) Anselm and the Background to Adam Wodeham's Theory of Abstract and Concrete Terms, *Rivista di storia della filosofia,* 43, 261–71.

SPECHT, F. A. (1885) *Geschichte des Unterrichtswesen in Deutschland von den ältesten Zeiten bis zur Mitte des 13. Jahrhunderts,* Stuttgart.

SPICQ, C. (1944) *Esquisse d'une histoire de l'exégèse latine au Moyen Age,* Paris.

STEINACKER, H. (1954) Die römische Kirche und die griechischen Sprachkenntnisse des Frühmittelalters, *Mitteilungen des Instituts für österreichische Geschichtsforschung,* 62, 28–66.

*Studies in Medieval Linguistic Thought* (1980) *S. i. M. L. T. dedicated to Geoffrey L. Bursill-Hall,* ed. by K. Koerner, H.-J. Niederehe and R. H. Robins (Amsterdam Studies in the Theory and History of Linguistic Science, Series III – Studies in the History of Linguistics, Volume 26 [ = *Historiographia Linguistica,* 7, 1–2]), Amsterdam.

*Studi Noniani* (1967–85), Genova (ten vols published so far).

SWIGGERS, P. (1988) Les premières grammaires des vernaculaires galloromans face à la tradition latine: stratégies d'adaptation et de transformation, *L'héritage des grammairiens latins de l'Antiquité aux Lumières,* Paris, 259–69.

TAVONI, M. (1984) *Latino, grammatica, volgare. Storia di una questione umanistica,* Padova.

THIEL, M. (1973) *Grundlagen und Gestalt der Hebräischkenntnisse des frühen Mittelalters,* Spoleto.

THOMPSON, A. H. (1935) *Bede, His Life, His Time and Writing. Essays in Commemoration of the Twelfth Centenary of His Death,* Oxford.

THUROT, CH. (1869) *Extraits de divers manuscrits latins pour servir à l'histoire des doctrines grammaticales au moyen âge,* Paris (reprinted Frankfurt a.M., 1964).

VÄÄNÄNEN, V. (1971) *Introduzione al latino volgare,* Bologna (Italian trans. of *Introduction au latin vulgaire,* Paris 1967², revised and corrected by the author).

VAN DE VYVER, A. (1929) Les étapes du développement philosophique du haut moyen âge, *Revue Belge de Philologie et d'Histoire,* 8, 425–52.

VAN DE VYVER, A. (1931) Cassiodore et son œuvre, *Speculum,* 6, 244–92.

VASOLI, C. (1961) *La filosofia medioevale* (Storia della filosofia, vol. II), Milano.

VERGER, J. (1973) *Les universités au Moyen Age,* Paris (Italian trans. Bologna 1982, with introduction by F. Bruni).

VERGER, J. (1982) Des écoles à l'université: la mutation institutionelle, *La France de Philippe Auguste. Le temps des mutations*, Actes du Colloque International organisé par le Centre national de la recherche scientifique. (Paris, 29 Sept.–4 Oct. 1980), Paris, 817–46.

VINEIS, E. (1988) Grammatica e filosofia del linguaggio in Alcuino, *Studi e saggi linguistici*, 28, 403–29.

VISCARDI, A. (1957) *Le origini* (Storia letteraria d'Italia, vol. I), Milano.

VLASTO, A. P. (1970) *The Entry of the Slavs into Christendom. An Introduction to the Medieval History of the Slavs*, Cambridge.

WATSON, F. (1908) *The English Grammar Schools to 1660: Their Curriculum and Practice*, Cambridge.

WEISHEIPL, J. A. (1964) Curriculum of the Faculty of Arts at Oxford in the Early Fourteenth Century, *Mediaeval Studies*, 26, 143–85.

WEISHEIPL, J. A. (1965) Classification of the Sciences in Medieval Thought, *Mediaeval Studies*, 27, 55–90.

WEISHEIPL, J. A. (1966) Developments in the Arts Curriculum at Oxford in the Early Fourteenth Century, *Mediaeval Studies*, 28, 151–75.

WEISHEIPL, J. A. (1969) The Place of the Liberal Arts in the University Curriculum during the 14th and 15th Centuries, *Arts libéraux et philosophie au moyen âge*, 209–13.

WEISS, R. (1950a) The Translators from the Greek of the Angevin Court of Naples, *Rinascimento*, I, 195–226.

WEISS, R. (1950b) The Greek Culture of South Italy in the Later Middle Ages, *Proceedings of the British Academy*, 37, 23–50.

WEISS, R. (1951) Per una lettera di Lorenzo d'Aquileia sullo studio del greco e delle lingue orientali a Parigi alla fine del Duecento, *Rivista di storia della Chiesa in Italia*, 5, 266–8.

WEISS, R. (1952) Lo studio del greco all'abbazia di San Dionigi durante il medioevo, *Rivista di storia della Chiesa in Italia*, 6, 426–38.

WHITE, C. L. (1898) *Aelfric. A New Study of His Life and Writings*, Boston.

WIERUSZOWSKI, H. (1966) *The Medieval University*, Princeton.

WRIGHT, R. (1976) Speaking, Reading, and Writing Late Latin and Early Romance, *Philologus*, 60, 178–89.

ZONTA, B. (1960) I codici GLPV dell'*Elementarium Papiae*: un primo sondaggio nella tradizione manoscritta ed alcune osservazioni relative, *Studi classici e orientali*, 9, 76–99.

# Index